JACOBITISM
and the English people
1688–1788

JACOBITISM
and the English people
1688–1788

PAUL KLÉBER MONOD

Assistant Professor of History
Middlebury College, Vermont

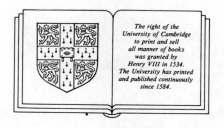

The right of the
University of Cambridge
to print and sell
all manner of books
was granted by
Henry VIII in 1534.
The University has printed
and published continuously
since 1584.

CAMBRIDGE UNIVERSITY PRESS

Cambridge
New York   Port Chester
Melbourne   Sydney

Published by the Press Syndicate of the University of Cambridge
The Pitt Building, Trumpington Street, Cambridge CB2 1RP
40 West 20th Street, New York, NY 10011, USA
10 Stamford Road, Oakleigh, Melbourne 3166, Australia

First published 1989

Printed in Great Britain at the University Press, Cambridge

British Library cataloguing in publication data
Monod, Paul Kléber
Jacobitism and the English people, 1688–1788
1. Great Britain. Jacobitism, 1603–1837
I. Title
941.06

Library of Congress cataloguing in publication data
Monod, Paul Kléber.
Jacobitism and the English people, 1688–1788/Paul Kléber Monod.
p.   cm.
Bibliography.
Includes index.
ISBN 0 521 33534 5
1. Jacobites.
2. England – Civilization – 18th century.
3. England – Civilization – 17th century.
4. Great Britain – Politics and government – 18th century.
5. Great Britain – Politics and government – 1689–1702.
I. Title.
DA813.M86 1989
941.507 – dc 19   88-36743   CIP

ISBN 0 521 33534 5

To my parents, and Jan

Contents

PART FOUR TWO FACES OF TREASON

Plates

Maps

Tables

Graph

Note for reader

Until 1752, England used the Julian calendar, which was ten days behind the continental Gregorian calendar down to 1700, and eleven days behind thereafter. Whenever a date before 1752 is followed by 'N.S.', it means that the Gregorian 'New Style' calendar has been used. In addition, the Julian calendar marked the New Year on 25 March, not 1 January. Thus, '30 January 1714' would be '1715' to us. Many contemporary writers, however, gave both the old year and the new for dates between 1 January and 25 March: hence, '30 January 1714/15'. I have standardized all dates before 1752 to this style, giving both the old year and the new, in order to avoid errors in dating periodicals and correspondence.

Acknowledgments

A host of acquaintances, friends and relatives on both sides of the Atlantic have assisted in the long process of producing this work. It began in 1980 as a Yale University doctoral dissertation, supervised by John Brewer. His patience and encouragement initially sustained this project, and he continued to provide much good advice even after leaving Yale for Harvard. The influence of my second adviser, Linda Colley, is evident on every page. Her careful readings have immeasurably improved my writing style, and have saved me from rash assumptions, too numerous to mention. I could not have hoped for a better mentor. Conrad Russell, my third dissertation reader, constantly reminded me that English history did not begin in 1688, and the rigour of his thinking weeded out many errors in my work. A fourth, informal adviser was Eveline Cruickshanks of the History of Parliament Trust, whose kindness and generosity in providing me with sources and suggestions cannot be properly thanked.

Before I started off to begin research in England, Douglas Hay spent much time in giving me archival references, which proved invaluable, Paul Fritz, J. P. Kenyon, Bruce Lenman and Nicholas Rogers replied to written enquiries with many useful comments. In England, I spoke with J. C. D. Clark and the late G. V. Bennett, both of whom supplied further enlightenment. Paul Chapman allowed me to read an unpublished paper on Jacobite rhetoric, Paul Hopkins discussed Jacobite politics in the 1690s with me and Daniel Szechi relayed material to me. David Hayton, John Styles and Joanna Innes spent hours listening to my fledgling ideas. At the Public Record Office, John Post guided me through grimy heaps of barely legible legal documents. Miss Jane Langton of the Royal Archives at Windsor was also extremely helpful to me; and I must thank Her Majesty Queen Elizabeth II for permission to use the Stuart Papers. James Mist, who works, ironically enough, for the Queen at Windsor, presented me with new facts about his ancestor Nathaniel. G. B. Seddon and R. J. Charleston allowed me to read the important Glass Society papers, and Richard Sartin of the Harris Museum, Preston, gave me access to the Walton-le-dale Corporation Book. A version of Chapter 8 was read in a seminar at King's College, Cambridge, in 1983; I am grateful to Lawrence Goldman for that opportunity. Without Fran and Coline Devine in Stockport, and Winnie and Margaret Monod in London, I would not have had such warm and pleasant places to live in while delving into the archives. Without the Social Sciences and Humanities Research Council of Canada, and the Ministère de l'Education du Québec, I might not have had the money to live in England at all.

Back in America, I have profited from my fellow graduate students at Yale, through the shared researches of Kathleen Wilson and John Ramsbottom, and from conversations with Bart Blankenfeld, Cathy Hamilton, Richard and Lynn Stewart, Marcia Wagner and others. Parts of Chapter 1 were presented as a paper to a seminar at the Folger Library in 1986, for which I must thank Nicholas Phillipson, J. G. A. Pocock and the staff of the Folger. To my family I owe special debts. My parents nurtured my interest in history, and gave me unstinting support in my studies for many years. My father did not live to see the final product, but I hope it would have pleased him. He and my mother and brother David contributed more to it than they knew. Last of all, and first of all, I thank my wife Jan; this is her book as much as mine. From beginning to end, through dismal archives and endless revisions, she has been there, sharing in my work as I share in hers, an intellectual partner whom I also love.

I am writing this on the two hundredth anniversary of the death of Charles Edward Stuart. It is not a date of great historical significance, but for one who has studied Jacobitism so long, it arouses mixed feelings of wistfulness and release. Now at last, Charlie is gone awa'. Yet the silence in which all history ends cannot tell us that he will never come again.

Middlebury, Vermont, 31 January 1988

Abbreviations

Add. MS	Additional manuscript
Assi.	Assizes
Beinecke	Beinecke Library, Yale University, New Haven, Connecticut
B.L.	British Library
Bloch	Marc Bloch, *Les Rois Thaumaturges* (Strasbourg, 1924)
Bodl.	Bodleian Library, Oxford
Bossy	John Bossy, *The English Catholic Community, 1570–1850* (London, 1975)
C.L.R.O.	City of London Record Office
Crawfurd	Raymond Crawfurd, *The King's Evil* (Oxford, 1911)
C.S.P.D., W.&M.	William John Hardy, ed., *Calendar of State Papers, Domestic Series, of the Reign of William and Mary* (13 vols., London, 1895–1924)
D.N.B.	Leslie Stephen and Sidney Lee, eds., *The Dictionary of National Biography* (63 vols., London, 1885–1900)
E.H.R.	*English Historical Review*
Garrett	Jane Garrett, *The Triumphs of Providence: The Assassination Plot, 1696* (Cambridge, 1980)
Grosart	Alexander Grosart, ed., *English Jacobite Ballads, Songs and Satires, etc. from the Mss. at Townley Hall, Lancashire* (Manchester, 1877)
H.J.	*Historical Journal*
H.M.C.	Historical Manuscripts Commission
J.B.S.	*Journal of British Studies*

J.S.A.H.R.	*Journal of the Society for Army Historical Research*
K.B.	King's Bench
L.R.O.	Lancashire Record Office
Luttrell	Narcissus Luttrell, *A Brief Historical Relation of State Affairs from September 1678 to April 1714* (6 vols., Oxford, 1857)
P.C.	Palatinate of Chester
P.D.	Palatinate of Durham
P.L.	Palatinate of Lancaster
P. & P.	*Past and Present*
P.R.O.	Public Record Office
R.A.	Royal Archives
Rawl.	Rawlinson Manuscripts
S.H.	*Social History*
S.P.	State Papers
Somers Tracts	Walter Scott, ed., *A Collection of Scarce and Valuable Tracts … particularly that of the late Lord Somers* (2nd edn, 13 vols., London, 1813)
T.H.S.C.	*Transactions of the Honourable Society of Cymmrodion*
T.L.C.A.S.	*Transactions of the Lancashire and Cheshire Antiquarian Society*
T.R.H.S.	*Transactions of the Royal Historical Society*
T.S.	Treasury Solicitor
V.C.H.	*Victoria County History*
Ward	W. R. Ward, *Georgian Oxford: University Politics in the Eighteenth Century* (Oxford, 1958)
W.H.R.	*Welsh Historical Review*

Introduction: defining Jacobitism

> He talked with regret and indignation of the factious opposition to Government at this time, and imputed it, in a great measure, to the Revolution. 'Sir, (said he, in a low voice, having come nearer to me, while his old prejudices seemed to be fermenting in his mind,) this Hanoverian family is *isolée* here. They have no friends. Now the Stuarts had friends who stuck by them so late as 1745. When the right of the King is not reverenced, there will not be reverence for those appointed by the King.
>
> Boswell's *Life of Johnson*, 21 March 1783[1]

James Francis Edward Stuart – to his friends King James III, the Old Pretender to his foes – gazes down at us with gentle eyes and a cryptic smile, like the benign young god of an ancient and forgotten religion. His portrait from the studio of Alexis Belle may also remind us of the enigmatic cult devoted to this royal deity: Jacobitism, named after *Iacobus*, or James in Latin. As elusive as the smile of the Pretender, Jacobitism has been more of an impression than a reality for those historians who have suspected its importance. Jacobitism has remained a hidden stream of political subversion, a mysterious shadowy presence, too vague to grasp, too volatile to define. From the first, therefore, it became a subject for superficial judgments, which tended to be either enthusiastically romantic or implacably hostile.

The romantic tradition was born before the bodies at Culloden were cold. It can still be deliciously savoured in the works of Sir Walter Scott, Andrew Lang and a host of lesser writers, who were usually addicted to the opium of reactionary nostalgia.[2] For them, the Stuarts were the heroes of a tragic drama, victims of the pitiless juggernaut of 'moder-

---

[1] George Birkbeck Hill and L. F. Powell, eds., *Boswell's Life of Johnson* (6 vols., Oxford, 1934–64), vol. i, pp. 164–5.
[2] See esp. Scott's *Redgauntlet. A Tale of the Eighteenth Century* (Edinburgh, 1824), and Lang's *Prince Charles Edward Stuart: The Young Chevalier* (London, 1903).

nity'. The work of the romantics was often based upon impeccable scholarship, but it conveyed little sense of the complexity of Jacobitism, of its causes, or of why it was abominated by English governments as the most heinous form of treason. This last point was amply explained by some of the foremost historians of the nineteenth century, including both Whigs like Macaulay and Whiggish Tories like Mahon.[3] They identified the cause of the exiled Stuarts with the evils of absolutism and Roman Catholicism, which for them were virtually interchangeable. In their minds, Jacobitism was the nemesis of all that was free, just and rational in English government and society.

The romantic view of Jacobitism persisted into the twentieth century in the works of the prolific Taylers and Sir Charles Petrie, which were addressed to general audiences.[4] Most scholars, however, continued to be unsympathetic towards what was seen as a regressive political phenomenon, whose appeal was limited to a small number of desperate conservatives. G. P. Insh depicted the Scottish Jacobites as the doomed defenders of a dying, pre-capitalist social order, while G. H. Jones examined the tangled threads of Jacobite plotting in a largely diplomatic context, paying little attention to the nature and extent of Jacobite sentiment.[5] Similar assumptions about Jacobitism can be detected in the more recent interpretations of Paul Fritz and G. V. Bennett, which emphasized the manipulation of Jacobite plots by Whig politicians seeking to enhance their own power.[6] Bennett adopted a sceptical attitude towards Tory Jacobitism, representing it as a hopeless political tactic that had no real chance of success.[7]

Nevertheless, scholarly interest in Jacobitism revived in the 1970s, primarily on account of the researches of Eveline Cruickshanks. Materials in French archives and in the Stuart Papers at Windsor

---

[3] Lord Macaulay, *The History of England from the Accession of James II*, ed. C. H. Firth (6 vols., London, 1913–15); Lord Mahon, *History of England from the Peace of Utrecht to the Peace of Versailles, 1713–1783* (7 vols., London, 1839–54).

[4] For example, Alistair and Henrietta Tayler, *The Old Chevalier* (London, 1934), and *1715: The Story of the Rising* (London, 1939); Sir Charles Petrie, *The Jacobite Movement* (2 vols., London, 1948–50).

[5] G. P. Insh, *The Scottish Jacobite Movement* (Edinburgh, 1952); G. H. Jones, *The Main Stream of Jacobitism* (Cambridge, Mass., 1954).

[6] Paul Fritz, *The English Ministers and Jacobitism between the Rebellions of 1715 and 1745* (Toronto, 1975); G. V. Bennett, 'Jacobitism and the Rise of Walpole', in Neil McKendrick, ed., *Historical Perspectives: Studies in English Thought and Society in Honour of J. H. Plumb* (London, 1974), pp. 70–92.

[7] G. V. Bennett, *The Tory Crisis in Church and State, 1688–1730: The Career of Francis Atterbury, Bishop of Rochester* (Oxford, 1975), and his 'English Jacobitism, 1710–1715: Myth and Reality', *T.R.H.S.*, 5th Series, 32 (1982), pp. 137–51.

convinced her that the Tory party had survived forty years of proscription after 1714 by adopting the Pretender's cause.[8] This thesis was strongly criticized by Linda Colley in her book on the Tory party under the first two Georges. She pointed out that the Tories had more options open to them than Jacobitism, and that they were never wholly committed to the Stuarts as a party.[9] Although Colley's views were not completely incompatible with those of Cruickshanks, their debate tended to polarize historical opinion; it also obscured the issue of Jacobite adherence by concentrating on certain types of evidence and avoiding the problem of definition. The political influence of Jacobitism continued to be stressed by historians like Daniel Szechi, Frank McLynn and Ian Christie, but their conclusions were cautious and tentative.[10]

A bolder and more controversial approach was propounded by J. C. D. Clark, who argued that Tory allegiance to the Stuarts could be made into a polemical lever with which to turn the prevailing interpretation of eighteenth-century English history on its head.[11] The strength and durability of Jacobitism, Clark argued, indicated the continued significance of kingship and religious principles, and the failure of 'Whig consensus' after 1714. Yet he also presented Toryism and Whiggery as ideological twins; both were essentially conservative, monarchist and Anglican. Clark's provocative picture of an English *ancien régime* was in some ways a useful corrective to orthodox historiography, but it rested on a new set of unproven assumptions about the nature of party ideology, and it complicated the question of what was distinctive in the Jacobite position.

If the role of Jacobitism in elite politics has engendered disagreement among historians, its impact on social relations has become an enigma.

---

[8] Romney Sedgwick, ed., *The History of Parliament: The House of Commons, 1715–54* (2 vols., London, 1970), vol. i, pp. 62–78; Eveline Cruickshanks, *Political Untouchables: The Tories and the '45* (London, 1979).

[9] Linda Colley, *In Defiance of Oligarchy: The Tory Party, 1714–60* (Cambridge, 1982), esp. ch. 2.

[10] D. Szechi, *Jacobitism and Tory Politics, 1710–14* (Edinburgh, 1984); F. J. McLynn, *The Jacobites* (London, 1985); Ian Christie, 'The Tory Party, Jacobitism and the "Forty-Five": A Note', *H.J.*, 30, 4 (1987), pp. 921–31.

[11] J. C. D. Clark, 'A General Theory of Party, Opposition and Government, 1688–1832', *H.J.*, 23, 2 (1980), pp. 316–18; 'The Politics of the Excluded: Tories, Jacobites and Whig Patriots, 1715–60', *Parliamentary History*, 2 (1983), pp. 209–22; *English Society, 1688–1832: Ideology, Social Structure and Political Practice during the Ancien Regime* (Cambridge, 1985), pp. 141–61; *Revolution and Rebellion: State and Society in England in the Seventeenth and Eighteenth Centuries* (Cambridge, 1986), pp. 111–16, 125–6, 174–7.

In Scotland, the 'culture clash' envisioned by Insh was rejected by Bruce Lenman, who found the Jacobite Highlands to be far more integrated into the national economy than had been supposed; he proposed religion, not 'modernization', as the key to Jacobite adherence.[12] In England, however, no similar social explanation emerged, due to the caution of historians who could not decide how seriously Jacobitism should be taken. Nicholas Rogers revealed the widespread use of Jacobite rhetoric and symbolism in riots and demonstrations between 1714 and the 1750s, but he was reluctant to portray affection for the Stuarts as a genuinely popular attitude.[13] Meanwhile, E. P. Thompson and his students had come across Jacobite connections with activities as diverse as poaching, smuggling and anonymous letter-writing.[14] Once again, however, they were hesitant to draw broad conclusions, and suggested, like Rogers, that the seriousness of popular commitment to the Stuart cause was virtually impossible to ascertain.

It is indeed difficult to judge the seriousness of something when we are not certain of what we should be judging. Most historians have taken it for granted that they can recognize 'real' Jacobitism, or that they could if it existed; but they have not made much of an attempt to explain their methods to others. Different notions about the definition of Jacobitism have generated much of the conflict about its significance. When are historians justified in describing an individual as 'a Jacobite'? Presumably, when it can be shown that he or she preferred a Stuart king of the exiled line to the ruling monarch or dynasty. It need not be assumed that all Jacobites maintained an unflagging, lifelong devotion to the Stuart family, or that they all would have laid down their lives, their estates or their money for the cause. A very wide range of commitment existed among Jacobites. Some loved the banished King only in their youth, or in their old age; some, like Bolingbroke, admired him on and off, and between bouts of interest hated him ferociously for leading them astray. Some were attracted to him for only a few months,

---

[12] Bruce Lenman, *The Jacobite Risings in Britain, 1689–1746* (London, 1980), and *The Jacobite Clans of the Great Glen, 1650–1784* (London, 1984). See also Paul Hopkins, *Glencoe and the End of the Highland War* (Edinburgh, 1986).

[13] Nicholas Rogers, 'Popular Protest in Early Hanoverian London', *P. & P.*, 79 (1978), pp. 70–100; 'Riot and Popular Jacobitism in Early Hanoverian England', in Eveline Cruickshanks, ed., *Ideology and Conspiracy: Aspects of Jacobitism, 1689–1759* (Edinburgh, 1982), pp. 70–88.

[14] E. P. Thompson, *Whigs and Hunters: The Origin of the Black Act* (Harmondsworth, 1977); Douglas Hay, Peter Linebaugh, John G. Rule, E. P. Thompson and Cal Winslow, *Albion's Fatal Tree: Crime and Society in Eighteenth-Century England* (New York, 1975), pp. 156–7, 225, 325.

particularly in the heady summer of 1715. Many would do no more for him than wish him well, but this too made a sort of Jacobite.

Jacobites may be identified by what they said and did, and by what others said about them. Unfortunately, most of the surviving evidence falls into the latter category – it consists of accusations, allegations and scraps of information from which inferences may be drawn. These types of material must be very carefully weighed, and few solid conclusions can be reached from them. Even direct expressions of Jacobitism may be difficult to interpret. Nevertheless, historians should not shrink from exploring the possibility of Jacobitism, which they have too often dismissed as absurd or implausible.

Consider two examples that illustrate the complexity involved in defining a Jacobite. John Byrom, the Manchester Nonjuror and poet, produced voluminous autobiographical remains, as well as substantial quantities of poetry and prose, that leave little doubt as to who he thought to be the rightful king of England.[15] Yet his Jacobite statements are veiled and ambiguous, as in his famous ditty which ends, 'But who Pretender is, and who is King, / God bless us all; – that's quite another thing!' When Charles Edward Stuart was in Manchester during the rebellion of 1745, Byrom acted circumspectly, allowing himself to be escorted to an interview with the Prince by an armed guard.[16] Should Byrom be regarded as one of the staunchest of Jacobites, or as a careful 'trimmer'? It should not be forgotten that his allegiance to the Stuarts, however quietly he maintained it, caused him to sacrifice a career in the Church or the law because he refused to swear oaths to a 'usurper'. He was no politician, but he was one of the most consistent and honest of English Jacobites.

In contrast to John Byrom, Francis Daughty left little trace of himself, other than in the records of Worcestershire Assizes for 1690. They tell us that he was a labourer of Bromsgrove, who was accused by three witnesses of having said that 'King James is the right King of England and none but he' on 3 May 1690. Was Francis Daughty a Jacobite? In this case, the opinion of the court cannot help us, because Daughty was released under a general pardon before judgment was passed.[17] Whatever decision is reached on the testimony will be as fallible as any rendered by a jury. If Daughty did speak these words,

---

[15] See Richard Parkinson, ed., *The Private Journal and Literary Remains of John Byrom*, Chetham Society, 32, 34, 40, 44 (4 parts in 2 vols., 1854–7).
[16] *Ibid.*, vol. ii, part ii, p. 394.
[17] P.R.O., Assi. 2/2, 20 Sept. 2 W. & M.; Assi. 5/12, Worcs. 1690, indt.

however, he was guilty of a serious crime. The names of King James II
and his heirs were officially anathematized; to proclaim their right to
the throne verbally was to run the risk of punishment by imprisonment,
fines, the pillory or a whipping. These were good reasons *not* to employ
Jacobite rhetoric, so that even the most drunken of blessings for the
Pretender implied a choice that must be explained. Francis Daughty
may not have believed what he was reputed to have said; but if he did
not, he was a very foolish man.

    John Byrom and Francis Daughty demonstrate the great variety in
Jacobite sentiment, and in the ways by which it was expressed. No clear
dividing line separates 'real' Jacobites from those whose commitment
was less 'serious'. To be sure, disgruntled Stuart adherents complained
at times about 'tippling' Jacobites who would do no more than toast
the Pretender's health, but this was an invidious distinction.[18] If a
willingness to die for a cause were the only true indication of resolve,
then few Englishmen or women in the modern age have been seriously
committed to anything. Gentry families of 'tippling' Jacobites often
kept their allegiance to the Stuarts alive for generations; they were not
less serious in their loyalty merely because they avoided recklessness.

    Dr Samuel Johnson might be imagined as an archetype of the
'tippling' or 'sentimental' Jacobite, because he spoke privately on the
right of the Stuarts to the throne, but did nothing publicly to promote
it, and even changed his mind about it periodically.[19] Johnson's
Jacobitism, however, was private by necessity. His reflections on the
Revolution and the Hanoverian Succession, which may seem innocuous today, could not have been publicized in his lifetime. Strongly
phrased and full of bitterness, they reflected 'old prejudices' Johnson
found impossible to renounce, in spite of frequent misgivings. He may
have been a timid, back-sliding Jacobite, but his attachment to the
Stuarts was no less profound for all that.

    Johnson's commitment was certainly emotional; but can allegiance
ever be separated from emotions? To write of Jacobitism, as the
romantics realized, is to explore preferences, sympathies, affections,
feelings, even love – all contradictory, misleading and unpredictable

[18] See Robert Patten, *The History of the Late Rebellion* (2nd edn, London, 1717),
p. 100, and [John Byrom and Robert Thyer], *Manchester Vindicated* (Chester,
1749), p. 16.
[19] See Hill and Powell, eds., *Boswell's Life of Johnson*, vol. i, pp. 37, 145–7, 429–31,
vol. ii, p. 320, vol. iii, pp. 155–7, 162, vol. iv, pp. 154–5, 170–1; and Howard
Erskine-Hill, 'The Political Character of Samuel Johnson', in Isobel Grundy, ed.,
Samuel Johnson: New Critical Essays (London, 1984), pp. 107–36.

factors. It might be argued that this messy display of emotions can be reduced to an analysis of 'interest'. Many who embraced the Stuart cause were motivated by blatant self-interest – desire for office, disappointed ambition, a wish to insure themselves with the other side. Yet interest, in spite of Namier, has never been a consistent, universal, self-evident category; obviously, not every disgruntled politician turned to Jacobitism as an option. Interest depends upon perceptions or points of view, which, in turn, are linked inextricably to beliefs, ideas, aspirations, loyalties, the whole welter of complex factors that comprise consciousness, and are usually summed up in a rhetoric of emotions. It is not misleading, therefore, to use terms like Jacobite sentiment, sympathy or attachment.

Jacobitism itself may be defined as both the idea and the expression of support for the claims of the exiled Stuarts. It has also been called a movement, and in J. C. D. Clark's work, an ideology. The first of these epithets implies a general coordination of Jacobite activities. In fact, Jacobitism was more organized than most historians have suggested, but the sphere of centralized direction was restricted; the adherents of the Stuarts were not all engaged in a single enterprise, and the Jacobite 'movement' was only a small part of the whole. A similar caveat applies to the term 'ideology'. If it means no more than a collection of ideas, beliefs or principles, then it is quite possible to cobble together a 'Jacobite ideology'; but if this set of ideas must be unified, distinguishable from others, and maintained with consistency as a 'world-view', then Jacobitism was an ideology for only a small number of devoted loyalists, most of them Nonjurors.[20] Jacobitism was compatible with a wide range of ideological positions, although most of its distinctive features were derived from the Toryism of the 1670s and early 1680s.

In searching for a general label for Jacobitism, it should be remembered that the most concrete evidence for its existence is found in records of expressions – words, images, forms of behaviour. These possess a certain coherence; they resemble each other sufficiently to be considered as an entity. Jacobitism can be seen as a system of expressions, or of signs. It might be imagined as a series of road-signs, extending in every direction. Once they are mapped out, it becomes clear that they follow similar patterns, and that their winding paths are not random or unplanned. This system of signs might be called a

[20] Almost all of the writers cited by Clark were Nonjurors. See also Bruce Lenman, 'The Scottish Episcopal Clergy and the Ideology of Jacobitism', in Cruickshanks, ed., *Ideology and Conspiracy*, pp. 36–48.

political culture, or perhaps more properly a 'subculture', a part of the cultural totality of seventeenth- and eighteenth-century England.

'Culture', however, is a diverse and ambiguous concept. As the subject of a branch of anthropological research, it has inspired a multitude of conflicting interpretations. An older school of thought regarded it as equivalent to the habits, customs and traditions of a society, a definition adopted by historians of 'popular culture' like Peter Burke or Robert Muchembled.[21] Today, however, culture has evolved to include human activity in all of its manifestations, and the term is often invoked without much sense of precision. Scholarly debate has centred on what determines culture – in other words, on that which must be outside it, and on which it depends. Thus, various Marxist or materialist writers have represented culture as governed by economic relations, although no agreement exists on the ways by which this sovereignty is exercised.[22] The structuralist anthropologist Claude Lévi-Strauss has presented the relationship between culture and 'non-culture', or nature, as both an 'opposition' and a dependency. Cultural phenomena like mythology, according to Lévi-Strauss, are 'not directly linked with a different kind of reality'; nevertheless, he argues that myths are objectifications of thought, just as thought is an objectification of nature.[23] Mythology, in other words, is indeed determined by a different reality, but at one remove, and 'if the human mind appears determined even in the realm of mythology, *a fortiori* it must also be determined in all of its spheres of activity'.[24]

The critic Jacques Derrida complained that Lévi-Strauss's stitching up of a supposed separation between culture and nature had created 'a scandalous suture'; for his part, Derrida rejected representational theories of meaning, and proposed the subversion of difference, so that

[21] See A. L. Kroeber and Clyde Kluckhorn, *Culture: A Critical Review of Concepts and Definitions* (Cambridge, Mass., 1952); Peter Burke, *Popular Culture in Early Modern Europe* (New York, 1978); R. Muchembled, *Popular Culture and Elite Culture in France, 1400–1750*, tr. by Lydia Cochrane (Baton Rouge, La., and London, 1985).

[22] See Marvin Harris, *Cultural Materialism: The Struggle for a Science of Culture* (New York, 1979); Maurice Godelier, *Perspectives in Marxist Anthropology*, tr. by Robert Brain (Cambridge, 1977); David Seddon, ed., *Relations of Production: Marxist Approaches to Economic Anthropology*, tr. by Helen Lacker (London, 1978). For a sociological perspective, see Raymond Williams, *Culture* (Glasgow, 1981).

[23] Claude Lévi-Strauss, *The Raw and the Cooked: Introduction to a Science of Mythology*, tr. by John and Doreen Weightman (New York and Evanston, 1964), pp. 10–11.

[24] *Ibid.*, p. 10. Lévi-Strauss has influenced some historians, notably Fernand Braudel, who depicted nature as a boundary or limit on cultural possibility in his work *Civilization and Capitalism, 15th–18th Century*, vol. 1: *The Structures of Everyday Life: The Limits of the Possible*, tr. by Sian Reynolds (London, 1981).

culture and 'non-culture' would become indistinguishable.[25] Similarly, if less radically, Michel Foucault maintained that the science of human culture was a recent innovation that had replaced a universalist conception of meaning (in which nature itself was a vast system of signs), and would eventually give way to language as a new focus for knowledge.[26] If culture is synonymous with language, however, the anthropological emphasis on 'non-cultural' determinants becomes problematic. Outside language is silence. The 'different kind of reality' on which cultural determinism relies becomes incomprehensible, because it lies beyond language. 'Nature' and 'the material world' are intelligible only as cultural concepts, subsumed within language, which names them and thus creates them.

Although the Derridean anti-programme resembles sophistry in its purest sense, Derrida and Foucault should not be ignored by historians dealing with culture. The identification of culture with language, that is, with all forms of communication or discourse, is convincing. Culture may therefore be seen as a self-creating universe, an endless dialectic between individual invention and existing conventions that are themselves artefacts.[27] The study of cultural behaviour is a reading of certain types of texts; as Clifford Geertz has put it, '[t]he culture of a people is an ensemble of texts, themselves ensembles, which the anthropologist strains to read over the shoulders of those to whom they properly belong'.[28] How does this apply to political culture? In a standard formulation, Sidney Verba has written that '[t]he political culture of a society consists of the system of empirical beliefs, expressive symbols, and values which define the situation in which political action takes place'.[29] This definition separates 'action' from 'situation' or context – but where is the dividing line to be drawn? The specific political act and its 'background' are blended together, so that political culture should present itself as a process of unification rather than differentiation.

The concept of culture is no stranger to eighteenth-century English history, thanks to a pair of fecund, if unfocussed, articles by E. P.

25 Jacques Derrida, *Of Grammatology*, tr. by Gayatri Chakravorty Spivak (Baltimore and London, 1976), pp. 103–5.
26 Michel Foucault, *The Order of Things: An Archaeology of the Human Sciences* (New York, 1973).
27 See Roy Wagner, *The Invention of Culture* (revised edn, Chicago and London, 1981).
28 Clifford Geertz, 'Deep Play: Notes on the Balinese Cockfight', in C. Geertz, ed., *Myth, Symbol and Culture* (New York, 1971), p. 27.
29 Sidney Verba, 'Comparative Political Culture', in Lucien Pye and Sidney Verba, eds., *Political Culture and Political Development* (Princeton, 1965), p. 513.

Thompson.[30] He did not attempt to define culture very clearly, but he indicated what he thought was *outside* culture: 'the purchase, *seriatim*, of . . . labour power', 'economic rationalization', in short, capitalism.[31] This suggested that 'naked' economic relations, particularly when they involved a change from customary practice, constituted 'non-culture'. Yet Thompson challenged this argument himself in a later article, in which he examined the economic definition of class:

> I am calling into question . . . the notion that it is possible to describe a mode of production in 'economic' terms, leaving aside as secondary (less 'real') the norms, the culture, the critical concepts around which this mode of production is organized . . . class is an 'economic' and it is also a 'cultural' formation: it is impossible to give any theoretical priority to one aspect over the other.[32]

Thompson acknowledged here the interdependence of cultural and material reality, but he did not admit their equivalence or unity. We may go further in asserting that the economic formation of class is itself a cultural construct, because the everyday experience from which it is derived cannot be detached from the 'norms' and 'critical concepts' of a specific culture. To separate them, only to recombine them in the idea of class, would indeed require a 'scandalous suture'.

How does this conception of culture relate to the study of Jacobitism? First, Jacobite political culture should be interpreted as a language, with its own internal logic or grammar, operating as a coherent system. Second, it is pointless to search outside political culture for the origins of this language; its causes and context are contained within it, and should be discussed as a series of interconnections rather than a hierarchy of external determinants. Third, Jacobitism cannot be wrenched out of the wider culture of which it was a part. As. J. C. D. Clark has pointed out, the appeal of Jacobite rhetoric compels us to reassess conventional historical views; but in return, the existence of Jacobitism must be reconciled with broader trends, not all of which are figments of the teleological imaginations of Whig historians.

This discussion of Jacobite political culture will deal only with England, omitting any detailed analysis of Jacobitism in the Celtic nations. Scotland and Ireland, although partly integrated into a British framework, remained to a large extent culturally distinct from England

---

[30] E. P. Thompson, 'Patrician Society, Plebeian Culture', *Journal of Social History*, 7, 4 (1974), pp. 382–405, and 'Eighteenth-Century English Society: Class-Struggle without Class?', *S.H.*, 3, 2 (1978), pp. 133–65.

[31] Thompson, 'Patrician Society', p. 382.

[32] E. P. Thompson, *Folklore, Anthropology and Social History* (Brighton, 1979), pp. 18, 21 (reprinted from *Indian Historical Review*, 8, 2 (1978)).

in this period, and it would be overly ambitious to include them, as well as risky in tempting the wrath of nationalist historians. Wales, with its different language, heritage and customs, also deserves particular attention. Happily, Welsh Jacobitism has inspired a number of excellent studies, and important new interpretations have emerged in the work of J. P. Jenkins.[33] Of course, strong links were forged between Jacobites in England and those in Wales, Scotland and Ireland, which cannot be ignored by historians. Celtic names and personalities will therefore figure in many of the following pages, but the conclusions reached about Jacobitism in England cannot be applied to its neighbours without modifications.

Jacobitism was born with James II's flight to France in December 1688. The threat of a restoration remained real as long as a viable Stuart candidate breathed, and a foreign power was prepared to advance his claims; political support in Britain was a desirable but not always essential factor. The English government was rocked by three great waves of Jacobite activity, in 1689–96, 1714–23 and 1745–53. The first of these generated most of the basic structures of Jacobite political culture; the second was the most widespread and the most dangerous; the third echoed its predecessor with less force, and ended with a whimper when the frustrated Prince Charles Edward Stuart became an alcoholic. Jacobitism never regained its initiative, although Charles Edward's vain attempts to revive his forlorn cause did not cease until his death in January 1788. At this point an almost moribund Jacobite political culture collapsed, with the defection of the Scottish Nonjurors as its last act.

The Revolution settlement of 1689, ratified and extended in 1701, and fulfilled in 1714 by the Hanoverian Succession, had as its primary purpose the exclusion of the Catholic Stuarts. This aim largely determined the development of the English state in the seventy years after the Revolution, influencing both the adoption of 'libertarian' policies like religious toleration, and the enactment of repressive legislation – the Riot Act, the Septennial Act, the Black Act. Jacobitism allows us to contemplate the nature of eighteenth-century English government and

[33] See J. Arthur Price, 'Side Lights on Welsh Jacobitism', *Y Cymmrodor*, 14 (1901), pp. 136–53; Herbert M. Vaughan, 'Welsh Jacobitism', *T.H.S.C.* (1920–1), pp. 11–39; Donald Nicholas, 'The Welsh Jacobites', *T.H.S.C.* (1948), pp. 467–74; P. D. G. Thomas, 'Jacobitism in Wales', *W.H.R.*, 1, 3 (1962), pp. 279–300; Philip Jenkins, 'Jacobites and Freemasons in Eighteenth-Century Wales', *W.H.R.*, 9, 4 (1979), pp. 391–406, his *The Making of a Ruling Class: The Glamorgan Gentry, 1640–1790* (Cambridge, 1983), esp. ch. 6, and his 'Tory Industrialism and Town Politics: Swansea in the Eighteenth Century', *H.J.*, 28, 1 (1985), pp. 103–23.

society from the perspective of its avowed nemesis. Whether England emerges as a 'liberal' or an *ancien régime* polity will be a major concern of this investigation.

The first part of the following work deals with Jacobite rhetoric and argument as it appeared in propaganda. Polemical prose, poetry and material artefacts provide relatively accessible means by which to appreciate the patterns of Jacobite political culture. Part Two examines the structural foundations of Jacobite activity, from the underground networks that promoted the cause to the denominational differences that weakened it. Popular politics – riots, demonstrations, seditious words cases – is the subject of Part Three. To paraphrase Horace Walpole, Jacobitism was the 'hidden mother' of decades of popular dissension; but how closely was plebeian unrest linked to Jacobite political culture? From here we turn in Part Four to contrasting forms of individual adherence to the banished Stuarts: the peaceable, sociable Jacobitism of the gentry, and the militant loyalty of the rebels of 1715 and 1745. Finally, we may arrive at a fuller understanding of the role of the 'Kings over the water' within the cultural systems of the late seventeenth and eighteenth centuries. They were the devils of William-ite and Hanoverian cosmology, but we will be contemplating them mainly as their supporters did, in the guise of sacred and mystical beings. If this characterization is impossible for us to regard without disbelief, it is because a great intellectual distance must be bridged between us and the world in which James Francis Stuart's smile was recognized as that of a vital and living god.

PART ONE

Jacobite rhetoric

Chapter 1

Laws of man and God: the moral foundations of Jacobite political argument

> Englishmen can have no pretence whatsoever to rise up against their *lawful*
> *King* because *The King* of England can do no Wrong.
>
> > *Robin's Last Shift*, 1715/16[1]

The association of Jacobitism with divine right theory once served as a reason for relegating its political writings to the dustbin of intellectual history.[2] Historians generally assumed that the Stuart conception of monarchy had been utterly discredited by the triumph of William and Mary, and that divine right held appeal thereafter only to a tiny residue of reactionary fanatics, particularly the Nonjurors. The political attitudes of the Nonjuring clergy were seen as 'preposterous' and ridiculously anachronistic.[3] Such Whiggish assessments illustrated a woeful lack of understanding of Jacobite political argument. As several more recent studies have shown, the formidable intellectual structure of monarchist theory retained considerable influence after 1688. George Cherry pointed out the legal strength of the Tory constitutional position, which he mistakenly labelled 'Jacobite', in the Convention of 1689, and Gerald Straka emphasized the importance of 'providentialist' thought in justifying the transfer of sovereignty to William and Mary.[4] Mark Goldie, H. T. Dickinson and J. A. W. Gunn have

---

[1] [George Flint], *Robin's Last Shift ... Part I* (London, 1717), no. 3, 3 March 1715/16, p. 83.

[2] By divine right, I mean the belief that the authority of government was derived solely from God. The old classic, J. N. Figgis, *The Divine Right of Kings* (2nd edn, New York, 1914; reprinted 1965), deals very cursorily with the period after 1688.

[3] L. M. Hawkins, *Allegiance in Church and State: The Problem of the Nonjurors in the English Revolution* (London, 1928), pp. vii, 53–4.

[4] George L. Cherry, 'The Legal and Philosophical Position of the Jacobites, 1688–1689', *Journal of Modern History*, 22, 4 (1950), pp. 309–21; Gerald M Straka, 'The Final Phase of Divine Right Theory in England, 1688–1702', *English Historical Review*, 77, 305 (1962), pp. 638–58. Providentialism, however, should not be equated with divine

examined the continuing appeal of Tory divine right theory in the post-Revolutionary period.[5] J. P. Kenyon has extended these views much further by maintaining that 'contract' theory, especially the Lockean variety, played little part in the debate over the legality of the Revolution, which centred on ideas of 'abdication' and 'vacancy', less offensive to Tory consciences.[6] The reappraisal of divine right has culminated in the claim of J. C. D. Clark that the English state after 1688 repeatedly invoked divine sanction as 'the most powerful (and, at that time, the only convincing) justification for monarchy'.[7] Far from being 'preposterous', divine right now seems ubiquitous and eminently reasonable.

Yet Kenyon's and Clark's revisionist interpretations may have obscured the definition of divine right, because they tone down the rhetorical differences between constitutional theories. Jacobites are distinguished from Williamites by little more than their choice of king, and the Revolution of 1688 is reduced to a power-shuffle. Historians who have dissented with revisionism, however, have concentrated on the limited achievements of radical Whigs as evidence of change under the Williamite regime.[8] In fact, the outraged Jacobites provide us with a much better perspective from which to assess the Revolution settlement. They insisted that the old constitutional framework had been smashed into pieces, and that monarchical legitimacy had been sacrificed to self-serving principles. The conservative image of the Revolution that has been highlighted by Kenyon and Clark did not convince the Jacobites; they looked beyond it at the moral foundations of sovereignty, and saw both illegality and weakness. Through their eyes, we can appreciate the revolutionary consequences of 1688.

Jacobite political argument, however, cannot be subsumed entirely

---

right. See also Straka's *Anglican Reaction to the Revolution of 1688* (Madison, Wisconsin, 1962).

[5] M. A. Goldie, 'Tory Political Thought, 1689–1714', unpublished Ph.D. dissertation, Cambridge University, 1977, esp. chs. 6 and 11; H. T. Dickinson, *Liberty and Property: Political Ideology in Eighteenth-Century Britain* (New York, 1977), ch. 1; J. A. W. Gunn, 'The Spectre at the Feast: The Persistence of High-Tory Ideas', in *Beyond Liberty and Property: The Process of Self-Recognition in Eighteenth-Century Political Thought* (Kingston and Montreal, 1983), pp. 120–93.

[6] J. P. Kenyon, 'The Revolution of 1688: Resistance and Contract', in McKendrick, ed. *Historical Perspectives*, pp. 43–69, and his *Revolution Principles: The Politics of Party, 1689–1720* (Cambridge, 1977), esp. ch. 2.

[7] Clark, *English Society*, p. 126.

[8] See Lois Schwoerer, *The Bill of Rights, 1689* (Baltimore, 1981); Gary S. De Krey, 'Political Radicalism in London after the Glorious Revolution', *Journal of Modern History*, 55, 4 (1983), pp. 585–617.

within the boundaries of divine right. As Paul Chapman demonstrated in his pioneering dissertation, Jacobite propaganda was remarkably diverse, and offered a wide-ranging and often radical critique of English government and society.[9] A distinctive Jacobite point of view developed through an alliance of divine right with Country principles; it reaffirmed the sanctity of monarchy, while upholding the rights of the people against injustice.[10] Howard Erskine-Hill has suggested that radicalism and conservatism were united within Jacobite argument by a consistent pattern of themes and images, such as the comparison of usurpation to violent rape.[11] Underlying this rhetoric was a sense of moral conviction, in which divergent and conflicting strains of political theory merged into a single ethical vision. Its subversive power hindered the Williamite and Hanoverian regimes from establishing themselves on a firm constitutional basis, and its effects could be detected even after 1760 in the awkward formulation of English sovereignty.

This chapter deals with Jacobite political argument as expressed in prose works; poetry is considered in the next chapter. The media for constitutional debates in this period were pamphlets and journals rather than verse. The Jacobite Muse, therefore, must await her moment, while the grandiose machinery of Jacobite political thought is paraded before us.

Divine right and the Nonjurors

It is fitting to begin with the Nonjurors, that long-suffering remnant of the Restoration Church. They were unflinching adherents of divine right; but it must be stressed at the outset that they did not advocate unbridled royal power. The belief that the authority of kings derived from God, and that they were consequently not to be resisted, did not entail support for the freedom of monarchs to do as they pleased. The notorious Robert Filmer may have been alone in his admiration for unrestricted or arbitrary monarchy; the apologists for royal power in the 1680s, as James Daly has shown, wrote of the King as absolute and

[9] Paul Chapman, 'Jacobite Political Argument in England, 1714–1766', unpublished Ph.D. dissertation, Cambridge University, 1983. In this context, 'radical' means that which questions the 'roots' of existing authority.
[10] See Paul Monod, 'Jacobitism and Country Principles in the Reign of William III', *H.J.*, 30, 2 (1987), pp. 289–310.
[11] H. Erskine-Hill, 'Literature and the Jacobite Cause: Was there a Rhetoric of Jacobitism?', in Cruickshanks, ed., *Ideology and Conspiracy*, pp. 49–69.

irresistible, but did not sanction arbitrary rule.[12] Filmer, in fact, was seldom cited by Jacobite writers, and never for his opinions on monarchical power; to represent divine right theory as Filmerian, an error many historians have fallen into, is like characterizing British socialism as Marxist-Leninist.

Jacobite propaganda drew a clear distinction between absolute and arbitrary monarchy. Charles Leslie, the most extreme divine right theorist among the Nonjurors, and their most prolific controversialist, asserted in his *Rehearsals*, a series of essays published in 1704–8, that '[t]he king is the only *fountain* of *power* in the *kingdom*. Neither *lords*, nor *commons*, nor any *other* have any *authority*, but what they derive *wholly* and *solely* from the *crown*; and the *crown* holds of none but God'.[13] Yet royal power was not unrestricted. On the contrary, the King

> is *bound* by all the ties that are possible to *bind* a *king*. He is *bound* by his *oath* to God at his *coronation*, as well as his *promise* to his *people*. He is *bound* by all the *laws* of *justice* and *honour*. And I will add, that he is *bound* by his *interest* too; which with some is the strongest tie. For it cannot be his *interest* to *provoke* his *people*, lest factions shou'd arise: of which there has been frequent and fatal *examples*.[14]

A 'contractualist' could not have asked for much more than all this. Nevertheless, according to Leslie, it was unlawful to resist the power of the monarch even if he broke these ties. The subject was bound to observe the rule of passive obedience towards his sovereign, even if the ruler violated all the laws and behaved arbitrarily.

Passive obedience is very difficult for modern observers to understand, and it would seem to make a mockery of the nice distinction between absolutism and arbitrariness. In spite of the Nonjuring insistence on it, however, it was more an ideal goal than a practical imperative. In fact, there were two ways around it. First, passive

---

12 James Daly, 'The Idea of Absolute Monarchy in 17th Century England', *H.J.*, 21, 2 (1978), pp. 227–50. The same distinction prevailed in France; see Roland Mousnier, *The Institutions of France under the Absolute Monarchy* (2 vols., Chicago and London, 1979), vol. i, pp. 659–65. For Filmer, see Peter Laslett, ed., *Patriarcha and other Political Works of Sir Robert Filmer* (Oxford, 1949); Gordon J. Schochet, *Patriarchalism in Political Thought: The Authoritarian Family and Political Speculation and Attitudes, Especially in Seventeenth-Century England* (Oxford, 1975), esp. chs. 7–8; J. W. Daly, *Sir Robert Filmer and English Political Thought* (Toronto, 1979).
13 'Philalethes' [Charles Leslie], *A View of the Times, their Principles and Practices: in the ... Rehearsals* (6 vols., London, 1750), vol. i, no. 37, 7 April 1705, pp. 227–8.
14 *Ibid.*, vol. ii, no. 140, 18 Sept 1706, p. 356.

obedience might become in practice a sort of passive resistance. The obvious example is the case of the Seven Bishops in 1688; they failed to comply with King James's orders regarding the Declaration of Indulgence, but they did not see themselves as resistors.[15] Secondly, as the Nonjuring cleric Jeremy Collier noted, 'though the Supream Magistrate is unaccountable, yet his Ministers are not'.[16] Everything objectionable in a monarch's behaviour could be represented as the fault of bad advice from wicked counsellors. If a king could do no wrong, his servants obviously could.

Their respect for sovereign authority, therefore, did not incline the Nonjurors towards despotism. They even saw themselves as defenders of lawful liberty. The liberties of the subject in a divine right monarchy were based not upon inalienable right but upon the free grace of the crown. The lay Nonjurors John Byrom and Robert Thyer argued in 1748 that 'most of our boasted Liberties, even the great Charter itself, are only so many *Concedimus*'s from the Crown, as appears by the very form of them'.[17] Once liberties had been granted, however, they should not be violated or revoked. The Nonjurors, like everyone else on the political scene, praised Magna Carta, *habeas corpus*, and the unrivalled beauty of that invisible goddess, 'the Constitution'. As Matthias Earbery put it in 1731, in reply to an attack on the Nonjurors made in *The Craftsman*, 'I know not of any of these Assertors of the Divine Right of Government, who suppose Men were born for Slavery: The Good of Society is the Freedom of Society'.[18]

If the Nonjurors were really promoters of 'Freedom', why was it thought necessary to impose such a rigid and restrictive construction on monarchical authority? Perhaps the best answer can be found in Leslie's *Rehearsals*, which represented divine right as the only alternative to anarchy and popular tyranny:

> To cure the *tyranny* of a *king*, by setting up the *people*, is setting 10000 *tyrants* over us instead of *one*. It is *hell* broke *loose*, and worse than the worst of *devils*. And besides, it admits of no remedy, we have no *prospect* of the *end*. There is nothing but eternal *revolution* and *confusion*, in advancing the power of the *people*. One *party* WORRYING *another*; and *another* UNDERMINING, and then WORRYING *that*, for each *party* are equally the *people*.[19]

[15] See J. R. Western, *Monarchy and Revolution: the English State in the 1680s* (London, 1972), pp. 231–4.
[16] [Jeremy Collier], *Vindiciae Juris Regii* (London, 1689), p. 40.
[17] [Byrom and Thyer], *Manchester Vindicated*, pp. 321–2.
[18] [Matthias Earbery], *The Occasionall Historian, No. II* (London, 1731), p. 72.
[19] [Leslie], *Rehearsals*, vol. i, no. 51, 21 July 1705, p. 313.

The lack of a divinely sanctioned authority, in short, would prevent the establishment of any sort of ultimate authority; the result must be party strife, an endless struggle for domination. Popular government would throw society back into a Hobbesian state of nature in which power-hungry individualism would rule. This 'kingdom of ME' was Leslie's nightmare — 'to reduce all to the *noble savage* again! to make *mob* the *supreme*, and *kings* and *queens* to *worship* us, and *wear* OUR *liveries*!'.[20] Force would replace justice, right and wrong would depend upon numbers. Popular sovereignty, therefore, would bring with it the negation of liberty. 'It is to me surprising', Earbery reflected, 'that Republicans, who pretend so much to Liberty, will not shew it by one Transaction, when they are in power.'[21]

The Nonjurors saw divinely sanctioned authority as the only safeguard for preserving the moral order of society, which reflected in microcosm the order of the universe.[22] Removing the ordained monarch meant overthrowing God, because kings 'stand before us, in the *person* of the GREAT GOD *himself*, and are *Gods* to us. And can the *people* create *Gods*!'[23] Of course not; rule by the people would lead to the confusion of good and evil, the dissolution of fixed meanings and properties, the disintegration of society. The Nonjurors of the 1690s reached heights of rhetorical zeal in evoking the consequences of this catastrophe. The lay Nonjuror Nathaniel Johnston conjured up 'a long Train of War, Famine, Want, Bloud and Confusion, entailed upon us and our Posterity' as God's punishment for rebellion.[24] An infamous pamphlet of 1693, whose publisher, William Anderton, was executed for high treason, lamented that 'the Gates of Heaven are barr'd against us, and instead of *Blessings* we have *Plagues* and *Judgments*'.[25] These Nonjuring jeremiads answered the 'providentialist' defence of the Revolution, and sought to capitalize on the economic hardship caused by King William's war against France.[26]

20 *Ibid.*, vol. i, no. 14, 4 Nov. 1704, p. 86.
21 [Earbery], *Occasionall Historian, No. IV* (1732), p. 79.
22 For the origins of this view, see Arthur O. Lovejoy, *The Great Chain of Being: A Study of an Idea* (New York, 1936, 1960); E. M. W. Tillyard, *The Elizabethan World Picture* (New York, 1944); Foucault, *The Order of Things*, ch. 2.
23 [Leslie], *Rehearsals*, vol. i, no. 54, 4 Aug. 1705, p. 328.
24 [Nathaniel Johnston], *The Dear Bargain, or, A True Representation of the State of the English Nation under the Dutch* (n.p., 1690?), p. 24.
25 *Remarks upon the Present Confederacy, and Late Revolution in England, etc.* (London, 1693), p. 45.
26 The classic 'providentialist' work was by that apostate from Nonjuring principles, Dean William Sherlock, *The Case of Allegiance Due to Sovereign Powers* (London, 1691).

'Providentialism', however, was not the sole justification for 1688. The seventeenth century had produced an alternative to theocentric political argument – namely, the myth of an 'original contract', which maintained that English history had known a period when sovereignty had resided in the people.[27] Although royalist scholars, among them Nathaniel Johnston, had demolished the historical basis for this claim, it survived in theoretical form in the works of John Locke and other Whig contractualists. To be sure, as J. P. Kenyon and others have stressed, the direct influence of these writers on the Revolutionary settlement was meagre.[28] Nevertheless, the first years of William's reign saw the appearance of a substantial number of contractualist pamphlets; most of them were vague or mild in their assertions, but they were enough to infuriate a Nonjuror.[29] The main impact of the contractualists after 1688 may have been negative; they became the 'straw-men' of Nonjuring invective, just as Filmer had been for Locke himself. Their response to contractualism drew the Nonjurors into the realm of legal and historical scholarship, resulting in some of their finest work, as well as some of their most tiresome. Their object was to prove that an indefeasible hereditary right to the crown was a fundamental doctrine of English law.

With this aim, John Kettlewell settled his 'duty of allegiance' in 1691 by demonstrating the concurrence of natural, human and divine law in the hereditary right of King James II.[30] Charles Leslie devoted several issues of his *Rehearsals* to the historical, legal and Biblical foundations of the principle of hereditary right.[31] In 1713, George Harbin presented a huge volume of impressive erudition to reinforce his view that 'there cannot be any reasonable Dispute, to whom the true Duty of Allegiance

---

[27] J. G. A. Pocock, *The Ancient Constitution and the Feudal Law: English Historical Thought in the Seventeenth Century* (New York, 1967); Corinne C. Weston and Janelle P. Greenberg, *Subjects and Sovereigns: The Grand Controversy over Legal Sovereignty in Stuart England* (Cambridge, 1981).

[28] If Kenyon has over-stated his case, so have his critics, as for example Lawrence Stone, 'The Results of the English Revolutions of the Seventeenth Century', in J. G. A. Pocock, ed., *Three British Revolutions: 1641, 1688, 1776* (Princeton, 1980), pp. 70–1. See also J. R. Jones, *The Revolution of 1688 in England* (New York, 1972), and John Miller, 'The Glorious Revolution: "Contract" and "Abdication" Reconsidered', *H.J.*, 25, 3 (1982), pp. 541–56.

[29] See Mark Goldie, 'The Revolution of 1689 and the Structure of Political Argument', *Bulletin of Research in the Humanities* (1980), pp. 473–564. Dr Goldie kindly sent me a copy of this article.

[30] [John Kettlewell], *The Duty of Allegiance settled upon its True Grounds, According to Scripture, Reason, and the Opinion of the Church* (London, 1691), pp. 16–21.

[31] [Leslie], *Rehearsals*, vol. i, nos. 56–61, 18 Aug. – 28 Sept. 1705, pp. 339–80, no. 66, 13 Oct. 1705, pp. 412–20.

is due, by all Laws, Reason and good Conscience'.[32] In a pamphlet
written after James II's death in 1701, and republished in the crucial
years 1714 and 1745, the Nonjuring bishop George Hickes stated
James III's case succinctly by asking whether a legitimate child was not
the rightful heir to its father.[33] In short, not only Scripture, but English
law, natural law, and history, designated who was the true king. The
Revolution, therefore, was an offence against nature and the constitution as well as against God.

The intellectual vigour of Nonjuring divine right theory can be
measured by its devastating effectiveness against opponents from Dean
Sherlock to Bishop Hoadly.[34] Yet it was unable to overcome a basic
shortcoming: it had little to say about the exercise of power. Passive
obedience and non-resistance were useless in dealing with a monarch
like James II, who was determined to pursue unpopular policies that
threatened the Church of England. The Nonjurors could not deny that
James had a right to act as he did, but few of them could stomach his
goal of reintegrating Roman Catholics into political life.[35] James's
religion was anathema to his Protestant subjects, and if his removal was
difficult to justify constitutionally, it was easy to see it as a practical
necessity. Nevertheless, if the Nonjurors failed to resolve this contradiction between theory and practice, they were constant reminders of
the contradictions that existed in the Revolution settlement. The thin
veil of constitutional conservatism fabricated by both Whigs and
Tories in the aftermath of 1688 afforded little protection against the
withering blows of the faithful adherents of divine right, and if English
politics had been a purely intellectual game, the Nonjurors would have
won it handily. Not until the 1760s, when Jacobitism had been reduced
to a ghostly shade, could the defenders of the existing order lay claim to
the legitimacy of divine sanction without fear of a furious counter-

32 [George Harbin], *The Hereditary Right of the Crown of England Asserted* (London, 1713), p. 15.
33 [George Hickes], *Seasonable Queries Relating to the Birth and Birthright of a Certain Person* (n.p., 1714), previously published as *The Pretences of the Prince of Wales Examin'd, and Rejected* (London, 1701), and as *Some Queries proposed to Civil, Canon and Common Lawyers* (n.p., 1712). For the 1745 version, see P.R.O., S.P. 36/68, fos. 90, 92.
34 For these controversies, see J. C. Findon, 'The Nonjurors and the Church of England, 1689–1716', unpublished D.Phil. dissertation, Oxford University, 1978, and Mark Goldie, 'The Nonjurors, Episcopacy, and the Origins of the Convocation Controversy', in Cruickshanks, ed., *Ideology and Conspiracy*, pp. 15–35.
35 The best accounts of this campaign are in John Miller, *Popery and Politics in England, 1660–1688* (Cambridge, 1973), chs. 10–14, and his *James II: A Study in Kingship* (Hove, 1978).

attack. After three-quarters of a century of uncertainty, and with the great Nonjuring polemicists safe in their graves, conservatives could pretend that the Revolution had been an example of the resilience of a sacred and 'organic' constitution; but their radical critics were more correct in seeing it as a severe, albeit unexploited, disruption.[36]

The 'Whiggish' Jacobites

Ironically, the efforts of the Nonjurors in the 1690s fuelled political developments that were anathema to them: bitter party rivalry, and the re-emergence of radical Whiggery.[37] If the situation threatened the Jacobites, however, it also offered them new opportunities. Radical Whigs could quickly become disillusioned with William III's resistance to change, and some of them found common ground with Jacobites in a Country programme. The ex-Leveller Major John Wildman, for example, was making overtures towards St Germain by 1690.[38] His dalliance was brief, but a trio of his radical Whig colleagues who turned to King James around the same time were able to bring about a significant alteration in Jacobite rhetoric.[39] These 'Whiggish' Jacobites were of diverse backgrounds, although all were outsiders in English politics. Sir James Montgomery was a prominent Scottish Presbyterian politician, who had plotted with William of Orange before the Revolution; he was propelled into Jacobitism in 1689 by William's failure to satisfy the demands of the Presbyterian party.[40] His fellow Scot Robert Ferguson had been an Independent minister under the Protectorate; ejected from his English living at the Restoration, he became a virulent Exclusionist pamphleteer, was privy to the Rye House Plot, and accompanied the invasions of the Duke of Monmouth in 1685 and the Prince of Orange in 1688. Shortly after the Revolution, Ferguson apparently underwent a conversion to Anglicanism, which combined

---

[36] See Clark, *English Society*, ch. 4; Dickinson, *Liberty and Property*, chs. 7–8.

[37] See Henry Horwitz, *Parliament, Policy and Politics in the Reign of William III* (Manchester, 1977); Caroline Robbins, *The Eighteenth Century Commonwealthman* (Cambridge, Mass., 1959), esp. ch. 4; Mark Goldie, 'The Roots of True Whiggism, 1689–94', *History of Political Thought*, 1, 2 (1980), pp. 195–236.

[38] Maurice Ashley, *John Wildman: Plotter and Postmaster* (New Haven, Ct, 1947), pp. 291–8.

[39] They have been discussed in Goldie, 'Roots of True Whiggism', pp. 228–9; Paul Hopkins, 'Aspects of Jacobite Conspiracy in the Reign of William III', unpublished Ph.D. dissertation, Cambridge University, 1981, ch. 6; and Monod, 'Jacobitism and Country Principles', pp. 297–301.

[40] See his entry in *D.N.B.*; also J. Halliday, 'The Club and the Revolution in Scotland, 1689–90', *Scottish Historical Review*, 45 (1966), pp. 143–59.

with poor treatment by King William and a paranoid personality to transform him into a violent Jacobite.[41] The third of the 'Whiggish' Jacobites was Charlwood Lawton, a barrister and friend of William Penn, the Quaker patriarch. His journey from Whiggery to Jacobitism was largely motivated by a concern for a 'civil comprehension' that would remove religious restrictions on office-holding.[42]

The political writings of these three men illustrate the mistake of associating Jacobitism too closely with the high-flying rhetoric of the Nonjurors. The 'Whiggish' Jacobites all saw William III as a greater enemy to liberty than King James. Montgomery asserted that William had made a contract with the English people in 1688, through the terms of his invasion declaration, which had called for the restoration of English liberties, but had explicitly renounced any designs upon the crown. Since then, according to Montgomery, 'King William's manifest infraction of that original contract which we made with him ... doth evidently and unanswerably dissolve and make void the obligations of our oaths' to him.[43] These infractions included the suspension of *habeas corpus*, restrictions on freedom of the press, a lack of respect for Parliamentary legislation, and the imposition of unjust taxes to support an unnecessary war.[44] Charlwood Lawton shared his apprehension about William's behaviour:

I think our present Conquerors have not reviewed many of our *good old*, or made many *New* advantageous *Laws* for us. It is by *Unreasonable Fines, Arbitrary Imprisonments, Pressing men contrary to Law*, &c. (against all of which things the P. of O. his own *Declaration* inveighed, and our *Bill of Rights* provided) that they maintain their Conquests.[45]

Just as Montgomery employed contract theory, Lawton used the Bill of Rights to condemn William's 'tyranny'. For his part, Robert Ferguson concentrated on the abuses of justice in the treason trials of the early

---

41 See *D.N.B.* and James Ferguson, *Robert Ferguson the Plotter* (Edinburgh, 1887), which mentions his religious conversion on p. 265.

42 See *D.N.B*; [Charlwood Lawton], *Civil Comprehension* (London, 1705), and his *A Second Letter concerning Civil Comprehension* (London, 1706). Although sympathetic to Quakerism, Lawton seems to have remained an Anglican. Paul Hopkins has kindly provided me with much information about him.

43 [Sir James Montgomery], *Great Britain's Just Complaint for her late Measures, present Sufferings, and the future Miseries she is exposed to* (n.p., 1692), in *Somers, Tracts*, vol. x, p. 468.

44 *Ibid.*, pp. 449–56.

45 [Charlwood Lawton], *A French Conquest neither Desirable nor Practicable* (London, 1693), p. 17.

1690s.[46] He also manufactured the outrageous theory that William was an agent of the Vatican, whose ultimate aim was the destruction of the Church of England.[47]

The Jacobite court encouraged the 'Whiggish' Jacobites, especially after the failure of the La Hogue expedition in 1692, because it saw them as an alternative to the Nonjurors, who had been unsuccessful in broadening Jacobite support in England. James II also wished to resurrect the alliance with the Whigs that had sustained his toleration policies in 1687–8.[48] Yet to what extent was 'Whiggish' Jacobitism distinct from Nonjuring Jacobitism? At first glance, they seem entirely different. Sir James Montgomery, for example, refused to justify King James's behaviour before the Revolution; monarchs, he believed, should be held accountable for their actions by their subjects.[49] No Nonjuror could have agreed with this. Lawton, who invented the term 'Whiggish' Jacobite, wrote scornfully of 'the high flights of some *Jacobites*' – clearly, the Nonjurors – who 'whilst they too much cajole Kings ... lose their Interest with the People'.[50] Ferguson, while noting in one pamphlet that Scripture enjoined obedience to existing powers, nevertheless added, 'I cannot say, that ... the King of Great Britain would be innocent, in the sight and esteem of the supreme sovereign, should he levy money of his people without their antecedent consent in parliament.'[51] Although carefully worded, this was the kind of individual judgment on monarchy that the Nonjurors deplored.

The differences between 'Whiggish' Jacobites and Nonjurors, however, were not insurmountable. Charlwood Lawton praised the courage of those who had refused the oaths, and had proved that 'they have not supple *time-serving-Providential Consciences*'; he was also

---

[46] [Robert Ferguson], *A Letter to Mr. Secretary Trenchard* ([London], 1694), and his *A Letter to the Right Honourable, My Lord Chief Justice Holt, occasioned by the Noise of a Plot* ([London], 1694).

[47] [Robert Ferguson], *Whether the Preserving the Protestant Religion was the Motive unto, or the End that was designed in, the late Revolution?* ([London], 1695), in *Somers Tracts*, vol. ix, pp. 549–69, and his *The History of the Revolution* (n.p., 1717).

[48] B.L., Add. MS 37,661, *passim*; James II, *His Majesties most Gracious Declaration to all his Loving Subjects ... April 17 S.N. 1693* (n.p., 1693); Rev. J. S. Clark, ed., *The Life of James the Second, King of England, &c. Collected out of Memoirs Writ of his Own Hand* (2 vols., London, 1816), vol. ii, pp. 498–514; J. R. Jones, 'James II's Whig Collaborators', *H.J.*, 7, 1 (1960), pp. 65–73.

[49] [Montgomery], *Great Britain's Just Complaint*, pp. 437–40.

[50] [Charlwood Lawton], *The Jacobite Principles Vindicated* (London, 1693), p. 11.

[51] [Ferguson], *Whether the Preserving ...* , p. 558.

much esteemed by the Nonjuring bishop George Hickes.[52] The idea of liberty, as has been seen, was not abhorrent to the advocates of divine right; and the 'Whiggish' Jacobites in fact espoused many of the basic assumptions of the Nonjurors. Lawton acknowledged that kings had a prerogative that should be inviolate, although he did not accept that it should be an 'unlimited and unexplained Dispensing Power'.[53] He vested great importance in 'our Ancient, Legal, Limited and Hereditary Monarchy', and exhorted James II to '[c]ome Home, *Great Sir*, to Restore our *Trade*, ... to Deliver *Us* from DUTCH Delusions ... and to Establish all the *Liberties* of the *English* subject'.[54] Sir James Montgomery deplored the results of the Revolution in having 'turned our hereditary monarchy into an elective', and the inimitable Ferguson could describe the King of England as 'a Sovereign Prince, whose Person ... is *Sacred* and Inviolable; who cannot legally be resisted, opposed or withstood, and much less be judged, deposed or abdicated by any Power on Earth, or any Pretence whatsoever'.[55] Charles Leslie himself could have written these words, which were penned by men who had resisted and opposed the Stuarts for decades.

The 'Whiggish' Jacobites often borrowed rhetoric from the Nonjurors. Lawton and Montgomery both described the Revolution as an act of conquest perpetrated upon a people seduced by false promises. As Montgomery put it:

truly few people did suspect that the prince did really design what he so seriously and solemnly declared against; and every man was struck into state lethargy by the suddenness of the prince's attempt, the wonderful success it met with in the beginning, and the charming wheedle of securing liberty and property, which we are sadly and severely roused from at last by unspeakable oppressions, by the expiring groans of liberty and property, and by the dreadful view of those miseries, which threaten us from all hands and in all events.[56]

The echo of the Nonjuring jeremiad was deliberate, although the moral tone was more forgiving – after all, Montgomery had himself been 'infatuated' in 1688. 'We have been pulling down destruction with both our hands upon ourselves,' Sir James warned, 'and unless we

---

52 [Lawton], *Jacobite Principles*, pp. 5–6; C. E. Doble, *et al.*, eds., *Remarks and Collections of Thomas Hearne*, Oxford Historical Society (11 vols., 1884–1918), vol. ii, p. 60.
53 [Lawton], *Jacobite Principles*, p. 5.   54 [Lawton], *A French Conquest*, p. ii.
55 [Robert Ferguson], *A brief Account of some of the late Incroachments and Depredations of the Dutch upon the English* ([London], 1695), p. 68.
56 [Montgomery], *Great Britain's Just Complaint*, p. 468; [Lawton], *Jacobite Principles*, pp. 19–21.

repent, and repair these errors, the punishments we deserve will certainly overtake us.'[57] In a similar but sterner passage, Ferguson denied that 'all that sea of blood spilt in Europe' would be enough to 'wash away the blots and stains' brought upon Protestantism by the Revolution; only when 'we have taken the ignominy and reproach upon ourselves ... and have charged and lodged it upon our own disloyalty, pride and covetousness' would the sin be forgiven.[58] In spite of the tinge of Calvinist rigour, this language was reminiscent of a High Church sermon for 30 January, the commemoration of the 'martyrdom' of Charles I.

The intellectual and rhetorical mutations of the 'Whiggish' Jacobites were typical of many disillusioned radicals of the 1690s. William's refusal to sponsor further reform, and the emergence of the Court or Junto Whigs as the dominant element in the party, drove numerous 'old Whigs', like Sir Robert Harley, towards a Country alliance which could accommodate both Tory scruples about the sanctity of monarchy and Whig concerns for the rights of the subject.[59] To a large extent, the 'Whiggish' Jacobite polemicists passed from Whiggery to Jacobitism over the bridge of Country principles. It is hardly surprising to find that Charlwood Lawton became a close friend and adviser to Harley, or that Robert Ferguson turned to writing Harleyite propaganda after 1700.[60] The Nonjurors joined them in the Country camp; by the mid-1690s, they too were bitterly denouncing the conduct of the war, the corruption of ministers, the influence of the Dutch and the perversion of justice in the courts.[61] Jacobite Country propaganda, whether of 'Whiggish' or Nonjuring hue, emphasized that these evils were symptoms of the moral disintegration of government and society under an illegal usurpation. In spite of their political differences Jacobite writers were agreed that legitimate kingship had a vital moral significance for the English people.

---

[57] [Montgomery], *Great Britain's Just Complaint*, p. 441.
[58] [Ferguson], *Whether the Preserving ...* , p. 558.
[59] Goldie, 'Roots of True Whiggism', pp. 229–36.
[60] H.M.C., *The Manuscripts of his Grace the Duke of Portland* (10 vols., London, 1891–1920), vol. iv, pp. 287–8, 448, 478, 561, 611–12; Ferguson, *Ferguson the Plotter*, pp. 380–5.
[61] See [Thomas Wagstaffe], *A Letter to a Gentleman elected a Knight of the Shire to serve in the present Parliament* (n.p., 1695?); [Samuel Grascome], *An Appeal to all True Englishmen (If there be any such left;) Or, A Cry for Bread* (n.p., 1695?); [Samuel Grascome], *An Account of the Proceedings in the House of Commons, In Relation to the Recoining the Clipp'd Money, and Falling the Price of Guineas* (London, 1696).

The Jacobite journals, 1714–53

By William III's death in 1702, Jacobite political argument had become a variety of Country rhetoric, and had drawn closer to the mainstream of Toryism. The accession of Queen Anne, however, put Jacobitism into temporary eclipse, as it appeared that High Church aspirations could be met without a restoration.[62] The party struggles of Anne's reign soon dampened Tory hopes, and the Nonjurors regained importance after 1704 as implacable opponents of compromise with Whiggery. The Tory triumph of 1710, and the revival of concern over the succession, inspired a new flood of Nonjuring polemics. The popularity of Toryism, manifested in the Sacheverell affair and in overwhelming electoral victories, emboldened the Nonjurors to adopt a new attitude; the exile of the Stuarts was now blamed on a malevolent Whig faction, not on the whole nation. Charles Leslie began to think it possible to rescue 'a giddy People ... [d]ebauch'd by crafty, insinuating Men' and by 1715, with a popular reaction to George I's accession in full swing, Leslie could surmise that providence had at last converted the English public.[63] Decades of Hanoverian rule transferred the burden of guilt entirely from the people to the Whig party – as a Nonjuror explained to an 'old Whig' in a pamphlet of 1748, taxes, standing armies, corruption, placemen, 'the whole lot has been brought upon you by the sole Direction and Management of the *Whigs*, and them only'.[64]

This change in the Nonjuring attitude towards 'the people' was accompanied by the emergence of a Jacobite periodical press, edited by laymen. The Jacobite journals that flourished after 1714 should be seen both as responses to popular sentiment, and as reflections of a profound transformation of English political discourse. Before the Revolution, the most widespread medium for political debate was the pamphlet, a self-contained tract or treatise, firmly rooted in constitutional theory, and usually laden with Biblical allusions. The 'institutionalization' of Parliament as a permanent political forum under William III, and the polarization of party politics under Queen Anne, infused English government with a sense of mutability and of

---

62 For an example of Jacobite despondency, see [Thomas Wagstaffe], *The Present State of Jacobitism in England. A Second Part. In Answer to the First* (London,1702).

63 [Charles Leslie], *The Right of Monarchy Asserted* (London, 1713), pp. 9–10; [Charles Leslie], *Mr. Lesley to the Bishop of Sarum* (n.p., [1715]), pp. 5–7.

64 *A Remarkable Dialogue, Which lately happened In the Gardens of Luxembourg at Paris, Between An Old Impartial English Whig, and a Nonjuror of the Church of England, Concerning the Young Chevalier* (Edinburgh, 1748), pp. 16–17.

recurrent flux. The fixed meanings, rigid logic and Scriptural legitimation that had characterized the Nonjuring pamphlet of the 1690s
were unsuited to this situation. The voice of the new politics was the
periodical press – brief, effervescent, ephemeral, popular. If Jacobite
newspapers and magazines were less weighty than pamphlets, if their
reasoning was simplistic and inconsistent, if they relied on innuendo
and sly allusions rather than overtly treasonable statements, they
nevertheless reached a wider audience, and proved to be more resilient.
The tracts of the Nonjurors could be silenced by force, but when a
Jacobite journal was cut down, it usually sprang up again.[65]

The longest running Jacobite newspaper was published by Nathaniel
Mist, who took over Robert Mawson's *Weekly Journal, or Saturday's
Post* in 1716; it ran for twenty-one more years, as *Mist's Weekly
Journal* in 1725–8, and *Fog's Weekly Journal* in 1728–37, after Mist
had been forced into exile. Mist's partner Doctor Gaylard printed the
Jacobite *Freeholder's Journal* in 1722–3, following it with *The Loyal
Observator Reviv'd; or, Gaylard's Journal*, while John Purser, who
worked for 'Fog', produced the *National Journal* in 1746. The other
main Jacobite periodical in the early years of George I was George
Flint's *The Shift Shifted*, succeeded by *Robin's Last Shift*, of March–
September 1716. Hints of Jacobitism can also be detected in Elizabeth
Powell's High Church women's journal *The Orphan Reviv'd* of
1718–19, in the Duke of Wharton's *True Briton* of 1723–4, and in
Charles Molloy's *Common Sense* of 1737–9, which was funded by the
Pretender. The Nonjuror Matthias Earbery was responsible for the
short-lived *Universal Spy: Or, the Royal Oak Journal Reviv'd* in 1732.
George Osborne edited the Jacobite magazine *Mitre and Crown* in
1748–50, as well as the *True Briton* of 1751–3, which contained
contributions by the Catholic Jacobite John Caryll.[66] Jacobitism in the

[65] For the periodical press in the early eighteenth century, see Michael Harris, *London
Newspapers in the Age of Walpole: A Study of the Origins of the Modern English
Press* (London and Toronto, 1987).

[66] For details, see *D.N.B.* (Mist; his relative James Mist of Windsor Castle kindly
provided me with more accurate details about his background); H.M.C., *Calendar of
the Stuart Papers Belonging to His Majesty the King, Preserved at Windsor Castle* (7
vols., London, 1902–23), vol. vi, pp. 551–2, vol. vii, p. 19 (Flint); Fritz, *English
Ministers and Jacobitism*, p. 88 (*Freeholder's Journal*); Lewis Melville, *The Life and
Writings of Philip, Duke of Wharton* (London, 1913), and Mark Blackett-Ord,
Hell-Fire Duke: The Life of the Duke of Wharton (Windsor, 1982); P.R.O., S.P.
36/28, and P.R.O., K.B. 33/5/6 (*Universal Spy*); R.A., Stuart 137/68, 190/12,
199/108, and G. H. Jones, 'The Jacobites, Charles Molloy, and *Common Sense*',
Review of English Studies, New Series, 4, 13 (1953), pp. 144–7; David Greenwood,
William King, Tory and Jacobite (Oxford, 1969), pp. 77–80 (*Common Sense*);

provincial press was mainly limited to reprints of Mist's seditious editorials, although a genuine strain of provincial Jacobite journalism can be found in Henry Crossgrove's *Norwich Gazette* (1715–43) and Elizabeth Adams of Chester's *Weekly Courant*, for which John Byrom and Robert Thyer wrote their 'Manchester Vindicated' essays in 1746–8.[67]

These Jacobite periodicals were very popular. Paul Chapman has estimated that Mist's papers sold about 10,000 copies every week in the 1720s; one printer ran off this many copies of the 1728 'Persian Letter' issue on his press alone. Around 1720, according to Chapman, the Jacobite journals may have had a combined weekly readership of 200,000, making them equal rivals to the government press.[68] Of course, these figures must be handled carefully; they do not reveal how many people read Jacobite newspapers simply to learn the news, to peruse the advertisements, or to see what that trouble-maker Mist was up to now. Nevertheless, the Jacobite press was certainly in the vanguard of commercial journalism, and reached a large audience, including persons of influence. Judging by its advertisements, clergymen and country gentlemen were particularly attracted to Mist's papers, while the Harley family were avid readers of *Robin's Last Shift*.[69]

The Jacobite journals, with the partial exception of Wharton's *True Briton*, were thoroughly Tory, and imbued with High Church religiosity. They vilified Dissent and championed Anglican orthodoxy against its Erastian and Latitudinarian foes. Mist, a self-described 'Foil to the Atheistical Host', printed High Church arguments against Bishop Hoadly during the Bangorian controversy; among his letter-writers was a Tory lady who suggested that King George himself was allowing

P.R.O., S.P. 44/83, fos. 508–13, 521–2 (*National Journal*); B.L., Add. MS 28,236, *passim*, and Add. MS 28,252, fos. 101–5, 172–226 (*True Briton*).

67 R. M. Wiles, *Freshest Advices: Early Provincial Newspapers in England* (Ohio, 1965), pp. 282–8, mentions four provincial newspaper printers of the period who were prosecuted for Jacobite libels: William Ayscough of the Nottingham *Weekly Courant* and Philip Bishop of *The Exeter Mercury* in 1716 (see B.L. Stowe 750, fos. 224, 234); Crossgrove in 1718 (see also B.L. Add MS 5,853, pp. 554–9); and Edward Farley of *Farley's Exeter Journal* in 1728 (see P.R.O., S.P. 44/81, pp. 526, 549; S.P. 44/83, p. 13). See also G. A. Cranfield, *The Development of the Provincial Newspaper* (Oxford, 1962), and Rev. O. M. Tyndale, '"Manchester Vindicated" and the Later Nonjurors', *T.L.C.A.S.*, 53 (1938), pp. 119–30. Francis Clifton's *Oxford Post* of 1719 was probably printed in London (P.R.O., S.P. 35/15/31).

68 Chapman, 'Jacobite Political Argument', pp. 198–211.

69 R. B. Walker, 'Advertising in London Newspapers, 1650–1750', *Business History*, 15, 2 (1973), p. 121 (I owe this reference to Kathleen Wilson); H.M.C., *Portland*, vol.v, p. 574.

the Dissenters to ruin the Church.[70] Dissent was closely associated in High Church demonology with republicanism, which was reviled as a far worse tyranny than 'Popery'. As George Flint – who was, interestingly, a former Roman Catholic seminarian – asked rhetorically:

Which is the greater Slavery, Presbitery or Popery? Which is the greater Slavery, Monarchy, or a Common-wealth? Both these Questions I take to be resolv'd in this one: Which is the greater Slavery, to have one Pope than Ten Thousand; to have one King or Seven Hundred; for every Preacher of the Presbitery is a Pope, and every Head of the Common-wealth is a King.[71]

Thirty–two years later, the *Mitre and Crown* took up the same theme in maintaining that Presbyterians, like ultramontane Catholics (but unlike most Catholic Englishmen), believed in the lawfulness of resistance to kings, and hated hereditary monarchy.[72] Even those Jacobite papers that contained little discussion of religion were hostile to Dissenters. Wharton's *True Briton* castigated them for narrow-mindedness, while the *National Journal* accused them of having abandoned King James II after he had sacrificed himself for toleration.[73]

Although their religious position remained unchanged, the constitutional attitudes of the Jacobite periodicals altered markedly between 1714 and 1753. At first, they adopted an old-fashioned, *jure divino* approach to government. *Robin's Last Shift* opined that kings were the vice-gerents of God, and should always be obeyed; Mist printed letters in support of non-resistance and passive obedience.[74] King James III, however, was seeking to cement some kind of alliance with dissident Whigs; he still preferred political unity to 'faction', and may have believed that the Whigs would favour a broader toleration. After 1720, this goal began to seem possible, initially through the Wharton–Cowper group in the House of Lords, then through the Earl of Sunderland, who turned to the Stuart court for assistance in over-

---

70 *The Weekly Journal, or Saturday's Post*, no. 33, 27 July 1717, p. 197; no. 95, 4 Oct. 1718, p. 565.
71 [George Flint], *The Shift Shifted*, no. 9, 30 June 1716, p. 51.
72 [George Osborne] *The Mitre and Crown; or, Great Britain's true Interest*, vol. i, 2 Jan. 1748/9, pp. 250–2.
73 [Philip Wharton, Duke of Wharton], *The True Briton*, no. 22, 16 Aug. 1723; also nos. 36–7, 42, 4, 7, 25 Oct. 1723; *A Collection of Political and Humourous Letters, Poems and Articles of News, Publish'd in an Evening Paper, intitled, The National Journal, or, Country Gazette* (London, 1748), no. 32, 3 June 1746, pp. 102–4.
74 *Robin's Last Shift*, no. 3, 3 March 1715/16, pp. 83–4; *Weekly Journal*, no. 33, 27 July 1717, p. 197; no. 94, 27 Sept. 1718, p. 562; no. 95, 4 Oct. 1718, p. 565.

coming his nemesis, Sir Robert Walpole.[75] Political reality, therefore, militated against the propagation of divine right theory, which might alienate Whig allies. A more practical constitutional stance was mapped out in the early 1720s by the *Freeholder's Journal*. 'The People obey the Law', it noted, 'when they obey the good Prince, and as much as they obey it, when they vindicate themselves from Tyranny and Oppression, and this, and this only is to be termed *true Loyalty*.'[76] Wharton's *True Briton*, written by an ostensible 'old Whig', vaguely suggested a popular foundation for government, proposing, for example, that ministers could be guilty of treason against the people.[77] At the same time, Mist's papers began casually dropping references to an 'original contract', and quoting freely from Locke. In 1722, *Mist's Weekly Journal* remarked with approval that whenever England had been oppressed by 'arbitrary and illegal Rulers', 'we have found the *Ability* and *Means* to throw off the Yoak that galled Us'.[78] This passage might have pleased Locke without offending Charles Leslie, because an arbitrary and illegal ruler could not claim divine right.

From 1726 until 1742, Tories and dissident Whigs supported each other in a Country opposition to Walpole, a strategy unceasingly advocated by Nathaniel Mist, by then a key figure in the coordination of Jacobite policy.[79] *Fog's Weekly Journal* echoed his advice, but was careful to maintain a delicate balance between the idea of resistance and the sanctity of monarchy. In a lengthy editorial published in 1732, 'Fog' allowed of the Glorious Revolution that 'the Cause was just, the People formed the Measures for their own Relief, and Providence concurred in the Means used for their Preservation'. The Nonjurors would have been appalled; they would have been shocked further by 'Fog's' acceptance of 'what is called the Original Compact of Government'. Yet he left the details of this 'Compact' deliberately obscure, and explained that when he justified the Revolution, he meant only the events of November–December 1688, not the actions of the Convention. He denied that the deposition of monarchs was necessary, suggesting instead the imposition of further limitations on the crown:

---

[75] See C. B. Realey, *The Early Opposition to Sir Robert Walpole, 1720–1727* (Philadelphia, 1931), pp. 81–5, 124; Sedwick, ed., *History of Parliament*, vol. i, pp. 108–9. Sunderland's protégé, the 'commonwealthman' John Trenchard, was elected at Taunton in 1722 with help from local Tories and Jacobites – P.R.O., S.P. 35/34/6.

[76] *A Collection of Political Essays and Letters in the Freeholder's Journal* (London, 1722), no. 24, June 13, 1722, p. 139.

[77] *True Briton*, no. 44. 17 Feb. 1723.

[78] *Mist's Weekly Journal*, no. 166, 3 Feb. 1722, pp. 994–5.

[79] See R.A., Stuart 120/30, etc.

What wou'd have been the Case had King *James* stood his Ground, and had nothing been under the Consideration of the Legislature but the past Miscarriages of his Reign, his Religion or Evil Counsellors is a point no one can now determine. It is not impossible, but there might have been formed such Limitations as wou'd have secured and satisfy'd the Nation in all these Points ... To secure the Enjoyment of our Laws and Liberties was the Justification of that Resistance; but who shou'd be the King, independent of any other Cause, I hope was never thought to be the Cause of the Revolution.

Resistance, in short, should not have extended as far as altering the succession. Had the restrictions proposed by the Tories in the Exclusion Crisis been accepted, 'Fog' implied, the Revolution would have been avoided.[80] This view was strikingly similar to that of Sir James Montgomery, who had also praised the Tory call for limitations in 1679 as a means of constraining rather than undermining the monarchy.[81]

If *Fog's Weekly Journal* represented the high tide of Tory accommodation with Whiggery, George Osborne's *Mitre and Crown* and *True Briton* can be seen as a reaffirmation of divine right constitutionalism. By the late 1740s, the Country alliance had broken up, and the isolated Tories were wavering between the Hanoverian and the Jacobite Princes of Wales.[82] Osborne's journals tried to counter the drift towards Prince Frederick by recalling the theories on which Toryism had been founded. Subjects were 'obliged to submit to the *uncontroulable* Power of their Governors', wrote Osborne; and like Filmer, he did not bother to distinguish between absolute and arbitrary power. He scorned 'the imaginary Natural Rights all Men are said to be equally entitled to', and condemned the notion of original contract as making the King 'the Servant of his People, and liable to be depos'd at the Mercy of the Mob'. Although he acknowledged that '*Particular* Forms of government may be alter'd, by the Consent of all interested', as had been attempted by the Tories in the Exclusion Crisis, there could be no questioning of the 'Divine and Hereditary Right of the English Monarchy'.[83] This was *jure divino* at its most dogmatic, without the careful logic of the Nonjurors.

The Tory party was stricken after 1745, and Osborne might be seen as the spokesman of a dying movement, trying to revive itself by recovering its past. Yet he and his journalistic collaborators – John

[80] *Fog's Weekly Journal*, no. 184, 13 May 1732.
[81] [Montgomery], *Great Britain's Just Complaint*, p. 432.
[82] Colley, *In Defiance of Oligarchy*, pp. 253–60.
[83] *Mitre and Crown*, nos. 15–17, July–Sept. 1749, pp. 509–20.

Caryll, Edward Gibbon (father of the historian) and General James
Oglethorpe (who had returned to his family's traditional Jacobitism) –
were involved with a vigorous popular movement that played an
important role in the politics of the late 1740s and early 1750s, the
Independent Electors of Westminster.[84] Osborne's *True Briton* strenu-
ously defended Alexander Murray, a Jacobite leader of the Independent Electors who was gaoled in 1751 for contempt of the House of
Commons. In language redolent of Country principles and 'liberta-
rianism', the *True Briton* maintained that the House had violated
Murray's constitutional rights, which

> ought to excite the Care of every Lover of Liberty, and the Constitution to
> quarel [*sic*] against all Encroachments which may possibly terminate in the
> Loss of our Liberties, and the ruin of our Constitution ... if in no Instance
> Persons committed by that House, can have redress elsewhere, then their Power
> is *absolute* and *arbitrary* in every Case, and over every Commoner in
> England.[85]

Was this 'libertarian' rhetoric compatible with divine right? The
Nonjurors had first argued that it was, that 'liberty' and constitutional
safeguards could coexist with absolute monarchical sovereignty.
Osborne was merely following in their footsteps.

In their changing constitutional stance, the Jacobite journals were
reacting to the fortunes of the Tory party from 1714 until the early
1750s. Three features, however, distinguished Jacobite publications
from the milder strains of 'conventional' Tory argument: a readiness
to blame the ruling monarch for ministerial policy, the use of an
historical or moral typology of restoration, and occasional veiled
references to the exiled Stuarts themselves. All were dangerous tactics;
the government was quick to prosecute any hint of treasonable libel.
The printers and publishers of *Fog's Weekly Journal*, for example,
were arrested in 1732 for characterizing William III as an enemy of
liberty, a promoter of standing armies, and the originator of the
national debt.[86] The *National Journal* was luckier in escaping the law
in 1746 when it replied to the assertion made in a Tory paper that
'Richard II' (i.e. George II) should not be held responsible for the

---

[84] For Osborne's contacts with Caryll, Gibbon, Oglethorpe and other Tory politicians,
see B.L., Add. MS 28,249. See also Nicholas Rogers, 'Aristocratic Clientage, Trade
and Independency: Popular Politics in Pre-Radical Westminster', *P.&P.*, 61 (1974),
pp. 70–106, and Chapters 3 and 5 below.

[85] [George Osborne and John Caryll], *The True Briton*, vol. ii, no. 8, 14 Aug. 1751,
pp. 163, 166.

[86] *Fog's Weekly Journal*, no. 177, 25 March 1732; P.R.O., S.P. 44/82, pp. 67, 84.

actions of his ministers. On the contrary, the Jacobite journal argued, the unfortunate Richard 'was no more than the Tool of his Ministers ... If a Tool be a Part of the Government, *Richard* was a Part ... the People call for the Punishment of the Ministers and their Tools; instead of being punished, they are skreaned, they are honoured, they are rewarded.'[87] In order to save the constitution, the people should turn against the King as well as his ministers.

The historical typology of restoration was less blatant but equally treasonable. In 1660, a Stuart king had been restored to a throne taken from his father by 'Dissenters' and 'republicans'. Not surprisingly, the Jacobite journals revelled in the commemoration of Restoration day on 29 May, and made great sport of the fact that George I's birthday was on 28 May. Crossgrove's *Norwich Gazette* gave an annual snub to King George by printing the taciturn comment that his birthday had been 'observ'd here with the Usual Demonstrations of Joy and Loyalty', while noting that the 'Anniversary of the Happy Royal Family' on 29 May had been marked by bell-ringing from morning until midnight, streets strewn with flowers, sprigs of oak in every hat or bosom, all to celebrate 'that Happy RESTAURATION, on which *Religion* and *Liberty* returned with our BANISH'D KING', ending 'a long and miserable Rebellion and Usurpation ... under a most Arbitrary Tyrannical Power of an Hypocritical Restless FACTION'.[88] It took little wit to see in this 'faction' the face of Whiggery, or to deduce who the present 'BANISH'D KING' might be. Coincidentally, James Francis Stuart's birthday was on 10 June, which allowed *Fog's Weekly Journal* to perpetrate an audacious stunt in 1730. In the week after Restoration day, four days before the Pretender's birthday, 'Fog' printed General Monck's 1659 speech to the army, in which he urged his troops to 'resolve upon the Restoration of our Lawful King'. The paper apologized for the late appearance of the article, claiming that it had arrived too late for inclusion in the previous issue.[89] The same trick was repeated in 1734 and 1735, and copied by the *True Briton* in 1751.

Restoration day had a moral as well as an historical significance. Mist, for example, employed 29 May as a symbol of universal regeneration in a thinly disguised piece of 1721:

---

[87] *National Journal*, no. 10, 12 April 1746. The word 'skreaned' alluded to the 'Screen-Master' of the South Sea Bubble affair, Sir Robert Walpole.

[88] *Norwich Gazette*, 2 June 1717. I owe this reference to Kathleen Wilson.

[89] *Fog's Weekly Journal*, no. 89, 6 June 1730. The government was not fooled, but could take no action because the speech had been quoted *verbatim* – P.R.O., S.P. 36/19, fo. 102.

After wickedness had received its utmost Perfection in the Destruction of the *King* [Charles I, or James II]; we groaned under the oppressive Force of a cruel, ill bred *old Tyrant* [Cromwell, or George I] and the drivelling *Fool* his Son [Richard Cromwell, or George, Prince of Wales], whilst the *Royal* progeny wandered from Court to Court to find Protection ... Upon the RESTORATION ... there was a Universal Change, from all that was wicked and detestable, to all that was good and desirable. This Change was effected in a most miraculous Manner, with very little human Interposition: They who wish'd well to it, were kept back from assisting the Promotion of it, that the Hand of God might appear more visibly in it: They who wish'd ill to it were restrain'd from obstructing its Advancement.[90]

The Restoration, in other words, evidenced the divinely sanctioned kingship of the Stuarts, and brought with it a general revival of morality; it was a cosmic event, modelled on Christ's resurrection. This typology of moral restoration reappeared in later Jacobite writings, although it was transformed from a purely Christian into a largely 'classical' image. The fear that the national spirit was in decay, and could only be saved by a return to past virtues, was passed down, as J. G. A. Pocock has shown, from Tacitus to Machiavelli, Harrington and Bolingbroke.[91] The *National Journal* warned in 1746 of the general spread of corruption: 'Luxury and Effeminacy have ever been the Daughters of Extravagance and Profusion, those in their Nature make way for Corruption, which will ... determine in downright Slavery and the overturning of the Constitution.'[92] The paper was suppressed for printing advice to Jacobites to mourn rather than celebrate on 10 June, 'when they behold their Country, at home, enervated with Luxury, involved in an excessive national Debt, and in Danger of being enslaved by Corruption'.[93]

The theme of a Jacobite 'restoration of virtue' was given enormous impetus by Dr William King's Latin oration at the opening of the Radcliffe Camera at Oxford in April 1749. King punctuated his litany of modern wickedness with cries of 'REDEAT ILLE MAGNUS GENIUS BRITANNIAE' (restore that great *genius* of Britain).[94] The speech had a great effect on Jacobite propaganda; it clearly inspired an article in *Adams's Weekly Courant* in March 1754, prefacing a poem on corruption:

[90] *Mist's Weekly Journal*, no. 130, 27 May 1721, p. 775.
[91] See J. G. A. Pocock, 'Machiavelli, Harrington and English Political Ideologies in the Eighteenth Century', in *Politics, Language, and Time: Essays in Political Thought and History* (New York, 1971), pp. 104–47, and his *The Machiavellian Moment* (Princeton, 1975).
[92] *National Journal*, no. 34, 7 June 1746.   [93] *Ibid.*, no. 35, 10 June 1746, p. 122.
[94] See Greenwood, *William King*, pp. 197–203; 'The Opening of the Radcliffe Library in 1749', *Bodleian Library Quarterly*, 1 (1915), pp. 165–72.

For as much as many of your Readers are, without doubt, extreamly well affected and intirely devoted to the *true Interest* of their KING and COUNTRY; and would be very glad to live (I dare say,) to see a RESTORATION – of *Religion*, – *Liberty*, – *Publick Virtue*, – *and of every Thing*, in short, that is *honest, lovely, and of good Report*: – I shall therefore, (with your Leave,) make bold to present them with the Following Rhapsody: ...[95]

'*Honest, lovely, and of good Report*' referred to the 'MAGNUS GENIUS BRITANNIAE' himself, Charles Edward Stuart. The 'restoration of virtue' theme, like the historical typology of 1660, converted a complex political situation into a simple moral problem, to which there was a panacea: 'REDEAT'.

In spite of their frequent appeals for a restoration, the Jacobite periodicals seldom invoked the image of the Pretender. An infamous exception was the 'Persian Letter', written by the Duke of Wharton and published in *Mist's Weekly Journal* in 1728:

He [James Francis Stuart] is a Prince whose gracious Behaviour is sufficient to win, his Majesty to awe, and his Courage to face the most inveterate of his Enemies. His Sufferings have added Experience and Patience to those endearing Qualities, in order to compleat the greatest Character that ever Eastern Monarch bore. The Misfortunes of his Subjects grieve him more than his own, such is his Public Spirit.[96]

The usurper 'Meryweis' (George I) and his son 'Esreff' (George II) were by contrast avaricious, vain, tyrannical and despised. This clever satire was imitated from Montesquieu's *Lettres Persanes*, an early example of the influence of French Enlightenment thought on Jacobitism. Its publication caused Mist to flee the country, and kept Wharton in exile until his death. Significantly, it was presented as a sort of fairy tale – the exiled Prince was the hero of a fable. In fact, a fairy tale atmosphere pervaded all Jacobite efforts to portray the Stuart claimants. A pamphlet of 1721 pictured James III as a jovial country gentleman, who ate 'only of the *English* Dishes, and made his Dinner of Roast-Beef, and what we call *Devonshire* Pye'.[97] After the '45, Charles Edward's exploits in Scotland quickly became the stuff of myth, and were popularized in works like *Alexis; or, The Young Adventurer, Ascanius* and *Young Juba*.[98] Like the 'Persian Letter', these fabulous accounts

[95] *Adams's Weekly Courant*, no. 1093, 26 March 1754.
[96] *Mist's Weekly Journal*, no. 175, 24 Aug. 1728.
[97] *A Letter from an English Traveller at Rome to his Father, of the 6th of May 1721* (n.p., 1721), p. 6.
[98] *The Chronicle of Charles, the Young Man* ([Edinburgh?, 1745?]); [Alan Macdonald of Kingsborough], *Alexis; or, The Young Adventurer* (London, 1746); 'J. Burton',

attributed Bonnie Prince Charlie with a magical personal charm; their intention was to create a legendary folk hero, a Prince for the people. 'How deeply he enters into the Interest of the People,' marvelled one pamphleteer in 1750, 'and how just his Notions are of kingly Duties.'[99]

This was a far cry from the ponderous phrases of Hickes and Leslie. Party conflict and the commercial press had buried the reasoned absolutism of divine right under waves of populism and emotionalism; the god-like sovereign had been replaced by the fairy tale Prince. Jacobitism had adapted to the new politics by embracing it, in all its vigour and superficiality. The Jacobite journals turned wherever the winds of opposition blew – towards radical Toryism, Country principles, a Whig alliance, 'patriotism' and 'virtue'. Yet they tended to avoid serious questions – above all, the question that had once plagued the Jacobites, of why a Roman Catholic king should be entrusted with the protection of the Church of England. That was left for James III and the ageing Nonjurors to answer, with promises and assurances – the King had been raised as a Gallican and was not subservient to Rome, he might be induced to become an Anglican, his religion was preferable to the Lutheranism of the Hanoverians.[100] The failure of the Jacobite press to address such issues illustrates the wish of many High Churchmen to forget the problems of the past and to seek consolation in the prospect of 'a Universal Change, from all that was wicked and detestable, to all that was good and desirable'.

Pseudo-Whigs and radicals, 1715–78

The Jacobite journals constantly chided the Whigs for having abandoned liberty in favour of 'arbitrary government'. *Robin's Last Shift* enquired sardonically in 1715/16 '[t]hree or four Years ago, who such zealous Patriots as the Whigs? Who appeared more inveterate and inveighed more against the horrid Curse of arbitrary Power ... ? The

Ascanius: or, The Young Adventurer; A True History (London, 1746); 'M. Michell', *Young Juba* (London, 1748). Ralph Griffiths, the friend of Johnson and Goldsmith, admitted to being the author of *Ascanius*, plagiarized from the novel *Alexis* – P.R.O., S.P. 36/93, fos 65–7. Charles Edward himself penned an autobiographical work in this genre – R.A., Stuart 307/173.

99   *A Letter from H[enry] G[oring], Esq., One of the Gentlemen of the Bed-Chamber to the Young Chevalier* (London, 1750), p. 13.

100 See [Leslie], *Lesley to the Bishop of Sarum*, pp. 5, 11–12; James III, *His Majesty's Letter to the Reverend Mr. Charles Lesley. Urbino, Nov. 29, 1717 N.S.* (n.p., 1717); 'A Letter to Richard Steele, Esq.' in Bodl. Rawl. MS D. 1081, fos. 9b–10, printed in London in 1715 by Mrs Powell's husband Edmund. Abel Boyer, *The Political State of Great Britain* (40 vols., London, 1711 – 40), vol. ix, p. 107.

Inference is easily drawn.'[101] George Flint's paper warned of impending legislation '1. To continue this present House of Commons during his Majesty's Pleasure. 2. To suspend Magna Charta ... 3. To give a vote for a Lecturer to every one in the Parish, Tag-rag and Bob-tail'; and if any should complain about this combination of tyranny and Dissenting 'Church-democracy', Walpole himself was said to have answered, 'we have an Army, and you must, like Children, have Physick cram'd down your Throats to do you good'.[102]

Yet not all Jacobite propaganda after 1715 was overtly anti-Whig. In fact, it became a favourite ploy for Jacobite writers to disguise themselves as Whigs. The Stuart court encouraged this subterfuge, because it nurtured, as always, the dream of a bipartisan restoration; and even George Flint saw it as a worthwhile ploy.[103] In 1716, one pseudo-Whig pamphlet, *To Robert Walpole Esq.*, propounded the idea of electing James III to the throne, because 'a King elected to it would receive it under such Restraints as we Electors should lay it under'.[104] This proposal revealed the confidence of the Jacobites in their own popularity, and exhibited a willingness to allow new limitations on the crown; but it did not signify an espousal of the notion of elective monarchy. A companion piece, purportedly a reply from Walpole to the first pamphlet, unabashedly described James as being 'of divine race, the Majesty of *Jupiter*, the valour of *Mars* and the charms of *Venus* have conspired to make him the delight of God and Man'.[105] The two works make up an elaborate joke: the Jacobite writer suggests an elected monarchy, the Whig minister rhapsodizes about James Stuart's divine right.

Like most eighteenth-century political humour, pseudo-Whig Jacobitism was based on inversion – the Whigs had become Tories, the Tories Whigs. The same observation inspired Jacobite publicists from the Duke of Wharton to John Byrom to write in the guise of 'old Whigs' – really new Tories – who were disgusted by the repressive and oligarchical tendencies of the 'modern Whigs'. The notorious Jacobite pamphlet of 1719, *Ex Ore Tuo Te Judico. Vox Populi, Vox Dei*, maintained that all legitimacy came from the people; but the first part of the title betrayed its real purpose. Since the populace obviously favoured King James over King George, the author observed, the

[101] *Robin's Last Shift*, no. 6, 25 March 1715/16, p. 162.
[102] *Ibid.*, no. 9, 14 April 1716, pp. 230–1.
[103] See H.M.C., *Stuart*, vol. vii, p. 239.
[104] 'William Thomas', *To Sir Robert Walpole Esq.* (n.p., 1716?), p. 7.
[105] 'Rt. W.', *To Mr. William Thomas* (n.p., 1716?), p. 4.

restoration of the Stuarts should be supported by the Whigs. The treatise was, however, a satire, as was revealed in its opening sentence, a statement not of popular sovereignty, but of indefeasible hereditary right:

From the Solemnity of the CHEVALIER'S Birth, the moral impossibility of putting an Imposter on the Nation after the Manner pretended, and the disappointment in the attempt of proving him so, I think its Demonstration [sic], If HEREDITARY RIGHT be any recommendation, He has that to plead in his favour; and all Assertors of Limited Monarchy must allow that ought to be preferr'd if the Person having it, is endow'd with other Qualities fit to Govern.[106]

The government suspected a Nonjuror of having penned the piece, and Thomas Hearne was informed that it had been written by Samuel Brewster, a Tory barrister of Lincoln's Inn.[107] The authorities were so infuriated by it that they executed one of its printers, the young John Matthews, for high treason.

Two years later, *A Letter from a Whigg at Rome* appeared. Its author was William Godolphin, Viscount Rialton, the Duke of Marlborough's grandson and a former Whig who had gone over to the Tories. He insisted in his pamphlet that he was not a Jacobite, but argued that the tyranny of George I and his ministers had left the nation with the choice 'either to open our Arms to the Chevalier *de St. George*, or resolve to live in a perpetual allarum and mistrust'. Fear of arbitrary power, 'which banished the Father, make us receive the Son'.[108] Rialton's logic was unclear – even if King George was a tyrant, why should the Stuart claimant be the only other alternative? The standard answer, of course, was hereditary right; but this was more of a Tory than a Whig principle. In spite of repeated efforts to break the mould, there remained a certain inevitability about the Toryism of Jacobite propaganda. Pseudo-Whig arguments, however, should not be dismissed as trivial exercises in irony. They arose from a sentiment that was strongly felt in both parties – that factionalism should cease and all Englishmen come together to guarantee the future happiness of the nation. At the heart of Jacobite pseudo-Whiggery lay a longing for a return to unity.

106 *Ex Ore Tuo Te Judico. Vox Populi, Vox Dei* (n.p., 1719), p. 1. The copy in Bodl., 4° Rawl. 563 contains important marginal corrections. See also R. J. Goulden, 'Vox Populi, Vox Dei: Charles Delafaye's Paperchase', *The Book Collector*, 28, 3 (1979), pp. 368–90.

107 Doble *et al.*, eds., *Collections of Hearne*, vol. iii, p. 80; Joseph Foster, *Alumni Oxonienses: The Members of the University of Oxford, 1500–1714* (5 vols., Oxford, 1891–2), vol. i, p. 178.

108 [Viscount Rialton], *A Letter from a Whigg at Rome* (London?, 1721?), pp. 3–4.

This was not merely a nostalgic or reactionary notion; it could motivate radicalism as well. The search for a new and more perfect stability preoccupied Tom Paine as much has it did the Nonjurors, and the illusion that a 'golden age' might have existed at some time in the past fascinated radicals from the Levellers to Friedrich Engels. Jacobite rhetoric, in fact, may have influenced radicalism long after the Stuart cause had become decrepit. *The Whisperer* was a weekly paper of the early 1770s, edited by William Moore. Some of Moore's pieces verged on republicanism, but his journal also appealed to a Jacobite audience. Charles Edward Stuart was a regular reader, and Robert Gordon, the last regular Nonjuring bishop in England, praised Moore's virulent attacks on George III and the house of Hanover.[109] When he called King George 'a tool of state, / The government arbitrary, / The c[row]n insolvent − Elective', Moore might have been writing for the *True Briton*.[110] Although he claimed to abominate 'Tories, Jacobites and Scotchmen', Moore expressed indifference about which family held the throne, and was polite enough to call James Francis Stuart 'the *old Chevalier*', a Jacobite epithet, in an article vilifying George III as 'the present Idiot' and rebuking the Earl of Mansfield for betraying his erstwhile Jacobite friends.[111] No wonder that Moore was disavowed by radicals as a renegade trying to force an end to liberty of the press, or that he was accused of Jacobitism by the government.[112]

He was not the only radical publicist whose work owed something to the Jacobites. On Ash Wednesday in 1774, the *Public Advertiser*, in which Junius's letters had appeared, published an extraordinary letter from 'A SOUTH BRITON' on the Glorious Revolution:

This day eighty-four years ... an herald was proclaiming two undutiful children K— and Q— of England, etc. But ... [t]hey in a short time afterwards were obliged to appear where rebellion, perjury, fraud, cunning and deceit would stand in no good stead ... If we look into morality, our governors since that period, by their wicked example of bribery, corruption, dissipation, gambling, and every species of wickedness that can be committed, have so debauched the morals of the people that morality is in the same deplorable

[109] Henry Paton, ed., *The Lyon in Mourning*, Publications of the Scottish Historical Society, 20-2 (3 vols., Edinburgh, 1895–6), vol. iii, pp. 248, 252; R.A., Stuart, Additional Papers, Box 6, no. 102.

[110] *The Whisperer*, no. 5, 17 March 1770, p. 25. The 'secret history' of the house of Hanover in no. 56, 9 March 1771, pp. 343–8, owed much to [Matthias Earbery], *An Historical Account of the Advantages that have Accru'd to England, by the Succession in the Illustrious House of Hanover* (London, 1722), and *The Second Part of the Historical Account ...* (London, 1722).

[111] *The Whisperer*, no. 42, 8 Dec. 1770, p. 266; no. 96, 14 Dec. 1771, p. 606.

[112] *Ibid.*, no. 7, 31 March 1770, p. 46; no. 56, 9 March 1771, p. 348.

condition of liberty, property, and religion, viz., almost vanished from these once happy isles.[113]

Bishop Gordon was delighted by this attack, which was in the grand style of the Nonjurors; his friend Bishop William Forbes distributed 1,000 copies of it in Scotland. The printers of the paper, the celebrated Woodfall brothers, were imprisoned and fined for treasonable libel.[114] The author of the piece remains unknown; but in 1778, the young antiquarian Joseph Ritson, who had many connections in radical circles, published a genealogical table of the Kings of England, prefaced by a diatribe on the Revolution that closely paralleled the Ash Wednesday letter. Ritson concluded that hereditary right had lawfully descended from James II to James III and his son, Charles III.[115] Evidently, the heirs of Jacobite political argument after 1760 did not all become conservative propagandists for the Hanoverian king. The old promises of unity and moral regeneration continued to appeal to the imaginations of English radicals even after the Stuart cause had collapsed.

Historians can perhaps discern a 'Victorian mentality' or an 'Edwardian mind'; the eighteenth century, however, was a period of intellectual confusion. It was not 'the age of Locke'; but it was not the age of Charles Leslie either. If we attempt to simplify the situation into a struggle between conflicting points of view – Whig versus Tory, Hanoverian versus Jacobite, radical versus conservative – we will find that what at first appeared to be clear contrasts soon become amorphous, until finally opposites seem to blend together. The Jacobites, for example, adopted 'Whiggish' or Country attitudes; they altered their constitutional position to allow popular resistance to oppression; they imitated Whig 'contractualists', and left a legacy to radicalism. Where does Jacobitism end, and 'Revolution principles' begin? Yet Jacobite political argument was not wholly amorphous. It floated around a fixed position, like fog around a lamp-post. It constantly reiterated the themes that had been established by the Nonjurors: the importance of monarchical sovereignty, the moral degeneration of illegitimate regimes, the hope of revival through a restoration of the rightful King.

---

113 Paton, ed., *Lyon in Mourning*, vol. iii, pp. 295–6.   114 *Ibid.*, pp. 306, 338–9.
115 Bertrand H. Bronson, *Joseph Ritson, Scholar-at-Arms* (2 vols., Berkeley, 1938), vol. i, pp. 57–60. George Osborne wrote a similar work in 1753 – B.L., Add. MS 28, 236, fo. 64.

These ideas reverberated through seventy years of English history, sounding out a drum-beat of condemnation that finally trailed off into both conservative and radical echoes. The Jacobite message, that government must rest upon secure foundations of legitimacy, was constant. From the Jacobite perspective, the Revolutionary settlement was a massive fortress built on sand; they would not have been surprised at how easily it collapsed in the early nineteenth century.

Nevertheless, Jacobitism itself was a ramshackle structure, gathered out of the wreckage of a great system of political thought. Shaped by medieval, Tudor and early Stuart theorists, this system had been decaying since the Reformation, due to the spread of a religious and intellectual diversity that was incompatible with the vision of a unified society. At the centre of the ancient edifice of divine right theory was the image of the king's two bodies – a natural and physical body, which grew old and died, and an immortal body politic, which encompassed his office, the state and the Commonwealth. The origin of royal dualism, as Ernst Kantorowicz has shown, was the two-fold nature of Christ.[116] From the time of Richard II until the Civil War, it was a matter of some contention in English history as to whether or not the king's two bodies could be separated. The Restoration of 1660 asserted that they could not; the Revolution seemed to prove that they could, but the victors sought emphatically to deny it.

The Jacobites undermined that denial, by insisting that the ruling monarch had no legal claim to the throne, and that power was replacing right. They recognized that the Revolution, in spite of the efforts of its partisans, and the arguments of recent historians, had in fact removed the certainty of monarchical sovereignty and hereditary succession. Consequently, the eighteenth-century state was never fully successful in finding a secure form of legitimation for itself. In times of crisis, like the rebellions of 1715 and 1745, the defenders of the Hanoverian regime usually fell back on anti-Catholicism as the primary justification for the existing order. Only after the fading of Jacobitism could the ruling monarchs claim a hereditary right without drawing attention to the claims of their rivals. This did not, however, fully answer the question of sovereignty. Even William Blackstone, an old Tory, had trouble deciding where sovereignty lay in the 1760s – was it in the king himself, or in Parliament, of which the king was a

[116] Ernst Kantorowicz, *The King's Two Bodies: A Study in Medieval Political Theory* (Princeton, 1957).

part?[117] The cult of monarchy that developed under George III was intoxicating but theoretically empty; to this day, monarchy in Britain has no clear basis, except tradition.

The appeal of Jacobite political argument is obvious; it offered an intellectual security that could be found nowhere else. In Jacobite propaganda, moreover, divine right gradually shed its association with absolutist government, and increasingly became a myth of moral legitimation rather than an excuse for royal power. In this form, it pursued a radical critique of the Revolution and the Hanoverian monarchy. Its strength, however, rested as much in imagery as in theory. To appreciate the images of the Stuart cause, it is necessary to turn to Jacobite verse, which unashamedly revealed the king's two bodies in all their glory and absurdity.

---

117 See William Blackstone, *Commentaries on the Laws of England* (reprint of 1765 edn, London, 1979), vol. i, book 1, ch. 2, pp. 142–3, where 'the sovereign power of the state ... is divided into two branches; the one legislative, to wit, the parliament, consisting of king, lords, and commons; the other executive, consisting of the king alone'. In ch. 7, p. 234, however, 'the law ascribes to the king the attribute of *sovereignty* or pre-eminence'. The king was infallible, perpetual, irresistible and absolute – pp. 238–44. Not surprisingly, Blackstone interpreted 1688 as legal because James II had abdicated – ch. 3, pp. 204–7.

Chapter 2

Jemmy's the lad that is lordly:
popular culture and Jacobite verse

> Appear Oh James! approach thy native shore
> And to their antient State thy Realms restore
> When thou arrivest this nauseous tribe will fly
> Right shall revive and usurpation dye
>
> Jacobite poem, c. 1720[1]

The century after 1660 was the great age of English political poetry.[2] Jacobite verse comprised a large part of the poetic output of the period, but it has not been much appreciated by posterity. The Jacobite Muse held few charms for later generations; she was clothed in doggerel, and her music was crude. Occasionally, it is true, she might inspire a Dryden or a Pope – there are numerous Jacobite references in poems like 'Alexander's Feast' or 'Windsor Forest'.[3] These were not propaganda works, however, and they contained a complexity and ambiguity not to be found in the scribblings of lesser versifiers. The buzzing horde of minor poets and balladeers were not set on immortality; they wrote for the Stuart cause, and for their own livelihood. Most of them remain completely unknown; unlike their Scottish and Irish counterparts, they were not rescued by nationalist antiquarians like Burns or Hogg. Their work was allowed to sink into oblivion, as an embarrassment rather than a national treasure.

Historians have not shown much interest in English political poetry either. Unlike prose, verse was not a vehicle for political argument; it

---

[1] 'Poems', Beinecke Osborn Shelves f. c. 58, p. 79.
[2] See George de F. Lord, gen. ed., *Poems on Affairs of State: Augustan Satirical Verse, 1660–1714* (7 vols., New Haven and London, 1963–75). For a guide to printed works, see D. F. Foxon, *English Verse 1701–1750* (2 vols., Cambridge, 1975).
[3] See Erskine-Hill, 'Literature and the Jacobite Cause', in Cruickshanks, ed., *Ideology and Conspiracy*, pp. 52–4; also his 'Alexander Pope: The Political Poet in his Time', *Eighteenth-Century Studies*, 15, 2 (1981–2), pp. 123–48.

did not usually admit the other side of a debate, and it approached most issues without much sense of 'reasonable' judgment. In short, it was irresponsible, loudly and even violently partisan, apparently lacking in self-consciousness, redolent of prejudice rather than principle. Yet its direct and forceful imagery could convey a sense of dynamism that was often missing from prose works; hesitation, doubt, vacillation were overwhelmed by a primitive music. Of course, it would be a mistake to interpret Jacobite poetry as a product of the heart rather than the mind; verse is an artificial medium, and even the most simplistic Jacobite doggerel was cunningly crafted for a desired effect. It aimed, however, to focus rather than to educate sentiments; it was designed to provoke, not to persuade.

Was it in some way a 'voice of the people', a reflection of the culture of those who were not part of the elite of aristocrats, gentlemen, great merchants or professionals? Similar claims have been made for the *Bibliothèque bleue* of Troyes, the popular French chap-books of the seventeenth and eighteenth centuries, and for early modern English almanacs.[4] The weakness of such arguments is obvious. 'The people' did not compose any of this material, and their understanding of it, or reactions to it, are debatable; besides, only a segment of the common folk had Jacobite sympathies. Yet the search for an 'authentic' popular culture is a quest for El Dorado; no source can provide a perspective uncontaminated by elite values and concerns. The popular *mentalité* was far from 'pure'; it constantly soaked up elements of the so-called 'great tradition' of elite culture. It is difficult to determine how these hybrid cultural forms should be interpreted, because plebeians rarely bothered to record the significance of their cultural milieu.[5] The common people, moreover, were as divided as their superiors by religious, political and geographical factors, from which their attitudes

---

[4] Robert Mandrou, *De la culture populaire au XVIIe et XVIIIe siècles: La Bibliothèque bleue de Troyes* (Paris, 1975); Geneviève Bolleme, *La Bibliothèque bleue: La littérature populaire en France du XVIe au XIXe siècle* (Paris, 1971); B. Capp, *Astrology and the Popular Press: English Almanacs 1500–1800* (London and Boston, 1979), and his 'Popular Literature', in Barry Reay, ed., *Popular Culture in Seventeenth-Century England* (New York, 1985), pp. 198–243. For chap-book readership in England, see V. E. Neuburg, *Popular Education in Eighteenth-Century England* (London, 1971), ch. 5; Pat Rogers, 'Classics and Chapbooks', in Isabel Rivers, ed., *Books and their Readers in Eighteenth-Century England* (New York, 1982), pp. 27–45, and his *Literature and Popular Culture in Eighteenth-Century England* (Brighton and Totowa, New Jersey, 1985), chs. 7–8.
[5] Carlo Ginzburg, *The Cheese and the Worms: The Cosmology of a Sixteenth Century Miller* (New York, 1979), manages to reconstruct one plebeian world-view, but his sources are exceptional.

cannot be detached. All that remains is to offer one's own reading of the 'impure' sources that may offer insight into popular culture – a presumptuous, difficult and controversial expedient. The alternative, however, is to remain mute.

To be silent on the subject of Jacobite poetry would be to ignore a whole industry. Long before the creation of a commercialized Jacobite periodical press, ballads and songs were dispersed by the friends of the Stuarts to a popular audience. In June 1693, for example, a printing press was seized by the authorities at Westminster, on which had been run off 'divers new songs, designed to be disperst among the weavers and other discontented persons, to animate them to rise in the holydayes'.[6] In the same month, the grand jury at the London Sessions presented all singers and sellers of ballads for publishing treasonable libels.[7] The problem was not solved in the provinces; at Bath in September 1693, the Marquis of Carmarthen was treated to a chorus of seditious verses sung under his window by some musical Jacobites, 'which they called serenading the marquese'.[8]

In 1716, an epidemic of Jacobite ballad-hawking in London prompted a proclamation by the Lord Mayor against the practice, which was allegedly 'stirring up Seditions and Riots'.[9] Jacobite songs were apparently popular among the artisans and labourers who took part in the disturbances of George I's early years; even seditious variations on Latin odes sold well, and at cheap prices.[10] The hawkers, mostly very poor women, enhanced the treasonable content of their wares by clever sales techniques; one cried out 'you may sing it but I dare not'.[11] They worked for a small number of extremely productive Jacobite printers, including the Irishman Andrew Hinde, John Lightbody and the greatest of them all, Francis Clifton. He was a Lancashire man, educated at Oxford, a convert to Roman Catholicism, who ran his press with the help of his indefatigable wife Catherine.[12] Frequently imprisoned, always in debt, Clifton led a precarious existence, and was not a trustworthy friend; yet he had connections with Bishop Atterbury

---

[6] Luttrell, vol. iii, p. 109.   [7] Ibid., p. 14.   [8] Ibid., pp. 188–9.

[9] Boyer, *Political State*, vol. xi, pp. 747–8; Bodl. B. 8. 23. Jur., no. 35.

[10] A four-page printed classical 'ode' of 1720 on Charles Edward's birth sold for 2d, about the price of a newspaper; see B.L., C. 131, f. 16, no. 7.

[11] P.R.O., S.P. 35/11/21; see also S.P. 35/11/14, (1)–(4), and S.P. 35/11/20.

[12] Foster, *Alumni Oxonienses 1500–1714*, vol. i, p. 292; Thomas Gent, *The Life of Mr. Thomas Gent, Printer of York; written by himself* (London, 1832), p. 85. Gent worked with both Hinde (p. 21) and Clifton; he later moved to York, where he wrote and printed religious chap-books – see Charles A. Federer, *Yorkshire Chap-Books* (London, 1889).

of Rochester, the Tory Jacobite leader.[13] He straddled the boundary between the elite and plebeian classes, and a large public among the latter kept him in business. His career virtually ended, however, with the severe crack-down on the Jacobite press that followed Atterbury's fall in 1722–3.

Jacobite verse was spread in the provinces after 1714 by itinerant 'singing men' who performed in alehouses and taverns.[14] As will be seen in later chapters, seditious ballads and poems fired the blood of provincial rioters, and enlivened the meetings of many Jacobite clubs, some of which had special songs and 'poets-laureate'. Here the distinction between high and low culture broke down, and the same phrases and images appeared in both popular and elite settings. Verses designed for genteel consumption may have been more 'serious' or 'poetic', but squires liked doggerel too, as numerous manuscript collections attest.[15] By the mid-1720s, however, the hiatus of Jacobite poetry was ended, in the provinces as in London. Although the '45 rebellion reinvigorated the tradition of treasonable verse with Scottish airs, English poems on the exploits of Bonnie Prince Charlie tended to be aimed at an elite public; it is unlikely, for example, that many labourers could have enjoyed William King's Latin perorations.[16] Nevertheless, papers like the *True Briton* or *Adams's Weekly Courant* contained some cautiously Jacobite pieces in a more popular idiom, and in 1752 Mark Farley of Exeter was imprisoned for printing a seditious song.[17] A trickle of Jacobite poetry appeared in the 1760s and 1770s, directed at the small remnant of die-hard loyalists. The last-pre-antiquarian compendium of Jacobite verse was *The True Loyalist; or*

---

13 Gent, *Life*, pp. 87–90; for an offer by Clifton to inform on his associates, see P.R.O., S.P. 35/27/33.
14 See P.R.O., S.P. 35/22/57 for the case of George Barker, a singing-man who toured the Midlands and Welsh borders performing Jacobite songs.
15 For example, B.L., Add. MS 29, 981, or Beinecke Osborn Shelves f. c. 58; see also Richard Rawlinson's massive horde of Jacobite ditties in Bodl. Rawl. MSS Poet. 155, 181, 203 and 207. An attempt to distinguish elite from plebeian language can be found in Carey McIntosh, *Common and Courtly Language: The Stylistics of Social Class in 18th-Century English Literature* (Philadelphia, 1986).
16 See Grosart. This chapter will not deal with works in Scots dialect, or those that reflected Scottish nationalist concerns, although some of them are found in English collections. For King's Latin poems, see Paton, ed., *Lyon in Mourning*, vol. ii, pp. 67–8, 78; for a printed Jacobite work in Latin, dated 1749, see B.L., c. 131, f. 16, no. 8.
17 [Alexander Jenkins], *Jenkins's Civil and Ecclesiastical History of the City of Exeter and its Environs, from the Time of the Romans to the Year 1806* (Exeter, 1841), p. 205. Jenkins misdates the case, and the Jacobite riots that broke out at the same time in the town.

Chevalier's Favourite of 1779, a mixture of doggerel and 'serious' pieces that was used by the members of the Edinburgh Royal Oak Society, and perhaps by other gentlemanly clubs south of the Tweed.[18]

In spite of their stylistic differences, elite and plebeian works do not diverge much in content, or even in imagery, and their political point of view was consistent in its rigid, uncompromising Toryism. Untainted by 'Whiggish', pseudo-Whig or any other conciliatory postures, Jacobite verse heartily championed the highest flying principles of divinely sanctioned hereditary monarchy.[19] It cannot be assumed that its aficionados shared these beliefs; but they evidently favoured staunch Toryism in the poems and ballads they read or listened to, and their preference is revealing. It indicates an acceptance of the purpose of polemical verse, which was designed to be simple, demotic and partisan, the expression of powerful desires that needed no justification. Jacobite poetry was not the real 'voice of the people', but an imaginary reconstruction of that voice, a fantasy world of political extremism that was eagerly embraced by many of the people themselves, and thus became part of their culture. They did not create Jacobite verse; they actively encouraged it to create them, like a patron who employs an artist to paint an exaggerated portrait, and who admires in the results precisely what he expects to see in himself.

Above all, the public saw three things in Jacobite poems and songs: a cyclical interpretation of history, a demonic representation of the ruling monarchs, and an evocation of the extraordinary God-man who was the just and lawful king. These were not separate themes, but they can be considered as the individual components of a basic cosmology. Examining them they will not illuminate the plebeian *mentalité* as it really existed; it will, however, show how some of the common people, and part of the elite, wished their world to be represented in verse.

The cycle of history

The circularity of human history was illustrated in Jacobite poetry by the association of the Revolution with the Civil War. Perhaps the earliest piece of anti-Revolutionary propaganda was a broadside

---

[18] See Paton, ed., *Lyon in Mourning*, vol. ii, pp. 330–1, 343, vol. iii, pp. 274–5; *Notes and Queries*, 2nd Series, 1, 14 (1856), p. 265.

[19] Early signs of this staunch Toryism can be found in a collection of the 1690s, 'Loyal Poems', Beinecke Osborn Shelves b. 111, pp. 68, 474–5, 476–8. The only possibly 'Whiggish' Jacobite piece known to me is 'To King William' in Lord, gen. ed., *Poems*

ballad, 'The Ungrateful Rebel', which appeared while William was advancing from the west in November or early December 1688. It concerns 'a disloyal Tutch / Now newly come from the Dutch', who had rebelled with Monmouth in 1685, and now bids his friends 'Stand up for the good old Cause.' Although he claims to act in the name of religion, he admits that 'I cry'd down the Pope, / But 'tis with that hope, / To get a good Booty by't.'[20] This atrocious ballad conveys the Jacobite view of seventeenth-century history as a recurring struggle between rightful monarchy and a set of malicious conspirators who masked their greed and ambition with false religiosity.

'King James's Sufferings Describ'd by Himself', a poem of the early 1690s that was probably composed by a court writer at St Germain, relates the history of the Stuart family as a chronicle of victimization:

> The same Disloyall Brood
> Did shed my Fathers sacred Blood
> Whilst he their hellish Black Designs withstood.
> Then the Rebellious Crew,
> Calls back his Sons again,
> Not for to reign,
> But to be scorn'd and dispossest a new.
> And that my Royall Parent should not be alone,
> I'm Heir both to his Suff'rings, and his Throne ...[21]

The Stuart family, like Christ, was entirely at the mercy of a powerful Satanic faction. Yet the people as a whole were absolved from complicity in the sin of rebellion – in marked contrast to the Nonjuring jeremiads of the same period. Another work of the 1690s portrayed the people as hoodwinked by the scheming William: 'Wee'l all joyn with a foreign Prince / Against our lawfull King / For he from all our fancy'd fears / deliverance will bring.'[22] The use of 'we' is significant; the poet identifies with the crowd even in its errors. Ultimate responsibility for the Revolution lay with the traditional figures of Anglican abuse:

> The *Baptist*, and the *Saint*,
> The *Schismatick*, and *Swearer*;
> Have ta'n the Covenant,

on *Affairs of State*, vol. v, pp. 174–6; the judgment of the editor, however, is that it is a 'traditional Whig' work that oversteps the boundaries of loyal criticism.
20 Frederick George Stephens, ed., *Catalogue of Political and Personal Satires Preserved in the Department of Prints and Drawings in the British Museum* (3 vols., London, 1870–7), vol. i, no. 1207, pp. 734–5. The work can be dated from internal evidence.
21 'Loyal Poems', Beinecke Osborn Shelves b. 111, p. 10.
22 'The Belgick Boar', Bodl. Rawl. MS Poet. 207, pp. 10–17.

That Jemmy comes not here S^r.
Whilst all this Pious Crew do Plot,
To Pull *Old Jemmy* down . . .[23]

Even at a time when King James was courting 'Whiggish' allies, and the
Nonjurors were blaming the English public for the Revolution, Jacobite verse focussed its enmity firmly on the Dissenters.

Underlying this approach was a populist notion that all men were
not wicked, but that a few knaves were in control of the government.
Inverting divine order, they called themselves 'Saints', and at their head
was the Satan-figure of Oliver Cromwell. After 1688, 'Old Noll' and
his 'Oliverian Crew' were almost exclusively the literary property of
Jacobite poets; so the publication in 1690 of an heroic emblematic
portrait of William III, based on an earlier portrait of Cromwell, was a
gift to pro-Stuart satirists. 'On the Late Metamorphosis of an old
Picture of Oliver Cromwell's into a New Picture of King William: The
Head Changed, the Hieroglyphics Remaining' is one of the finest of all
Jacobite poems. It puzzles, in mock innocence, over 'Whether the
graver did by this intend / Oliver's shape with William's head to mend, /
Or grace King William's head with Cromwell's body, / If I can guess his
meaning I'm a noddy.' The author affects pity for Cromwell: 'This is a
punishment he never dreaded; / What did his Highness thus to be
beheaded?'[24] The Lord Protector had in fact been addressed as
'Highness', but the ironic comment on his beheading was a reference to
the execution of Charles I.

The analogy between Cromwell and William seemed to imply that
history did not change. In that case, however, its moral purpose would
be lost. Each situation had to be worse, or better, than its predecessors,
because the cycle of history was moving towards a final end. Thus,
Oliver was a lesser tyrant than William, as 'A paralel between Two
Noses' pointed out – after all, the Lord Protector 'did preserve us from
French & from Dutch. / Only rode us himself (he lov'd us so much) / A
French Refugee he did never admitt / Nor suffer a Duchman in Counsell
to Sitt.'[25] A generation later, the same point was made in 'Jotham's
Parable', which lampoons 'Nassau the Archer Cromwell of the two'.[26]
After 1714, a new villain could be added to the list, and in 'The Three

---

[23] *Ibid.*, p. 60. This poem is a variant on a popular song of the Exclusion Crisis, 'Old
Jimmy'; see Maurice Ashley, *James II* (London, 1977), p. 142.
[24] Lord, gen. ed., *Poems on Affairs of State*, vol. v, p. 149.
[25] Bodl. Rawl. MS Poet. 169, fo. 8.
[26] P.R.O., S.P. 35/7/67.

Olivers' it was suggested that George I was the worst Cromwell of the lot.[27]

The reign of the first Hanoverian seemed to be bringing the cycle of history to its culmination. Jacobite poetry began to trumpet a High Church challenge to its old enemies:

> We are not of the King-killing train:
> The Seed of old *Oliver* we defy,
> For High-Church for ever shall be my Cry,
> So drink to my Love o'er the Main.[28]

Cromwell's 'Seed' was of course the Whig party. Its Dissenting supporters were not spared the most vituperative attacks. Richard Savage, whose poetic fame rests mainly on Johnson's biography of him, wrote a series of Jacobite pieces in 1716, in which he castigated the 'Saints, that Curse and fflatter when they pray.'[29] A poem of 1722 challenged all '*Whigs*! *Atheists*! *Presbyterians*! *Sectarists*! / *Hell's Squadrons*! *We will* meet you hands to fists.'[30] The helplessness that characterized the seditious verse of the 1690s now gave way to a confrontational pugnaciousness, because the plebeian voice of Jacobitism was at last being heard.

The detested Whigs regained at this time a poetic nickname that was to plague them for many years. As an 'Address to Brittania' (*sic*) put it in 1716, they were 'those Rumpers for thy ruin bent'.[31] The identification of Whiggery with the Rump Parliament, which had been fairly common in the 1680s, returned after 1715, as an apt description of the domination of the state by a remnant or faction that had expelled or excluded the representatives of most of the nation – the royalists and moderates of 1648, the Tories of 1715. The Rump had killed a Stuart king in 1649; but a decade later, its brief revival and rapid collapse signalled the end of the Commonwealth and the return of Charles II. The cry 'Down with the Rump', therefore, was a call for a second Stuart restoration, and for the completion of another historical cycle.

In a spirit of supreme optimism, the Jacobite poets of George I's reign showed much more interest in the myth of restoration than had their

---

27 Beinecke Osborn Shelves f. c. 58, p. 13.
28 'The Church-Man's New Health', Nov. 1721, P.R.O., S.P. 35/29/23.
29 'A Litanny for the Year', P.R.O., S.P. 35/7/78; also Clarence Tracy, ed., *The Poetical Works of Richard Savage* (Cambridge, 1962), p. 25.
30 'A Prophetick Congratulatory Hymn to his Sacred Britannick Majesty King James the III', P.R.O., S.P. 35/40/60, verse xxxvi.
31 P.R.O., S.P. 35/7/66. For earlier Rump references, see Lord, gen. ed., *Poems on Affairs of State*, vol. iii, pp. 356, 503.

forebears. They revelled in the glorious 29th of May, and exhorted 'Kind Heaven, our Rightful Sovereign to restore; / K—g J—s the th—d, as he did Charles before.'[32] They appropriated the day as an antidote to Whig commemorations, and linked it inextricably with the Pretender:

> Let Whigs remember the fourth of November
> And sing of the Pope and ye Devill that day
> Wee'l burn our Bonnets and sing loyall Sonnets
> In praise of the Twenty ninth of May
> I wish e'er many more Years are come
> The same may bring in the tenth of June ...

The 29th of May was not, however, merely a day of remembrance and hope; it was also an impetus to action. The same poem depicted a restoration as a religious duty:

> It is but a folly to talk of your Holy
> Religion till you give Caesar his due
> For to plunder Princes to gloss your pretences
> Is serving of Christ like a Turk or a Jew
> Then pray return what you've taken away
> And make another restoring day
> Or else you as wicked as faction are grown
>   And Tho' to the Skies
>   You lift up your Eyes
> You but barter the Church which you own.[33]

The tone of admonition is striking; it clashes with the pretence of a popular voice, and reminds us of the distance between the author and his audience. At the moment of action, the poet emerges from his disguise, revealing himself as an agitator rather than simply one of the crowd.

The moment passed; action was not taken. Whether or not the crowd was willing is a question addressed in later chapters. In any case, the culmination of the cycle of history was deferred, and for three decades, Jacobite versifiers continued to wait for change. They saw signs of it in dates, personalities and events that seemed to correspond to those of the Civil War and Interregnum. In 1751, for example, the *True Briton* expressed its wishes for a Stuart return in the form of a poem allegedly written by a Cavalier in 1651.[34] 'Great Britain's

[32] 'On the 29th of May', Beinecke Osborn Shelves f. c. 58, p. 101. See also 'An Hymn to the Restoration', in versions printed by Clifton and Lightbody, P.R.O., S.P. 35/49/74, (2) and (3). Clifton's edition includes a woodcut showing George I as Cromwell.
[33] Bodl. Rawl. MS D. 400, fo. 95.
[34] *True Briton*, vol. i, no. 22, 29 May 1751; also vol. iii, no. 22, 3 June 1752.

Remembrancer' recalled in 1753 that exactly a century before, 'Britain was blest with a curs'd Lord Protector, / And Satan's pure saints too whined many a D—mn'd lecture.' Since then, the English Church and state had been progressively degraded at the hands of 'the Rump, – and the Dutchman, – the German, – the Jew'. The Jewish Naturalization Bill was seen as the final chapter of 'a strange, tragi-comical story' that must end with the restoration of a Stuart.[35] The bill failed, but so did the Jacobites; the millennium never came.

In this failure can be observed the fundamental contradictions of the Jacobite interpretation of history, and of the strategy of Jacobite verse. A divinely ordained cycle of events required no human intervention, just as a poetic voice that echoed the will of the people should not have to entreat them to act. The necessity of action, however, could not be avoided; and here the pretences of Jacobite poetry collapsed, as the possibility emerged that history might not be circular, and that the anonymous poet might not be the incarnation of the people. The self-fulfilling cycle, like a self-generating popular poetic language, was a fiction – the sort of fiction that might happily be accepted as truth, but could never be forced into reality.

Devils and Carnival kings

The cyclical view of history was characterized by moral outrage. The nation had fallen from a pristine, sanctified order into a realm of injustice and depravity; wickedness was rewarded, and goodness oppressed. 'Great Britain's Remembrancer' depicted both the Commonwealth and the Hanoverian age in these terms:

> How did Anarchy then, & the wildest confusion
> demonstrate an Hellish Usurper's intrusion!
> how did all honest Subjects, & faithful good folk,
> then Grievously groan, Sirs, beneath the sad Yoke![36]

If the psychological basis of Whiggery was anti-Catholic paranoia, the foundation of Toryism might be called anarchophobia. Hell was disorder, and the agents of the devil – Cromwell, William of Orange or the Hanoverians – were sowers of confusion, whose immoral

35 Grosart, pp. 110–11. For the Bill, see T. W. Perry, *Public Opinion, Propaganda and Politics in Eighteenth-Century England: A Study of the Jew Bill of 1753* (Cambridge, Mass., 1962).
36 Grosart, p. 111.

behaviour was all the more disgraceful because they occupied the place of God's anointed.

The early attacks on William III were the most savage and personal of any Jacobite diatribes, partly because the unfortunate Nassau was a vulnerable target. He was ugly and ungainly; he had fathered no children; and he was rumoured to be homosexual. These unpardonable faults were crassly exploited by Ralph Gray, a Nonjuring priest, in his 'Coronation Ballad' of 1689:

> He has gotten in part the shape of a man
> But more of a monkey deny it who can
> He has the tread of a goose and the legs of a swan.
>   A dainty fine King indeed ...
>
> He is not qualified for his wife
> Because of the cruel midwife's knife,
> Yet buggering of Benting doth please to the life.
>   A dainty fine King indeed ...
>
> An unnatural beast to his father and uncle;
> A churl to his wife without e'er a pintle [i.e. a penis];
> But excuse me in this for I hate to dissemble.
>   A dainty fine King indeed ...[37]

The point of this execrable exercise was to emphasize William's 'unnaturalness'. He looked like an animal, he behaved like a beast to James II, and, most extraordinary of all, he was both castrated and a sodomist! 'Unnatural' meant Satanic; anything that violated the laws of creation must be alienated from God. Gray's satire, therefore, was not just physical; it was moral and religious.

William and Mary's greatest crime was 'parricide'. Mary was anathematized in Jacobite verse as 'The Female Parricide', a 'monster' unique in history except for the Roman Tullia and King Lear's daughter Goneril.[38] Arthur Mainwaring, a Jacobite poet who later converted to Whiggery, was the author of 'Tarquin and Tullia', a mythic story of usurpation set 'In times when Princes cancell'd nature's law ... / When children used their parents to dethrone.'[39] Murdering one's father was no simple crime, even before Freud's Oedipus. It was associated, by Mainwaring as by Freud, with a legendary pre-Christian

---

[37] Lord, gen. ed., *Poems on Affairs of State*, vol. v, pp. 41–2, 43–4.
[38] *Ibid.*, pp. 156–7.
[39] *Ibid.*, p. 47; for another 'Tarquin' reference, see 'The Belgick Boar', Bodl. Rawl. MS Poet. 207, p. 10.

past, when human passion was unbridled by morality. For the Jacobite poet, however, it was an unnatural act; 'nature's law' stipulated obedience to fathers. Patriarchy was a divine rather than a human institution, and violating it was an offence against God.

Of course, James II had not been murdered, but as 'The Duchess of York's Ghost' succinctly put it, 'Had he been murdered, it had mercy shown, / 'Tis less to kill a King, than to dethrone.' This poem unfolds the full meaning of the deed through a series of references to a Biblical scenario:

> How boldly did some villains sell their King
> Engaging to the next Sanhedrim to bring
> Substantial proof of warming-pan intrigue, ...
> These blessed reformers have the King dethroned;
> Under such Pharisees Judaea groaned.[40]

The symbolic parricide of William and Mary's rebellion is transformed here into a reenactment of the killing of Christ, the greatest of all crimes in Christian typology.[41] Tarquin and Tullia were pagans, and 'The Duchess of York's Ghost' mentions the 'pagan doctrine' by which the Revolution was justified; it also calls Holland 'The very sink and plague of Christendom', and accuses the rebels of 1688 of having 'no God but trade'. Deposing the father-king was therefore the ultimate anti-Christian impiety, a result of paganism and materialism.

The effects of parricide are laid out in 'A Panegyrick' of 1696/7, which, in spite of the doubts of the editors of Poems on Affairs of State, is evidently a Jacobite poem, written either by Henry Hall, the Nonjuring organist of Hereford Cathedral, or by the politician John Grubham Howe.[42] The poem lists the consequences of William's usurpation, beginning with lack of filial devotion:

> Hail happy William, thou art strangely great!
> What is the cause, thy virtue or thy fate
> For thee the child the parent's heart will sting;
> For thee the Favourite will desert his King; ...
> Thy loyal slaves love thy oppression more
> Than all their wealth and liberty before.
> For thee, and tyranny, they all declare –
> And beg the blessing of eternal war.

40 Lord, gen. ed., Poems on Affairs of State, vol. v, pp. 299–300.
41 For the persistence of Christian and pagan typology in eighteenth-century literature, see Paul J. Korshin, Typologies in England, 1650–1820 (Princeton, 1982).
42 For Howe's Jacobitism, see Hopkins, 'Aspects of Jacobite Conspiracy', p. 285.

William has turned things into their opposites; in his Orwellian kingdom, war becomes peace, and love is hate. The source of his power is compared to that of the devil over his intimates: 'Rebels, like witches, having signed the rolls / Must serve their masters, though they damn their souls.'[43] As in witchcraft, rebellion reversed the natural order of things, subverted the meaning of words and set the world upside down.[44]

Historians have examined inversion, particularly as it was manifested in the European Carnival, as a feature of popular culture. In Carnival week, the beggar is crowned king, and the poor, like rebels or witches, temporarily reverse the social order.[45] England had no Carnival by the eighteenth century, and its popular festivals were less bacchanalian, but fairs and feasts and Merry Andrews preserved an English version of 'misrule'.[46] The Satanic figure of William III may therefore seem like an attempt to impose elite cultural values, which were hostile to inversion. Carnival, however, was the joyful expression of a whole society, and its effects were usually palliative. William was demonic because he acted alone, for selfish purposes; he was the grand seducer, who made the English oppose their own interest and duty, who brought confusion rather than pleasure. Seventeenth-century plebeians would have recognized the difference between Carnival and rebellion or witchcraft, even if modern historians sometimes do not.

George I, on the other hand, was depicted in Jacobite poetry as a fool, a second-rate substitute for a king, whose despotism was akin to farce. The turnip was the symbol of his mediocrity. According to a widespread rumour, George had been hoeing turnips in his garden at Hanover when the news of Queen Anne's death arrived; he was ever afterwards associated with the lowly root. The turnip is sometimes represented as a product of the Agricultural Revolution, a sign of material progress; but in fact, this interesting vegetable had been known in England for at least two centuries before it became a celebrity

---

[43] Lord, gen. ed., *Poems on Affairs of State*, vol. v, pp. 456–7.

[44] See Emmanuel LeRoy Ladurie, *The Peasants of Languedoc*, tr. by John Day (Urbana, Ill., 1976), pp. 203–10; Stuart Clark, 'Inversion, Misrule and the Meaning of Witchcraft', *P. & P.*, 87 (May 1980), pp. 98–127.

[45] See Burke, *Popular Culture*, ch. 7; Natalie Zemon Davis, *Society and Culture in Early Modern France* (Stanford, Cal., 1975), ch. 4; Emmanuel LeRoy Ladurie, *Carnival in Romans*, tr. by Mary Feeney (New York, 1980).

[46] See Robert Malcolmson, *Popular Recreations in English Society, 1700–1850* (Cambridge, 1973).

among agrarian reformers.[47] In Jacobite poetry, it was a symbol of poverty, not of advancement: 'No Root so fit for barren / H[anove]r can be found; / For the Turnip will grow best / When 'tis sown in poorest Ground.'[48] The turnip-hoeing story indicated that George was a prince of low birth, not fit to be ruler of England, and the continental origin of the turnip pointed to George's foreignness. William III had also been criticized for his nationality, and christened 'the Dutch Hogan Mogan', a term used by Marvell in the 1660s.[49] 'What's the difference between an Orange and a Turnip?' a Jacobite song asked rhetorically, answering 'like to like as the devil said to the Collier, both pernicious to England'.[50]

Nevertheless, the two were not alike; the Netherlands were serious economic rivals of England, while Hanover was simply ridiculous. William III was threatening, so the Jacobite poets sexually castrated him, but they gave George I an insatiable libido: 'Those Turnips have a King if we may credit Fame, / His Scepter is his Hoe, and Priapus is his Name.'[51] George's mistress, Melusine von der Schulenburg, whom he created Duchess of Munster in 1716 and Duchess of Kendal in 1719, was very fat, like her lover, and their size was a source of much Jacobite hilarity. In 'The Bed-Tester's Plot', George and Munster fall through a bed while fornicating when the structure collapses under their combined weight; the unhappy monarch cries out that it must be a Jacobite plot![52] The other side of George's sex life was his cuckoldry; his wife Sophia Dorothea had been caught in an affair with the dashing Count Königsmarck, and was incarcerated by her husband for the rest of her life.[53] As the survival of the charivari and Skimmington ride in England demonstrated, wifely infidelity was popularly regarded as the fault of the husband, who was treated with public

[47] See Conrad Russell, *The Crisis of Parliaments: English History, 1509–1660* (London and New York, 1971), p. 186.

[48] 'The Turnip Song: A Georgick', Bodl. Rawl. MS Poet. 207, fo. 109.

[49] 'Hogan Mogan' was derived from *hoogmogendheien* or high mightinesses, applied to members of the Dutch Estates-General. See 'The Character of Holland', in Elizabeth Story Donno, ed., *Andrew Marvell: The Complete Poems* (Harmondsworth, 1981), p. 114, l. 80, and note on p. 264; also Eric Partridge, *The Penguin Dictionary of Historical Slang*, abridged by Jacqueline Simpson (Harmondsworth, 1980), p. 447.

[50] P.R.O., S.P. 35/66/65.   [51] Bodl. Rawl. MS D. 400, fo. 91.

[52] *Ibid.*, D. 383, fo. 77.

[53] Ragnhild Hatton, *George I: Elector and King* (London, 1978), pp. 54–60. Sophia Dorothea was sometimes defended in Jacobite verse, as in 'The Lady's Case: or, a Letter from an Injur'd Wife beyond Sea to a Munster Crack', P.R.O., S.P. 35/28/62. She was approached in 1718 by Jacobite agents who wished to use her against her husband; Hatton, *George I*, p. 61.

scorn.[54] George's disgrace became so well known that it was not even necessary to name him when cuckolds were mentioned – 'Kind Heaven assist our Heir & banish Strife / In driving every Cuckold to his wife.'[55] 'Cuckoldy George' wore the symbols of his failure as a husband on his head: 'Exalt his horns above his fellows', bade one doggerel poet, adding unhumourously, 'And make his body grace the Gallows.'[56]

George I's image in Jacobite poetry bore a resemblance to the Lord of Misrule, the central figure in Carnival, who upsets the existing order and suspends conventional morality. A foolish ruler, however, was actually the opposite of a Carnival king. George was inverting the world from the wrong direction, for his own purposes rather than for the benefit of the people. His turnip-hoeing, sexual appetite and cuckold's horns were negative attributes because they denoted a mean-spirited and selfish character; one ditty called him 'a King of great Spight / For he Set up all wrong & pull'd down all Right.'[57] His foibles were not always funny, and could bring damaging consequences: 'A King like George was Heaven's Severest Rod / The utmost Vengeance of an Angry God.'[58] If he was sometimes clownish, he could also be tyrannical, a 'Nero the Second' who gloried in his country's ruin and was merciless in his butchery of Jacobite patriots.[59]

Like William III, George I was a devil in Jacobite cosmology; but he was more of a mischievous, saturnalian imp than a sinister Satan. He was the sort of devil who could be found in the woodcut illustrations to chap-book literature.[60] George II was depicted in precisely the same way; he was a fool, a tyrant, a 'German Savage' and a servant of the devil, and at times he even inherited the turnip-hoe and cuckold's horns. A song of 1747 invents a conversation between the second Hanoverian and his infernal master:

54 See E. P. Thompson, '"Rough Music": le charivari anglais', *Annales: Economies, Sociétés, Civilizations*, 37 (1972), pp. 285–312; Martin Ingram, 'Ridings, Rough Music and "The Reform of Popular Culture" in Early Modern England', *P. & P.*, 105 (1984), pp. 79–113; John Gillis, *For Better, For Worse: English Marriages, 1600 to the Present* (New York and Oxford, 1985), pp. 79–80.
55 'Might overcomes Right', Bodl. Rawl. MS C. 986, fo. 20.
56 P.R.O., S.P. 35/55/30.
57 'An Excellent New Ballad to a True Old Tune', Bodl. Rawl. MS D. 383, fo. 142.
58 *Ibid.*, fo. 64.
59 'Nero the Second', in Grosart, pp. 6–8, and Bodl. Rawl. MS D. 383, fo. 111. See also 'Cato's Ghost', a commentary on Addison's play and an appeal to Britons to assassinate the tyrant, in Bodl. Rawl. MS D. 383, fo. 106, and Grosart, pp. 101–4.
60 See, for example, 'The Witch of the Woodlands' or 'The History of Dr. John Faustus' in John Ashton, ed., *Chap-Books of the Eighteenth Century* (reprint, New York, 1966), pp. 35–52.

Old Beelzebub turned at a voice he well knew,
And Stoping cry'd oh! Brother George is it you, ...
of all my good Servants North, East, South & West,
I speak it sincerely George thou art the best.

George pleased with the Compliment, smiled like a fool
And bowing said Sir I hope you don't flatter your Tool,
Tho' the trouble I give you is not much I must own,
For as to religion you know I have none.[61]

The bitterness of this kind of satire had largely worn off by the 1740s; the old formulae were no longer infused with anger, urgency or confidence. A more venomous treatment was reserved for George II's son, the Duke of Cumberland, victor of Culloden and scourge of Jacobitism. He was 'Billy my Darling and Blood thirsty boy, / He'll ravish, and plunder, burn, kill & destroy.' This was the Butcher of Jacobite legend.

If the historical Cumberland had some virtues, mercy was certainly not one of them, as his refusal of aid to the rebel wounded at Culloden showed.[62] His enemies, of course, were prone to extreme exaggeration, making the Duke into the 'Butcher of the Northern Clime / Thy fame descends to future time, / Your Massacres & Murders more / Than e'er were known in days of Yore.'[63] No figure since William III had aroused such Jacobite hatred, and it was almost certainly a Stuart supporter who penned the epitaph published in the *London Chronicle* soon after the Duke's death in 1765:

Here lyes a victim to all-conq'ring death;
The man who conquer'd on Culloden's heath.
What else he was, or what his victims were,
The groans of weeping Scotland best declare.[64]

The Jacobite evocation of Cumberland's 'crimes' was suffused with pathos: 'The little Babes for mercy cryed, / Their bleeding Mothers were denyed / The lives of Husbands and their own.'[65] Sentiment was emerging as an important literary trend at this time, and Jacobite poetry was fully attuned to it.[66] Although the sentimentalist vogue was

[61] Grosart, pp. 5–6.
[62] For an attempt to rehabilitate Cumberland, see W. Speck, *The Butcher: The Duke of Cumberland and the Suppression of the '45* (Oxford, 1981).
[63] Grosart, pp. 78–9.   [64] Paton, ed., *Lyon in Mourning*, vol. iii, p. 214.
[65] Grosart, p. 79.
[66] On the rise of sentiment, see Northrop Frye, 'Towards Defining an Age of Sensibility', in James L. Clifford, ed., *Eighteenth-Century English Literature: Modern Essays in Criticism* (New York, 1959), pp. 311–18; W. F. Wright, *Sensibility in English Prose*

most pronounced in novels and poems read by the upper and middle classes, it cannot be assumed that 'feeling' was a purely elite phenomenon; folk tales contained a good deal of exaggerated misery, weeping and gnashing of teeth. Jacobite verse can therefore be placed at the intersection between a new fashion in elite literature and an old theme in popular culture.

Cumberland's character had a less gruesome side; he could be an obese, dim-witted 'Lump of Lead', well matched with his brother Frederick, the 'pratting Monkey'.[67] Frederick, Prince of Wales, attained a modicum of respect in Jacobite poetry; he was, after all, a self-proclaimed 'patriot', and many Tories were prepared to support him in the late 1740s, while keeping the Jacobite option open as well.[68] When Frederick died in 1751, his Jacobite epitaphs were mild:

> Here lies Fred'rick the Silly.
> I'd rather it had been Willie.
> The whole generation
> Would been no loss to the nation.
> But since God's ta'en the best,
> May the D—l take the rest.[69]

If Frederick's caricatures were rather bloodless, political strategy was not the only reason. Life was slowly being sapped from Jacobitism itself after 1745; and in the end, there remained only a formalized rejection of the ruling monarch, and a bitter memory of defeat.

As has been shown, King George III was not the first of his line to undergo savage criticism; his predecessors had suffered a hundred Juniuses. Their weapons, however, were not forged from the mythology of English constitutionalism; they were shaped from the images of popular culture. Tarquin the parricide, the turnip-hoeing cuckold, the bloody butcher of Culloden, were as much folk villains as King Herod or the Sheriff of Nottingham. Yet they did not spring from an oral tradition; they were manufactured by educated men like Henry Hall and Francis Clifton, and they seem to have first appeared in writing. As representatives of the middling and upper classes, familiar

Fiction, 1760–1814 (New York, 1937); and R. F. Brissenden, *Virtue in Distress: Studies in the Novel of Sentiment from Richardson to Sade* (New York and London, 1974).

67 Beinecke Osborn Shelves f. c. 58, p. 132.

68 For Frederick and the Tories, see Aubrey Newman, ed., 'Leicester House Politics, 1750–60, from the Papers of John, Second Earl of Egmont', in *Camden Miscellany xxiii*, Camden Society, 4th Series, 7 (1969), pp. 124–73; Colley, *In Defiance of Oligarchy*, pp. 253–60.

69 Paton, ed., *Lyon in Mourning*, vol. iii, p. 89.

with the literature of the elite, Jacobite poets might be seen as accomplices in the co-opting of popular culture from above; but this would distort their role in vitalizing old forms. Certainly, they bent traditions out of shape by enlisting them in a partisan cause, and it is not difficult to point out the limits of their plebeian rhetoric. Nevertheless, traditional images remained recognizable in their work, and their adopted language was convincing enough to the crowd as well as to gentlefolk. They were not cultural outsiders intruding in a plebeian sphere. Perhaps historians should begin to question the assumed opposition of popular and elite culture, of oral and written media, of Carnival and Lent.

The 'lost lover'

Popular culture produced heroes as well as villains, and the exiled Stuarts could draw upon heroic models from their own family history as well, particularly the royal martyr Charles I.[70] The image of 'our Injur'd King' was derived from an even more powerful religious icon, the crucified Christ, so that the sufferings of the sacred monarch paralleled those of his God.[71] Christian typology, however, was often mixed with classical references, as in Henry Hall's poetic eulogy to King James:

> The Great, good Man, whom Fortune does displace,
> May fall to want, but never to disgrace.
> He holds his value with the wise and good,
> And prostrate seems as great as when he stood.
> His sacred person, none will dare profane,
> Poor he may be, but never can be mean.
> So ruined Temples Sacred Awe dispence,
> They lose their height but keep their reverence
> The pious crowd the deformed Pile deplore
> And what they ne're can raise they still adore.[72]

The juxtaposition of grandeur and misery, of lamentation and panegyric, establishes a theme of duality that is sustained through a series of contrasts – James is both human and divine, overturned and inviolable,

---

[70] Folk heroes are discussed in Burke, *Popular Culture*, pp. 150–5; Mandrou, *De la culture populaire*, pp. 146–63; for Charles I, see Kenyon, *Revolution Principles*, pp. 75–6.
[71] See Korshin, *Typologies in England*, pp. 117–22.
[72] Grosart, p. 86; Bodl. Rawl. MS Poet. 203, p. 5.

ruined and venerated. He is compared to Christ as well as to the standard example of classical virtue, Cato. Hall's poem, in short, is about the king's two bodies.

This work was evidently designed for elite consumption, and it may be wondered whether 'the pious crowd' it mentions was any more than a pious hope. Was an audience of artisans and labourers prepared to accept the religious and political content of Stuart kingship? Clearly, they demanded a different language and approach, such as in 'Old Jemmy', a doggerel piece of 1692. The banished monarch was represented as 'a Lad, / From English Blood Descended, / No *Dutchman* Born or Bred / Nor for a Whig suspended.' His attractions, however, went further than chauvinism or anti-Whiggery; he was also 'a Prince / Of Noble Resolutions; / Whose Powerful Influence, / Will end all our Confusions'; and in battle, 'No force can him withstand; / No God of war but must give place, / When *Jemmy* leads the *Van*.'[73] Here was a popularized version of sacred kingship, exerting a mystical 'Influence' that cannot be withstood, making order out of confusion, leading 'the Van', a nice pun on the slang word for a Dutchman.

James II, however, was too controversial to inspire many affectionate portrayals during his lifetime. His son James Francis, on the other hand, was an enigmatic personality, although the little that was known about him in England was generally positive. He lacked judgment and vigour, but he was brave, pious, chaste, tolerant in his religious views, and generous to the poor.[74] After 1714, the Jacobite bards lavished attention on him, moulding him into a fairy tale monarch, and popularizing his image through familiar forms that lent themselves to infinite variations. The most important of these was the 'lost lover' ballad, a common medium for non-political verse. Unrequited love was an excellent metaphor for Jacobitism, and the habits of the 'lost lover' perfectly suited James III. Of course, the amorous shepherds and shepherdesses of these pieces had classical origins, and their Virgilian forebears had inspired a host of Elizabethan versifiers, from Sidney and Spenser to Ralegh and Marlowe. The earliest of Jacobite 'lost lover' poems was a mock-classical work in which the nymph 'Phillis' refuses to be Queen of the May because 'I'll never were [*sic*] a Garland whilst *Pan* is away.' The shepherds rebuke her, but she

---

[73] 'Loyal Poems', Beinecke Osborn Shelves b. 111, p. 59.
[74] The best biography of him remains Alice Shield and Andrew Lang, *The King over the Water* (London, 1907).

is supported by the nymphs.[75] The style may be genteel, but May-day, the pagan god Pan and the adoring women would reappear in later demotic forms. Once again, the elite and popular traditions were not separate; they ran together in the rustic fantasies of 'lost love'.

James III was represented in the 'lost lover' ballads as an heroic and virtuous young prince, unlike his rival George I:

> He does not make his Country poor
> Nor spend his Substance on a Whore,
> His loving Wife he does adore,
> For he is brisk and Lordly.

> He looks not like a Country Clown,
> Nor their [sic] grows no Thorns upon his Ground,
> Nor keeps no Whore of forty Stone,
> For he is brisk and Lordly.[76]

The plebeian voice resonates loudly in this poem. The emphasis on James's marital fidelity reflected the popular disapproval of male adultery noted by Keith Wrightson in the seventeenth century, and the 'Country Clown' insult would have amused any Londoner.[77] The Pretender's 'lordliness' is reminiscent of the chivalric heroes of popular romance; his 'briskness' may have had a sexual connotation, as his wife had just given birth to Prince Charles Edward. The idea of the king's two bodies appeared in the 'lost lover' ballads in the guise of procreative power; the king was able to bring fertility, to regenerate nature, because he was divine as well as human. The white rose was often used to symbolize this theme of rebirth. In Clifton's 'The Sheppards Holliday, or the Maidens Opinion of the Rose', James III's birthday is celebrated as a spring festival: 'All you that ever lov'd my Sheppard here / In harmless Mirth rejoyce and Sing, / And briskly Sport and play.'[78] Their 'brisk' merry-making will reinstate the rightful king.

The 'harmless' quality of their gaiety, however, stands out as an incongruous bit of moralizing; it reminds us that the Jacobite crowd was sympathetic to High Church piety. The 'lost lover' poems often depicted James III's divine attributes through a Christian typology. A ballad entitled 'The Happy Pair' was headed by a woodcut showing a

---

75 'Loyal Poems', Beinecke Osborn Shelves b. 111, p. 80. This poem may have been written in the Commonwealth period, but was easily adapted to Jacobite use. For Pan as a type of Christ, see Korshin, *Typologies in England*, pp. 5, 309, and plate 8.

76 'The Highland Lasses Wish', P.R.O., S.P. 35/29/60, (1).

77 K. Wrightson, *English Society, 1580–1680* (New Brunswick, N.J., 1982), pp. 99–100.

78 P.R.O., S.P. 35/22/62.

knight and a lady holding a pierced heart – a symbol of love, of Christ and of the Pretender, who is described in the work as 'Lordy', 'Godlike' and 'the Master of my Heart'. 'When will my lovely Shepherd dear, / To his lost Sheep again return?' queries the poet, likening James Francis to the Biblical shepherd, Christ himself. A similar parallel is found in 'The Happy Lady', where the sufferings of Christ are compared with James's plight; 'his Friends hold him in Scorn, / They give him Honey mixt with Gall, / They turn'd him out in Grief and Thrall / ... they do my Love disown.' Christ too was scorned, given a sponge soaked in vinegar at his crucifixion, and disowned by Peter; but he rose again, just as James, who is 'sweeter than the Rose in June', will return again.[79] Like Christ, James will become a risen god, a god of vegetation, the rose of June.

The religious strain in Jacobite verse sometimes clashed with the sexual implications of the king as procreator, as in this charming ditty:

> To see gued Corn grow on the Rigs,
> And banishment to all the Whiggs.
> And things restor'd as they sh.d be
> Oh! this wd. do mickel for to wanton me;
> To wanton me, To wanton me,
> Oh this wd. do mickel to wanton me.[80]

Sexual awakening and spring have always been connected; what is May-day but a celebration of fertility? As will be seen in Chapter 7, the attributes of May-day were often transferred to the Jacobite holidays of 29 May or 10 June, and women were central to their commemoration:

> When Dames of Britain shall espouse
> The royal Cause with verdant Boughs,
> Gather'd from the propitious Tree
> Sacred to Jove and Monarchy:
> When in the Month of June the Roses,
> Shall give Offence to wiggish Noses,
> Nor Lady's Breast yield them from protection,
> Against the fury of a Faction
> The Rose so virgin white before,
> Now blusing [sic] with the stain of Gore
> Then, not till then the Injur'd Nation,
> May hope to see a Restoration.[81]

[79] P.R.O., S.P. 35/31/154. For other examples of Christian typology, see Richard Savage's 'An Other Litany for the Year', P.R.O., S.P. 35/7/78, and Tracy, ed., *Works of Savage*, p. 26; also S.P. 35/6/21, and the pretentious 'Prophetick Congratulatory Hymn' in S.P. 35/40/60, which compares James to Phoebus-Apollo as well.
[80] Beinecke Osborn Shelves f. c. 58, p. 125.
[81] *Ibid.*, p. 125; see also P.R.O., S.P. 35/11/85.

The oak leaves and white roses point to the completion of a cycle of nature, but this can only be accomplished through the symbolic rape of James Stuart's female acolytes. The link between regeneration and sex was obvious, and in the 'stain of Gore' can perhaps be seen a small reflection of the violent sacrifice that was necessary, in ancient myths, to bring back the 'corn-god' and the spring.[82]

The cycle of nature resembled the cycle of history; both were beyond human control, and culminated in the restoration of the nation's happiness. Nature, however, was associated with paganism and sexuality, while history operated according to strict moral rules. The use of sexual as well as Christian imagery in the 'lost lover' poems indicated a tension within Jacobite literature between its secular and religious heritage. The libertine populism of the Cavalier poets and the stern religiosity of High Church divines were sometimes uneasy partners. The first looked back to the England of Charles II, to May-day and 'cakes and ale'; the other venerated the royal martyr, trembled for the fate of the Church of England, and observed a rigorous Laudian sobriety. Yet they were never entirely separate tendencies, and most Jacobite poetry, elite and plebeian, displayed a mixture of Cavalier and High Church elements. Moral righteousness and pagan celebration merge in the flowery 'Imitation of the Fifth Ode of Horace', which pictures James III freeing the royal palace from 'Curst Incest, and Vile Sodomy; / Triumphant *Caesar* by divine Command, / Shall purge the Errors of a guilty Land.' This High Church reverie, however, was followed by a vision of bucolic merriment: 'The Lads with curling Ivy bound / The Maids with flowry Garlands crown'd, / To their great Pan shall yearly Honours pay, / And consecrate with Mirth, the *Restoration* Day.'[83] The cycles of history and nature merge harmoniously; Caesar and Pan are united in the restored monarch.

The stilted rural merry-making of this work prefigures the idealist rusticity of John Gay, which has been linked with the nostalgic political writings of Bolingbroke.[84] Through poets like Gay, elite literature reclaimed the 'lost lover' theme in the eighteenth century, and reinfused

---

82 Although the universality of such myths is no longer accepted, there is still much of interest in Sir J.G. Frazer, *The Golden Bough: A Study in Magic and Religion* (abridged edn, New York, 1930).

83 P.R.O., S.P. 35/65/116, fo. 50; another imitation of the Fifth Ode is in Grosart, pp. 3–4. For the original, see James Michie, ed., *The Odes of Horace* (Harmondsworth, 1976), p. 222.

84 See Isaac Kramnick, *Bolingbroke and his Circle: The Politics of Nostalgia in the Age of Walpole* (Cambridge, Mass., 1968), pp. 226–7; Sven M. Armens, *John Gay: Social Critic* (New York, 1954), ch. 1.

it with classical allusions. This was not the only example of literary foreshadowing in Jacobite verse; Pope was to begin his work on Horace only a few years after the treasonable 'Imitation of the Fifth Ode' appeared. In most ways, however, 'serious' Jacobite poetry was far from innovative; rather, it reiterated old forms. The comparison of England with Augustan Rome, which had long been favoured by English monarchist poets, and had flourished under Queen Anne, survived in Horatian Jacobite works like the 'Prophetick Congratulatory Hymn' of 1722, in which James III becomes 'Britain's Phoebus', who 'Gilds with his Presence like a God our Sphere' – Horace's Fifth Ode had likened Augustus to the sun.[85] Christian typology, however, was never lost sight of, and the Jacobite Apollo of this piece was also an imitation of Christ; he 'comes of all Mankind the first', and enlightens the world, as does Christ in John 1:15 and 19. The 'Hymn' is reminiscent of Pope's 'Messiah' of 1712, and hearkens back to an 'Augustan moment' under Queen Anne that had already passed.

Plebeian Jacobite verse contributed little to the 'great tradition'; most of it would have made Pope cringe. After the collapse of the Atterbury Plot, however, the Jacobite ballad press disappeared. Its demise meant that Charles Edward Stuart hardly ever appeared in doggerel; although prints and pictures of him were marketed commercially after 1745, few songs were written about the Prince in England. Plebeians turned to Scottish ditties about 'Charlie-O', or dredged up old verses about his father.[86] The gentry, meanwhile, were treated to pompous evocations of Charles as a Christian Hercules battling against the monsters of 'an impious age', or as the victor of Prestonpans casting off 'th'oppressive weight of Slavish reigns', or as the 'Glorious TYPE of Heaven'.[87] These unimaginative pieces mimicked the moral tone and classical erudition of Pope, but they lacked even the pretence of a plebeian voice. Commercialization had made the 'little tradition' dangerous in the eyes of the government; it was allowed to continue as harmless folklore, but was suppressed whenever it stepped into the political sphere. Seditious verse in a genteel poetic style circulated privately, while the crowd had to borrow its tunes from the Scots. A rift had developed between the

[85] See Howard Erskine-Hill, *The Augustan Idea in English Literature* (London, 1983); and, for a different view, Howard D. Weinbrot, *Augustus Caesar in 'Augustan' England: The Decline of a Classical Norm* (Princeton, 1978). The poem is in P.R.O., S.P. 35/40/60.

[86] 'Charlie-O' was sung by some bricklayers at Shrewsbury in 1750, which occasioned a fight with a group of soldiers; fragments of 'Old Jemmy' and 'Prince Charles's Restoration' were overheard during a riot in Walsall in 1751. See Chapter 7.

[87] Grosart, pp. 99, 43, 128–9.

languages of high and low Jacobitism, due to the intervention of the government. If the eighteenth century witnessed a growing alienation between elite and popular culture in England, its causes may perhaps be sought in the political fears of the nation's rulers.

The effects on Jacobitism of this linguistic divorce were damaging. Although the Stuarts retained a large plebeian following long after 1722, the prospect of co-ordinated action receded; the abortive insurrection at Walsall in 1750, which is described in Chapter 7, was the last attempt by the Jacobite gentry to mobilize the people, but it deteriorated into a bewildering muddle. Decades of defeat had inculcated reticence and timidity in genteel Jacobites, while the crowd remained vocal and audacious. The upper-class friends of the exiled family gradually retreated into clubs and secret gatherings, where they dreamed hopefully of a Prince who would magically convert his enemies: 'Thy person & thy words infuse delight, / They who oppose, inward confess thy right.'[88] They continued to sing the old tunes for many years, but in the end they were singing only to themselves.

For all his bravado, Charles Edward Stuart never succeeded in entering the pantheon of English folk heroes, as James Francis Stuart had through the 'lost lover' ballads. They had summed up a popular ethos, in which the millennium was just around the corner. In a world of confusion and injustice, James III was the saviour whose arrival was endlessly deferred; he was the *logos* who would one day give proper meaning back to a language of politics that had been subverted by usurpation. Yet the image of the 'lost lover' was contradictory – he appeared as a pagan vegetation god, a paragon of Christian morality, a man of sorrows, a triumphant Caesar. He was a pastiche of conflicting features, a motley product of the different strands that ran through the fabric of popular culture; nevertheless, in all his incarnations, he was the beloved object of a fervent and yearning affection.

The interplay between elite and popular discourse in Jacobite verse can be imagined, not as a series of oppositions, but as a process of communication. The elite voice was didactic, moralistic, classical, lofty; its plebeian equivalent was joyful, religious, sociable and combative. In seditious poetry, the two idioms were often indistinguishable, because they shared an outlook that was Anglican, xenophobic, respectful of monarchy and concerned with order. Did they mirror 'authentic' strains in elite and popular culture? This chapter has

[88] *Ibid.*, p. 121.

frequently implied that they did, by citing their similarity to trends in genteel literature and to the social practices of the common people; but the final answer to the question is more complicated. No social class has a perfectly 'authentic' voice; the media through which cultural values are expressed control their form, and it is impossible for historians to reach beyond the sources into a pristine class consciousness. Empirical research, the reconstruction of 'objective' conditions, the application of theoretical models, have failed to penetrate far into the mind of the crowd. Like the 'lost lover', an ideal popular culture cannot be retrieved; we can only describe, in general terms, the traces that have been left by plebeians themselves and by those who sought to speak for them. Jacobite verse supplies a myriad of these traces, and for this reason alone, its shifting voices should be heard.

Chapter 3

Look, love and follow: images of the last Stuarts in Jacobite art

> The CHRISTIAN HERO's Martial Looks here shine,
> Mixt with the SWEETNESS of the STUART's Line,
> Courage with Mercy, Wit with Virtue join'd.
> A beauteous Person, with more beauteous Mind.
> Verses attached to a print of Charles Edward Stuart's 1745 medal[1]

Visual imagery seems to operate by rules different from those of writing.[2] Above all, an art that depends upon vision has been able to claim an immediacy and universality that are lacking in written forms. To understand a Jacobite poem, the reader must be aware of poetic conventions, literary allusions and a whole repertoire of symbols. To appreciate a picture of the Pretender, on the other hand, one has only to look at it – or so it was maintained by Jacobite propagandists:

> What Britton can survey that heavenly face?
> And doubt his being of the Martyrs Race
> Ev'ry fine feature does his birth declare,
> The Monarch and the Saint are shining there.[3]

If Britons could only *see* King James's face, even in effigy, they would all agree on his legitimacy, no matter what their previous inclinations. The Oxford poetry professor Thomas Warton made the same point in 1717–18 in a piece addressed to Pope's friend William Cleland, 'occasioned by His Present of His Majesty's King James III's Picture'. In the royal image, Warton observed the king's two bodies – 'The King,

---

[1] Unprinted broadside, B.L., C. 131, f. 16, no. 9; also printed in the *True Briton*, vol. v, no. 20, 6 June 1753, p. 471.
[2] For discussions of some of these rules, see E. H. Gombrich, *Meditations on a Hobby Horse and Other Essays on the Theory of Art* (London and New York, 1963), and John Brewer, *The English Satirical Print, 1600–1832: The Common People and Politics, 1750–1790s* (Cambridge, 1986), introduction.
[3] 'By a Lady Looking on the Chevalier's Picture', Beinecke Osborn Shelves f. c. 58, p. 6.

the Hero, and Y^e Christian shine / Awfully blended in ye Germ Divine' – and even an atheist must 'humbly learn from hence, / To own a God, and see a Providence!'.[4] Seeing the king's picture, in other words, would result in an instant recognition, and a sudden conversion. 'Look, love and follow' was a favourite device of Jacobite artists; it expressed a confidence in the mystical power of vision.

Of course, this power was an artistic deception. The significance of King James's image was enhanced by Warton's rapturous verses; were we simply to look at the picture without the aid of the poem, we might miss the king, or the hero, or the Christian in it. The visual language of Jacobite propaganda, furthermore, was not more direct or approachable than writing. Its message was hidden behind a similar symbolic rhetoric, and deciphering it requires the same sort of referential guides. The broadside ballad 'An Outlandish Present', printed by Francis Clifton in 1720, was accompanied by woodcut illustrations showing a lady and a gentleman, roses, flaming hearts, a ship on the water, an empty throne, a crowned king hiding in an oak tree and a butler. Although the verses exhort us merely to 'see' their meaning, it is impossible to grasp what the work is about unless we are able to recognize the 'lost lover', the Jacobite rose, the Boscobel oak or the pun on James Butler, Duke of Ormonde.[5] Pictures did not provide a wholly open mode of communication, and their magical qualities failed to transform everyone; the eighteenth-century atheist was not likely to have seen Providence in the face of the Pretender.

Yet the insistence on visual immediacy and power should not be dismissed. It had a long connection with Christian revelation. No monotheistic religion had vested such importance in visual imagery as western medieval Christianity; indeed, Judaism and Islam eschewed, at least in principle, pictures of their God. The Christian deity was supposed to have been actually seen in the person of Christ, and the typological conversion of the New Testament, that of St Paul, was centred on the concept of sight. Medieval worshippers could look upon their Man-God in every church, along with his mother and all the host of saints. Protestantism, however, asserted the supremacy of the word, or the Bible, over visual experience. The Reformation initiated an iconoclastic reaction, resulting in the unadorned simplicity of Dissenting chapels; but the Church of England was not fully purged of religious statues, stained glass windows, frescoes and rood-screen

---

[4] P.R.O., S.P. 35/68/1. The poem clearly inspired the verses that head this chapter.
[5] P.R.O., S.P. 35/21/122b (2).

Calvaries.[6] High Churchmen were less uncomfortable with these survivals than their Low brethren, and it is no coincidence that the only examples of early eighteenth-century church paintings mentioned by Norman Sykes both led to accusations of Jacobitism.[7] An irate Whig cleric responded to the altar-piece set up by Reverend Richard Welton at Whitechapel by pointing out that 'the Homilies of the Church of England declare against all Images or Pictures in Churches'.[8]

During the Commonwealth and Protectorate, royalist propagandists combined the religious iconography that had survived the Reformation with the new medium of printed engravings perfected by the Dutch, in spreading the image of the martyr-king Charles I. A multitude of widely circulated pictures represented Charles as 'the man of sorrows', a convention that directly referred to his divine nature and resemblance to Christ. The depiction of Charles II in the oak tree was a different sort of icon, more light-hearted and perhaps more pagan, but it too had Christian significance; the smiling king in the flowering tree was the reverse of the suffering king on the barren cross. Charles II was the risen Christ, a king in triumph.[9] The notion of 'hiding the king' was also a metaphor for Stuart propaganda, in which the identity of the monarch was disguised, and he was recognizable only to those who loved him. The visual images of Charles the martyr and of the king in the oak tree later provided Jacobites with contrasting models on which a repertory of graphic propaganda could be based.

The iconography of the 1650s appealed to the concerns and aspirations of the royalist gentry; it humanized, sentimentalized and to an extent popularized Stuart monarchy. The art of the Stuart court, however, was quite different; it emphasized the grandeur and unapproachability of sovereignty. Sir Anthony Van Dyke's Charles I was

---

[6] For iconoclasm in the 1640s, see David Underdown, *Revel, Riot and Rebellion: Popular Politics and Culture in England, 1603–1660* (Oxford and New York, 1987), pp. 139–40, 177–8, 181.

[7] Norman Sykes, *Church and State in England in the Eighteenth Century* (Cambridge, 1934), p. 236. For the altar-piece at St Clement Danes, reputed to contain portraits of the Pretender's wife and children, see Ronald Paulson, *Hogarth: His Life, Art and Times* (abridged edn, New Haven, 1974), pp. 63–5.

[8] Bodl. Rawl. MS B. 376, fo. 46. In the painting, showing the Last Supper, Judas Iscariot was recognizable as Bishop White Kennett of Peterborough, who was detested by Jacobites for his support of William and Mary. Welton became a Nonjuror in 1715.

[9] For representations of both Charles I and II, see Richard Ollard, *The Image of the King: Charles I and Charles II* (New York, 1979); for Charles the martyr, and popular imagery in general, see Peter Karsten, *Patriot-Heroes in England and America: Political Symbolism and Changing Values over Three Centuries* (Madison, Wisc., 1978).

a resplendent demi-god, not a 'man of sorrows', and Sir Peter Lely's powerful Charles II can hardly be imagined hiding in a tree. Stuart court art did not expire in 1688; it survived at St Germain, and later in Rome and Florence, until the 1780s. It was circulated in England in the form of medals, prints and copies of paintings. In fact, the Stuart court controlled the visual imagery of Jacobitism to a far greater extent than it did Jacobite political writings or poetry. The principal aim of this chapter will be to explore the relationship between 'populist' iconography and court art, a mixture of tension and symbiosis which typified the ambiguities and divergences within Jacobitism. The character of their cause was summed up in the different faces the exiled Stuarts showed to the world.

Lineage and sovereignty, 1688–1745

James II took little interest in his own public image after 1688, and only one painting of him without his family is known to have been executed while he was in exile.[10] His son, however, was painted several times between the Revolution and his father's death in 1701. In the most charming of these portraits, by Nicholas de Largillière, the young Prince of Wales appears in a lush garden with his sister, Princess Louise Marie, 'La Consolatrice'; he stands regally above the little Princess, who points at him with her finger.[11] His hand is stroking the head of a large dog, who looks at him with affection. The viewer is clearly supposed to regard him as his sister and the dog do, with respect, devotion and deference. The family portrait painted by Pierre Mignard in 1695 depicts the Prince as a bold and majestic youth, standing apart from the trio of his parents and sister; he gestures towards a crown and sword in the foreground of the picture.[12]

These two works illustrate the main theme of court art at St Germain in the 1690s: the hereditary right of the Prince of Wales. James II did not want the throne back for his son more than for himself; he reportedly rejected an offer by William III in 1697 to allow the Prince to succeed after William's death.[13] Nevertheless, he was determined to

---

[10] It is in the National Portrait Gallery, NPG 366. A useful, but not comprehensive, guide to Jacobite portraits can be found in Richard Ormond and Malcolm Rogers, eds., *Dictionary of British Portraiture*, vol. i (London, 1979).

[11] NPG 976.

[12] Not mentioned by Ormond and Rogers, the painting is in the Royal Collection.

[13] Clarke, ed., *Life of James the Second*, vol. ii, p. 574. The veracity of this story has been questioned.

refute the 'warming-pan' myth and assert the legitimacy of his heir. Thus, James Francis was depicted with his sister (whose birth proved that Mary of Modena was not barren), and with his father, whom he strongly resembled. Hereditary right was further stressed in a set of medals issued in 1699, some showing King James and his son on opposite sides of the piece, others with the two of them together on the obverse side.[14] Lineage, after all, was the basis of the Stuart claim to the throne, and it was the principal focus of court propaganda until the 1740s.

A secondary theme of court art was sovereignty; not the rather distant variety defended in Jacobite political writings, but a full-fledged monarchical authority. This was represented through images of martial prowess and comparisons with classical heroes. In 1697, the brilliant medallist Norbert Roettiers, whose family had previously served King William, executed a series of medals to protest the French renunciation of the Jacobite cause in the Treaty of Ryswick. On the obverse of these medals is a magnificent portrait of the Prince of Wales; in one version, he wears a Roman costume with a shining sun on his breast. The reverses show ships tossed by waves, rising and risen suns, exploding mines, doves carrying olive branches – contrasting images of adversity and triumph, war and peace, to remind the viewer that all hopes are united in the Prince.[15] The Augustan references, particularly the use of sun imagery, seem to foreshadow the Jacobite 'Horatian Odes' of a later period; but they were derived from French court art rather than from English classicism. These medals, in fact, are very French in inspiration, and they imply a kind of absolute sovereignty that is closer to the rule of Louis XIV than to that of Charles II.[16] In spite of his espousal of Country doctrines in his proclamations and political tactics, King James continued to promote an authoritarian visual image for his heir.

James II's death in 1701 was commemorated by Roettiers with a

---

14 The standard guide to medals before 1760 is E. Hawkins, *Medallic Illustrations of the History of Great Britain and Ireland* (2 vols., London, 1885; reprinted 1969); the photographic version (Lawrence, Mass., 1904, reprinted 1979) eliminates most of the descriptive text but includes some medals not found in the original. The medals referred to here are in Plate CXI, nos. 3–6 of the latter version.

15 *Ibid.*, Plate CIX, no. 6, Plate CX, nos. 1–6; Duke of Manchester, *Court and Society from Elizabeth to Anne. Edited from the Papers at Kimbolton* (2 vols., London, 1864), vol. ii, p. 114. See Plate 2. For Roettiers, see *D.N.B.* and J.R.S. Whiting, *Commemorative Medals* (London, 1972), p. 18. Two concealed hordes of these medals were discovered in London in the 1860s.

16 For a comparison of English and French monarchy in the seventeenth century, see John Miller, 'The Potential for "Absolutism" in Later Stuart England', *History*, 59 (1984), pp. 187–207. For sun imagery, see Tillyard, *Elizabethan World Picture*, p. 87.

medal showing the heads of both the late King and his successor on one side, and a second portrait of James III, in Roman armour, on the other.[17] Lineage and sovereignty were united graphically and obviously in this piece. Seven years later, Roettiers used the same head of James III on pieces issued in connection with the Scottish rebellion of '08. These were James's first visual propaganda statements, and they established an interesting balance between command and persuasion. The obverse bore the Biblical motto 'CUIUS EST', meaning both 'Whose is it?' and 'He whose it is', derived from Christ's order to 'render unto Caesar' the tribute money in Mark 12:16–17. On the reverse was a map of Great Britain and Ireland, with Scotland and England labelled separately – a comment on the unpopular union – and the words 'REDDITE' (restore) or 'REDDITE IGITUR' (therefore restore). To look at the medal is to see that he is 'whose it is', so therefore give it back to him and unite the two bodies, natural and spiritual, that are shown on the two sides of the piece. It is a powerful statement of visual immediacy; loyalty and logic compel us to restore him. Yet it is also an admission that the King cannot regain his kingdoms alone, and it offers a simple argument for supporting him. The medals were mainly distributed in Scotland, where the Duchess of Gordon presented one to the Edinburgh Faculty of Advocates in a notorious incident, but some English Jacobites owned copies, like the Nonjuring antiquarian Richard Rawlinson and the Catholic Widdringtons of Northumberland.[18]

The 1708 medals were James's first attempt to communicate with his subjects through court art. They were designed to encourage action rather than simply to display the lineage and sovereignty of the monarch. As in many later Jacobite works, the obverse presented an 'ideal' portrait, while the reverse was engraved with the 'real', albeit allegorical, situation, in which the King did not enjoy his own. The subtle compromise between an image of authority and an appeal to the public was in keeping with the Jacobite attempt to win support among English Tories and Scottish opponents of the union. After 1710, as will be seen in Chapter 6, the popularity of the exiled monarch grew rapidly, aided by fortuitous circumstances, and by the last years of

---

[17] *Medallic Illustrations*, Plate CXIII, nos. 6–7.

[18] See Plate 3. The medal is in Hawkins, *Medallic Illustrations*, Plate CXXVI, nos. 4–10. For the '08 see George Lockhart, *Memoirs Concerning the Affairs of Scotland* (London, 1714), pp. 339–81. The Duchess's gift is discussed in Shield and Lang, *King over the Water*, pp. 163–4, and in Lord, gen. ed., *Poems on Affairs of State*, vol. vii, pp. 491–503. See also Bodl. Rawl. MS D. 1489, fo. 26, and F. J. A. Skeet, ed., *Stuart Papers, Pictures, Relics, Medals and Books in the Collection of Miss Maria Widdrington* (London, 1930), p. 73.

Queen Anne, a thriving trade in pictures of James III was being carried on across the Channel.[19] The exiled King's adherents, however, did not always interpret Stuart court art as it was intended they should. Bishop Atterbury of Rochester owned a small ink and wash drawing of James III in full military regalia, an image of sovereign power. He pinned to it a copy of some Horatian verses – not the bombastic Fifth Ode, but the gentler Third Ode, Book Three, praising 'the just and steady-purposed man'.[20] In visual art, as in verse, Jacobites saw their King as more human and less warlike than the court painters and medallists envisaged him. At the same time, an indigenous strain of Tory Jacobite visual propaganda was developing in England, creating images of King James III that differed markedly from court art.

Tory Jacobite iconography is beautifully summed up in a painted fan, dating from around 1720, now owned by the Victoria and Albert Museum.[21] It shows James III in an oak tree, his head circled by three crowns; next to him, Queen Anne ascends to heaven amid dark clouds of grief and winged cherubs. Beneath her, Britannia mourns, leaning on a table on which the orb, crown and sceptre are placed. To relieve her distress, a cherub lifts a curtain to reveal the arms of the house of Stuart, surmounting a large white rose. The popular imagery of the 1650s has been revived here in a Jacobite context, with Queen Anne playing the role of Charles I, and her half-brother representing Charles II. Significantly, James III is depicted not as a figure of authority or power, but as the successor to his sister, whose sovereignty he had never acknowledged. Britannia will have to give him the trappings of monarchy, because he cannot take them himself. This picture is a gentle fantasy, in which the real problems of a restoration are forgotten. The return of the rightful king will be as simple as it was in 1660. Like Britannia, the viewer is led merely to recognize the face hiding in the tree (or the lady behind the fan). Look, love and follow – but there is no exhortation here to act.

The fan picture epitomized a certain type of Jacobite mentality that flourished after 1715, and has already been observed in the Restoration day visions of Mist and Crossgrove, or the 'lost lover' poems. It was nostalgic and emotional, pervaded by an absolute certainty of final victory, and by trust in the justice of Providence. After the collapse of

---

[19] P.R.O., S.P. 34/22, fos. 54–7, 71: S.P. 44/79A, pp. 2–3, 4, 5–6.
[20] P.R.O., S.P. 35/40/47. The drawing was found in Atterbury's papers by government agents.
[21] Victoria and Albert Museum, T. 160–1970.

the Atterbury Plot in 1722, this sort of Jacobitism could easily become passive; it retreated into drinking clubs and associations and nurtured loyalty to the Stuarts as a family tradition. Visual culture was important in fossilizing family loyalty. Medals, glassware, fans and other artefacts were constant reminders of the allegiance of one's forefathers, and numerous gentry families, like the Leghs of Lyme in Cheshire, the Bedingfields of Oxburgh Hall in Norfolk or the Joneses of Chastleton in Gloucestershire, owned large collections of Jacobite paraphernalia. The habit of accumulating these objects is discussed in Chapter 8.

The first generation of Jacobite collectors has not left many of its possessions to posterity. Only about a dozen engraved glasses of the 1720s are known to exist; they are called 'Amen' glasses, because they are inscribed with a Jacobite version of 'God Save the King', ending with an 'Amen'. The poem is ambiguous, because the king is not named, and only the monogram 'JR' reveals his identity.[22] Like the Victoria and Albert fan, the 'Amen' glasses present a simple game of guessing the identity of the king. They are meant to encourage Jacobite feelings, but not to promote human intervention in the process of restoration; they are engraved with a prayer for divine action, not with a battle cry. The same approach can be seen in Jacobite jewellery. Putting icons of the exiled Stuarts on rings or pendants was not a new idea in 1715; the 1697 Roettiers portrait of James Francis appears on an early 'tongue-piece', so called because Jacobite agents carried them under their tongues, and monogrammed mourning rings appeared after the death of James II.[23] In James III's mature portrait rings, however, he looks like a country gentleman; he wears an ordinary coat, with the ribbon of the Garter, and gazes forward without any distinguishing air of majesty. Nothing betrays him as a king.[24] This was visual propaganda at its most exclusive, so disguised as to be inaccessible to anyone who does not know its secret.

[22] G. B. Seddon, 'The Jacobite Engravers', in R. J. Charleston, Wendy Evans and Ada Polak, eds., *The Glass Circle*, 3 (Surrey, 1979), p. 40; Albert Hartshorne, *Old English Glasses* (London and New York, 1897), p. 347; Joseph Bles, *Rare English Glasses of the XVII and XVIII Centuries* (London, 1924), p. 86; Christie's catalogue, *English and Continental Glass: Wednesday 4 June 1980* (London, 1980), no. 153, pp. 26–7; Sotheby's *Catalogue of English, Continental Glass and Paperweights: Tuesday, 6th March 1984* (London, 1984), pp. 36–7.

[23] Hawkins, *Medallic Illustrations*, Plate CX, no. 7; Victoria and Albert Museum, Harman-Oates Collection, M.21–1929, on display in the jewellery room, Case 34, Board E, no. 13.

[24] Victoria and Albert Museum, Waterton Collection, 6–1889 and 926–1871, on display in Case 34, Board E, nos. 14–15; see also British Museum, Franks Bequest

A more commercialized form of English Jacobite art could be found
in the unsophisticated woodcuts on ballad sheets and broadsides, or in
the cryptic illustrations that headed Jacobite newspapers.[25] The title of
Mist's Weekly Journal in its most belligerently treasonable phase, from
1720 to 1723, was surrounded by a woodcut showing a post-man and
a figure of Britannia, standard journalistic devices; but behind the
post-man is a handsome male profile casting out rays of light, with the
caption 'Advenit Ille Dies' (that day is coming), and behind Britannia is
a rising sun containing some undecipherable symbol. The young
sun-god was James III, in an incarnation evidently inspired by court art
and the Fifth Ode of Horace, which indicates that court propaganda
could influence 'populist' imagery. Mist's assistant Doctor Gaylard
published a newspaper in 1723 whose head-piece depicted a woman
holding a baby under a benign sun – the infant is Prince Charles
Edward, the sun his father – and a tree stump next to which a sapling is
springing up. The latter was borrowed from prints of the 1650s, and
represented a Stuart heir rising from the ruin of his house.[26] Once
again, courtly and 'populist' images were mixed together in an allegorical composition.

How did Stuart court art respond to the growth of an indigenous
English Jacobite iconography? To some extent, it embraced the development, and adopted a more 'populist' approach to visual propaganda,
but this was tempered by the persistence of traditional courtly themes.
The magnificent 1721 medal designed by the Papal engraver, Otto
Hamerani, shows a warlike and confident James, a brilliant sun
beaming on his breast-plate, with the motto 'UNICA SALUS' (the only
safety, or way to health, welfare, prosperity). The idealized portrait
exuded power and authority. On the reverse side, however, can be seen
the 'real' state of the English nation; in front of a very accurate and
minutely detailed view of London, the Hanoverian horse tramples on
the British lion and unicorn, while Britannia weeps.[27] Here again was a
nationalistic appeal to the public – particularly, to the people of

1897, Catalogue of Finger Rings, nos. 1373 and 1374; *T.L.C.A.S.*, 40 (1922–3),
facing p. viii.
25 The only attempt to produce a Jacobite satirical print or cartoon in this period was
quickly suppressed around 1716. The print, an absurdly complicated allegory of
Hanoverian viciousness, was engraved but probably never published – see P.R.O.,
S.P. 35/68/112.
26 *The Loyal Observator Reviv'd; or, Gaylard's Journal*, no. 17, 30 March 1723; the
issue also included a letter decoration showing Charles II in the oak tree.
27 Hawkins, *Medallic Illustrations*, Plate CXLV, no. 3. See Plate 4.

London, who were expected to support the planned rising that was part of Atterbury's Plot.

The 'populist' tendency in Jacobite court art after 1715 affected the representation of James Francis's wife, Clementina Sobieska. An exotic Polish princess, with an impressive pedigree – her grandfather had saved Vienna from the Turks in 1683 – she had been kidnapped and imprisoned by the Emperor on her way to meet her husband in Italy in 1718, on the instigation of George I, who had a penchant for locking up inconvenient women. Rescued by the daring Irish adventurer Charles Wogan, her dramatic ride out of captivity was celebrated by numerous Jacobite writers and medallists. Her portrait on Hamerani's medal commemorating her escape shows a dynamic and bold young woman, her hair fashioned to resemble the crest of a helmet, her bosom raised to show her strength of character.[28] Unfortunately, this fairy tale heroine soon became merely a consort; on her later medals, she looked plump and childlike, or grave and matronly, while her husband is depicted on the same pieces as a manly Greek god in armour.[29] The cult of Clementina that became widespread among Catholics in the 1720s probably owed more to her early images than it did to those that subordinated her to her husband.

Clementina gave birth to Charles Edward Stuart in 1720 and Henry Benedict Stuart in 1725; by then, her excessive Catholic piety and dissatisfaction with her position had fired the quarrels with her husband that led to their two separations. James's popularity in England had already waned. By the 1730s he had largely conceded defeat for his own ambitions, and was negotiating with Tory leaders for the separate succession of his son.[30] As in the 1690s, the Prince of Wales became the central figure of Stuart court art, in which the themes of lineage and sovereignty were again paramount. As a baby, he was extolled as 'SPES BRITANNIAE' (the hope of Britain); by 1735, he was being depicted as a handsome young warrior, clad in armour, flanked by the star that had supposedly appeared at his birth, under the motto

---

[28] *Ibid.*, Plate CXLIII, no. 7, and no. 10. For paeans to her, see *The Whole Life and Character of that beautiful, pious and illustrious Princess Sobieski who is by Proxy espous'd to the Chevalier* (London, 1720?), in P.R.O., S.P. 35/24/68, and the narrative of her escape in S.P. 35/40/51; and John T. Gilbert, ed., *Narratives of the Detention, Liberation and Marriage of Maria Clementina Stuart* (Shannon, 1894, 1970).

[29] Hawkins, *Medallic Illustrations*, Plate CXLIII, nos. 8–9.

[30] See Eveline Cruickshanks, 'Lord Cornbury, Bolingbroke and a Plan to Restore the Stuarts, 1731–1735', *Royal Stuart Papers*, 27 (1986).

'MICAT INTER OMNES' (he shines among all).[31] Christ's nativity, according to St Luke, was similarly heralded by a star, as was that of Alexander the Great. Charles Edward's dashing and heroic image was created visually long before the '45, especially in his portraits by Antoine David, Louis-Gabriel Blanchet and the young Catholic Englishman Giles Hussey.[32] The double portraits by David and Blanchet depict Henry Benedict as a sort of side-kick, a placid, dependable companion. It may not be far-fetched to suggest, as Margaret Forster has, that the roots of Charles Edward's self-destruction lay in the idolization of him as a youth.[33] Yet who could have foreseen his unhappy future in the determined gaze of the beautiful young Prince?

Romans and Highlanders, 1745–88

After the rebellion of 1745, Prince Charles Edward Stuart made a concerted effort to promote his own image in England through visual propaganda. This was one of the first English examples of an orchestrated campaign to publicize the political character of an individual. It was made possible by the development of new commercial techniques in the early part of the eighteenth century.[34] Far from opposing the trend towards a 'consumer society', Jacobitism encouraged it, at least in the political arena. Nevertheless, the options that were open to treasonable propaganda were limited; except in very rare circumstances, Jacobites could not advertise their wares.[35] They depended on a network of clubs, loyal printsellers and probably pedlars, rather than on a broad-based 'mass marketing', and they aimed their appeal mainly at the gentry and middling sort.

Prince Charles directed much of this publicity himself. In an undated memorandum, for example, he ordered medals of himself as a child to be recast; a package containing some of these pieces was intercepted on

---

31 Hawkins, *Medallic Illustrations*, Plate CXLIV, nos. 15–16, Plate CL, nos. 3–4.
32 NPG 434–5 (David); Royal Collection (Blanchet); Hussey's drawing of the Prince is in the British Museum, and a miniature by Hussey is at Blair Castle.
33 Margaret Forster, *The Rash Adventurer: The Rise and Fall of Charles Edward Stuart* (St Albans, Herts., 1973), p. 296. For a recent biographical assessment of Charles Edward, see L. L. Bongie, *The Love of a Prince: Bonnie Prince Charlie in France, 1744–1748* (Vancouver, 1986).
34 See Neil McKendrick, John Brewer and J. H. Plumb, *The Birth of a Consumer Society: The Commercialization of Eighteenth-Century England* (Bloomington, 1982).
35 Among the exceptions was Hannah Ashburn, a London glass-seller and fanmaker, whose bill-head of 1745 showed Jacobite roses – G. Bernard Hughes, *English, Scottish and Irish Table Glass, from the Sixteenth Century to 1820* (New York, 1956), p. 242.

its way to Bristol in 1747.[36] In the summer of 1750, in preparation for the visit he was to make to London, he commissioned a new medal, two pictures by Baudouin, a miniature by Le Brun père and a bust by Le Moine.[37] These items were quickly copied in England. Imitations of the bust, which had been displayed in Paris and was much admired, were available from a shop in London within three months. When Charles met Dr William King in the English capital in September 1750, a servant who did not know his identity remarked upon his extraordinary resemblance to the heads on sale in Red Lion Street![38]

Charles Edward's public image in the period 1745–52 differed markedly from the court art of his father and grandfather. He was more of a 'populist' than they were, but he was also fortunate in living amidst the intellectual experimentation that has been called the Enlightenment. One of its features was the revival of interest in classical antiquity; another was the concept of 'natural man', the so-called 'noble savage' who was untainted by social vices.[39] Through both of these avenues, the writers of the Enlightenment sought to escape what they saw as the corruption and tyranny of their own day. The Jacobite cause was attractive to some of them, because it seemed to offer a monarchical solution to modern decadence. Voltaire, the great proponent of the '*thèse royale*', wrote one of the declarations prepared for Charles Edward during the abortive French invasion attempt of 1743–4.[40] In Jacobite iconography, Enlightenment ideas were manifested in two different but complementary figures: the Roman and the Highlander.

It is interesting that so many of the important figures in early classical antiquarianism – the Abbé Grant, James Dawkins, Charles Towneley and others – were Jacobites.[41] By restoring the legacy of Greece and

[36] Helen Farquhar, 'Some Portrait Medals Struck between 1745 and 1752 for Prince Charles Edward', *British Numismatic Journal*, 17, New Series, 7 (1923–4), p. 218; P.R.O., S.P. 36/95, fos. 136–7.
[37] R.A., Stuart 308/45, /93.
[38] William King, *Political and Literary Anecdotes of His Own Times* (London, 1819), p. 199; Farquhar, 'Some Portrait Medals', pp. 215–17. The original bust is now in the Scottish National Portrait Gallery.
[39] For a broad treatment of these themes, see Peter Gay, *The Enlightenment: An Interpretation* (2 vols., New York, 1966–70).
[40] Cruickshanks, *Political Untouchables*, p. 97; Laurence Bongie, 'Voltaire's English, High Treason and a Manifesto for Prince Charles', *Studies on Voltaire and the Eighteenth Century*, 171 (1977), pp. 7–29. See also Peter Gay, *Voltaire's Politics: The Poet as Realist* (New York, 1965), esp. chs. 1 and 7.
[41] See Lesley Lewis, *Connoisseurs and Secret Agents in Eighteenth Century Rome* (London, 1961).

Rome, they were commenting on the degeneration of their own day, and urging a return to the 'patriotic' values of antiquity. 'Patriotism' was of increasing importance in the politics of the 1740s and 1750s; it bore a nonpartisan tinge, and was used both to justify opposition Whiggery and to bolster the ailing Tories. Hugh Cunningham has argued that 'patriotism' in the eighteenth and nineteenth centuries should not be identified with conservatism; yet the radical 'patriot' was always dissatisfied with what was seen as a decline from pristine glory, and the spread of self-interest.[42] In this way, 'patriotism' was critical of the very process of commercialization that often sustained its propaganda. The contradiction could be resolved by elevating commerce into a 'patriotic' duty; and perhaps it is in this concept, rather than in Mandevillian self-interest, that historians should look for the origins of English commercialization.

Charles Edward's image of a Roman 'patriot' originated in the '1745' medal engraved by Norbert Roettiers the younger, probably in 1748. As Helen Farquhar has shown, the piece was modelled on a small medal of 1735 depicting Charles as a boy; but the portrait on the later work is unique.[43] In it, Charles seems to be much older than his actual age, and his physical attributes are engagingly realistic. He is balding, his chin is weak, he is bare-shouldered, without armour. This is an 'authentic' portrait, typical of Roman republican sculpture; the Roman reference is strengthened by the heightening of relief and the incision at the shoulder, which give the impression of a bust. The Roettiers portrait appeared in many other forms of visual propaganda. It was used in jewellery, including gold, onyx, silver gilt and coloured glass versions. Watch-cases bearing the portrait and the motto 'Look, Love and Follow' were brought from France by Jacobite agents, and one Catholic supporter used the Roettiers head as a letter seal in the 1760s.[44] In June 1750, Charles asked George Waters junior, his Paris banker, to have more medals made; he was informed that the mould

---

[42] Hugh Cunningham, 'The Language of Patriotism, 1750–1914', History Workshop, 12 (1981), pp. 8–33. For a similar viewpoint, see Gerald Newman, The Rise of English Nationalism: A Cultural History, 1740–1830 (New York, 1987), esp. chs. 4 and 7.

[43] Hawkins, Medallic Illustrations, Plate CLXV, nos. 10–11; Farquhar, 'Some Portrait Medals', pp. 173–86, 195–7. See Plate 5.

[44] Hawkins, Medallic Illustrations, Plate CLXV, no. 12; Victoria and Albert Museum, Waterton Collection, 932–1871, on display in Case 34, Board E, no. 16; Andrew Lang, Pickle the Spy or the Incognito of Prince Charles (London, 1897), pp. 107–10; Farquhar, 'Some Portrait Medals', pp. 190, 194–5; P.R.O., S.P. 78/237, fo. 62; B.L., Add. MS 28,235, fo. 158.

had been broken, but that the engraver could make a new piece with the same head. An account later appears in the Stuart papers for 300 medals and an unspecified number of medalets.[45]

The purpose of this transaction may have been to supply a Jacobite club that had been organized in 1749 by the Sussex recusant John Caryll, who later funded the *True Briton*. The medals distributed by Caryll's 'Oak Society' had the Roettiers portrait on the obverse and the Cavalier emblem of a withered tree, from whose roots a sapling springs, on the reverse, along with the slogan 'REVIRESCIT' (it revives, or grows green again) and the date 1750. The members of the club were mainly Roman Catholics, and included many women, like Lady Molyneux (Caryll's mother-in-law), Lady Newburgh, Mrs Towneley, Mrs Anderton, Lady Bellew and Lady Mostyn. Several of them purchased a number of medals, and it is likely that they were bought for further circulation. The engraver Thomas Pingo was reimbursed for striking the medals; although he produced commissions for the Hanoverians, he was Italian, and probably had few scruples about English politics.[46] The aim of the Oak Society was almost certainly to raise money for Charles Edward's projected attempt of September 1750, of which more will be told in Chapter 7.[47]

One member of the Oak Society was 'Mr Bickam Engraver'. This was George Bickham of Mays Buildings, St Martin's-in-the-Fields, one of the most prolific engravers of prints and cartoons in Westminster. He may have sold copies of the print, ascribed to the Scottish Jacobite artist Robert Strange, showing the '1745' medal over the poem 'The CHRISTIAN HERO's Martial Looks here shine', verses which also appeared in Caryll and Osborne's *True Briton*.[48] In the summer and autumn of 1749, Bickham was implicated in the sale of a series of Jacobite cartoons.[49] One of them, which is untitled, associates Charles

[45] R.A., Stuart 308/93, 315/215–215A.
[46] B.L., Add. MS 28,249, fos. 308–97; Hawkins, *Medallic Illustrations*, Plate CLXXIV, no. 1; Seddon, 'The Jacobite Engravers', p. 40; Grant Francis, *Old English Drinking Glasses: Their Chronology and Sequence* (London, 1926), pp. 187–8; Farquhar, 'Some Portrait Medals', pp. 186–90.
[47] The standard reconstruction of the plots of 1750–3 is in Petrie, *The Jacobite Movement: The Last Phase*, pp. 140–59, which reproduces his article 'The Elibank Plot', *T.R.H.S.*, 4th Series, 14 (1931), pp. 175–96.
[48] See the quote at the beginning of this chapter, as well as Farquhar, 'Some Portrait Medals', p. 183; R.A., Stuart, Printed Papers, Box 6, no. 37. The last lines of the poem appear in *Mitre and Crown*, May 1749; see also R.A., Stuart 300/135.
[49] P.R.O., S.P. 36/111, fos. 165–76, and Herbert M. Atherton, *Political Prints in the Age of Hogarth* (Oxford, 1974), pp. 76–8. Bickham also sold seditious maps of Culloden, engraved by a friend of Caryll's – P.R.O., S.P. 36/116, fos. 21, 23, 25; S.P. 36/117, fo. 316; B.L., Add. MS 28,231, fos. 81, 92–5.

Edward with the Roman emblem of a liberty cap.[50] Another, called
'The Agreeable Contrast between the Formidable John of Gaunt [i.e.
the Duke of Cumberland] and Don Carlos of Southern Extraction',
depicts Charles as a thoughtful youth reading in a well-stocked library.
What are the books on his shelves? Leslie, perhaps, or Hickes or
Harbin? No; they are 'The Original Laws, the Original Contract',
Thucydides, Machiavelli, *De L'Esprit des Lois*, Livy, Tacitus, Sueto-
nius, Harrington and Locke![51]

Like the liberty cap, Charles's library is meant to convey his devotion
to 'patriot' principles, classical virtue and the English constitution. Its
Whiggish tenor hints at the Jacobite efforts to unite the opposition in
London and Westminster behind the Stuart banner, which culminated
in the activities of the Independent Electors of Westminster, described
in Chapter 7, and the plot of 1752, 'laid and transacted by Whiggers',
according to Charles himself.[52] In that year, another medal was
executed by Roettiers, bearing on the reverse the same scene that
appeared on the '1745' piece, a ship sailing towards Britannia, but with
the mottoes 'O DIU DESIDERATA NAVIS' (O long awaited ship) and
'LAETAMINI CIVES' (rejoice citizens), with the date 23 September
1752.[53] The term 'CIVES' has a strong Roman connotation, but it also
may refer to the citizens of London, who were supposed to rise up in
support of the Young Pretender, according to the scheme concocted by
Alexander Murray, the darling of the Independent Electors.

The obverse of the 1752 medal carries the '1745' head under the
slogan 'REDEAT ILLE MAGNUS GENIUS BRITANNIAE', Dr King's famous
cry at the Radcliffe Camera oration of 1749.[54] It was suggested earlier
that King was the spokesman for a Jacobite 'Machiavellian moment' in
the 1740s and early 1750s, which produced a vocal critique of the
'luxury' and 'decadence' of Hanoverian England. This would explain
the presence of Tacitus, Machiavelli and Harrington in the library of

---

50 Stephens, ed., *Catalogue*, vol. iii, no. 2834, pp. 627–8.
51 *Ibid.*, vol. iii, no. 3042, pp. 753–4. See Plate 6. Although it was swiftly suppressed,
   this cartoon must have had some impact, because it elicited at least two government
   replies – no. 2790, pp. 599–600, and no. 2832, pp. 626–7.
52 Lang, *Pickle the Spy*, p. 178. The chief Whig in the plot was Alderman George
   Heathcote.
53 Hawkins, *Medallic Illustrations*, Plate CLXXV, no. 11.
54 See Chapter 1. King's famous line may have been derived from Thomas Warton's
   poem, 'The Eighth Ode of the Second Book of Horace Imitated. To Sir Robert
   Walpole', verse i, lines 7–8: 'Poor *Britain* might appease her Griefs, and smile, /
   And hope her Genius had not left her Isle' – Thomas Warton the elder, *Poems on Several
   Occasions* (New York, 1930), p. 47. This would connect the Augustan theme of
   Jacobite poetry with King's 'Machiavellianism'.

'Don Carlos', as well as the use of devices like the liberty cap or the references to Roman republican sculpture. As J. G. A. Pocock has shown, a 'neo-Harringtonian' tradition of political discourse survived into the eighteenth century, and can be traced in the works of writers like Bolingbroke.[55] Yet the Jacobites were not advocating a republican solution to Britain's distress; Charles Edward was more of a Sulla, a Caesar, an Augustus, than a Cicero or Brutus. He resembled Bolingbroke's 'Patriot King', a monarch who would repair the damage wrought by decades of self-interest in government.

In his pictorial representations, Charles Edward retained the god-like aura of Stuart royalty. One of the 1749 cartoons shows him as the restorer of nature, standing beneath a leafy tree chanting 'Mercy & Love Peace &c.', while his nemesis Cumberland is placed next to a bare tree, muttering 'B[loo]d & W[oun]ds'. A woman in a tartan dress with a basket of roses under her arm (Flora Macdonald) stares at the princely flower-child and his pet, a greyhound (symbol of loyalty), saying 'Oh, the Agreeable Creature W^t a Long tail he has'; on the other side, an angry woman (his Savoyard mistress) shakes her fist at Cumberland and his retainer, an elephant, declaring 'Let no body like Me be Deceiv'd W^{th} such a pittiful tail'.[56] The sexual reference to the 'tails' recalls the importance of fertility, and of women, in the Jacobite cycle of commemoration, and provides another example of the 'vegetation god' idea. The mottoes on the 'Don Carlos' cartoon extol his 'Sacred Feet' and ascribe his parentage to '*Mars* and *Venus*'; in spite of his republican book collection, there can be no doubt that this young Prince is divine.

The title of 'Patriot Prince' was not monopolized by Charles Edward Stuart. Frederick, the Hanoverian Prince of Wales, was presenting himself in the same light at this time, and it is debatable as to who was copying whom. A rumour that Frederick had appeared in plaid at the Middlesex election of 1750 seemed to imply that he was imitating his Stuart rival.[57] At any rate, Frederick's 'Patriot Prince' image was inherited by his son, George III, with tumultuous consequences for the English political system. Ironically Charles Edward's 'patriotic' persona also prefigured the image of George III's arch-critic, John Wilkes, who sought, like 'Don Carlos', to attract adherents of all political persuasions by symbolizing a legitimacy that was consti-

[55] See Chapter 1, n. 91.
[56] Stephens, ed., *Catalogue*, vol. ii, no. 2833, pp. 626–7. See Plate 7.
[57] W. S. Lewis, gen. ed., *The Yale Edition of Horace Walpole's Correspondence* (41 vols., New Haven, Ct., 1937–84), vol. xx: *Correspondence with Sir Horace Mann*, iv, p. 131.

tutional and 'republican'. Wilkes did not appropriate divine sanction for himself, but his supporters sought to establish a hero-cult around a man – a sprightly fertility figure, perhaps? – who stood, like Charles Edward Stuart, outside the channels of conventional politics.[58] The Wilkites resorted to a commercial campaign that was markedly similar to that of the Jacobites two decades earlier, although it was maintained on a larger scale and more openly. The Independent Electors of Westminster may have provided a link between the two political movements.[59]

The Wilkites, however, abominated the other incarnation of Charles Edward Stuart: the man in plaid. After 1760, of course, this figure was associated with the Earl of Bute, who had always been a strong Hanoverian, and was a man of order rather than a rebel; but the Jacobite implication remained. The image of the Prince in plaid was an historical reality, as he had worn Highland dress during the '45, although most of the English depictions give only the roughest approximation of the bonnet and tartan or trews.[60] Nevertheless, the costume of the clans was instantly recognizable. In the anti-Cumberland cartoon 'John of Gant in Love, or Mars on his Knees', a tiny figure in the background, garbed in rather ludicrous plaid, is shown saying 'No Swines for me', referring to the obese Hanoverian Prince; this barely noticeable detail betrays the Jacobite import of the print.[61] The Highland Prince appeared in all the artistic media of Jacobite propaganda. Medals were emblazoned with him carrying an enormous sword; book illustrations and prints depicted him as a bold Scottish adventurer.[62] Some of these artistic interpretations are rather comical; in one mezzotint, Charles wears an outfit that makes him look like a Cavalier, with long flowing hair and a bagpipe under his arm.[63] A

---

[58] For the image of George III, see Linda Colley, 'The Apotheosis of George III: Loyalty, Royalty and the British Nation, 1760–1820', *P.& P.*, 102 (1984), pp. 94–129; for Wilkes, see John Brewer, *Party Ideology and Popular Politics at the Accession of George III* (Cambridge, 1976), ch. 9, and Linda Colley, 'Eighteenth-Century English Radicalism before Wilkes', *T.R.H.S.*, 5th Series, 31 (1981), pp. 1–19.

[59] See John Brewer, 'Commercialization and Politics', in McKendrick, Brewer and Plumb, *Birth of a Consumer Society*, pp. 197–262. The *North Briton* attacked the Jacobitism of the Independent Electors in nos. xxxvi and xxxviii, 5 and 19 Feb. 1763; but the later Wilkites cultivated ties with the old Tories, as Linda Colley has shown.

[60] For Scottish costume, see John Telfer Dunbar, *History of Highland Dress* (2nd edn, London, 1979).

[61] Stephens, ed., *Catalogue*, vol. iii, no. 2834, pp. 627–8.

[62] Hawkins, *Medallic Illustrations*, Plate CLXV, no. 13, Plate CLXVI, no. 2, Plate CLXXIII, no. 16; Farquhar, 'Some Portrait Medals', p. 212; frontispiece to the 1746 edition of *Ascanius*, in Yale University, Sterling Library, Bz27 31u.

[63] Stephens, ed., *Catalogue*, vol. iii, no. 2674, pp. 535–6.

curious Staffordshire porcelain model of 'Fame on the Crest of the Wave' shows 'a gingerbread-like Prince Charles', in bonnet and tartan, 'shaking the paw of the British lion flanked by two pug dogs'.[64]

Many versions of the Prince in plaid were derived from an engraving attributed to Robert Strange, who had joined the '45 rebellion and fled to France. This depiction of Charles Edward was even copied on imported Chinese porcelain mugs – for those of different sympathies, similar mugs were made showing the Duke of Cumberland.[65] The portrait also appeared on Jacobite glassware. Of two hundred Jacobite glasses in English collections located by Dr G. B. Seddon, twenty bear engraved heads of Charles Edward. The majority show the Prince in bonnet and plaid, with the motto 'AUDENTIOR IBO' (I go more boldly).[66] A punch bowl has survived with the same inscription, suggesting that the glasses were made for a Jacobite club.[67] A few glasses present a side view of Charles, in which his balding head, long Stuart nose and weak chin are evident; the source may be the '1745' Roettiers medal, although the glass engraver has added a plaid coat.[68]

Highland dress became a stigma in the iconography of the 1760s, but it had a more positive connotation for some in the decade after 1745. Unlike costume armour, it had a real, not an artificial, military air. The Highlander did not have the genteel look of an eighteenth-century English army officer; he was a wild, brutal type of soldier whose courage lay in his recklessness. The Highlander was a barbarian, not a Roman. His romantic character was not invented by Sir Walter Scott. When we contemplate the brightly enamelled salt-glaze jug in the Harris Museum at Preston, showing a tartaned warrior with targe and claymore, we should consider the strangeness of such an image for contemporary English eyes. In 1750, only one British regiment wore Highland dress, and it had rarely appeared south of the Tweed. The Highlands were isolated, their people virtually unknown, except as primitive warriors and rebels. For the Lancashire family that owned the

---

64 Peter Bradshaw, *Eighteenth Century English Porcelain Figures, 1745–1795* (Woodbridge, Suffolk, 1981), p. 226 and plate 131; now in the Katz Collection, Boston Museum of Fine Art.
65 For the print, see James Dennistoun, *Memoirs of Sir Robert Strange* (2 vols., London, 1855), vol. i, pp. 48–50; Francis, *Old English Drinking Glasses*, Plate LXVIII; Farquhar, 'Some Portrait Medals', pp. 203–6. The Chinese mug is in the British Museum, Department of Oriental Antiquities, Franks Collection, no. 809.
66 Seddon, 'The Jacobite Engravers', p. 40, Figure 3, pp. 52–3, and Figure 12, pp. 70–1. See also Plate 8.
67 British Museum, Catalogue of English Pottery, No. E 113.
68 Seddon, 'The Jacobite Engravers', Figure 9, pp. 64–5.

jug, the little man on it must have seemed as bizarre as James Boswell did when he entered a fancy dress party in 'Corsican' costume; and the romantic fascination that later glorified Pasquale Paoli had much in common with the popularity of Prince Charlie in plaid.[69]

The comparison with Paoli points towards a reconciliation of the Roman and barbarian Charles, the classical and romantic images of the Prince. Both were united in the 'patriot', the man of dignified Roman virtue who longed for the simple life and unbridled freedom of his rustic ancestors. The dreams of the embattled Augustan were fulfilled in the rude Highlander, just as the ideal of American republicanism was to be enshrined in the primitive rectitude of the 'backwoodsman'. This concept of the 'patriot' was embryonic in the 1740s and early 1750s; the second half of the century would bring it to fruition through the influence of the Enlightenment, with its twin visions of neo-classical purity and the 'natural man'. Jacobitism was in the vanguard of these intellectual developments, and Charles Edward's visual propaganda must have seemed very up-to-date in the decade after the '45, particularly in comparison with the tired and stilted court art that was favoured both by the Old Pretender and by George II.

Yet all this was to change with astonishing rapidity. The Elibank Plot disintegrated in 1753, amidst rumours of Charles's drunkenness and suspicions of his mistress, Clementina Walkinshaw, whose sister was in the household of the Princess of Wales. Within little more than a year, Charles's reputation had been ruined. The Jacobite cause never recovered from the fall of its idol. In 1760, when Clementina abandoned him, taking with her their daughter Charlotte, the Prince went into a long depression. His succession to his father's titles in 1766 did not stimulate a new propaganda campaign; he failed even to issue a medal, although his brother Henry, now a powerful Cardinal, commissioned one of himself.[70] In 1769, however, the ever-loyal John Caryll began sending Charles sensible advice about reinvigorating his cause. Caryll became Jacobite Secretary of State in 1770, and for the next five years he steered his master along a steadier path.[71] His greatest achievement was Charles's marriage in 1772 to Louisa of Stolberg-Gedern, a minor

[69] See Frederick A. Pottle, *James Boswell: The Earlier Years, 1740–1769* (New York, 1963), p. 425. Boswell toyed with the idea of making Charles Edward King of Corsica – Frank Brady and Frederick A. Pottle, eds., *Boswell on the Grand Tour: Italy, Corsica and France, 1765–1766* (New York, 1955), pp. 245, 324–5. Highland dress was a favourite costume in masquerades of the 1760s and 1770s.

[70] It is reproduced in Alice Shield, *Henry Stuart, Cardinal of York and his Times* (London, 1908), facing p. 264.

[71] See R.A. Stuart 448–52 for Caryll's correspondence.

German princess, whose dowry was provided by the French government.

The marriage to Louisa resuscitated Jacobite iconography. Charles was fortunate in having found a witty and dynamic wife, who reportedly captivated a string of English admirers, notably Thomas Coke of Holkham, the future agricultural reformer. He escorted her to Rome to meet her husband, danced with her at a costume ball, and was given by his paramour a portrait of himself in fancy dress, with an amorous statue of Ariadne gazing upon him.[72] Louisa was Charles's last propaganda asset, and he used her well as long as Caryll was advising him. Although their wedding medal was a rather shoddy piece of old-fashioned court art, most of Louisa's pictures are informal and charming.[73] The intimate portrait of 1772, depicting the Stuart Queen playing a guitar, flatters her with a delicate prettiness; it was owned by the English College at St Omer, and is now at Stonyhurst College in Lancashire.[74] The English artist Ozias Humphrey made a pair of miniatures of Charles and Louisa around 1775; she is graced with an intriguingly romantic expression and he looks intelligent and dignified, clearly a match for the ponderous George III.[75] A print of 'The Consort of the Chevalier Stuart, Commonly Called the Pretender' circulated in Britain in the mid-1770s. Like the wedding medal, it portrays Louisa as grand and splendid, with a magnificent *bouffante* hair-do and a dazzling display of jewellery; but this courtly image is framed by the old Jacobite device of a lover's knot, a hint of indigenous 'populist' symbolism. Beneath the picture is an allegorical scene, where Providence directs the gaze of a seated Louisa towards a ship approaching a rocky island, above which hangs a crown held by a celestial hand.[76] This is an aggressive piece of propaganda, not simply a curio; it reflects the same confidence expressed in the con-

[72] A. M. W. Stirling, *Coke of Norfolk and his Friends* (London, 1912), pp. 65–6. For her other admirers, see Chapter 9.

[73] For the medal, see Farquhar, 'Some Portrait Medals', p. 201, and Herbert M. Vaughan, *The Last Stuart Queen: Louise Countess of Albany: Her Life and Letters* (London, 1910), facing p. 10. The couple are shown garbed in togas.

[74] It is reproduced in Forster, *The Rash Adventurer*, as well as other places.

[75] See George C. Williamson, *Life and Works of Ozias Humphrey, R.A.* (London, 1918), p. 50, and facing illustration, for Charles's portrait; Louisa's, which is now at Burghley House, Northamptonshire, is reproduced as the frontispiece to Vaughan, *The Last Stuart Queen*.

[76] See Plate 9 for this print. Bishop Gordon mentioned it as being sold in London in 1773, and in the following year, Bishop Forbes gave one to the Catholic Lady Linton, wife of the future Earl of Traquair – Paton, ed., *Lyon in Mourning*, vol. iii, pp. 287, 304–6.

temporary portrait of Charles in armour, gesturing towards a ship at sea.[77]

Charles's petulant and vindictive character, however, ruined whatever hopes he had of regaining a political role. In May 1775, he dismissed John Caryll when the diligent Englishman disobeyed him by asking the Pope to recognize the Stuart King's titles.[78] Within two years, new reports of Charles's dissipation and his cruel treatment of his wife began to circulate.[79] Worst of all, the couple still had not produced an heir. On a St Andrew's day binge in 1780, Charles assaulted his wife physically, which caused her to leave him, first for a convent, then for her lover Alfieri. They were formally separated in 1784. As a last resort, the ailing Charles summoned his long-neglected daughter Charlotte to his side. Growing up in obscurity and relative poverty in Paris, Charlotte was a thorough *bourgeoise*, and she may not have taken very seriously her father's attempts to promote her as the ultimate incarnation of the Stuart cause. He legitimized her, made her Duchess of Albany, and commissioned medals for her, bearing figures of Hope, maps of England, the Stuart arms and storm-tossed ships, with mottoes like 'SPES TAMEN EST UNA' (there is still one hope).[80]

Charlotte may have had little intention of carrying on her father's pretensions, but she did not mind being idealized by artists. The Scot Gavin Hamilton drew her in chalk in a severe neo-classical style, while his compatriot H. D. Hamilton painted her as a beautiful young woman wearing a tiara.[81] These striking representations carry echoes of the Roman and romantic conceptions of Charles Edward Stuart, reminding us of how advanced Jacobite iconography had once been. In his own final portrait, however, Charles reverted to an older tradition of iconography. Commentators have often said that this work, executed by H. D. Hamilton in 1785, shows the Young Pretender's

---

77 The painting, purchased by Lady Braye from Cardinal York's estate, is now at Stamford Hall, Leicestershire.
78 R.A., Stuart, 480/110.
79 A supporter in London angrily rebuked him in 1777 for his behaviour towards Louisa – *ibid.*, 490/57.
80 H.M.C., *Tenth Report, Appendix, Part VI. The Manuscripts of the Lord Braye* (London, 1887), p. 236. Charlotte meant to send 200 of the medals to Paris, but was concerned that the title on them, 'Charlotte, Duchesse d'Albanie, fille de Charles III., Roi de la Grande Bretagne, de France et d'Irlande, défenseur de la Foi', would cause difficulties with the authorities – Henrietta Tayler, *Prince Charlie's Daughter: Being the Life and Letters of Charlotte of Albany* (London, 1950), p. 74.
81 The drawing is in the collection of Lord Primrose; the painting is in the Scottish National Portrait Gallery.

physical and moral decadence; but this is to read life into art falsely. He does not look drunk, or sick, or disheartened; he merely seems tired and sad. His large drooping eyes, pouting lower lip and sagging chin convey a sense of pathos, and his coat, in spite of the Garter ribbon, is very plain. The painting recalls the image of the 'man of sorrows', the royal martyr Charles I. At the last, Charles Edward had returned to the most venerated of Stuart myths. The portrait struck a responsive chord in the hearts of the 'faithful remnant', and there are more copies of it in British collections than any other picture of the exiled Stuarts.[82]

When Charles Edward Stuart died in January 1788, Jacobitism died with him. His daughter began almost immediately to negotiate the sale to the Hanoverian Prince of Wales of a jewel worn by Charles I on the scaffold.[83] Her uncle Henry Benedict, Cardinal York, or Henry IX as he was in the Stuart succession, made only one effort at visual propaganda in his nineteen-year 'reign', and it was no more than a reissue of his 1766 medal, a fine but uninspiring example of court art. The motto on the reverse was 'NON DESIDERIIS HOMINUM, SED VOLUNTATE DEI' (not by the desire of men, but by the will of God).[84] It was an admission of a century of failure, a renunciation of 'populism' and a reaffirmation of the narrow divine right doctrines that had never been enough to sustain the cause. As a political statement, it was so inoffensive as to lack any real seditious import; nobody could be offended by it. The piece was handed out to anyone who visited the Cardinal, including the banker Thomas Coutts, who carried one back to his patron, King George III.[85]

Propaganda was the vital heart of Jacobite political culture, feeding the many arteries of the cause with infusions of ideas and images that made action possible. To be sure, propaganda did not create Jacobite political behaviour; but without ideas or images, there would have been no Jacobitism at all, and discontent with the Revolutionary settlement would have taken another form. The Jacobite voice was not undivided, however, and the differences between Nonjuring and 'Whiggish' principles, between elite and demotic poetry, between court

[82] Two versions exist in England, the original (NPG 376) and one owned by the antiquarian Charles Towneley, now at Towneley Hall, Lancashire; three copies can be found in Scotland (SNPG 622, Dundee Art Gallery and Lennoxlove, Lothian).

[83] Beinecke Osborn Files, 'Lavington Box', letter of Ralph Payne to Prince of Wales, 28 May 1788. The unfortunate Charlotte died of liver cancer in November 1789.

[84] The medal is reproduced in Shield, *Henry Stuart*, facing p. 264.

[85] E. H. Coleridge, *The Life of Thomas Coutts, Banker* (2 vols., London, 1920), vol. i, p. 271.

art and 'populist' iconography, have been central to the preceding chapters. Nevertheless, the basis of Jacobite propaganda was always a moral statement: tampering with the legitimate succession had brought about a national malaise. This conviction arose from an acceptance of the sacred or mystical character of monarchy, no matter how vaguely it might be expressed; and the conception of sacred monarchy was itself derived from the medieval theory of the king's two bodies. The Revolution of 1688 had violently separated the two bodies, allowing an invasion of immorality and vice. The weak were oppressed by self-interested minorities – Whigs, Dissenters, foreigners – who were no longer restrained by the influence of a unifying kingship.

This was the standard Tory nightmare, produced by fear of a new and unpredictable existence. Yet it would be a mistake to picture Jacobitism as no more than a reactionary attitude, a yearning for the order and stability of a mythical past. The restoration of the Stuarts also offered the promise of a better future, of an end to war and social strife. The repressive laws passed since the Revolution were to be repealed, and Parliament was to be made free of corruption and manipulation. For some, Jacobitism even meant an extension of religious toleration. These aspirations must not be ignored. The appeal of Jacobite propaganda cannot be explained simply in terms of an atavistic urge; in fact, the rhetoric of the Stuart cause was flexible enough to absorb many of the 'progressive' intellectual trends of the eighteenth century, and it would not be difficult to construct an interpretation of Jacobitism as a kind of 'radicalism'. Of course, this approach would undervalue the divine right, High Church, anti-republican side of the cause, upon which Jacobite 'radicalism' often fed. Historians should recognize that Jacobitism was not a static ideology; it was a vibrant, disunified, often contradictory collection of arguments, a cacophony of variations on the recurring tune of kingship.

PART TWO

Structures of Jacobitism

Chapter 4

Jacobite underworlds: the practice of treason

> I hope some Patriot will rouze the People to shake off this Arbitrary Government, and Animate them with the Saying of the *Noble Roman* who defended the Capitol.
>
> Livy, *Quosque tandem*, &c.
>
> — HOW LONG WILL YOU BE
>
> IGNORANT OF YOUR STRENGTH
>
> COUNT YOUR NUMBERS
>
> *Sure you ought to fight with more Resolution for Liberty than your Oppressors for Dominion.*
>
> COUNT YOUR NUMBERS. *Vox Populi, Vox Dei* (1719)[1]

Organized political movements are often studied through the history of institutions – clubs and associations, legislative bodies and trade unions. Jacobitism cannot be examined in this light. It had no institutional existence, except at the Stuart court, which exercised only minimal control over its supporters. Although the Jacobite gentry formed a wide variety of clubs, as will be seen in Chapter 9, their main purpose was sociable rather than conspiratorial. In order to understand the vast range of Jacobite treasonable practices, from espionage and recruiting to sabotage and petty acts of defiance, we must look not at institutional structures, but at patterns of behaviour. Every example of treason, including many that might otherwise be regarded as unimportant, made a statement about the attitudes of its perpetrators, and was defined by characteristics that linked it to a broader political framework. For these reasons, treasonable behaviour can be examined as part of the culture of Jacobitism.

Few of these practices were attributable to 'spontaneous' feelings, generalized causes or unfocussed discontent. They were usually the

---

[1] *Vox Populi, Vox Dei*, p. 7; also found in a letter dropped in a street in a Surrey market town in 1724 – P.R.O., S.P. 35/53/13.

expressions of what might be called Jacobite communities – ex-army officers, Irish immigrants, Nonjurors, English recusants. Together, these groups comprised a widespread clandestine network for the propagation of the Jacobite gospel – in effect, a series of interlocking Jacobite underworlds, founded on religious and social solidarities. The term 'underworld' is doubly appropriate, because a professional criminal element could be found among those who promoted the interests of the exiled Stuarts. The Jacobite underworld, however, was not confined to secret activities. Its denizens also publicized the cause, and themselves, through commercial media. Newspapers avidly followed the exploits of Jacobite heroes, or villains, and brought to their readership a vivid awareness of the moral issues involved in the struggle over the succession. The Jacobites were constantly frustrated in their attempts to infiltrate English institutions; but they were masters of publicity, and they turned their vicissitudes into a profusion of evocative stories and images. This chapter will consider five aspects of the Jacobite underworld: the tavern culture of ex-army officers, the social basis of conspiracy, military recruitment among the Irish, the role of criminal gangs and the significance of individual acts of protest. The correspondences between them illustrate the ways by which behaviour could become a means of communication.

The theatre of the ex-officers

The first Jacobite group to catch the imagination of the public, albeit in a negative way, was composed of a small circle of discontented gentlemen, displaced functionaries and cashiered army officers. The most reckless and audacious of these men were the ex-officers, who delighted in outrageous displays of their treasonable allegiances. John Childs has recently estimated that one third of James II's army officers followed him to France and Ireland, and another third retired or were dismissed from service.[2] Many of the latter became Jacobite agents. The government press represented them as wild, desperate individuals of no fortune or credit – the same caricature that Macaulay later sought to perpetuate in his portrayal of these 'restless and unprincipled men'.[3] This view reflected the fear of a sort of Jacobite *lumpenproletariat* of demobilized soldiers and professional criminals. In the eyes of their enemies, Jacobites were of 'the dangerous classes', persons without

[2] John Childs, *The Army, James II, and the Revolution* (Manchester, 1980), p. 206.
[3] Macaulay, *History of England*, vol. v, ch. 21, pp. 2504–6.

honour or scruples, often outsiders like the hated Irish, always ready to engage in detestable crimes.

It was a ridiculous parody of James II's officers. Many of them were proprietors of large estates, like Sir Theophilus Oglethorpe of Godalming, Surrey; others were minor but no less respectable gentlemen like Lionel Walden of Huntingdon. Younger sons of the aristocracy and gentry often chose military careers, and James was served by many such men, including Colonel James Grahme, brother of Lord Preston, and Sir John Talbot. The notorious Sir John Fenwick had been obliged to sell his Northumbrian properties for debt, but he was still a gentleman and had formidable connections. All of these officers were Anglicans, and had been Members of Parliament; all became active Jacobite agents.[4] Roman Catholic and Irish officers were often poorer, but they were not desperadoes. Edward Sackville, a recusant younger son of a junior branch of the Earl of Dorset's family, was a professional soldier who owned some land in Kent, had served as an M.P., and obtained for his son a post in the household at St Germain.[5] Like his ex-army colleagues, he was no penniless adventurer.

Nevertheless, some former officers fit the Macaulayesque stereotype. The most infamous of them was Captain George Porter, grandson of the royalist diplomat and poet Endymion Porter. The eldest of Endymion's five sons defected to the Parliamentarians; his third son was a 'swashbuckler of the worst type'; the fourth was a playwright who killed two men in duels and abducted the daughter of the Earl of Newport. George Porter was the offspring of this union, and he took after his father and uncles. In 1684, he murdered a man who had accidentally struck him with a cane at the theatre; he may also have killed an upholsterer some years earlier. He has rightly been called 'almost pathologically aggressive'. After losing his captaincy in Slingsby's Horse at the Revolution, he lived on a small annuity, but was, naturally, deep in debt.[6]

Porter's background was exceptional; his social life was not. Jacobite ex-officers were inclined to display a flamboyant zeal, modelled on the behaviour of the Cavaliers.[7] They congregated in taverns in London and Westminster, close to the centre of political power. A raid in March

---

[4] See their biographies in Basil Duke Henning, ed., *The History of Parliament: The House of Commons, 1660–1690* (3 vols., London, 1983).
[5] *Ibid.*, vol. iii, pp. 377–8.
[6] See *D.N.B.* for Endymion Porter, and Garrett, pp. 32–4.
[7] For the activities of Cavalier officers under the Commonwealth, see David Underdown, *Royalist Conspiracy in England, 1649–1660* (New Haven, 1960).

1690/1 on the Blue Posts and the Dog in Drury Lane, and the Bear in Holborn, turned up Captains Throgmorton, Abercromby, Dowdwell and Scudamore, along with Sir Roger L'Estrange, the pamphleteer, and a certain Father Francis.[8] These taverns were the settings for some serious plotting, as in May 1695, when the Earl of Ailesbury and Viscount Montgomery met with Fenwick and Captain Robert Charnock at the King's Head, Leadenhall Street, to discuss a restoration scheme.[9] Important Jacobite anniversaries were marked with drunken tavern revels, which were unfailingly reported by the Williamite press. To commemorate the day James Francis Stuart's birth had been announced, the disaffected gathered in their dens to drink his health in February 1691/2.[10] Warrants were issued in October 1693 for persons who had celebrated James II's birthday in Drury Lane by making a bonfire and proposing toasts like 'Box it about, it will come to my father'.[11] In 1695, the ex-officers decided to turn their observance of the Prince of Wales's birthday into a full-scale riot, with disastrous consequences, as will be shown in Chapter 6. The prosecutions that followed did not stop the Jacobite ex-officers, who commemorated King James's birthday in October 1695 'in their utmost gayety', and marked 10 June 1696 with healths and music at the Tun tavern in the Strand.[12] Only the Treaty of Ryswick, which buried James II's hopes, put an end to this Jacobite 'gayety'.

The tavern culture of the Jacobite ex-officers was a conscious affront to the supposedly 'puritan' sobriety of the Williamite regime, a way of suggesting, however erroneously, that the Saints were again in power.[13] Taverns were also the stages for the extravagant theatre of the ex-officers. They aimed to capture the attention of the public by their escapades; they were in a sense showmen or players, and it was no accident that their close associates included the actor Cardell Goodman and the 'singing-men' Reading and Pate.[14] They exhibited their sympa-

8 Luttrell, vol. ii, p. 189.
9 Garrett, pp. 28–32; [W. E. Buckley, ed.], Memoirs of Thomas, Earl of Ailesbury. Written by Himself (2 vols., Westminster, 1890), vol. i, p. 354. Ailesbury was scandalized by the place, which he believed to be a brothel.
10 Luttrell, vol. ii, p. 353.
11 Ibid., vol. iii, p. 207. For the source of the expression, see the anecdote about Sir Walter Ralegh and his son in Andrew Clark, ed., 'Brief Lives,' chiefly of Contemporaries, set down by John Aubrey, between the Years 1669 & 1696 (2 vols., Oxford, 1898), vol. ii, p. 185.
12 Luttrell, vol. iv, p. 71.
13 For the culture of drink, see Peter Clark, The English Alehouse: A Social History, 1200–1830 (London, 1983).
14 Bodl. Carte MS 329, fo. 146; Garrett, pp. 24–8.

thies at every opportunity, even when confined – some Irish prisoners in the Savoy illuminated their windows for King James's birthday in 1691.[15] Oglethorpe and Fenwick were mentioned in the papers the same year for cocking their hats at Queen Mary in public places, a gesture of contempt.[16] Violence often marked the private lives of these men. One of the rioters of 1695 fought a duel over a woman he had met at a playhouse; he killed his opponent, but died of his own wounds.[17] At Norwich in 1697, a Captain Ogilby who 'hath some years sculk'd here with a certain widdow woman of this countrey that kept him to serve her purposes', was killed by an Irish Jacobite companion after an evening of heavy drinking and plotting.[18]

The theatrical life-style of the ex-officers was not engendered by a consistent political viewpoint. Oglethorpe and Fenwick were prominent 'Middletonians', who favoured concessions to the Church of England. Other ex-officers, particularly Roman Catholics, were opposed to any conciliation. Colonel John Parker, an Irishman, wrote to Lord Melfort from Lancashire in 1692, advising him and King James to 'Waft yourselves ouer & we will throw ourselues at your feete with the 2 Idols Liberty and Property'; he counselled against coming to terms with the High Church and 'Whiggish' Jacobites.[19] The infamous Assassination Plot of 1696 was concocted primarily by so-called 'Noncompounders' like Parker. This conspiracy, however, was not a sinister and half-mad plan concocted by a gang of impecunious villains. It was linked to the scheme of Sir William Parkyns, a former Clerk of Chancery, for an insurrection in the north and Midlands.[20] According to a paper sent to the French government, the Duke of Beaufort and the Earls of Ailesbury, Exeter, Chesterfield and Yarmouth, all of them Nonjurors, were prepared to rise in support of a landing by French troops.[21] Louis XIV sent an army to Calais and waited for a change in the weather to launch an invasion. The plan for William's assassination may have been unknown to him and to most of the English plotters, but it was part of a wider conspiracy, not a desperate attempt.

[15] Luttrell, vol. ii, p. 294.   [16] Ibid., p. 204.   [17] Ibid., vol. iii, p. 489.

[18] E. M. Thompson, ed., Letters of Humphrey Prideaux sometime Dean of Norwich to John Ellis sometime Under-Secretary of State, 1674–1722, Camden Society, 15 (1875), p. 188.

[19] Rev. T. C. Porteous, 'New Light on the Lancashire Jacobite Plot, 1692–4', T.L.C.A.S., 50 (1934–5), p. 31.

[20] Garrett, p. 103; T. B. Howell, ed., A Complete Collection of State Trials (33 vols., London, 1816–26), vol. xiii, col. 82.

[21] Pierre Burger, 'Spymaster to Louis XIV: A Study of the Papers of the Abbé Eusèbe Renaudot', in Cruickshanks, ed., Ideology and Conspiracy, pp. 124–6.

The assassins themselves were not shady characters, with the exception of Porter. Parkyns was rich; so was the London brewer Sir John Friend. Ambrose Rookwood's father had an estate at Stanningfield in Norfolk; Thomas Keyes's family were settled at Glatton in Huntingdonshire. Robert Lowick was of an ancient Yorkshire family of gentry, and Thomas Pendergrass's forebears had lost their Irish properties to Cromwell. Only Pendergrass was poor, and none of them was indigent or rootless.[22] Their conspiracy, however, was hardly respectable. Assassination was universally abhorred; contrary to popular belief, it was not sanctioned by the Roman Catholic Church. Rookwood and Keyes may have shared the convictions of their ancestors, who were executed for taking part in the Gunpowder Plot of 1605, but other Catholics, like Lowick and Pendergrass, had real qualms about killing William, and some of the assassins, like Parkyns and Friend, were Anglicans.

The explanation for the Assassination Plot lies not in the principles of the ex-officers, but in their lives – their tavern culture, their flamboyant gestures, their love of intrigue and violence, all of which expressed an ardent and intemperate loyalty. The assassins were products and victims of a swashbuckling Cavalier mentality, and their plot was the finale of a drama they had been acting out for years. It had a clear message: that the times were out of joint, and that murder could be legal. Unhappily for the plotters, they were thwarted in the last act, and their play ended as tragedy, with a final scene on the gallows. These men, who had called James II their 'father', and had behaved like disinherited children with nothing more to lose, served even in death as human propaganda for the notion that there could be no justice until the King returned.

They were not the last of their ilk. James's ex-officers lingered on for decades as agents in the Stuart cause, and when George I disbanded a number of Tory regiments in his first years as king, he contributed a flood of new recruits to the pool of Jacobite military men. After 1715, however, their public image was quite different, as the case of Captain James Lennard demonstrates. Probably cashiered in the spring of 1715, Lennard was at Preston with the rebels in November. When the recusant squire Richard Towneley was tried for his part in the rising, he

---

[22] Lowick and Pendergrass are noticed in *D.N.B.*, Rookwood and Keyes in Joseph Gillow, ed., *A Literary and Biographical History, or Biographical Dictionary of the English Catholics* (6 vols., New York and London, 1885).

offered the far-fetched defence that the witnesses had mistaken Lennard for him. Towneley was acquitted, which reveals much about the sympathies of his jurors.[23] Captain Lennard had escaped to Calais, where he joined a large group of exiles, and 'pretended himself a Catholic'.[24] He drank loud healths to James III at the Golden Spur, a Calais tavern owned by an English spy, and paraded with a friend through the town, carrying a sword inscribed *'that they would lose the last Drop of their Blood to restore King James the Third'*.[25] Against the advice of his friends, Lennard boldly returned to London in March 1717/18, where he was immediately arrested and imprisoned.[26]

Mist's *Weekly Journal*, which chronicled Lennard's life over the next year, reported that he had escaped from custody along with John Matthews, the printer and future boy-martyr. Retaken at Gravesend a month later, the Captain was transported to Lancashire, where he was acquitted of a charge of highway robbery; he was then tried in the same court for high treason in joining the rebellion.[27] His sister appeared at the trial to testify that this was another case of mistaken identity; the real rebel had been his twin brother! Incredibly, the jury again found him not guilty.[28] He was still at liberty in London in 1719, when he visited his old prison-mate John Matthews, soon to be executed for printing *Vox Populi, Vox Dei*.[29]

Captain James Lennard was a brave Jacobite officer of the old school, who liked to make dramatic gestures and trumpeted his sentiments. In 1696, men of his type were considered utter villains, and nine of them lost their lives for complicity in the Assassination Plot. By 1718, however, the mood of a large part of the nation had altered; Lennard was found innocent of being a common criminal and a rebel, and was guaranteed wide publicity by the *Weekly Journal*. While he may not have achieved the status of a popular hero, he was clearly not regarded as a scoundrel. In the end, the violent and emotional tavern culture of the ex-officers had been tamed and absorbed by the commercial media.

---

[23] Albert Nicholson, 'Lancashire in the Rebellion of 1715', *T.L.C.A.S.*, 3 (1885), p. 83.
[24] H.M.C., *Stuart*, vol. vii, p. 21.   [25] P.R.O., S.P. 35/13/37; S.P. 35/12/192–4.
[26] H.M.C., *Stuart*, vol. vi, p. 228.
[27] *Weekly Journal*, no. 74, 10 May 1718, no. 84, 19 July 1718, no. 79, 14 June 1718, no. 93, 20 Sept. 1718.
[28] A transcript of the trial, doubtless intended for publication, is in Bodl. Rawl. MS C. 376.
[29] Goulden, 'Vox Populi, Vox Dei', pp. 376, 378.

Agents and operatives

The Assassination Plot and the story of Captain Lennard exemplify the amateur nature of Jacobite operations. The ex-officers tended to act on their own initiative, without coordinating their plans with the representatives of the Stuart court. They were typical Jacobite agents. The deep-set divisions and animosities among the adherents of the exiled King were constant obstacles to efficiency, as Daniel Szechi has shown.[30] Jacobites seldom took a broad view of the path to success; they usually preoccupied themselves with narrow projects that did not always serve the interests of the cause as a whole. This was in part the result of a Country mentality, hostile to the idea of centralized organization. It was also partly attributable to religious and ethnic diversity – Protestants did not much trust Catholics, the English and Scots were always suspicious of the Irish.

It may seem incredible that this ramshackle structure was able to plan two rebellions and countless conspiracies without complete discovery by the government. In fact, the post-Revolutionary state was never as competent as its enemies feared. The authorities were not capable of strict surveillance or massive repression; they depended, as the Jacobites did, on the individual talents of their operatives. Paul Hopkins has pointed out that William III was often uninformed about the schemes of his opponents, and the dalliances of his own ministers.[31] Sir Robert Walpole constructed a formidable system of intelligence to counter the Jacobite threat, but it was soon infiltrated by a highly placed Stuart agent, John Lefebure, who was in charge of intercepting seditious letters at the Post Office.[32] The Pelhams, in spite of their indispensable spy 'Pickle', or Alaistair Macdonald of Glengarry, were often baffled by the erratic plotting of Charles Edward Stuart. The successes of the Jacobites, however, did not rest solely on the mistakes of their foes. Their agents were protected by bonds that linked them to wider groups and communities. Jacobite operations can therefore be considered from a social as well as a political angle; and the former may provide a better understanding of how the cause survived for so long.

Religion, class and sociability were the three main ingredients in

---

30 Szechi, *Jacobitism and Tory Politics*, ch. 2.
31 Paul Hopkins, 'Sham Plots and Real Plots in the 1690s', in Cruickshanks, ed., *Ideology and Conspiracy*, p. 92.
32 Fritz, *English Ministers and Jacobitism*, ch. 10, and 'The Anti-Jacobite Intelligence System of the English Ministers, 1715–1745', *H.J.*, 16, 2 (1973), pp. 265–89; Cruickshanks, *Political Untouchables*, p. 47.

successful clandestine work. The religious factor was obvious in the higher echelons of Jacobite operatives. Catholic priests were prominent in many of the plots of the 1690s. The Anglican bishop Atterbury and Reverend George Kelly helped to formulate the great conspiracy of 1721–2, and Reverend Thomas Carte was James III's principal liaison with the Tory party in the 1730s and 1740s. Roman Catholic gentlefolk, who were long accustomed to sheltering priests in attics, cellars and secret rooms, proved no less welcoming to Jacobite agents of their own religion. A Scottish veteran of the '45 was caught in Dorset in 1751, living off the charity of local recusant families; he was found to be carrying a list of English military forces.[33] This is but one of many similar examples, over a period of seventy years. As the next chapter will argue, religion was central to the Jacobite cause, and it was crucial in sustaining the activities of the Pretender's agents.

Social status is a more complex issue. Unlike France, England in the late seventeenth and eighteenth centuries was a society stratified more by class than by order or 'estate'. Although landowners dominated politics, theirs was not a 'one-class' nation; the existence of a separate 'middling sort' of people was generally recognized, and industrious artisans were thought of as different from the 'indigent poor'. Land, money, birth and occupation defined this system, much as they did in later periods.[34] The English were acutely aware of social gradations, and the Jacobite gentry was very reluctant to put its fate in the hands of low-born agents. Some bad experiences in the early years seemed to justify this attitude. The infamous William Fuller, who had risen from skinner's apprentice to Mary of Modena's page, with the assistance of some Herbert relatives and a timely conversion to Catholicism, became a carrier of letters to and from St Germain in 1689, hiding the documents in his buttons. After eleven successful journeys, Fuller was captured at the Half-Moon tavern in Cheapside, and was persuaded to change sides, a sudden transfer of allegiance that was facilitated by reconversion to Protestantism.[35] Like the equally plebeian John Lunt, who is discussed in Chapter 10, Fuller became an inveterate informer, concocting wild accusations against prominent politicians. No

---

33 P.R.O., S.P. 36/117, fos. 7, 409, 465–70.
34 The idea of a 'one-class' society is proposed in Peter Laslett, *The World We Have Lost Further Explored* (New York, 1984), ch. 2. An interesting, if questionable, approach to class in this period is found in R. S. Neale, *Class in English History, 1680–1850* (Totowa, N.J., 1981).
35 George Campbell, *Imposter at the Bar: William Fuller, 1670–1733* (London, 1961), pp. 13–54.

wonder, then, that Jacobite landowners preferred to deal with operatives of their own class.

Genteel agents were not always more competent. The bumbling Colonel Cecil, who managed Jacobite affairs in the 1730s, was duped by Walpole into believing that the Great Man himself sympathized with the exiled monarch, and thereupon took to delivering treasonable correspondence directly to the delighted first minister.[36] Nevertheless, an operative who was also a gentleman could count on strong support from those of his class. Lieutenant Thomas Anderson, a Yorkshire recusant whose father owned an estate at Gales near Richmond, had deserted Ligonier's dragoons in 1749; two years later, he was arrested in Perthshire when someone mistook him for Prince Charles himself. Luckily, he avoided identification, and was released, only to be taken up again in 1752 at Perth on suspicion of treasonable practices. He was tried at Worcester in November for desertion and for attempting to enlist men for the Pretender; he confessed to the former charge, but was found guilty of both and was sentenced to be shot at Shrewsbury. King George was deluged with petitions of mercy on his behalf from Yorkshire, Lancashire, Worcestershire and Shropshire; he was championed in the last of these counties by Anne Kynaston of Hardwick, who had carried money to Prince Charles in Flanders. The *True Briton* and *Adams's Weekly Courant* published detailed reports on his case. He was finally executed, however, revealing his true allegiance before death by praying 'to protect and guard the dearest P[rince] wherever he goes'.[37] In spite of his religion, Anderson had received a great deal of aid from the Tory gentry.

Agents of lesser descent had to form their own solidarities, often based on forms of sociability. In October 1757, the government discovered a small gang of Stuart operatives in Deptford, led by William Dunster, a Wiltshire tailor who had served in the French army. He was in contact with Thomas Tiggins, an Irish shoemaker and owner of a 'stopshop' or hardware store in Portsmouth, who was engaged in mapping the harbour there in preparation for a French landing. Dunster's little band included two of his journeymen, a coachman and a dockyard labourer; they drew up coded articles which they signed and then burned, took oaths of secrecy on a prayer book and swore to

36 King, *Political and Literary Anecdotes*, pp. 36–9; also Sedgwick, ed., *History of Parliament*, vol. i, pp. 113–14.
37 Hugh Owen and J. B. Blakeway, *A History of Shrewsbury*, vol. i (London, 1825), pp. 507–8; *Adams's Weekly Courant*, no. 979, 12 Dec. 1752; *True Briton*, vol. iv, no. 15, 19 Nov. 1752, p. 357, vol. v, no. 2, 17 Jan. 1753, pp. 43–4.

join the French invaders. Their Jacobitism was very indiscreet. Dunster went about the streets singing 'Over the Water to Charley'; he and his friends openly drank healths to the exiled Stuarts; and on one occasion, a member of the gang 'rehearsed one of the most treasonable Songs as Tongue could express' in an open field behind the parish church in Woolwich. Not surprisingly, they were soon infiltrated by a government spy, and arrested.[38]

Dunster and his cabal resemble a friendly society more than a nest of secret agents. Ritual and sociability cemented their resolve; coded rules, oaths, songs and treasonable toasts bonded them together in their risky enterprise. The clubs and associations of the landed and monied elite are discussed in Chapter 9; the Deptford gang was a similar body on a different social level. Its purpose of reinforcing the loyalty of plebeian Jacobite operatives through sociability was not unique, although the medium for this was usually a tavern rather than a club. The tavern, alehouse or inn could provide a refuge from the world, a safe-house in which dreaming and plotting thrived under the intoxicating influence of drink. As with the ex-officers, the tavern was a stage on which Jacobite fantasies could become reality. A whole system of Jacobite public houses was established in London in the 1690s, built upon an existing structure of Roman Catholic taverns, like the Half-Moon in Cheapside, where Fuller was taken.[39] These places were hard to suppress; when the government closed down the imaginatively named Orriginal Bromfield's Jacobite coffee-house in Buckingham Court in 1690, he simply continued to sell coffee and liquor illegally in his home.[40]

After 1714, the number of Jacobite houses expanded as Tory hostelries followed their clients into King James's camp. The Portuguese proprietor of Ozinda's coffee-house, once the haunt of Jonathan Swift, was arrested in his establishment in September 1715, along with Sir Richard Vyvyan and one Captain Forde, who were involved in the plan for a rebellion.[41] An informer in 1723 revealed the names of a dozen taverns in London and Westminster where 'disaffected clubs' were held, adding four in the provinces at Wrexham, Chester, Stafford and Bakewell, Derbyshire, where men had been recruited for the Pretender in the shadow of Chatsworth![42] Stuart agents clearly had a

---

[38] P.R.O., S.P. 36/138, fos. 99–100, 109–12, 115–17, 159–71, 186–215.
[39] Bryant Lillywhite, *London Coffee Houses* (London, 1963), p. 255.
[40] C.L.R.O., MJ/SR 1754, warrant of Board of Green Cloth for Bromfield. He may have been related to the Quaker William Bromfield, a Jacobite agent.
[41] Lillywhite, *London Coffee Houses*, p. 432.   [42] P.R.O., S.P. 35/47/25.

broad choice of shadows in which to lurk, from the fashionable
Ozinda's to the lowly Horse Shoe in Whitechapel. The revelation of the
Atterbury Plot, however, temporarily shattered the tavern system, and
in 1724 even the resilient Ozinda family was induced to retire to
France.[43]

Refuges for Jacobite agents reemerged by the 1740s, when a government spy reported on eleven houses for the disaffected in the capital,
each with a different clientele. Sir Watkin Williams Wynn congregated
with the Welsh Jacobites at the Somerset coffee-house; the Nonjurors
rendezvoused at the Nag's Head, Westminster; and the Irish Catholics
met at the Highland Man in Queen's Street.[44] In 1751, Jacobites coming
over from France could find safety at Hamilton's coffee-house near
Leicester Gardens or Patrick Hoare's at Charing Cross.[45] Twenty-four
years later, treasonable letters were found at Mrs Leslie's coffee-house
in Prince's Street, Leicester Fields; they referred to a landing at Milford
Haven and to the movements of 'His Highness'. Mrs Leslie had been
heard to claim, falsely or erroneously, that Charles Edward Stuart had
recently visited her.[46] By 1775, hers must have been one of the last
Jacobite houses in England, and the agents who used it as a post office
were probably in the service of France.

Jacobites never tried to separate business and sociability. Like
religion and class, tavern life was part of the social framework on
which Jacobite organization was constructed. Clearly, this was symp-
tomatic of a 'pre-bureaucratic' mentality, in which the agencies of
authority did not see themselves as detached from a specific cultural
milieu. On the contrary, Jacobite operatives immersed themselves in
social affiliations, using their religion, status and even drinking habits
to uphold their treasonable activities. Their enemies, on the other hand,
constructed an increasingly bureaucratic state apparatus, extending
from the excise to the army, in order to exclude King James's adherents
from any institutional power. At the same time, the government
attempted to discredit the Jacobites by associating them exclusively
with unloved minorities – Roman Catholics, Scots, the Irish. The last of
these were in fact very active in the cause, and they deserve particular
attention.

43 Lillywhite, *London Coffee Houses*, p. 433.
44 B.L., Add. MS 32,703, fos. 522–3.
45 P.R.O., S.P. 78/240, fos. 126, 182; S.P. 78/241, fo. 220.
46 H.M.C., *Fourteenth Report, Appendix, Part X. The Manuscripts of the Earl of Dartmouth* (2 vols., London, 1895), vol. ii, pp. 368–9.

The Irish regiments

The history of the Irish in England in the eighteenth century has been unjustly neglected. Dorothy George commented on their large numbers in London, but their numerical strength is difficult to determine.[47] Their real significance rested in their impact on English consciousness, not on the size of their community. For almost a century after 1689, the Irish were regarded as the most determined of Jacobites. Although Jacobitism in Ireland is largely unexplored, L. M. Cullen has suggested that there was a perceived threat to the other island until the 1760s, and the English government feared the possibility of a rising in favour of the Stuarts until the late 1770s.[48] The French considered sending Cardinal York to head an Irish rising as late as 1796, to Wolfe Tone's annoyance.[49]

Irish Jacobitism was bolstered by the 'Wild Geese' regiments in French service. Formed in the early 1690s from veterans of James II's Irish campaign, they included six infantry regiments – Bulkeley, Clare, Dillon, Rooth, Berwick and Walsh (founded 1776) – and Fitzjames's regiment of horse. Their flags bore the cross of St George, as well as English crowns, Irish harps and British lions. The *régiment Rooth*, nicknamed 'the Pretender's body-guard', marched to 'The King shall enjoy his own again'.[50] The Irish and British characteristics of the regiments were clearly emphasized. Recruiting for these units soon became a serious problem in both Ireland and England. The first person executed for treasonable practices under William III was an Irish recruiter, Patrick Harding.[51] In the last years of Queen Anne's reign, the Tory administration was outraged by stories of men recruited in Ireland with promises that they 'would see the young King'. In June 1714, the Kelly brothers, a pair of Irish gentlemen, were taken in Kent

---

[47] M. Dorothy George, *London Life in the Eighteenth Century* (New York, 1925, 1965), esp. pp. 113–25.
[48] L. M. Cullen, *The Emergence of Modern Ireland, 1600–1900* (London, 1981), pp. 195–200. See also Arthur O'Leary, *Loyalty Asserted; or, The New Test Oath Vindicated* (n.p., 1779).
[49] R. Barry O'Brien, ed., *The Autobiography of Theobald Wolfe Tone, 1763–1798* (2 vols., Dublin, 1910), vol. ii, pp. 12, 83. Lord Cloncurry, a prominent United Irishman, was a frequent guest of the Cardinal in 1803, and pleased the old man by addressing him as 'Majesty'. *Personal Recollections of the Life and Times, with Extracts from the Correspondence, of Valentine Lord Cloncurry* (Dublin, 1849), pp. 199–201.
[50] See L. and F. Funcken, *L'Uniforme et les Armes des soldats de la guerre en dentelle* (2 vols., Tournai, 1975–6), vol. i, pp. 57–85; P.R.O., S.P. 35/64/13a.
[51] Luttrell, vol. ii, p. 8; Howell, ed., *State Trials*, vol. xii, cols. 645–6.

for enlisting men; they had a letter of certification from Lord Middleton, James III's Secretary of State. Within a month, an Act was passed making it high treason to recruit for the Pretender.[52]

That a government so embroiled in Jacobite conspiracy would enact such legislation shows the level of distrust of the Irish, who were seen as tools of France and of international Catholicism. Yet the measure did not end recruiting in England. In fact, the problem increased sharply under George I, particularly between 1719 and 1727, due to a peacetime drive to replenish the French army. The recruits were usually told that they were to serve King James rather than Louis XV, and were sometimes assured that they would soon return to England with the Pretender.[53] Jacobitism provided a strong enticement; some recruiters in Wapping in 1723 carried a picture of James III in order to encourage enlistment.[54] Of course, loyalty to the Stuarts was not the only reason for joining up; most of the recruits were very poor, and were attracted by the prospect of steady pay. One had been rejected from the Foot Guards because he was too small, and thought 'it is better for me to go thither than to starve'; another was approached while walking through St James's Park without shoes, by a recruiter who pitied his miserable condition.[55] Nevertheless, even in their poverty, many Irishmen were discriminating about whom they would serve.

Almost all the recruits were recent Irish immigrants, but they were not all Roman Catholics. A list of some men recruited in 1724 in St Giles-in-the-Fields included twelve Protestants and only seven Catholics. Among them were nine servants, two soldiers, two tailors, a barber, a shoemaker, a tide-waiter, a fencing-master and a Scottish gentleman; few of these were skilled or 'respectable' occupations. Most of the men were southerners, from Dublin, Leinster and Munster; only three were northerners, one of them an Ulsterman. Like other recruits, they were enlisted in London and transported through a string of Irish inns to Gravesend or Deal, from whence they were smuggled over to France.[56] The recruiters themselves were generally veterans of the French army, like Michael Berford or Bedford, arrested in 1724, who had served King James in Ireland, then joined a French cavalry

---

52 Boyer, *Political State*, vol. vii, pp. 62, 91–5, 546–8, 562–3, 611; P.R.O., S.P. 78/159, fos. 72, 77, 83, 87, 179; S.P. 44/116, pp. 5–9, 68–9, 81–2, 108–9; S.P. 34/23/71–2, 79–82, 84; S.P. 35/1/11.

53 For example, P.R.O., S.P. 35/58/80, fo. 163; S.P. 35/64/13a; S.P. 35/16/8; S.P. 35/3/70. One recruit said he would serve King Louis, but not the Pretender; this was a unique scruple. P.R.O., S.P. 35/27/68, fo. 268.

54 P.R.O., S.P. 35/48/8.   55 P.R.O., S.P. 35/57/14; S.P. 35/53/51.

56 P.R.O., S.P. 35/20/54.

regiment.[57] Some, however, were not military men; John Harrold was a tobacco merchant, and Sir William Kennedy was both a priest and a baronet.[58]

Irish recruiting was less evident in the early years of George II's reign, although in 1732 a recruiter for the Rooth regiment was arrested in London.[59] The War of the Austrian Succession revived the practice temporarily, and in 1745 an important recruiting gang was revealed; its organizers were George Fitzgerald, chief agent for the French tobacco monopoly, and Richard Child, Viscount Castlemain, a former Tory politician who had retired to his Essex estates. The recruits had been obliged to swear an oath of fealty to James III.[60] Enlistments into the French Irish regiments continued until the 1750s, but records of cases investigated then do not mention the Pretender.[61] It is likely that Charles Edward's expulsion from France in December 1748 dispelled the myth that the Irish regiments served the Stuarts rather than the King of France.

Their military role, combined with the English stereotype of them as semi-barbarians, made the Irish into the shock-troops of Jacobitism. Expatriate Irishmen were viewed by English Jacobites as willing cannon-fodder in any insurrection. A number of them were recruited in Lancashire in 1689–90 to take part in a rising in that county.[62] In October 1715, three Irish soldiers in the Foot Guards were executed for trying to fill up their company with loyal Jacobites who would support the Duke of Ormonde's projected landing.[63] A Spanish merchant ship, ironically named *The Revolution*, was seized at Genoa in 1722, and found to be carrying Irish recruits who were to take part in an invasion of England.[64] Letters found on board led to the arrest in England of Catherine Lucas on suspicion of recruiting; she was discovered to

---

57 P.R.O., S.P. 35/54/46.
58 P.R.O., S.P. 35/61/35; S.P. 35/63/84–7. For the Harrold family, see Jacob M. Price, *France and the Chesapeake: A History of the French Tobacco Monopoly, 1674–1791, and of its Relationship to the British and American Tobacco Trades* (2 vols., Ann Arbor, 1973), vol. i, pp. 259, 535.
59 P.R.O., S.P. 36/28, fo. 17.
60 P.R.O., S.P. 36/79, fos. 98–100. For Fitzgerald, see Price, *France and the Chesapeake*, vol. i, pp. 557–62; for Castlemain, see Sedgwick, ed., *History of Parliament*, vol. i, p. 549.
61 See P.R.O., K.B. 33/5/1.
62 William Beamont, ed., *The Jacobite Trials at Manchester in 1694*, Chetham Society, 28 (1853), p. 77.
63 Boyer, *Political State*, vol. x, pp. 354, 385–8, vol. xi, p. 504.
64 *The Whole Proceedings upon the Arraignment, Tryal, Conviction and Attainder of Christopher Layer, Esq; for High Treason in Compassing and Imagining the Death of the King* (London, 1722; Dublin, 1723), Dublin edn, Appendix, pp. 24–38.

possess declarations of James III and letters from Bishop Atterbury's associate, Dr John Freind.[65] As might be expected, the French sent Irish troops to Scotland during the '45, and a number of Irishmen joined Prince Charles's army in Manchester – they are discussed in Chapter 10.

The rift between Charles Edward and France in 1748 ended the involvement of Irish regiments in Jacobite plots. Nevertheless, the sentiments of recruits did not change much; in 1771, an Englishman who had served in an Irish regiment claimed to have been privy to a plot by recruiters in England to murder George III, which they imagined would bring about a Stuart restoration.[66] The expatriate Irish community also maintained a strong attachment to the exiled family, if an extraordinary memorial sent to the government in 1779 can be believed. It was written by Thomas Buttson, an Irish handloom weaver living in London, who was clearly disturbed mentally, and had been confined in St Luke's hospital. If his ravings about the Jesuits fomenting the American Revolution are ignored, however, his testimonial reveals a remarkable picture of Irish life in the capital in the early years of George III. Buttson recorded several instances of 'malicious Speeches against the king and Royal family', and conversations 'about the Stuards family and about Religion'. He recalled 'when I was a Boy in dublin I heard Such people as they Say the king was a usurper a murderer a Rober'. He was convinced that his employers were engaged in a plot against the King, in league with their friends the radical aldermen George Hayley, Frederick Bull and John Wilkes.[67]

The story is ridiculous, but it may accurately reflect the conjunction of Jacobite and radical sympathies among the Irish population in London. Peter Linebaugh has recently discovered a connection between the Irish strikers of 1768, who supported Wilkes, and the Whiteboys, a Catholic gang that terrorized landowners in Ireland in the 1760s and 1770s.[68] Jacobitism may have supplied a crucial link here. The Whiteboys were founded during the French invasion scare of the late 1750s; their name came from the colour of their coats, a colour associated with the Bourbons and Stuarts. In the first major Whiteboy trial in 1767, a number of the accused testified that they had sworn

---

[65] Lucas denied the charges, and attempted to solicit the assistance of the Duchess of Tyrconnel, the former French officer Viscount Dillon, and the 'Duke of Worton'. P.R.O., S.P. 35/44/143, 146, 180; S.P. 35/45/107, 125; S.P. 35/78, part 1, fo. 1.

[66] *The Whisperer*, no. 90, 2 Nov. 1771.   [67] P.R.O., S.P. 37/13, fos. 202–7.

[68] Peter Linebaugh, 'Eighteenth-Century Crime, Popular Movements and Social Control', *Bulletin for the Study of Labour History*, 25 (1972), p. 15.

oaths to the King of France and to Charles Edward Stuart, and that their aim was to prepare for a French landing.[69] Irish support for Wilkes originated in the same rebellious spirit that animated the Whiteboys, and both may have owed their impetus to Jacobitism. ✓

Jacobitism and crime

Like the Jacobite ex-officers, the Irish were often portrayed in the Whig press as a criminal class, determined to undermine the law and social order as well as the Williamite regime. In most ways, this caricature was grossly misleading. Jacobitism did not explicitly threaten the rule of law or the social hierarchy; on the contrary, it stressed the importance of obedience to legal powers and respect for status. Yet the Jacobite belief that values had been turned topsy-turvy by the Revolution was certainly conducive to the disruption of what was seen as illegitimate authority. This subversive aspect of Jacobitism may have been particularly attractive to those who ordinarily had little influence on the institutions of government: the poor and labouring classes. Subversion, however, was legitimized by allegiance to the rightful ruler. The demonstrative loyalty of plebeian Jacobites must not therefore be written off as a mere facade; in fact, it was a crucial factor in justifying acts of protest, even crimes.

Jacobitism was connected with several types of criminal behaviour, most notably highway robbery, smuggling and poaching. These varieties of crime might be interpreted as 'social banditry', implying that they were undertaken by plebeians motivated by social grievances, and were sanctioned by other plebeians.[70] The concept of 'social crime' has been criticized, however, for distorting the nature of criminal activities. As John Styles has pointed out, 'social bandits' were usually motivated by greed rather than necessity; they operated in gangs indistinguishable from professional criminal groups; and their support in the plebeian community depended on the extent to which their actions affected common people.[71] Nevertheless, some criminals clearly saw themselves

---

[69] Sir Richard Musgrave, *Memoirs of the Different Rebellions in Ireland* (3rd edn, 2 vols., London, 1802), vol. ii, pp. 207–20.
[70] The concept of 'social crime' is discussed in E. P. Thompson's contribution to 'Eighteenth-Century Crime, Popular Movements and Social Control', *Bulletin for the Study of Labour History*, 25 (1972), p. 9. See also the essays in Hay *et al.*, *Albion's Fatal Tree*.
[71] John Styles, ' "Our Traitorous Money Makers": The Yorkshire Coiners and the Law, 1760–83', in John Brewer and John Styles, eds., *An Ungovernable People? The*

as 'social bandits', and their attitude towards their own activities, while it may have been delusory, must be explained.

The prosecution of crime, whether 'social' or 'regular', tended to increase whenever harsh economic conditions followed the end of a war, and troops released from service were unable to find employment.[72] The disbandment of James II's much criticized army had similar effects. Of James's 35,000 troops, only about 10,000 continued to serve King William.[73] At Ipswich in 1689, some units loyal to James mutinied, but most of his soldiers, including many Irishmen and Catholics, were simply 'demobbed'.[74] The government intercepted a letter in 1689 from one of these men, who wrote that his regiment at Chester had been purged of seven or eight Roman Catholics, and that the Lieutenant-Colonel 'swore that all the whole regiment must take an oath to fight against King James and all popery. Upon that I laid down my arms and four more.' Twenty-four men finally quit the regiment, and were abused by a Williamite crowd.[75]

The presence of some 25,000 uprooted, impoverished and disaffected former soldiers in England soon became a serious social and political problem. Whether or not a real increase occurred in the number of crimes committed is debatable, but there was undoubtedly a greater apprehension of crime in the early years of William III's reign, which grew as the economy worsened after 1692. The press gave prominence to reports of Jacobite sentiments among criminals, scandalizing Williamite observers like Narcissus Luttrell, who did not fail to note cases of felons who drank to King James on the gallows, money clippers who were apprehended with copies of James's declarations, or highway robbers who forced their victims to drink healths to the exiled King while being relieved of their money.[76] Although Luttrell admitted that some criminals might be 'pretending to be Jacobites', he accepted most of these stories, and with good reason – the ranks of criminal gangs were filled with James II's former troops, like the highwayman

English and their Law in the Seventeenth and Eighteenth Centuries (New Brunswick, N.J., 1980), pp. 245–9.

[72] See J. M. Beattie, *Crime and the Courts in England, 1660–1800* (Princeton, 1986), pp. 213–35, and his 'The Pattern of Crime in England, 1660–1800', *P. & P.*, 98 (1974), pp. 93–5; Douglas Hay, 'War, Dearth and Theft in the Eighteenth Century: The Records of the English Courts', *P. & P.*, 95 (1982), pp. 117–60; Peter Linebaugh, 'The Tyburn Riot Against the Surgeons', in Hay *et al.*, *Albion's Fatal Tree*, p. 89.

[73] Luttrell, vol. i, pp. 494–5, 505.

[74] See Charles D. Ellestad, 'The Mutinies of 1689', *J.S.A.H.R.*, 53, 213 (1975), pp. 4–21.

[75] *C.S.P.D., W. & M.*, vol. i, pp. 141–2.   [76] *Ibid.*, vol. ii, pp. 103, 610, 613, 630.

taken on Hounslow Heath in 1695 who admitted to being an ex-soldier in the banished King's army.[77] Jacobitism also gave criminals a way to legitimize their defiance of the law, as when a captured member of the infamous Golden Farmer's gang of highwaymen told Chief Justice Holt that 'he did not own him for a judge, King James being his lawful sovereign'.[78]

The underworlds of crime and Jacobite plotting were not far apart, and poor drifters like John Lunt might turn from carrying secret messages to robbery on the highway without compunction.[79] The relationship could work both ways, and criminals could become conspirators. James Whitney, the leader of the Golden Farmer's gang, while in prison in 1692–3, offered to reveal a plot to kill King William, in which he had been deeply involved; but the government refused him a pardon, and he was hanged.[80] Lunt later repeated Whitney's allegations during the Manchester trials of 1694.[81] Although it may not have been true, the story indicates a future development, the use of Jacobite connections with criminal gangs to advance the interests of the exiled King. This was most evident among the smugglers of Kent and Sussex.

The south-coast smugglers had sound financial reasons for liking the Stuarts, because their trade was dependent on the connivance of the French authorities, the allies of King James. The transportation of Jacobite agents across the Channel, furthermore, was a brisk and profitable business; William Fuller was carried over by the owlers of Romney Marsh more than twenty times in 1689.[82] Of course, treasonable contraband could be very dangerous, and in 1690 an innkeeper of Lydd, near Rye, was hanged, drawn and quartered for conveying letters to the French fleet.[83] This example was not forgotten; three years later, the notorious 'Farmer' Hunt, smuggler of French brandy and English Jacobites, announced to one of his human cargoes 'that he would not be hanged for any B— in Christendom'. Hunt made over £3,000 in 1689–96 by running Jacobites, and the Earl of Ailesbury paid him 10 guineas to be smuggled over in 1693; for his money, the Earl spent ten days and nights in hiding, subsisting on little food and 'a runlet of thin gut wine from Calais, and sour, so I was forced to boil

[77] Luttrell, vol. iii, p. 537.   [78] Ibid., vol. ii, p. 252.
[79] Beamont, ed., Jacobite Trials, p. 81.
[80] Luttrell, vol. iii, pp. 26–7.   [81] Beamont, ed., Jacobite Trials, p. 22.
[82] Campbell, Imposter at the Bar, pp. 42–3.
[83] Luttrell, vol. ii, pp. 124, 135.

it', before an owler arrived to convey him to France.[84] 'Farmer' Hunt's motives were entirely mercenary, as in all probability were those of the other smugglers who carried agents, money and even political pamphlets back and forth throughout the reigns of William, Anne and George I.[85] Smuggling, after all, was a business, carried on by entrepreneurs seeking to maximize their own profits, not by romantic 'social bandits'.

The smugglers became vital to Jacobite hopes in the mid-1740s. The French expedition of 1743–4 was to be piloted by two masters of contraband vessels, Thomas Harvey and Robert Fuller, who were married to Frenchwomen; as they were not regarded as very trustworthy, the authorities kept them under guard at Boulogne, although they were treated 'in a very handsome manner as they express it'.[86] The invasion was cancelled in March 1744 due to storms, but communications were maintained with England through the owlers, who transported several officers of the Comte de Lally-Tollendal's Irish regiment to spy on the troops guarding London.[87] As Charles Edward advanced to Derby, the French prepared another fleet, and the Jacobites in London, headed by Lord Barrymore and Sir Watkin Williams Wynn, sent a letter to the Prince, promising him £10,000 if he reached the capital. The message, carried by Richard Barry, arrived too late at Derby – Charles received it at Stirling in January.[88] A copy was sent to France, in the care of James Bishopp, an officer in the French army and brother of Sir Cecil Bishopp of Parham, a Sussex M.P., but he was arrested while trying to find an owler to take him across the Channel.[89] For once, the smugglers had failed their Jacobite allies.

Nevertheless, the contrabanders themselves were showing signs of a stronger allegiance to the Stuarts. This was due to the decline of lone entrepreneurs like 'Farmer' Hunt, and the rise of smuggling gangs,

---

[84] [Buckley, ed.], *Ailesbury Memoirs*, vol. i, pp. 316–19. Hunt was kidnapped by the Jacobites in 1696 and brought to France, because they feared he would reveal too much if captured – *ibid.*, vol. ii, p. 397.

[85] See Manchester, *Court and Society*, vol. ii, pp. 113, 131; H.M.C., *Stuart*, vol. iii, p. 184.

[86] Cruickshanks, *Political Untouchables*, pp. 62–3; Cal Winslow, 'Sussex Smugglers', in Hay *et al.*, *Albion's Fatal Tree*, p. 147.

[87] Cruickshanks, *Political Untouchables*, pp. 90, 96, 99, 102.

[88] Sedgwick, ed., *History of Parliament*, vol. i, pp. 442, 618.

[89] R.A., Stuart 296/24; W. V. Crake, 'The Correspondence of John Collier, Five Times Mayor of Hastings, and his Connections with the Pelham Family', *Sussex Archaeological Society Collections*, 45 (1902), pp. 81–3; Sedgwick, ed., *History of Parliament*, vol. i, p. 463.

composed mainly of ordinary labourers.[90] Jacobitism strengthened the
bonds of loyalty on which the success of these gangs depended. In
1744, it was reported that some of the smugglers of Romney Marsh
had drunk the healths of King James and his two sons, and a gang at
Hastings was alleged to have taken oaths of allegiance to the King of
France.[91] The Duke of Richmond, a West Sussex Whig magnate who
loathed both Jacobites and smugglers, informed the Duke of Newcastle
in 1746 that local contrabanders had begun to 'declare themselves
rebels'.[92]

In the following year, a group of smugglers attacked the Customs
House at Poole and recovered some confiscated tea. According to a
letter in the Stuart Papers, this 'Insurrection' was 'attempted by Lally's
influence on one Wilson, a smuggler in Sussex'; the latter was probably
Samuel Wilson, a grocer who had previously been involved in smuggling.[93] The gang later murdered a revenue officer and a witness who
had informed on them; they dumped one of the bodies in a well at
Ladyholt in West Sussex, and two of them took shelter with a local
gardener, William Comleach. The owner of Ladyholt, and Comleach's
former employer, was none other than John Caryll, the indefatigable
Jacobite; the arrest of his erstwhile employee for assisting the smugglers caused Caryll great distress, and it took considerable effort to
obtain Comleach's release.[94] Caryll's concern suggests that, like the
Comte de Lally-Tollendal, he had more than a passing interest in the
contraband business; he was apparently part of a broad nexus of
Jacobite-smuggling connections.

The smugglers were not a coherent group; but their endeavours were
often tied closely to the Jacobite cause, and some of them even absorbed
a measure of Jacobite political culture. The same conclusion applies to

[90] See Winslow, 'Sussex Smugglers', in Hay et al., Albion's Fatal Tree, pp. 150–4. For
    more on smuggling in the period, see Edward Carson, The Ancient and Rightful
    Customs: A History of the English Customs Service (London, 1972), ch. 5; Paul
    Muskett, 'Military Operations against Smuggling in Kent and Sussex, 1698–1750',
    J.S.A.H.R., 52, 210 (1974), pp. 89–110.
[91] Winslow, 'Sussex Smugglers', in Hay et al., Albion's Fatal Tree, p. 157.
[92] Ibid., p. 140.
[93] R.A., Stuart 301/5; Journal of the House of Commons, vol. 25 (1745),
    pp. 104–5; Winslow, 'Sussex Smugglers', in Hay et al., Albion's Fatal Tree,
    pp. 136–9, 160–6. The Comte de Lally-Tollendal later became governor of Boulogne,
    a major smuggling port.
[94] B.L., Add. MS 28,231, fos. 19–30, 31, 35; 'A Gentleman of Chichester', A Full and
    Genuine Account of the Inhuman and Unparalleled Murders of Mr. William Galley,
    A Custom-House Officer, and Mr. Daniel Chater, A Shoemaker, by Fourteen
    Notorious Smugglers (6th edn, Chichester, n.d.), pp. 18–22, 32.

the so-called Blacks, bands of poachers in the deer forests of Berkshire and Hampshire in the early 1720s who blackened their faces as a disguise. They have stirred the interest of several historians, and no fewer than three interpretations of their activities have been proposed. Pat Rogers represented the Blacks as a dangerous gang of cut-throats, not much different from the organized criminals of Jonathan Wild's London; E. P. Thompson, however, depicted them as 'social bandits', trying to recover lost forest rights from rapacious and despotic Whig governors.[95] Most recently, Eveline Cruickshanks and Howard Erskine-Hill have suggested that the Hampshire Blacks were embroiled in Jacobitism, and that the savagely repressive Black Act was designed to combat a political threat.[96]

The story filled in by Cruickshanks and Erskine-Hill is complex, and need only be summarized here. Philip Caryll of North, a cousin of the Ladyholt family, was taken up by the government in March 1723 for drinking the Pretender's health in the house of James Francis Stuart's former nurse at Portsea.[97] An innkeeper of Horndean testified that Caryll held meetings at his establishment with Sir Henry Goring, a former Tory M.P., the lawyer James Tooker of Woodhouse, a 'Farmer Port', who sounds like a smuggler, and a mysterious gentleman without a hand, who 'screwed into something fastened to the Stump of his Arm, an Iron Thing with which he help'd himself at Dinner'.[98] This exotic character should have been a smuggler, if not a pirate. Sir Henry Goring fled to France in August 1722, when the Atterbury Plot was discovered. It was soon known to the Dutch ambassador that Goring had approached the Blacks for assistance in the conspiracy, and 'en avoit formé une compagnie pour le service du prétendant'.[99] According to the ambassador, the Blacks had originally been a group of smugglers; their Jacobite affiliation, he wrote, was the primary reason for the passage of the Black Act.

This account is verified by a letter from Sir Henry Goring to James

95 Pat Rogers, 'The Waltham Blacks and the Black Act', H.J., 17, 3 (1974), pp. 465–86; Thompson, Whigs and Hunters. For earlier forest riots, see Buchanan Sharp, In Contempt of All Authority: Rural Artisans and Riot in the West of England, 1586–1660 (Berkeley and Los Angeles, 1980), chs. 6–9.
96 Eveline Cruickshanks and Howard Erskine-Hill, 'The Waltham Black Act and Jacobitism', Journal of British Studies, 24 (1985), pp. 358–65.
97 P.R.O., S.P. 35/42/154–5.
98 Whole Proceedings, London edn, Appendix, pp. 4–6.
99 B.L., Add. MS 17,677, kkk. vol. 5, fos. 548–9.

III, dated 6 May 1723. He vilified Caryll as a 'wolf in sheep's clothing', but was thankful that he had not trusted his recusant colleague with the most secret of his plans:

I had settled an affair with five gentlemen of that country who were each of them to raise a regiment of dragoons well mounted and well armed which I knew they could easily do for the men had horses and homes of their own, and were, to say the truth most of them, the persons who some time since robbed the late Bishop of Winchester's Park, and have increased in their number ever since. They go by the name of the Waltham Blacks (tho few of them live there) which is a most loyal little town ... I once saw two hundred and upwards of these Blacks in a body within half a mile of my house. They had been running brandy. There was 24 customs officers following them who they abused heartily and carried off their cargo. I am told there is no less than a thousand of them and indeed I believe they have now taken loyalty into their heads, and will I hope prove very useful.[100]

The incident described here was a pitched battle in 1720 between customs officers and the Mayfield gang of smugglers at Goring in Sussex. As early as 1716, this gang was reported to have distributed copies of the Pretender's declarations and to have drunk his health publicly; so their Jacobitism was not of recent vintage.[101] The Hampshire Blacks, in short, grew out of a group of smugglers with long-standing Jacobite ties.

In Berkshire, the Jacobite relationship with Blacking was less pervasive. James Barlow, whose inn near Cranborne was a meeting-place for Blacks, was a former gamekeeper and a Tory; in 1723, he was indicted at Berkshire Assizes for destroying a fish-pond and for saying 'God damn the King and all his Posterity I hope to have a new Master in a little time'.[102] Charles Rackett of Hall Grove, Wingham, a Roman Catholic squire and brother-in-law to Alexander Pope, was taken up with his son Michael and two servants in May 1722 for poaching deer. Michael fled overseas; his father, who was worth £20,000, was bailed at King's Bench, with the Jacobite agent Colonel James Butler as a surety.[103] A government list of accused Blacks was drawn up in 1723, on which some names are marked 'Jacobites', including Rackett,

[100] R.A., Stuart 67/16.
[101] Muskett, 'Military Operations against Smuggling', pp. 98–9.
[102] Thompson, *Whigs and Hunters*, pp. 90–1; P.R.O., Assi. 2/8, Berks., Qua. 10 G. I, and every Assize thereafter until Aut. 3 G. II; P.R.O., S.P. 44/81, p. 335.
[103] Thompson, *Whigs and Hunters*, pp. 92–3, 278–94. Butler styled himself 'Viscount Galmoy'. See [G. E. Cokayne], *The Complete Peerage* (14 vols., London, 1910–59), under 'Galmoy'.

Barlow and Richard Fellows, a butcher of Dorney, near Maidenhead, who was alleged to have enlisted men as poachers.[104]

This information could be construed to mean that the Racketts were undertaking the same role of Jacobite liaison with the Blacks that Goring and Caryll performed in Hampshire. Yet even this would not fully explain Blacking, which was not a thoroughly coherent phenomenon. If the largest and best organized gang of Blacks were Jacobites and former smugglers, others may not have been, and some Blacks did not belong to gangs at all. 'King John', who led a group of Hampshire Blacks, declared his loyalty to George I, and the Berkshire Blacks were more likely to have been foresters than smugglers.[105] An element of 'social banditry' may in fact have infused Blacking, which was in part a protest against the monopolization of forest resources by the state and the great landlords. At the same time, the ties between Blacking and Jacobitism were undeniably strong, and they apparently persisted; in March 1746, while Charles Edward was still undefeated in Scotland, newspapers reported that the Blacks had reemerged in Hampshire, robbing parks and stealing deer or sheep.[106] This was about the time that the Sussex smugglers began calling themselves 'rebels'.

The examples of highwaymen, smugglers and Blacks suggest that the Whigs were not entirely wrong in associating Jacobitism with crime. All sorts of groups on the fringes of criminality were accused of harbouring Jacobite sentiments, like prostitutes, who were alleged to have a particular affection for the Stuarts, or debtors in the Mint.[107] Beggars or 'Gypsies', who were always imagined to be potential criminals, were often depicted as susceptible to Jacobitism, because they were ruled by an 'absolute monarch', their elected king.[108] Interestingly enough, one of the beggar kings, the eccentric Bampfylde Moore Carew, marched with Prince Charles's army from Edinburgh to Derby in 1745. He was an unusual beggar, the son of a clergyman of the Devonshire Carew family, and he did much soliciting from the West Country Tory gentry.[109]

To some extent, the congruencies between crime and Jacobitism may

[104] Thompson, *Whigs and Hunters*, p. 157; P.R.O., S.P. 35/43/23.
[105] Thompson, *Whigs and Hunters*, chs. 3 and 5.
[106] *St. James's Evening Post*, no. 5638, 8–11 March 1745/6.
[107] Joseph Addison, *The Freeholder*, ed. James Leheny (Oxford, 1979), pp. 24–6, 48 and n. 4, 52 and n. 3; P.R.O., S.P. 35/55/3, (1)–(3).
[108] Henry Fielding, *The History of Tom Jones, A Foundling*, ed. Martin C. Battestin and Fredson Bowers (2 vols., Oxford, 1975), vol. ii, pp. 666–73.
[109] 'An Apology for the Life of Bampfylde Moore Carew', in C. H. Wilkinson, ed., *The King of the Beggars: Bampfylde Moore Carew* (Oxford, 1931), pp. 267–70.

have been founded on intellectual compatibility. 'Social bandits' and adherents of the Stuarts shared a desire for the restoration of lost rights and the revival of true justice. This parallelism, however, should not be taken too far. The concept of 'social banditry' remains too vague to support any definite ideas about its goals; besides, most criminal groups were more concerned with making quick profits than with righting wrongs. For their part, the purveyors of Jacobite propaganda never promised the full restitution of popular privileges or the elimination of poverty, and if the exiled King had ever returned, footpads, smugglers and poachers might have continued to operate as they had before.

Symbolic acts and anonymous letters

The Jacobite underworlds so far considered were self-contained communities, not at all representative of the mass of 'ordinary' people. Were treasonable practices common among the broader English public? This is a difficult question, because there is no clear line of division between the semi-organized underworlds of Jacobitism and the nation at large. In July 1736, for example, a bomb went off in the lobby of Westminster Hall, scattering copies of a printed paper condemning five recently passed Acts of Parliament, including the Gin Act, which had aroused much plebeian discontent. It might be conjectured that this was a 'genuine' act of popular protest. In fact, it was the work of a cranky Nonjuror, Robert Nixon, who headed a small band of ardent Jacobites, among them a Southwark innkeeper named Samuel Killingbeck and the printer Doctor Gaylard. They produced another paper, proclaiming the legitimacy of James Francis Stuart, which they fixed on horses, cows and railings at Spa Fields. In the end, they were all arrested, and Nixon was sentenced to a hefty fine, five years in prison and to provide sureties for life.[110] Were these men a club of low-level Jacobite agents, or a collection of 'ordinary' individuals bent on displaying their sentiments?

The closer one examines Jacobitism, the more one doubts the

[110] P.R.O., T.S. 11/1027, no. 4315; William Coxe, *Memoirs of the Life and Administration of Sir Robert Walpole, Earl of Orford* (3 vols., London, 1798), vol. iii, pp. 346–9; Cambridge University Library, Cholmondeley (Houghton) MSS, 70/2, fos 7, 9, 14–15; John, Lord Hervey, *Some Materials Towards Memoirs of the Reign of George II*, ed. Romney Sedgwick (3 vols., London, 1931), vol. ii, p. 566. For Jacobitism and the Gin Act riots, see George Rudé, ' "Mother Gin" and the London riots of 1736', *Guildhall Miscellany*, 10 (1959), p. 62.

existence of 'ordinary', 'typical' or 'average' people in eighteenth-century England. Every case of Jacobite protest seems to fit into a framework of communal solidarities; each individual adherent of the Stuarts was also a member of some sub-section of English society. The assumption of community support and protection underlay most treasonable acts. In January 1748/9, the heads of the rebels Thomas Deacon and Thomas Syddall were removed from the Exchange in Manchester. The perpetrators were sheltered by their Jacobite neighbours, and never apprehended; they remained unknown until 1828, when the aged Miss Frances Hall confessed on her deathbed that her brother Edward, later an eminent surgeon, had taken the heads with some friends and buried them.[111] At York, two rebel heads were stolen from Micklegate Bar in 1754. A large reward for the offenders was offered by the Rockingham Club, but it loosened no tongues. Although a drunken cooper publicly proclaimed that he was the culprit, the authorities were finally able to trace the crime to William Arundell, a Roman Catholic merchant tailor in Swinegate. Arundell, who had allegedly fought with the rebels in the '45 and later been a highwayman, boasted of the deed to his friends, and gave one of the heads to Edward Drake, son of the Nonjuring antiquarian Francis Drake. Nevertheless, he was arrested only after his journeyman was interrogated and confessed to assisting him.[112] Like Edward Hall, Arundell's identity was safeguarded by his religious and political affiliations.

If treasonable practices were communally based, they were also meant to convey messages from Jacobite groups to the authorities. The exhibition of rebel heads was a symbolic humiliation for adherents of the Stuarts. Against this sort of public insult, individual Jacobites waged a guerilla war of counter-symbolism, aimed primarily at desecrating images of the ruling monarch's authority. In 1689, the picture of William III at the Guildhall was defaced when someone cut out the crown and sceptre; a Westminster butcher was accused in the following year of hanging effigies of William and Mary on the gallows at Tyburn.[113] After 1714, the distinction between symbol and reality became blurred, as Jacobite defiance was directed at the royal family itself. An Irish chairman in St James's Park in 1719 spat three times in the face of the Princess of Wales, and in October 1745, a Catholic priest

111 J. H. Nodal, ed., *City Notes and Queries* (7 vols., Manchester, 1879–88), vol. ii, pp. 88, 106–7, vol. vii, p. 81.
112 P.R.O., Assi, 45/25, part 2, York 1754, infos. nos. 1–10, 125–6; P.R.O., S.P. 44/134, pp. 250–1, 291–2; S.P. 36/126, fos. 19–24, 63–5, 165–74.
113 Luttrell, vol. i, pp. 606–7; C.L.R.O., MJ/SR 1754, rec. no. 40.

threw a seditious paper, sealed with the Pretender's head, at King George II, who was reviewing the City militia.[114] These overt attacks may have been the result of over-exposure to the fantasy world of Jacobite propaganda, in which the Hanoverians were made to appear contemptible.

The government, however, did not make allowance for fantasists. Worried by the plethora of treasonable writings, it increasingly equated words with actions. The execution of John Matthews for printing *Vox Populi, Vox Dei* was an extreme example of this policy; but it had been preceded by the even more shocking case of James Shepheard, an eighteen-year-old London coach-painter's apprentice. In January 1717/18, he wrote a letter to the Nonjuring cleric John Leake, in which he vowed to '*smite the Usurper in his Palace*'. Fearing it was a trick, the anxious Leake reported the letter to a Whig alderman, who induced Shepheard to rewrite it in his presence. On this evidence, Shepheard was tried for high treason. It was revealed at his trial that he was well educated, and that he had resolved as early as 1715 to kill King George.[115] He became an instant celebrity among Jacobites; Lord Oxford claimed to know his family, and the Nonjuror Robert Orme ministered to him in captivity. When the young man was executed in March, Orme wrote his dying speech.[116] The Nonjuring priest may also have penned the 'Hymn to the Trinity' attributed to Shepheard; it was widely distributed, as were portraits of the youth dressed in robe and turban, pointing to his 'Hymn' and the letter to Leake.[117] An enraptured Jacobite agent described him as 'one of the noblest spirits that ever England bred, and beautiful like an angel . . . Never man went through his sufferings with more fortitude and sedateness.'[118]

The veneration of James Shepheard testified to the importance of writing for the Jacobites. His crime was composing a letter; he was represented, somewhat falsely, as an author; and his whole life was viewed as a work of art. Shepheard was the incarnation of Jacobite propaganda. It is not surprising that an eternally frustrated cause would turn to writing as a shrine for its aspirations – it was easier to

---

[114] Boyer, *Political State*, vol. xvii, pp. 340–1, 446; P.R.O., S.P. 36/72, fos. 348–50.

[115] Boyer, *Political State*, vol. xv, pp. 114–17, 344–56.

[116] H.M.C., *Stuart*, vol. vi, p. 328; Boyer, *Political State*, vol. xv, pp. 358–71; P.R.O., S.P. 35/65/162, (1); S.P. 35/11/41.

[117] *An Hymn to the Holy and Undivided Trinity, Written by James Shepard, During his Imprisonment in Newgate* (London, 1718), P.R.O., S.P. 35/11/53; S.P. 35/11/64. A copy of the print is in Bodl. Rawl. MS D. 383, fo. 74; see also Plate 10. For its suppression, see P.R.O., S.P. 44/79A, pp. 146, 148.

[118] H.M.C., *Stuart*, vol. vi, p. 328. See also Boyer, *Political State*, vol. xv, pp. 438–40.

write than to act. The most important of all Jacobite underworlds was that of printers and publishers. As James Shepheard demonstrated, however, seditious writing was not confined to a professional sphere. In London and Westminster, it was usual for individuals to register their vexation at the frequent fast-days proclaimed by William and Mary by posting angry papers on church doors.[119] These written protests against the 'puritan' nature of fasting or the unworthiness of the royal couple were more effective than burning or tearing up the official proclamations, although one group of malcontents found a merrier expedient by holding a dance on a fast-day.[120] Seditious writing appears in the fast-day papers as a form of popular protest, a voice for the disenfranchised.

The problem of defining an 'authentic' popular voice, however, has been discussed in Chapter 2, and it must be admitted that most seditious letters do not provide insight into a plebeian consciousness. E. P. Thompson, of course, has argued otherwise in his article on anonymous threatening letters; he has published one fascinating example, found in 1766 in the market-place at Woodbridge, Suffolk, in which threats of destruction to workhouses, warehouses, mills and gentry estates are combined with the wish that 'our exiled King could come over or send some Officers with a few [illegible] Troops as we are all sold for the National Debt'.[121] While the letter was motivated by economic grievances, its political content was borrowed from Jacobite propaganda, and may reflect knowledge of the invasion plan of 1759 or of Charles Edward's recent succession to the royal title. The writer had been exposed in some way to a broader political culture, which he was turning to his own purposes; for him, a Stuart restoration meant relief from oppression.

Unfortunately, this is by no means a typical Jacobite anonymous letter. Most of them were privately directed at a specific person, and were entirely political in purpose. They were usually sent to politicians or local magistrates, and contained wild promises, vague menaces, Stuart manifestoes, propaganda essays, even seditious poetry.[122] The authors of these epistles were mainly over-zealous Jacobite agents or

119 C.L.R.O., MJ/SR 1754, rec. for Elizabeth and Jane Wilcox, rec. no. 12, indt. no. 42; Luttrell, vol. ii, pp. 59, 231.
120 Luttrell, vol. ii, pp. 449–50, vol. iii, pp. 87–8; Beinecke Osborn Files, 'Seers'.
121 E. P. Thompson, 'The Crime of Anonymity', in Hay et al., Albion's Fatal Tree, p. 325.
122 P.R.O., S.P. 35/1/10, (1)–(3); S.P. 35/26/16, fos. 34–5; S.P. 35/27/3, fos. 3–5; S.P. 35/33/141; S.P. 36/18, fo. 3; S.P. 36/59, fos. 257b–h; S.P. 36/121, fos. 76–7, 87, 99–100.

Nonjurors; this was also true of the few anonymous letters that were posted publicly.[123] These efforts failed miserably in eliciting favourable reactions, even from individuals who were drifting towards the Stuarts.[124] Anonymous letters could not be trusted, and many of them were not genuine, such as one sent to various mayors in 1713, which was designed to throw suspicion on the Tory government; similar hoaxes were perpetrated in Leicester in 1738 and Nottingham in 1747.[125] The most controversial of these cases was that of a poem to Prince Charles found in a laundry basket in Carfax, Oxford, after the bitter county election of 1754. Although it was probably planted by the Whigs, their intentions back-fired, and at least four people who saw the poem – three mercers and the treasurer of Christ Church – eagerly made copies for their private edification.[126]

In short, the study of anonymous Jacobite letters is not very enlightening. Only a handful of interesting examples have survived, all dating from during or after the rebellion of 1745, when there was more enthusiasm than coherence in the Jacobite cause. A paper fixed on the door of Bristol Cathedral in November 1745, shortly after Carlisle fell to the rebels, cursed King George 'and all in Authority; the Quakers, Presbyterians, and all the Protestants in general', and went on to threaten that the residence of a Whig magistrate 'should be Fired by the Friday following unless he put Fifty Guineas under his House'.[127] Like the Woodbridge letter, this might be considered as an indication of widespread popular discontent; but it is more likely the work of an angry Catholic, charged by the advance of a Jacobite army into England. By the time they reached Staffordshire, the situation was very tense, and an anonymous Jacobite in that county was moved to write a

---

123 In 1761, for example, Charles Edward's remaining supporters stuck up protests against George III's accession in London and Westminster – R.A., Stuart 405/65. Other cases of public letters are discussed in Chapters 6 and 7.

124 For example, George Heathcote in 1743, who turned a letter sent to him over to the government – P.R.O., S.P. 36/60, fos. 131–7. So did the Duke of Argyll in 1742 – Sedgwick, ed., *History of Parliament*, vol. i, pp. 72, 114.

125 P.R.O., S.P. 34/21/133–4; S.P. 34/22/1, fos. 22–4; Doble *et al.*, eds., *Collections of Hearne*, vol. iv, p. 227; *V.C.H. Leicestershire* (4 vols., London, 1907–), vol. iv, pp. 125–6; R. W. Greaves, *The Corporation of Leicester, 1689–1836* (Leicester, 1970), pp. 93–4; P.R.O., S.P. 44/130, pp. 299–302, 310–12; S.P. 36/102, fos. 105–14.

126 B.L., Egerton 3440, fos. 71–158; R. J. Robson, *The Oxfordshire Election of 1754: A Study in the Interplay of City, County and University Politics* (London, 1949), pp. 128–34.

127 *St. James's Evening Post*, no. 5592, 16–19 Nov. 1745. An information was later given concerning the perpetrator – John Latimer, *The Annals of Bristol in the Eighteenth Century* (Bristol, 1893), pp. 257–8.

threatening missive to Swynfen Jervis, a Gowerite Tory who had taken a prominent part against the rebels. 'Reflect on your late Behaviour', Jervis was advised, 'what Punishment does it not deserve your Disloyalty will suck you into eternal Perdition.'[128] Clearly, someone in Staffordshire had been deeply influenced by the Nonjuring jeremiads of the 1690s.

In fact, Jacobite anonymous letters are full of literary references. They applied the rhetoric of propaganda to particular circumstances, as can be appreciated in an ingenious and amusing note sent to the Kays, a Presbyterian family of south-east Lancashire, in January 1745/6:

> Notice is hereby given that his Rumpish Highness the Second Pretender [John Kay of Manchester], and Prince of the Presbyterian Territories [Samuel Kay of Manchester] has given an Order for the raising of a new Regiment of Rossendale Plunderers under the Emphatical Distinction of Oliverian Murderers ... they shall receive no Pay nor Cloathing but every Man a rusty Sword, an old Stick, and a long Pike and roasting Spit, and all Things fitting to compleat a Gentleman Plunderer and an Oliverian Murderer, out of whose Hands, God save the true born King.[129]

The local wit who wrote this was evidently familiar with Tory and Jacobite satire. Like other anonymous letter-writers of the '45, he was partly compensating for the silence of the Jacobite press, which had been effectively stifled by the government. When pamphlets and newspapers could no longer battle with the 'Oliverian Murderers', individuals had to take up their pens.

Anonymous letters, of course, could not reach a wide audience, and they represent an increasing desperation among adherents of the Stuarts. Within a few years of the '45, the emptiness of Jacobite threats had become obvious. In 1753, the publisher David Mallet was sent an anonymous warning not to publish Bolingbroke's anti-Jacobite *Letter to Sir William Wyndham*. 'A Man *like You*, when he reads this will *tremble*', fulminated the indignant letter-writer; but Mallet did not tremble, 'nor did he ever hear more of them [the Jacobites], their wrath being as impotent on this as on all other occasions'.[130] Words were no substitutes for actions, and anonymous letters were a sort of wish-fulfilment rather than a real weapon. The last Jacobite example was

---

128 B.L., Add. MS 29,913, p. 12.
129 Dr W. Brockbank and Rev. F. Kenworthy, eds., *The Diary of Richard Kay, 1716–51, of Baldingstone, near Bury, a Lancashire Doctor*, Chetham Society, 3rd Series, 16 (1968), pp. 105–6.
130 Beinecke Osborn Files, 'Mallet'.

sent to the commanding officer of Pendennis Castle at Falmouth in March 1779, when a French invasion was considered likely. Signed 'Orlovin, Duc de Haro', the letter begins as a mock proclamation, denouncing 'the Erastian Heretics called Protestants' for their 'continued Treason & Rebellion', and goes on to order the commander to proclaim Charles Stuart as King. It then digresses into a confusing passage about 'the Credentials of Monsieur St Remi', whoever he was, and 'the Correspondence of Madame de Mont Carmel with the Duke of Norfolk'.[131] These were the tangled fantasies of a misguided zealot, and they summed up what Jacobitism had become – a rambling, disgruntled, disembodied voice, trailing off into incoherence.

The underworlds of Jacobitism handled the everyday business of the cause – hatching conspiracies, transporting agents, recruiting. They also engaged in special acts of publicity, defiance and sedition. In these pursuits, they were protected and encouraged by the communities – Roman Catholic, Irish, Nonjuring etc. – to which they were attached. The denizens of the Jacobite underworlds were not 'ordinary' people. They were generally members of strictly defined occupational groups, like ex-officers or smugglers, or of minority religions. Their commitment to the Stuart cause was unusually strong, and they made little attempt to conceal their sentiments, often indulging in bold displays of loyalty. In their taverns and clubs, they cultivated a Jacobite sociability that was a means of strengthening their political cohesion. Yet if these habits set the Jacobite underworlds apart from the mainstream of 'ordinary' attitudes, they also made Jacobitism a reflection of English social life. Riven by religious divisions, stratified by occupation and class, late seventeenth- and eighteenth-century England was not a unified culture. The Jacobite underworlds were products of this disjointed society, and their behaviour was a form of protest against it. Through their tavern theatre, seditious acts and anonymous letters, they propounded a dream of unity and peace that attained, as will be seen, a wide appeal among 'ordinary' folk. At that point, the underworlds of Jacobitism and a large segment of English society seemed to merge into one.

[131] P.R.O., S.P. 37/13, fos. 44–5.

Chapter 5

Religion and loyalty: Jacobitism and religious life

[B]ut sure we have not so un-learnt Religion and Loyalty, as now to neglect those Inquiries and Principles, which (under God) wrought our Deliverance from the long Darkness of Popish Errors by the Reformation, and freed us from the long, long Cruelties and Usurpations of the Republicans, and Cromwell by the happy, happy Restoration.   *Mitre and Crown* (1748)[1]

The central importance of religion in English political affairs in the late seventeenth and eighteenth centuries is at last being recognized by historians.[2] Previous chapters have argued that religious beliefs saturated Jacobite rhetoric, and that religious affiliations supported the existence of Jacobite underworlds. Yet what effect did adherence to the Stuarts have on religious institutions, and on religious practice? In the last chapter, it was suggested that Jacobitism was incapable of penetrating the institutions of government, partly because of proscription, and partly on account of an anti-organizational or Country bias among the Jacobites. The Church of England was one of the nation's most powerful institutions, perhaps the only one whose influence extended into the remotest corners of the kingdom. In spite of the Jacobite sentiments of large numbers of Anglican ministers, however, the Catholic Stuarts were never able to regain solid support among the clergy. Instead, the leaders of the Church sold it into further bondage to the state.

Jacobitism was more successful among the Roman Catholics, who had a natural attachment to a king of their own faith, and whose

---

[1] *Mitre and Crown*, vol. i, Oct. 1748, p. 25.
[2] See Bennett, *Tory Crisis*; Clark, *English Society*; Geoffrey Holmes, *The Trial of Doctor Sacheverell* (London, 1973), esp. ch. 2; Gary S. De Krey, *A Fractured Society: The Politics of London in the First Age of Party, 1688–1715* (Oxford, 1985), ch. 2; and Jan Albers, 'Seeds of Contention: Society, Politics and the Church of England in Lancashire, 1689–1790', unpublished Ph.D. dissertation, Yale University, 1988.

religious survival depended more on the recusant gentry than on centralized structures. The anti-Erastian Nonjurors remained constantly loyal, and a Jacobite strain among the factious Quakers endured for decades. Each of these denominations will be considered in this chapter; but it would be a mistake to overlook the sole religious institution that was under the control of the exiled court, namely the Stuart monarchy itself. English kings were religious figures, the high-priests of a state cult. While the sacerdotal attributes of kingship declined in England, the exiled line attempted to keep up its priestly image, particularly through the supposed ability to cure scrofula by the laying-on of hands.

The royal touch

The supreme manifestation of the theory of the king's two bodies was the royal touch. Marc Bloch's magnificent work on 'the healing kings' showed how the practice of touching for scrofula probably originated in England in the reign of Henry II; it remained a powerful form of propaganda for English monarchs who wished to demonstrate their sacred character.[3] In the twenty-five years of his reign, Charles II touched around 100,000 people; interestingly enough, the largest number of these were stroked in 1682–3, just after the Exclusion Crisis.[4] James II, whose rival the Duke of Monmouth performed cures of his own, also did a great deal of touching in three years on the throne, and tried to restore the Catholic service used in the healing ceremony.[5]

After the Revolution, William III discontinued the practice, calling it a 'silly superstition'; on the only occasion when he agreed to lay hands on a scrofulitic, he reputedly told him 'God give you better health, and more sense'.[6] Queen Anne revived the royal touch as a means of asserting her legitimacy, which she may sometimes have doubted herself; she bestowed her thaumaturgic power on Samuel Johnson, but he had a relapse. King George I refused to use the touch, although a Whig lady once kissed his hand in hope of a cure. The first Hanoverian was more apprehensive of failure than he was repulsed by 'superstition', however, and he kept the prayers for healing in the liturgy

[3] Bloch, pp. 41–9.   [4] Ibid., pp. 377–8; Crawfurd, p. 112.
[5] Crawfurd, pp. 131–8; Helen Farquhar, 'Royal Charities. Part III. Continuation of Touchpieces for the King's Evil. James II to William III', British Numismatic Journal, 14, New Series, 4 (1920), pp. 89–113.
[6] Macaulay, History of England, vol. iv, ch. 14, p. 1746.

throughout his reign.[7] None of his descendants has yet attempted to resurrect the custom.

The supernatural powers of the kings of England do not make much sense to us today, but it would be wrong to classify the royal touch as a 'silly superstition'. The term 'superstition' has always been more abusive than analytical, and all too often, one person's 'superstition' or 'magic' turns out to be another's religion. Keith Thomas has pointed out that the line between religion and magic in the early modern period was a thin one indeed; even the Reformation did not succeed in separating the two.[8] The royal touch was not regarded as magical by its defenders – on the contrary, it was consistent with the religious teachings of the Church of England, and the healing ceremony was included in the Prayer Book. The effectiveness of the touch could be upheld empirically, because so many had seemed to be cured. 'To dispute the matter of fact', wrote Jeremy Collier, 'is to go to the excesses of skepticism, to deny our senses, and be incredulous even to ridiculousness.'[9] Opposition to the touch was usually based on theological rather than 'rational' or political grounds. William III saw it as Roman Catholic, an interpretation shared by James I, who had touched only reluctantly.[10] Neither monarch was inclined towards religious scepticism or the diminution of monarchical power; James I was a great believer in witchcraft, and both he and William were jealous of their prerogatives.

In exile, James II continued to use the touch as evidence of his mystical gifts and as an affront to his rival. He may have issued touch-pieces, small medals which supposedly carried healing power from the fingers of the monarch, in Ireland in 1690; he certainly touched at St Germain in the following decade.[11] Among those who sought a cure was Maria Shireburn, a Lancashire recusant who later married the eighth Duke of Norfolk.[12] After King James's death in 1701, the intercession of his spirit was credited with the performance of several miracles, and there was an abortive attempt to have him canonized.[13] His son reportedly touched in Paris before 1713, and

[7] Bloch, pp. 390–2; Crawfurd, pp. 144–53.

[8] Keith Thomas, *Religion and the Decline of Magic* (New York, 1971), pp. 253–79, 636–40.

[9] Quoted in Bloch, p. 391, n. 1.   [10] Crawfurd, pp. 82–5; Bloch, pp. 336–9.

[11] Farquhar, 'Royal Charities, Part III', pp. 113–17.

[12] C. D. Sherborn, *A History of the Family of Sherborn* (London, 1901), p. 50.

[13] James Macpherson, ed., *Original Papers; Containing the Secret History of Great Britain, from the Restoration to the Accession of the House of Hannover* (2 vols., London, 1776), vol. i, pp. 597–9.

issued touch-pieces in 1709.[14] Of course, he had not been crowned yet; but English kings had never seen their thaumaturgic power as dependent on consecration by the Church. In this opinion, they differed from many clerical writers, like Charles Leslie, who argued that 'kings are anointed by the priests of God and receive their *crowns* from *them*, that is from *God*, as *holding* from *him*'.[15] James Francis Stuart may in fact have been crowned at Perth on 23 January 1715/16, in a makeshift ceremony, but his use of the touch in Scotland was not tied to his anointment.[16]

After the '15, James touched at Avignon, Lucca and Rome.[17] In 1718, Anne Oglethorpe wrote to the Duke of Mar, requesting a touch-piece for a relative of Sir William Wyndham who was suffering from the King's evil. She wrote that he 'has such faith he can be cured that it is barbarous to oppose him'.[18] A certain reluctance to employ the King's supposed power can be detected here. The touch, after all, was controversial; to some it was redolent of Catholicism or 'superstition', to others it could only be practised by a consecrated king. The Stuart court, furthermore, had no desire to hazard James's reputation on the success of his cures. Consequently, his touching was not much advertised in England. A pamphlet appeared in London in 1721, recounting some remarkable cures of scrofula in the vicinity of Rome, but it carefully avoided mentioning who was performing them. 'Can human Reason ever pretend to in[v]estigate such supernatural Power?' asked the enraptured author. 'Ought we not rather to suffer our selves to be wrap'd up in Admiration, when we consider the transcending Effects of Miracles!'[19] The Whig surgeon William Beckett was not so wrapped up; in a strong reply to this pamphlet, he maintained that the touch was a recent innovation, and had not always worked.[20] James III had little to gain by stirring up such controversies.

---

14 Helen Farquhar, 'Royal Charities. Part IV. Continuation of Touchpieces for the King's Evil. Anne and the Stuart Princes', *British Numismatic Journal*, 15, New Series, 5 (1921), pp. 161–3.

15 [Leslie], *Rehearsals*, vol. ii, p. 295, 31 July 1706, no. 126; Bloch, pp. 216–24.

16 Martin Haile, *James Francis Edward, The Old Chevalier* (London, 1907), p. 210, suggests that a coronation took place; Shield and Lang, *The King over the Water*, p. 251, cast doubt on it. See also Farquhar, 'Royal Charities. Part IV', p. 166.

17 Farquhar, 'Royal Charities. Part IV', pp. 167–70.

18 H.M.C., *Stuart*, vol. vi, p. 287. Mar had been made a Duke by James III in 1715.

19 'M.T.', *A Letter from a Gentleman at Rome, to his Friend in London; Giving An Account of some very surprising Cures in the King's Evil by the Touch, lately Effected in the Neighbourhood of that City* (London, 1721), p. 17.

20 William Beckett, *A Free and Impartial Enquiry into the Antiquity and Efficacity of Touching for the Cure of the King's Evil* (London, 1722).

Belief in the touch quietly persisted among Jacobites in England. The grandson of the Nonjuror Thomas Brett went to France in 1736 to be touched by Louis XV, and some of James II's touch-pieces were being used by the nuns of the Micklegate convent in York to treat skin diseases among the local poor in the 1760s. The recusant Mrs Elizabeth Tankred of York included in her will in 1765 'my great Medall of James II ... in a silver Box', one of that monarch's touch-pieces.[21] The danger of making the use of the touch too public, however, was revealed in the furious response to Thomas Carte's infamous note to his 1747 *History of England,* in which he related the cure by James III's touch of a Bristol labourer named Christopher Lovel, who had been sent to the continent by some philanthropic Jacobites. The story was immediately assailed in the Whig press by numerous letter-writers, who denounced the presumptuous Nonjuror and claimed that Lovel had suffered a relapse – his benefactors had raised a second subscription to send him back again, but he died on the journey. The intense outcry against Carte caused the aldermen of London to withdraw their patronage from his *History,* and the result of the episode was nothing but humiliation for the Jacobites.[22]

This did not deter the supporters of Charles Edward Stuart. He had touched at Edinburgh in 1745, in spite of the fact that he was only Prince of Wales; like Monmouth, he suspended the rules of the game in order to promote his cause.[23] In 1751, the Jacobite press took its revenge for the embarrassment of Christopher Lovel by publicizing an outrageous fable about a Birmingham iron-box maker named David West, who was allegedly cured of scrofula through an encounter on Restoration day, 1749, with a stranger, 'the most comely Person he had ever beheld'. Aficionadoes of Jacobite propaganda will immediately recognize Prince Charles in this handsome apparition. The stranger laid his hands on West after reciting a Latin (!) prayer, and intoning the words '*I touch, but God healeth*'; he then instructed the happy man not

---

[21] Henry Broxap, *The Later Non-Jurors* (Cambridge, 1924), p. 335; J.H.C. Aveling, *Catholic Recusancy in the City of York 1558–1791* (St Albans, Herts., 1970), p. 115, and his *Northern Catholics: The Catholic Recusants of the North Riding of Yorkshire 1558–1790* (London, 1966), p. 404, n. 2. It is a significant reflection on the loyal association of 1745 that both Mrs Tankred and the superiors of the York convent subscribed to it.

[22] Farquhar, 'Royal Charities. Part IV', p. 167; John Nichols, *Literary Anecdotes of the Eighteenth Century* (6 vols., London, 1812), vol. ii, pp. 495–504; Crawfurd, pp. 155–7.

[23] Farquhar, 'Royal Charities. Part IV', p. 173; Crawfurd, pp. 157–8.

to reveal the encounter for twelve months.[24] As Chapter 7 will show, Restoration day in 1750 was marked by a major riot at Walsall that soon spread to Birmingham; so this charming anecdote had a connection with wider events. Well-informed Jacobite readers of the Chester *Courant*, the *True Briton* or the *London Evening Post* must have inferred that the revelation of this miracle had brought about an equally prodigious insurrection in the West Midlands.

The stories of Lovel and West indicate that the debate over the royal touch was empirical rather than 'rational'; it was based on the efficacy of the practice, not on the possibility of miracles. The Enlightenment introduced a new scepticism about revealed religion, and sought to undermine the intellectual foundations of 'superstition', but the influence of these ideas was limited. A few doubters like David Hume or Conyers Middleton were not enough to change the general acceptance of divine intervention in human affairs, as the panic caused by the earthquake of 1750 demonstrated.[25] Ironically, the English Jacobites were quick to assimilate 'enlightened' notions, a process discussed in Chapter 3, although they continued to represent Prince Charles as a divine being. Charles Edward himself was not prepared to abandon the family tradition of laying-on hands; after his father's death, he used the touch on Italian sufferers in 1770 and 1786. His brother Henry issued touch-pieces during his 'reign', one of which was credited with the power to cure scrofula in Ireland as late as 1901.[26]

By the time Charles died, however, belief in the royal touch appears to have been extinct in England. It was killed, not by the spread of 'rationalism' after 1688, but by political necessity. It was hard to uphold the sanctity of a royal succession that had been altered by Parliamentary manipulation, and monarchs whose legitimacy was so easily challenged could not afford to take the risk of trying to perform miracles. Although every English ruler claimed to be sacred, and Queen Anne went so far as to act the part, they were highly vulnerable to Jacobite competition. Williamite and Hanoverian supporters, therefore, were obliged to heap scorn on the royal touch as 'superstitious' and ineffectual. The sacredness of English monarchs was no longer

---

[24] *Adams's Weekly Courant*, 16 July 1751; *True Briton*, vol. ii, no. 9, 21 Aug. 1751, pp. 198–201; *London Evening Post*, no. 3718, 17 Aug. 1751; R.A., Stuart, Printed Papers, Box 6, no. 82, for a broadside version.

[25] See Clark, *English Society*, p. 171.

[26] Farquhar, 'Royal Charities. Part IV', pp. 174–80; Crawfurd, pp. 158–9; Lord Mahon, *The Decline of the Last Stuarts. Extracts from the Despatches of British Envoys to the Secretary of State* (London, 1843), pp. 36, 93.

expected to give evidence of itself, and their priestly role was gradually replaced by the symbols of 'patriotic' kingship. This development had far-reaching consequences. The touch had been more than a political gimmick; as Marc Bloch put it, 'the idea of the royal miracle was related to a whole conception of the universe', according to which the sacred monarch typologized the Christian God.[27] When the touch was abandoned, a great deal of the mystery of divine kingship wore off, and a secular image of monarchical authority slowly crept up the backstairs, to cover the royal nakedness.

The Roman Catholics

The idea of a priest-king who acted as an intermediary between God and the people may have held particular attraction for those whose religion called for the constant mediation of ministers, like Roman Catholics. Of course, recusants had a further reason for remaining loyal to James II and his descendants. King James lost his throne because he tried to give his coreligionists a measure of power within the English state, a policy that was totally unacceptable to most Anglicans.[28] The importance of Jacobite allegiance for English recusants, however, has been a difficult issue for historians sympathetic to their plight. By the late eighteenth century, most Catholic leaders in England had adopted an assimilationist view; they maintained that the majority of their faith had never been concerned with politics, and were patiently awaiting toleration. An echo of this can be found in John Bossy's otherwise excellent study of the English Catholic community, in which Jacobitism is barely mentioned.[29]

The political docility of recusants seemed to be demonstrated by the efforts of the Dominican Thomas Strickland to formulate an oath of submission to the Hanoverians after 1715. This incident, however, has generally been misinterpreted. While Strickland himself was plainly anti-Jacobite – he was later known as 'Walpole's priest' and became Bishop of Namur through the influence of George I – others involved in the submission plan did not share his political opinions.[30] They were

27 Bloch, p. 385. For a discussion of whether or not magic should be regarded as a 'world-view', see Hildred Geertz and Keith Thomas, 'An Anthropology of Religion and Magic', *Journal of Interdisciplinary History*, 6, 1 (1975), pp. 71–109. The royal touch, however, was part of a religious system, not an autonomous magical practice.
28 See Miller, *James II*, pp. 241–2; Ashley, *James II*, pp. 293–5.   29 Bossy, *passim*.
30 For Strickland, see Gillow, *Biographical Dictionary of English Catholics*, vol. v, pp. 533–5, and *D.N.B.*.

alarmed at the prospect of the destruction of their community by a vengeful Whig administration in the aftermath of the '15 rebellion, and they wished recusants to have the same advantage as Anglican Jacobites, who could take the oaths and live without molestation. These attitudes are clearly stated in a letter of December 1716 from the Chief Superior of the English Jesuits to Mary of Modena's Jesuit chaplain, Thomas Lawson, concerning a conference held by Bishop Gifford:

> The occasion of his desiring to meet us was to consult on the impending danger Catholics were under at present of the ruin of their religion and of their estates, to avoid which there was framed an oath of submision to King George and the present Government of living peaceably and quietly ... I did not approve of some expressions as 'an entire submission,' for which I put 'sincere submission,' because I think an entire submission to George I implies a duty as well of acting for him as of being barely passive under him, and thus it will come to be looked upon as an Oath of Allegiance, which I never could allow of.[31]

The purpose of the oath, in short, was to safeguard Catholics against persecution, not to make them loyal to George I. It failed because its backers could not agree on how far it should go.

The submission plan exemplified the terrible dilemma of English recusants: maintaining allegiance to the Stuarts led to further persecution, but disowning the exiled line meant a betrayal of their deepest sentiments. This problem racked the Howard clan after the Revolution, and helped to tear apart the marriages of two Dukes of Norfolk. The seventh Duke had become a nominal Protestant and a Williamite; his wife, the daughter of the staunchly Jacobite Earl of Peterborough, remained a Catholic. During their messy divorce in the 1690s, the Jacobites aligned behind the Duchess, although she may have offered secretly to inform on her father.[32] The Duke was succeeded by his Catholic nephew, whose father, Lord Thomas Howard, had been drowned while sailing to Ireland to join King James in 1689. The eighth Duke sent £2,000 to the Pretender in 1715 to support the rebellion, but he soon after became associated with Thomas Strickland's submission scheme, to the horror of his Jacobite wife Maria. She left him

---

[31] H.M.C., *Stuart*, vol. iii, pp. 348–50. Father Lawson sent this letter to James III, adding that the Jesuits had nothing to do with Abbot Strickland's scheme – *ibid.*, pp. 466–7.

[32] J. M. Robinson, *The Dukes of Norfolk* (Oxford, 1982), pp. 145–7; G.P.R. James, ed., *Letters Illustrative of the Reign of William III. From 1696 to 1708. Addressed to the Duke of Shrewsbury, by James Vernon, Esq. Secretary of State* (3 vols., London, 1841), vol. ii, pp. 346–7.

and returned to her father's Lancashire estate, where she lived with a lover, Peregrine Widdrington, who had been 'out' in the '15.[33] The plan of submission was defeated partly through the efforts of Norfolk's cousin, Henry Charles Howard of Greystoke. After its abandonment, the poor Duke had to write a cringing letter to James III, defending his conduct: 'I have always aimed in all my actions to serve you ... I flatter myself that If my enemys should asperse me that you woud not believe me capable of anything prejudicial to your interest.'[34] He was arrested in 1722 for complicity in the Atterbury Plot, but even this did not fully redeem him in the eyes of the Jacobite court; in 1731, a year before his death, Nathaniel Mist complained to Rome that Norfolk was rich enough to contribute much more money to the cause.[35] His title was inherited by his brother, who had been a rebel in 1715. This augured well for the Jacobites; but the ninth Duke was married to a strong-willed woman with collaborationist views. She took her husband to court in January 1732/3, and became a friend of the Prince of Wales, whose first child was born in Norfolk House. Yet the Duke quietly kept up his Jacobite ties; when he went back to court in 1745, it was partly because his Yorkshire estate agent, Andrew Blyde, was 'out' with Prince Charlie, and he later employed a prominent rebel, John Sanderson, as his master of horse.[36] After his wife's death in 1773, the aged Duke may have reverted to his old allegiance; he was probably the 'D.N.' mentioned in the Jacobite letters found in Mrs Leslie's coffee-house in 1775, which were discussed in the last chapter.

The political troubles of the Howard family illustrate the complexity of Jacobite sentiment among recusants, as well as its persistence. Historians of English Catholicism have often underestimated the latter. J. H. C. Aveling's seminal works do not ignore Jacobitism, but they suggest that loyalty to the Stuarts was declining by 1715 and had become almost irrelevant by 1745.[37] In fact, the recusant response to the '15 in the north was overwhelming, as Chapter 10 will show. Their bitter experience of defeat, however, convinced most Catholics that they could not rise again. Yet it was pretty clear where their sympathies

---

[33] Robinson, *Dukes of Norfolk*, pp. 147–50; Jones, *Mainstream of Jacobitism*, p. 107.
[34] R.A., Stuart 47/79.   [35] *Ibid.*, 142/141–2.
[36] Robinson, *Dukes of Norfolk*, pp. 154–5, 160; Cruickshanks, *Political Untouchables*, p. 91; B.L., Add. MS 28,231, fo. 179.
[37] Aveling, *Northern Catholic*, pp. 367–70, and his *The Handle and the Axe: Catholic Recusants in England from the Reformation to Emancipation* (London and Tiptree, Essex, 1976), pp. 253–5.

lay in 1745. As the rebels advanced into England, Thomas Maynott, a Catholic gentleman of Mountnessing in Essex, was arrested for wishing success to Prince Charles's attempt; Harry Wells, a Hampshire recusant, allegedly drank 'A health to him that was turn'd out; Not to Him that turn'd him out, And the Devil turn him inside out, that will not put this health about.'[38] To be sure, some Catholics in Yorkshire subscribed to the loyal association; Lord Fairfax of Gilling drank King George's health with an officer who was searching his house for arms, and Sir Edward Gascoigne of Parlington wrote to Lord Irwin, condemning the rebels as 'wild animals scampering on the hills'.[39] These sudden manifestations of recusant allegiance to George II were produced by fear; anti-Jacobite measures were particularly strict in Yorkshire, because the county was dominated by Whigs, and the large Catholic population was not trusted.[40] Lord Fairfax owned a set of Jacobite glasses, decorated with the family crest – if the soldiers had found them, it would have meant trouble.[41]

John Bossy's depiction of the English Catholics as a religious community centred on the gentry is important to understanding the survival of recusant Jacobitism. An institutionalized Church structure would have been more susceptible to government pressure, and it is worth noting that the main architects of submission and collaboration were the bishops (or 'Vicars Apostolic') and members of religious orders. Adherence to the Stuarts could survive more easily in isolated country houses than in churches or chapels. It also fared better in the north, where Catholics were numerous, than in the Midlands and south, where they were a tiny minority among landowners. Of the hundreds of Catholics who went into exile with James II in 1688–9, a disproportionate percentage were southerners.[42] They included two Sussex gentlemen who became Secretaries of State – Henry Browne, later Viscount Montagu, and John Caryll, created Baron Durford – as well as Richard Bulstrode of Astley, Warwickshire, George Holman of

---

38 P.R.O., S.P. 36/73, fos. 52–4; S.P. 37/83, fos. 9, 11, 200.
39 Aveling, *Northern Catholics*, pp. 368–9; Aveling, *The Handle and the Axe*, p. 254.
40 See Cedric Collyer, 'Yorkshire and the "Forty-Five"', *Yorkshire Archaeological Journal*, 38 (1955), pp. 82–5.
41 Aveling, *Northern Catholics*, p. 368. Sir Henry Bedingfield of Oxburgh Hall, Norfolk, insisted in a letter of 1745 to the Earl of Hardwicke that he was in no way disloyal to King George. He never informed the Earl that he owned the most magnificent collection of Jacobite glassware in existence. J. H. Pollen, S. J., ed., 'Bedingfield Papers', in *Miscellanea VI*, Catholic Record Society Publications, 7 (London, 1909), pp. 162–5.
42 Aveling, *The Handle and the Axe*, pp. 242–3.

Warkworth, Northamptonshire, Bevil Skelton of Ravely, Huntingdonshire, a Fermor of Oxfordshire and an Arundell of Wiltshire.[43]

Many southern recusants, particularly younger sons, went to
London rather than St Germain, and took up a trade. The Catholic
bookseller William Canning, a member of a gentry family of Warwickshire, was thrice arrested for distributing seditious works, and was
pilloried in 1693.[44] Canning's assistant was Francis Dormer, a relative
of Baron Dormer; his descendants were involved with Jacobite
publishing in London until the 1730s.[45] Richard Stafford of Thornbury,
Gloucestershire, a convert to Catholicism, had a shorter career in the
London propaganda industry; after writing some incoherent Jacobite
tracts in 1690, he was committed for lunacy by his Anglican family.[46]
Another genteel trade that attracted recusants was banking. Henry
Jerningham, son of a Norfolk baronet and brother of a leading Jacobite
diplomatic agent, was a goldsmith in Covent Garden, who raised
money for King James during the Swedish Plot.[47] One of his servants
was caught distributing copies of *Vox Populi, Vox Dei* in 1719.
According to Thomas Hearne, the notorious pamphlet was published
by John Lewis, a Welsh recusant bookseller in Russell Street, close to
Jerningham's shop – interestingly, the young Edward Gibbon became a
Catholic in 1753 through a priest recommended by a Mr Lewis,
bookseller, of Russell Street.[48]

The rebellion of 1715, however, left the Catholic community shaken
and demoralized. Although most southern recusants did not take an
active part in the rising, they were affected by its outcome. The
imposition of new taxes on Catholics and stronger enforcement of
penal laws in the period 1715–22 were dire threats to the vulnerable
southerners, and it is not surprising that they were the main supporters

---

43 See the Marquis of Ruvigny and Raineval, *The Jacobite Peerage, Baronetage, Knightage and Grants of Honour* (Edinburgh, 1904), pp. 216–18.
44 Luttrell, vol. ii, pp. 308, 626; vol. iii, pp. 104, 138–40; H.M.C., *Report on the Manuscripts of Allan George Finch* (5 vols., London, 1913–), vol. iii, p. 364; Gillow, *Biographical Dictionary of English Catholics*, vol. i, pp. 395–6.
45 See Boyer, *Political State*, vol. x, p. 329; P.R.O., S.P. 44/80, p. 38; P.R.O., T.S. 11/424, no. 1292 (John Dormer); P.R.O., S.P. 44/82 (Edward Dormer).
46 He is noticed in *D.N.B.*; see also Luttrell, vol. ii, p. 27, and C.L.R.O., MJ/SR 1752A, indt. Richard Stafford.
47 Fritz, *English Ministers and Jacobitism*, pp. 16, 43; H.M.C., *Stuart*, vol. iii, pp. 102, 436, 530, 538, vol. iv, p. 109.
48 Goulden, 'Vox Populi, Vox Dei', p. 372; Gillow, *Biographical Dictionary of English Catholics*, vol. iv, pp. 209–11; Doble *et al.*, eds, *Collections of Hearne*, vol. iii, pp. 30–1; Edward Gibbon, *Memoirs of my Life*, ed. G. A. Bonnard (London, 1966), p. 61.

of the submission oath. By the middle of the century, many of them had converted to Protestantism, and the Catholic gentry community was shrinking.[49] The Stuarts could still look to a few unbending loyalists among southern recusants, like John Caryll of Ladyholt; his *True Briton* was read by some of his Catholic neighbours in Hampshire, like his uncle Edward, the Matthews family of Heath House, near Petersfield, and Ralph Sheldon of Winchester.[50] Yet few English recusants were left at the Stuart court after 1715. Caryll's cousin was a gentleman usher to James III, as was Sir John Gifford of Burstall, Leicestershire, but most of the Pretender's servants were Scottish or Irish.[51] When Charles Edward wanted a new shadow-Secretary of State in 1769, he commissioned John Caryll to ask one of the Mannocks, a Catholic family of Suffolk; inheritance problems, however, prevented him from leaving his estate, and Caryll himself became the Secretary.[52]

By this time, the Stuart Pretender was no longer recognized as King of England by the Pope. The death of James III had allowed Rome to make a conciliatory gesture towards England by snubbing Charles Edward. In fact, the Stuarts had never been able to count on the support of the Catholic hierarchy. Although James II and his son enjoyed the right to make episcopal nominations, their choices sometimes disappointed them – Bishop Stonor, for example, was an enthusiastic backer of submission.[53] Jacobite sentiment was more pronounced among the lower clergy. Father Thomas Southcott was the principal revenue collector for the Stuarts in 1715–18, and the newspaper writer George Flint took minor orders at the English College in Rome before bad health and 'a weak head' obliged him to return to England.[54] Even the withdrawal of official recognition did not alter the allegiance of some Catholics in religious orders. The rectors and students of the English, Scottish and Irish Colleges in Rome, and the superiors of two Irish convents, defied the Papal ban on honours for Charles III in April 1766, and received their King in state, with full ceremonial robes, a sung *Te Deum* and kissing of hands. The outraged Vatican banished the rectors and superiors, and Abbé Grant, agent for the Scottish Catholics, lost his pension.[55] Recusants in England were

[49] Bossy, pp. 324–5.   [50] B.L., Add. MS 28,231, fos. 143v, 144, 149.
[51] Ruvigny, *Jacobite Peerage*, pp. 218–20.
[52] R.A. Stuart 448/83A, 450/83A.
[53] For their ecclesiastical nominations, see Ruvigny, *Jacobite Peerage*, pp. 226–31; for Stonor, see Aveling, *The Handle and the Axe*, pp. 254, 325–6.
[54] Jones, *Mainstream of Jacobitism*, p. 127; Fritz, *English Ministers and Jacobitism*, p. 16; H.M.C. *Stuart*, vol. vii, p. 19.
[55] Mahon, *Decline of the Last Stuarts*, p. 31.

often no more obedient in renouncing the Stuarts. Charles Edward retained the famous Catholic jurist Francis Plowden as his lawyer in the 1780s, and his daughter Charlotte dined with Mrs Standish of Standish, Lancashire, in 1788.[56] The harmless Cardinal York was revered by English Catholics; as late as the 1820s, the Jerninghams of Norfolk kept a picture of him in their house at Cossey.[57]

Jacobitism was an identifying feature of Anglocentric Catholicism, and became a banner of resistance to the ultramontane tendencies of the late eighteenth century. The exiled Stuarts were an alternative source of authority within the Church, the symbolic leaders of a gentry-oriented rather than institutionalized religion. Nevertheless, the Pope won in the end. His ultimate weapon was a religious tenet more powerful than English Catholic nationalism: the necessity of unity. Among the papers of the Jacobite Lord Nairne is a list, written in the 1690s, of the 'Grounds of a true Catholick'. It insists that '[a]ll Catholick good consists of Unity ... All diabolical Art tends to violat Unity.'[58] The Catholic desire to find a source of unity ended in the concept of a sacred monarchy, which was applied to both the Church and the state. The English recusant community remained faithful to the divinely ordained line of Stuart kings from the Revolution until 1766, and often longer still; but its loyalty to the sacred monarchy of Rome proved even more enduring.

The Nonjurors

If the English Catholics were headed by the gentry, the Nonjuring communion was based on clergymen. Yet the Nonjurors were not an institutionalized Church: they were a loose confederation of ministers, perhaps the most erudite collection of clerics ever to grace an English denomination. Unfortunately, their learning and piety has obscured their place in history. Reacting to the invective thrown at them by Whig historians, ecclesiastical scholars have often denied that the Nonjurors had any real interest in politics. Canon J. H. Overton, the greatest proponent of this view, explained the differences between the Nonjurors and the body of the Church of England as the result of an inclination 'to prefer the old order of things to the new', and of an

---

56 Beinecke Osborn Files, 'Lavington Box'; Tayler, *Prince Charlie's Daughter*, pp. 119–20.
57 Egerton Castle, ed., *The Jerningham Letters (1780–1843)* (2 vols., London, 1896), vol. ii, p. 185.
58 Bodl. Carte MS 208, fo. 224a.

admiration for the Stuart period, 'an age of less grossness' than that of William III and George I. Overton tried to separate Nonjuring from Jacobitism, arguing that they 'were not convertible terms;... there were Nonjurors who were in no active sense of the term Jacobites, men who were content to live peacefully and quietly without a thought of disturbing the present government'.[59]

There is some truth in this. Obviously, most Nonjurors were not Jacobite agents or conspirators; but they were also not all patristic scholars. The vast majority of them were ordinary, working clergymen. What they all had in common was a refusal to swear oaths to the ruling ✓ monarchs, a rejection of the legitimacy of the new regime. In no uncertain way, they affirmed that William and Mary, Anne and the Georges had less right to their allegiance, and to the throne, than the exiled Stuarts. In an age that took oaths very seriously, Nonjuring was a very strong political statement. Reverend Thomas Brett, who became a Nonjuror only in 1715, described his conversion as a gradual process of political awakening; 'my eyes were at last opened', he wrote, when he became convinced that James Francis Stuart was really James II's son. The Sacheverell trial made him doubt Queen Anne's legitimacy, and 'to believe that I had taken oaths which I ought not to have taken'. Finally, soon after George I's accession, he gave up his benefice and was received into the Nonjuring communion.[60] For most Nonjurors, the decision to remain loyal to the Stuarts had been taken less gradually, in the feverish atmosphere of 1689–90; but the logic of their choice was the same. Whether or not they were active in the cause, the Nonjurors were Jacobites by definition.

From the beginning, of course, some of the four hundred or so Nonjuring clergy wished only to retire into seclusion. The spiritual mentor of these 'passive' Nonjurors was the saintly Bishop Ken, and they included influential laymen like Robert Nelson and Francis Cherry. Their quietism, however, should not be misconstrued as acquiescence; they never intended to give up the Stuarts. An apocryphal story about Francis Cherry may cause us to wonder just how 'passive' he really was; allegedly, he met King William while hunting one day, and tried to coax the royal steed down a precipitous bank, hoping its rider would break his neck.[61] In 1710, Cherry, Nelson and

[59] J. H. Overton, *The Nonjurors: Their Lives, Principles, and Writings* (London, 1902), pp. 14, 417. See also Thomas Lathbury, *A History of the Nonjurors: Their Controversies and Writings* (London, 1845), and Findon, 'The Nonjurors and the Church of England'.

[60] Broxap, *Later Non-Jurors*, pp. 19, 24–5.   [61] See Cherry's biography in *D.N.B.*

Reverend Henry Dodwell returned to the regular communion of the Church of England, but they still declined to take oaths. Nelson, in fact, adopted the habit of rising from his knees and taking snuff when prayers were read for Queen Anne.[62] It should also be remembered that Cherry was the close friend of the carbuncular Jacobite Thomas Hearne.

The 'active' Nonjurors, by far the majority of deprived clergymen, saw themselves as comprising the true Church of England, and rejected all talk of reconciliation. George Hickes wrote in 1691 that the Nonjurors

are still as much Friends of the Church, and Enemies of Schism, as ever; but then by the Church they understand the *True Old Church* of England, with all her venerable Doctrines of Faith, Justice and moral Honesty, and all her strait Decrees against the *resisting, deposing* and *forfeiting* Doctrines ... you have separated from her, and them, and not they from you.[63]

Laurence Howell plagiarized these words from Hickes in *The Case of Schism* of 1716 (Howell was not a very imaginative writer), adding that 'the odious Name of *Separatist* belongs to those, who departed from the Church's true Communion in the Year 1688; and not to the *Chast Few*, who for the Preservation of a good Conscience quitted their then present Support, and prospect of further Promotion'.[64] Thus, the Nonjurors could convince themselves that they had not violated the principle of ecclesiastical unity; like the 'proto-Protestants' of the Middle Ages, they were preserving the true faith as guardians of Christ's promise that his Church would be forever visible. Robert Gordon, the last regular Nonjuring bishop in England, was to the end an uncompromising opponent of reunion; in the mid-1770s, he condemned Thomas Brett the younger as a 'lukewarm and moderate man' for proposing a plan of reconciliation with the juring majority.[65] Gordon died believing that his was the only true Church of England.

By 1693/4, however, the Nonjurors had been compelled to set up their own episcopal structure, to keep the 'Chast Few' alive until the return of the rightful king. This was the first step towards the creation of a distinct denomination. The Nonjuring search for religious purity advanced the process of separation when they came close to removing

---

62 Paton, ed., *Lyon in Mourning*, vol. iii, p. 199.
63 [George Hickes], *An Apology for the New Separation* (London, 1691), p. 10.
64 [Laurence Howell], *The Case of Schism in the Church of England truly Stated* (n.p., 1716), p. 1.
65 Paton, ed., *Lyon in Mourning*, vol. iii, pp. 305, 308, 317.

themselves from even a liturgical resemblance to the established Church. Between 1717 and 1733, they were bitterly divided by a dispute over the so-called 'Usages' of Edward VI's first Prayer Book, which included the mixing of wine with water in communion, and the addition of various prayers and oblations to the service. Although a compromise was eventually reached, the 'Usagers' controversy made the Nonjurors appear to be crypto-Catholic, because the first Prayer Book was less strongly Protestant than later versions.[66] The 'Orthodox British Church' founded by Reverend Thomas Deacon in Manchester in the 1720s represented the fulfilment of the dreams of the 'Usagers'. Deacon himself was entirely a Nonjuring product; his stepfather was Jeremy Collier, he had been ordained by Henry Gandy and was consecrated irregularly in 1733 by the fanatical 'Usager' Bishop Archibald Campbell. Deacon's *Complete Collection of Devotions*, published in 1734, was a thorough revision of the Anglican liturgy, which adopted not only the 'Usages' but many other 'pure' practices associated with the early Christian Church.[67]

His enemies called Deacon's new liturgy 'Papist'. In fact, while he was certainly a ritualist, Deacon was not a Catholic in disguise. Like those Nonjurors who sought a union with the Greek or Russian Orthodox Churches, he was immensely ambitious, and aimed at finding a 'primitive' form of worship that would have universal appeal. His disciple, the learned Manchester barber Thomas Podmore, who was 'out' in the '45, wrote a remarkable treatise comparing the Roman Catholic, Anglican and Eastern Orthodox versions of Christianity; he rejected all three, and was especially critical of their common fault of uniting Church and state.[68] Clearly, the Deaconites were straying far from all established varieties of Christian belief, into a radical 'primitivism' and anti-Erastianism. Nevertheless, they did not sever all links with the established Church. Many Anglican clergymen subscribed to Deacon's *Collections*, of which 1,400 copies were sold, and one of the Nonjuring Bishop's closest friends was Reverend John Clayton of the Manchester Collegiate Church. Through Clayton, a former member of the Holy Club, Deacon was acquainted with John Wesley, whom he advised not to separate from the Church of England.[69]

66 See Overton, *The Nonjurors*, pp. 290–308.
67 Henry Broxap, *A Biography of Thomas Deacon, The Manchester Non-Juror* (Manchester, 1911). For his portrait, see Plate 11.
68 Thomas Podmore, *The Layman's Apology for returning to Primitive Christianity* (Manchester and London, 1747); Broxap, *Thomas Deacon*, pp. 156–8.
69 Broxap, *Thomas Deacon*, pp. 75–6, 100, 172–3, 176, 180.

The Deaconite connection with the Collegiate Church persisted until 1798, when Bishop Thomas Garnett of the 'Orthodox British Church' sent the fellows there copies of the Nonjuring liturgy and prayers, which they approved of, but were unable to introduce without episcopal consent.[70] By then, the Manchester Nonjurors had apparently given up their allegiance to the Stuarts. They survived only a few more years. Macaulay's story that their last bishop, Charles Booth, emigrated to Ireland in 1805, is probably false; he was still listed in trade directories until at least 1819.[71] The regular Nonjurors were already extinct. The last reference to John Mansfield, Bishop Gordon's successor in London, was in 1789, and the Bowdlers' chaplain at Bath died in 1798. Both men were Jacobites to the last, to the annoyance of their Scottish Episcopal brethren, who accepted the Hanoverians after Charles Edward's death.[72]

About 4 per cent of the clergy became Nonjurors after the Revolution. Macaulay described them as 'preachers without hearers', a highly inaccurate label.[73] At least ten English peers became Nonjurors after 1688 – the Duke of Beaufort and the Earls of Chesterfield, Clarendon, Exeter, Gainsborough, Huntingdon, Salisbury, Thanet, Winchelsea and Yarmouth – as well as about sixty present and former Members of the House of Commons.[74] Some gentry families unconnected with recent Parliaments, like the Cottons of Conington, Huntingdonshire, the Yallops of Bowthorp in Norfolk, or the Yarboroughs of Snaith Hall, Yorkshire, also refused the oaths.[75] In all, there were perhaps one hundred Nonjuring gentry families in the 1690s, from the Pomeroys of Devon to the Wyats of Kent, the Lutwyches of Shropshire and the Tempests of Durham. Not all were strict Nonjurors; most of them probably attended the established Church. Nevertheless, their

[70] Broxap, *Later Non-Jurors*, p. 288.
[71] Macaulay, *History of England*, vol. iv, ch. 17, p. 2010; collection of Manchester trade directories, 1804–19, in Institute for Historical Research, London. For the last stages of the Deaconite church in Shrewsbury, see William Phillips, ed., 'William Cartwright, Nonjuror, and his Chronological History of Shrewsbury', *Transactions of the Shropshire Archaeological and Natural History Society*, 4th Series, 4 (1914), pp. 1–70.
[72] Richard Sharp, '100 Years of a Lost Cause: Nonjuring Principles in Newcastle from the Revolution to the Death of Prince Charles Edward Stuart', *Archaeologia Aeliana*, 5th series, 8 (1980), pp. 49, 52, 54 n. 70, 55 n. 87.
[73] Macaulay, *History of England*, vol. iv, ch. 14, p. 1729.
[74] For Nonjuring lords, see Cokayne, *Complete Peerage*; for M.P.s, see Henning, ed., *History of Parliament*, vol. i, p. 100.
[75] For the Cottons, see P.R.O., S.P. 36/76, fos. 110–11; for the Yarboroughs, Overton, *The Nonjurors*, p. 496; for the Yallops, Thompson, ed., *Letters of Humphrey Prideaux*, pp. 172, 177.

actions excluded them from any public office, and could have a severe effect on family fortunes. It is hardly surprising that after the death of James II in 1701, many lay Nonjurors agreed to take the oaths. Others were more persevering, and the Hanoverian Succession added to their ranks John Byrom and his fellow poet Edward Holdsworth, Charles Jennens, the librettist of Handel's *Messiah*, and the eminent physician Sir Richard Jebb.[76] Most of the Nonjuring gentry had died or rejoined the Church of England by the accession of George III, although as late as 1761, Byrom's brother-in-law, John Houghton of Bagguley, Cheshire, refused to take the office of sheriff on the grounds that he would not abjure the Stuarts.[77]

The oaths were seldom administered to those of the lower and middling classes, but it was they who from the first provided the bulk of worshippers in Nonjuring conventicles. A sermon in London by Charles Leslie on 30 January 1689/90 was attended by sixty people, which was 'a great auditory at this time'.[78] Government raids on the Nonjuring meetings in the capital in 1691–2 discovered forty people gathered in a house in Holborn, and one hundred at a conventicle in Fleet Street.[79] After 1715, more than a dozen Nonjuring meetings, some of them of considerable size, could be found in London. Two hundred people attended Reverend Robert Orme in Aldersgate Street in May 1715, and Reverend Richard Welton was preaching to almost two hundred weavers and artisans in Whitechapel when his conventicle was raided in November 1717.[80] The plebeian Nonjurors of London could create a lot of trouble for the government; they swung elections in City wards, infiltrated the small-arms arsenal, and together with the high-flyers of St Andrew's Holborn, they could make up a formidable mob.[81]

In the provinces, the Nonjurors met in congregations at Ashbourne

76 Overton, *The Nonjurors*, pp. 268, 341–4.
77 Parkinson, ed., *Remains of Byrom*, vol. ii, part ii, pp. 624–9.
78 Samuel Weller Singer, ed., *The Correspondence of Henry Hyde, Earl of Clarendon, and his brother, Laurence Hyde, Earl of Rochester* (2 vols., London, 1828), vol. ii, p. 303.
79 Luttrell, vol. ii, pp. 386–7, 398, 438.
80 P.R.O., S.P. 35/12/50; S.P. 44/116, pp. 289–91; S.P. 44/117, p. 199; *The Weekly Journal, or, British Gazeteer* (known as *Reed's Weekly Journal*), 15 March 1718, pp. 998–1000; Overton, *The Nonjurors*, pp. 282–4.
81 William Matthews, ed., *The Diary of Dudley Ryder, 1715–1716* (London, 1939), pp. 155–6 (City politics); P.R.O., S.P. 35/77, part 1, fo. 66; S.P. 44/79A, pp. 193–205 (small-arms arsenal). Nicholas Rogers found none of Welton's congregation tried for riot in 1715–16, but few rioters were actually taken up. Rogers, 'Popular Protest', p. 91.

in Derbyshire, at Manchester and at Newcastle.[82] In 1717, Reverend Abraham Yapp was arrested at the house of a Newcastle surgeon, while officiating to nineteen male hearers and an unspecified number of women.[83] In the late 1720s, when the Newcastle meeting split over the Usages controversy, they averaged thirty weekly communicants, and totalled sixty-five adults as well as the children of fourteen families. As late as 1764, twenty people were confirmed at Newcastle by Bishop Forbes, and Nonjuring continued in the town for another two decades.[84] The Deaconites at Manchester increased from around twenty in the late 1720s to sixty in 1746–7 to perhaps one hundred by the time of their founder's death in 1753. Deacon's successor Kenrick Price had seventy communicants in 1757, and Bishop Garnett was still administering to a congregation of thirty in 1804.[85] These were small but not insignificant numbers; they show that the Nonjurors did not lack an audience in the middling and lower classes. If they had been able to proselytize openly, the 'faithful remnant' might have been very successful.

The Nonjurors did in fact achieve a minor success in drawing laymen of humble backgrounds directly into the work of their Church. Edward Hart, a London bricklayer and friend of Thomas Brett, published Nonjuring polemical works; he was beaten to death by some constables at Chatham while trying to convert a group of dockyard workers. Lee Carrick, the well-educated son of an army officer, was compelled by poverty to take up shoemaking as a trade, but through his Nonjuring connections became secretary to the Society for the Propagation of Christian Knowledge.[86] Most of the Deaconite clergy were tradesmen: Kenrick Price was a grocer, William Cartwright of Shrewsbury was an apothecary and Charles Booth was a watchmaker. The erudite barber Thomas Podmore has already been mentioned. Lay and plebeian involvement in Church life was made necessary by the gradual extinction of the original Nonjuring clergy and the decline of gentry support. It was a trend reminiscent of Dissenting groups like the Baptists or Quakers, and it foreshadowed the Wesleyan Methodists. These are apt comparisons. Separated from the juring Church by their

---

[82] For Thomas Bedford's Ashbourne conventicle, see Overton, *The Nonjurors*, pp. 339–40.
[83] P.R.O., S.P. 35/8/112, (1) and (2); S.P. 35/10/95; Sharp, '100 Years of Nonjuring Principles', pp. 38–9.
[84] Sharp, '100 Years of Nonjuring Principles', pp. 43, 46, 50–1.
[85] Broxap, *Thomas Deacon*, pp. 99–100; Broxap, *Later Non-Jurors*, pp. 257, 289.
[86] Broxap, *Later Non-Jurors*, pp. 310, 312.

1 Portrait of James Francis Edward Stuart, studio of Alexis Belle, 1712

2 Medal with portrait of James, Prince of Wales, by Norbert Roettiers the elder, 1697

3 Medal with portrait of James Francis Stuart, by Norbert Roettiers the elder, 1708

4 Medal with portrait of James Francis Stuart, by Otto Hamerani, 1721

5 Medal with portrait of Charles Edward Stuart, by Norbert Roettiers the younger, 1745

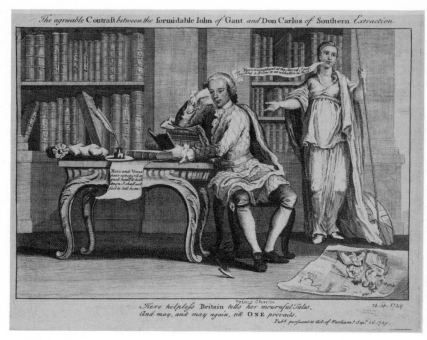

6 'The Agreeable Contrast between the Formidable John of Gant and Don Carlos of Southern Extraction', 1749

7 'The Agreable Contrast', 1747

8 Jacobite glass with portrait of Charles Edward Stuart and motto 'AUDENTIOR IBO'

9 Portrait of Louisa Stuart, artist unknown, *c.* 1774

10 Portrait of James Sheppard or Shepheard, artist unknown, 1718

11 Portrait of Thomas Deacon, artist unknown, *c.* 1745

12 *Benn's Club of Aldermen*, by Thomas Hudson, 1752

13 Jacobite glass with rose, thistle and 'FIAT' motto;
Prince of Wales feathers on base

14 Portrait of Thomas Syddall, artist unknown, *c*. 1745

uncompromising allegiance, their anti-Erastianism, their religious 'purity' and even their liturgy, the Nonjurors transformed themselves into a Nonconformist sect. They would not have admitted it, but their strict loyalty alienated them further and further from the ecclesiastical establishment which they both loved and hated.

The Church of England

We *knew King James* must *be ruined*, or *we*, & we *allowed Charity to begin at Home*. For the *Rest, between ourselves*, I *am not for justifying all that is past: for the main Engines in all great Transactions are ill Men*, & *it is a great Chance if they do good Things*. But the *debating* of *this*, I *leave to others*, & *content myself* with *praying God* to *pardon* what *has been*, & *is amiss*.[87]

The letter was from a clergyman of the Church of Ireland, James Bonsell, to the English antiquarian John Strype, dated April 1691; but it was typical of the sentiments of most ministers of the Church of England. William Cole, who edited Strype's correspondence, opined that the letter was '*fairly giving* up the *Revolution*'. This was an exaggeration; in fact, however unhappy Bonsell and other clergymen may have been about the legality of the Revolution, they were not prepared to gamble the fate of their Church, and their own careers, on the restoration of an unrepentant James II. The religious and political climate of the next two decades altered the attitude of many High Churchmen towards the Stuart claimant, and by 1715 a substantial number of clergymen were prepared to embrace the Jacobite cause; but they were crushed by the power of the Whig state. With the destruction of clerical Jacobitism, the Church effectively ceased to be an independent political force, except on a local level.

A small but vocal minority of Anglican ministers loudly condemned the Revolution from the first. As early as May 1689, a parson in the Whig bastion of Hull preached against 'King Ninie [William] and the apostate bastard [Queen Mary]'.[88] In November, Bishop Cartwright of Chester's former chaplain was pilloried for writing and publishing a seditious ballad on the coronation, and four months later a Northamptonshire cleric was pilloried and fined £200 for saying William and Mary were not lawful monarchs. The penalties in these cases were heavy; a judge even warned the last-mentioned offender that he might have been executed for his crime.[89] The government was worried about

[87] B.L., Add. MS 5,853, p. 375.   [88] Bodl. Carte MS 79, fo. 218.
[89] Luttrell, vol. ii, p. 24.

containing clerical disaffection, and it did not hesitate to prosecute ministers for seditious words. In 1689–90, clergymen were tried in Monmouthshire, Shropshire and at Prestbury, Cheshire, where the curate allegedly said King James 'was Ordained King by the Arch bishops and all the Nobles of the Land & found to be the right heir to the Crowne'. His accuser called him 'noe better than a papist'.[90]

The Nonjuring schism by no means eliminated the Jacobite element among the clergy. Two Suffolk parsons were tried at King's Bench in 1691 for drinking confusion to William and Mary on a recent fast-day; apparently, 'one of them carried a pidgeon pye to church under his cassock, and after to the place of meeting among them, where one wish'd king Williams heart was there, and he could make a good dinner thereof'. They were heavily fined and pilloried.[91] Other recalcitrant compliers included the minister at Midhurst, Sussex, seat of the recusant and Jacobite Browne family, who was bound over to Assizes for drinking to King James and the Prince of Wales.[92] The West Midlands clergy were particularly abusive to the new rulers in 1692–3, and clerics were prosecuted for seditious words in Herefordshire, Shropshire and Worcestershire.[93] By 1693, however, most clerical opposition to the Revolution had been stifled by severe punishments or cast out into the Nonjuring wilderness. Perhaps the last instance of a cleric prosecuted for Jacobitism in William's reign was Reverend William Cox of Quinton, Gloucestershire, who was accused of saying, shortly after the revelation of the Assassination Plot, 'I see there is a plott & that he [King William] ... has narrowly escaped the hand of justice but vengeance will overtake him he will die the death of a Tyrant, there will a Raveillac arise.'[94] A 'little gentleman in black velvet' did arise to topple William, but this Ravaillac was a mole, not a clergyman.

A major reason for the dwindling of clerical Jacobitism was the lack of episcopal protection. After the ejection of the Nonjuring bishops, most of whom were replaced by Whigs, the heads of the Church

---

90 P.R.O., Assi. 5/10, Monmouth 1690, indt. Nicholas James, Salop 1690, indt. John Wagstaffe; P.R.O., P.C. 24/145, part 1, Spring 2 W. & M., infos. R. Day, N. Byolin.
91 Luttrell, vol. ii, pp. 309–10, 356, 391; Bodl. Carte MS 233, fos. 252–3, 264, 270; Carte MS 76, fo. 291.
92 Luttrell, vol. ii, p. 352.
93 P.R.O., Assi. 5/12, part 1, Hereford Qua. 1692, info. no. 12, rec. no. 5, indt. Hugh Pugh; Assi. 5/12, part 2, Salop Aut. 1692, info. no. 4; Assi. 5/13, Civ. Worcs. 1693, info. John Glover, rec. for Daniel Kendrick (see also Chapter 8 for this case); Luttrell, vol. iii, p. 38.
94 P.R.O., Assi. 5/17, Gloucs. 1697, info. no. 5, indt. Wm. Cox.

maintained apparent unanimity in their allegiance to William. In fact, not all of them were as loyal as they seemed. Jonathan Trelawny of Exeter and John Hough of Oxford endorsed a letter sent in December 1693 to Louis XIV, asking him not to tamper with the Church of England if James II were restored.[95] The Jacobitism of Nathaniel Crew, Bishop of Durham, was widely suspected, and the government excepted him from the general pardon of 1690. Crew could not prevent the deprivation of the Nonjuring Dean of Durham, Bernard Granville, and in 1697/8 Granville's relative Sir George Wheler, a prebend of the Cathedral, was tried for sending money to King James, speaking against the government, and having his servant forge his name on the Association of 1696.[96] The political impotence of Bishop Crew illustrated the dangers of episcopal adherence to the exiled line.

James II's death, however, led to a sudden alteration of Jacobite policy towards the Church of England. Influenced by the Nonjurors and by his Secretary of State, Lord Middleton, James III sent an extraordinary set of 'Instructions' in March 1701/2 to Charles Leslie. He promised that he would never attempt to change the 'legal rights, privileges and immunities' of the Church, which meant no repeal of the Test and Corporation Acts, although he explicitly opposed any persecution of Dissenters or Roman Catholics. More astonishing still, he agreed to 'waive during our own reign our right of nomination to bishopricks and all other dignities and benefices'; he would appoint an Archbishop of Canterbury and four other bishops, who would have the authority to propose candidates for episcopal posts. Finally, he was willing to remit all first fruits and tenths paid by the clergy to the crown.[97] This remarkable document was calculated to appeal to the anti-Erastian temperament of the High Church clergy, which had turned the Convocations of the early 1700s into political battlegrounds.[98]

The strategy worked. Obsessed by resentment of Whig bishops and fear of 'the Church in danger', High Church clerics began to drift, almost inexorably, towards Jacobitism. By 1704, James III's chief Nonjuring spokesman, Charles Leslie, was recognized as a leading

[95] Hopkins, 'Aspects of Jacobite Conspiracy', pp. 369–70. The fourteen other peers who sponsored the letter were all Nonjurors or known Jacobites. For Trelawny, see also Monod, 'Jacobitism and Country Principles', p. 302.
[96] D.N.B. (Crew, Granville and Wheler); James, ed., Vernon Letters, vol. ii, pp. 55–7.
[97] Macpherson, ed., Secret History, vol. i, pp. 606–7.
[98] See Bennett, Tory Crisis, chs. 3–4; Mark Goldie, 'The Nonjurors, Episcopacy, and the Origins of the Convocation Conspiracy', in Cruickshanks, ed., Ideology and Conspiracy, pp. 15–35.

propagandist for the Tory cause.[99] Six years later, the trial of Dr Henry Sacheverell brought the issue of religious crisis into dramatic focus. Sacheverell's attack on 'False Brethren', that is, Low Churchmen, contained a veiled condemnation of the Revolution that did not go unnoticed.[100] As has been seen, clergymen had often been prosecuted under William III for seditious words and sermons, and if Sacheverell's treason was less overt, it was equally obnoxious to the government. His light sentence encouraged High Churchmen to greater boldness, at least in private company, as a letter of 1713 to Thomas Brett reveals:

> Dr Sacheverell preached before the Sons of the Clergy ... afterwards a gathering took place where Dr Bisse, Bishop of Hereford, and the Bishop of Rochester honoured us with their presence ... we drank a great many loyal healths and the musicians were so foolish as to play a tune which they say is called 'The King shall enjoy his own again.' However, it was received with universal acclamations and was often repeated and when they offered at another tune they were as universally hissed.[101]

Clearly, many High Churchmen, including Bishop Atterbury of Rochester, were on the path to Jacobitism long before Queen Anne died.

The fall of the Tory party from power in 1714–15 expanded the scope of disaffection among High Churchmen. The riots of the following years were often abetted by the clergy, as the next chapters describe. Ministers were prosecuted for seditious words in 1715 in Berkshire, Devonshire and Derbyshire; in 1716 in Yorkshire, Norfolk, Dorset, Gloucestershire and Shropshire; in 1718 in Cornwall and Suffolk; in 1719 in Herefordshire; and in 1722 in Westmorland. They now had answers to the accusation that they were 'noe better than a papist' for espousing Jacobitism. George Read of Chilton, Berkshire, claimed that 'the Pretender was a good Protestant and had been so for three years then past'.[102] Thomas Dorsett of Worthen, Shropshire, was less misinformed when he said:

99 See Goldie, 'Tory Political Thought', chs. 6 and 11.
100 See Holmes, *Trial of Doctor Sacheverell*, esp. chs. 3, 6–8.
101 Quoted in Broxap, *The Later Non-Jurors*, p. 4. For Bishop Bisse, see also H.M.C., *Stuart*, vol. vi, p. 385. Atterbury reportedly asked Bolingbroke to proclaim King James on Queen Anne's death in 1714 – see Joseph Spence, *Observations, Anecdotes and Characters of Books and Men Collected from Conversations*, ed. James M. Osborn (2 vols., Oxford, 1966), vol. i, p. 284. Bennett, *Tory Crisis*, p. 182, denies this story, citing Dr Stratford's disbelief in H.M.C., *Portland*, vol. vii, p. 337; but Stratford stated that he would credit the tale if it came from Lord Harcourt, which it apparently did.
102 P.R.O., Assi. 5/37, part 2, Berks. Qua. 3 G. I, info. no. 3, rec. ad pros. no. 4, indt. G. Read.

Admitting he was A papist why might he not maintaine our libertys and Rights of the Church as Well as it was Done in King Charles the Seconds time, who it was well known lived and Dyed a papist ... why might not the p^{r}tend^r as he is Called change his religion for the Sake of a Crown as well as he that is now in poss[ess]ion of the thrown.[103]

These were good questions, and extremely dangerous ones for the government, which was quick and severe in punishing erring clerics. Theophilus Jones of Stretton, Herefordshire, was fined £20 and imprisoned without bail for saying 'itt was hard upon the young Gen^t on the other side of the Water for itt was not yett proved against him but that he was King James's son'. Jones could not pay the fine, and languished in gaol for eight years.[104]

Heavy penalties did not deter all disaffected ministers. Mimicking Sacheverell, Jacobite clergymen entertained the populace with frequent seditious sermons. Huge crowds in Bishopsgate and St Pancras heard Willoughby Mynors, curate of Shoreditch, preach on the degeneration of the nation under 'usurpers'; he was ejected from his living in 1716 after delivering a Jacobite diatribe from the pulpit on 10 June.[105] Charles Humphreys, curate of St Mildred's Breadstreet, shocked his loyalist rector in October 1715 by praying for those 'now deprived of their just Rights; and that God would please to restore them'.[106] The minister of Gray's Inn chapel prayed for the rebel lords in February 1715/16, as he had formerly done for executed Jacobite recruiters.[107] In 1718, the clergyman at Weston, Nottingham, preached that 'the Nation was Governed by Fools, encouraged by Knaves, and carried on by Madmen and Usurpation'; three years later, the rector and curate of Bedale, Yorkshire, were accused of delivering treasonable orations during services.[108] The most spectacular example of Jacobite sermonizing, however, was that of Edward Bisse, rector of Portbury, Somerset, and St George's, Bristol, who progressed through the West Country,

---

103 P.R.O., Assi. 2/5, Salop Aut. 1, 2 G. I, Qua. 2 G. I; Assi. 5/36, part 1, Salop Qua. 2 G. I, infos. nos. 33–4.
104 P.R.O., Assi. 2/6, Hereford Aut. 5, 6 G. I; Assi. 5/39, part 2, Hereford Aut. 5, 6 G. I, info. no. 11, indt. T. Jones. For other cases, see P.R.O., Assi. 2/5, Gloucs. Qua. 3 G. I; Assi. 2/6, Gloucs. Qua. 3 G. I; Assi. 4/18, pp. 10, 406; Assi. 5/36, Gloucs. 2 G. I, info. G. Curtis, info. no. 34; Assi. 23/5, Devon Aut. 2 G. I; P.R.O., S.P. 35/12/60 (Suffolk), S.P. 35/13/60 (Cornwall), S.P. 35/41/36, 149, S.P. 35/45/177 (Westmorland); S.P. 44/117, pp. 353–4 (Derbyshire), 492 (Devon); S.P. 44/118, pp. 205–6 (Norfolk), 226–7 (Dorset); St James's Evening Post, no. 198, 1–4 Sept. 1716 (Yorkshire).
105 P.R.O., S.P. 44/118, pp. 48–9; St James's Evening Post, no. 163, 12–14 June, 1716; Boyer, Political State, vol. xii, p. 470.
106 Boyer, Political State, vol. xii, pp. 595–605.   107 B.L., Stowe 750, fo. 170.
108 P.R.O., S.P. 44/79A, pp. 23–4, 238; S.P. 35/25/122.

assuring his audiences that 'GEORGE ... has no Business here. We have had no Laws these Thirty Years, never since the Time of King *James* the Second, nor shall till King *James* ... comes.' Apprehended at last during a sermon at Bristol in 1718, Bisse was rescued by his congregation; after his recapture, he was tried and sentenced to the pillory, £800 in fines and four years in prison. When he was pilloried at Charing Cross, nothing was thrown at him, and the crowd abused a man who called him a villain.[109]

Like Sacheverell, Bisse became a popular hero; but this was not enough to sustain clerical Jacobitism. By 1722, the Anglican clergy and Church-affiliated bodies like the London charity schools had been rigorously purged of malcontents.[110] As always, the main agency of government control was the preferment system; Jacobite clerics could hope for nothing from a Hanoverian king and loyal bishops. Even a small transgression could wreck a career. When John Thomlinson, rector of Rothbury, Northumberland, prayed for King James in 1716, he quickly corrected himself by telling the congregation it was a mistake, 'and so read a prayer for King George, so that they could not make any thing of it'.[111] By 1722, the number of seditious words cases and treasonable sermons had been reduced to a trickle. The body of Jacobite opinion within the clergy had been cowed; then, at one stroke, it was decapitated by the arrest and imprisonment of Francis Atterbury, Bishop of Rochester. The lower clerical ranks rumbled – the curate of Fordwich, Kent, was taken up for a seditious sermon, and the minister of St Alban's Woodstreet, who reportedly kept a picture of James III in his room, preached on 'Imprisonment in a good Cause'.[112] It was not much; nothing really could be done.

After 1722, the conciliatory efforts of High Churchmen like Bishop Gibson of London led to peaceful coexistence with the Whig administration. Jacobitism survived among the clergy only in isolated instances, and in small independent pockets. In London, where it had

---

109 Boyer, *Political State*, vol. xvi, pp. 489–501; J. C. Hodgson, ed., *Six North Country Diaries*, Surtees Society, 108 (1910), 'Diary of John Thomlinson', p. 151. For more on Bisse, see P.R.O., S.P. 35/7/83; Doble *et al.*, ed., *Collections of Hearne*, vol. vi, p. 258.

110 For the charity schools, see Boyer, *Political State*, vol. xii, pp. 366, 470–1; *St James's Evening Post*, no. 213, 6 Oct. 1716.

111 Hodgson, ed., *Six North Country Diaries*, 'Diary of John Thomlinson', pp. 66, 93; see also p. 89, where Thomlinson prayed for King Charles instead of King William. A similar incident occurred in 1715 at Derby, a nest of clerical Jacobitism. See John Stevenson, *Popular Disturbances in England, 1700–1870* (London, 1979), pp. 22–3.

112 P.R.O., S.P. 35/33/1; S.P. 35/43/94.

been so vigorously excised, it was virtually dead; when the minister of Poplar Church, Islington, prayed for the 'Right Heir to the Crown' in 1726, he voiced the last echo of Sacheverellite zeal in the capital.[113] Several years later, however, a bizarre manifestation of Jacobite sentiment appeared at the Reverend John Henley's celebrated oratory in Lincoln's Inn Fields. A former propagandist for Walpole who had separated from the Church of England to found his own 'primitive' sect, Henley treated the butchers of Clare Market and other hearers to a series of seditious harangues between 1743 and 1754. From his pulpit, Henley denounced William III and the Hanoverians, praised James II, celebrated the rebel victory at Prestonpans and declared that 'The King of the North shall return'. When he was arrested during the rebellion, his loyal butchers accompanied him to prison in mourning garb, carrying marrow-bones and cleavers.[114] Henley's strange sermons reveal that Jacobitism could reemerge in London – but only outside the established Church.

The old cause breathed a little more freely in the provinces. At Durham, it had been implanted by the long tenure of Bishop Crew, who died in 1721 exhorting those around him '*don't you go over to them – don't you go over to them*', meaning the Hanoverians.[115] His protégé, Sir John Dolben – ironically, the son of the Whig M.P. who moved for Sacheverell's impeachment – held the so-called 'golden prebendary' at Durham, and paid an annuity to the exiled Atterbury; in the 1740s, he happily accepted the gift of Charles Edward Stuart's portrait from Philip Thicknesse.[116] No wonder that Dolben was 'reckoned a staunch friend to the Pretender, or, at least, to hereditary right'.[117] Another Jacobite enclave was the Collegiate Church of Manchester, where an attempted purge by the Whig Bishop Peploe of Chester was defeated in 1726 by a writ of *mandamus* forbidding him from exercising wardenship. The case centred on a chaplain, Richard Assheton, who refused to pray for King George and baptized children on only one non-holy day – 10 June.[118] The Collegiate Church became a haven for

---

113 P.R.O., S.P. 35/62/69–70.
114 Graham Midgely, *The Life of Orator Henley* (Oxford, 1973), pp. 229–45.
115 Philip Thicknesse, *Memoirs and Anecdotes of Philip Thicknesse, late Lieutenant Governor of Land Guard Fort, and unfortunately Father to George Touchet, Baron Audley* (2 vols., n.p., 1788), vol. i, p. 13.
116 D.N.B.; Thicknesse, *Memoirs*, vol. i, pp. 209–11.
117 Hodgson, ed., *Six North Country Diaries*, 'Diary of Thomas Gyll', p. 200.
118 Samuel Hibbert-Ware, *History of the Foundations in Manchester of Christ's College, Chetham's Hospital, and the Free Grammar School* (2 vols., Manchester, 1830), vol. ii, pp. 72–5.

Jacobites thereafter, and in 1745 its chaplains and fellows greeted Charles Edward Stuart enthusiastically; they hid the arms of the local militia, read prayers to the rebels on St Andrew's day and were granted private audiences by the Prince. John Clayton, a chaplain, fell on his knees before Charles Edward as the Scots marched through Salford.[119]

As at Manchester, the clerical fellows of Oxford University were able to preserve a Jacobite tradition for decades. Their speciality was commemorative preaching; Thomas Warton senior, the poetry professor, compared Cromwell to George I in a Restoration day sermon in 1719, and George Coningsby of St Mary's Hall, Dr King's college, was suspended from preaching for delivering a similar lecture on 30 January 1726/7.[120] Nathan Wetherall of University College, a Hutchinsonian, was accused of advocating passive obedience in a sermon on 30 January 1756.[121] Perhaps the last Oxford Jacobite sermon was preached by Dr Pusey on 5 November 1837; it condemned the Glorious Revolution as the cause of current troubles in Church and State.[122] The Oxford Movement was in fact the last of a series of religious societies based at the University, most of which had Jacobite connections, from Francis Cherry's Nonjuring circle, to the Holy Club, of which John Clayton was a member, to the Hutchinsonians.[123] Religious independence and Jacobitism were often symbiotic strains.

In the West Midlands, Jacobite sentiment survived among the clergy only through lay protection. In the 1720s, Reverend John Taylor alienated his patron, Edward Owen of Cundover, Shropshire, by refusing to drink a toast to the exiled Stuarts on his knees.[124] Time altered the politics of this region little, and in 1749 a West Bromwich cleric was tried at King's Bench for criticizing the illumination of houses to celebrate the victory at Culloden.[125] The curate of Colton in Staffordshire was arrested in 1750 for writing a letter to a local gentleman, recommending an itinerant Scot as 'a sincere and hearty

---

119 Beatrice Stott, 'The Informations Laid Against Certain Townsmen of Manchester in 1746', *T.L.C.A.S.*, 42 (1925), pp. 27–39; Parkinson, ed., *Remains of Byrom*, vol. ii, part ii, pp. 393–4.
120 P.R.O., S.P. 35/16/131, 143; S.P. 35/17/1, 44, 57; Ward, pp. 134–5.
121 Ward, pp. 134–5.
122 *The Royalist*, vol. 4, no. 7, 30 Oct. 1893, pp. 110–11.
123 For a discussion of some of these groups, see John Walsh, 'Religious Societies: Methodist and Evangelical, 1738–1800', in W. J. Shiels and Diana Wood, eds., *Voluntary Religion*, Studies in Church History, 23 (Oxford, 1986), pp. 279–302.
124 Nichols, *Literary Anecdotes*, vol. iv, pp. 491, 662.
125 P.R.O., K.B. 1/10, Trinity 22/23 G. II, Salop, affids. Phillips, Baddison and Dalloe, fo. 33.

well wisher to the king and prince, and one who has received several wounds in his service, at the battle of *Preston Pans*, and at that most unfortunate one at *Culloden*'; the man would be 'a great entertainment' at 'the jubilee' on 10 June. The cleric was sentenced to two years' imprisonment and a huge fine of £900.[126] Ministers in the smuggling area of Romney Marsh in Kent were also occasionally prone to Jacobite tendencies. Thomas Coppock, briefly curate of Snave, became chaplain to the Jacobite regiment raised in Manchester in 1745; John Kirkby, rector of Blackmanstone, was chaplain to the Jacobite Edward Gibbon of Putney, until he imprudently omitted the name of the King in prayers during the '45 rebellion, and was dismissed by his fearful patron.[127]

These examples affirm that Jacobitism did not perish among the clergy in 1722, but they also show that allegiance to the Stuarts could only persist beyond the authority or the notice of episcopal authorities. Although High Church sympathy for the exiled monarchs may have been widespread long after Atterbury's fall, it is difficult to interpret silence. Hints of hidden loyalties, however, can be detected in some rather unlikely individuals. Reverend Richard Graves, for instance, was a friend of the impeccable Whig Ralph Allen of Bath, and led a very quiet clerical life. Yet an important character in his novel *The Spiritual Quixote* is a sympathetic Jacobite shoemaker, who combines charity and good nature with the habit of wearing a white rose on 10 June. In 1771, moreover, Graves christened one of his children with the evocative name John Charles Edward.[128] The strictly Nonjuring Bowdlers of Bath considered Graves's principles upright enough to entrust their sons to his charge at the small school where he taught in his parish.[129] The evidence is slight, but compelling.

Graves was a figure of little influence in the Church; so were all Jacobite clergymen after 1722. The ecclesiastical leaders of high-flying Anglicanism had made peace with the government in the 1720s, and never deviated from the Erastian line. They allowed the suspension of Convocation, acquiesced in the return of occasional conformity and assisted in the virtually complete subordination of the bench of bishops

---

[126] *Gentleman's Magazine*, vol. xx, Aug. 1750, p. 343; vol. xxi, Aug. 1751, p. 375. This incident was connected with the Walsall riot of 29 May 1750, which is discussed in Chapter 7.

[127] Beatrice Stott, 'Parson Coppock', *T.L.C.A.S.*, 40 (1923), pp. 50–1; Gibbon, *Memoirs*, p. 31.

[128] Richard Graves, *The Spiritual Quixote, or The Summer's Ramble of Mr. Geoffrey Wildgoose*, ed. Clarence Tracy (London, 1967), pp. xxvi, 24.

[129] [Thomas Bowdler], *Memoir of the Late John Bowdler, Esq.* (London, 1825), p. 23.

to ministerial power. As a reward for loyalty, the government agreed not to meddle with the political and financial privileges of the Church. Ultimately, it proved a poor exchange. If the High Church clergy was belligerent and intolerant before 1722, it was also free and popular. By shackling themselves to Walpole's administration, the High Church-men gradually lost contact with their plebeian constituency, which was far less prepared to accept Whig rule. A century later, when the confessional state began to collapse around it, the Church of England found itself powerless in the face of change, still fettered to a govern-ment that was now prepared to scrap the legislative basis of Anglican dominance. Perhaps Pusey was not wrong after all in seeing 1688 as the origin of the Church's nineteenth-century agonies.

The Dissenters

The exiled Stuarts never delivered themselves up wholly to the High Churchmen. They remained Roman Catholics, at least until Prince Charles belatedly, and temporarily, accepted Anglican communion at St Mary-le-Strand during his visit to London in September 1750.[130] They did not hesitate to employ non-Anglicans in Jacobite business; one of their chief agents in London in 1715 was a Jewish merchant, Francis Francia.[131] James II and his son consistently espoused a wider toleration for Protestant Dissenters as well as Catholics. During his reign, James's Declaration of Indulgence had gained considerable support from Dissenters.[132] The passage of the Toleration Act of 1689, however, combined with their dislike of Roman Catholics to ensure the firm loyalty of most Nonconformists to William and Mary. Neverthe-less, some did not renounce James, particularly among the smaller sects, who gained less security from the new Act than did the Presby-terians.

The Dissenting Jacobites included some extraordinary characters. Edward Roberts, who had been instrumental in the negotiations with Nonconformists and Whigs in 1687–8, was a Baptist and former Cromwellian who went to St Germain after the Revolution and became

---

130 See Lang, *Prince Charles Edward Stuart*, pp. 451–2; Peter de Polnay, *Death of a Legend: The True Story of Bonny Prince Charlie* (London, 1952), p. 165.

131 Howell, ed., *State Trials*, vol. xv, cols. 898–994; Cecil Roth, *A History of the Jews in England* (3rd edn, Oxford, 1964), p. 208. Francia may in fact have been a double agent. For James II's good relations with the Jewish community, see Roth, *A History of the Jews in England*, pp. 173–84.

132 See Miller, *James II*, pp. 167–87; Jones, 'James II's Whig Collaborators'.

James II's envoy to the anti-Williamite Dutch republicans in 1692.[133] Edward Nosworthy of Ince Castle, Cornwall, was a very hot Whig and member of the Green Ribbon Club during the Exclusion Crisis. Probably an Independent or Baptist in religion, Nosworthy became a gentleman of the privy chamber to James in 1688, and retained his office in exile. Active as a Jacobite agent in 1695–6, he identified with Lord Melfort's Catholic party, which was more inclined towards toleration than the Anglican followers of Lord Middleton.[134] Most Jacobite Dissenters, however, were Quakers. They objected to the oaths and doctrinal strictures imposed by the Toleration Act, and John Bossy has suggested that they had an affinity with Roman Catholics, reflected in their amiable relations on a local level.[135] Although most Quakers were loyal to King William, a significant minority retained ties with St Germain through their leader, William Penn.

Penn's recent biographers, reacting to the venomous comments of Macaulay on the revered patriarch, have denied that he was ever an active Jacobite.[136] Admittedly, while Penn was to some extent a courtier, he was not a politician, and he lacked the temperament of a conspirator. The government, however, would not have arrested him four times in 1689–91 without cause. His last arrest, in January 1690/1, was a result of the apprehension of Richard Grahme, Viscount Preston, who was caught on a boat in the Thames carrying two letters from Penn to James II, and a commission from the Quaker for the use of two vessels.[137] Preston later revealed that Penn, the Earl of Clarendon, the Countess of Dorchester, Bishop Turner of Ely, Penn's friend Charlwood Lawton, a Quaker named Leighton and others had been involved in a restoration plot; his testimony was corroborated by Matthew Crone, a Jacobite agent.[138] Penn's denials of complicity were disingenuous, but it should be noted that Preston's accomplice John Ashton was executed for the plot, and the Quaker leader was undoubtedly terrified.[139]

---

[133] Hopkins, 'Aspects of Jacobite Conspiracy', pp. 128–9.
[134] Henning, ed., *History of Parliament*, vol. iii, pp. 165–6.
[135] Bossy, pp. 392–4.
[136] See, for example, Vincent Buranelli, *The King and the Quaker: A Study of William Penn and James II* (Philadelphia, 1962), pp. 171–6.
[137] William C. Braithwaite, *The Second Period of Quakerism* (London, 1919), pp. 151–2, 161–3; Howell, ed., *State Trials*, vol. xii, cols. 646–822. The sloop on which Preston was sailing belonged to a Quaker woman of Wapping – [Buckley, ed.], *Ailesbury Memoirs*, vol. i, p. 276.
[138] H.M.C., *Finch*, vol. iii, pp. 308–45.
[139] For his statements, see Braithwaite, *The Second Period of Quakerism*, pp. 164–6.

Penn was not alone among the Quakers in his dogged allegiance. A letter was issued at Yearly Meeting in 1692, urging the cessation of party strife within the community: 'Away with those upbraiding characters of Jacobites and Williamites, Jemmites and Billites, &c., so used by the world's people against one another ... Let us have no such upbriding distinctions in God's camp.'[140] Among the Quaker Jemmites was William Bromfield, a merchant and shipowner, who transported agents, recruits and supplies to Ireland and England in 1689–90.[141] Another Quaker kept the house in Goodman's Fields which served as a refuge for Jacobite fugitives.[142] In 1696, however, the Friends obtained an Act of Parliament allowing them to make an affirmation rather than taking the oaths. The affirmation undermined Jacobite Quakerism, and by February 1697/8 the Abbé Renaudot, French agent at St Germain, could write that the Friends 'were at first very much attached to the legitimate King and were of great use to him, especially Mr. Penn, their Patriarch: but some time ago they changed their ways, and Mr. Penn betrayed him'.[143]

Nevertheless, Quakers continued to be persecuted by both Whigs and Tories. Their sufferings may have reactivated Jacobite sentiments, and in 1712 Lord Nairne wrote to an English operative 'that the King was glad to hear that La[w]ton and Pen were still honest'.[144] The exiled court wanted to use Lawton and his friend Penn in sounding out the Earl of Oxford, a plan that came to nothing. By this time, Penn was old and sick, but there were other Quakers who were more suitable for plotting, especially those with mercantile connections. Robert Gerard, a Quaker merchant at Rotterdam, handled Jacobite letters and sheltered agents passing through the Netherlands in 1716.[145] A Quaker shipmaster named Day was executed for high treason in 1722 for transporting recruits from Ireland to Spain in connection with the Atterbury Plot.[146] Other Friends were less active, but more expressive,

---

140 Ibid., p. 179.
141 Burger, 'Spymaster to Louis XIV', in Cruickshanks, ed., Ideology and Conspiracy, pp. 114–15; Beaumont, ed., Jacobite Trials at Manchester, pp. 12–13; P.R.O., P.L. 28/1, p. 27. That Bromfield was not a 'pretended Quaker', as the government agent Richard Kingston suggested, is proved by his begging letters in the Carte Manuscripts.
142 G. H. Jones, Charles Middleton: The Life and Times of a Restoration Politician (Chicago, 1967), p. 247.
143 Burger, 'Spymaster to Louis XIV', in Cruickshanks, ed., Ideology and Conspiracy, p. 115; Braithwaite, The Second Period of Quakerism, pp. 182–90.
144 Macpherson, ed., Secret History, vol. ii, pp. 277, 293.
145 H.M.C., Stuart, vol. iii, pp. 53, 68, 502.
146 P.R.O., S.P. 44/81, p. 109.

in displaying their loyalty. The Quaker almanac writer George Parker was prosecuted in Anne's reign for including James III in a list of European sovereigns; in 1723, his almanac predicted an imminent restoration.[147] Elizabeth Penn, possibly a relative of the patriarch, wrote to the Pretender in 1716/17, advising him to send letters 'to the whole Parliament of England concerning thy just right and forgiveness to them', which 'would be to them, as though thou spoke'. She claimed to be acquainted with some Tory Jacobites.[148] This was not a unique relationship – at Hertford, the Quakers supported High Church candidates in the 1690s, and voted after 1715 for Charles Caesar, the Jacobite Tory M.P. for the borough.[149]

The politics of toleration made strange alliances. As late as 1777, the American loyalist Samuel Curwen lodged in Manchester with a woman who was 'a Quaker in religion and a Jacobite in political principle'.[150] Very little can be ascertained about the depth of Dissenting sympathy for the Stuarts; but it is clear that the same exiled King whose Anglican followers killed a Quaker in Bristol in 1714, destroyed a Quaker meeting-house in Oxford in 1715, and threatened Quaker grain merchants in Warwickshire in 1756, could depend upon the allegiance of some Friends. Nothing could illustrate better the complexity of the relationship of Jacobitism to religion.

The religious diversity of late seventeenth- and eighteenth-century England was both an obstacle and an opportunity for Jacobitism. Competition between denominations violated the myth of unity that was fundamental to Jacobite attitudes, but it also allowed the exiled monarchs to exploit sectarian divisions and gain new allies. The Stuarts were assured of the loyalty of the Catholics and Nonjurors, and they catered to the religious concerns of High Church Anglicans and Quakers in order to gain their trust. Their approach was realistic in admitting the impossibility of religious uniformity, although by courting all sides they risked offending everyone. Their judicious use of the controversial royal touch demonstrated a sensitivity to differences of opinion among their supporters. Of course, the refusal of James II and his son to change their religion inhibited their success in winning over

[147] Parker is noticed in *D.N.B.*; see also Chapman, 'Jacobite Political Argument', p. 21 n. 50.
[148] H.M.C., *Stuart*, vol. iii, pp. 470–1.
[149] Sedgwick, ed., *History of Parliament*, vol. i, p. 261.
[150] Andrew Oliver, ed., *The Journal of Samuel Curwen, Loyalist* (Cambridge, Mass., 1972), p. 366. I owe this reference to Douglas Hay.

Protestants, but High Church clerics were clearly able to circumvent this problem in their own imaginations.

In spite of the merits of their religious policy, however, the banished Stuarts were constantly frustrated by the conservatism of institutionalized religious bodies. The Catholic Church was reluctant to commit itself wholeheartedly to a restoration, and the Church of England was too vulnerable to state control. Jacobitism had to rely on the Catholic gentry, the Nonjurors, independent or isolated Anglican clergymen and Quakers. This gave the Stuart cause an extra-institutional religious character that blended well with its Country rhetoric, and bolstered its criticism of the growing Whig state. Yet Jacobite opposition to the subordination of the Church to the state could lead to the extreme anti-Erastianism of the Deaconites, who advocated a separation of religious from secular institutions. Although most High Churchmen could not subscribe to this view, it was shared to some extent by Roman Catholics and the other-worldly Quakers. For these oppressed religious minorities, survival required that the Church and government exist apart, except at the highest level, in the person of the sacred and divinely ordained king.

PART THREE

Popular Jacobitism

Chapter 6

The torrent: riots and demonstrations, 1688–1715

And you may as well stop the Tide at *Gravesend*, with your *Thumb*, as oppose the Torrent of the Inclinations of the People, now their Eyes are open'd.

Charles Leslie, 1715[1]

How can the popularity of a political phenomenon be judged? In the first chapter, it was shown that Jacobite propaganda had a large circulation; this does not prove, however, that it reached the common people. The plebeian voice of Jacobite verse had some appeal, but its success is difficult to measure. The commercialized art of the 1740s was confined to the capital, and was often too costly for labourers and artisans. Although the Jacobite underworlds were representative of broader groups, it would be a mistake to identify them with 'the people'. The last chapter, moreover, argued that Jacobitism was unable to maintain the support of an important constituency, the High Church clergy. Should it then be concluded that consistent Jacobite sentiment was confined to ethnic and religious minorities, and to a small band of Tory loyalists? The evidence of collective popular action – riots, demonstrations, commemorations – suggests otherwise. For forty years, Jacobitism helped to motivate, inform and direct plebeian protest. No seditious political cause at any time in English history had such a prolonged or widespread effect on the public.

The use of riots to assess the views of the common people, however, involves considerable methodological difficulties. Recent scholarship on popular protest is deeply indebted to the researches of George Rudé. In his able hands, the wild, sinister 'mob' composed of the dregs of the people, a constant stereotype of previous historiography, was transformed into the disciplined 'crowd' of respectable tradesmen and

[1] *Lesley to the Bishop of Sarum*, p. 13, in Bodl. Rawl. MS D. 383.

artisans, expressing its discontent with an inequitable social and economic system. Unlike the 'mob', the 'crowd' was not a malleable, mindless mass, easily manipulated by scheming politicians; it was an autonomous entity with its own specific goals.[2] Rudé's 'crowd' has become a firmly established orthodoxy; in particular, historians have accepted that 'crowds' acted more or less spontaneously, without elite direction, that they consisted of people with similar outlooks and perceptions and that the actions of 'crowds' typified the opinions of plebeians, that is, small traders and labourers.

These assumptions have made the 'crowd', like the 'mob', into a meta-historical entity. When blindly applied, they impose a dreary conformity on analyses of riots and demonstrations. Although the following discussion is deeply indebted to Rudé, it will treat the 'crowd' warily. To begin with, the ruling elite of eighteenth-century England was often not averse to encouraging, abetting or countenancing riots by their social inferiors. Is a crowd not *the* 'crowd' if it accepts bribes, or if it is spurred on by upper-class agitators? To affirm that it is not may be simply to echo the absurd prejudices of eighteenth-century observers about the 'mob'. Crowds that were incited or even paid by others were not merely hired pawns. The behaviour of an angry mass of people is not easily controlled by outside agents; it is highly unlikely, moreover, that rioters should have no interest in the object of their demonstration. If they are guided by agitators, it is almost always because they are willing to listen to what the agitators have to say.

E. P. Thompson has employed the Gramscian term 'cultural hegemony' to describe the influence of the ruling classes of eighteenth-century England over the common people.[3] 'Hegemony' does not imply total control; it allows for plebeian protest, and in fact rests partly on the idea that the common people will defend their rights if the 'hegemony' of their rulers infringes too much upon them. It therefore differs from the more rigid system of obedience and obligation depicted

[2] See especially George Rudé, *The Crowd in History: A Study of Popular Disturbances in France and England, 1730–1848* (London, 1981), and his *Paris and London in the Eighteenth Century: Studies in Popular Protest* (New York, 1971). For Jacobite rioting, see his *Hanoverian London 1714–1808* (London, 1971), pp. 113–14, 187, 206–8. Peter Linebaugh, in 'Eighteenth-Century Crime, Popular Movements and Social Control', pp. 11–15, sees the 'crowd' as less respectable than Rudé, but this impression may be created by the incredible muddle of eighteenth-century social description.

[3] Thompson, 'Patrician Society', pp. 387–90; see also Quintin Hoare and Geoffrey Nowell Smith, eds., *Selections from the Prison Notebooks of Antonio Gramsci* (London, 1971), p. 12.

by J. C. D. Clark, although there are many striking similarities between
the two conceptions.[4] 'Cultural hegemony' is a useful idea, but it should
be noted that many cultural values, like anti-Catholicism, were shared
rather than imposed, and that some values were indigenous to the
lower classes. Furthermore, no single, monolithic elite political culture
predominated in the eighteenth century; divisions within the privileged
classes could easily break social solidarity, and segments of the elite
might assist popular action against those to whom they were opposed.
England's rulers feared and hated the 'mob' only when they perceived it
to be against them; hostile rioters were 'sturdy beggars', friendly ones
were 'the voice of the people'. In these circumstances, there was plenty
of scope for the development of what might be called a 'subversive
hegemony' – an elite political culture that was aimed against the
government, upon which rioters could draw to legitimize their
behaviour.

The idea of 'cultural hegemony' makes the 'spontaneity' or 'auton-
omy' of the crowd impossible to ascertain, and largely irrelevant.
Similarly, the ideological homogeneity of different types of rioters is
open to question. Like their rulers, eighteenth-century crowds spoke
with many tongues. Which was the 'real crowd' of 1792, the London
radicals or the Birmingham loyalists? Rudé has argued that both were
expressing the constant antipathy of plebeians to those who held
wealth and power; but was Joseph Priestley's money more important
than his religion or his politics to the 'Church and King' rioters who
pulled down his house?[5] The rioters did not say so, and their stated
objectives should not be ignored. The beliefs and prejudices of those
involved in such demonstrations have often been winked at by historians who refuse to take them seriously. Yet no matter how much one
would like to interpret the Gordon Riots, for example, as economically
motivated, they remain fundamentally anti-Catholic in character.[6]
However difficult it may be, we must try to understand intolerance on
its own terms. The task is complicated by the fact that different crowds
frequently had contradictory biases. This diversity may reflect a
multiplicity of crowds, separated by ethnic, religious and political
cleavages that extended from top to bottom of the social scale.

If the homogeneity of the 'crowd' is not accepted, its role as a mirror
of public opinion becomes suspect. The actions of rioters may reveal
what large numbers of people in certain areas felt about an issue at a

[4] Clark, English Society, ch. 2.   [5] Rudé, The Crowd in History, pp. 135–8.
[6] See Rudé, Paris and London in the Eighteenth Century, pp. 268–92.

particular time, but the majority was always mute. Almost all Jacobite protesters were shopkeepers, artisans and labourers residing in cities or towns. The rural cottagers and agricultural labourers who comprised most of England's population took very little part in either Jacobite protest or Hanoverian celebration; their political opinions are a matter of pure conjecture. Butchers, bucklemakers and urban weavers should not be allowed to speak for them. George Rudé has warned against Michelet's tendency to equate crowds with 'the people'; historians should also avoid identifying demonstrators with the labouring classes in general.[7]

These observations are particularly relevant to a discussion of Jacobite crowds. A Jacobite crowd is a group of people who employ Jacobite rhetoric or symbolism in a riot, public commemoration or open demonstration. The actions of Jacobite crowds were not necessarily 'spontaneous', or their rhetoric 'autonomous'; they were often distinct from other types of crowds, and they cannot be seen as typical of public opinion in England. Nevertheless, they expressed the sympathies of a large portion of the English population, over a remarkable period of time.

The genesis of popular Jacobitism, 1689–1714

Jacobite crowds did not spring up suddenly after the Hanoverian Succession, as might be imagined from a cursory study of political protest in the years before 1714. Their development was long and complex, and can only be understood in relation to the movements of plebeian politics in the last half of the seventeenth century. The attention of almost all historians of popular unrest has focussed on London, where crowds appeared at every upheaval of the 1600s, and where politics seem to have oscillated more wildly than elsewhere. In the early 1640s, as Brian Manning has shown, demonstrators in London precipitated the execution of Strafford, attacked the bishops and helped convince an alarmed Charles I to quit the capital.[8] Yet London crowds also greeted with enthusiasm the restoration of Charles II, an image Jacobite propagandists never tired of evoking.[9] By 1679,

---

[7] Rudé, *The Crowd in History*, p. 7.
[8] Brian Manning, *The English People and the English Revolution, 1640–1649* (London, 1976), chs. 1–4.
[9] For a discussion of the coronation celebrations, see Gerard Reedy, S.J., 'Mystical Politics: The Imagery of Charles II's Coronation', in Paul J. Korshin, ed., *Studies in*

however, the capital had turned, if not against the King, at least against his heir, and the popular Pope burnings held on Queen Elizabeth's accession day during the Exclusion Crisis seemed to show that the City was a Whig stronghold.[10]

An insightful explanation of these events has been presented by Tim Harris.[11] In 1660, he argues, the major religious groups were united in welcoming back the King; within a few years, however, the Dissenters had become alienated by persecution, and it was they who formed the nucleus of Whig support in the Exclusion Crisis. Harris sees two crowds in Restoration London – one comprised of Dissenters or Whigs, the other made up of Tory Anglicans. From the perspective of later events, Harris's views are very convincing. It should be emphasized, however, that Dissent before 1689 was an amorphous entity; the distinction between a Dissenting and a Low Church Anglican position was not yet clear, and Dissenters did not see themselves as a minority, or as sectarian schismatics. Furthermore, religious strife did not necessarily entail constitutional disagreement. Even in 1642, most dissentient Londoners did not question the king's sovereignty; as in 1679, they sought merely to change the king's mind, or to replace his wicked ministers, not to topple him from his throne.

The differences between Whig and Tory crowds were not absolute. For many in both camps, a good deal of common ground could be discovered – in anti-Catholicism, for example. The point is important in interpreting the actions of crowds in the capital between 1688 and 1714, as popular support for the Whigs gradually disintegrated. Gary De Krey has represented this change as the effect of Whig abandonment of populist principles; their 'apostasy', combined with their strengthened grip on wealth and power in London, turned the common people away from the Whigs, towards the Tories.[12] De Krey's analysis is perceptive, but it may over-simplify the situation. Harris has shown

---

Change and Revolution: Aspects of English Intellectual History, 1640–1800 (Menston, Yorks., 1972), pp. 19–42.

[10] See J. R. Jones, *The First Whigs: The Politics of the Exclusion Crisis, 1678–1683* (London, 1961), pp. 88, 112–13; David Ogg, *England in the Reign of Charles II* (2 vols., Oxford, 1956), vol. ii, pp. 595–6. For an overview of London politics from 1679 to 1742, see Henry Horwitz, 'Party in a Civic Context: London from the Exclusion Crisis to the Fall of Walpole', in Clyve Jones, ed., *Britain in the First Age of Party, 1680–1750: Essays Presented to Geoffrey Holmes* (London and Ronceverte, 1987), pp. 173–94.

[11] Tim Harris, *London Crowds in the Reign of Charles II: Propaganda and Politics from the Restoration until the Exclusion Crisis* (Cambridge, 1987); also his 'The Bawdy House Riots of 1668', *H.J.*, 29, 3 (1986), pp. 537–56.

[12] De Krey, 'Political Radicalism', pp. 606–15, and his *A Fractured Society*, ch. 5.

that the Whigs never had a monopoly on the affections of Londoners. The Tory appeal, moreover, was not merely negative; it had a strong attraction for those who favoured unity, security and peace. The decline of Whig popularity was due in part to the sharpened definition of sectarianism under the Toleration Act. Anglicans who might have supported Exclusion were now separated from the Dissenters by the wall of denominationalism, and fear of Nonconformity replaced anti-Catholicism as a cause for riots. Defection to Toryism took place across the common religious and political ground shared by all Churchmen.

Historians have not given much prominence to Jacobitism in discussing this transition. They have assumed that James II fled London under a cloud of popular disapproval in 1688, and that he and his son remained unloved by the people in the capital at least until 1714. The events of December 1688 do not bear out this view. On the nights of 12–14 December, having learned that King James had left the capital, rioters in London sacked Roman Catholic houses and chapels.[13] On Sunday, 16 December, however, James reluctantly returned to the capital, and to his utter surprise was greeted by a tumultuous welcome reminiscent of 1660:

as soon as he returned there, he was hugely surprized with the unexpected testimony of the peoples affection to him, it is not to be imagined what acclamations were made, and what joy the people express'd at his Majesty's return; such bonefires, ringing of bells, and all immaginable [sic] marks of love and esteem, as made it look liker a day of triumph than humiliation; and this was So universall among all ranks of people, that the King, nor none that went with him had ever seen the like before, the same crowds of people and crys of joy accompanying him to Whitehall, and even to his Bed Chamber door itself.[14]

What had happened? The hated policies of the Papist court had been washed away by the attacks on Catholic conventicles; now it was safe for the sovereign to return. The crowd had acted on the old belief that the king could do no wrong – but his ministers could. Although the London populace had frightened James, they did not drive him from the throne. His own lack of judgment, and the advance of William's army, accomplished that.

After James II's 'abdication', the salvation of the nation, the Church

13 William L. Sachse, 'The Mob and the Revolution of 1688', *J.B.S.*, 4, 1 (1964), pp. 23–40.
14 Clarke, ed., *Life of James the Second*, vol. ii, p. 262; [Buckley, ed.], *Ailesbury Memoirs*, vol. i, pp. 214–15.

and the crown rested in William and Mary. In spite of the vicissitudes of his reign, and the death of his consort in 1694, William III was upheld by his image of Protestant hero until his death. Nevertheless, the long war with France brought hardship and disillusionment, which congealed into discontent in the mid-1690s. Even in London, where the possibility of a French-supported restoration was generally equated with economic ruin, William's popularity began to wane. In July 1693, when the Catholic printers Canning and Dormer were pilloried at Charing Cross for printing King James's 'Whiggish' declaration, they 'were favourably used by the mob'.[15] No doubt the generous promises from St Germain, inspired by Melfort's correspondence with Charl-wood Lawton, had something to do with this friendly reception.

King William's war, however, continued. In April 1695, a crowd released 200 impressed soldiers from the house of an army provost marshal in Holborn, and sacked another recruiter's house in Drury Lane. Robert Ferguson regarded this incident as evidence of plebeian disaffection to William.[16] The Jacobite ex-officers and their friends took great encouragement from the event; later in the same month, they broke into the Savoy prison, allowing some of their comrades to escape. On 26 May, they attempted to rescue prisoners from a messenger's house in the Haymarket, and conducted a drunken demonstration there on the following day.[17] Finally, on 10 June, they tried to turn one of their tavern revels into a full-scale riot. As a Whig commentator described it:

We had anothere Ryot last night in Drury Lane by some who had appointed a Meeting at the dogg Taverne to Celebrate the Prince of Wales's Birth day which they did with Trumpetts Hautbois and Loud Huzzas in the Evening. They gave mony for a Bonfire and were present at forcing such as past by to Drink K James his health and his Sons and those that refused it they abusd Several ways at last it came to drawing up of Partys on each side of the way but the Williamites being Strengthend by the Butchers from Clare Market they fell very foul upon the Ryoters and soon put them to their Shifts some being first well beaten and some were taken.[18]

Most of the rioters were military men, like George Porter and Sir John Fenwick; they used trumpets, kettle-drums and flags to proclaim their

[15] Luttrell, vol. iii, p. 140.
[16] Ibid., vol. iii, pp. 460–1; [Robert Ferguson], *Whether the Parliament be not in Law dissolved by the Death of the Princess of Orange?* ([London], 1695), pp. 56–7.
[17] C.S.P.D., W. & M., vol. v, pp. 435, 479–80, 483, vol. vi, p. 341; Luttrell, vol. iii, pp. 489, 495.
[18] Bodl. Carte MS 239, fo. 146, also fos. 30–1; Luttrell, vol. iii, pp. 488–9, 495–6, 509.

insurrectionary intentions. A few months later, many of them were deeply involved in the Assassination Plot.

The people of London were not much inclined to join in the treasonable festivities. The behaviour of the Clare Market butchers is worth remembering, because they had altered their politics dramatically by 1715. Robert Ferguson's dream of a popular uprising against William in the capital remained unrealized; Londoners may not have been happy about the war, but few were willing to join notorious characters like the ex-officers in restoring an unrepentant James II. If his conciliatory declarations had earned him some sympathy, they had not completely altered his image. While a tradition of Jacobite commemoration was maintained in London by James's adherents, they were always a tiny minority.

In the provinces, however, popular politics had followed a very different path. In a brilliant study, David Underdown has argued that the English countryside in the early seventeenth century was divided by two contrasting cultures, one of them festive, communal and ultimately royalist, the other 'puritan', capitalistic and Parliamentarian.[19] Although his identification of these two cultures with, respectively, arable and wood-pasture or clothworking regions is not entirely persuasive, his emphasis on geographical differences is not misguided. Seventy-two years after the outbreak of the Civil War, most of the royalist areas were still Tory, and witnessed Jacobite rioting in 1714–15. Unlike London, where popular politics had a tortuous and contradictory history, the provinces present a remarkable picture of continuity.

Nevertheless, the politics of the early eighteenth century give the impression that 'puritan' England had shrunk, at least if Dissent and Whiggery are seen as its offspring. The county electorate was overwhelmingly Tory, as were the market towns, most of the larger cities and many industrial regions like the Black Country.[20] In fact, the Restoration era may have struck a much harder blow at 'puritanism' in the provinces than it did in London. The complete separation of Nonconformity from Anglicanism that took hold only after 1689 in London may have been evident much earlier in provincial England.[21] To be sure, the Exclusion Crisis swept the countryside as it did the capital, but it faded quickly in places where Dissenters were few. The

19 Underdown, *Revel, Riot and Rebellion*, esp. chs. 1–4.
20 See Colley, *In Defiance of Oligarchy*, ch. 5.
21 For the condition of Dissent under the Restoration, see Michael Watts, *The Dissenters: From the Reformation to the French Revolution* (Oxford, 1978), ch. 3.

Duke of Monmouth's popularity was largely based on Nonconformity; he was warmly received in towns with strong Dissenting traditions on his 'progresses' through the south-west, the West Midlands and the north-west in 1681–2.[22] Although Robin Clifton has suggested that. Monmouth's rebels in 1685 were not mainly Dissenters, this is not easily proved – arguably, he had been abandoned by most of his Anglican admirers by then.[23]

James II's religious policies were no better received in the provinces than in London. As in the capital, the Revolution was signalled by anti-Catholic demonstrations; but these tended to take place in the larger towns like Newcastle and Hull, where a significant number of Dissenters and Low Churchmen lived.[24] The acceptance of William and Mary's succession to the throne was not universal. At Stamford, for example, the mayor and parson, who were creatures of the Jacobite Earl of Exeter, tried to stop celebrations led by Whig aldermen by bringing out the militia and the 'water engine' against them.[25] Throughout William III's reign, rumblings of discontent could be heard periodically in the provinces, particularly in the north and west. A crowd of recusants and disaffected persons broke open Morpeth gaol in 1690 and freed some state prisoners.[26] The witnesses against some Catholic gentlemen accused of receiving military commissions from James II were insulted and almost stoned by a Mancunian mob in 1694.[27] The acquittal of these suspects inspired bell-ringing and rejoicings in Oxford, where a few months later the news of Queen Mary's death led to festivities among the scholars and some Scottish pedlars.[28] A crowd at Carlisle in 1697 threatened to break down windows that were illuminated to mark the Treaty of Ryswick – they had also been offered money to drink King James's health.[29]

The centre for public demonstrations against William's rule, however, was Bristol, where the merchant community was bitterly

---

22 J. N. P. Watson, *Captain-General and Rebel Chief: The Life of James, Duke of Monmouth* (London, 1979), pp. 128–32, 143–5; Ogg, *Charles II*, vol. ii, pp. 645–6.
23 See Robin Clifton, *The Last Popular Rebellion: The Western Rising of 1685* (London and New York, 1984), pp. 272–6; Peter Earle, *Monmouth's Rebels: The Road to Sedgemoor, 1685* (London, 1977), pp. 5–17.
24 Sachse, 'The Mob and the Revolution', pp. 31–5, 39.
25 *C.S.P.D., W. & M.*, vol. i, p. 61.
26 Luttrell, vol. ii, p. 86, vol. iv, p. 71.   27 Beamont, ed., *Jacobite Trials*, p. 49 n. 1.
28 Andrew Clark, ed., *The Life and Times of Anthony Wood, Antiquary of Oxford, 1632–1695, Described by Himself*, Oxford Historical Society, 24–6 (3 vols., 1892–4), vol. iii, pp. 471, 476.
29 Max Beloff, *Public Order and Popular Disturbances, 1660–1714* (London, 1963), p. 46.

divided into Whig and Tory factions. The wealthy Hart family were leaders of the High Churchmen, and remained loyal to the exiled Stuarts; William Hart, prebendary of the Cathedral, became a Non-juror, and Sir Richard Hart, M.P. for the town from 1681 until 1695, was involved in the Jacobite conspiracy of 1695–6.[30] His partner as borough representative in the 1689 and 1690 Parliaments was Sir John Knight, a fanatical Tory who was in close touch with Stuart agents from 1693 onwards, and who organized a Jacobite cabal in Bristol that included Hart and other local merchants.[31] The town's Jacobitism was manifested early in the new reign; in 1690, Bristol clergymen refused to ring bells for William's successes in Ireland.[32] The following year saw the exacerbation of political tensions through a series of customs disputes; resentment of heavy taxation caused the mayor, Sir John Knight, to refuse payment of charges for the circuit judge, who was met in the town by an angry mob throwing dirt at his coach.[33] When the news of Queen Mary's death arrived in December 1694, the Jacobites, among them some customs officers, 'made publick rejoycings', ringing church bells and dancing through the streets to the tune of 'The King shall enjoy his own again'.[34]

The political turmoil in Bristol in the 1690s demonstrated that alienated Tories could easily turn to Jacobitism, and suggested that they could count on some popular support. Like Bristol, Manchester and Oxford saw severe Jacobite riots in 1714–15 that had been foreshadowed by the events of William's reign. Although it cannot be claimed that the exiled Stuarts had widespread popular support in the decade after the Revolution, they were not wholly reviled by the English people, at least in certain areas. London, where the power of Dissent lasted longer, was far more hostile to the banished monarchs. It had lagged behind other towns in the development of popular Toryism; while Bristol, Norwich and Newcastle mostly elected High Churchmen to Parliament, London continued to be dominated by Whigs. This Whig hegemony in the capital began to alter only in the last years of Queen Anne. The apostle of change was Dr Henry Sacheverell.

[30] Latimer, *Annals of Bristol*, p. 19; Henning, ed., *History of Parliament*, vol. ii, pp. 502–3. See also Jonathan Barry, 'Popular Culture in Seventeenth-Century Bristol', in Reay, ed., *Popular Culture*, pp. 59–90.

[31] Henning, ed., *History of Parliament*, vol. ii, pp. 696–7; H.M.C., *The Manuscripts of the Marquess of Downshire. Papers of Sir William Trumbull* (1 vol., 2 parts, London, 1924), part i, pp. 446–8, part ii, p. 680; Monod, 'Jacobitism and Country Principles', pp. 301–2.

[32] Latimer, *Annals of Bristol*, p. 19.   [33] Luttrell, vol. ii, pp. 255, 277, 575.

[34] *Ibid.*, vol. iii, pp. 423–4.

Sacheverell did not create a revolution in London politics; he was merely the spokesman for it. At its root was hatred of Dissent. After thirty years of howling in the wilderness, the Dissenters had been rescued by toleration in 1689; but they were thereby set further apart from the Anglican mainstream. As sectarian outsiders, they became the source of High Church dread, and their supposed power and wealth fuelled popular paranoia. The Whig party was seen as no more than the political arm of Nonconformity, and Low Churchmen were 'False Brethren' who assisted in the corrupting work of the 'Roundheads'. These malcontents were thought to be aiming at the destruction of the Church of England, and the enslavement of the people under a republican despotism. Memories of Cromwellian rule, of military tyranny and religious fragmentation, added to Anglican hostility towards the heirs of the 'puritans'. In 1710, these sentiments found expression in the slogan 'High Church and Sacheverell'. The extra-ordinary popularity of the high-flying doctor has been discussed in Geoffrey Holmes's excellent studies of the London riots of 1 March, when meeting-houses were pulled down throughout the City.[35] This 'night of fire' marked a violent turning-point in London politics; when the Whigs tried to organize counter-demonstrations on Queen Eliza-beth's accession day in 1711, they met with rebukes from Londoners still warm for Sacheverell.[36] To the sound of breaking windows and burning pews, the capital had finally aligned itself with most of the rest of the country.

Of course, the Whigs were quick to accuse Jacobites of making hay in the doctor's sun. Not all of these allegations can be satisfactorily assessed, but they are not unlikely. Colonel Clifford, one of James II's ex-officers, was reportedly seen among the London rioters.[37] On his triumphant 'progress' through the West Midlands, Sacheverell was attended at Worcester by an Irish Nonjuring lord, a writing-master recently turned out of his position for seditious words and a Jacobite printer.[38] At Shrewsbury Assizes, a lay Nonjuror of Whitchurch,

[35] Holmes, The Trial of Doctor Sacheverell, pp. 156–78, and his 'The Sacheverell Riots: The Crowd and the Church in Early Eighteenth Century London', P. & P., 72 (1976), pp. 55–85.
[36] [Delariviere Manley], A True Relation of the several Facts and Circumstances of the intended Riot and Tumult on Queen Elizabeth's Birth-day (London, 1711), pp. 8–9. The author was a notable female writer, companion of the Jacobite alderman John Barber.
[37] P.R.O., S.P. 34/12/17.
[38] Abel Boyer, The History of the Reign of Queen Anne, Digested into Annals (11 vols., London, 1703–13), vol. ix, pp. 205–9.

Thomas Yewde, led a crowd that tried to compel the grand jury to present a Sacheverellite address to Parliament, and when refused committed some disorders.[39] This evidence does not prove that support for Sacheverell was concomitant to Jacobitism; but they were congenial partners, and the crowds that embraced the doctor's message might easily adhere to the exiled King, if they believed he was sincere in his promises to protect the Church. High Church politicians were influenced by the same logic. As Daniel Szechi has shown, the Tory landslide in the elections of 1710 produced an energetic group of Jacobites in the House of Commons. Furthermore, although their outward behaviour was circumspect, the Tory leadership in the next four years became enmeshed in conspiracy with the Pretender's court.[40]

Wafting through this atmosphere of renewed Jacobitism came the strains of the notorious Civil War song 'The King shall enjoy his own again'. In September 1711, Captain John Silk, commander of a company of the London militia, had the tune played by his hautboys while leading a march of the trained bands through the City.[41] A year later, in Chester, the town's sheriff rode with some other gentlemen and alehouse keepers in a cart from the maypole at Northgate to the maypole at Handbridge across the Dee, playing the famous song and encouraging the crowd to shout for them.[42] The last chapter mentioned the attendance of Sacheverell, Atterbury and Bishop Bisse of Hereford at a Sons of the Clergy meeting in 1713 where 'The King shall enjoy his own again' was performed.

In spite of these cases, Tory Jacobitism in the years 1710–14 should not be exaggerated. Most High Churchmen had not made up their minds about the succession; if James III had become a Protestant, they might have gone over to him entirely, but his refusal to convert made them willing to accept the prospect of a Lutheran king. Nevertheless, most Tories would only countenance the Elector Georg Ludwig on certain conditions: he must retain a Tory government, preserve the safety of the Church, keep peace in Europe and pursue only English national interests. In short, he must not reverse the Sacheverellite

[39] *Ibid.*, p. 185; P.R.O., S.P. 34/12/45.
[40] Szechi, *Jacobitism and Tory Politics*, chs. 3, 7; Edward Gregg, *Queen Anne* (London, 1980, 1984), ch. 14.
[41] *The Ballad of the King shall enjoy his own again: with a Learned Comment thereupon, at the Request of Capt. Silk* (London, 1711).
[42] Rev. Gibbs Payne Crawfurd, ed., 'The Diary of George Booth of Chester and Katherine Howard, his Daughter, of Boughton, near Chester, 1707–1764', *Journal of the Chester and North Wales Architectural, Archaeological and Historic Society*, New Series, 28, part 1 (1928), pp. 17–18.

revolution. If Hanover failed them, the Tories might give the Stuart King a chance to enjoy his own again; but few in power thought such a step necessary in August 1714, and King George, unaware of the strength of English public opinion, gave little attention to the possibility of a popular Tory reaction against him. He was proclaimed as Queen Anne's successor by a High Church government that thought, naively, he would keep them in office. The mood of London's populace was understandably confused. In the first week of August, Oxford and Bolingbroke, whose quarrels had wrecked the Tory ministry, were insulted by a crowd in the capital, but the Duke of Ormonde was cheered, and the Duke of Marlborough was more hissed than hurrahed.[43] Within a month, however, King George had begun to purge his government from top to bottom of High Churchmen. As their party leaders fell from power, or rather slid, the Tory crowds remembered their other king.

The coronation riots of October 1714

When did the allegiance of a Tory crowd begin to wander away from the Hanoverians? The historian of Congleton in Cheshire has recorded that in August 1714, the Dissenting chapel there was attacked by a High Church mob incensed by the ringing of the church bells to mark the death of Queen Anne.[44] This may have been the first outbreak of anti-Hanoverian unrest in England. Two months later, on 20 October 1714, King George I was crowned. In over twenty towns in the south and west, loyalist observances of the coronation were disrupted by rioters, some of them chanting seditious slogans. Charles Leslie's 'torrent' had been unleashed.

These disturbances were seldom overtly Jacobite. Their inspiration was Sacheverellite and High Church; only in a few cases were treasonable words spoken. Nevertheless, the shrieks of Whig outrage were not without foundation; to disrupt celebrations on that particular day was to throw a pretty direct affront at the new King himself. The people of many English towns were giving notice to the Hanoverian monarch that they did not consider him inviolate, and that he had better heed the wishes of the Tory part of the nation. The Tory gentry and aristocracy

[43] Bennett, *Tory Crisis*, p. 186; Harold Williams, ed., *The Correspondence of Jonathan Swift* (6 vols., Oxford, 1965), vol. ii, pp. 102–4.
[44] W. B. Stephens, ed., *History of Congleton* (Manchester, 1970), p. 230. There may be some confusion as to the date of this riot; the meeting-house was certainly attacked in July 1715. P.R.O., P.C. 24/152/3, indt. of Thos. Gillimore *et al.*

fully supported the rioters; they stayed away from the coronation festivities, and in some instances arrived with their supporters to smash up the proceedings. Eleven weeks before, the accession had been marked by almost unanimous declarations of loyalty to Hanover. By 20 October, in many provincial towns, Tory Hanoverianism was nowhere to be seen.

The main accounts of these riots were written by government officials and Whig propagandists; they may distort events, and should be used cautiously. Nevertheless, they all tell a similar story, repeated over and over in different towns: the loyalists were holding balls, making bonfires or drinking at taverns when the rioters broke up their merriment, sacked their houses and assaulted their persons.[45] The name of Sacheverell, who had been making a 'progress' through the West Country, was on everyone's lips. 'Sacheverell and Ormond, and damn all foreigners!' cried the crowd at Bristol.[46] At Taunton, the good news was 'Church and Dr. Sacheverell'; at Birmingham, 'Kill the old Rogue [King George], Kill them all, Sacheverell for ever'; at Tewkesbury, 'Sacheverell for ever, Down with the Roundheads'; at Shrewsbury, 'High Church and Sacheverell for ever'. At Dorchester and Nuneaton, the doctor's health was drunk. Sacheverell's old enemies, the Dissenters, were not spared. The Tucker Street meeting-house in Bristol was pillaged, and a Quaker who tried to persuade the mob to desist was killed by them. The meeting-house in Dorchester was 'insulted'. A clear preference for Tory politicians was expressed – 'Hardress and Lee' at Canterbury, 'Bene and Berney' at Norwich, 'No Hanover, No Cadogan, but Calvert and Clarges' at Reading.[47]

It is not likely that anyone who rioted on George I's coronation day failed to understand that they were boosting the hopes of his Stuart rival. According to Whig reports, some people were much more explicit. At Taunton, Francis Sherry allegedly said on 19 October that 'on the morrow he must take up Arms against the King'.[48] The Birmingham rioter John Hargrave apparently urged his comrades to 'pull down this King and Sett up a King of our own'.[49] Who was to be the people's king? The Dorchester crowd was in no doubt about it; they

---

[45] The main published source is *An Account of the Riots, Tumults, and other Treasonable Practices; since His Majesty's Accession to the Throne* (London, 1715). It has been attributed to Defoe.
[46] Latimer, *Annals of Bristol*, p. 106.
[47] *An Account of the riots*, pp. 5–14; Rev. Peter Rae, *The History of the Rebellion* (2nd edn, London, 1746), p. 108.
[48] P.R.O., S.P. 35/74/2.   [49] P.R.O., S.P. 35/74/4.

Map 1 Coronation day riots, 20 October 1714

tried to rescue an effigy of James Francis Stuart that was to be burned by the local Dissenters, and voiced the strange question 'Who dares disowne the Pretender?'.[50] The bargemen of Tewkesbury wished to have money to drink to Sacheverell and the King; reprimanded by loyalists for putting the doctor first, they replied 'it should be the King if they would have it so'. Again they were refused, no doubt because they had not named the King – was it to be James or George? At this, they attacked their prospective benefactors, shouting 'Sacheverell for ever, Down with the Roundheads'.[51]

In two places, the Tory crowds expressed themselves through a theatre of their own, as well as by undermining the theatre of the Whigs. At Bedford, the maypole was put in mourning on coronation day, and remained so for almost a month.[52] The Chester revels of 1712 had pointed to the Jacobite significance of the maypole; it symbolized the 'vegetation god' motif of Stuart kingship, and recalled the relationship between May-day and Restoration day. These themes were discussed in Chapter 2 – but treasonable verse did not inspire the Bedford demonstrators, who had in mind a particular political memory. The 'puritans' of the Civil War had taken down maypoles, and the Commonwealth outlawed them. They had reappeared in 1660, when James, Duke of York, helped to set up a gigantic one in London.[53] Remarkably, this aspect of the Restoration was still remembered fifty years later, and was quickly adapted to imply that Hanoverian rule was no different from that of the 'puritans'. The other example of popular theatre was at Frome in Somerset, where the coronation rioters 'dressed up an Idiot, called *George*, in a Fool's Coat, saying, Here's our *George*, where's — '[54] This happy conceit drew upon another popular custom mentioned in Chapter 2, the mockery of authority at fairs or carnivals. The 'Fool George' was a 'Lord of Misrule', precisely the character that George I was later to assume in Jacobite poetry. Jacobite propaganda may in fact have imitated the theatre of the people.

The social origins of the 20 October rioters are obscure, because very few of them were prosecuted. Whig characterizations are so hostile as

---

[50] Lady Newton, *Lyme Letters, 1660–1760* (London, 1925), p. 264.
[51] P.R.O., S.P. 35/74/5.
[52] *An Account of the Riots*, p. 12.
[53] Underdown, *Revel, Riot and Rebellion*, pp. 54–6, 60, 68, 88–90, 177–8, 269, 274–5; Christopher Hill, *Society and Puritanism in Pre-Revolutionary England* (New York, 1964), pp. 184–6; Dennis Brailsford, *Sport and Society: Elizabeth to Anne* (London and Toronto, 1969), p. 202.
[54] Rae, *History of the Rebellion*, p. 109.

to be useless; the crowd at Frome, for example, was described as consisting of 'Kennel Rakers, and Bailiffs Followers', when it was probably made up of weavers. The same source, however, noted that the Bristol demonstrators included Kingswood colliers 'hired for the purpose', and the Tewkesbury mob was reportedly led by bargemen, watermen, troughmen and butchers.[55] Among the rioters at Canterbury, the government was informed, were a gentleman, two maltsters, a tailor, a silkweaver and a cordwainer; at Shrewsbury, the mob contained a justice of the peace, a draper, a butcher, a baker, two tailors, five cordwainers, three 'yeomen' and a 'labourer'.[56] The seven rioters tried at Bristol were a tailor, a gardiner, a weaver, a sugar-baker, a barber, a saddler and a cordwainer.[57] These may have been only the ringleaders; they were certainly a 'respectable', and very male, collection. They also represented a fair cross-section of the trading and artisanal classes of market towns, leavened with skilled labourers like colliers and bargemen. The gentry and 'middling' presence among them was notable. At Taunton, the Tory mayor, his son, the recorder, headborough, constable and the son of the Stamp Duty officer all took part in the riot.[58] At Norwich, Tory gentlemen stood by a local tailor in the vanguard of the mob.[59]

The Whig press blamed not only Tory magistrates but also 'the Pulpit' for sowing the disorders of 20 October. Clerical involvement, however, was not so obvious. A rumour had been spread at Taunton that 300 clergymen were to appear with white napkins to protest the burning of Dr Sacheverell in effigy; but the doctor was not burned, and the parsons did not show themselves. At Newton Abbot, the minister removed the bell-clappers so that the coronation could not be rung in; Newton Abbot, however, was some distance from the nearest riot.[60] The clergy mainly kept their heads low, their typical political stance. Nevertheless, the most important figure in the 20 October riots was a cleric. Sacheverell was aware of this, and proud of it, as his incredibly cocky open letter of 31 October demonstrated:

The Dissenters & their Friends have foolishly Endeavour'd to raise a Disturbance throughout the whole Kingdom by Trying in most Great Towns, on the Coronation Day to Burn Me in Effigie, to Inodiate my Person & Cause with the Populace: But if this Silly Stratagem has produc'd a quite Contrary Effect, &

[55] An Account of the Riots, p. 14; Latimer, Annals of Bristol, p. 107; P.R.O., S.P. 35/74/5.
[56] P.R.O., S.P. 35/74/6a.   [57] Boyer, Political State, vol. viii, p. 489.
[58] P.R.O., S.P. 35/74/2.
[59] An Account of the Riots, p. 8.   [60] Rae, History of the Rebellion, p. 109.

turn's upon the First Authors, & Aggressors, and the People have Express'd their Resentment in any Culpable way, I hope it is not to be laid to my Charge, whose Name ... they make Use of as *the Shibboleth of the Party*.[61]

The fault, in short, lay entirely with the Whigs and Dissenters – a brazen charge indeed!

The coronation day riots were essentially Sacheverellite, but they incorporated some disturbing new elements into the High Church theme. The demonstrators insulted the ruling monarch, and at times they spoke or acted in favour of the Pretender. The Tory leaders who instigated the riots may not have fully intended this; their purpose of impressing Tory popularity upon the new King may have been pushed further by the exuberance of their supporters and the existence of a strong current of High Church Jacobitism that could not now be controlled. Significantly, the first major blossoming of popular Jacobite sentiment took place outside London, where affection for the exiled Stuarts had never completely subsided.

The map of political protest on 20 October has a distinct southern and western orientation; no riots took place in the north, although the rebellion was soon to break out there. On the other hand, some towns that were disturbed on coronation day, like Bedford or Chippenham, were not later known for disaffection. The distribution of rioting indicates an overall strategy. The north was known to be infested with Catholic Jacobites; disturbances there would not impress King George, or King James, with the seriousness of the situation. The south and west, however, were High Church bastions, relatively free of recusants, and much closer to the capital. Many of the Tory leaders, men like Ormonde, Lansdowne, Bathurst, Beaufort and Wyndham, who were imperilled by the actions of the new monarch, had power bases in the West Country. The coronation riots, in short, may have been concentrated in the Tory provincial heartland by design, so as to emphasize the dire consequences of George I's preference for Whigs.

The prosecution of the rioters turned into a fiasco. Not trusting local judges and juries, the government brought five offenders from Taunton up to the capital to be tried, but eventually released them on bail.[62] The decision to try seven rioters at Bristol by a Special Commission was a disastrous mistake; it inspired an attack on the Duke of Richmond at Chichester, and prolonged disorders in Bristol itself.[63] The judges were

[61] Bodl. Rawl. MS B. 376, fos. 59–60.   [62] Boyer, *Political State*, vol. viii, p. 469.
[63] *An Account of the Riots*, p. 15.

met with cries of '*No Jeffrey, no Western Assizes*' – the policies of James II were still unpopular, even if his son was not. The mob's slogans soon changed to 'A Cheverel, A Cheverel, and down with the Roundheads ... up with the Cavaliers'. William Hart, a Tory tobacco merchant and son of the Jacobite Sir Richard, was accused of being a ringleader on 20 October. He escaped indictment, but one of the accused rioters was whipped, the others fined and imprisoned for three months.[64] The sentences were comparatively light, and the major effect of the trials was to conjure up in the town all the conflicts of the seventeenth century.

A similar tension prevailed in the little town of Axminster in Devon. On 5 November, anniversary of the Gunpowder Plot and of William of Orange's landing at Torbay, a crowd in Axminster rescued effigies of the Pope and Pretender from the flames, and proclaimed the latter as James III, King of England.[65] It was a strange turn of events that had produced this scene, on this day of all days, in a thoroughly Protestant county, and a town that had once welcomed Monmouth. The memory of the Revolution was now odious to many Englishmen, and a Catholic king was for some preferable to a king who ruled through a Whig Parliament.

28–9 May and 10 June 1715

The Whigs won the elections of 1714/15 with ease. The polling was accompanied by numerous riots, but the note of disaffection was muffled. Although seditious cries were heard in the night at Hertford, and more open ones at Leicester, the Tory candidates had no wish to damage their chances of election by allowing their supporters to voice treasonable sentiments.[66] With the King against them, of course, they were bound to lose, which made their victories in over 200 seats, including many of the most open constituencies, all the more impressive.[67] Many old Jacobites were reelected, but the Tory party as a whole was still divided, unable to choose between George and James. By the spring of 1715, however, the continued extension of proscription and the impeachment of former ministers reduced the Tories to desperation. Sir William Wyndham, Lord Lansdowne and other

---

[64] Boyer, *Political State*, vol. viii, pp. 484–96.
[65] *An Account of the Riots*, pp. 12–13.
[66] *Ibid.*, pp. 16–26; Rae, *History of the Rebellion*, p. 121.
[67] Colley, *In Defiance of Oligarchy*, pp. 120–1, 186–7.

prominent party leaders approached the Pretender with an offer of support for a rising in the west of England.[68]

Almost immediately, popular unrest flared up again. The disorders of the spring and summer of 1715 were so complicated and numerous that no brief account can do them justice; fortunately, the London riots have been admirably described by Nicholas Rogers, who has also provided some insightful remarks on the meeting-house attacks of May–August.[69] The following argument, however, differs from Rogers's interpretation in emphasizing the Jacobite content of the disorders. Popular Jacobitism took longer to develop in London than elsewhere, as has been seen. Once they had been initiated, however, seditious riots took place regularly in the capital for eighteen months, from April 1715 until November 1716. This chapter will consider only the period before 1 August 1715, by which time the transition from a Tory to a Jacobite rhetoric was complete.

The earliest public demonstrations in London to awake the concern of the government were intended to prevent the ejection of the Tories from office. As early as November 1714, a French newsletter noted that at the Lord Mayor's Banquet 'la populace cria *Ormond point de Marlborough*'. Ormonde's birthday on 29 April 1715 was celebrated by bonfires near Newgate Market.[70] The beloved general symbolized the Tory peace policy, and he enjoyed a reputation for probity, unlike the rapacious Marlborough. The memory of Queen Anne, that pillar of the Church, received similar veneration, with bell-ringing, flag-waving and closed shops on the anniversary of her accession day, 8 March – of course, this was also the date of King William's death.[71] On Anne's coronation day, 23 April, a crowd met at Snow Hill to make a bonfire under a banner with the Queen's picture and the inscription 'Imitate her who was so Just and Good, / Both in her Actions and her Royal Word'. The reference to 'her Royal Word' may have hinted at the rumour that she had promised to restore her brother. In any case, the crowd burned a picture of King William, broke unilluminated windows near St Andrew's Holborn, and proposed 'to sing the Second Part of the

68 See Elizabeth Handasyde, *Granville the Polite: The Life of George Granville, Lord Lansdowne, 1666–1735* (Oxford, 1933), pp. 139–50.

69 Rogers, 'Popular Protest', *passim*, and 'Riot and Popular Jacobitism', in Cruickshanks, ed., *Ideology and Conspiracy*, pp. 76–81. Also useful are James L. Fitts, 'Newcastle's Mob', *Albion*, 5, 1 (1973), pp. 41–9; Sir Charles Petrie, 'The Jacobite Activities in South and West England in the Summer of 1715', *T.R.H.S.*, 4th Series, 18 (1935), pp. 85–106.

70 B.L., Add. MS 22,202, fo. 212; Boyer, *Political State*, vol. ix, p. 333.

71 Boyer, *Political State*, vol. ix, p. 241.

Sacheverell-Tune, by pulling down Meeting Houses'. They were restrained, but the local clergy did not interrupt their revelry on the following day, although it was a Sunday.[72] Interestingly enough, the rector of St Andrew's Holborn was none other than Dr Sacheverell himself.

Jacobitism was not blatant in these well-controlled demonstrations. On 28–9 May, however, it broke its bonds and shook the City of London. A powerful grass-roots Tory movement had emerged there after 1710, at the heart of which was animosity for Whig and Dissenting merchants, a sentiment shared by Tory bankers and High Church artisans alike. Stock-jobbing was seen as the immoral and parasitical expression of Whig principles, so it is not surprising that the crowds gathered on 28 May at the Stock Exchange shouting 'High Church and the Duke of Ormonde'.[73] One passer-by was brave enough to cry 'Long live King George' – because 28 May was the Hanoverian King's birthday – but he was beaten by the angry mob. Insults to the sovereign went further at Cheapside, where the rioters cried 'No Hanoverian, No Presbiterian government', and it was in the same place on the next day – for George I was unlucky enough to have been born on the eve of Restoration day – that Jacobitism began openly to show its face. The cries were 'A Restoration, a Stewart, High Church and Ormonde', 'A Stewart, a second Restoration', and even 'No King George, King James the third'. A coachman shouting for King James 'was hollowed through the Mob'. Whiggish windows were broken, and in Queen Street a battle raged between the rioters and the trained bands, from whose ranks Captain Silk had long since been purged.[74] At Smithfield, according to Abel Boyer, 'a large mob burnt Cromwell (some say Hoadly) in effigy'.[75] Cromwell and Hoadly, like King William, were symptoms of the same disease, which had to be bled by violence from the body politic.

London was not the only town to experience riots on 28–9 May, and it is likely that they were coordinated. Restoration day had not been a popular festival between the Revolution and 1715; John Evelyn had complained in the 1690s that its commemoration had been forgotten, and the Tories do not appear to have tried to revive it in 1710–

[72] *Ibid.*, pp. 333–41; Rae, *History of the Rebellion*, p. 135; *Flying Post*, no. 3638, 28–30 April 1715.
[73] See P. G. M. Dickson, *The Financial Revolution in England: A Study of the Development of Public Credit, 1688–1756* (London and New York, 1967), ch. 2.
[74] P.R.O., S.P. 35/74/9; B.L., Add. MS 17,677, I.I.I., fo. 235.
[75] Boyer, *Political State*, vol. ix, p. 421.

14.[76] The reappearance of Restoration day celebrations in many English towns in 1715 was clearly an aspect of spreading disaffection and may have been connected with the plans for a Jacobite rising. Places where 29 May had been no more than a minor Church holiday suddenly burst into festivity in 1715. Henry Crossgrove, the Jacobite newspaper editor, chortled that Norwich had witnessed 'the greatest Rejoicings that ever were known here' on Restoration day.[77] At Bristol, Jacobites wore rue and thyme on 28 May, because they rued the day King George was born, and longed for time to pass until the morrow, when they decorated their houses and persons with oak leaves, and hummed 'The King shall enjoy his own again'.[78] In the spring of 1715, Jacobitism appropriated the popular custom of displaying the leaves of Charles II's tree, a claim that was not wholly relinquished for decades.

At Oxford on 28 May, a crowd of undergraduates and townsfolk, stirred up by the rumour that Queen Anne, Bolingbroke, Ormonde and Sacheverell were to be burned in effigy, beat up the loyalists celebrating the day, broke into the Presbyterian meeting-house, and made a bonfire of its pulpit, pews and windows, to which was added an effigy of the chapel's minister. Their slogans were 'An Ormond, an Ormond, a Bolingbroke, down with the Roundheads, no Constitutioners [members of the Whig Constitutional Club], no Hanover; a new Restoration'. On the following day, the Baptist and Quaker meeting-houses were treated in a similar fashion.[79] The method of destruction of the chapels had symbolic overtones; aside from being good firewood, the pulpit and pews of a meeting-house were almost the only features that defined it as a place of worship, and they set it apart from Anglican churches, because the pulpit was more prominent and the pews arranged differently. From a social viewpoint, the Oxford rioters were even-handed, victimizing not only the wealthy Presbyterians, against whom most High Church rage was directed, but also the more plebeian Baptists.

Manchester was another trouble spot on 28–9 May. It had been experiencing disturbances for weeks, set off by a group of gentlemen who pelted the 'New Chapel' on Cross Street with dirt; they were presented at the March Assizes, but the charges were dropped.[80] Cross Street chapel was to be the focus of Jacobite protest in Manchester in

---

[76] E. S. de Beer, ed., The Diary of John Evelyn (London, 1959), pp. 955–6. Sermons were still given on the day, however; Evelyn attended one by Dean Sherlock in 1696 – ibid., p. 1024.
[77] B.L., Add. MS 5,853, p. 558.   [78] Latimer, Annals of Bristol, p. 110.
[79] Rae, History of the Rebellion, p. 140; P.R.O., S.P. 44/116, pp. 293–7, 302–3.
[80] P.R.O., P.L. 28/1, p. 230.

1715. In early May, James III was proclaimed in the town by a disaffected mob.[81] On King George's birthday, observant loyalists were dispersed by the Jacobites, and the sympathies of local magistrates were glaringly displayed by their decision to indict, not the riotous disrupters, but the loyalists themselves, who were charged with 'disturbing subjects of the King's Anglican Church with a bonfire'![82] On 29 May, oak leaves appeared on hats and houses in Manchester, and two days later the destruction of Cross Street chapel was begun.[83]

In most towns, there was a lull in disturbances between 29 May and the Pretender's birthday on 10 June. The celebration of this day, the highest of all political holidays for Jacobites, was an unmistakable sign that Sacheverellite protest had merged with a newly formed popular attachment to the exiled King. London saw the demolition on 9–10 June of Wright's Presbyterian meeting-house, which had been attacked by Sacheverell's supporters in 1710.[84] Twenty years before, on the same day, the butchers of London had quashed Jacobite celebrations. By 1715, butchers were being represented by Whig propagandists as particularly susceptible to Jacobitism.[85] What sanguine Jacobite would have predicted in 1695 that two decades later the birth of James II's son would be marked by bonfires in the City, bell-ringing in Whitechapel, flags in Clerkenwell, and cockades everywhere?[86]

At Bristol on 10 June, the Jacobites bedecked themselves with white ribbons.[87] The church bells were rung at Norton St Philip and Wolverton, near Frome in Somerset; people drank openly to James III, and a crowd was narrowly dissuaded from visiting its wrath upon the local meeting-house.[88] At Marlborough, revellers broke into the church and rang the bells, thus legitimizing the holiday in spite of the parson.[89] In Norwich, to Henry Crossgrove's delight, many of the streets were strewn with flowers and oak leaves, as they had been on 29 May, and the church bells chimed.[90] Further north, in Warrington, bells were rung, green boughs were worn, and a crowd crying 'Down

[81] *Flying Post*, no. 3660, 18–21 June 1715.   [82] P.R.O., P.L. 28/1, p. 236.
[83] *Flying Post*, no. 3660, 18–21 June 1715.
[84] Rogers, 'Popular Protest', p. 73.
[85] See 'The Butcher Woman; or, the *Tòry* Evidence', in *Mughouse Diversion: Or, A Collection of Loyal Prologues and Songs, Spoke and Sung at the Mug-houses* (3rd edn, London, 1717), pp. 37–9.
[86] *Flying Post*, no. 3657, 11–14 June 1715, P.R.O., S.P. 35/3/58, fo. 131.
[87] Latimer, *Annals of Bristol*, pp. 110–11.
[88] *Flying Post*, no. 3658, 14–16 June 1715; Rae, *History of the Rebellion*, p. 151.
[89] *Flying Post*, no. 3662, 23–5 June 1715.
[90] B.L., Add. MS 5,853, p. 558. For disturbances in Norwich, see Kathleen Wilson, 'The Rejection of Deference: Urban Political Culture in England, 1715–1788', unpublished Ph.D. dissertation, Yale University, 1985, ch. 5.

Map 2 Riots and demonstrations, 29 May and 10 June 1715

with the Rump' was barely prevented from attacking the meeting-house. At Leeds, a bonfire was made, and a man was later indicted for threatening the meeting-house.[91] That these were planned demonstrations is obvious. The clergy urged the people on in most places by ringing the church bells, and there were leaders in the crowds who sought to prevent violent rioting. The 10th of June was everywhere an occasion for public joy, for celebration by the Church and people. No doubt many plebeian participants would have liked to have gone further, but the meeting-houses were spared, except in London and, most dramatically, at Manchester.

Between 1 June and 30 July 1715, Cross Street chapel was systematically annihilated, piece by piece. The windows were broken on 5–6 June; the surrounding wall, pulpit, clock and furniture were destroyed on 9 June; and on the celebrated 10th of June the slate was pulled off the roof and broken. The next day, the lead was torn from the roof. On 12 June, during services, most of the rest of the building was wrecked, and the whole structure appears to have been flattened on 30 July.[92] This methodical destruction must have passed on to Dissenters the chilling message that the Manchester Jacobite crowd wanted their presence totally extinguished, in all its outward manifestations. It was a violent call for a return to the uniformity of Charles II's reign, and a harbinger of more severe rioting.

The meeting-house riots, June–July 1715

The summer of 1715 saw a worsening of the crisis of the Hanoverian Succession. The Tory plot for a rising in the west was crystallizing. Meanwhile, the West Midlands and Lancashire witnessed a series of riots that resulted in the ransacking of over thirty Nonconformist chapels. Nicholas Rogers has noted that the centres of disorder did not coincide with the places where a rebellion or a French landing was expected; he has therefore surmised that the riots were not connected with the Tory conspiracy.[93] This interpretation ignores the fact that widespread rioting always drew troops into an area. Northumberland and the west remained quiet, as did all coastal towns; thus, they did not attract the army. The disorders caused military units to be moved into

[91] *Flying Post*, no. 3660, 18–21 June 1715; P.R.O., Assi. 41/1, York 6 Aug. 1715, 10 March 1715/16. This man may have been arrested for a later attack.
[92] *Flying Post*, no. 3660, 18–21 June 1715.
[93] Rogers, 'Riot and Popular Jacobitism', in Cruickshanks, ed., *Ideology and Conspiracy*, p. 72.

the interior, far from the centres of the projected uprising. If there had been a plan to divert government forces into the Midlands and north-west, it could not have been more smoothly executed.

The involvement of the local gentry in the Midlands riots lends credibility to the idea of a general design. Numerous Tory gentlemen, justices and magistrates were accused of abetting the disturbances. The most notorious example was at Newcastle-under-Lyme, where Ralph Sneyd, former M.P. for the borough, was indicted for joining the rioters, and the mayor and two justices were imprisoned for refusing to interfere with them.[94] Eleven gentlemen were taken up among the accused rioters at Dudley, Cleobury Mortimer, Whitchurch, Wem and Stafford; one of them, John Ghent of Whitchurch, was along with Ralph Sneyd a member of the 'Mock Corporation of Cheadle', a Staffordshire club whose suspicious activities are detailed in Chapter 8. Henry Wagstaffe, parish clerk of Wolverhampton, was also arrested.[95] At West Bromwich, two prisoners alleged that they had been told a pair of gentlemen were to give 60 guineas apiece to encourage the mob, and one of the gentlemen was to direct them.[96] The evidence of collusion between rioters and local gentry in Lancashire is vague, but some gentlemen reportedly drank to James III at an inn by Salford bridge during the riots, and a J.P. was said to have given the crowd directions to nearby chapels.[97]

Nevertheless, if the Tory gentry gave a green light to the crowds, they did not motivate or lead them. A butcher headed the rioters at Newcastle-under-Lyme, and the Shrewsbury mob, according to Rogers, was spurred on by a skinner named 'Captain Ragg', otherwise Henry Webb.[98] At Wolverhampton, the ringleaders included the town crier and bailiff, John Wild, who was the brother of the infamous 'thief-taker general', Jonathan Wild.[99] The Manchester rioters, as will

[94] J. H. Y. Briggs, 'The Burning of the Meeting House, July 1715: Dissent and Faction in Late Stuart Newcastle', North Staffordshire Journal of Field Studies, 14 (1974), pp. 70–3; B.L., Stowe 750, fo. 272; P.R.O., Assi. 4/18, p. 240.

[95] P.R.O., Assi. 4/18, pp. 235, 240; Assi. 2/5, Staffs. Aut. 2, 3 G. I. Ghent may have been a relative of the printer Thomas Gent, who had relations in Staffordshire – see Gent, Life, pp. 114–15. Only one of the eleven gentlemen, Walter Craven or Craydon of Keele, was found guilty; he was fined 40s and imprisoned.

[96] The Historical Register (2 vols., London, 1724), vol. i, p. 329.

[97] Flying Post, no. 3667, 5–7 July 1715.

[98] Rogers, 'Riot and Popular Jacobitism', in Cruickshanks, ed., Ideology and Conspiracy, p. 77; P.R.O., Assi. 4/18, p. 315; Briggs, 'Burning of the Meeting House', p. 72.

[99] Gerald P. Mander and Norman W. Tildesley, A History of Wolverhampton to the Early Nineteenth Century (Wolverhampton, 1960), p. 111; P.R.O., Assi. 4/18, p. 247; Assi. 2/5, Staffs. Qua. 2 G. I, Aut. 2, 3, G. I.

be seen, were guided by a blacksmith and a shoemaker. Furthermore, the riots did not always spread by careful concert; they were often carried from town to town by rumour, by itinerant individuals and by the crowds themselves. The result was simultaneous outbreaks in widely separated places – for example, on 8 July, meeting-houses were attacked at Whitchurch, Stone, Leek, Shrewsbury, Burton-on-Trent, Walsall, Dudley and Stourbridge. A seditious words case tried at Worcester Assizes revealed how some riots may have started. Edward Conway, a peripatetic shoemaker, had come looking for work at the home of a Worcester shoemaker, William Smith, on 2 July 1715. He said he had been at Holywell in North Wales, where the mob was up and had pulled down all the meeting-houses. According to a witness, Conway claimed 'ye whole cry of ye Mobb was if ye King molested them they'd fire him'; another person testified that Conway said 'they'd pull down ye meeting houses there as well as they were in other places ... & y^n sd God Bless ye King I doe not name w^t King but sd. ye King shall enjoy his Rights again'.[100]

Conway's words, however, did not spark off a riot in Worcester – he was arrested, and the meeting-house there was spared until 12 July. The time may not have been right; the populace was ready for action, but the Tory gentry and magistrates were not. The crucial signal that would release the crowds was still red. The destruction of the meeting-houses depended on a combination of elite indulgence and plebeian fervour; the former may have been part of a plan, while the latter could almost be taken for granted in many parts of the country. The same formula brought the West Midlands rioting to an end, not gradually, but abruptly. Instead of spending themselves out, the disorders came to a sudden halt on 1 August 1715, the anniversary of Queen Anne's death and King George's accession. The signal had changed again, and the crowds responded.

This does not imply that the West Midlands rioters were a hired mob; they were simply aware of the political situation. Their large numbers and varied composition suggest that they represented a broad segment of the local population. About 500 people were arrested for the riots in Shropshire, Staffordshire and Worcestershire – the Warwickshire Assize records, unfortunately, have not survived. About 2,000 individuals may have participated in the unrest in these three counties, and several hundred more in Birmingham. Most of them lived

---

[100] P.R.O., Assi. 5/35, part 2, Civ. Wigorn Aut. 2 G. I, info. no. 1; Assi. 2/5, Worcs. Qua. 2 G. I. Conway was found guilty, gaoled for a month and pilloried three times.

in towns of fewer than 1,000 inhabitants, where a riot involving 100 or 200 persons was an impressive affair. In the smaller towns, those arrested were mainly tradesmen and artisans. At Wem, for instance, they included a miller, four tailors, three shoemakers, a 'yeoman' and a solitary 'labourer'. Further south at the mining village of Cleobury Mortimer, a gentleman, a mercer, a pipemaker, a butcher, a blacksmith and a carpenter were apprehended.[101] These 'respectable' types were not typical of the people of rural Shropshire; the absence of 'labourers', 'husbandmen' and even miners among them is notable. Of course, it is possible that only ringleaders were taken up by the constables.

In the industrial villages of the Black Country, on the other hand, the crowds were drawn from the major occupational groups. At Walsall, for example, twenty-seven out of forty-three accused rioters were bucklemakers.[102] Scythemakers dominated the mob at Stourbridge, and at Dudley several of Lord Ward's colliers joined in wrecking the chapel.[103] Those arrested for the Stafford riot of 15 July formed a pretty accurate cross-section of a market town: three gentlemen, five 'middling men' (two maltsters, a chandler, an apothecary, a gunsmith), four shopkeepers (three butchers and a blacksmith), twenty-two skilled artisans (six cordwainers, four tailors, two skinners, two coopers, a mason, a glover, a roper, a carpenter, four weavers), seven 'yeomen', thirteen 'labourers' and a 'drummer'.[104] By the constable's estimate, this group made up over half the total number of persons involved in the riot.

The evidence of court records should be treated carefully. The social background of rioters who were not arrested remains unknown, and there may have been many more unskilled labourers among the crowds than the Assize Books suggest. Efforts at classifying rioters according to rank, furthermore, are based on guesswork, because the records do not reveal whether an individual was rich or poor, a master craftsman or an apprentice. Nevertheless, on the basis of limited and imperfect information, some general points can be derived. The West Midlands crowds were townsfolk, drawn from the non-agricultural sections of the local economy. Rural labourers or 'husbandmen' rarely appear among the apprehended rioters, which indicates a higher level of High Church political consciousness in the trading and industrial classes.

101 P.R.O., Assi. 4/18, pp. 311–12.
102 Ibid., pp. 237–8. For the industries of the Black Country in this period, see Marie B. Rowlands, Masters and Men in the West Midlands Metal Trades before the Industrial Revolution (Manchester, 1975).
103 P.R.O., Assi. 4/18, pp. 167–9.   104 Ibid., pp. 242–4, 249.

Oldham
Blackley • Failsworth
Eccles • Manchester
Stand •
Platt •

Congleton
•

Leek
•

Newcastle-
• under-Lyme

Stone •
Uttoxeter
•

Stafford •
Burton-
• on-Trent

Lichfield
•

Wolverhampton
•
Walsall
•

Kingswinford
•
West Bromwich
Oldbury
Dudley •
• Birmingham
Halesowen
Stourbridge •
• King's Norton

Worcester
•

Leeds
•

Manchester •
Sheffield •

Congleton •

Wrexham •
Whitchurch •
Stamford •

Wem •
Peterborough •
Shrewsbury •
Bridgnorth •
Cleobury Mortimer •
Nuneaton •

Worcester •

Bath •

Yeovil •

Map 3 Meeting-house riots, 11 June–1 August 1715

Almost all of those taken up were men, but this may reflect the mentality of the constables rather than the quiescence of women.

In Lancashire, the crowds were different. As might be expected, they included large numbers of textile workers; but they also attracted many so-called 'husbandmen'. Very few 'middling' men appear in the lists of arrests. The fifty-one people who appeared at Assizes or Quarter Sessions for rioting included thirteen skilled tradesmen or artisans from outside the textile trade (three shoemakers, four tailors, two brick-layers, a tanner, a joiner, a skinmaker and a blacksmith), seventeen persons involved in the textile industry (four tapeweavers, three weavers, three fustian cutters, two pattenmakers, two Inceweavers, a feltmaker, a calendarman and a dyer), fifteen individuals who may have been in rural occupations (two shearmen and thirteen 'hus-bandmen'), four 'labourers', a badger or hawker of provisions, and a 'singing-man'.[105] These meeting-house rioters can be contrasted with the loyalists who were prosecuted for making a bonfire on 28 May. They included two dyers, two mercers, a chapman, an apothecary and a Dissenting gluemaker who was indicted at Assizes for words against the Church of England.[106] The loyalists were a very 'middling' crowd, while the Jacobite mob was more plebeian. Manchester seems to have been politically divided along social and occupational lines.

The court records, however, may be misleading. A 'husbandman' presented at Quarter Sessions appeared later at Assizes as a tailor, demonstrating that occupational descriptions were not always reliable. All of the arrested 'husbandmen' gave Manchester as their place of residence; perhaps they were weavers or unskilled workers rather than agricultural labourers. The prejudices of the Tory magistracy must also be taken into account. They may have rounded up the most prominent loyalists, while arresting only the more insignificant High Churchmen. It is interesting, moreover, that the leaders of the Manchester mob were not textile workers – they were Thomas Syddall, a blacksmith, and William Ward, a shoemaker. Tradesmen like Syddall and Ward may have been more numerous among the rioters than the court records imply. A further deficiency in the legal sources is illustrated by an agreement reached in Oldham between a J.P. and the parents and masters of some youths involved in the attack on Greenacres meeting-house. The older generation paid 20 shillings apiece to atone for the

---

[105] P.R.O., P.L. 28/1, pp. 234, 237; L.R.O., QJI/2/10, pp. 522–3. An Inceweaver specialized in the type of cloth produced at Ince, near Wigan.
[106] P.R.O., P.L. 28/1, pp. 233, 236.

sins of the younger. This document contains two facts not conveyed by other material: many of the Oldham rioters were young, and some of them, one third of those named on the agreement, were women.[107]

Names and occupations tell nothing about motives. It is evident, however, that religion was still the main ingredient in High Church unrest. The West Midlands were not foreign to Sacheverell; he had made a 'progress' through them in 1710, and had ministered early in his career to a congregation near Birmingham. The meeting-house attacks were clearly Sacheverellite. The level of animosity directed against Dissenters, particularly Presbyterians, was often astonishing. After the riots, as the meeting-house at Whitchurch was being rebuilt, a local carpenter named Samuel Ratcliffe, who had helped in its demolition, was overheard damning the Presbyterians and vowing that 'all the Dissenters in a little time should be flying for their lives' when the chapels were again pulled down.[108] At the height of the disturbances, a paper was posted around Shrewsbury:

We Gentlemen of the Loyal Mob of *Shrewsbury*, do issue out this Proclamation to all Dissenters from the Church of *England*, of what Kind or Denomination soever, whether Independent, Baptists or Quakers: If you, or any of you, do encourage or suffer any of that damnable Faction called Presbyterians, to assemble themselves amongst you, in any of your Conventicles, at the time of Divine Worship, you may expect to meet with the same that they have been treated with. Given under our Hands and Seals the 11th Day of July 1715. *God save the King.*[109]

This shows the specificity of High Church hatred, which singled out the powerful Presbyterians as an especially 'damnable Faction'.

The Shrewsbury proclamation was also Jacobite in tone. It mimicked a royal edict, but blessed an unnamed king. While it declared that the mob was 'loyal', it did not say to whom. In the heat of action, the West Midlands rioters had not been so evasive. At Wolverhampton, a bucklemaker was alleged to have shouted 'God damn King George, and the Duke of Marlborough' from the roof of the meeting-house, and a suspected spy was forced by the crowd to bless King James III on his knees. Robert Holland of Bilston, a bucklemaker, urged his Wolver-

---

[107] Manchester Central Library, Archives Room, LI/55/5/15. I owe this reference to Jan Albers.

[108] P.R.O., Assi. 5/36, part 1, Salop Qua. 2 G. I, info. no. 17. The Birmingham rioters spared one meeting-house on the condition that it be converted to a private residence. See Robert K. Dent, *The Making of Birmingham: Being a History of the Rise and Growth of the Midland Metropolis* (Birmingham, 1894), p. 60.

[109] Rae, *History of the Rebellion*, p. 152.

hampton comrades, 'Now boys goe on we will have no King but James the third & he will be here in a month and wee will drive the old Rogue into his Country again to sow Turnipps'.[110] In Walsall, the Stuart claimant received the benedictions of a tailor.[111] At Leek, a cordwainer drank 'an health to King James the Third, and wee hope in a short time too wee shall have him amongst us'.[112] The revival of the Church was no longer imagined to be possible without the restoration of a Stuart king, an event that was seen as imminent.

The crowds in Lancashire hammered out the same message. After wiping out Cross Street chapel, the assiduous Manchester rioters roamed around the area, eliminating other offensive hostels of presbytery at Blackley, Greenacres, Monton, Stand, Platt and Failsworth. The troops sent to Manchester at the end of June failed to stop the disorders, and the mob was reportedly on its way to Yorkshire when its energy ran out and it dispersed.[113] Tom Syddall and William Ward were quickly arrested, and were tried for seditious words as well as riot. Syddall was pilloried and imprisoned for damning King George; Ward's indictment was found *ignoramus*, but the shoemaker had confessed to taking part in the destruction of Monton meeting-house near Eccles, so he too was imprisoned.[114]

Meanwhile, the plans that had been so carefully laid by the Tory leaders were coming to fruition. At Oxford, Bath, Bristol, along Tyneside and in Scotland, the Jacobites were ready to act. Suddenly, in September and early October, the government pounced on them. Wyndham and several other Tory M.P.s were arrested, the nests of insurgents at Oxford and Bath were flushed out by troops, and the arms being stored at Bristol were seized. Only in Northumberland was the rebellion able to start; a force composed mainly of Catholics rode around the county for weeks, vaguely threatening Newcastle, before heading across the Scottish border and south again into Lancashire. Syddall and Ward were still in Lancaster gaol when the Jacobite army arrived there, and both men joined it. After the crushing defeat at Preston, they were recaptured. Ward was able to convince a jury that he had been forced to join the rebels, and was acquitted, but Syddall was executed for high treason.[115] Months before, in the wake of the

110 *Historical Register*, vol. i, p. 330; P.R.O., Assi. 4/18, pp. 230, 232.
111 P.R.O., Assi. 4/18, p. 230.
112 *Ibid.*, p. 248.   113 Rae, *History of the Rebellion*, p. 151; P.R.O., S.P. 35/3/68.
114 P.R.O., P.L. 28/1, pp. 232, 233, 238.
115 See Petrie, 'Jacobite Activities in South and West England', pp. 95–101; Handasyde, *Granville the Polite*, pp. 139–50; and Chapter Ten.

meeting-house riots, the government had passed the Riot Act, imposing the penalty of death on rioters who refused to disperse when ordered to do so by a magistrate. Men like Tom Syddall, it seemed, were now doomed one way or the other.

Walking through central Manchester today, it is hard to envision the distance that once separated the church of St Ann's from the former Collegiate Church, now Manchester Cathedral. They have been connected by rows of shops and warehouses since the tremendous expansion of the town at the end of the eighteenth century. The old Manchester has been swallowed up by a vast conurbation, and the outlying places once visited by the Jacobite mobs are now parts of an urban continuum. In 1715, however, St Ann's stood outside the limits of the town, and the Presbyterian chapel around the corner on Cross Street was further out still. Between them and the Collegiate Church lay a wide cultural divide, separating the Dissenters and their Whig friends from the gestures and rituals that defined the High Church.

It was not always an unbridgeable gulf; after all, the Nonjuror John Byrom, who mingled with the high-flyers of the Collegiate Church, occasionally attended the low services at St Ann's. Yet in the Sacheverellite tempest of 1710, the bridges were blown down. On either side were left groups of people of every social class, united by their perception of themselves and their relationship to those on the other side. One group was characterized by its concern for the preservation of the national Church and the sanctity of monarchy, which were seen as the twin foundations of prosperity and harmony. On the other side were those who did not have a place in this scheme of religious and political unity – Dissenters, Whigs, Low Churchmen, stock-jobbers, atheists and other supposedly unprincipled rogues. From their point of view, their opponents were crypto-Catholics and Jacobites. When adherence to the exiled Stuarts mushroomed among the High Churchmen after 1710, it did not surprise their adversaries, and it seemed natural even to themselves.

What caused the breakdown of communication between the two segments of English society? Nicholas Rogers has pointed to the effects of the long wars with France, which engendered national economic distress and divided those who suffered on account of the conflict from those who profited by it.[116] Although there is some truth in this

---

[116] Rogers, 'Riot and Popular Jacobitism', in Cruickshanks, ed., *Ideology and Conspiracy*, pp. 78–9.

interpretation, it tells only part of the story. The mid-1690s had also been years of deprivation, of grain crises and shortages of specie due to the war, but the Jacobites were wrong in assuming that they could exploit popular discontent. William III remained the bulwark of Protestantism for most High Churchmen as well as Low; except in a few isolated cases, Jacobite agitation could not arouse much opposition to him. By 1714, however, conditions were different. George I had proved himself far worse than his alternative in the minds of many High Churchmen, by turning out the Tories and showing favour to their enemies. Geoffrey Holmes has pointed out that the Sacheverell mobs did not express a desire for the end of the war; similarly, the Jacobite crowds of 1714–15 did not say much about maintaining the peace.[117] Nevertheless, the issue was bound up in the High Church vision that infused them. The Tory party, symbolized by Ormonde, stood for peace and stability, while the Whigs, typified by Marlborough, represented war and disorder.

Popular Tory rage, however, centred on religious rather than secular objects – in particular, on the hated meeting-houses. Why was the protection of the Church of England so important to plebeian Englishmen and women? No doubt because it embodied a powerful myth of unity that had great appeal to 'respectable', settled and skilled tradesmen or artisans. The alternative to the Church was feared to be a cruel universe in which exploitation of the many by the few ran rampant. The denizens of this dark other world were corrupt and greedy men like Marlborough, scheming minorities like the Presbyterians, sectarians and infidels of all types, who squabbled for power in an imaginary Gehenna. The nightmare had once become real, at least in the historical memory of Toryism. Between 1649 and 1660, legitimate authority had been abolished and supposedly replaced by naked force. From highest to lowest, anarchic individualism was thought to have taken hold, resulting in oppression and chaos. The Hanoverian Succession threatened to revive that situation, and the only remedy seemed to be a restoration of the Stuarts. In this context, Jacobitism excited, between October 1714 and August 1715, the most widespread political disturbances of any comparable period in English history.

117 Holmes, 'Sacheverell Riots', pp. 67–8, and *Trial of Doctor Sacheverell*, pp. 177–8.

Chapter 7

The day will be our own: the tradition of Jacobite protest, 1715–80

[T]here will be no good times 'till King James the 3ʳd come again .. you may kiss my Arse & King George too, the day will be our own.
Allegedly spoken by William Price of Hereford, butcher,
on 10 June 1718.[1]

If Jacobite riots and commemorations had ceased with the defeat of the rebels in November 1715, or even with the end of the Hanoverian Succession crisis in 1722–3, they would provide only a brief episode in the history of eighteenth-century popular culture. After its assimilation into the mainstream of plebeian protest, however, Jacobitism did not fade away for at least four decades. To be sure, it did not retain the strength it had enjoyed in the summer hiatus of 1715. By the early 1720s, the Jacobite beast had been temporarily tamed by the government, except in a few places like Norwich and Bristol. The revival of popular Jacobitism in the 1740s and early 1750s was more restricted than the torrent of 1715, and was confined mostly to Lancashire, the West Midlands, East Anglia and the south-west, although it is likely that Jacobite sentiment lingered elsewhere in less strident forms.

Nicholas Rogers has tried to explain the longevity of plebeian Jacobitism by arguing that the Stuart cause provided a 'language of political blasphemy ... designed to draw Whig anger, to tease and unsettle the Court'.[2] For the government, however, Jacobite ritual and rhetoric were neither 'teasing' nor 'blasphemous'; they were expressions of treasonable disaffection, and were treated quite differently from simple insults against authority or attacks on the Whig party. It presumes a very low level of political sophistication on the part of ordinary Englishmen and women to suggest that they did not realize

[1] P.R.O., S.P. 44/79A, pp. 156–7.
[2] Rogers, 'Riot and Popular Jacobitism', in Cruickshanks, ed., *Ideology and Conspiracy*, pp. 83, 85.

the seriousness of Jacobite protest. The circumstances of seditious rioting, moreover, offer strong evidence of the specificity of plebeian Jacobitism. Crowds did not call upon the Stuarts in all situations; on the contrary, such behaviour was restricted to clearly defined areas of protest, which implies that Jacobitism was not merely a form of legitimation. White roses, oak boughs and blessings for James III were positive political statements that must be analysed with the same attention that has been devoted to the number 45 or Captain Swing.

Between the plebeian mobs and the mass-market publishers like Clifton or Mist was carried on a complicated and undocumented dialogue. It would be ludicrous, of course, to portray Jacobite crowds as passive receptacles for Stuart propaganda; yet it is equally simplistic to write of the appropriation of Jacobite political culture by plebeians for their own purposes. As much as they absorbed the language, it infused them. Rioters took literary images – horns, turnips, roses – and made them real, by translating them into communal action. The images, however, transformed reality into the dramatization of a political cosmology. Jacobite crowds were actors in an elaborate morality play, whose script was written partly by others, partly by the players themselves, and was often improvised. As with seditious verse, it is vain to search for an 'authentic' plebeian voice in political riots and demonstrations; the cultural mixture of these events prevents the historian from separating what is borrowed from what is indigenous. Everything is at once 'authentic' and derivative. When William Price of Hereford reportedly said 'the day will be our own', his words meant that 10 June was a day of plebeian triumph, but they also echoed the slogans of Jacobite propaganda. The two connotations were not mutually exclusive.

Jacobite sympathizers did not attempt to make every day their own, because not all occasions lent themselves to political theatre. It is important to recognize that politics did not occupy a constant place in the lives of eighteenth-century plebeians, and that political riots were exceptional episodes. The following section considers some of the riotous contexts in which treasonable themes did emerge, so as to delineate the parameters of Jacobite protest.

Strikes, elections and chapel-breakings

Popular Jacobitism was not a catch-all for discontent; it was aroused by particular circumstances, and pursued specific aims. It was an

aggressive champion of Tory principles and Anglican religious hegemony, but had little to contribute to the resolution of economic
problems. With its rosy vision of social harmony, Jacobitism was not of
much use to disgruntled workers involved in labour disputes, unless
some further political or religious factor was present. Even then, it was
inadvisable for strikers to resort to a treasonable rhetoric that could do
a great deal of harm to their cause by inviting the wrath of the
government.

The silk weavers of London understood this point well. In 1719, a
Stuart sympathizer tried to turn a weavers' strike into an insurrection in
support of the rebellion in Scotland.[3] His failure illustrates the good
sense of the strikers, who had nothing to gain from politicizing their
grievances. Five years later, however, some serge weavers at Culmstock
in Devon destroyed pictures of George I and his family when they broke
into the house of their employer during a strike. Their anger had been
aroused by this sergemaker's close connections with the government
and his Nonconformity.[4] This was a rare example, as was the incident
in 1750 when some striking Newcastle keelmen proclaimed 'Prince
CHARLES King [sic] of England, France & Ireland, Defender of the
Faith'. Some of these men were Scots, who had been encouraged to
proclaim the Young Pretender by a Jacobite lawyer from Edinburgh.[5]

Although Jacobite political culture was imbued with a moral vision
that could have social consequences, it was vague in describing the just
society that would follow a restoration. Consequently, Jacobitism was
connected only in general ways with the idea of 'moral economy' that
spurred on economic protesters in the eighteenth century.[6] In 1756,
some food rioters in Warwickshire refused to disperse 'til the Pretender
came to stop them'; but this was an isolated case, and it was inspired by
the fact that the grain merchants at Nuneaton and Tamworth were
Quakers.[7] In the following year, another social issue awakened the
diminishing strain of Jacobite protest. The Militia Act was feared by
many plebeians as a ploy to send them overseas to fight. During the
ensuing disturbances, a mysterious gentleman was observed posting
copies of a paper at Halifax and Harrogate. Addressed to 'the most

[3] Boyer, Political State, vol. xviii, pp. 44–7.
[4] P.R.O., S.P. 35/49/52 (2), S.P. 35/50/61.
[5] Newcastle Courant, no. 2941, 5 May 1750. I owe this reference to Kathleen Wilson.
  See also P.R.O., S.P. 36/112, fos. 331, 333, and Chapter 10.
[6] For this concept, see E. P. Thompson, 'The Moral Economy of the English Crowd in
  the Eighteenth Century', P. & P., 50 (1971), pp. 76–136.
[7] P.R.O., S.P. 36/135, fo. 272; B.L., Add. MS 32,867, fos. 3–4.

honest & industrious part of the People usually called – The lower sort', the paper insisted that the rumours of imminent conscription were true, and exhorted Yorkshiremen to '[r]emember your legal native King'.[8] The recommendation may not have had much effect on the anti-militia rioters in the West Riding, who 'talk of nothing but a Leveling Scheme'; nevertheless, in the East Riding, the mob avoided harassing the estates of Roman Catholics.[9] Meanwhile, Tory militia officers in Suffolk were denounced to the government for toasting the return of King James.[10]

The Militia Act arose from a knotty political situation in which a declining Tory party had lent its support to the Whig ministry of Pitt and Newcastle. Historians have suggested that the 1750s witnessed an increasing unity among England's political elite, and the gradual disintegration of the two-party system.[11] Popular Jacobitism, which had been born from Whig–Tory strife, was bound to decay along with partisan animosities. Yet the Tory party had rarely allowed Jacobite sentiments to interfere with elections, because this might have divided thair supporters and allowed the government to level accusations against Tory candidates. Until 1747, only a few incidents can be cited of Jacobitism at the hustings. At a Lichfield by-election in 1718, William Sneyd, cousin of the alleged instigator of the 1715 Newcastle-under-Lyme riot, was elected M.P. 'by a very great mob with papers in their hats resembling white roses, headed by the same person that was captain of the famous riots at West Bromwich'.[12] In 1722 at St Albans, Thomas Gape, who later became M.P. for the town, made some musicians play 'The King shall enjoy his own again' during an election riot.[13] Jacobite hopes were running high in that year, and caused disorders at Coventry , where Lord Craven led a procession of 2,000 Tory supporters into the town, crying 'Down with the Rump! .. No Hanoverians!'[14] Thomas Carte reported with glee of the Coventry

---

[8] B.L., Add. MS 32,874, fos. 274–5; B.L., Egerton 3436, fos. 154–5, 159.
[9] B.L., Add. MS 32,874, fo. 222; B.L., Egerton 3436, fo. 153. See also J. R. Western, *The English Militia in the Eighteenth Century* (London, 1965), pp. 290–302.
[10] B.L., Add. MS 32,884, fo. 383.
[11] See J. C. D. Clark, *The Dynamics of Change: The Crisis of the 1750s and English Party Systems* (Cambridge, 1982); W. A. Speck, *Stability and Strife: England, 1714–1760* (Cambridge, Mass., 1979), ch. 6, dates this change from an earlier period.
[12] Josiah C. Wedgwood, *Staffordshire Parliamentary History from the Earliest Times to the Present Day*, vol. 2, William Salt Archaeological Society (London, 1922), p. 215, note 2.
[13] H.M.C., *Report on the Manuscripts of the Earl of Verulam* (London, 1906), p. 119; Sedgwick, ed., *History of Parliament*, vol. ii, p. 59.
[14] Sedgwick, ed., *History of Parliament*, vol. i, p. 340.

rioters 'you never saw Fellows of such Mettle, so well Train'd, so fit for Business'.[15] With equal mettle, a mob of Welsh colliers employed by Sir Watkin Williams Wynn went about Chester during a mayoral contest in 1733, beating those who cried out for King George.[16]

After the disastrous elections of 1747, the Tory party in the West Midlands, determined to set itself apart from the treacherous Gowerite defectors, began to encourage large-scale Jacobite demonstrations. At the Lichfield races of 1747, Sir Thomas Gresley and Sir Charles Sedley appeared with 'the Burton Mobb, most of 'em in Plaid Wastcoats [sic], Plaid ribbons around their Hatts, and some with white Cocades'. Sir Lyster Holte, Sir Watkin Williams Wynn, Sir Walter Wagstaffe Bagot and the Earl of Uxbridge also attended, to drink the Pretender's health and to sing treasonable songs. A symbolic blow was struck at Lord Gower, and a real series of blows was laid upon the unfortunate Duke of Bedford, Gower's cousin, by a dancing-master of Burton-upon-Trent, appropriately named Christopher Sole. The other rioters included the son of a sheriff of Lichfield, a sheriff's officer, servants of the Earl of Uxbridge and the Hill family of Shenston, some 'middling' men and tradesmen, a schoolmaster and a few labourers.[17] According to the Stuart Papers, Prince Charles's adviser Sir James Harrington was present at the meeting, and only the timorousness of the Tory baronets prevented the demonstrations from becoming a general uprising.[18] The 1753 Lichfield by-election stirred up the bold Jacobitism of the Staffordshire squires for the last time; Sir Thomas Gresley, who was returned as M.P., rode into the town attended by 200 gentlemen and 500 freemen wearing blue (Tory) and white (Jacobite) ribbons.[19] In the general elections of 1754, however, the West Midlands were quiet, and the only treasonable demonstration was at Leicester, where the Tory candidates brought up a mob of colliers from Coleorton who terrorized local Whigs by singing anti-Hanoverian songs.[20]

The accession of George III almost brought about the final extinction of the old Tory party. A group of die-hard 'independent country gentlemen', however, stuck to their High Church principles on the

15 The Whole Proceedings upon ... Christopher Layer, E. 7.
16 Sedgwick, ed., History of Parliament, vol. i, p. 204.
17 Wedgwood, Staffordshire Parliamentary History, vol. 2, pp. 253–4; P.R.O., S.P. 36/102, fo. 80.
18 Lang, Pickle the Spy, p. 90.
19 Wedgwood, Staffordshire Parliamentary History, vol. 2, p. 254.
20 V.C.H., Leicestershire, vol. iv, p. 127. William Gardiner, Music and Friends (2 vols., London and Leicester, 1838), vol. i, p. 207, which is the source of the V.C.H. account, does not mention the songs.

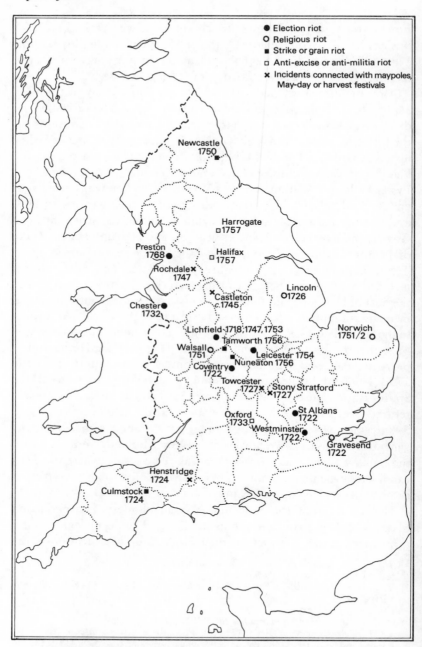

Map 4 Riots and demonstrations involving Jacobitism after 1715

back-benches, and they were supported in their constituencies by the familiar crowd of tradesmen and artisans. Among these plebeian Tories, Jacobitism lingered long after it had ceased to be a Parliamentary issue. At Preston in 1768, the old Tories Sir Peter Leicester and Sir Ralph Standish were cheered on by mobs of in-burgesses, who allegedly rallied to cries of 'Down with the Rump', 'No King George', 'Prince Charles', 'King James' and 'White Cockades'.[21] These charmingly anachronistic slogans (King James was dead, and Charles was no longer a Prince) proclaimed Preston's legacy of independence from Whig and Hanoverian domination. As at Lichfield in 1747, Jacobitism was a sign of Tory difference, a 'glorious memory' that distinguished the High Church party from its rival, especially in difficult times.

Religious distinctions lay at the heart of party conflict, and contributed to many Jacobite disorders. Church politics sometimes stimulated Jacobite responses. The dismantling of a church spire in Lincoln, the election of a churchwarden in Gravesend, or of a lecturer in St Giles-in-the-Fields, might generate treasonable cries from the crowds.[22] The anti-Dissenting mood of the summer mobs of 1715 did not quickly disappear, as two cases from the early 1750s demonstrate. The half-finished Presbyterian meeting-house at Walsall was demolished in May 1751 by a crowd of bucklemakers from the area known as the Hill Top. They reportedly shouted 'King James leads the Van', a pun derived from the ditty 'Old Jemmy' which was discussed in Chapter 2, and sang 'Prince Charles's Restoration' as they went about their work.[23] The rioters were motivated by a sense of territorial right, but it is important to note that they were defending the religious character of their locality, which indicates the survival of Sacheverellite prejudices. In a similar riot at Norwich in March 1751/2, a Methodist congregation was attacked by the Tory 'Hell fire Club'; the crowd called themselves 'Jemmy's men', sang treasonable songs, and chanted 'Church and King, and no law!' (i.e. no Toleration Act). One of them was accused of saying 'Now is the time, or never, let us throw off G—e and bring in Jemmy', while others allegedly chanted 'King

21 William Dobson, History of the Parliamentary Representation of Preston (2nd edn, Preston and London, 1868), p. 34.
22 Sir Francis Hill, Georgian Lincoln (Cambridge, 1966), pp. 27–8; P.R.O., S.P. 35/31/2; S.P. 36/16, fo. 217; S.P. 36/17, fo. 41.
23 P.R.O., Assi. 5/71, part 2, fos. 27–9; Ernest James Homeshaw, The Corporation of the Borough and Foreign of Walsall (Walsall, 1960), p. 94. I am grateful to Douglas Hay for discussing the Walsall disorders with me.

James *for ever*; *King* James *for ever*'.[24] As in the West Midlands, the Methodists in Norwich were perceived to be Dissenters, although in other places they were accused of Jacobitism.[25]

Most Jacobite disturbances were not connected with specific economic, political or religious issues. They took place on commemoration days, occasions associated with the Stuart or Hanoverian dynasties; they focussed on the conception of kingship and the question of legitimacy. The next three sections will explore the significance of Jacobite rhetoric and ritual on the two great Jacobite holidays, 29 May and 10 June, and the development of a counter-theatre of protest to undermine Hanoverian festivals.

Restoration Day

Popular Jacobitism was often associated with the festivals of the plebeian calendar, whose dominant theme was the cycle of the seasons. It was appropriate that Jacobite unrest should accompany seasonal change, because the High Church view of history was envisioned as a cycle of disruption and restoration. As was shown in Chapter 2, the Stuart king, whether Charles II or James III, became a sort of vegetation god, whose return would bring back the spring. He was also endowed with the attributes of the Christian god, whose cycle of death and resurrection heralded the renewal of nature.

In some areas, seasonal change was celebrated in autumn, the time for harvesting. At Rochdale in Lancashire, for example, the annual rush-bearing in August was an important feast, in which townships in the parish vied with each other in gathering crowds of revellers and exhibiting magnificent harvest garlands. After the rebellion of 1745, in which a few local men took part on the Jacobite side, the Rochdale rush-bearers formed themselves into two parties, christened 'Blacks' and 'Jacks' by a Whig J.P. – the Hanoverian cockade was black. In 1747, while the 'Jacks' were meeting at the Union Flag Inn, they were attacked by the 'Blacks' and some soldiers, who broke into the building and ransacked it. According to the 'Blacks', their rivals had the

---

[24] *A True and Particular Narrative of the Disturbances and Outrages That have been committed in the City of Norwich, Since November to the present Time* (London, 1752), pp. 27, 31.

[25] See John Walsh, 'Methodism and the Mob in the Eighteenth Century', in G. J. Cuming and Derek Baker, eds., *Popular Belief and Practice* (Cambridge, 1972), pp. 213–28. Anti-Methodist riots took place at Walsall and Wednesbury in 1743–4 – Homeshaw, *Walsall*, p. 92.

effrontery to hang a plaid handkerchief out of the window of the inn, and destroyed some garlands dressed up with orange ribbons to cries of 'Down with the Rump'. More shocking still, when the Whigs had tried to sing a song in praise of the Duke of Cumberland, the Tories threw stones and piss-pots at them from the inn's balcony.[26] Although this affair took on a tone of levity – after all, seasonal feasts were supposed to be fun – it had serious complications. A man was almost killed, fifteen or twenty 'Jacks' were arrested and fined, and the innkeeper brought an action of trespass against the 'Blacks' in the court of King's Bench.[27]

Antic frivolity characterized another seasonal holiday, the spring feast of 1 May. This celebration of fertility and youth occasionally led to Jacobite outbursts, as at Henstridge in Somerset, where a confront-ation between the landlord and villagers over the erection of a maypole led to the singing of treasonable songs on May-day in 1724.[28] Maypoles played a part in a number of Jacobite incidents, including those at Chester and Bedford that were noted in the previous chapter. The maypole, of course, was a shrine to fertility, and it does not require faith in Freud to see it as a phallic symbol, or to interpret the garlands and plates with which it was usually decorated as representations of female sexuality. The Puritans, Dissenters, Methodists and moralists who tried to stamp out May-day revels were in no doubt as to their sexual connotations. Maypoles therefore may have always been a little suspect to the Whig authorities. Perhaps this explains the story that appeared in *Mist's Weekly Journal* in June 1727, recording the decoration of maypoles at Stony Stratford, Buckinghamshire, and Towcester, Northamptonshire, ostensibly to celebrate the accession of George II. The government reacted negatively, and troops were sent to prevent the desecration of crown forests by the merry-makers.[29] Was there some hint of disloyalty in this apparently pro-Hanoverian event? Were the villagers really rejoicing at the death of George I?

In his interesting study of popular recreations, Robert Malcolmson remarks upon the eighteenth-century practice of transferring the ceremonies of May-day to Restoration day.[30] The two feasts were

26 Chetham Library, Manchester, Raines MSS, vol. 14, p. 441; Alfred Burton, *Rush-bearing* (Manchester, 1891), pp. 66–7.
27 In 1745, the rebels had requisitioned a horse from Adam Robinson, the innkeeper, 'but upon his Application to one of their Chiefs he was restored'. Chetham Library, Raines MSS, vol. 34, p. 80.
28 Thompson, 'Eighteenth-Century English Society', p. 159.
29 *Mist's Weekly Journal*, no. 115, 1 July 1727.
30 Malcolmson, *Popular Recreations*, pp. 30–1.

clearly regarded as so similar in content that the rituals of one were perfectly suited to the other. This transferal may have been inspired by Jacobitism. All known cases of the shift to 29 May occurred after 1715, and most in the aftermath of the '45. At Castleton in the Peak District, May-day ceremonies are still annually observed on Restoration day. The decoration of the church steeple with garlands on 29 May originated in the 1740s; later, a more elaborate ritual involving a 'Garland King' and a procession was developed.[31] The king was Charles II, and the ceremony was a playing-out of the vegetation god role of the Stuarts. In the wake of the rebellion of 1745, in a village so close to the rebel path, and to the Whig stronghold at Chatsworth, this evocation of Stuart theo-kingship must have carried political overtones.

Before the 1760s, Restoration day was a highly partisan occasion, and it was not easy for a Whig to show joy at its observance. At Oxford in 1716, some Whigs attempted to share in the event by wearing oak boughs, but the Jacobite gownsmen struck up 'The King shall enjoy his own again' on fiddles and pipes, and the people threw 'Squibs and Serpents' at the hapless Hanoverian loyalists.[32] On the same day in London, a profusion of oak boughs, some of them gilded or silvered, appeared on hats and breasts; before long, the familiar cry of 'High Church and Ormonde' had been raised, along with 'No Hanover'.[33] The Whigs lost their patience. In 1717 and 1718, people were arrested in London simply for sporting a sprig of green.[34] This remained the standard Whig response to Restoration day for the next four decades. In 1747 in Manchester, Bland's dragoons removed oak leaves from hats and stays, and beat some recalcitrant women in the streets.[35]

Clearly, 29 May was not a bipartisan holiday. In fact, nobody before 1760 called it by the innocuous name 'Oak Apple day'; it was always Restoration day, an appellation that carried strong Jacobite overtones. At Norwich in 1728, revellers wore gilded roses as well as oak boughs on 29 May, to emphasize the Jacobite connection.[36] The Whigs sought to counter this sort of behaviour by boosting 28 May, George I's birthday, as an occasion for loyal commemoration; but the attempt

---

31 Bob Bushaway, *By Rite: Custom, Ceremony and Community in England, 1700 – 1880* (London, 1982), p. 57.
32 Boyer, *Political State*, vol. xi, pp. 644–7.   33 *Ibid.*, pp. 643–4.
34 *Weekly Journal*, no. 25, 1 June 1717, p. 147; Boyer, *Political State*, vol. xv, p. 634.
35 *Manchester Vindicated*, p. 234.
36 *Norwich Gazette*, 4 June 1728. I owe this reference to Kathleen Wilson.

often failed. At Cambridge on 28 May 1716, a mob destroyed the loyalist bonfire at Clare College, crying 'Down with the Rump', and on the morrow, a crowd of townsmen and gownsmen attacked Trinity College, beat up Whigs, broke unilluminated windows and burned the pews and the clock of the meeting-house.[37] The next year, a wag at the Cambridge market-place announced that the rejoicings of 28 May were to be postponed until the following day.[38]

At Watton in Hertfordshire, a large crowd appeared with flags, green boughs on their hats and horns on their heads on 29 May in 1717. A gardener, William Brotherton, was bound over to Quarter Sessions for leading this demonstration.[39] The horns, symbols of cuckoldry, were meant to lampoon the marital troubles of George I, and this incident seems very much like a 'Skimmington ride'. Yet it would be a mistake to interpret Jacobite commemorations purely in terms of folk-culture; they always bore a political significance. Mist hinted that the Watton affair had been concocted by the 'Oaken-Bough Gentry', who had intended 'something Extraordinary' to take place, but had been prevented by a J.P. who dispersed the demonstrators.[40] This 'something Extraordinary' may have been an insurrection. Charles Caesar, M.P. for Hertfordshire, was the principal organizer of the Swedish Plot of 1716–17, and he may have intended to show the strength of local support for the Stuarts by creating a major incident. In 1718, as will be seen below, Caesar's close friend and ally the Earl of Oxford may have encouraged similar demonstrations in Hereford on 29 May and 10 June.

The most alarming of all 29 May celebrations took place in the Jacobite heartland of the Black Country in 1750. A crowd of about 300 people, mostly bucklemakers, gathered at the Hill Top in Walsall, carrying with them, in the words of a military officer who witnessed the event:

an Image or Figure dressed up in the likeness of a Man, his Head was a Barber's Block with an Old Wig upon it, and there was fixed to the hinder part of it a Horse Tail which reached down all along the Back; That he had upon his Hands white Gloves, and upon his Legs white Stockings, that his Cloathing appeared to be chiefly Rags or anything else that could make it look mean and disgraceful; that about the Breast was a paper or Label expressing these Words, Evil to him that Evil think, it is this that makes the Nation Stink; in one hand

---

[37] B.L., Stowe 750, f. 194.
[38] Hodgson, ed., *Six North Country Diaries*, 'Diary of John Thomlinson', p. 122.
[39] W. J. Hardy, ed., *Hertford County Records: Notes and Extracts from the Sessions Rolls* (2 vols., Hertford, 1905), vol. ii, p. 50, no. 23.
[40] *Weekly Journal*, no. 26, 8 June 1717, p. 154.

was an Orange, and in the other a bunch of Turnips. They raised and fixed a Gibet they hung by the Neck the aforesaid Figure or Image, with a pair of Horns set upon the Head.[41]

The attributes of this effigy were those formerly ascribed to George I in Jacobite propaganda – ragged clothing denoting poverty, the lustful 'Belly', the turnips, the cuckold's horns. In fact, the whole 'usurping' line was on display here, as the orange, for William III, indicated. The ritual mockery of the 'Lord of Misrule' culminated in a public execution. The white gloves and stockings, as Peter Linebaugh has shown, were often worn by criminals on their way to a 'wedding' with the gallows at Tyburn; they may also have been ironical touches, as white was the Stuart colour.[42]

The Walsall riot began as a commemoration, but it soon became much worse. The crowd did not disperse; disorders continued until 8 June, when a bucklemaker named William Wiggin went about the streets of Walsall, singing treasonable songs in preparation for the Pretender's birthday.[43] The next day, the government despatched the experienced agent Nathaniel Carrington to the town, and began sending troops into the area.[44] Carrington reported on 23 June, almost a month after the initial disturbances, that a mob of 500 or 600 was again in the streets, waiting to be joined by local colliers. They were dispersed by the authorities, but that night some agitators, including one 'who is an apothecary and a Jacobite Fellow, and alway's at the head of Parties', were arrested while trying to raise another riot.[45] Unrest, however, was spreading. On 10 July, Richard Leveson Gower wrote to the Secretary of War requesting more soldiers to quell 'the Confusion that now reigns in the Towns of Birmingham, Walsall and Wednesbury'. Six troops of horse were despatched to the area.[46] Nine days later, a letter printed in the Gentleman's Magazine spoke of 'the report of a great insurrection in Birmingham', and mentioned rumours of a clash between dragoons and rioters in which several soldiers had been killed.[47] The carnivalesque romp at Walsall had turned into a regional uprising.

41 P.R.O., S.P.44/81, pp. 192–3; S.P. 36/113, fos. 88–101, 128–9, 137–43; Homeshaw, Walsall, pp. 92–4.
42 Linebaugh, 'The Tyburn Riot Against the Surgeons', in Hay et al., Albion's Fatal Tree, pp. 112–15. White gloves were worn in October 1716 by mourners at the London funeral of Thomas Bean, who was executed for leading the Jacobite attack on the Salisbury Court Mug-house – Boyer, Political State, vol. xii, pp. 238, 440–4, 448.
43 P.R.O., Assi. 4/20, Staffs. Sum. 24 G. II, indt. W. Wiggin.
44 P.R.O., S.P. 44/81, pp. 189–90, 197–9; S.P. 36/113, fo. 145.
45 P.R.O., S.P. 36/113, fo. 194.   46 P.R.O., S.P. 44/318, p. 52.
47 Gentleman's Magazine, vol. xx, July 1750, p. 331.

The insurgents were finally suppressed by force. Some of the Walsall rioters absconded, and were 'Sheltered by Gentlemen that are there friend's in this Country'.[48] Eight of them, including two women, were later arrested; four of the prisoners were members of the same bucklemaking family of James, and another was Eleanor Wiggin, no doubt a relative of the tuneful William.[49] Their case was conveyed from Assizes to King's Bench, a frequent tactic in areas where the political sympathies of judges and juries were not trusted by the government. In January 1750/1, several persons testified that collections of money had been raised at Walsall, Sutton Coldfield, Wolsley Bridge and Lichfield races for the support of the accused, who eventually admitted that 'several Charitable Persons' had sent them donations. The government questioned Sir John Astley, who swore himself innocent of any fund-raising.[50]

Meanwhile, the Walsall affair had taken an intriguing turn. The letter of 9 June 1750, written by Reverend Taylor of Colton to John Webb of Hamstall Ridware, was discussed in Chapter 5. It was carried between the two villages, which are only a few miles from Walsall, by a former Scottish rebel who was later arrested in Herefordshire for highway robbery.[51] The letter mentioned 'the jubilee' to be held at Hamstall Ridware on 10 June; and on that day, according to an informer, John Webb was visited by a number of gentlemen from Staffordshire, Warwickshire and Cheshire, among them Sir Edward Littleton, William Meredith of Henbury, one of the Bagots, a Sneyd, a Kynnersley of Loxley and a Lichfield attorney named Frogard.[52]

Thomas Daniel, a relation of Reverend Taylor and curate of Stow and Gayton, was also taken up at this time; he was warned of his impending arrest while attending the Bowling Green Club at Uttoxeter.[53] The government took an interest in this organization, which boasted Sir Walter Wagstaffe Bagot, Ralph Sneyd and an assortment of Fitz-herberts, Kynnersleys, Bowyers and Fieldhouses among its members. It had been formed on 15 May 1750, exactly two weeks before the Walsall riot, and was to disband on the Tuesday before Michaelmas.[54] Two weeks before Michaelmas in 1750, Prince Charles Edward briefly visited London in connection with a murky conspiracy. He had recently arranged for the purchase of 26,000 muskets in Antwerp.

[48] P.R.O., S.P. 36/113, fo. 196.   [49] P.R.O. Assi. 2/15, Staffs. Sum. 24 G. II.
[50] P.R.O., K.B. 1/10, part 1, Hilary 24 G. II, Rex vs. James & others.
[51] *Gentleman's Magazine*, vol. xx, August 1750, p. 343, vol. xxi, August 1751, p. 375.
[52] P.R.O., S.P. 36/114, fo. 83.   [53] *Ibid.*, fos. 98–100, 102–3.
[54] *Ibid.*, fo. 87. Members of five of the twelve families on the Hamstall Ridware list were in the club.

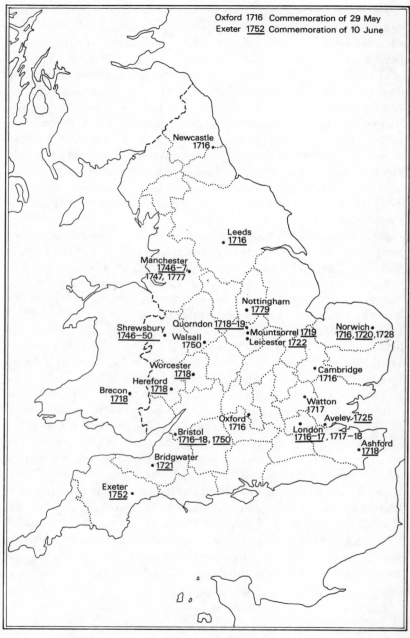

Map 5 Notable commemorations of 29 May and 10 June 1716–79

Arriving in the capital on 16 September, he met with Dr King, the Duke of Beaufort, the Earl of Westmorland and other Tory leaders, who dissuaded him from making any rash attempt. Prince Charles left London on 22 September – the Tuesday before Michaelmas.[55]

It seems very likely that the Uttoxeter Bowling Green Club had been formed to incite the disorders that broke out at Walsall on 29 May, and that the 10 June meeting at Hamstall Ridware was held to lay plans for some wider insurrection. The 26,000 muskets may have been destined for the Black Country. Certainly, the week before Michaelmas had a crucial importance in Prince Charles's scheme; the Lichfield races, which had seen previous Jacobite demonstrations, were held then. Two years later, Charles Edward issued a medal with the date 23 September 1752; it may have been a promise to return on the day after the anniversary of his last departure. All of this is speculation, but it makes sense out of the numerous scraps of enigmatic evidence, and it points towards the conclusion that the last great Jacobite gambit took place in 1750, not 1745.

The Walsall riot shows that 29 May was a day for real as well as symbolic rebellion. Its Jacobite character was not merely ritualistic or commemorative; it was actively treasonable and insurrectionary. Restoration day was a time for an aggressive affirmation of loyalty to the exiled Stuarts, not for wistful remembrance. After Walsall in 1750, however, little is known about the Jacobite 29 May. The day undoubtedly continued to be observed, but its political import may have faded along with Prince Charles's hopes. The last mention of Jacobitism on Restoration day was made by Samuel Curwen, an American Loyalist who was passing through Manchester on 29 May 1777. His Jacobite landlady informed him that all those 'in the abdicated family's interest, which is here openly professed' were in the habit of 'putting up large Oak boughs over their doors on 29 May to express joy at the glorious Event of the restoration of the Stuart family to the English throne; many such I saw'.[56] Manchester, of course, was exceptional in its enduring Jacobitism. Elsewhere, Restoration day was becoming 'Oak Apple day', a harmless festival of spring. Nevertheless, in many places the practice of attacking 'Whigs' who refused to wear oak boughs on 29 May survived.[57] This custom was the last vestige of the vigorous Jacobite politics of Restoration day.

[55] Petrie, *The Jacobite Movement: The Last Phase*, pp. 142–5; King, *Political and Literary Anecdotes*, pp. 196–7; Mahon, *Decline of the Last Stuarts*, p. 76.
[56] Oliver, ed., *Journal of Samuel Curwen*, p. 366. I owe this reference to Douglas Hay.
[57] Bushaway, *By Rite*, pp. 74–5.

The 10th of June

Important as 29 May was to popular Jacobitism, it was often only a prelude to the central event of the Jacobite year, the birthday of James III on 10 June. Like Restoration day, 10 June was a day of festive celebration – popular Jacobite commemorations always stressed joy rather than regret, and it is interesting to note that 30 January, the Tory day of mourning, never inspired much interest in the plebeian public. The symbol of 10 June was the white rose. This unambiguous badge of disaffection for the ruling regime was also a token of love and of the spring; if it was often provocative, and could lead to violence, its connotations were at the same time amorous and gentle. Wearing the white rose was an essentially individual gesture, even when large numbers were involved. Although communal rituals were sometimes introduced on 10 June, it remained a day for personal expressions of loyalty. Plebeian protesters, after all, were not merely faces in a crowd; they were individuals who were making their own decisions about allegiance.

In some places, of course, white roses were costly items, and were worn primarily by persons of substance. In London, for example, the economics of market gardening made 10 June a rather genteel holiday. The capital was flooded with white roses in 1716, and the flower sellers reaped a fine profit from them, increasing the price of a corsage from 2d in the morning of June 9 to 10d in the evening. Labouring folk could not afford such prices. Nevertheless, several people were arrested for resisting soldiers assigned to remove the offensive flowers, and a lawyer named Musgrave was wounded by a half-pay officer who tried to pluck off his button-hole favour.[58] In 1717, more clashes took place in London between soldiers and Jacobite gentlemen on 10 June, but in the next year the government was able to suppress the white roses.[59]

Outside London, flowers were less expensive, and 10 June was observed as a plebeian festival, especially in the years after 1715. The white rose was so popular in Norwich that it was adopted on a variety of political occasions. On 10 June 1716, the Norwich Jacobites strewed the streets with sand and flowers; four days later, they appeared at the town guild day wearing white roses.[60] The Pretender's birthday in

[58] Boyer, *Political State*, vol. xi, pp. 742–4.
[59] *Weekly Journal*, no. 27, 15 June 1717; Boyer, *Political State*, vol. xv, p. 634; P.R.O., S.P. 35/16/104.
[60] *Flying Post*, no. 3819, 23 June 1716; *Norwich Gazette*, 16 June 1716. I owe this and the two following references to Kathleen Wilson.

1720 was observed with both white roses and 'clean White gloves', a wedding day custom that made reference to the recent marriage of James III to Clementina Sobieska.[61] Roses also appeared in Norwich on 29 May 1728, and a few days later at the election of a Tory mayor.[62] This was, however, the last known example of Jacobite roses in the town, although the anti-Methodist riots of 1751/2 suggest that the popular mood did not alter much in the next two decades.

Bristol, and the whole rose-covered West Country, had an equally strong tradition of plebeian celebrations on 10 June. In 1716, and again in 1718, revellers marked the day with a bonfire on Brandon Hill; there were so many white roses in the town on the latter occasion that the magistrates had to issue two proclamations against them.[63] The intervening year, 1717, saw 'some idle Sluts' appear at the main guard-house in Bristol with white roses in their bosoms. They were marched off to gaol by the soldiers 'in a sort of Mock-Triumph, beating the Whore's March, as they call it, before them'. That night, a bonfire was made on the College green.[64] It was fitting that the commemoration of James III, the 'lost lover', should be observed by (notoriously promiscuous?) women wearing tokens of affection. The women, and men, of Bristol kept up their love for the Stuarts through the next three decades. The town saw an ostentatious display of white roses on 10 June 1736, following the town magistracy's celebration of the marriage of the Hanoverian Prince of Wales; and 1750, that year of wild Jacobite dreams, saw another heavy turnout of Jacobite blooms.[65]

Large towns did not have a monopoly on the commemoration of 10 June. In the little village of Mountsorrel, Leicestershire, two women garlanded the cross with white roses on the happy day in 1719. At nearby Quorndon, where a villager had been fined in the previous year for wearing the notorious flowers, twenty people met in 1719 to fire off a gun; on the next 10 June, a man was reported to have walked about the village sporting a white rose, and making speeches about James III's right to the throne.[66] This small corner of Jacobite zeal was typical of a county dominated by gentlemen like Sir Cloberry Noel and Francis Mundy, who promised to raise 2,000 horsemen in Leices-

[61] W. Massey, 'Acta Norvicensia, 1720–1729', Norwich Record Office, MS. 217.
[62] Norwich Gazette, 4 June 1728; Norwich Mercury, 8 June 1728.
[63] Latimer, Annals of Bristol, p. 113.
[64] St. James's Evening Post, no. 321, 13 June 1717.
[65] Latimer, Annals of Bristol, pp. 196–7, 258.
[66] P.R.O., S.P. 35/16/101; S.P. 35/16/133; S.P. 35/21/111.

tershire to support a rising in 1718.[67] The town of Leicester was a hotbed of disaffection; on 10 June 1722, some of its citizens proclaimed James III at the market cross, an action probably linked to the Atterbury plot.[68] The local Whigs, headed by the Duke of Rutland, were outraged by this incident, and demanded a government enquiry. It is amusing to note that Rutland himself had been suspected of disaffection to Hanover. His father had once expressed guarded sympathy for the exiled Stuarts to Bishop Atterbury, and his father-in-law, Lord Lexinton, who had been accused of treasonable words against William III, was included on a list of Jacobite supporters sent to James III in 1721.[69]

Elite sponsorship of popular Jacobitism on 10 June was widespread. At Aveley, near Hornchurch in Essex, parishioners gathered in the church on the Pretender's birthday in 1725. The bells were rung, the villagers wore white roses, and one enthusiast hoisted a flag in his garden.[70] This was the sort of peaceful confirmation of community solidarity that was supposed to be typical of Tory government. It was an example not of 'teasing' but of ignoring the naughty Whiggish world. James III's friends, however, were often more boisterous in their loyalty. At Ashford in Kent on 10 June 1718, some tradesmen decided to go on a spree; they ran about the streets, drank the Pretender's health, rang the church bells on their knees (which must have been difficult), and honoured one of their number with a paper crown inscribed 'King James the 3rd'.[71] The main difference between this case and the orderly celebration at Aveley was that the Essex folk were abetted by their parson, while the Kentish men had to make their own fun, and supply their own bell-ringing legitimation.

The celebration of 10 June was not always peaceful or purely commemorative; it could be violent, and at times it had insurrectionary implications. The remainder of this section will consider five such incidents for which a considerable body of information has survived. They took place at Hereford in 1718, Bridgwater in 1721, Shrewsbury in 1750, Exeter in 1752 and Nottingham in 1779. All of these riots reflected a national political context, but they also provide insight into the local conditions that brought about Jacobite unrest.

The Hereford affair was a baffling episode. On 29 May 1718, a

---

67 Sedgwick, ed., *History of Parliament*, vol. ii, p. 296.
68 P.R.O., S.P. 44/123, pp. 113, 229–30, 341–2.
69 H.M.C., *Stuart*, vol. v, p. 118, vol vi, p. 288; H.M.C., *Eleventh Report, Appendix, Part VII*. (London, 1889), p. 35.
70 P.R.O., S.P. 35/57/8.   71 P.R.O., S.P. 44/79A, pp. 162–4, 293.

group of riotous youths demonstrated in the town; among them was the apprentice to a tanner named Benjamin Crow.[72] At 1 a.m. on the morning of 10 June, according to his own testimony, a clothworker, Charles Awbrey, was woken by the sound of the town crier making a proclamation; later, he heard a solemn voice intoning something behind the Greyhound Inn. The next day, Benjamin Crow allegedly came to Awbrey with a white rose in his hand and 'in a sneering way' asked if he had heard the Pretender proclaimed the previous night; when Awbrey replied that he had, Crow assured him that he was mistaken, that it had been declared against the Pretender. This must have been hard to believe from a man carrying a white rose. A second witness deposed, however, that he too had heard noises at 2 a.m. on 10 June, and that someone in By Street had been reciting poetry. A shoemaker claimed to have encountered two gentlemen near the Chain Causeway who were bellowing things like 'down with the Round heads' and 'God bless the King & God send him safe home'.[73]

Although Benjamin Crow's friends tried to defend him by accusing Charles Awbrey himself of proclaiming James III, his case was damaged by an accusation made by Anne Lewis, the wife of a local gentleman. She had been standing at the vicarage, talking to the parson's wife, at midnight on 10 June, when William Preece or Price approached her, reproved her for not wearing a white rose in her bosom, and told her he had been at the Market House drinking the Pretender's health with 100 others; he then spoke the words quoted at the beginning of this chapter. Presented for seditious words at Hereford Assizes, Price was bailed by Benjamin Crow, who provided a surety in £50, a massive sum for a tanner. Eventually, Price was acquitted of his crime, which may show the confusion of the jury – what was Anne Lewis doing at the vicarage at midnight? – or perhaps its political sympathies.[74] Hereford was Harley territory, and in the spring and summer of 1718 the Earl of Oxford was busily raising money among his family and friends to finance what was left of the Swedish Plot.[75] The spectral gentlemen on the Chain Causeway may have known something of the Earl's efforts. Worcester and Brecon, two other towns within the domains of the Harley–Foley clique, also saw disturbances on 10 June 1718 – at Brecon, Bishop Hoadly was attacked by an angry mob.[76] The

[72] Ibid., pp. 159–60.   [73] Ibid., pp. 157–9.
[74] Ibid., pp. 156–7; P.R.O. Assi. 2/6, Hereford Aut. 4, 5 G. I, Qua. 5 G.I.
[75] H.M.C., Stuart, vol. v, p. 456.
[76] P.R.O., S.P. 44/79A, pp. 180–1; S.P. 35/12/75.

Hereford incident may have been part of a broad conspiracy, but it was also marked by petty rivalries, like the animosity between Charles Awbrey and Benjamin Crow.

The great riot at Bridgwater in 1721 had no obvious connection with Jacobite plotting. The roots of unrest in the town lay in local tensions between an aggressive group of Whigs and a Tory-dominated corporation whose members did not disguise their Jacobite tendencies. Of course, the truth about the situation in Bridgwater is clouded by the biases of the Whigs who provided most of the evidence against their rivals – they included the historian John Oldmixon, a customs officer in the town.[77] A Whig councillor accused the Tory mayor in 1716 of drinking to James III and having 'The King shall enjoy his own again ' played at a tavern; in the folowing year, some dragoons shot at the innkeeper of this tavern, who had refused to drink damnation to Sacheverell.[78] In the summer of 1721, the Secretary of State was deluged with reams of confusing and contradictory testimony about an alleged riot at Bridgwater on 10 June.[79] The dragoons stationed in the town claimed that they had been attacked by the townspeople, who responded with assertions that the dragoons had beaten several of them at random, without provocation.

On the morning of 10 June, according to the soldiers, a patrol in the Shambles, while trying to remove a white rose from a woman's bosom, was pelted with stones and dirt by a crowd led by a butcher's son. That evening in Eastover, across the river, another group of dragoons attempting to take white roses from some washerwomen was also attacked by 'a great many women'. A large crowd then followed them through the streets, calling out names at them, and vowing they would wear white roses 'in spite of King George and all his Rogues'. The dragoons later returned in greater strength and assaulted several men who were wearing Jacobite tokens. Lionel Farley, an overseer of the poor, whose maid was sporting one of the favours, was arrested for brandishing a loaded pistol. That night, when Lieutenant Colonel Hamilton went to Eastover to question the butcher whose son had led the first riot, he was threatened with knives and cleavers and had to fight his way back across the bridge.[80]

---

[77] His reports are in P.R.O., S.P. 35/27/23 and 35/27/59. See also J. P. W. Rogers, 'John Oldmixon in Bridgwater 1716–30', *Proceedings of the Somersetshire Archaeological and Natural History Society*, 113 (1968–9), pp. 86–98.

[78] I. M. Slocombe, 'A Bridgwater Riot, 1717', *Proceedings of the Somersetshire Archaeological and Natural History Society*, 106 (1961–2), pp. 66–76.

[79] P.R.O., S.P. 35/27/52–4, fos. 218–44.

[80] P.R.O., S.P. 35/27/15; S.P. 35/27/42a; S.P. 35/27/52, fos. 220–1; S.P. 35/27/57.

The townspeople denied these stories, maintaining that there had been no white roses, and that the soldiers had made unwarranted attacks on them. It is clear that the dragoons were excessively violent – they beat several people mercilessly – although they were restrained from firing on the crowd. On the other hand, it is hard to credit the total innocence of the inhabitants of Eastover, whose testimony was blatantly orchestrated by the town's Tory magistrates in order to bewilder the government with masses of conflicting evidence. If the riots did take place, as seems certain, they conformed to patterns of Jacobite disorder that have been observed elsewhere. They resembled a series of street fights between rival gangs; the people of Eastover were guarding their own province, whose boundaries were demarcated by white roses, against the hated occupying troops. The mayor of Bridgwater's wife had taunted the dragoons by daring them to go into the Shambles.[81] The rioters were not simply territorial, however; they kept to the traditions of the day by wearing Jacobite flowers, and by festooning the Cornhill and the officers' quarters with garlands of roses, oak and horns. The soldiers took these rituals seriously enough to counter them by carrying warming pans around the town.[82]

Women were in the forefront of the Bridgwater riots. The mayor's wife herself reportedly appeared on 10 June 'Stuck over with White Roses'.[83] This female prominence imparted the message that the Pretender's birthday was a love-feast. Yet the women were accused of considerable violence, and they were backed up by a formidable phalanx of butchers. This was neither the first nor the last time that a Jacobite riot was played out to the accompaniment of the rough music of marrow-bones and cleavers. The burly, well-armed butchers were natural leaders of crowds; their High Church politics were rooted in the trade itself, with its links to farming, its close corporate organization and its pride in a rather unpleasant profession, which engendered a hostility to 'outsiders' and to those who threatened the established order. Butchers, it seems, have always been Tories.[84] It is

81 P.R.O., S.P. 35/27/23.
82 P.R.O., S.P. 35/27/53, fos. 235–6; S.P. 35/27/54, fo. 244.
83 P.R.O., S.P. 35/27/23.
84 See J. R. Vincent, *Pollbooks: How Victorians Voted* (Cambridge, 1967), pp. 10–11, 16, for nineteenth-century examples. Vincent provides no explanation of the conservatism of butchers; perhaps he should poll some of his readers in the *Sun*. For an international dimension to the politics of butchers, see John Merriman, 'Incident at the Statue of the Virgin Mary: The Conflict of Old and New in Nineteenth-Century Limoges', in J. M. Merriman, ed., *Consciousness and Class Experience in Nineteenth-Century Europe* (New York, 1980), pp. 129–48.

not surprising to find that almost no Bridgwater butchers joined Monmouth's Rebellion in 1685, although the town provided a large number of recruits for the Duke.[85]

The Bridgwater riot involved violence on both sides. The Shrewsbury brawl of 1750, on the other hand, was entirely the fault of some zealous dragoons. After the '45, 10 June became a popular event in Shrewsbury; the maypoles were adorned with white roses every year on the happy day, and in 1749 white flags were carried about the town, emblazoned with 'Long Live Prince Charles'.[86] The troops stationed there were aware of the sympathies of the inhabitants, and they were looking for trouble on the night of 9 June 1750, when a patrol happened to pass the house of a master bricklayer named Richards. He was paying his labourers and, as was his custom, enjoying a mug of ale with them. In anticipation of the glorious tenth, they were singing lustily:

> Charley's red & Charley's white
> and Charley is bonny O,
> He is the Son of a Royal King
> and I love him the best of any O.
>
> When he came to Darby Town
> Oh, but he was bonny O
> The Bells did ring, & the bagpipes play
> And all for the love of Charley, O.

'This is a rebellious Song, and they are Rebels that sing it', one of the dragoons sagely remarked, to which a woman sitting at the door of a nearby almshouse replied, 'You are Rebels, & they are the true Subjects'. The enraged troopers chased off the woman, broke into the house, and beat several of the bricklayers. A case against the dragoons was later brought before King's Bench by several of their victims, who must have had powerful friends, but it was unsuccessful.[87]

In Shrewsbury, 10 June was apparently a day for the relaxation of social divisions, for the master to drink with his labourers. It was a day for serenading a lost love, the bonny Highland Laddie dressed in plaid. It was a day for singing rebellious Scottish airs about the 'young adventurer'; and it was Charlie's day more than his father's. The transposition of the romantic cult of Prince Charles onto his father's birthday represents the passing of an older tradition of Jacobite

---

[85] Earle, *Monmouth's Rebels*, p. 204.   [86] P.R.O., S.P. 36/113, fo. 183.
[87] P.R.O., T.S. 11/926; P.R.O., K.B. 1/10, part 2, Michaelmas 24 G. II. The song 'Charley O' is a variation on a Scottish ditty with the same refrain – see Nodal, ed., *City Notes and Queries*, vol. iv, pp. 118, 119, 122.

political culture and the birth of a new one. The references to the rebellion may also have had an immediate significance. The insurrection that had begun two weeks earlier at Walsall may have been spreading to Shrewsbury. This was certainly the purpose of a paper posted throughout the town on 11 June:

> Honest Lads of Shrewsbury do not be frighted at the Insult you received last Night it was base & cruel it was contrary to the Laws of God and Nature therefore stand on your own Defence you have as great a Right to wear a Broad Sword as any Man whatever Wear your Swords and use them as Men as Englishmen as Men of Courage and Not against the Naked, the Decrepid the Defenceless – .[88]

This notice, reminiscent of the Shrewsbury 'Loyal Mob' proclamation of 1715, was written by someone familiar with Nonjuring literature: the phrase 'contrary to the Laws of God and Nature' might be from Kettlewell's *Case of Allegiance Settled*. The 'Honest Lads', however, did not rise, and the West Midlands plot fizzled out.

It was followed in 1752 by an even more audacious scheme, the brainchild of Charles's adviser Alexander Murray. Although the central feature of the so-called Elibank Plot was a popular uprising in London, it also called for a rebellion in Scotland, and perhaps an insurrection in the English provinces as well.[89] It is possible that the Exeter riots of 10–12 June 1752 had some connection with Murray's plans. A powerful strain of plebeian Jacobite sentiment had continued to exist in the West Country, and was aggravated by the effects of war and the quartering of soldiers in many towns. On the afternoon of 10 June 1752, two dragoons were approached at an inn in the Eastgate district of Exeter by three men who shook white roses at them, saying '*Damn you, we wear these for those we love, & will wear those in spight of you or your Master*'. Later, the trio joined a dozen townsmen who assaulted a soldier at the bowling green. That evening, a large crowd appeared in St Sydwell's parish at Nicholas Payne's Pollimore Inn, where they decorated the inn-sign with white roses. Payne cried out at some soldiers that '*he would drink Prince Charles's health forever*'. The following day, 11 June, was the anniversary of George II's accession. It was celebrated by the officers of the regiment, but not by the corporation or townspeople. On 12 June, a crowd gathered at St Sydwell's crying '*God damn the Soldiers, knock them down; knock them on the head*'. A rich maltster beat a soldier with a stick, while the

[88] P.R.O., S.P. 36/113, fo. 184.
[89] Lang, *Pickle the Spy*, p. 126; Petrie, *Jacobite Movement: The Last Phase*, pp. 145–9.

rioters roared '*God damn you, & your King too, we shall see who shall be King by & by*'.

The government eventually indicted nine men for taking part in these disturbances. They included the three who initiated the rioting in Eastgate – William Lloyd, a cordwainer, Nicholas Layton, a stay-maker, and William Fenwick or Phenix, a tailor – along with Nicholas Payne, the maltster John Burrow, a cordwainer named Edward Rice, a barber, a mariner, a pressman and Ambrose Penny, a serge weaver. As at Bridgwater in 1721, the town magistrates were clearly on the side of the Jacobite crowd, and showed their sympathies by laying a case before King's Bench against several loyalists and soldiers who had resisted the rioters.[90] The resemblance between the Exeter and Bridgwater riots goes further than this; both were attempts to defend territorial boundaries against the encroachments of King George's troops. Like Eastover in Bridgwater, or the Hill Top at Walsall, St Sydwell's parish was outside the town centre, and beyond government control – it was also the poorest and most populous area of Exeter.[91]

The St Sydwell protesters sought to extend their territory, however, by invading Eastgate, and attacking soldiers with an unusual ferocity. They wore white roses 'for those we love', but violence rather than amorousness characterized their behaviour, and women were conspicuously absent from their vanguard. Their aggressiveness, and their words – 'we shall see who will be King by and by' – suggest that the Exeter rioters may have had some inkling of the developing plan for a Jacobite rising. Sir John Astley had visited France in March to consult with Prince Charles, accompanied by his son-in-law, Anthony Langley Swymmer, M.P. for Southampton. Swymmer journeyed on to Boulogne and to Rome, where King James conferred a military commission on him in September.[92] Around the same time, Charles Edward issued the mysterious medal dated 23 September 1752. If the Exeter rioters had known about the conspiracy, they must have been very excited at the end of September. In fact, on 26 September, Nicholas Layton, William Fenwick, Ambrose Penny, Edward Rice and Humphrey Thomas, a cordwainer, met at an Exeter inn, where they

90 P.R.O., T.S. 23/21; [Jenkins], *History of Exeter*, p. 205.
91 W. G. Hoskins, *Industry, Trade and People in Exeter, 1688–1800* (Manchester and Exeter, 1935, 1968), pp. 112–13, 115–21.
92 Sedgwick, ed., *History of Parliament*, vol. i, p. 424, vol. ii, p. 459; Lang, *Pickle the Spy*, pp. 190, 213; R.A., Stuart 336/7, 337/162, 338/69, 338/137; Ruvigny, *Jacobite Peerage*, p. 245.

drank to James III and thrashed two loyalists who refused the health.[93] Their celebration was premature. The arrest of the Jacobite agent Thomas Anderson at Perth may have delayed the anticipated rising, and when Dr Archibald Cameron was taken in Scotland in March 1753, Murray's plot was indefinitely postponed.

After 1753, there were no more grand conspiracies, and Jacobitism entered its long twilight. Yet it would be erroneous to assume that after forty years, the cause of the exiled Stuarts simply vanished. Evidence of its lingering effects has been presented in previous chapters, and the stubborn survival of Jacobite sentiment in Lancashire until the late 1770s was noted above. For die-hard adherents of Charles Edward, the spring of 1779 must have seemed more promising than any time in the last twenty years. Defeats in America had embarrassed George III and broadened the war; France now controlled the Channel, and an invasion seemed imminent. The indefatigable John Baptist Caryll was again approaching an unreceptive French government with plans for a Jacobite attempt in Scotland.[94] In Parliament, the old Tory country gentlemen were drifting away from Lord North's ministry and into opposition. Among them was Sir Charles Sedley, M.P. for Nottingham, who had marched with the Lichfield mob of 1747. In national politics, he was friendly to Rockingham, but in his constituency he was 'the darling of the high church party', which was 'headed by butchers, who .. taught their dogs to bark at a signal, against their opponents, which they called barking *Sedley only!*'. After Sedley's death in 1778, Whigs and Tories in Nottingham elected a compromise candidate to represent the framework-knitting industry.[95]

In 1779, the Nottingham hosiers reduced wages for the framework-knitters, who responded by petitioning Parliament for a raise. The Tory butchers led the subscription effort; but in June 1779, the petition was rejected by the House of Commons. 'This news arrived in Nottingham', Gravenor Henson informs us, 'on the 10th of June, which was then a great holiday amongst the Tories or Jacobites, who wore white roses, in honor of the Pretender, who was said to have been born on that day.' Without doubt, these Tories or Jacobites included many

[93] P.R.O., T.S. 23/21; B.L., Add. MS. 39,923, fos. 144–5.
[94] Paul de Perugia, *La Tentative d'Invasion de l'Angleterre de 1779* (Paris, 1939), pp. 50–1; see also R.A., Stuart 497/122.
[95] Sir Lewis Namier and John Brooke, eds., *History of Parliament: The House of Commons, 1754–90* (3 vols., London, 1964), vol. iii, p. 419; Gravenor Henson, *The Civil, Political and Mechanical History of the Framework-Knitters, in Europe and America ... Vol. i* (Nottingham, 1831), pp. 383–401.

stalwart butchers. That night, their allies the framework-knitters, infuriated by the rejection of their plea for just wages, attacked the houses of the hosiers, destroying hundreds of frames. They also damaged the mills owned by Richard Arkwright, who, ironically enough, had voted for the Tory-Jacobite candidates in the 1768 Preston election.[96]

If 10 June was still 'a great holiday' in Nottingham in 1779, was it also preserved in other towns? Nothing is known of this. Yet the relationship between Sir Charles Sedley, the butchers and the unhappy framework-knitters exemplifies the preservation of a coalition of Tory gentlemen and tradesmen with skilled labourers, the same coalition that had sustained Jacobitism under the first two Georges. This political alliance had been strong in many of England's expanding industrial areas, like Lancashire and the West Midlands, and it contributed to the growth of a plebeian political consciousness that expressed itself after 1790 in popular radicalism. Preston, Manchester, Leeds, Walsall, Birmingham, Leicester, Nottingham and Norwich witnessed considerable Jacobite unrest between 1715 and 1760 – sometimes even later. After 1780, all of these industrial towns were centres of radicalism. The links between the two political phenomena remain obscure. The roses of 10 June had withered to ashes by the time the English working class was born; but their sweet aroma may have wafted around the cradle. In the reigns of the first two Hanoverians, they had been in full bloom, and had provided a heady scent of defiance. The men and women who wore them, however, did not just proclaim their dislike of King George, his Whig ministers and his dragoons; they declared an allegiance 'to those we love', to a different party and another king.

Jacobite counter-theatre

The commemoration of 29 May and 10 June evolved into an elaborate theatre of Jacobite ritual; anti-Hanoverian demonstrations, by contrast, relied on a counter-theatre of mockery and satirical imitation to deflate and debunk ceremonies honouring the ruling house. Of course, Jacobite festivals made use of derision, as at Walsall in 1750, and anti-Hanoverian protests often involved affirmations of loyalty to the Stuarts, so that the distinction between theatre and counter-theatre was

[96] Henson, *Civil, Political and Mechanical History*, pp. 401–10; Dobson, *Representation of Preston*, p. 38.

never absolute. Nevertheless, anti-Hanoverian incidents were rarely as elaborate or as politically explicit as Jacobite commemorations; they tend to resemble sporadic outbursts rather than settled traditions.

The observance of George I's accession day on 1 August elicited minor, localized reactions from his detractors. Gentlefolk might appear in mourning, wearing black cloaks or symbolic plants like rue and thyme to show their regret at the passing of Queen Anne and the reign of her successor. Plebeian Jacobites seldom stirred on this day, except in London. The Bridewell boys attacked a loyalist household in Blackfriars on 1 August 1715; in 1716, and again in 1718, Thomas Lister of St Leonard's, Shoreditch, was abused by his neighbours for illuminating his windows on the accession day.[97] At Halesworth in Suffolk, the pillory was decorated with a pair of bullock's horns hung with turnips on 1 August 1717.[98]

The only major riot on George's accession day took place at Harwich in 1724, when 200 or 300 fishermen appeared at the town hall, where the mayor and other loyalists were making merry. Led by 'a Person Dressed up with Horns and Crying out here is your King George', who was carried on a chair, the fishermen later ushered Daniel Smith senior, a Tory alderman, back to his house. Two days later, Daniel Smith junior and Captain George Fairlie bedecked a fisherman with ribbons and a drum, and sent him about the streets to beat up a crowd. As he passed the mayor, he 'turned up his Backside & Clapt his Hand on it & drummed roundhead Cuckolds &c.'. The Smiths and Captain Fairlie denied that there was any harm in their sport; they were supported by twenty Tory corporation members, and sixteen owners or masters of fishing vessels, who signed certificates blaming everything on the hysteria of the mayor.[99] Yet the government was justly suspicious; the M.P. for Harwich, and ally of the Smiths, was Humphry Parsons, a London brewer who was one of James III's chief contacts in the capital.[100] Parsons, who owed his considerable fortune to the beer trade with France, may have been involved in smuggling, a major activity for Essex fishermen. Significantly, the Whig interest at Harwich was based on the customs office there.

The disorders at Harwich, however, cannot be wholly understood in

[97] Rogers, 'Popular Protest', p. 76; Fitts, 'Newcastle's Mob', p. 46; P.R.O., S.P. 35/4/34; S.P. 35/7/11; S.P. 35/12/96; S.P.35/12/96 (i).
[98] P.R.O., S.P. 44/79A, pp. 111, 114–15.
[99] P.R.O., S.P. 35/51/3; S.P. 35/51/41; S.P.35/54/56–8; S.P. 44/124, pp. 65–8, 114–32.
[100] P.R.O., S.P. 44/124, p. 18; S.P. 35/51/3; Sedgwick, ed., History of Parliament, vol. i, p. 242, vol. ii, p. 326.

terms of local politics or the economics of contraband. They also involved a popular counter-theatre that drew upon the concept of the 'Lord of Misrule'. The horned cuckold 'king' was the centre of the Carnival on 1 August. He was a living effigy of misrule, a ludicrous reminder of George I's unfitness as a monarch. Two days later, a second 'Lord of Misrule' appeared, who poked fun at authority with his saucy gestures. The ambiguous symbolism of the two events was deliberate. A real king should not be a fool – this was the message of the 1 August antics – but a plebeian 'king' could turn up his backside at the mayor, to show his contempt for unjust authority. An ideal of 'good government' can be detected through the anarchic appearance of 'misrule'; the Carnival king can be seen as embodying a notion of order as well as legitimizing disorder. The perfect ruler was certainly not 'your King George'; more likely, he was 'our Jemmy'.

George I's coronation day, which had produced so many riots in 1714, witnessed further disorders on its first anniversary. In London, some members of the Honourable Artillery Company were insulted on their way to a loyalist celebration by a High Church mob.[101] A loyalist bonfire in Birmingham was attacked to cries of 'Down with the Roundheads, and the Rump, no Kingkillers, Sacheverel for ever'; one rioter bet a shilling that 'he'll come yet', meaning James III, and another burned a beef heart, saying it was King George's own.[102] A similar incident occurred at Abingdon in the following year, and at Ellesmere in Shropshire a cobbler, a shoemaker and two other men assaulted loyal revellers by 'shooting peas' at them.[103] These were violent demonstrations, whose counter-theatre was largely restricted to defiance. It soon became evident, however, that coronation festivities could not be stopped, and 1716 saw the last attempts to silence loyal celebrations on 20 October.

Hanoverian birthdays, on the other hand, were less widely observed by Whigs, and could more easily be subverted by Jacobites. As has been shown, 28 May was deliberately ignored by George I's adversaries, who saved their energies for the following day. The Prince of Wales's birthday on 30 October brought disorders to Oxford in 1716; soldiers marking the event were threatened by a crowd in Eastgate that threw 'dirty Turnip-Tops' at them, The outraged troops then went on their

---

101 *Flying Post*, no. 3768, 25 Feb. 1715/16.
102 *St James's Evening Post*, no. 63, 22 Oct. 1715.
103 *Flying Post*, no. 3872, 23 Oct 1716; P.R.O., Assi. 2/5, Salop, Qua. 3 G. I; Assi. 5/37, part 2, Salop, Qua. 3 G. I, indts. Joseph Jeffry *et al.*, John Rogers, Richard Tydder, Thomas Bowker.

own terrorist spree, breaking unilluminated windows, threatening townspeople and firing on the mayor, who tried to stop them. A number of Tory peers, not all of them Jacobites, lodged a protest against the soldiers in the House of Lords, pointing out quite rightly that few people celebrated the Prince of Wales's birthday anyway, so that the broken windows might have belonged to Hanoverian supporters.[104]

Jacobite counter-theatre was developing into a response to extraordinary manifestations of Hanoverian loyalty. It continued to menace unusually zealous Whig celebrations until well into the reign of George II. In Bristol, Whig attempts to observe royal holidays with unprecedented displays of fireworks were violently undermined in 1735. On George II's accession day, a crowd of Kingswood colliers and local artisans, joined by two brewers and a gentleman, ransacked the houses of loyalists, and publicly burnt fireworks in the form of a dragon and crown, as well as 50 pounds of tallow candles. The rioters, who included several weavers, did not hesitate to pilfer the loom and tools of a Whig artisan, demonstrating that trade solidarity did not extend across political lines.[105] The loyalists tried again with elaborate fireworks on George II's birthday, depicting the King's cypher above an orange, from which issued a spear wounding a dragon; the Jacobite mob pelted the magnificent scenario with dirt and stones, and destroyed it.[106]

These special commemorations, and the anti-Hanoverian reactions to them, took place in the wake of the uproar caused by the Excise Bill and the elections of 1734. The two rebellions produced similar rises in the political temperature, and inspired short-lived waves of anti-Hanoverian violence. In London, a crowd assaulted loyalists in Holborn on 7 June 1716, the thanksgiving day for the suppression of the '15.[107] Manchester Jacobites, led by one of the Dickinsons, at whose house Prince Charles Edward had lodged in 1745, manhandled their rivals on the Duke of Cumberland's birthday in 1746.[108] The circumstances of these disturbances, however, were exceptional, and they did not succeed in preventing future celebrations of Hanoverian victory over the Stuarts.

Anti-Hanoverian protest had fizzled out by 1760. Although George III

---

[104] Boyer, *Political State*, vol. xii, pp. 419–44, 505–31.   [105] P.R.O., K.B. 33/5/3.
[106] Latimer, *Annals of Bristol*, p. 193.   [107] *Flying Post*, no. 3818, 21 June 1716.
[108] P.R.O., T.S. 20/37, fo. 8. The Dickinson house in Market Street was ever afterwards known as 'the Palace'.

Map 6 Anti-Hanoverian riots, 1715–80

was later much reviled by the Wilkite press, his commemoration days never inspired the sort of popular counter-theatre that had marred the feasts of his predecessors. This suggests that the monarch was not a 'natural' target for plebeian demonstrators. The anti-Hanoverianism of 1715–60, moreover, should not be regarded as mere 'political blasphemy'; like the anti-monarchism of the 1790s or of 1815–20, it was closely tied to a broader political culture, namely Jacobitism. Interestingly, one of the few anti-Hanoverian disorders of the early reign of George III occurred at Nottingham in 1780, where a crowd clashed with guard officers and broke no fewer than 168 sash windows on 4 June, the King's birthday.[109] The incident becomes more comprehensible when it is recalled that on 10 June 1779, Nottingham was host to the last known Jacobite commemoration. As in former times, anti-Hanoverianism and Jacobitism went hand-in-hand.

London and Westminster

Between 1715 and 1722, popular Jacobitism disturbed the peace of almost every important English town. Only a few naval ports like Portsmouth or Plymouth were untouched by it. It died out quickly, however, in places where Whig political or economic power was strong, like Liverpool, Hull or Sheffield, and it survived only fitfully in towns that had much to lose from rebelliousness, like Newcastle-upon-Tyne. By 1722, it had been weeded out of the provincial south-east, the East Midlands and Yorkshire; it remained strong in Lancashire, the West Midlands, East Anglia and the south-west. The Atterbury debacle stunned plebeian Jacobites into quiescence, as it did their elite counterparts; only at Bristol and Norwich did seditious disorders continue with frequency into the late 1720s and 1730s. In the strongholds of Stuart sentiment, however, unrest lurked just below the surface of stability. The '45 brought it out again, and the next decade was disturbed by Jacobite riots and demonstrations at Manchester, Lichfield, Oxford, Bristol, Newcastle, Walsall, Shrewsbury, Norwich, Exeter and Leicester. Yet the situation of 1715 was not recreated; Jacobitism was confined to larger towns, where Whig control was less easily exercised. By 1754, the revival had ended, although the vestiges of popular adherence to the exiled family did not disappear until at least 1780.

These neat generalizations do not apply to London, which must be

[109] Geoffrey Trease, *Nottingham: A Biography* (London, 1970), p. 158.

treated as a special case. Nicholas Rogers has compiled an exhaustive account of the many Jacobite disturbances of 1715–16 in the capital and its suburbs, Westminster and Southwark, which culminated in the street fights between gangs of 'Jacks' and 'Muggites', members of Whig-sponsored Mug-houses.[110] By the end of 1716, this period of almost continuous rioting had passed. Jacobite holidays were observed by a few people until 1719, but serious disorders had subsided in London, and never resurfaced. Why did this happen?

The capital of England was, to a large extent, a self-contained world. In the early eighteenth century, it was still a remarkably medieval city, and the foundations of its economic, religious and social life were corporate institutions of considerable antiquity. The government of the City operated along the rudimentarily democratic lines of a commune of the Middle Ages. Trade solidarities were of the utmost importance; the aldermen were backed by trade guilds, and Common Councilmen relied for support on organized groups of artisans and tradesmen in the wards. The religious role of the guilds was particularly important; they had their own churches and chose their own ministers. The Church of England had always been very active in the capital, even in the difficult days of the 1680s; its power and prestige were visible not only in the innumerable City churches, but also in charitable concerns like the hospitals and infirmaries. The growth of the great trading Companies had strengthened the corporate character of London, because they too were centralized regulatory bodies, that blocked the spread of individual enterprise. Of course, similar institutions were found in other English towns; but the influence of local gentry families, the weakness of civic government, and the decline of the ancient guilds and Companies allowed more independence to persist in the provinces than in the capital.

The ferment of the seventeenth century demonstrated the peculiarities of London's politics. London was as divided as anywhere in the realm, but those who ran its institutions were able to sway its politics in certain directions: for Parliament in 1642, for the King in 1660, against Popery in 1679, for the King again in 1681–2, for William of Orange in 1688. The centralization of City institutions led to the deceptive appearance of unanimity. Political movements supported by

110 Rogers, 'Popular Protest'. See also Fitts, 'Newcastle's Mob'; [John] Doran, *London in the Jacobite Times* (2 vols., 1877), vol. i; John Timbs, *Clubs and Club Life in London* (London, 1872), pp. 38–47; Robert Chambers, ed., *The Book of Days* (2 vols., Edinburgh, 1863), vol. ii, pp. 109–12.

the big merchants could quickly win control in the capital; but as Charles II discovered in 1682, mastery of Common Hall, of the guilds and the City churches could put an abrupt end to opposition. Like any medieval town, London's political identity was vested in its corporate structures, and the City would not fight against itself. In this way, however, it differed from a polarized nation where rebellion and civil war were always possible.[111]

In 1715, one of London's corporate foundations, the Church of England, was largely alienated from the new regime. Most of the popular preachers in the capital – Atterbury, Sacheverell, Welton, Mynors – were Jacobites. Richard Welton's congregation at Whitechapel rioted against a Whig preacher in October 1714; the boys of Bridewell, where Atterbury had been lecturer, became notorious for taking part in Jacobite demonstrations; and the restive crowds in Sacheverell's parish of St Andrew's Holborn were discussed in the last chapter.[112] The vestry of St Martin's-in-the-Fields was accused of raising money for the encouragement of riots.[113] In June 1716, the curate of St George's Southwark was dismissed when his rector and a nearby Whig Mug-house were attacked by a High Church mob.[114] A month later, a former Bridewell boy named Daniel Vaughan, who had been awarded the Locke gift to start his own small-coals business, was shot dead at the head of the rioters storming the Salisbury Court Mug-house in Fleet Street.[115] Jacobitism was equally apparent in City government. A Whig club listed twenty-three former, current and future Common Councilmen as 'disaffected' in 1715, shortly before the Tories won an overwhelming majority on the Common Council.[116] This victory was greatly aided by Jacobite elements in the Church. In Portsoken ward, Peter Monger, a rabidly Jacobite brewer, was elected by the votes of Dr Welton's congregation, in spite of a warrant for his arrest on a charge of high treason.[117]

[111] For a comparison of London with provincial towns that differs from the views proposed here, see Nicholas Rogers, 'The Urban Opposition to Whig Oligarchy', in M. and J. Jacob, eds., The Origins of Anglo-American Radicalism (London and Boston, 1984), pp. 132–48.

[112] Account of the Riots, p. 13; Boyer, Political State, vol. viii, pp. 438–9; Fitts, 'Newcastle's Mob', p. 46; E. G. O'Donoghue, Bridewell Hospital, Palace, Prison, Schools, from the death of Elizabeth to Modern Times (London, 1929), pp. 180–3.

[113] Flying Post, no. 3772, 13 March 1715/16.   [114] Ibid., no 3821, 28 June 1716.

[115] O'Donoghue, Bridewell Hospital, p. 186.

[116] Henry Horwitz, W. A. Speck and W. A. Grey, eds., London Politics 1713–1717, London Record Society Publications, 17 (1981), pp. 7, 47–51.

[117] Matthews, ed., Diary of Dudley Ryder, pp. 155–6.

Its very success, however, brought about the decline of Jacobitism in London. Disaffection could infiltrate the institutions of the capital, but it could not survive in organizations that were so susceptible to government pressure. The churches, charity schools and hospitals were purged with ruthless thoroughness by the summer of 1716. The Common Council evinced more concern for narrow City interests than for assisting the Pretender, and in 1725 its powers were curbed by Walpole.[118] The guilds and the trading Companies had never wavered in their loyalty to King George, and they became bulwarks of Hanoverianism in the capital. Government intervention also took the form of anti-Jacobite violence or state terror. The creation of the Mug-houses, situated, as James Fitts has pointed out, in areas of extreme unrest, was a brilliant stroke.[119] It need not be assumed that the Whig mob was more genteel than the plebeian 'Jacks'; Dissenting or Low Church weavers and tradesmen were plentiful enough to provide a crowd of lower-class loyalists.[120] The victory of the 'Muggites' was aided by the Riot Act, under whose provisions five 'Jacks' were executed for the attack on Read's Salisbury Court Mug-house in July 1716.[121] The whole force of the law, the army and the 'Muggites' was mustered against Jacobitism in London; moreover, the friends of the Stuarts were forced to rely on institutions that were designed to preserve corporate unity above all else.

After its popular moment had passed, Jacobitism in the capital was forced to adopt a variety of different strategies. Within City politics, it became elitist, infusing the politics of wealthy aldermen like Humphry Parsons, John Barber, Francis Child, George Heathcote and William Benn. It also clung to shadowy groups like the clandestine printers or the remnants of the Nonjurors, and it lingered among Irish immigrants. Finally, it moved outside the walls. This was a common enough occurrence; as has been seen, popular Jacobitism tended to migrate into populous suburbs — Eastover, the Hill Top, St Sydwell's — where it

118 For London politics in this period, see C. J. Henderson, *London and the National Government, 1721–1742* (Durham, North Carolina, 1945), and Nicholas Rogers, 'Resistance to Oligarchy: The City Opposition to Walpole and his Successors, 1725–47', in John Stevenson, ed., *London in the Age of Reform* (Oxford, 1977), pp. 1–29.

119 Fitts, 'Newcastle's Mob', pp. 44–5.

120 This interpretation differs from Rogers, 'Popular Protest', p. 78. His own statistics on page 86 show that eleven out of sixty Jacobite rioters were gentlemen or genteel tradesmen — were the 'Muggites' more elitist than this?

121 Boyer, *Political State*, vol. xii, pp. 227–35; *The Case of the Five Rioters* (London, 1716), Bodl. fol. θ 662.

could less easily be suppressed. In Westminster, Jacobite sentiment was able to find a more secure popular base.

Nicholas Rogers has argued that the 'independence' of Westminster tradesmen, particularly those involved in victualling, offered fertile ground for opposition politics; but it should be added that many Tory magnates like the Duke of Ormonde or the Grosvenors had important interests in the borough.[122] Atterbury had used his influence as Dean of Westminster to return two Jacobites for the constituency in 1722, amidst scenes of rioting at the hustings; they were unseated on petition.[123] Using the powerful lever of Whig patronage, the Court was able to dominate Westminster politics for almost two decades thereafter. In 1741, however, the candidacy of the tremendously popular opposition Whig Admiral Edward Vernon led to fresh disorders at the polls and a blatant Court attempt to rig the election. A club called the Independent Electors of Westminster was formed to promote a petition to Parliament calling for an annulment of the returns. Although not at its inception a Jacobite body, the Independent Electors may have inspired a plan devised around 1743 by the Nonjuror Thomas Carte for setting up local clubs to support Jacobite candidates at elections.[124] Sir Watkin Williams Wynn and Sir John Hynde Cotton were prominent early members of the Independent Electors, and the Jacobite rebel David Morgan was supposed to have been connected with the organization.[125]

In 1747, the stewards of the Electors' anniversary feast included the Earl of Lichfield, the Earl of Orrery and George Heathcote, all Jacobites. Thinly veiled healths were drunk to an unnamed king, who was toasted 'over the water', and 'To all those that dare to be honest'. A man was caught making notes of the meeting; identified as an innkeeper who was lodging a witness against Lord Lovat, he was beaten and thrown out.[126] Accusations of disaffection, however, contributed to a heavy defeat for the Electors at the 1747 election, when one of their candidates was the Jacobite Sir Thomas Dyke. Two years later, Lord Egmont estimated that only 1,000 of Westminster's 7,000 voters were Jacobites; but this conservative estimate was still a substantial

---

[122] Rogers, 'Aristocratic Clientage'.
[123] Sedgwick, ed., *History of Parliament*, vol. i, p. 286.
[124] Rogers, 'Aristocratic Clientage', pp. 74–5; R. W. Greaves, 'A Scheme for the Counties', *English Historical Review*, 48, 192 (1933), pp. 630–8.
[125] Rogers, 'Aristocratic Clientage', p. 75; Stephens, ed., *Catalogue*, vol. iii, no. 2859, p. 646.
[126] *Gentleman's Magazine*, vol. xvii, March 1747, pp. 150, 152.

number.[127] The Independent Electors may have become an exclusively Jacobite club by this time. When a Scottish Nonjuror attended one of their meetings in May 1749, he was distressed by their low status, but delighted by their toasts and songs:

The 1st toast was prosperity to Ch— and King; the 2d to the Prince; the 3d to the Independent Electors of Westminster . . . The 4th toast was to the P— again; the 5th to the next Royal visitation; . . . and the last that I witness'd was in these words: May the late ridiculous undertaking of fireworks illuminate the minds of every true Briton. Betwixt the toasts we were entertain'd with some songs, such as the 'Highland Ladie,' 'A Hero from fair Clementina,' 'The Character of a Whig', etc.[128]

The last 'Royal visitation' had been in 1745, the illuminations referred to were in commemoration of the victory at Culloden, and 'The Character of a Whig' was a Jacobite song of the 1690s.

The fortunes of the Independent Electors were reversed later in 1749, when a by-election united all the anti-Court factions behind an opposition Whig candidate. Although the government won a narrow victory, the Independent Electors, led by Lord Elibank's brother, Alexander Murray, organized a petition against the returning officer. Murray himself was called to the bar of the House of Commons, however, on a charge of intimidation at the polls. Appearing in February 1751, he refused to kneel at the bar, and the offended House ordered him confined to Newgate. He was released from prison in June, and was accompanied to his house by a huge crowd of sympathizers, headed by twelve butchers 'in white, with blue Favours', and a flag inscribed with 'Murray and Liberty'.[129] Only a month after his release, Murray sent Charles Edward a plan for a rising in London, and in November he fled to the continent, where he became one of the Prince's closest advisers.

Murray's insurrectionary schemes never came to fruition, but the Independent Electors maintained close contact with the Jacobites. In February 1752, Samuel Johns, an attorney of Lyons Inn who was described as 'the Field Marshall & Commander in Chief' of the organization, wrote to John Caryll about a meeting of 'our friends' at the Crown and Anchor tavern in the Strand. Johns informed Caryll that 'I shall bring the Remainder of my Medals & an Account of w^t remains due to me.'[130] The medals were probably the pieces struck for Caryll's

127 Newman, ed., 'Leicester House Politics', p. 145.
128 Paton, ed., *Lyon in Mourning*, vol. iii, pp. 282–3.
129 Sedgwick, ed., *History of Parliament*, vol. i, p. 287; Rogers, 'Aristocratic Clientage', pp. 77–8; *True Briton*, vol. ii, no. 1, 26 June 1751, p. 22.
130 Rogers, 'Aristocratic Clientage', p. 95; B.L., Add. MS 28,249, fo. 396.

Oak Society, which Johns may have been distributing. Two years later, the opposition candidate in Westminster was General James Edward Oglethorpe, who had supplied funds for Caryll's Jacobite paper, the *True Briton*.[131] He polled a miserable 261 votes, however, indicating that the strength of the Independent Electors had finally been broken.

Opposition politics in Westminster revived with the Wilkite clamour of 1763; but the connection of the Independent Electors with the new radicals was complex. While the *North Briton* condemned the Electors as Jacobites, Tory blue became the colour of Wilkes's supporters.[132] In the City of London, meanwhile, Jacobitism had caused no demonstrations since 1719; the '45 had not resuscitated popular disaffection in the capital, as it had elsewhere.[133] The old Jacobite group of aldermen was gone by 1763; their position had been inherited by the non-Jacobite Tory William Beckford and his followers. Caryll believed that Beckford was contemplating a turn to the Stuarts before his sudden death in 1770, but there is no firm evidence of this.[134] Ten years later, in the Gordon Riots, the London crowds acted on an anti-Catholic prejudice that seems very far indeed from Jacobitism. Nevertheless, some peculiar traces of former times faintly coloured these disturbances. The Protestant Association decided to march on Parliament in a meeting held on 29 May – Restoration day – and its procession to Westminster was led by a contingent of Scots playing martial music, a strange echo of 1745.[135] The rioting ended on 5 June, but six days later, on the notorious 10th, John Wilkes himself ordered the arrest of William Moore, former editor of *The Whisperer*, who was handing out seditious papers in Fleet Street.[136] While these are minor details, they indicate the strange transformations of popular protest in London after 1760.

The exceptional violence of the Gordon rioters may have reflected their realization that unrest could not be long sustained in the capital; crowds had to make their point quickly and sharply before order was reimposed. Medieval corporatism still dominated the City; even the

131 Namier and Brooke, eds., *History of Parliament*, vol. i, p. 335; B.L., Add MS. 28, 236, fos, 30, 48–9, 61–2, 65.
132 *North Briton*, no. xxxviii, 19 Feb. 1763, p. 125; Colley, 'English Radicalism before Wilkes', p. 16.
133 A. A. Mitchell, 'London and the Forty–Five', *History Today*, 15, 10 (1965), pp. 719–26; Nicholas Rogers, 'Popular Disaffection in London During the Forty-Five', *London Journal*, 1, 1 (1975), pp. 5–27.
134 R.A., Stuart 450/95A.
135 Robert Watson, *The Life of Lord George Gordon* (London, 1795), p. 20.
136 Hill and Powell, eds., *Boswell's Life of Johnson*, vol. iii, Appendix F, pp. 538–9.

Wilkites had barely shaken it. Wilkes himself had been absorbed into the unchanging governmental structure of the capital. By the end of the century, however, London was no longer an anachronism; on the contrary, it was a model of 'modern' social control. The same institutional forces that had stymied the Levellers, Exclusionists, Jacobites and Wilkites went on to crush the Jacobins, radicals and Chartists, but by then the corporate bodies of London seemed to be aspects of 'modern' urban order. The City had pioneered in the marginalization of political dissent, a tactic that was to work well in the industrial cities of the nineteenth century. If Paris was the mother of revolutions, London was the grandfather of stability.

In a sense, London had passed from the Middle Ages into 'modernity' without much experience of the 'early modern', a period characterized by embryonic plebeian political awareness combined with inadequate means of government repression. Jacobitism was the preeminent product of 'early modern' English popular politics. It thrived because the state was not strong enough to root it out, and because it was perfectly suited to the High Church mentality of its age. It appealed both to the atavistic longing for religious unity, and to the timeless desire for legitimate, moral government. Its social basis rested on an alliance of local gentry with tradesmen and artisans. In many provincial towns, this coalition succeeded in preserving for forty years a tradition of Jacobite protest, based on popular rituals, religious prejudice and the heady myth of Stuart kingship.

Chapter 8

All for the lawful heir? The problem of Jacobite seditious words

> Thomas Saunders
> did call King William
> Rogue and glorifyed dog
> and said he was No King
> but Prince of Orange.
> Information in State Papers, December 1704[1]

Between 1689 and 1760, a large number of seditious words cases were prosecuted in common law courts throughout England. Almost all of them were connected with Jacobitism. This may indicate widespread sentiment in favour of the restoration of the Stuarts; but it may also represent something quite different, such as the settling of disputes through false accusations, or a popular hysteria similar to the witch-craft scares of the seventeenth century. In fact, the last person put to death for witchcraft in England, albeit by a mob rather than a court, was also reputed to have spoken words in favour of Prince Charles Edward during the rebellion of 1745. Unfortunately, this interesting fact does not solve the problem of how to interpret seditious words cases. It is relatively certain that Ruth Osborne, who died from a ducking in Buckinghamshire in 1751, was not a witch; it is far less evident that she never spoke seditious words.[2]

Historians have sometimes been compared to detectives or lawyers; they also often sit as judges, especially when accounts conflict or there is reason to doubt testimony. In these instances, no judgment is infallible. The historian must fall back on strategies of interpretation, informed not only by the alleged facts, but also by a knowledge of their contexts, and an awareness of the law. This chapter will consider Jacobite seditious words from all of these vantage points.

[1] P.R.O., S.P. 34/5/19.   [2] She is noticed in *D.N.B.*

Evidence and its contexts

It was the law that defined words as treasonable, and that created the rules for judging whether or not such words were spoken. The term 'seditious words' referred only to verbal expressions, not to writing, which was 'seditious libel'. Occasionally, spoken words were called 'treasonable', and the famous treason statute of 25 Edward III (1362) had drawn no distinction between speaking and writing. The Edwardian law had been strengthened and extended by Richard II and Henry VIII, but their statutes were soon repealed.[3] Nevertheless, it was not until 1628, in Pine's case, that the common law definitely and finally decided that seditious words were not to be tried as high treason.[4] They constituted thereafter a crime of misdemeanour, with penalties ranging from flogging and pillorying to imprisonment and fines. Cases were tried at Quarter Sessions, Assizes and King's Bench, with transferal to a higher court depending on how seriously examining justices considered the crime to be, and whether or not local juries were seen as politically trustworthy.

The records of these courts are far from complete, and it is easy to lose sight of a case due to the loss of documents, the illegibility of existing ones or the haphazard methods of some clerks. Judging whether or not accusations were justified also poses enormous difficulties. Many prosecutions were clearly malicious. William Munden, a churchwarden of Ashford, Middlesex, was accused in 1718 of speaking against King George and in favour of King James. Thirty of his friends, however, signed a certificate declaring him to be well-affected to Hanover, and no fewer than seventy villagers supported a declaration that his main accuser was a litigious and quarrelsome person, who had been arrested on Munden's orders for not repairing his fences. Furthermore, Munden's foe had been involved in a tythe dispute, had insulted the vicar of Ashford and had sworn revenge against the churchwarden; a woman who upheld his accusation had been taken up for a bastard child by Munden, who had also threatened to hang her husband for having three wives.[5]

The evidence provides fascinating insight into the petty feuding of village life; but does it prove that Munden was innocent? Nicholas

---

[3] Isobel Thornley, 'Treason by Words in the Fifteenth Century', *E.H.R.*, 32, 128 (1917), pp. 556–61; see also Roger B. Manning, 'The Origins of the Doctrine of Sedition', *Albion*, 12, 2 (1980), pp. 99–121.
[4] Howell, *State Trials*, vol. iii, cols. 359–68.   [5] P.R.O., S.P. 44/79A, pp. 152–6.

Rogers had no doubt that he was, and used the case to support a
suggestion that Jacobitism 'became the classic frame-up of the early
eighteenth century'.[6] Malicious motivations, however, should not
disqualify testimony. The government, which was extremely scrupulous in its handling of seditious words cases, always recognized this
rule. As Charles Delafaye put it in a letter to a justice at Newark-upon-
Trent, who was concerned by the presence of malice in a local seditious
words prosecution: 'Accusations of all kinds are sometimes rather
owing to Malice & Revenge than to Conscience and a publick Spirit,
and yet tho ye Motive is not virtuous the Complaint may be true.'[7] Even
today, many people see justice as a kind of vengeance; the prosecution
of one's enemies may serve a public as well as a private purpose. While
personal conflicts are significant, so is the social or political background against which they take place. In Munden's case, the historian
should not ignore the level of High Church disaffection at this time, or
the possibility that those who signed the certificates in his favour were
as anti-Hanoverian as their churchwarden.

The discovery of personal conflicts, in short, does not make seditious
words accusations any easier to judge. This was clearly demonstrated
in a horrendously complicated case from Staffordshire in 1692.
Thomas and Ellen Peake of Keele informed a J.P. that one Henry Perry
had promised them money and land if they would falsely swear
seditious words against a certain Thomas Hemmings, with whom Perry
was involved in a dispute over some property. Perry, however, denied
arranging this 'frame-up', and retaliated by prosecuting the Peakes for
perjury. Although the outcome of this manoeuvre is unknown, a writ of
capias was issued against Ellen Peake and her daughter, apparently in
connection with the perjury case, as late as 1718, which would make
this one of the longest running Assize cases of recent centuries.[8] In this
bewildering story, it is almost impossible to sort out who was seeking
revenge on whom.

As a guide through the judicial labyrinth, historians may turn to the
records of central government. Especially after 1714, the Secretaries of
State and the Attorneys General took an active interest in many diverse
cases of seditious words. Contrary to what one might expect, they were
careful in gathering and assessing information, and made every effort

[6] Rogers, 'Riot and Popular Jacobitism', in Cruickshanks, ed., *Ideology and Conspiracy*,
p. 71.
[7] P.R.O., S.P. 44/81, p. 116.
[8] P.R.O., Assi. 5/12, part 1, Stafford 1692, infos. 5–8, and indts. of Ellen Peake of
Chebsey and Ellin Peake of Keele; Assi 5/38, part 1, Stafford Qua. 4 G. I (1718).

to be 'fair' in their recommendations – they did not carry on an orchestrated vendetta. Yet the government was often suspicious of local authorities, because it felt that guilty persons were being set free by disaffected judges and juries. Richard Morlborne, for example, was bound over to Assizes in 1742 for proclaiming King James at Derby, but he was set free by the Tory mayor; on his release, he went about the town, crying 'Down with the Rump'. Although he was taken up again for this offence, the town sessions at which he was to appear were not held, because the mayor said he was ill and refused to depute anyone to replace him. The outraged government decided to prosecute both Morlborne and the mayor at crown expense.[9] Seven years later, the Attorney General advised the transfer of the trial of some Cirencester artisans from Gloucester Assizes to the court of King's Bench, because he did not believe a local jury would find the men guilty of seditious words. His assumption was correct; the bills against all five men were found *ignoramus* at Gloucester, and the cases were never brought to Westminster.[10] The verdict of a jury, petty or grand, was regarded as sacrosanct by every administration, even when it seemed biased.

Occasionally, the government intervened when it believed a person being held for trial was innocent. In 1711, the Attorney General, Edward Northey, recommended bail for John Franklin, a Portsmouth lawyer who was alleged to have defended the claim of the 'Prince of Wales' to the throne. Northey pointed out that Franklin was a Dissenter, 'a quiet Man and not likely to have spoken such Words', while his accuser had a bad reputation; besides, it was unbelievable that Franklin could have been 'so mad as to speak such Words in a publicke Room where Persons were, who were not known to him'.[11] It is significant, however, that this case occurred under a Tory administration, which was somewhat reluctant to prosecute Jacobite offenders. The Whig government that followed it was less inclined to sympathize with the accused. Nevertheless, it was sometimes willing to acknowledge mistakes. Timothy Cecilion, a Venetian merchant, was sentenced to the pillory and imprisonment at Durham Assizes in 1756 for drinking the Pretender's health at Monkwearmouth, near Sunderland. The justice who passed the sentence was later convinced that Cecilion had been found guilty only because he was a foreigner; an

---

[9] P.R.O., S.P. 36/60, fos. 117, 144.
[10] P.R.O., S.P. 44/133, p. 467; P.R.O., Assi. 2/15, Gloucs. Lent 22 G. II (1748/9), Summer 23 G. II (1749); Assi. 4/20, Gloucs., Lent 22 G. II (1748/9).
[11] *Ibid.*, S.P. 34/15/154–5; S.P. 35/15/158–9; 34/15/160.

Englishman had been acquitted of the same charge, although Cecilion's friends alleged that he, not the Venetian, had spoken the seditious words. The government was convinced, and the King remitted the punishment.[12]

Although the central authorities rarely acted in favour of a defendant, they were assiduous in gathering information on both sides. This can be observed in the tortuous case of Theophilus Levett of Lichfield, a friend of Dr Johnson's family. In 1718, he reportedly prevented the parish clerk of the town from saying 'Amen' to the final 'God Save the King' when a brief was read in church, when he 'clapt his Hand upon this Depon[ts] Mouth', and the clerk 'Blubbered' to the amusement of the congregation.[13] No action was taken, but three years later Levett, then a candidate for coroner and town clerk, was accused of wearing white roses on 10 June and of drinking toasts to the Pretender 'with other Gentlemen who were recconed the Jacobites of the Town'. Fortunately for him, all of his accusers were persuaded to retract their statements, testifying that they had been tricked into making them by Levett's enemies, who appear to have been local Whigs. Alice Hayes, 'a poor servant girl', claimed that one of these Whig gentlemen had promised to marry her if she swore a false affidavit against Levett![14] The government may have doubted these retractions – after all, Lichfield was infamous as a Jacobite stronghold – but it did not pursue the matter, and Levett was not brought to trial.

The Levett case involved party rivalry over a local office. This was not a common scenario; only a small number of Tory placemen, magistrates or politicians were accused of seditious words, and no person of national importance ever appeared in a courtroom to answer such charges. In 1690, the government quietly stifled an accusation against Robert Sutton, Lord Lexinton, because it did not wish to encourage informations against peers.[15] The same reasoning was apparently applied in 1720 concerning a charge against Lord Craven's

---

[12] P.R.O., P.D. 16/1, 18 Aug. 1756, nos. 9–10, Kalendar 1756; P.D. 17/8, indts. of Jeremiah Abbs, Timothy Cecilion, recs. for Charles Hanson, James Hodgson *et al.*, P.R.O., S.P. 36/136, fos. 1–6, 30–4; S.P. 44/134, pp. 389, 394, 431.
[13] P.R.O., S.P. 35/12/21. Dr Johnson's correspondence of 1743–4 with Levett is printed in R. W. Chapman, ed., *The Letters of Samuel Johnson* (3 vols., Oxford, 1952), vol. i, pp. 18–20.
[14] P.R.O., S.P. 35/27/48; S.P. 35/28/1; S.P. 35/28/12; S.P. 35/28/68; S.P. 35/30/17; S.P. 35/30/22; S.P. 35/30/29; S.P. 35/48/27.
[15] H.M.C., *Eleventh Report, Appendix, Part VII*, p. 35. Lexinton would have had to be tried by his peers, which would have posed great difficulties.

brother Robert, which was dropped.[16] The most notorious politically motivated accusation of seditious words was made against the Solicitor General, William Murray, the Prince of Wales's tutor Andrew Stone and the Bishop of Gloucester by Christopher Fawcett, recorder of Newcastle, in 1753. He alleged that the three men had drunk the healths of James III and of the Jacobite Secretary of State, the Earl of Dunbar, who happened to be Murray's brother, at a mercer's house in London in 1732. Although the story was probably true – Murray had been a raging Jacobite in his youth – the administration managed to discredit Fawcett's confused testimony.[17] Only one Member of Parliament was ever arrested for seditious words. During the '45 rebellion, Sir John Glynne of Hawarden, Flintshire, was taken up with the village rector for drinking the health of Prince Charles on the bowling green of a local inn. They were sent to London for trial, but were pardoned when the principal witness, intimidated by a riot in which her house was wrecked, failed to appear in court.[18]

Seditious words charges were no more fruitful in resolving political struggles on a local level. The Tory mayor of Nottingham was deprived of his office and committed to prison in 1715 for drinking to the success of the Pretender; but he turned his incarceration into a show of Tory solidarity by entertaining supporters in his cell, and after his release, his prison bed-curtains were used as a banner by his party.[19] Complaints of treasonable healths drunk by the mayor of Bridgwater in 1716 or the corporation of Marlborough in 1745 did not lead to action by the authorities, in spite of the Jacobite reputations of both boroughs.[20] The government may have discouraged politically motivated prosecutions, because they had a tendency to back-fire and embarrass the accusers.

The foregoing examples provide some insights into the problem of how to deal with conflicting testimony. They reveal a variety of malicious motives that should make historians wary; they also remind us, however, that malice is not a certain indicator of fabrication. They show that the government was very concerned about possible disaffection, but that it was never inclined to sanction political witch

---

16 P.R.O., S.P. 35/21/48; S.P. 35/21/82; S.P. 35/22/55, i–iv.
17 B.L., Add. MS 33,050, fos. 200–367. For Murray's earlier Jacobitism, see R.A., Stuart 85/21, 87/38, 89/40.
18 W. E. B. Whittaker, *The Glynnes of Hawarden*, Flintshire Historical Society Publications (Chester, 1906), pp. 24–5. For accusations made at a 1724 Lincolnshire by-election, see Hill, *Georgian Lincoln*, pp. 26–7.
19 John Blackner, *The History of Nottingham* (Nottingham, 1815), p. 379.
20 Slocombe, 'A Bridgwater Riot, 1717', p. 74; P.R.O., S.P. 36/72, fo. 26. Sir John Hynde Cotton was M.P. for Marlborough in 1745.

hunts through seditious words charges. The central authorities always took accusations of seditious words seriously and were generally scrupulous in dealing with them. No evidence exists in the State Papers of hysteria within the national government. Seditious words accusations should not therefore be viewed as the products of an organized campaign to weed out Tories; nor were they attributable to an exaggerated paranoia. On the other hand, we should be aware that not all of them were truthful.

Even if we could know with certainty that seditious words were spoken, we would not necessarily have a better idea of what they meant. Can drunken or angry or antagonistic expressions be interpreted as evidence of political sentiments? Is a toast to King James always a sign of Jacobitism, or is it sometimes a playful jest without serious content? Should every damnation of King George be read in terms of disaffection, or might some of them be no more than blasphemous growls from irate or inebriated tempers?

As in judging the reliability of testimony, context is essential in evaluating the meaning of seditious words. Yet in very few circumstances is much information available about the persons involved or the background to the situation. In a small number of cases, enough is known about the main players to allow an understanding of their motives. In October 1693, for instance, three soldiers gave informations to a Worcester J.P. against Daniel Kendrick, a clergyman who had been in their custody. He was alleged to have announced in a Worcester tavern that he was for King James, and later at his lodgings he reportedly drank the exiled King's health, telling his guards 'you may drinke to your King and I will drinke to my Kinge'. Kendrick was bailed, and did not come to trial.[21] The ecclesiastical records of Worcester, however, reveal that he had been a protégé of Sir Walter Blount, the Roman Catholic high sheriff of the county under James II, who had chosen him to preach an Assize sermon in 1688 urging the repeal of the Test Act and penal laws. This had outraged Bishop Thomas and Dean Hickes of the cathedral chapter, who believed Kendrick was guilty of incest in marrying his late wife's sister. For this offence, and for drunkenness, Kendrick was excommunicated by the Consistory court in 1689, and deprived of his living.[22] By 1693, Bishop

[21] P.R.O., Assi. 5/13, Civ. Worcs. 1693, info. John Glover, rec. D. Kendrick.
[22] I owe all this information to the kindness of John Ramsbottom. His sources are Bodl. Ballard MS, vol. 12, no. 21; Kendrick's *Sermon preached in the Cathedral Church, Worcester* (London, 1688), and Worcestershire Record Office, 'Correction of Clerks', BA 2638: 795.61.

Thomas and Dean Hickes had been ejected as Nonjurors and Kendrick, a broken man with nothing left to lose, was being watched by the army. His seditious words undoubtedly reflected his real hopes.

Reverend Kendrick was a far more important man than Walter Tate, an itinerant Irish labourer who arrived at the house of Matthew Reynolds of Clint, West Yorkshire, in February 1689/90. Thinking Reynolds was a Roman Catholic, Tate revealed that he had come over from Dublin, 'sent by King James to fight for him in England'. Under examination, Tate admitted that he had been a soldier under James II, but claimed to have been drunk when he spoke the words.[23] The case disappeared from the court records; Tate may have enlisted in the Williamite army to escape punishment, because a year later, a labourer of his name was tried at Berkshire Assizes for saying near Reading 'God damn mee I will never serve King William as a Soldier any more, I will be one that will help to bring in King James if there be any occasion'. He was judged not guilty.[24] Perhaps the jury would have decided the case differently if they had known about the West Yorkshire accusation, or if they had heard the testimony of John Wilson, one of the witnesses in the famous Lancashire recusant trial of 1694. Wilson claimed that around February 1689/90, Edmund Threlfall, a Jacobite agent, told him the names of several Irish labourers he had recruited at London to fight in the insurrection that was being planned in Lancashire; among the dozen men whom Wilson remembered was a certain Walter Tate.[25]

It is improbable that an obscure character like Tate would have appeared in so many court cases unless he was a fairly determined adherent of King James. He was, however, merely a small-fry in the crowded pond of Jacobite Lancashire. Among the Roman Catholic gentlemen who were presented for seditious words at the Palatinate Assizes in the early 1690s was Cuthbert Threlfall of the Ashes, Goosnargh, brother of the conspiratorial Edmund. His fine of 13s 4d did not dissuade him from joining the rebel army at Preston twenty-three years later.[26] George Carus of Halton was acquitted of toasting King James and 'the confusion of all Protestants' in 1693.[27] He and his father, Christopher, had been ordered to surrender themselves to the

---

[23] P.R.O., Assi. 45/15, part 4, no. 119.
[24] PRO., Assi. 2/2, Berks. 9 March 3 W. & M.; Assi. 5/10, Berks. 1690, indt. Walter Tate.
[25] Beamont, ed., *Jacobite Trials*, p. 77.
[26] P.R.O., P.L. 28/1, p. 36; Joseph Gillow and Anthony Hewitson, eds., *The Tyldesley Diary* (Preston, 1873), pp. 22–3.
[27] P.R.O., P.L. 28/1, pp. 57, 65; P.L. 26/27, 2, indt. G. Carus.

authorities in 1690 on suspicion of having received commissions from King James – in fact, Christopher Carus was one of the principal officers in James's 'secret army'.[28] His son Thomas and two of his grandsons joined the rebels in 1715.

In the south-west there were few Catholics, but several Anglican gentlemen were accused of seditious words. One of them, Henry Brydges of Keynsham in Somerset, the brother of Lord Chandos, was presented to the county Assizes in 1690/1. He petitioned the government against this prosecution, on the grounds that it was based on the false witness of a man who had tried to break into his house. The Attorney General stayed proceedings on the indictment; but two weeks later, a new request arrived from Brydges to remove two other indictments against him. The Attorney General may now have become suspicious of Harry Brydges, because his petition was not granted, and in April 1691 he was found guilty on two counts of seditious words and one of uttering false news.[29] The government's caution was vindicated in the summer of 1694, when an Irish officer who had been a liaison between St Germain and the Bristol Jacobites disclosed that Henry Brydges was one of King James's strongest supporters in the area.[30]

Individuals accused of seditious words in the 1690s tended to represent groups that had the reputation of being sympathetic to the Stuarts – the high-flying clergy and gentry, Nonjurors, Roman Catholics, the Irish. Perhaps many of them were innocent, or did not really hold the principles they were supposed to have professed. The examples noted above, however, suggest that some accusations had a good deal of weight behind them. The situation became far more complex after 1715, because the majority of seditious words prosecutions were now being made against artisans and tradesmen whose backgrounds are difficult to trace. Little is known about Thomas Syddall, the Manchester blacksmith who led the mob that pulled down local meeting-houses in the summer of 1715, and who was pilloried for saying 'God damn King George'.[31] He gave the impression of having been a committed Jacobite, because he joined the rebels after they liberated him from Lancaster gaol, and was eventually executed for high treason. His 'lieutenant' in the riots, the young shoemaker William Ward, was presented at Assizes in 1715 for saying 'King

---

[28] C.S.P.D., W. & M., vol. ii, pp. 272, 302; Bodl. Carte MS 181, fo. 561; V.C.H. Lancashire (8 vols., London, 1906–14), vol. viii, p. 121.
[29] P.R.O., Assi. 23/3, Somerset Hiernal, 3 W. & M., 4 April 1691, fo. 166; C.S.P.D., W. & M., vol. ii, pp. 272, 302. Brydges was sentenced to fines totalling £26 13s 4d.
[30] H.M.C., Downshire, vol. i, part i, pp. 446–8.   [31] P.R.O., P.L. 28/1, pp. 232, 238.

George hath broke the peace, now we'll bring in a King of our owne'. Like Syddall, he followed the Jacobite army to Preston, but he claimed he had been forcibly recruited, and was acquitted, probably on account of his youth.[32] Unfortunately, the backgrounds of these two interesting men remain in shadow.

In only a few rare instances after 1715 are we privileged with some snippets of information about the accused. In 1746, a jeweller of Durham named Joseph Swallow was fined £20, imprisoned for a year and ordered to put up £100 in security for saying in November 1745, 'Here is King James's Health ... Damne King George'.[33] In March 1749/50, James III received a letter from Joseph Swallow, who related 'how that by his two years imprisonment in England & Fine ... on Acct. of the Royal Cause, together with his loss of Business & the Non Payment of his Wife's Jointure at Milan, have oblig'd him to come into Italy for the recovery of the same'. The 'Chicaneries' of his creditor in Milan, together with the loss of a parcel of silver foil from Paris, had ruined him financially. He begged for relief, and James, always generous, sent him £50.[34] Clearly, 'Giuseppe Svvallovv', as James Italianized him, was no ordinary Durham jeweller. He was a Roman Catholic, with an Italian wife and extensive continental business connections. Attachment to the Stuarts must have come naturally to him, and it is not surprising to find him writing to the Jacobite court at Rome.

One of the last cases investigated by the government was redolent of conspiracy. In November 1752, three soldiers at Reading swore seditious words against a young gentleman whose identity was at first uncertain. By the following April, it was known that he was Richard Price Astley, son of the Tory M.P. Sir John Astley; he had since made his escape to France.[35] His father is already familiar to us as the benefactor of the Walsall rioters in 1750 and the chief intermediary in the plot of 1752–3. His son's knowledge of the developing conspiracy may have prompted his rash insulting of King George and the royal family in the presence of hostile witnesses. As a young man steeped in Jacobitism, there is every reason to believe that Richard Astley meant what he said about the Hanoverians.

Hundreds of other seditious words cases prosecuted after 1715, however, must be analysed according to more general criteria, without

---

32 *Ibid.*, pp. 233, 238.
33 P.R.O., P.D. 17/5, indt. J. Swallow; P.D. 17/6, Assi. 22 G. II (1748), release order for Swallow, dated 12 Aug. 21 G. II (1747).
34 R.A. Stuart 305/11.   35 P.R.O., S.P. 44/85, pp. 318–20, 346.

the benefit of biographical details. They may point to real disaffection for the ruling monarch, and attachment to the Stuarts; or they may represent nothing more than attempts to shock, irritate or impress other people. The law, of course, did not recognize treason as a pose or affectation. Loyal judges and juries were not often swayed by pleas of drunkenness or play-acting; it was enough for them that the words had been spoken. This is important to remember, because it demonstrates, once again, the seriousness with which Jacobitism was regarded. Nevertheless, historians may search for some further grounds for discrimination in the facts of the case, and their general context.

Consider the concrete – or rather vaporous – example of Christopher Fuller of Old Romney, Kent, a yeoman who, 'being very much in liquor', sat down with three dragoons in an alehouse in the spring of 1717 and tore one of their cloaks. When told that this was a crime against King George's cloth, he allegedly replied, 'God dam you & King George Booth [both]'. The magistrates of New Romney, who examined Fuller, noted that when sober he claimed to have no recollection of having said anything.[36] Fuller's drunkenness and forget-fulness, however, were irrelevant to the law, and his defence would not stand up against three witnesses, unless the jury felt sorry for him. Historians who seek to resolve whether or not Fuller realized what he was saying will have to look at the testimony itself. The man obviously had some grudge against soldiers. He mentioned no personal grievance in his examination, and nothing in his words implies that he had imbibed the anti-army, Country principles associated with Toryism, and particularly with Jacobites like William Shippen.[37] Fuller's rage probably stemmed from a more localized issue. The soldiers had been sent to the edge of Romney Marsh to guard the coast against smugglers and Jacobites, two groups that were closely connected, as was shown in Chapter 4. Christopher Fuller's seditious words, therefore, put him on the side of the smugglers, and of their friends, the Jacobites. In spite of his inebriation, his political position was remarkably coherent.

Factors such as location and time period can be very helpful in determining the possible motivations for seditious words. Although virtually nothing is known about hundreds of individuals like Christo-pher Fuller, the meagre facts of their alleged crimes often provide

---

[36] P.R.O., S.P. 35/9/1, i–iii.
[37] See William Shippen et al., *Three Speeches against Continuing the Army* (n.p., 1718); Lois G. Schwoerer, *No Standing Armies! The Anti-Army Debate in Seventeenth Century England* (Baltimore, 1974).

enough information to place them within the broad outlines of Jacobite political culture. Together, these cases present a remarkable variety of religious, occupational and political experiences. Christopher Fuller had little in common with the Manchester rioter Tom Syddall or the wandering Irishman Walter Tate. The distinctions between them may be less important to an understanding of Jacobitism, however, than the fundamental similarities in the words they spoke.

Numbers and patterns

The sense of context is unfortunately lost when we move from consideration of specific cases to the overall features of seditious words prosecutions. In examining statistics, trends, chronologies, wide geographical areas and social classes, there is a danger of forgetting that each example must be judged individually in order to determine its reliability and meaning. Nevertheless, a general overview is critical to any understanding of the dimensions of the seditious words problem.

From various Quarter Sessions, Assize and King's Bench records, the names of more than 700 persons who were accused of seditious words have been culled.[38] Nicholas Rogers discovered about 250 others in the London area in 1715–16 and 1745–6.[39] The rough total of about 1,000 names may represent more than half of the nationwide total of all persons prosecuted for this offence – assuming that the unexamined London and Middlesex records (for 1689, 1691–1714, 1717–44 and 1747–60), the two missing Assize Circuits (Norfolk and Home) and

[38] The Assize records used were: P.R.O., Assi. 2, 4, 5 (Oxford Circuit), 23 (Western Circuit), 35 (South-Eastern Circuit, 1690, 1715–16, 1745–6), 41, 45 (Northern Circuit); P.R.O., P.L. 26–8; P.R.O., P.D. 16–17; P.R.O., P.C. 24 (1690, 1715–16, 1745–6). The unpublished Quarter Sessions records consulted were: L.R.O., DDke/2/2, QJI/2/10, QSI/1/89–120 (Indictment Books and Indictments, 1686–1746); C.L.R.O., MJ/SR 1751–67 (Sessions Rolls, 1690); Oxfordshire Record Office, Quarter Sessions Minute Books, 1688–1768, and Quarter Sessions Rolls, 1687–1783, both transcribed by Canon J. Oldfield. In addition, the following published Quarter Sessions records were used: William LeHardy and Geoffrey L. Reckitt, eds., *County of Buckingham: Calendar to the Sessions Records* (5 vols., Aylesbury, 1936–58), vols. ii, iv, v (1694–1724); J. H. E. Bennett and J. C. Dewhurst, eds., *Quarter Sessions Records with Other Records of the Justices of the Peace for the County Palatine of Chester 1559–1760*, Record Society of Lancashire and Cheshire, 94 (1940); William John Hardy, ed., *Notes and Extracts from the Sessions Rolls, 1581–1850*, Hertford County Records, vols. i–ii (2 vols., Hertford, 1905); and H. C. Johnson and N. J. Williams, eds., *Quarter Sessions Records, Easter 1690 to Michaelmas 1696*, Warwick County Records, vol. ix (Warwick, 1964). P.R.O., K.B. 10/15–17 (Indictments, 1715–21) was also examined. Unless otherwise noted, the records used covered the period 1689–1760.

[39] Rogers, 'Popular Protest', p. 86, and 'Popular Disaffection', pp. 5–27.

the remaining Quarter Sessions rolls contain fewer cases than have already been discovered. This means that about 2,000 individuals were subjected to criminal allegations of seditious words in the years between 1689 and 1760. The figure is substantial, but not huge; by comparison, almost 550 persons were accused of witchcraft in Essex alone between 1560 and 1680.[40] Of course, this number does not provide a sense of the true scale of verbal disaffection, because it does not include unreported crimes. A West Yorkshire diarist mentioned one such incident, recounted to him during the '45 rebellion:

I was at Holmfirth at Josh Wilson's the Shopkeeper. He tells me that some time before the last Rebellion [the '15] he was with one Bouker, Mr. Thompson and Mr Kaye of Netherthong at Cavehull well and they drank the Pretender's health; and he charged Dr Wilson his Brother not to keep company with them for if he did he would be hanged.[41]

It is impossible to estimate how many examples of this sort occurred.

Although seditious words charges were only a tiny percentage of the criminal cases handled in English courts in this period, they required a disproportionate amount of attention from justices, because they were frequently complicated and were very seriously regarded.[42] Most of them were sent up to Assizes, and they were often reported in newspapers.[43] Accusations of seditious words, however, were not evenly spread across the seventy years after the Revolution. They were concentrated into three main periods: 1689–97, 1714–24 and 1745–52. The graph showing the distribution of cases on the Oxford Circuit Assizes demonstrates this. Seventy cases, or about 30 per cent of the total, occurred in the first eight years of William III's reign; one hundred and seven, about 47 per cent of the total, were reported in the first decade of George I's reign; and nineteen, or about 8 per cent, clustered in the years 1745–51. Only twenty-one other cases were heard in the remaining forty-seven years from 1689 to 1760. Almost

[40] A.D.J. Macfarlane, *Witchcraft in Tudor and Stuart England* (New York, 1970), pp. 23, 66.
[41] C. E. Whiting, ed., 'The Diary of Arthur Jessop', in *Two Yorkshire Diaries*, Yorkshire Archaeological Society Record Series, 107 (1951), pp. 119–20.
[42] For eighteenth-century criminal statistics, see Beattie, *Crime and the Courts*, chs. 2–5; also his 'Pattern of Crime', pp. 47–95, and 'Crime and the Courts in Surrey 1736–1753', in J. S. Cockburn, ed., *Crime in England 1500–1800* (Princeton, 1977), pp. 155–86; and Hay, 'War, Dearth and Theft', pp. 117–60.
[43] For the elaborate theatre of Assizes, see J. S. Cockburn, *A History of English Assizes, 1558–1714* (Cambridge, 1972); Douglas Hay, 'Property, Authority and the Criminal Law', in Hay et al., *Albion's Fatal Tree*, pp. 17–63, and the response to this in J. H. Langbein, 'Albion's Fatal Flaws', *P. & P.*, 98 (1983), pp. 96–120.

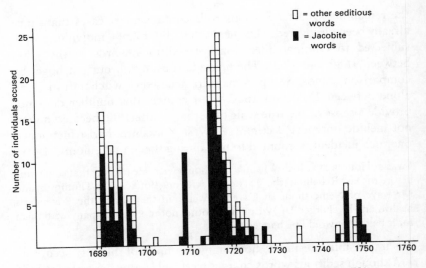

Graph 1 Oxford Circuit seditious words accusations, 1689–1751

every case on the Oxford Circuit was related to the threat of a Jacobite invasion or rebellion, including the eleven persons indicted in 1709 – they were all Tory town leaders in Gloucester who were prosecuted for drinking treasonable healths in the aftermath of the '08.[44]

Were Hanoverian loyalists simply more vigilant in these years, or did more incidents of seditious words take place in times of invasion or rebellion scares? The latter view carries more credibility. Jacobite activity in most spheres – propaganda, riots and demonstrations, the work of spies and agents, anonymous letters – flourished in the same periods that saw proliferations of seditious words cases. The government and its friends, furthermore, were vigilant even when Jacobitism was dormant, as the trickle of cases in quiet years illustrates. In some years, such as 1743–4 or 1759, when invasions were widely rumoured, but the Jacobites were being cautious or quiescent, there was no increase in seditious words prosecutions. It seems, therefore, that the distribution of cases represents an actual increase in the expression of disaffection, and that people were more inclined to speak treason when they felt there was a good chance they might be vindicated.

Two-thirds of the cases heard on the Oxford Circuit definitely

44 P.R.O., Assi. 5/29, part 2, Civ. Gloucs. 1709, indts. Thomas Smith, James Lander, James Lander senior, recs. 2–15; H.M.C., *Portland*, vol. x, p. 78. The three cases in 1727–8 followed the accession of George II.

Table 1. *Seditious words cases: conviction rates, 1689–1752*

	Percentage	Total no. of accused
Oxford Circuit		
Berkshire	18	11
Oxfordshire	30	20
Worcestershire	35	26
Gloucestershire	17	55
Herefordshire	30	27
Monmouthshire	21	14
Shropshire	40	29
Staffordshire	26	45
Average	27	Total 227
Palatinate of Lancaster	30	59

involved Jacobite words. The extant records do not inform us of the exact words spoken in about 8 per cent of the cases, so it is possible that as many as 75 per cent of allegations concerned specifically Jacobite words. Many of the non-Jacobite examples had Jacobite implications, because they took place during seditious riots or demonstrations. With one or two exceptions, moreover, non-Jacobite seditious words cases occurred in the same periods, the same places and among the same occupational groups as Jacobite words cases. A tiny number of prosecutions – six on the Oxford Circuit, and about a dozen in all the records studied – were made against anti-Stuart words, republican words or attacks on the Royal Supremacy. These interesting cases deserve some attention, but they have been eliminated from consideration in the graphs and tables.

Conviction rates, as shown in Table 1, were comparatively low. Although they varied from county to county, the averages of 27 per cent on the Oxford Circuit, or 30 per cent in the Palatinate of Lancaster Assize, are considerably lower than the 50 per cent rates found for many other crimes. The government felt that juries were more reluctant to convict in seditious words cases, and often suspected that this reflected sympathy with the political views of the accused. Many juries, however, may simply have been cautious in assessing accusations that rested on malicious motives. It is worth adding that one third of all cases could not be traced to the stage of final judgment, either because the records are incomplete, or because the accused disappeared from them, for one reason or another.

The social backgrounds of accused persons in three counties are shown in Table 2. Under William III and Anne, a large number of gentlemen were among those prosecuted. In Lancashire, most of these gentlemen were Roman Catholics, but in Gloucestershire they were all Anglicans. The two 'wives' on the Staffordshire list may have been of gentry status; one of them was a recusant. If 'yeoman' and 'husbandman' are assumed to refer to agrarian occupations, then only in Staffordshire were the majority of accusations made against farming folk, while tradesmen, artisans and shopkeepers predominated in Lancashire and Gloucestershire. The influence of Roman Catholicism accounts for the wide social spread of suspects in Lancashire, as well as for the over-representation of the gentry. The political influence of the Nonjuring Duke of Beaufort in Gloucestershire explains the number of gentry and clergymen accused there – one of the two clerics on the list was the chancellor of the diocese of Gloucester. Many of the townspeople prosecuted in this county were probably also connected with the Somerset interest. In addition, the environs of Bristol produced several accusations against Tory gentlemen who were allies of Sir John Knight. In Staffordshire, the lack of any prominent Jacobite interest is reflected in the small number of scattered, rural cases. In short, accusations in the 1690s were not random; they were directed against political and religious groups with known Jacobite sympathies, and against individuals who might be expected to have spoken treason.

The change in social background of the accused after 1714 is dramatic. Gentlemen diminished greatly in number, although clergymen did not. Almost all of the defendants were of the 'middling' or lower social orders. From bucklemakers to shoemakers to butchers to locksmiths, they were the artisans and tradesmen who formed the mainstay of the Tory party in the towns of provincial England, the same sort of people who rioted in 1714–15 and maintained for decades a tradition of Jacobite unrest. In Lancashire and Staffordshire, many of them were in fact rioters, and the limited amount of rioting in Gloucestershire may account for the fact that only there were fewer cases reported in 1715–52 than in 1689–1714. The decline in the number of gentlemen accused may seem strange. The Lancashire Roman Catholic gentry were undoubtedly more circumspect following the disaster of the '15 rebellion, but a far greater proportion of the High Church gentry was sympathetic to Jacobitism after 1714. Yet this

Table 2. *Seditious words cases: social backgrounds of accused persons*

Lancashire	Staffordshire	Gloucestershire
1689–1714		
6 gentlemen	1 'yeoman'	9 gentlemen
1 doctor	2 'husbandmen'	2 clergymen
1 shipmaster	1 widow	2 maltsters
1 joiner	2 'wives'	1 apothecary
1 cooper	1 unspecified	1 silversmith
1 innkeeper		2 glaziers
1 flaxman		1 victualler
1 tailor		1 grocer
1 shoemaker		1 baker
1 carrier		1 mercer
1 farmer		1 tailor/woolcomber
1 'yeoman'		1 cordwainer
2 'husbandmen'		1 exciseman
2 'labourers'		1 bailiff
1 unspecified		1 'yeoman'
		2 'labourers'
		4 unspecified
Totals 22	**7**	**32**
1715–52		
1 gentleman	1 locksmith	2 gentlemen
1clergyman	1 miller	2 clergymen
1 schoolmaster	1 joiner	2 apothecaries
1 barber	1 butcher	1 glover
4 chapmen	1 baker	1 barber
1 innkeeper	1 tailor	1 mason
1 baker	1 feltmaker	1 grocer
1 tailor	1 bodicemaker	1 carrier
1 flaxdresser	1 filemaker	1 exciseman
4 weavers	2 cordwainers	3 woolcombers
1 whitster	4 bucklemakers	1 stocking weaver/barber
4 shoemakers	1 scotch-pedlar	1 seaman
1 blacksmith	10 'yeomen'	1 'yeoman'
1 mariner	2 'labourers'	1 'husbandman'
3 'husbandmen'	2 'wives'	2 'labourers'
2 'labourers'	1 spinster	1 unspecified
9 unspecified	7 unspecified	
Totals 37	**38**	**22**

actually explains their absence from the courts. When Jacobite gentlemen were a small minority, it was both easy and relatively safe for their opponents to single them out for prosecution. After 1714, however, with Jacobitism so widespread in the Tory party, Hanoverian supporters apparently felt that it was better not to stir up trouble by bringing gentlemen to court for verbal indiscretions. The rarity of allegations against political figures further supports this interpretation.

Women of all social groups were prosecuted for seditious words, but cases involving women tended to cluster together in particular places and periods – for example, Staffordshire in the 1690s, Berkshire in 1715 or Buckinghamshire in 1715–19.[45] Some counties, like Gloucestershire, never saw the presentment of a woman for seditious words. Because they were seen as less of a political threat than men, women became targets of accusations mainly in counties where there was little fear of widespread disaffection. Women could be as stridently disaffected as men in expressing their political sentiments. When the constable of Stone came with a warrant to requisition her husband's horses, the recusant Magdalen Pyott of Hilderston in Staffordshire yelled at him 'God Damn the sheriffe he is a Rogue & sends Rogues about the Country to undoe us God Damne them all there is noe King but King James & if my horses were to serve King James they should goe'.[46] The courts, however, treated women more leniently than men. Elizabeth Bennett, a spinster of Cuddington, Buckinghamshire, presented to Quarter Sessions on a charge of threatening to poison King George, was released on a recognizance that was respited until 1724, and seems never to have come to trial.[47] For words no more serious than these, albeit written rather than verbal, James Shepheard was executed for high treason in 1717/18.

The social background of the accusers, in the few cases in which this is known, bore no fixed relation to that of the accused. Gentlemen could be informed against by their servants, although this was uncommon.[48] Allegations against gentlemen were usually supported by other gentlemen, even when someone of lower rank was the chief witness.

---

45 Women were accused in three out of seven cases in Staffordshire in the 1690s, two out of three in Berkshire in 1715, and all four cases in Buckinghamshire between 1715 and 1719. Jan Albers has informed me that women were far more numerous than this in defamation cases tried by the Consistory Courts.
46 P.R.O., Assi. 2/2, Staffs. 12 March 2 W. & M.; 5/10, Staffs. 1690, info. 10 and indt. of Magdalen Pyott.
47 LeHardy and Reckitt, eds., *Buckingham Sessions Records*, vol. v, pp. 59–60.
48 For example, see P.R.O., S.P. 35/20/89, information of Sarah Smith against her master, Gilles Chambers of Horsley, Gloucestershire.

Clergymen, on the other hand, could be denounced by anyone, without the assistance of upper-class allies.[49] Tradesmen and artisans were almost always accused by other of their own rank, or by soldiers.[50] Aware of their own unpopularity and of the extent to which their interests were those of the government, soldiers acted in this period like a police force, and were particularly conscientious in reporting sedition wherever they saw or imagined it. They certainly incited, directly or indirectly, many examples of seditious words. Soldiers often had problems, however, in prosecuting offenders, because judges and juries were often ill-disposed towards their testimony.[51] Usually, the accusations made by soldiers were supported by the testimony of civilians, a practice that added weight to allegations. Customs and excise officers, who made a small number of accusations, sometimes encountered the same difficulties with the courts.[52] For its part, the government appreciated the watchfulness of its agents, but made no attempt to organize them systematically as spies.

Seditious words incidents frequently occurred in alehouses or inns. These places where drink was sold were the primary centres of social life, of conviviality and local politics, for most of the male population and many women.[53] Drunkenness, however, was a factor in only a minority of cases. So too, apparently, was personal enmity. In the most common situation, the accused had some previous acquaintance with the accuser, and the two were initially on friendly terms. This is significant as an indicator of the political polarization that existed on every social level, and could divide those who were not otherwise hostile to one another.

The regional distribution of seditious words cases in certain critical years can be observed in Table 3, which shows the number of cases presented in each county at Assizes, and in various London and Middlesex courts, in 1690, 1715–16 and 1745–6, the peak years for prosecutions. It is immediately obvious that there were more cases in the London area than in the rest of the nation combined. In fact, one third of all cases discovered in the period 1689–1760 took place in the capital. As the centre of government, a metropolis humming with

---

49 George Read, minister of Chilton, Berkshire, was prosecuted in 1716 by a farm labourer and his wife – P.R.O., Assi. 5/37, part 2, info. 3, rec. 4, indt. G. Read; Assi. 4/18, p. 10.

50 See Rogers, 'Popular Disaffection', pp. 19–22.   51 See P.R.O., S.P. 35/53/57.

52 For example, P.R.O., S.P. 35/17/60, a report on the information of a customs searcher at Marazion against certain local figures. Women were also discriminated against by the courts, and their accusations generally had to be corroborated by men.

53 See Clark, English Alehouse, ch. 10.

Table 3. *Seditious words cases: regional distribution*

	1690	1715	1716	1745–6
London & Middlesex Sessions	53 (24)[a]	— 156 (89)	—[b]	97[c]
ASSIZES				
South-eastern Circuit				
Kent	5 (2)	1 (–)	2 (1)	4 (2)
Sussex	3 (3)	—	—	1 (1)
Surrey	6 (5)	2 (–)	1 (1)	4 (3)
Hertfordshire	1 (1)	1 (1)	—	—
Essex	—	—	4 (4)	4 (3)
Suffolk	2 (1)	(n.a.)	(n.a.)	(n.a.)
Western Circuit				
Hampshire	—	2 (1)	—	1 (1)
Wiltshire	—	1 (1)	4 (2)	—
Dorset	—	1 (1)	1 (1)	—
Devon	3 (–)	1 (1)	2 (1)	1 (–)
Cornwall	—	2 (1)	2 (2)	2 (1)
Somerset	—	1 (–)	3 (2)	3 (–)
Oxford Circuit				
Oxfordshire	—	—	8 (5)	—
Berkshire	2 (1)	3 (3)	—	—
Gloucestershire	—	2 (2)	4 (3)	2 (2)
Worcestershire	1 (1)	3 (2)	4 (1)	—
Herefordshire	4 (–)	—	5 (5)	1 (1)
Monmouthshire	3 (2)	1 (–)	—	—
Shropshire	4 (4)	—	6 (3)	—
Staffordshire	3 (3)	13 (12)	2 (2)	4 (4)
Northern Circuit				
Yorkshire	4 (4)	2 (1)[d]	4 (1)[d]	8 (7)
Northumberland	2 (2)	1 (–)[d]	—[d]	1 (1)[d]
Cumberland	2 (2)	—[d]	—[d]	—[d]
Westmorland	—	1 (–)[d]	—[d]	—[d]
Palatinates				
Lancashire	5 (2)	5 (4)	1 (1)[d]	8 (6)
Cheshire	3 (2)	5 (4)	—	—
Durham	—	1 (1)	2 (2)	3 (3)
Total Assizes	53 (35)	49 (35)	55 (37)	47 (35)

[a] Includes Middlesex Sessions only.
[b] From Rogers, 'Popular Protest'; includes Middlesex and London.
[c] From Rogers, 'Popular Disaffection'; includes Middlesex, London, Southwark and some K.B. cases.
[d] Signifies incomplete records.
(n.a.) Denotes records not available.
Note: the numbers refer to individuals, not cases; numbers in brackets are accusations of specifically Jacobite words; the last column covers autumn 1745 to spring 1746.

Jacobite plots, both real and imagined, and the largest concentration of people in the country, London's predominance in seditious words cases is understandable. The frequency of Sessions held in the London area may also have encouraged litigiousness – in 1690, the Middlesex Sessions met no less than seventeen times. Malicious accusations may have been more common in the capital on account of overcrowding and social tensions. For example, in 1690 a tenement landlord, Thomas Rowland of Dartmouth Street, Westminster, was accused of saying 'Come boys let us drink King James health & I will sell my houses to vindicate him'. He was also prosecuted for being a highwayman, for allowing overcrowding in his buildings, for keeping disorderly persons, especially pregnant women, in his house, and for pestering one Hester Cooper, widow.[54] Clearly, a number of people, including Hester Cooper, did not like Thomas Rowland, and it is probable that many of his enemies were also his tenants.

The high number of cases in London and its environs in 1715–16 was not unprecedented; if the City Sessions, the Surrey Sessions and the King's Bench records were included, they might result in a total of around seventy-five prosecutions for 1690, compared to an average of seventy-eight annually in 1715–16. This suggests that the political climate in the capital early in William and Mary's reign was not as mild as has been assumed by historians. Nicholas Rogers has argued that there was little Jacobite activity in London in 1745–6, but the number of seditious words accusations during the '45 rebellion was higher than in any other period. Although Rogers points out that many of the accused were Irish or Catholics, showing a more limited range of suspects than in 1715–16, disaffection was evidently still considered to be a problem in the capital.[55]

The level of seditious words cases in provincial England usually bore some relationship to political divisions within each county, but the number of cases during the two rebellions did not necessarily correspond to the presence of Jacobite gentry families. In 1715–16, for example, Wiltshire, Oxfordshire and Hertfordshire had plenty of gentlefolk loyal to the Stuarts, but none of these counties saw many seditious words cases. The Tory gentlemen of Kent tended towards Hanoverianism, but as late as the '45 common people were being presented in the county for seditious words – they may have been influenced by the smuggling trade. The effects of the riots of 1715–16

---

[54] C.L.R.O., MJ/SR 1751, rec. 129, indt. 5; MJ/SR 1764, recs. 5, 37, 257, indt. 38, and gaol calendar.
[55] Rogers, 'Popular Disaffection', pp. 18–21.

can be seen in the figures for the West Midlands and Lancashire, and the fears of a rising in Essex, Somerset and Cheshire in the same period led to several prosecutions in those counties. The invasion scare of 1745 is registered in the number of cases for Kent, Essex and possibly Somerset. In most of the counties through which Prince Charles retreated in 1745, like Staffordshire and Lancashire, he left seditious words cases in his wake.[56] Panic over the rebellion also spread into Yorkshire, Durham and Northumberland. Some of those accused of seditious words were actually out with the rebels, like James Sparks, a stocking weaver of Derby, who went to greet the Jacobite army near the town, saying 'I am Glad to see you, I have long wish'd for you I Care not who the D—l knows it'.[57] Poor Sparks, who deserted during the retreat, was captured and executed.

Most examples of seditious words in the provinces can be explained in terms of local political and religious factors – resentment against Whigs and Dissenters, the strength of High Church sentiments, the spread of popular Jacobitism. Only in certain parts of Yorkshire do social problems appear to have played a role in a number of incidents. Quarrels over land generated several prosecutions in the East and West Ridings, including one in 1719 involving a certain Thomas Banks, a gentleman who was accused both of seditious words and of menacing his neighbours with a pistol and whip. In spite of his rank, Banks was sentenced to be whipped for stealing poultry from a widow, and was fined for the charges of assault, but was acquitted of seditious words.[58]

Statistics are often ambiguous, and in many counties we are dealing with such a small number of cases that a general analysis seems absurd. The combined impression given by the statistical evidence, however, is consistent. In their chronological, social and geographical dimensions, seditious words cases provide an adequate reflection of the overall patterns of Jacobitism, both as a real and as a perceived threat. They emphasize the recurring features of popular Jacobite political culture.

---

[56] Six further cases in Cumberland are mentioned in the Treasury Solicitor's Papers, P.R.O., T.S. 20/112, no. 7.

[57] P.R.O., T.S. 20/25, fo. 16; T.S. 20/91, fo. 23. For similar cases, see P.R.O., Assi. 5/65, part 1, info. no. 32; P.R.O., S.P. 36/82, fo. 171; P.R.O., P.C. 24/161/9, rec. John Cupid; P.R.O., T.S. 20/23, fos. 15–16, 28–30, 35; and P.R.O., P.L. 26/35, part 4, indt. J. Tomlinson.

[58] P.R.O., Assi. 45/18/1, nos. 26–32; Assi. 4/2, fo. 13v. For another land dispute that provoked seditious words allegations in West Yorkshire, see P.R.O., Assi. 45/16/3, nos. 5–12.

What was said?

The final aspect of seditious words cases that must be considered here is in many ways the most important – the words themselves. Some of them at least can be taken as serious expressions of political sentiments; further examination of what was said strengthens the impression that these cases do indicate widespread popular disaffection. Few of the statements that resulted in prosecutions can be described as casual or conversational. Almost all of them are pronouncements of one sort or another, declarations of loyalty, of Stuart legitimacy, or of the infamy of the ruling monarch. They show a general preoccupation with precisely those issues that were broadcast by Jacobite propaganda, but they ignore the subtleties and ambiguities of written argument. They are not meant to persuade – on the contrary, they are more like magical incantations, pronounced to conjure up good spirits or to banish the bad. In this sense, they can be interpreted as the remnants of a traditional politics that vested great significance in oral culture. Yet they also reflect the impact of written sources, especially poetry and songs, on the common people. They reinforce the impression that oral and written culture were not separate streams.

The central issue in seditious words cases, as in all Jacobitism, was legitimacy. Thomas Pritchard, a labourer of Stepney, put it concisely when he allegedly asserted in September 1715 'King George has no right to the Crown No by God King George has no right to the Crown'.[59] Six years later in Westminster, a glazier named Smith summed up the other side of the case when he told two men, strangers to him, in the kitchen of the Angel, Longditch, 'how can they call him a pretender the nation could never call prove [sic] him a pretender, that all the nation knew he was lawfully boarn [sic], and was the reall Sone of the Late K: James'.[60]

These two themes echoed in almost every seditious words case from 1689 until 1760: the ruling King or Queen had no right, the lawful King was King James. In 1691, William Colley of Tewkesbury, a labourer, confessed to having said 'There is no king in England but King James. And where is one for King William there is two for King James in England if there were occasion'.[61] Peter Webb of Wolver-

---

59 P.R.O., K.B. 10/15, part 3, Michaelmas 1715, indt. T. Pritchard. I have used the term 'indictment' for true bills of this court in order to maintain consistency, although they were really called 'informations'.
60 P.R.O., S.P. 35/33/154.
61 P.R.O., Assi. 2/2, Gloucs. 13 Aug. 3 W. & M.; Assi. 5/11, part 2, Gloucs. 1691, indt.

hampton was only a nailer, but in December 1689, while singing Christmas carols in Albrighton, Shropshire, he demonstrated considerable knowledge of hereditary right when he told a weaver friend that 'wee ought to live in a rule and obedience under Kinge James as well as where hee is as if hee were amongst us & that hee that is yor King Meaninge Kinge William is a Usurper to the Crowne, & has noe more to Doe with it then I have.'[62] No Nonjuror ever put the case for James II any better than this obscure artisan, who was pilloried, fined and gaoled for his opinions.

Under Queen Anne, Jacobites usually asserted that James Francis Stuart was the lawful Prince of Wales rather than King, and that he should succeed his sister. For saying 'I doe declare for the Prince of Wales whose right it is to be here but he is kept out by the psent Governm'', David Roach was pilloried at Westminster in 1706/7.[63] Any right George I claimed was of course roundly denounced by the Jacobites; they even denied his existence. 'There is no such person as king George Englishmen are all fools to believe him as such he is a usurper & you have no king but king James the third', maintained James Blacko in Paignton, Devon, in 1723. For these words, he was fined and gaoled for two years.[64]

The riots of 1715 awakened interest in the question of hereditary right in the West Midlands, even among people who were not entirely sure of James Francis Stuart's family relationships. In August 1715, Thomas Jones, nailer and headborough of Cradeley, near Stourbridge, Worcestershire, while conversing with two friends about the late disturbances, defended the rioters, one of whom he had in custody, and stated that King George 'was not right heir to the Crown'. Who then was? Jones answered 'his Brother'.[65] These remarks, however ignorant, are particularly interesting because they came from a local official. Three years later, a feltmaker of Newcastle-under-Lyme named Thomas Birkes demonstrated more learning in genealogy when he said

62 P.R.O., Assi. 5/10, Salop Qua. 1690, info. 3, indt.; Assi. 2/2, Salop 15 March 2 W. & M. (1690).
63 P.R.O., Assi. 23/4, Southampton Hiernal 5, 6 Anne, 5 March 1706/7, fo. 188.
64 *Ibid.*, Devon Aut. 9, 10 G. I, 13 Aug. 1723. Blacko was suspected of being a Catholic priest, and had boasted of being at the battle of Preston – P.R.O., S.P. 34/33/6, i, ii. For other self-proclaimed rebels of the '15, see P.R.O., S.P. 35/11/112, 113; S.P. 35/16/58, i; P.R.O., Assi. 2/6, Salop Aut. 5, 6 G. I; Assi. 4/14, p. 328; and P.R.O., S.P. 35/32/98.
65 P.R.O., Assi. 5/35, part 2, Worcs. Aut. 1, 2 G. I (1715), rec. ad pros. nos. 31, 32, info. 10, indt. Jones absconded after being accused of these words, and his prosecutors spent so much money trying to find him again that they dropped the charges – P.R.O., Assi. 4/18, p. 166, Worcs. Aut. 1, 2 G. I.

'I believe King James is the son of King James, and I believe that King James will be our Kinge yett.'[66] He was whipped, fined £1 and imprisoned for this.

Thirty years of Hanoverian rule did not erase the feeling that they were not rightful kings. John Sheerer of Newcastle-upon-Tyne pleaded guilty to having said in March 1745/6, while the rebellion in Scotland was still undefeated, that 'it was time King George was gone home for that he loved the Pretender And he hoped he would wear the Crown and that he (meaning the Pretender) had a better Right to the Crown of England than King George or words to that Effect'. He was fined only 1s – he must have been very poor – but he was imprisoned for a full year.[67] A month later, at Bury in Lancashire, Jeffrey Battersby, a shoemaker, allegedly said:

That no Hanoverian had any right to the Crown of England and that King James the third had the only right to the Crown of England ... it belonged to the Stuarts ffamily and that ... King George has no more right to the Crown than you or I have and that King James had the only right thereto And you shall see he will come to the Throne and then we shall have fflourishing times.[68]

The combination of an assertion of hereditary right with hopes for a restoration was typical of seditious words cases in 1745–6.

From the verdicts or the internal evidence in each of the cases mentioned above, it can be surmised that the words were actually said. If they reflected the sentiments of the offenders, then it may be concluded that concern about the legitimacy of the ruling monarch was found among common people in a wide variety of occupations and locales. It was not difficult for them to understand the principles of lawful succession. Margaret Steene, a Roman Catholic of Burslem, Staffordshire, and wife of a yeoman or gentleman farmer, was asked by her neighbour in 1689 to return a shearing hook that had been loaned her. Steene replied that if she had the hook, 'she would keepe it by the same Right as King William kept his Crowne, ffor itt was none of his owne, for he was an outcomling a Rouge [sic] & A Bastard, And that they would have his head as soone as the [sic] Could'.[69] Everybody could grasp the reference to the supposed 'right of conquest', and the

---

[66] P.R.O., Assi. 2/6, Staffs. Aut. 4 G. I: Assi. 5/38, part 1, Stafford Lent 1718, info. 2, rec. 2, rec. ad pros. 3, indt.
[67] P.R.O., Assi. 45/23, part 2, nos. 101B–G; Assi. 41/3, Newcastle 4 Aug. 1746.
[68] P.R.O., P.L. 26/35, part 4, indt. Battersby pleaded the Act of Grace of 1747 and was acquitted.
[69] P.R.O., Assi. 2/2, Staffs. 12 March 2 W. & M.; Assi. 5/10, Staffs. 1690, info. no. 15, indt.

implication that if William was a rightful king, then anybody might take whatever they wanted, by force.

William was often called a 'Rogue', meaning that he was a thief who had stolen the crown. Simon Lynch, a gentleman of St Andrew's Holborn, and probably an Irishman, was fined and gaoled in 1690 for saying King William was 'a Rogue & a Sonne of a Whore & that he tooke his ffather's Right from him'.[70] The family relationship between James and William, which made the latter's 'crime' even more heinous, was a frequent subject for Jacobite commentary. In 1690, Henry Ellyott of St Paul's, Covent Garden, was pilloried five times, fined and imprisoned for calling William 'no king I'll Justify it, he is an outlandish Curr, a Son of a Whore, he eats the bread out of his fathers mouth'.[71] These remarks are reminiscent not only of the poetry directed against William on account of his foreignness and unkingly behaviour, but also of the poetry of 'parricide' that depicted him as an ungrateful son-in-law.

The extent to which poetic and literary images influenced seditious words is difficult to assess, but in some cases the connection was clear. Often the speakers added some touches of their own to the allusions. The 'turnip-hoer' slur against George I, for example, was wittily adapted by one Richard Terrill in 1717:

God damn King George for when news came to him that he was to be king of England he was howing Turnips and when he Came to England he Rap't his old Coat with an old Cheeney woman for Cheeney and forgot to take his Turnip seed out of his pockets so the old woman got all his Turnip seed.[72]

'Cheeney' was China-root, a supposed cure for syphilis, and the turnip-seed in the pocket of the coat was an obvious sexual reference, as well as a strong suggestion of degrading poverty. King George's supposed indigence and cupidity also disgusted Daniel Wood of Sittingbourne, Kent, who allegedly grumbled in 1716 that 'Wee have a King and as soone as he comes he [asks?] a maintenance for his children It's like a person comeing into Towne with a Coach and six horses and then flinging himselfe on the parish It's not to be borne, Wee will not have such a Cuckoldy king'.[73] George's marital state was perhaps the most popular subject for invective against him. Andrew Roberts was fined and gaoled in Devon in 1718 for saying 'The King is a Blockhead &

70 C.L.R.O., MJ/SR 1755, indt. 33; MJ/SR 1766, gaol calendar. See also the curious collection of 'Jacobite Papers' in B.L., Add. MS 39,923, fo. 6.
71 C.L.R.O., MJ/SR 1753, indt.   72 P.R.O., S.P. 35/10/94.
73 P.R.O., Assi. 35/156/12, Kent 24 July 1716, indt.

a Cuckold'.[74] A year earlier, Wilmott Mitchell had been whipped at Launceston, Cornwall, for announcing 'Good news is come to Dover they are all a comeing over Weell bring him in & crown him king & send the Cuckold to hannover'.[75]

This was obviously a song, and demonstrates the spread of Jacobite verse into a remote county. Songs were probably important sources for ✓ seditious expressions, although it is not always easy to decide whether or not specific words were inspired by verse. For example, it was a widespread hope that George I should drown on his way to Hanover. As early as August 1714, Alice Hunt of Lambeth allegedly said 'I wish the Bottom of the Ship may come out, that is to bring the King over so no other poor Soul should come to any harm for it'.[76] Two years later, John Purse was whipped, fined and gaoled in Dorset for saying 'I wish the Shipp (meaning the Shipp that carried the king into holland) had sunk'.[77] At least one song about George's drowning on a journey to Hanover is known. An innkeeper of Leominster was accused in 1719 of singing a song 'to this Effect that the King and all that were with him might be drowned'.[78] Alice Hunt's words were spoken so early that she could not have derived them from this song, but John Purse may have been inspired by it. On the other hand, the song may have developed out of a popular motif expressed in these seditious words cases.

Rumours provided another source of seditious expressions. William and Mary were particularly vexed by 'false news' from Ireland in 1689–91, including reports that William was dead or defeated.[79] A nationwide rumour circulated in the years after the Revolution to the effect that William had stolen treasures from royal palaces and sent them to the Netherlands. This story combined the 'Rogue' motif with an anti-foreign strain. Robert Jefferson of Hexham, Northumberland, was accused in 1689 of saying that the Prince of Orange had purloined King James's 'rich Hangings', and that he had 'Rob'd Whitehall of King James Plait & had Smelted itt and some of itt had Coyned into money and the rest he made into Piggs Like Lead and sent it into Holland'.[80] Thirteen years later, after William's death, Richard Salt of Lichfield, a labourer, was tried at Gloucester Assizes for alleging that

---

[74] P.R.O., Assi. 23/5, Devon Hiernal 4 G. I, 28 March 1718.
[75] *Ibid.*, Cornwall Hiernal 3 G. I, 25 March 1716/17.
[76] P.R.O., Assi. 33/155/9, Lent 1714/15, General Home Circuit, Surrey, indt. 8.
[77] *Ibid.*, Dorset Aut. 2, 3, G. I, 25 July 1716.
[78] P.R.O., S.P. 35/17/9. He was judged not guilty at Hereford Assizes – P.R.O., Assi. 2/7, Aut. 6, 7 G. I; Assi. 2/7, Aut. 6, 7 G. I; Assi. 2/6, Qua. 6 G. I.
[79] See C.L.R.O., MJ/SR 1752, indts. 37, 45.
[80] P.R.O., Assi. 45/15, part 3, info. 37.

William 'robbed Windsor Castle ... and sent from Windsor to holland a large silver Cisterne'.[81] After Queen Anne's death, a rumour was circulating to the effect that she had recognized James Francis Stuart as her successor before her demise. John Chepple of Tring, Hertfordshire, a yeoman, was pilloried, gaoled and fined for asserting 'that the Pretender was Queen Anne's Brother and that the Queen owned him to be her Brother, and sent for him before she dyed'.[82]

It is difficult to decide at times whether a seditious words case was echoing a rumour or creating one. What, for example, is to be made of the elaborate pornographic stories recounted in 1714/15 by Leonard Paddock of Ashby-de-la-Zouche, Leicestershire, an attorney and legal adviser to the Nonjuring Earl of Huntingdon?

That King George has no more right to the Crowne than my Arse. That King George has the pox and has pox'd the Court and that the Court pox'd the Prince and princess and that they would pox the Nation. That the prince was a Shitten dog and run Out ... that the Prince beshit himself and the Princess every night and further Said that the Prince Whored so much that the Princess took him to bed so Soon as he had dined, that when his Nailes were pared he might goe where he pleased ... that there is Guineas Coining in the Mint but that ther was a deficiency in King George's head upon them (to wit) there wanted a pair of horns upon the said Guineas before they would pass Courrent among Englishmen.[83]

Paddock was probably adding much of his own imagination to the familiar tales of degradation. His luxuriantly detailed rumours illustrate that the Jacobite image of the Hanoverian royal family was already well formed only eight months after the succession of George I.

Under George II, as was noted in Chapter 2, there was a deterioration in Jacobite creativity. In seditious words cases, as in poetry, the second Hanoverian was usually lampooned in ways invented for his father. 'King George is nothing but a Hannover turnep Hoe-er and if the Pretender was to come I wou'd join along with him', Thomas Savill of Low Layton, Essex, a labourer, allegedly declared in the summer of 1746.[84] In Gloucestershire in 1749/50, a yeoman named Samuel Vaughan was fined and jailed for saying 'God damn Great George our King — Long live great James our King God bless great James our

81 P.R.O., Assi. 4/17, Gloucs. Aut. 1 Anne; Assi. 5/22, part 1, Gloucs. 1702, indt.
82 P.R.O., Assi. 35/155/10, Summer 1715, General Home Circuit, Hertfordshire, indt.
83 P.R.O., S.P. 44/117, pp. 204–5; S.P. 44/79A, p. 23; H.M.C., *Report on the Manuscripts of the Late Reginald Rawdon Hastings, Esq.* (4 vols., London, 1928–47), vol. ii, pp. 214, 216–18, 220.
84 P.R.O., Assi. 35/186/12, General Home Circuit, indt.

King'.[85] This parody of the future national anthem was not original; 'Long live great James our King' was a Jacobite song dating from the 1720s, which can be seen inscribed on the famous 'Amen' glasses.[86] The Hanoverian version was apparently derived from it.

More ancient than any song or rumour was the sentiment that 'there have been no good times in old England since ...'. A Westminster chairman named Humphrey Watson was pilloried in 1690 for asserting that there had been no good times since the coming of King William and there would be no good times until King James returned.[87] Thirty-two years later, in a bookshop in St Paul's churchyard, a certain Phillip Jones was heard complaining 'of the unhappy times, and said That when our lawful and rightful Sovereign Lord King James the third came the times would be altered ... we shall have no good times till we see King James the third in England'.[88] This was the gist of much Jacobite propaganda, but it was also a very ancient form of grumbling. In 1591, for example, an Essex labourer was pilloried for saying that 'we shall never have a mery world while the queene lyveth'.[89]

These complaints were very general. Seditious words did not usually refer to specific policies of the Hanoverian government. Attacks on the Whig ministers or on local officials fell into the category of scandal rather than sedition. Scandalous words cases were rare, but they indicate that there were many options open to those who wished to do no more than annoy the authorities. Sometimes, the distance between scandal and sedition was debatable. Agnes Tuckwell, a cutler's wife from Aylesbury, Buckinghamshire, was fined in 1716 for disrupting the commemoration of the thanksgiving day for the suppression of the '15 rebellion. She had attacked a Whig gentlewoman named Ann Mead, calling her 'Presbiterian bitch, salt bitch, fat-arst bitch', and seizing Mead's commemorative candles, saying 'she wished she could burn the Whiggs in like manner as these candles'.[90] In other cases, however, scandalous words bore no directly treasonable overtones. Francis Springate, a trooper in the Life Guards,

---

85 P.R.O., Assi. 4/20, Civ. Gloucs. Lent 23 G. II (1749/50); Assi. 2/15, Civ. Gloucs. Lent 23 G. II.
86 The text of the song is given in Hartshorne, *Old English Glasses*, p. 347. See also Chapter 3.
87 C.L.R.O., MJ/SR 1764, indt. 28.   88 P.R.O., S.P. 35/32/23.
89 J. S. Cockburn, ed., *Calendar of Assize Records: Essex Indictments, Elizabeth I* (London, 1978), p. 373, no. 2245.
90 LeHardy and Reckitt, eds., *Buckingham Sessions Records*, vol. iv, pp. 157, 160, 175, 230.

should not be assumed to have had Jacobite sympathies merely beccause he allegedly called the Whig government of 1715 'a pack of Presbyterian villains'.[91]

Seditious words were distinctive. They did not dwell upon the political or religious situation of the nation, and they seldom gave voice to developed arguments. They mocked the ruling monarchs, but gave no justification for Jacobitism beyond the fundamental issue of heredi- tary right, or the vague promise of good times when the King enjoyed his own again. Within these verbal boundaries, however, treasonable expression flourished in great variety. Justices recognized the differ- ences between types of seditious words, and were always more severe in punishing those who claimed to be ready to act on their sentiments. John Owen, a gentleman of Bristol, confessed in 1692 to having said 'King James hath sent a Declaration into England wherein he declares That when he Comes into England, he will Take off half the Excise & the Customs shall not be halfe so much paid as it is now.' For this relatively innocuous 'false news', he was fined £6 13s 4d. Thomas Dowst of Bristol, gentleman, was indicted at the same Assizes for saying 'I have been in Towne & heard a Letter that Came from King James & have put my Sword & Pistolls forth to be in good Ord[r] & am resolved To go & meet him & he shall be Welcome to me.' He was fined £20 and committed until he paid it.[92] His heavier sentence was apparently due to the audacity of his words.

Most seditious words were not complaints or even threats. They were assertions of one king's right and another's lack of it. They did not constitute attacks on authority so much as avowals of a higher authority by which existing powers might be judged. This could be expressed in a very simple way – a blessing on King James, invective against the 'Rogue' seated on the throne – but it was always a dangerous principle. No greater treason was known to the law than what Thomas Cooke said in Wiltshire in 1715, for which he was thrice whipped and gaoled for three years without bail: 'I believe King James the third is right heir to the Crown'.[93]

The century after the Restoration witnessed recurring outbreaks of seditious words prosecutions, against republicans in the 1660s, radical

[91] P.R.O., K.B. 10/15, part 3, Michaelmas 1715, indt.; S.P. 44/118, p. 37.
[92] P.R.O., Assi. 5/12, part 2, Gloucs. 1692, indts.; Assi. 2/2, Gloucs. 20 July 4 W. & M., 31 March 5 W. & M.
[93] P.R.O., Assi. 23/5, Wiltshire Aut. 2 G. I, 5 Aug. 1715. This may have been the equivalent of a death sentence.

Whigs in the Exclusion Crisis, supporters of Monmouth under James II and Jacobites from 1689 until the accession of George III. Jacobite seditious words accusations ended on the Western Circuit in 1747; on the Oxford Circuit, in 1751. Interestingly, the last allegation sent to the government under George II was made in 1756 by the scholar Eugene Aram, who was later hanged for murder, against the political pamphleteer William Guthrie.[94] In Lancashire, North Yorkshire and Durham, the final cases of Jacobite words took place during the invasion scare of 1757. At Beverley in the East Riding, an Irishman allegedly damned King George in 1759, again while an invasion was feared; the same sentiment was voiced by an anti-militia rioter at Hexham in 1761.[95] After this came a long silence broken only by an occasional Catholic who denied the Royal Supremacy. The last outbreak of seditious words prosecutions in England occurred in the 1790s, directed once more against republicans.[96]

If political riots and seditious words are used to measure 'political stability', it can be suggested that, in spite of quiet periods, the English monarchy was never wholly secure from the 1640s until the 1830s. The restoration of royal prestige after the cataclysm of 1649 was not fully accomplished until the accession of Victoria, by which time there had been a considerable shift in constitutional authority. This interpretation, however, assumes that those who participated in Jacobite unrest, or who voiced seditious words, seriously threatened the settlements of 1689 and 1714. The preceding chapters have argued that those who rioted or spoke out in favour of the Stuarts did believe that the exiled family should be brought back to the throne. Their commitment to a restoration, of course, had its limits, but this observation is equally true of James Francis Stuart himself, who was never willing to risk everything on a reckless gamble. Jacobitism offered a great deal to those who longed for traditional social order, justice and legitimacy. It is not surprising that it had a popular appeal.

Yet popular Jacobitism thrived mainly in periods when the conventional Tory alternative was in temporary limbo, as in 1714–23 or 1747–52. Toryism prescribed many of the same remedies as Jacobitism, and it was largely the confusion of the Tories that produced the burgeoning of seditious unrest. Popular Jacobitism, moreover, was not

[94] P.R.O., S.P. 36/136, fos. 75–7. Both men are noticed in *D.N.B.*
[95] P.R.O., Assi. 45/26, part 4, nos. 39–40; Assi. 45/26, part 5, nos. 1A–D.
[96] See Clive Emsley, 'An Aspect of Pitt's "Terror": Prosecutions for Sedition during the 1790s', *S.H.*, 6, 2 (1981), pp. 155–84.

very effective. The Stuart court was never much interested in it, and it depended on the encouragement of local gentry and clergymen, or, as in London, on Tory grass-roots organization. It tended to become submerged without such support. Nobody, even in the most panicky Whig administration, ever believed that the populace was going to bring about a Stuart counter-revolution. What was feared was that disorder would create a chaotic situation, facilitating an insurrection among the gentry or an invasion from abroad. The most minor cases of seditious words were seen as contributing to the creation of such disorder.

It is difficult to compare the numbers of Jacobite supporters to those who adhered to other forms of popular protest. They were certainly more disruptive than the republicans of the 1660s, or the Monmouth-ites of the 1680s. The boundaries of Wilkite sentiment or of Jacobitism in the 1790s are vague, but it is likely that neither movement was more substantial than Jacobitism in its heyday. Only the vast demonstrations of the period after 1815 dwarf the unrest caused by the Jacobites; but they make all that came before look insignificant. Contemplating the huge numbers at Peterloo should remind historians not to exaggerate the scope of any previous popular political cause. The eighteenth century was developing towards a society in which mass politicization was possible, and Jacobitism definitely promoted this trend; but it took the economic changes of the period after 1760, and the effects of a long and arduous conflict between 1792 and 1815, to mobilize huge segments of the population.

Indeed, it is impossible to know what the political sentiments of the majority of the English people were in the eighteenth century. Most of the population worked in agriculture, but very few farmers or farm labourers became involved in rioting or seditious words cases. Even in the towns, only a minority of inhabitants expressed their political beliefs. It is probable that Jacobites outnumbered Hanoverian support-ers in most English towns in 1714–16 – many contemporary observers believed this to be the case. Their advantage was soon lost, however, and by the 1740s popular Jacobitism was restricted to a few of the larger urban centres and industrial villages. In the countryside, evi-dence of Jacobite sympathy is too fragmented to form a coherent picture. Edmund Burke, while staying in a village near Bradford in Wiltshire, supposed that most of the rural folk of the county were 'hearty Jacobites' as late as 1752, but he based this mainly on the disaffected opinions of his landlady.[97] Historians should be more careful in their conclusions.

The bulk of public sentiment was probably indifferent, and the weight of neutrality worked generally in favour of the *status quo*. Nevertheless, indifference was of little use in fighting a rebellion, as several commentators noted in 1745.[98] Lack of popular enthusiasm for the ruling monarch always worried the authorities. In 1695, a Post Office official wrote nervously from Warrington that 'when we had the good news of the surrender of the castle of Namur, our loyal town made never a bonfire but one that I made myself and all the companions I had was one mercer and two butchers'.[99] Such signs were regarded as ominous.

Uncertainty over which way the uncommitted would turn in periods of political upheaval lasted for almost a century. It allowed Samuel Johnson, discoursing with his Whig friend Dr John Taylor in September 1777, to make some remarks about popular Jacobitism that even Boswell called outrageous:

Sir, the state of the country is this: the people knowing it to be agreed upon all hands that this King has not the hereditary right to the crown, and there being no hope that he who has it can be restored, have grown cold and indifferent upon the subject of loyalty, and to have no warm attachment to any King. They would not, therefore, risk any thing to restore the exiled family. They would not give twenty shillings a piece to bring it about. But, if a mere vote could do it, there would be twenty to one; at least, there would be a very great majority of voices for it.

This claim may have been quite preposterous, but Johnson, who knew that there was still some popular Jacobitism alive in England in the late 1770s, was playing with the fact that no 'mere vote' of the adult population had ever been taken on the succession issue. His opponent had no better idea than Johnson what most of the common people felt about the Stuarts, and was induced to admit

that if the question as to hereditary right were to be tried by a poll of the people of England, to be sure the abstract doctrine would be given in favour of the family of Stuart; but he said, that the conduct of that family, which occasioned their expulsion, was so fresh in the minds of the people, that they would not

---

[97] Thomas W. Copeland, ed., *The Correspondence of Edmund Burke* (6 vols., Cambridge, 1958), vol. i, pp. 113–14.
[98] See B.L., Add. MS 29,913, p. 14.
[99] H.M.C., *Downshire*, vol. i, part ii, p. 544. The Williamite butchers are worth noting.

vote for the restoration. Dr. Johnson, I think, was contented with the admission as to the hereditary right, leaving the original point in dispute, *viz.* what the people on the whole would do, taking in right and affection; for he said, people were afraid of a change, even though they think it right.[100]

[100] Birkbeck-Hill and and Powell, eds., *Boswell's Life of Johnson*, vol. iii, pp. 156–7.

PART FOUR

Two faces of treason

Chapter 9

Lives of the gentry: Jacobitism and the landed elite

> I was born and bred a servant of your ffamily: my affection for it began with my Life, and shall end with it: It is the only part of my Inheritance which Violence and Power has not been able to break into: But whilst . . . I retain that Passion, I shall continue very little concernd for the rest.
>
> George Granville, Lord Lansdowne, to James III, 9 April 1720[1]

Ironically, the least explored area of Jacobite political culture is that which encompasses the behaviour of the landed elite. Plebeian Jacobitism is far more accessible to historians, because it was prosecuted in the courts. The aristocracy and gentry rarely appeared before judges or juries to answer for their political actions or statements. Moreover, Jacobitism did not often play an open role in Parliamentary politics. To some extent, this explains why Eveline Cruickshanks, studying the elaborate plots that pervade the Stuart Papers, proposed that the Tories were a Jacobite party, while Linda Colley, concentrating on Tory organization and structure, concluded that Jacobitism was only a minor phenomenon. The political life of the Tory landed classes, however, was not restricted either to clandestine conspiracy or to elections and Parliaments. Politics were integrated into the tissue of everyday life; Whiggery and Toryism describe different social outlooks as well as party affiliations. Individuals could wander from one camp to the other, but they were obliged to take on the cultural baggage associated with their new party. Only a handful of hugely ambitious magnates like the Duke of Marlborough, self-appointed arbiters like Robert Harley or eccentrics like the Earl of Shrewsbury could afford to detach themselves from the party cultures of their day.

This chapter will consider Jacobitism as a factor in the social lives of the landed classes. It will range over topics like education, marriage,

[1] R.A., Stuart 46/66.

careers, fashions, habits and death; at its centre is sociability, which brought together men of similar politics to drink and carouse. The influence of Jacobitism on these aspects of everyday life may reveal much about the nature of loyalty to the exiled Stuarts among the elite. How deeply did disaffection penetrate ordinary life? What political purposes were served by gentry sociability? Should this kind of Jacobitism be contrasted with the commitment of those who actually rose in rebellion, and whose sacrifices are examined in the next chapter?

To begin with, the limits of the landed elite should be determined. It included the aristocracy and the approximately 16,000 minor and major gentry families of England. It also comprised those who may not have owned land, but who claimed gentility through a close connection with a landed family. Into this category fell lawyers like Christopher Layer, merchants like William Benn and scholars like John Byrom. Finally, monied or professional men who purchased land and attained quasi-genteel status can also be seen as part of this elite. Few notable Jacobites, however, were self-made men; the importance of government patronage meant that an individual who was trying to advance himself on the national stage would hardly be attracted to a treasonable cause. Jacobite families whose wealth was based on trade, commerce or industry generally moved up into the elite under the Restoration monarchy, when High Church principles were more conducive to financial success. Nevertheless, on a local level, minor figures can be found who prospered as manufacturers, merchants or lawyers through connections with Jacobites in the county elite.

It is not easy to calculate the number of Jacobites in the elite – neither the English government nor the Stuart court was able to do it with any precision. In Chapter 5, however, it was argued that almost all Roman Catholics retained some allegiance to the banished monarchs until the 1760s; this would mean that between 7 and 10 per cent of the landed classes were disaffected throughout the period from the Revolution to the accession of George III. The Nonjurors never numbered more than a couple of hundred gentry families, or about 1 per cent of the elite. As for juring Anglican Jacobites, any estimate of their strength must rest on guesswork. Between 1714 and 1754, a consistent third of Tory M.P.s showed some definite sign of attachment to Jacobitism.[2]

---

2 This calculation is primarily based on the biographies in Sedgwick, ed., *History of Parliament*. I have tried to assess the reliability of evidence in each case. See also Christie, 'Tory Party', which arrives at a similar figure.

Whether or not this figure is indicative of Jacobite support in the nation at large is debatable. A haphazard attempt at estimating gentry Jacobitism on a county basis, using diverse sources of information from 1689 until 1760, turns up a variety of numbers, from 11 per cent in Sussex to about 40 per cent in Lancashire. In summation, it may be conjectured that about one in four English aristocrats and gentlemen harboured Jacobite sympathies under the first two Hanoverians, while a smaller number, perhaps one in six or seven, adhered to Jacobitism under William III and Queen Anne.

These disaffected patricians constituted a substantial market for Jacobite propaganda; they gave tacit encouragement to rioters and demonstrators, and they can often be connected with outbreaks of seditious words cases. They were the motor that powered the Jacobite cause. Yet they suffered for their actions less than any other group, and their behaviour has often been interpreted as empty posturing. This chapter, by pursuing diverse avenues of investigation, will suggest why elite Jacobitism should be taken seriously.

The making of a Jacobite

All lovers of eighteenth-century literature are familiar with Fielding's Squire Western, that boorish, blustering, brutal caricature of a West Country Tory squire, whose own sister cannot abide him:

'Your Ignorance, Brother,' returned she, 'as the great *Milton* says, almost subdues my Patience.' 'D—n *Milton*, ' answered the Squire, 'if he had the Impudence to say so to my Face, I'd lend him a Douse, thof he was never so great a Man ... Do you think no one hath any Understanding, unless he hath been about at Court? Pox! The World is coming to a fine Pass indeed if we are all Fools, except a Parcel of Roundheads and *Hannover* Rats. Pox! I hope the Times are a coming that we shall make Fools of them, and every Man shall enjoy his own. I hope to *zee* it, Sister, before the *Hannover* Rats have eat up all our Corn, and left us nothing but Turneps to feed upon.'[3]

Linda Colley has demolished the quaint idea that the Tory party was composed entirely of Squire Westerns; but ever since his invention, this unsympathetic gentleman has been the standard type of the Jacobite landowner. His ignorance, 'backwardness', hostility to the court and religious intolerance are often represented as characteristic of the Jacobite gentry, those 'diehards prepared to risk being permanent

---

[3] Fielding, *Tom Jones*, vol. i, pp. 321–2.

castaways', as one historian has recently called them.[4] It would be happy indeed if this were a true picture, because Jacobitism would then require little explanation. Unfortunately, reality was much more complicated. The Jacobite elite was not uneducated, 'backward' or parochial; it was as varied in background and aspirations as its Whig rivals, and included figures as different as the Duke of Wharton and Peter Legh of Lyme. Among those who inherited their Jacobite principles, however, certain recurring features of upbringing and training can be discerned.

Because religion was fundamental to the born Jacobite, it was fitting that many infants first encountered the Stuart cause in a religious ceremony: their christening. Proud Jacobite parents sometimes chose to give their children a lifelong distinction, or stigma, by naming them after a member of the disinherited line. The most famous example of this was Sir Theophilus Oglethorpe's son James Edward, who later founded the colony of Georgia.[5] Frances Sobieski Ince, daughter of a Lancastrian recusant family, was christened with the name of James III's queen around 1730.[6] 'Clementina' and 'Henry Benedict' were more popular with Catholics than among Anglicans, but 'Charles Edward' gained general acceptance. Five generations of Yorkshire Radclyffes, Protestant relatives of the Earls of Derwentwater, bore the names Charles Edward.[7] One wonders how many other infants were named 'Charles' or 'James' after the Pretenders. Did the ex-Tory Henry Fox merely wish to vaunt the Stuart ancestry of his Lennox wife when he named his son Charles James?

Having the Pretender as a godfather was a considerable honour for a Jacobite child. Hearne once met a Mr King of Hertfordshire, who was James III's first godson.[8] Christopher Layer sought a similar favour for his daughter at Rome in 1721, but had to settle for a proxy.[9] No ceremony abroad, however, could have been as elaborate as the 'extraordinary christening supper at Manchester' described by a scandalized Whig in 1746, at which the Hanoverians and Prince Charlie 'were present at the same table ... in paste or in plaster':

---

[4] Roy Porter, *English Society in the Eighteenth Century* (Harmondsworth, 1982), p. 129.

[5] Patricia Kneas Hill, *The Oglethorpe Ladies and the Jacobite Conspiracies* (Atlanta, 1977), p. 9.

[6] *V.C.H. Lancashire*, vol. iv, p. 105; Joseph Foster, *Pedigrees of the County Families of England*, vol. 1: *Lancashire* (London, 1873), under 'Atherton'.

[7] Charles P. Hampson, *The Book of the Radclyffes* (Edinburgh, 1940), pp. 257–60.

[8] Doble, *et al.*, eds., *Collections of Hearne*, vol. viii, p. 268.

[9] See Layer's biography in *D.N.B.*

there was his present Majesty in the centre of a dish of chickens with their rumps turned towards him, his late Majesty in a dish of unbuttered turnips, the Prince of Wales in a hasty pudding, and the Duke in a blood pudding ... the elegant treat closed with the young chevalier in the centre of a pyramid of sweetmeats. The young lady was baptised in a plaid mantle, and her name was Sobieski. I presume the clergyman who officiated was an excellent person, and well qualified to succeed Bishop Cappock [Reverend Thomas Coppock, a rebel of the '45].[10]

This delectable joke must have afforded great mirth in the Jacobite bastion of Manchester.

The atmosphere of Jacobite family life was predictably pious. John Dawnay of Cowick Hall, Yorkshire, a Tory M.P., had prayers read twice daily to everyone in his household, but never allowed King George I to be mentioned in these devotions.[11] Edward Gibbon noted in his memoirs that his grandfather retired after the Atterbury Plot to his house at Putney, where 'in the daily devotions of the family the name of the King, for whom they prayed, was prudently omitted'.[12] During the rebellion of 1745, however, when the family chaplain, John Kirkby, neglected to mention the King's name in morning prayers, Gibbon's father dismissed him – a revealing illustration of the sheer panic evinced among the Tory Jacobite gentry by Charles Edward's foolhardy attempt.[13] The situation passed, however; by the early 1750s, Gibbon senior was helping to finance the *True Briton*, and may have returned to his cautiously Jacobite orisons.[14] Understandably, some children rebelled against daily doses of legitimist piety. Edward Gibbon junior outraged his father by becoming first a Roman Catholic, then a freethinker, while John Dawnay's son Henry, Viscount Downe, defected to the Whigs.[15] Not all offspring were so refractory; the Bowdlers of Bath successfully transmitted their Nonjuring principles through three generations.[16] The bowdlerization of Shakespeare was the outcome of a century of strict Jacobite piety.

The daughters of Jacobite families were brought up to lead tradi-

[10] Quoted from Philip Doddrige's *Correspondence* in *Palatine Note-Book*, vol. iii (1883), p. 277.
[11] H.M.C., *Manuscripts of the Earl of Egmont. Diary of Viscount Percival, afterwards Earl of Egmont* (3 vols., London, 1920–23), vol. i, pp. 191–2; Sedgwick, ed., *History of Parliament*, vol. i, p. 607.
[12] Gibbon, *Memoirs*, p. 17.
[13] *Ibid.*, p. 31, and Chapter 5. For Gibbon senior's involvement in the conspiracy of 1743–4, see Cruickshanks, *Political Untouchables*, p. 40.
[14] B.L. Add. MS 28,236, fos. 2, 7, 12.
[15] Gibbon, *Memoirs*, pp. 59–61; Sedgwick, ed., *History of Parliament*, vol. i, p. 607.
[16] See [Bowdler], *John Bowdler*, *passim*.

tional lives as wives and mothers. Catholic women might become nuns – John Caryll, in fact, was ruined partly on account of the large sums he had to pay out to aunts who had entered convents in Belgium and France. Few Jacobite women attained more than a rudimentary education, although the cause attracted some notable female intellectuals. Mary Astell, the famous feminist writer of the 1690s, associated with the Nonjurors and with Bishop Atterbury, and made veiled references to hereditary right in her polemical works; she also advocated the creation of Protestant nunneries in which women could devote themselves to learning and piety.[17] She was not the only woman of Jacobite inclinations who took an interest in female education. In 1752, the Marquise de Mezières, formerly Eleanor Oglethorpe, established, with the aid of James III, a refuge for recusant women who had been forced to flee England, and for Protestant girls under the age of seven. The latter were admitted, according to the Marquise, because Protestant families cared only about the religious education of their sons![18]

Those Protestant Jacobite sons might be taught at home by a suitable tutor, like the Nonjuror William Law who instructed Gibbon's father; or they might be sent away to school. John Ellis, another Nonjuror, ran a school at Conyhatch near Highgate where he educated the sons of the Earl of Dartmouth, Earl Ferrers, Sir Charles Bagot, Sir Christopher Musgrave, Sir John Mordaunt and Sir John Cotton.[19] Of the great national schools, Winchester and Westminster were the Jacobite favourites. Disaffection thrived at the latter institution under the headmastership of Dr Robert Freind, brother of the Jacobite M.P. and physician John Freind. The rebel Earl of Mar's son was enrolled in the school in 1716, and Dr Freind was said to be 'as careful of him as if he were his own son', encouraging the boy to head the Jacobite party among his schoolmates.[20] Winchester was even more notoriously hostile to the Hanoverians; in March 1716/17, the wardens, fellows,

---

[17] See Ruth Perry, *The Celebrated Mary Astell: An Early English Feminist* (Chicago, 1986); Joan K. Kinnaird, 'Mary Astell and the Conservative Contribution to English Feminism', *J.B.S.*, 19 (1979), pp. 53–79; Bridget Hill, 'A Refuge from Men: The Idea of a Protestant Nunnery', *P. & P.*, 117 (1987), pp. 107–30; Paul Monod, 'The Politics of Matrimony: Jacobitism and Marriage in Eighteenth-Century England', in Eveline Cruickshanks and Jeremy Black, eds., *The Jacobite Challenge* (Edinburgh, 1988), pp. 31–6.

[18] Hill, *Oglethorpe Ladies*, pp. 121–4.

[19] P.R.O., S.P. 35/65/136. On schoolmasters in this period, see Geoffrey Holmes, *Augustan England: Professions, State and Society, 1680–1730* (London, 1982), ch. 3.

[20] H.M.C., *Stuart*, vol. iii, p. 143.

masters, usher and children of the school were presented by the grand
jury of Hampshire Assizes 'for their known disaffection and corruption
of manners'.[21] The tactic did not work, for on 1 August 1718, the boys
'came into the Church in the middle of the Service with Rue and Time
in theire breasts, and others with Crape hatt bands in their hatts'.[22]
Secretary Craggs himself ordered that 'these poor children' be
whipped. Yet as late as 1753, the college warden, John Coxed of
Bucknell, was referred to as one of 'the honestest Jacks in Hampshire'.[23]

Although University enrolments shrank in the century after 1660,
the upper ranks of the landed classes continued to favour some higher
learning for their sons.[24] For Jacobite fathers, the advantages of
Oxford over Cambridge were obvious. The Whiggery of Cambridge
should not be exaggerated, but Jacobitism was treated harshly there.
Several of the fellows of St John's College, Cambridge, were summarily
ejected for refusing the oaths in 1690; a second purge in 1716/17
removed the college's remaining Nonjurors.[25] Students were less easily
intimidated; some of them fought with soldiers in January 1691/2 over
a royal toast proposed by the vice-chancellor, and in 1715 a group of
Johnsians loudly celebrated the Pretender's birthday at the Three
Tunns tavern.[26] The serious attacks by townsmen and gownsmen on
Trinity and Clare Colleges on 28–9 May 1716 were described in
Chapter 6, but after 1717, Cambridge was pretty tranquil. A young
Jacobite on the banks of the Cam must have felt himself to be a lonely,
isolated and persecuted individual. In 1749, two undergraduates,
Charles Amcotts, who later became M.P. for Boston, and Edward
Parker, were expelled for drinking the Pretender's health.[27] The
University dealt with this last flourish of legitimism in characteristically
severe fashion.

The situation at Oxford was much more congenial. No mass refusals
to swear oaths took place there, and the occasional Nonjuror, like

[21] V.C.H. Hampshire and the Isle of Wight (5 vols., London, 1900–12), vol. ii, p. 344.
[22] Ibid., and P.R.O., S.P. 35/12/97; S.P. 44/79A, pp. 212–13.
[23] B.L., Add. MS 28,231, fo. 142.
[24] On the decline in numbers at the Universities, see Lawrence Stone, 'The Size and Composition of the Oxford Student Body, 1580–1910', in L. Stone, ed., The University in Society (2 vols., Princeton, 1974), vol. i, pp. 37–59.
[25] Overton, The Nonjurors, pp. 187–8.
[26] Luttrell, vol. ii, p. 330; P.R.O., S.P. 35/3/63, (1)–(2).
[27] Namier and Brooke, eds., History of Parliament, vol. ii, p. 19; Ellen d'Oench, The Conversation Piece: Arthur Devis and his Contemporaries (New Haven, Ct, 1980), p. 61.

Thomas Hearne, was allowed quietly to remain in residence. A recent historian of the University has fumed at the injustice done to it by malicious Whigs after 1714, but his own account makes it evident that government fears of disaffection were not groundless.[28] The vicious rioting of 28–9 May 1715, detailed in Chapter 6, resulted in a reprimand for the vice-chancellor, and there was more unruliness at Oxford before the year ended, with a messenger attacked by a large crowd in August, and the descent of General Pepper to disperse the Jacobite conspirators in October.[29] One of the plotters boasted of raising 1,000 scholars to support the rising – doubtless, an inflated estimate, but suggestive of undergraduate opinion.[30] The arrival of King George's troops did not put a stop to disorder. In December 1715, two Balliol scholars were arrested for calling some soldiers 'Rebells', and in February 1715/16, two Exeter College undergraduates were beaten by officers for playing 'The King shall enjoy his own again' on a hautboy.[31] The riots of 29 May and 30 October 1716, which were discussed in Chapter 6, mainly involved townspeople, but it is significant that, in contrast to Cambridge, none of the colleges was attacked.

The passage of time cured none of Oxford's disloyalty to the Hanoverians. Gownsmen were accused of reviving Jacobite slogans during the celebrations for the dropping of the Excise Bill in 1733.[32] Three undergraduates were presented at Assizes for breaking windows at Whiggish Exeter College, and crying 'Down with King George … King James for ever', on 10 June 1747.[33] Prince Henry Benedict's birthday in February 1747/8 was commemorated by five undergraduates who gathered at Balliol; after drinking too much, they boldly marched to Exeter College, and threw dirt at the windows, shouting 'God bless King James, God damn King George'. When the Whig scholar Richard Blacow tried to disperse them, he was greeted with the memorable words, 'I am the man that dare say God bless King James

28 Ward does not mention the (apocryphal?) story that the garden gates of Trinity College were to be closed until the Stuarts returned. Conrad Russell believes, alas, that he saw them open in 1960 to admit a load of beer. Jonathan Clark, however, maintains that they are fixed shut.
29 P.R.O., S.P. 44/116, pp. 293–7, 302–3; S.P. 35/2/18; S.P. 35/3/29; and Chapter 10.
30 *St. James's Evening Post*, no. 76, 22–4 Nov. 1715; Boyer, *Political State*, vol. x, pp. 585–6.
31 P.R.O., Assi. 5/36, part 2, Oxon. Qua. 2 G. I, infos. 8–11, 15.
32 Coxe, *Memoirs of Sir Robert Walpole*, vol. iii, p. 137; but see Ward, pp. 149–50.
33 P.R.O., S.P. 36/103, fo. 171. To the government's disgust, the bills against them were found *ignoramus*.

the 3d and tell you my name is Dawes of St. Mary Hall. I am a man of independent fortune and therefore am afraid of *no one* or *no man*. James Dawes was later indicted at King's Bench, along with his friends John Whitmore and Charles Luxmoore; the vice-chancellor was also prosecuted, for refusing to take the testimony of witnesses. This did not prevent the unrepentant Dawes and Whitmore from rioting again, with a musical band, outside Balliol gates in October. A month later, the pair were sentenced to a fine and two years' imprisonment; Luxmoore and the vice-chancellor were acquitted.[34] Yet when William Pitt visited Oxford in April 1749, for the opening of the Radcliffe Camera, he heard undergraduates singing treasonable songs, saw pictures of Charles Edward for sale in the market and witnessed Dr King's rousing Jacobite oration.[35]

Although Jacobitism was alive at Oxford after the '45, it was more constrained. None of the incidents of 1747–8 was very large, and the demonstrators were swiftly punished. Exeter was by this time a Whig stronghold, and Jacobite sentiment had withdrawn into certain other colleges; at Magdalen in 1752–3, for example, Edward Gibbon found that 'the constitutional toasts were not expressive of the most lively loyalty for the house of Hanover'.[36] In December 1754, after the disastrous Oxfordshire election, five scholars of Corpus Christi, including a future college president, were fined for hanging a picture of Charles Edward Stuart in the undergraduate common room.[37] In an earlier age, they might not have been punished at all.

In its heyday, Oxford's well-deserved Jacobite reputation rested not only on the undergraduates, but on academics like Dr William King of St Mary's Hall. Its Parliamentary representation was almost entirely Jacobite in sympathy from 1698 until the 1760s; the only Hanoverian Tory who sat for the University was George Clarke, who was challenged by the 'downright Jacobite' Dr Peirce Dod of All Souls in 1717 and by Dr King himself in 1722.[38] Oxford was perhaps the sole constituency in England where a staunch Tory could be opposed on the basis of his not being enough of a Jacobite. As late as 1762, in the

---

[34] *Mitre and Crown*, vol. i, Nov. 1748, pp. 105–8; Richard Blacow, *A Letter to William King, D.D.* (London, 1755); Ward, pp. 169–71; P.R.O., S.P. 44/84, pp. 206–7; S.P. 44/133, pp.408–9, 415–17, 423.

[35] Horace Walpole, *Memoirs of the Reign of King George the Second*, ed. by Lord Holland (2 vols., London, 1846), vol. i, p. 413. Ward, p. 199, shows that this must have taken place in April 1749, not in 1754 as Pitt implied.

[36] Gibbon, *Memoirs*, p. 53.

[37] Petrie, *The Jacobite Movement: The Last Phase*, p. 160.

[38] Ward, pp. 123–8.

election to choose a successor to the Jacobite chancellors Arran and Westmorland, the candidacy of Lord Lichfield, a Tory who had gone to court, was opposed by Lord Foley, who was backed, according to Henry Fox and Dr King, by the remnants of the Jacobite party.[39] With so much to recommend it, the University's appeal to adherents of the exiled monarchs is easy to appreciate. Oxford could give birth to, as well as nurture, friends of the Stuarts; it transformed Sir John Philipps, the son of a Whig M.P., into an arch-Jacobite Tory.[40] Of course, not every corner of the place was hostile to Hanover; the vice-chancellors and most heads of colleges, whatever their private views, did not actively seek to promote disaffection. Jacobitism prospered because of the encouragement of some academics, because of the Tory traditions of the institution and because so many undergraduates had been raised in it.

After Oxford came the Grand Tour; but the son of a Jacobite family had to be very circumspect abroad, because England's ambassadors were careful to watch the behaviour of young travellers. Sir Justinian Isham in 1719 warned his son, who was making the Grand Tour, to use discretion when at Rome on account of the number of spies there.[41] A personal interview with the Pretender, furthermore, could cause a young man to do and say extraordinary things. The Duke of Wharton met James III at Avignon in 1716, and never really recovered.[42] William Godolphin, Viscount Rialton, also renounced his Whig patrimony after seeing James at Rome in 1721.[43] The Whig Thomas Coke, who fell in love with Louisa of Stolberg while making his Grand Tour in 1772, returned to England and joined the Cocoa Tree Club.[44] His father was outraged, but young Coke may have been following the example of his grandsire Richard, who was said to have spoken disparagingly of King George while on the Grand Tour in 1715.[45] Travelling Whig grandees did not even have to set eyes on the Stuarts in order to be transformed; John Newport, heir to the Earl of Bradford, fled his tutor and installed himself with the exiled Duke of Ormonde at

---

[39] Ibid., pp. 221–2. Although he was defeated, Foley won the support of William Blackstone, a Tory of very complicated politics, and gained a majority of votes at New Inn Hall and four colleges.

[40] Colley, In Defiance of Oligarchy, p. 86.

[41] Sedgwick, ed., History of Parliament, vol. ii, pp. 169–70. For a general discussion of touring, see Jeremy Black, The Grand Tour (Edinburgh, 1986).

[42] See H.M.C., Stuart, vol. ii, p. 473.

[43] Sedgwick, ed., History of Parliament, vol. ii, pp. 67–8, and Chapter 1.

[44] Stirling, Coke of Norfolk, pp. 65–6, 87–8; see also Chapter 3.

[45] B.L., Add. MS 38,507, fo. 174.

Avignon in 1739.[46] One can imagine what effects the Grand Tour might produce on a Tory; Viscount Cornbury's visit to Rome in 1731 actually resulted in the concoction of a new restoration plot.[47] The son of Sir Rowland Hill, a Hanoverian Tory, may have had similar intentions when he and an unnamed companion sought out Charles Edward in Flanders in 1758.[48] Some Tory youths deliberately avoided the Stuarts so as to steer clear of embarrassing themselves; the second Sir Watkin Williams Wynn side-stepped the Pretender at Rome in 1768, although he paid a call on the Jacobite antiquarian Abbé Grant.[49]

Home again, the frivolity of Oxford and the irresponsibility of the Grand Tour left behind, the young Jacobite must consider marriage and a career. As I have argued elsewhere, politics was important in marital choice.[50] Religious endogamy among Roman Catholics and Nonjurors virtually ensured that marriage partners had the same politics, although mis-matches were possible, as in the case of the eighth Duke of Norfolk, whose wife left him for 'truckling with the usurper'.[51] Tory M.P.s tended to marry within party lines, although Jacobite Tories did not wed exclusively among themselves. Nevertheless, a successful marriage usually required political compatibility, as the irate Williamite Tory Reverend Samuel Wesley informed his Jacobite wife Susanna in 1701, when he told her 'we must part, for if we have two Kings, we must have two beds'.[52] Like almost all eighteenth-century husbands, Jacobite men subscribed to vague patriarchal views of marriage, although they were often remarkably affectionate towards their wives and children. High Church piety may have mitigated male domination and heightened the emotional content of Jacobite marriages, just as it inspired feminist writers like Mary Astell to argue for an end to the absolute power of husbands.[53]

---

[46] P.R.O., S.P. 36/48, fo. 170.

[47] Cruickshanks, *Political Untouchables*, p. 12, and her essay 'Lord Cornbury'.

[48] de Polnay, *Death of a Legend*, p. 188. From evidence in *D.N.B.*, it seems likely that these youths were Richard Hill, the future evangelical, and Lord Elgin.

[49] T. W. Pritchard, *The Wynns at Wynnstay* (Caerwys, 1982), p. 11; for Grant, see Chapter 5.

[50] Monod, 'The Politics of Matrimony', in Cruickshanks and Black, eds., *Jacobite Challenge*.

[51] Robinson, *Dukes of Norfolk*, p. 150.

[52] Rebecca Lamar Harmon, *Susanna: Mother of the Wesleys* (Nashville, 1968), p. 47. Their reconciliation on King William's death led to the birth of their son John.

[53] For differing interpretations of English marriage, see Lawrence Stone, *The Family, Sex and Marriage in England, 1550–1800* (New York, 1977), and Alan Macfarlane, *Marriage and Love in England: Modes of Reproduction, 1300–1840* (Oxford, 1986).

The choice of a career, like that of a spouse, was partly a political issue for Jacobites, because some of them scrupled at taking oaths. Those who did not might go into the legal profession. Among the Inns of Court, the Middle Temple was preferred by Jacobites; Christopher Layer practised there, and George Gordon, who wrote for the *National Journal*, gave it as his address.[54] William King and the publicist George Osborne both resided in 'the Temple'.[55] Jacobite lawyers could do a brisk business; Layer had a huge practice, and Sir Constantine Phipps made a fortune from defending men like Sacheverell and Atterbury.[56] Roman Catholics and Nonjurors could not enter the law, but some were connected with it; John Bowdler the elder became a chamber conveyancer in 1770, and the recusant Francis Plowden, descendant of an eminent jurist, was the most famous legal expert of the late eighteenth century. Plowden's clients included Charles Edward Stuart, whom he advised on the recovery of Mary of Modena's jointure in the 1780s, and the Whig leader Charles James Fox.[57]

Medicine was a career open to all Jacobites, and a few of them were in the vanguard of change in the profession. One of the leaders of the London Society of Apothecaries in its struggle against the hegemony of the Royal College of Physicians was James St Amand, who became a Nonjuror and Jacobite agent after the Revolution.[58] Dr John Radcliffe, whose Jacobite proclivities were as well known as his medical expertise, was the wealthiest and most influential physician in England under William III and Anne; his huge London practice was matched after 1714 by the Jacobite John Freind.[59] As an undergraduate at Oxford, the famous anatomy lecturer Frank Nicholls had been fined and forced to beg the pardon of the University Convocation for crying out 'An Ormond for ever' during a Jacobite incident in January 1715/16.[60] Most Jacobite medical men, however, were cut off from the mainstream of institutional patronage, and pursued modest careers serving like-minded gentlefolk. They included the Lancashire Nonjuror Roger

For child-rearing, see Linda A. Pollock, *Forgotten Children: Parent–Child Relations from 1500 to 1900* (Cambridge, 1985).
54 For Layer, see *D.N.B.*; for Gordon, P.R.O., S.P. 44/83, pp. 521–2. On the legal profession, see Holmes, *Augustan England*, ch. 5.
55 Greenwood, *William King*, pp. 374–5. Osborne's *Mitre and Crown* was 'By a Gentleman late of the *Temple*.'
56 He is noticed in *D.N.B.*
57 See *D.N.B.* and Beinecke Osborn Files, 'Lavington Box'.
58 Henning, ed., *History of Parliament*, vol. iii, pp. 379–80. For the medical profession, see Holmes, *Augustan England*, chs. 6–7.
59 See C. R. Hone, *Life of Dr. John Radcliffe, 1652–1714* (London, 1950); Sedgwick, ed., *History of Parliament*, vol. ii, pp. 53–4.
60 P.R.O., Assi. 2/5, Oxon. Qua. 2 G. I; Ward, p. 62.

Kenyon and the Nonjuring Bishop Thomas Deacon, whose practice was supported by the Lever family of Alkrington.[61]

The Jacobite elite had no compunctions about making money through business, trade, finance and manufacturing, although they disliked stock-jobbing, which they saw as parasitical.[62] Jacobites were especially prominent in industry. The rebel warehousemen of Manchester will be considered in the next chapter. John Crowley, who owned the largest ironworks in England, was arrested for his part in the conspiracy of 1715, and offered £20,000 for the Pretender's service during the Swedish Plot. One of his sisters married Sir Humphry Parsons, the wealthy Jacobite brewer; another wed Sir John Hynde Cotton.[63] Crowley and Parsons were both London aldermen, members of a strong Jacobite group that emerged in the upper body of City government in the 1720s, and deserves special notice here. One of its members was Sir Francis Child of Osterley Park, owner of Child's Bank, who received a note of thanks from James III for drawing up a violently objectionable Common Council address on the accession of George II.[64] Six other London aldermen – Robert Willimot, Robert Westley, George Heathcote, Edward Gibbon, William Benn and Daniel Lambert – conferred with a French agent in 1743 on the feasibility of a restoration attempt.[65]

Most of these City merchants, however, were scared back into Hanoverian loyalty by the discovery of the invasion plan of 1743–4, and they cringingly supported a loyal address to George II. Nevertheless, several of them fled London during the '45, fearing arrest, and took shelter at Alderman John Blachford's house on the Isle of Wight. In 1752, a painting by Hudson was presented to the Goldsmiths' Company, where it still hangs, showing the fugitive aldermen – William Benn, in a plaid waistcoat, John Blachford, Edward Ironside, Henry Marshall, Robert Alsop and Thomas Rawlinson – drinking a toast, while at their feet lies a letter franked by Sir Watkin Williams Wynn, a copy of the famous epistle sent to Derby.[66] This painting was a

---

[61] Overton, The Nonjurors, pp. 266–7; Broxap, Thomas Deacon, p. 87.
[62] For Tory criticism of stock-jobbers, see Dickson, Financial Revolution, ch. 2; Kramnick, Bolingbroke and his Circle, chs. 2–3.
[63] See M. W. Flinn, Men of Iron: The Crowleys in the Early Iron Industry (Edinburgh, 1962), pp. 58, 67–73.
[64] Sedgwick, ed., History of Parliament, vol. i, p. 549.
[65] Cruickshanks, Political Untouchables, pp. 40–1, 139–47.
[66] Ellen Gross Miles, 'Thomas Hudson (1701–1779): Portraitist to the British Establishment', unpublished Ph.D. dissertation, Yale University, 1976, vol. i, pp. 82–4; Greater London Council, Thomas Hudson: 1701–1779, Portrait Painter and Collector (London, 1979), plate 52 and notes. See also Plate 12.

visual vindication of its subjects from the charge of having done nothing to help the cause during the rebellion. In fact, Benn and George Heathcote were central to Charles Edward's insurrectionary schemes of 1750–2, and Alderman Daniel Lambert, a wine merchant, apparently channelled money to Irish Jacobite recruiters in the late 1740s.[67]

Almost all of the Jacobite aldermen could trace their origins to the gentry. Benn's family came from Hertfordshire, Henry Marshall was related to the Drakes of Buckinghamshire and Thomas Rawlinson's ancestors had lived in Lancashire.[68] They were mainly involved in the higher levels of commerce and finance, where it was not necessary to have a background in a particular trade. Child, Blachford and Ironside were goldsmith-bankers, and even the solitary self-made man among the Jacobite City politicians, the printer John Barber, transferred from the Stationers' to the Goldsmiths' Company. They were a very charitable group, and they dominated the management of several foundations, including the hospitals of Bridewell and St Bartholomew's.[69] For two decades, the Jacobite aldermen were a potent force in the economic and social life of the City; but after William Benn's death in 1755, they were led by the Hanoverian Tory William Beckford away from the Stuarts and into the arms of William Pitt. By the 1760s, they had disintegrated; Beckford became a radical reformer, but he did not bring his old colleagues with him.[70]

If trade or the professions were not suitable careers, a Jacobite gentleman could turn to the navy. The army, which was more strictly scrutinized by the government and more strongly resented by Tory landowners, was out of the question, but the royal navy was manned over the years by a sizeable crew of Stuart supporters. It was, after all, King James's own service, and many of his old colleagues at the Admiralty, including Samuel Pepys, Sir Anthony Deane and Thomas Bowdler, became Nonjurors after the Revolution.[71] In exile, James

67 R.A., Stuart 296/24; Lang, *Pickle the Spy*, p. 178; P.R.O., S.P. 36/112, fos. 137–8.
68 See B.L., Add. MS 62,558, fo. 55 (Benn of Westmell); Sedgwick, ed., *History of Parliament*, vol. ii, p. 243 (Marshall); Foster, *Lancashire Pedigrees*, 'Rawlinson'. For the social backgrounds of London aldermen, see Nicholas Rogers, 'Money, Land and Lineage: The Big Bourgeoisie of Hanoverian London', *S.H.*, 4, 3 (1979), pp. 437–54.
69 For the commercial, charitable and livery affiliations of the Jacobite aldermen, see Alfred B. Beaven, *The Aldermen of the City of London Temp. Henry III.–1912* (2 vols., London, 1908–13), pp. 124–9; O'Donoghue, *Bridewell Hospital*, pp. 272–3.
70 Colley, *In Defiance of Oligarchy*, pp. 270–83.
71 Pepys and Deane are noticed in *D.N.B.* and in Henning, ed., *History of Parliament*, vol. ii, pp. 200–1, vol. iii, pp. 226–8; for Bowdler, see Overton, *The Nonjurors*, pp. 254–5.

managed to seduce Admirals Sir Ralph Delaval, Henry Killigrew and Edward Russell to his side, although they were fickle friends.[72] Peregrine Osborne, second Duke of Leeds, followed a naval career until 1715, when he revealed his Jacobite allegiance and went into exile.[73] The Hanoverians failed to purge the navy as efficiently as the army, and as late as 1744, the French sought assistance in their invasion attempt from two British naval commanders, Christopher O'Brien and the Honourable Fitzroy Lee. Lord Barrymore's son, Lieutenant Richard Barry, was at Dunkirk with the invasion fleet; when the scheme collapsed, his father, then under arrest, had the audacity to request a promotion for him from the Duke of Newcastle! Amazingly, it was granted, so that Commander Richard Barry carried the letter to Derby in December 1745.[74]

Like Pope's Man of Ross, the Jacobite gentleman might have no wider ambition than the peaceful cultivation of his estates.[75] Yet many other careers were open to him, from law and medicine to commerce, banking or the navy. Jacobitism was never merely the prejudice of a poor, isolated, uneducated petty squirearchy; it infiltrated every section of the landed elite, and became, for many enterprising and active individuals, not so much a bad habit as a way of life.

Maintaining the cause

How was Jacobitism preserved in the lives of the elite? Immediately, one thinks of organized politics and the Parliamentary opposition to Whig rule. Yet these were often peripheral to the Jacobite life-style. King James's adherents in England were frequently reluctant to involve themselves too deeply in a political system whose legitimacy they doubted, and which branded them as outcasts. Roman Catholics and Nonjurors were excluded from office-holding; they supported the Tory party at elections, but they did not insist on Jacobite purity from candidates. Neither did Tory Jacobite voters; as Daniel Szechi has shown, even the most disaffected of them, like Peter Legh of Lyme,

---

[72] Jones, *Mainstream of Jacobitism*, p. 54; Macpherson, *Secret History*, vol. i, pp. 420, 457, 459–60; D.N.B.

[73] Henning, ed., *History of Parliament*, vol. iii, p. 185.

[74] Cruickshanks, *Political Untouchables*, p. 55; Sedgwick, ed., *History of Parliament*, vol. i, p. 442.

[75] For Pope's 'country house ideal', see Howard Erksine-Hill, *The Social Milieu of Alexander Pope: Lives, Examples and the Creative Response* (New Haven, Ct, 1975), esp. ch. 1.

were willing to work for the return of any sort of High Churchman.[76] About one third of Tory M.P.s throughout the period 1715–54 clearly exhibited Jacobite sympathies, making the Jacobites the largest pressure group within Tory ranks under George I and II; but the majority of party leaders wavered in their allegiances, and it would be misleading to describe the Tories as dominated by Jacobitism. In fact, most Tory Jacobite M.P.s were back-benchers, and the fiercest of independents; a number of them retired in disgust from politics, like Sir Thomas Dyke and Lord Digby in 1696, or Ralph Sneyd, Henry Campion and Francis Scobell in 1715. Prominent Tory leaders who became entangled with the exiled Stuarts tended to tailor their loyalties according to the dictates of the Parliamentary politics that were their main concern. Although there were exceptions, like the Dukes of Beaufort, it can be said that the steadiness of a statesman's allegiance was usually in inverse proportion to his political significance.[77]

The most loyal of Stuart supporters could find little to delight them in party politics; so some of them sought consolation through direct contacts with the Stuart court. None of the exiled monarchs was ever lonely for English company. Their shadow courtiers were mainly Roman Catholics, but a few Protestants could always be found among them, such as James II's Lord Chancellor Edward Herbert, Baron Griffin, Sir Thomas Higgons and the post-1715 exiles Bolingbroke, Ormonde, Lansdowne, Strafford, North and Atterbury.[78] Heneage Finch, the future Earl of Winchelsea, was arrested in 1690 while trying to flee to St Germain, and was obliged to remain in England for the rest of his life.[79] Temporary visitors often came in times of peace. After the Treaty of Ryswick, a succession of Tory M.P.s filtered over to St Germain; among them were William Bromley, Sir Thomas Twisden, Charles Aldworth, John Pitt, Sir Nathaniel Napier, Sir John Parsons, Sir Henry Johnson and Francis Scobell. Lady Grosvenor, the Roman Catholic wife of a Tory M.P., also spent much time at the Stuart court.[80]

Few Tory M.P.s visited the courts of James III, because of the dangers involved, although the Whig Robert Pigott, whose family was

---

[76] Szechi, *Jacobitism and Tory Politics*, pp. 61–2.
[77] This paragraph is based mainly on the biographies found in Henning, ed., *History of Parliament*, and Sedgwick, ed., *History of Parliament*.
[78] For their positions at court, see the appendices to Ruvigny, *Jacobite Peerage*.
[79] Henning, ed., *History of Parliament*, vol. iii, p. 324.
[80] Ward, p. 13; Sedgwick, ed., *History of Parliament*, vol. i, p. 181 n. 3, vol. ii, p. 488; Manchester, *Court and Society*, vol. ii, pp. 113–20, 138, 186–7.

staunchly Tory, made the trip, and was presented with the Pretender's portrait.[81] An opposition Whig, Robert Nedham, came to Rome with William King in 1736.[82] 'Charles III' began to receive court visitors only after John Baptist Caryll went to England in 1769 to revive Jacobite support. John Hampden, a descendant of the famous Parliamentarian, was despatched in 1770 by those Caryll had contacted, in order to assess Charles's character. Hampden was an ally of George Grenville, many of whose supporters were ex-Tories.[83] A Grenvillite of Tory lineage, Henry Seymour, became Louisa Stuart's lover in 1775, reportedly with the approval of her husband.[84] Another admirer of the Stuart Queen was Henry Herbert, Earl of Pembroke, who admitted to little regard for her spouse, but 'liked her exceedingly, so well, that I should be happy to endevor [sic] to prevent the extinction of the Stuart line'.[85] The Earl resided at Rome in 1784–5 with Charles and his daughter Charlotte; she became enraptured with 'Mylord Pimbrocke', although his only surviving comment about her was cruel.[86] Among the last Englishmen to visit Charles Edward was the playwright Bertie Greatheed, a friend of Charles James Fox.[87] It might be assumed that a call on the Pretender was no longer a political act; yet all of his visitors were supporters of the opposition, and even those who dropped in through curiosity might suffer strange effects. The radical Silas Neville saw Charles Edward and Cardinal York on a trip to Italy in 1779; he returned to England much less of a republican, and was even allowed to see the Duchess of Gordon's private collection of Stuart artefacts.[88]

---

81 He is noticed in *D.N.B.* and in Sedgwick, ed., *History of Parliament*, vol. ii, p. 374.
82 P.R.O., S.P. 36/95, fo. 5; R.A., Stuart 191/168; Sedgwick, ed., *History of Parliament*, vol. ii, pp. 290–1.
83 R.A., Stuart 450/48; Namier and Brooke, eds., *History of Parliament*, vol. ii, pp. 575–6. George Grenville was Sir Watkin Williams Wynn's father-in-law.
84 Lewis, ed., *Walpole Correspondence*, vol. xxiv, pp. 94, 102. Sir Roger Newdigate was at Rome later in 1775, but there is no evidence that he saw Charles at Florence – *ibid.*, p. 144.
85 Lord Herbert, ed., *Henry, Elizabeth and George (1734–80): Letters and Diaries of Henry, Tenth Earl of Pembroke and his Circle* (London, 1939), pp. 44–5.
86 He suggested that she should marry his house steward – Lord Herbert, ed., *Pembroke Papers (1780–1794): Letters and Diaries of Henry, Tenth Earl of Pembroke and his Circle* (London, 1950), p. 265. See also R.A., Stuart Add. 5/1, transcripts of Bodleian Library letters of Charlotte Stuart, vol. ii, no. 68, an unnumbered letter of 14 Feb. 1787. Nevertheless, Pembroke was instrumental in promoting Charles's request for Mary of Modena's dowry – *Gentleman's Magazine*, vol. lxxvii, part 2, Sept. 1807, p. 883.
87 Robert Chambers, *History of the Rebellion of 1745–6* (London and Edinburgh, 1869), pp. 504–5.
88 Basil Cozens-Hardy, ed., *The Diary of Silas Neville 1767–1788* (London, 1950), pp. 269–70.

Jacobites who could not make the trip to France or Italy could still send money. In 1699, Colonel Henry Slingsby reputedly brought £1,300 to King James from his friends in London.[89] Catholics in Lancashire took up collections for the Pretender under Queen Anne, and in 1715–16, the spirited Catherine, dowager Lady Petre, offered £1,000 to support the rebellion, while the Dukes of Marlborough and Norfolk remitted £2,000 each.[90] Father Thomas Southcott and Bishop Atterbury raised £18,000 in five months to finance the Swedish Plot of 1716.[91] A regular remittance system existed by 1731, when Nathaniel Mist advised the Stuart court that the Dukes of Norfolk, Bedford and Beaufort, the Duchess of Buckingham and the Marquis of Blandford were all rich enough to pay what was being asked of them.[92] The Duke of Beaufort led a Jacobite Tory group known as the Remitters after the '45; Godfrey Bagnall Clarke explained to James Boswell that the English Jacobites had 'cleared up' their failure to rise in the rebellion by sending money.[93] Charles Edward received small amounts from the Nonjurors until 1765, and in 1761 the recusant Lady Mary Webb paid 1,695 French *livres* into the Prince's account at Paris.[94] Donating money to the Stuarts was not a form of charity; the exiled family was never desperate for funds, and remittances from England can be seen as 'freely granted taxation' that cemented the relationship between subject and monarch. Like all taxes, these grants were often resented; the enormously wealthy Sir Watkin Williams Wynn, for example, excused himself from contributing anything in 1743 because he was too poor![95] Yet many others – and probably Wynn himself, after 1745 – gave sums great and small as assurances of their allegiance.

The preservation of elite Jacobitism did not depend on direct contact with the Stuarts. It often centred on personal pursuits, especially

---

89 Manchester, *Court and Society*, vol. ii, p. 118.
90 P.R.O., S.P. 34/12/138; S.P. 34/12/141; S.P. 34/12/150; S.P. 34/12/151; H.M.C., *Stuart*, vol. i, p. 348; Jones, *Mainstream of Jacobitism*, p. 107; Edward Gregg, 'Marlborough in Exile, 1712–1714', *H.J.*, 15, 4 (1972), p. 617.
91 Sedgwick, ed., *History of Parliament*, vol. i, p. 62; Fritz, *English Ministers and Jacobitism*, pp. 14–18; H.M.C., *Stuart*, vol. v, p. 456.
92 R.A., Stuart 142/141–2. He also mentioned that the Duchess of Marlborough might send money too.
93 Lord Fitzmaurice, *Life of William, Earl of Shelburne* (2 vols., London, 1912), vol. i, p. 38; Brady and Pottle, eds., *Boswell on the Grand Tour*, p. 67.
94 R.A., Stuart 409/128, 428/136. John Caryll reported in 1769–70 that money might again be sent from England, but no more was heard of this – R.A., Stuart 448/83A–C, 450/83.
95 Colley, *In Defiance of Oligarchy*, p. 34.

intellectual interests, such as antiquarianism or poetry writing. Anti-quarianism, in particular the exhumation of 'feudal law', had once been the preserve of critics of Stuart policy, but the final demolition of the idea of an 'ancient constitution' shifted antiquarian research into the royalist camp.[96] By the mid-eighteenth century, the congruence of antiquarianism and Jacobitism was notorious. Horace Walpole promised Richard Bentley in 1753 that 'my love of abbeys will not make me hate the Reformation till that makes me grow a Jacobite, like the rest of my antiquarian predecessors'.[97] In fact, the list of Jacobite antiquarians is astonishing – it includes Nathaniel Johnston, Thomas Baker, Thomas Hearne, Richard Rawlinson, Thomas Carte, Francis Drake (all Nonjurors), Sir Robert Atkyns, John Burton, Thomas Gent, Francis Gwyn, Thomas Tonkin and Browne Willis. Some produced significant studies, like Elizabeth Elstob, a protégé of George Hickes, who was one of the earliest Anglo-Saxon scholars.[98] Joseph Ritson was the saviour of the medieval Scottish ballad, and 'the last professed Jacobite in England', according to Southey.[99]

Jacobites were by no means regressive in their antiquarian interests. The 'new' antiquarianism of classical art collectors and 'virtuosi' had Jacobite roots – it is unlikely that Charles Towneley could have collected his famous marbles without the aid of his family's political associates in Italy.[100] James Dawkins and John Bouverie, co-authors of the seminal work of classical antiquarianism, *The Ruins of Palmyra*, both carried out Jacobite diplomatic missions in the late 1740s and early 1750s.[101] Whether their fixations were medieval charters or Roman statues, however, Jacobite antiquarians shared a love for the minute study of the past, which symbiotically sustained an affection for the hereditary line of rulers. Change always appeared to them as decline. Ritson may be allowed to speak for them all in his condemnation of the Glorious Revolution, written in 1779: 'the Constitution appears to

---

96 See Pocock, *Ancient Constitution*.
97 Lewis, ed., *Walpole Correspondence*, vol. xxxv, p. 146.
98 See Myra Reynolds, *The Learned Lady in England, 1650–1760* (Gloucester, Mass., 1920, 1964), pp. 208–11; Mary Elizabeth Green, 'Elizabeth Elstob: "The Saxon Nymph" (1683–1756)', in J. R. Brink, ed., *Female Scholars: A Tradition of Learned Women Before 1800* (Montreal, 1980), pp. 137–60.
99 See Bronson, *Joseph Ritson, passim*. Unlike most Jacobite antiquarians, Ritson came from a middle-class rather than a landed background.
100 See Sir Henry Ellis, *The Townley Gallery* (London, 1836), vol. i, pp. 2–3.
101 Lewis, *Connoisseurs and Secret Agents*, p. 134; Lang, *Pickle the Spy*, pp. 224–5; Namier and Brooke, eds., *History of Parliament*, vol. ii, pp. 304–5.

have suffered so violent and total a Change, that the very nature of things should seem to have been perverted along with it, and reduced to the original Chaos'.[102]

This attitude reflected the same moral preoccupations and atavism that permeated so much of the poetry of the late seventeenth and eighteenth centuries. The two greatest poets of the period – John Dryden and Alexander Pope – had Jacobite sympathies, as did several minor versifiers, like Jane Barker, Richard Savage, William Oldisworth and William Shenstone.[103] Among amateur Jacobite poets may be mentioned Lord Lansdowne, the Earl of Orrery, the Duke of Buckinghamshire, William King, John Byrom, Elijah Fenton and Bishop Ken. Poetry had a strong attraction for well-born adherents of the Stuarts. Jacobitism may have provided inspiration for certain poetic approaches; for example, Howard Erskine-Hill has suggested that Pope's 'country house ideal' had overtones of the nostalgic moralism of Jacobite propaganda.[104] Shenstone proposed a different view in a letter of April 1746 to Richard Graves, when he wrote: 'as for politics, I think *poets* are *tories* by nature, supposing them to be by nature poets. The love of an individual person or family, that has worn a crown for many successions, is an inclination greatly adapted to the fanciful tribe.'[105] In other words, Jacobitism appealed to poets because it was romantic.

Most gentlemen, however, were neither poets nor antiquarians; the vitality of their Jacobitism mainly lay in ordinary aspects of their lives. Allegiance to the Stuarts manifested itself in fashion and dress, in the planning of houses and gardens and in various types of collecting. The prize for Jacobite eccentricity must go to D'Oyly Michel of Shilvington, Dorset, a former gentleman usher to Mary of Modena, who refused to shave his beard until his master and mistress returned, a resolution he kept for some time before giving in to the objections of his friends.[106] Similarly, the Jacobite M.P. Sir William Whitlock always dressed in the style of the Restoration.[107] More up-to-date Jacobite fashions were popular during and after the '45. John Byrom's daughter Beppy bought

102 Bronson, *Joseph Ritson*, vol. i, p. 58.
103 For Barker, see Reynolds, *Learned Lady*, pp. 161–5. See Chapter 2 for Savage. Oldisworth is noticed in *D.N.B.* For Shenstone, see Richard Graves, *Recollections of Some particulars in the Life of William Shenstone, Esq.* (London, 1787), p. 16.
104 Erskine-Hill, *Social Milieu*, esp. ch. 9; also his 'Literature and the Jacobite Cause', in Cruickshanks, ed., *Ideology and Conspiracy*, pp. 49–55, and 'Alexander Pope', pp. 123–48.
105 Duncan Mallam, ed., *Letters of William Shenstone* (Minneapolis, 1939), p. 78.
106 *Weekly Journal*, no. 68, 29 March 1718, p. 404.
107 Sedgwick, ed., *History of Parliament*, vol. i, p. 183 n. 118; vol. ii, p. 535.

a blue and white dress to celebrate the rebel victory at Prestonpans in October 1745, and according to tradition she wore plaid garters after the rebellion.[108] Examples of the latter intriguing accoutrements have survived; they are stitched in bright colours with charming mottoes like 'OUR PRINCE IS BRAVE OUR CAUSE IS JUST'.[109] Scottish plaid became fashionable in Manchester among 'Apprentices, and other pretty Youths', many of them the younger sons of gentry families.[110] A Scottish manufacturer was producing so-called 'Betty Burke's gowns' in 1748, modelled on the tartan dress worn by Charles Edward while hiding in the Highlands. Bishop Forbes distributed several of them to 'worthy ladies' in York, including the wife and daughter of the physician John Burton.[111] Jacobite fashion was verging here on the 'commercialization' associated with the Wilkites, who may have inherited much from these plaid waistcoats and tartan gowns.[112]

A gentleman did not have to wear his politics on his face or back; he could safely root them in his garden or board them in his house. At Kirtlington Park, Oxfordshire, the estate of Sir James Dashwood, and at Henry Jones's house at Chastleton, Gloucestershire, clumps of Scottish firs, a very rare shrub in eighteenth-century England, alerted Jacobite agents that here was a friendly place of refuge.[113] The entrance to Alexander Pope's grotto at Twickenham was surmounted by a stone inscribed 'JR 1696', a cryptic reference to the year of the Assassination Plot.[114] Lullingstone Castle in Kent, home of Percival Hart and Sir Thomas Dyke, contained a room with a large rose on the ceiling, with the motto 'Kentish True Blue / Take this for a Token / That what is said here / Under the Rose is spoken'.[115] Peter Legh of Lyme Hall, Cheshire, held meetings of a Tory club in his 'Stag Parlour', where the chairs were covered with parts of the cloak worn by Charles I on the scaffold, and the Stuart arms were emblazoned on a wall.[116]

In the alcove of his drawing room, Legh kept a set of portraits of the

[108] Parkinson, ed., *Remains of Byrom*, vol. ii, part ii, p. 386.
[109] Victoria and Albert Museum, T. 107 & A–1938, and T. 121–1931.
[110] [Byrom and Thyer], *Manchester Vindicated*, p. 21.
[111] Paton, ed., *Lyon in Mourning*, vol. ii, pp. 62, 105, 178.
[112] See also the discussion of Charles Edward's image in Chapter 3.
[113] Robson, *Oxfordshire Election*, p. 11; Hartshorne, *Old English Glasses*, p. 370; Vaughan, 'Welsh Jacobitism', p. 20.
[114] Maynard Mack, *The Garden and the City: Retirement and Politics in the Later Poetry of Pope, 1731–1743* (Toronto, 1969), pp. 63–5 and note, pp. 287–8.
[115] M. T. Steevenson, 'Some Jacobite Clubs', Circle of Glass Collectors, Paper no. 59 (1945), p. 5. I am grateful to Dr G. B. Seddon for pointing these out to me, and to R. J. Charleston for allowing me access to them.
[116] The National Trust, *Lyme Park, Cheshire* (Hertfordshire, 1981), pp. 15–16.

Stuart family, from Mary Queen of Scots to Anne. James III was prudently omitted, but so were William and Mary. Portraits of the exiled family could bring trouble, as in 1722/3 when the Nonjuror Robert Cotton was arrested for informing a government messenger that a painting on his wall was that of the Queen of England, Clementina Sobieska.[117] In spite of the risks, Jacobite portraits were highly prized. Thomas Hearne, who was reprimanded for showing a picture of James III, that 'beautifull young Man', to an anatomy class in 1712/13, paid half a guinea for a print of the Pretender in 1715.[118] John Byrom admired a double portrait of James and Clementina in 1737, which was valued at the princely sum of £10.[119] The prices of these items reflected the difficulty incurred in obtaining them. Mary Caesar, wife of the Tory Jacobite Charles Caesar, solicited a recent print of James III from the exiled King himself in 1717, with the aid of Lord Oxford, Anne Oglethorpe and the Earl of Mar.[120] Jacobite medals were no easier to acquire. They were valued possessions at Oxford in 1711, when Dr Gardiner of All Souls proudly showed Hearne a piece depicting James III in copper or brass.[121] Richard Rawlinson may have acted as a purveyor of Jacobite medals for his Oxford friends in the 1720s, when he purchased a considerable number of them on his travels abroad.[122] Caryll's Oak Society medals of 1749–50 cost about £4 each in gold, and £1 4s 9d in silver.[123]

Because they were expensive and difficult to procure, Jacobite pictures and medals were cherished, and had striking effects on viewers. When Lord Cowper, an opposition Whig, saw Mrs Caesar's picture of James III through a glass in her closet, he was awe-struck, saying 'it had Not Only a Sweet but a Sensible Countenance, and a Likeness to both Parents More than Equal'.[124] No wonder, then, that objects associated with Charles Edward and the '45 became sources of

---

[117] Boyer, *Political State*, vol. xxiv, p. 187, vol. xxv, pp. 184–6, 344.
[118] Doble *et al.*, eds., *Collections of Hearne*, vol. iv, pp. 92–3; see also vol. vii, p. 164. St John's College, Oxford, still possesses a portrait of James Francis's sister Louisa – Mrs Reginald Lane Poole, *Catalogue of Portraits in the Possession of the University, Colleges, City and County of Oxford*, vol. iii, Oxford Historical Society, 82 (1926), p. 175, no. 53.
[119] Parkinson, ed., *Remains of Byrom*, vol. ii, part i, p. 122.
[120] H.M.C., *Stuart*, vol. v, pp. 124, 556, 570.
[121] Doble *et al.*, eds., *Collections of Hearne*, vol. iii, p. 212.
[122] Bodl. Rawl. MS D. 1128, fo. 17; Rawl. MS D. 1251, fo. 260; Rawl. MS D. 1179, fos. 9, 30; Rawl. MS D. 1489, fos. 23–6.
[123] The prices were calculated by Edward Hawkins in *Notes and Queries*, 2nd Series, 125 (1858), pp. 417–18.
[124] B.L., Add. MS 62,558, fo. 29.

veneration. The Prince reputedly presented a small snuffbox to Miss Pedder, daughter of a Tory merchant family, at a ball in Preston in 1745; the Pedders preserved it lovingly for generations.[125] The Dickinsons of Manchester, at whose house (known thereafter as 'the Palace') Charles Edward stayed, were given in return a silver christening spoon that became a treasured heirloom.[126] When Richard Barry died in 1783, he left a glass engraved to the effect that Charles Edward had drunk from it in 1745 on a fictitious visit to Marbury; it was sold for the incredible sum of £26.[127]

A substantial number of less singular Jacobite household items have survived. They range from the snuffbox that supposedly belonged to John Byrom, showing a portrait of Prince Charlie, to pin-cushions embroidered with slogans like 'Down with the Rump and God bless King Charles', one of which was owned by the Mosleys of Manchester.[128] Beppy Byrom possessed a teapot decorated with a white rose and the monogram 'C*R' – it clearly dated from after 1766.[129] Another teapot, with Charles Edward's portrait on it, can be seen in the Pottery Museum at Stoke-on-Trent. These artefacts may point to the existence of Jacobite women's sewing circles (who else produced the plaid garters?) and tea groups. Such organizations might have been the counterparts of male drinking clubs, for which much more evidence exists. As late as 1771, Dewsbury and Co. sent to Philip Egerton of Oulton an invoice for an order of Derby-Chelsea china, '2 Quart Jugs with the word Fiat and rose & thistle 2.2.0'. The Egertons kept their Jacobite pieces in a walnut cabinet which opened to reveal a framed bust of Prince Charles in armour.[130] These items, like the glassware found at Lyme, Wynnstay and Oxburgh Hall, were relics of Jacobite clubs and societies; and they bring our attention to the important issue of male sociability.

[125] It is now on display at the Harris Museum. For the Pedders, and Preston in the '45, see Edward Baines, *The History of the County Palatine and Duchy of Lancaster*, ed. James Croston (6 vols., Manchester, 1893), vol. v, p. 313; H. Clemesha, *A History of Preston in Amounderness* (Manchester, 1912), p. 302.
[126] William Axon, *The Annals of Manchester* (Manchester, 1886), p. 84; Manchester Central Library, Archives Room, LI/60/7/38.
[127] Earl Egerton of Tatton, 'The Cheshire Gentry in 1715: Drawn from the Ashley Hall Portraits at Tatton', *Journal of the Architectural, Archaeological, and Historic Society for the County and City of Chester and North Wales*, New Series, 15 (1909), p. 13.
[128] W. H. Thomson, ed., *Beppy Byrom's Diary* (Manchester, [1945]), pp. 11, 13; Parkinson, ed., *Remains of Byrom*, vol. ii, part i, p. 60; Sir Oswald Mosley, *My Life* (London, 1968), p. 2; Victoria and Albert Museum, T. 120–1931.
[129] W. H. Thomson, *History of Manchester to 1852* (Altrincham, 1967), pp. 178–9.
[130] Hartshorne, *Old English Glasses*, pp. 368–9.

Jacobite sociability

In his brilliant work on sociability in southern France, Maurice Agulhon distinguished an older form of corporate mutuality, centred on confraternities, from the newer, more 'democratic' structure of Freemasonry.[131] In England, both types of sociability can be found within the same organizations. The idea of the club combined ritual, hierarchy and corporate solidarity with a sense of individualism and open expression. Jacobite political culture fostered a sociability that was neither entirely 'conservative' nor wholly 'democratic', based on a dazzling variety of formal and informal gatherings – occasional group meetings, sporting activities, specialized clubs and secret societies, 'mock corporations' and Masonic lodges. Like the political sentiments that nourished it, Jacobite sociability was ambiguous and complex. Within its boundaries thrived every conceivable type of elite comradeship.

At the least organized end of the sociability scale can be placed private celebrations. Tom Hearne and five friends repaired to Foxcombe to commemorate 10 June in 1715; John Byrom marked the same day in 1729 by drinking with Messrs Lewis and Dickinson at the King's Arms in Manchester.[132] In times of trouble, friends might assemble to discuss the situation. Numerous allegations of 'cabals' among recusants in Northumberland were made in 1689–90, as will be seen in Chapter 10. A 'very dangerous Caball', which included several Roman Catholic gentlemen, was reported to be meeting at the London house of Dr Radcliffe in 1708.[133] The invasion scare of that year both excited and worried adherents of the Stuarts. In Lancashire, Nicholas Blundell went with other recusant gentleman to a bowling match on 10 June 1708, the only year in Queen Anne's reign when he celebrated the Pretender's birthday.[134]

Sporting events were often used to cover Jacobite plotting. The rebellion of 1715 began in Northumberland under the guise of a

131 M. Agulhon, *Penitents et Franc-Maçons de l'ancienne Provence* (Paris, 1968), abridged from his *La Sociabilité Meridionale. Confréries et associations dans la vie collective en Provence orientale à la fin du XVIIIe siècle* (2 vols., Paris, 1966).
132 Doble *et al.*, eds., *Collections of Hearne*, vol. v, pp. 65–6; Parkinson, ed., *Remains of Byrom*, vol. i, part ii, p. 372.
133 P.R.O., S.P. 34/9/88.
134 Frank Tyrer and J. J. Bagley, eds., *The Great Diurnall of Nicholas Blundell of Little Crosby, Lancashire*, vol. i, Lancashire and Cheshire Record Society, 110 (1968), p. 174.

hunting meet, and in April 1746 a group of Northumbrian recusants seemed to be repeating history when they appeared 'with their Servants, Fowling Pieces and Musick,... upon Pretence of Shooting upon the Moors'.[135] Many ephemeral sporting associations with Jacobite overtones can be mentioned. According to family tradition, the Duke of Beaufort held Jacobite meetings on a bowling green at Hawkesbury Upton near Badminton, and Thomas Carte wrote to the Pretender about a Jacobite hunt club in Durham in 1740–1.[136] In Staffordshire in the late 1740s, the Blue Coat Hunt tracked a fox dressed in red with hounds clad in tartan, while at Burton-on-Trent in 1747, a bull decorated with orange ribbons was baited by dogs garbed in plaid.[137] The mysterious Gorvin Hunt in North Devon even provided Jacobite glassware for its members; in fact, the only evidence of its existence is a short glass engraved with its name and a Stuart rose, dated 1769.[138]

In the aftermath of the '45, as Chapter 7 suggested, some sporting events became places of rendezvous for conspirators, like the Lichfield Races or the Uttoxeter Bowling Green Club. At the Leghs' pocket borough of Newton in November 1748, a gang of forty or fifty Jacobite gentlemen, including Peter Legh, Sir Thomas Egerton, Sir Robert Gwillym and Legh Masters, met at an inn for the annual hunt; after too much drinking, they marched out to the market cross, proclaimed King James, and offered money to 'any likely Fellow' who would enlist with Prince Charles. In the next two days, they processed through the town crying 'a Legh, a Legh, and down with the Rump', and dressed up their servants in plaid waistcoats with white hat ribbons, while the townspeople, who did not much appreciate these antics, pelted them with stones. The arrival of a Whig mob from Wigan ended the festivities.[139] This silly display typified the boldness and desperation of Tory Jacobites after the disastrous elections of 1747.

J. H. Plumb's happy picture of the spread of gentry amusements

[135] P.R.O., S.P. 36/85 fo. 37; see also Chapter 10.
[136] Hartshorne, *Old English Glasses*, p. 352; L. Eardley-Simpson, *Derby and the Forty-Five* (London, 1933), pp. 84–5.
[137] Maud Wyndham, ed., *Chronicles of the Eighteenth Century* (2 vols., Boston, 1924), vol. ii, p. 162; Beinecke, Lee Family Papers (Hartwell), Box 4A T–2. I owe the latter reference to Eveline Cruickshanks.
[138] M. T. Steevenson, 'More Clubs', Circle of Glass Collectors, Paper no. 107 (n.d.), p. 2.
[139] P.R.O., K.B. 1/10, part 2, Trinity 22/23 G. II, Lancs, affidts. of Ashton *et al.*; Parkinson, ed., *Remains of Byrom*, vol. ii, part ii, pp. 477–81; Sir William Blackstone, ed., *Reports of Cases determined at the Several Courts of Westminster Hall, from 1746 to 1779* (Dublin, 1781), vol. i, pp. 47–8.

through the 'commercialization of leisure' takes little account of the political polarization manifested in the Lichfield Races or the Newton Hunt.[140] Although Whigs and Tories enjoyed the same recreations, they did so separately. The profusion of Assembly Rooms built in this period may indicate the desire of one party to segregate itself from the other in its own recreational space. Of course, it was not always easy for revellers to keep their opponents away. At Manchester in February 1748/9, a private ball was given at the town Assembly Room by the Cheshire gentleman William Meredith, who was present at the Hamstall Ridware Jacobite meeting in June 1750, and John Wagstaffe, brother-in-law of the executed rebel James Bradshaw. A group of army officers stationed in the town invited themselves to this function, but the fiddlers treated them to 'Sir Watkins Jig', possibly a variant on 'The King shall enjoy his own again', and the crowd cried out 'Down with the Rump'. Wagstaffe was later beaten by some soldiers for his part in this demonstration.[141]

The private club offered the possibility of talking and drinking in an exclusive and secretive atmosphere. It met regularly, had formal rules and powers to enforce them, and concentrated on conviviality. Clubs with Jacobite associations existed at both of the Universities – the High Borlase at Oxford, the mysterious Family at Cambridge.[142] Linda Colley has shown that Tory party strategy was formulated in two London clubs, the Cocoa Tree and the Honourable Board of Loyal Brotherhood; she has also argued that neither of them was a Jacobite organization.[143] Indeed, both had to accommodate the whole gamut of Tory opinion, from Sir Walter Wagstaffe Bagot to William Beckford. Nevertheless, Jacobite Tories, including Westmorland and Beaufort, may have used the Cocoa Tree Club in September 1750 for a meeting with Charles Edward.[144] As late as 1774, at the height of the Quebec Act agitation, a newspaper reported that strains of 'Charlie's my

---

[140] J. H. Plumb, 'The Commercialization of Leisure in Eighteenth-Century England', in McKendrick, Brewer and Plumb, *Birth of a Consumer Society*, pp. 265–85.

[141] Parkinson, ed., *Remains of Byrom*, vol. ii, part ii, pp. 496–7, 508–14; *Mitre and Crown*, vol. i, April 1749, pp. 409–11. The note in Byrom's *Remains* wrongly identifies William Meredith with his grandfather, the third baronet, who would not have been called 'Mr. Meredith'.

[142] In 1738, the High Borlase Society adopted a motion proposed by Henry Perrot, M.P. for Oxfordshire, to negotiate a new restoration attempt. Sedgwick, ed., *History of Parliament*, vol. ii, p. 340. For the Family, see Clark, *English Society*, p. 157.

[143] Linda Colley, 'The Loyal Brotherhood and the Cocoa Tree: The London Organization of the Tory Party, 1727–1760', *H.J.*, 20, 1 (1977), pp. 77–95. The founders of the Loyal Brotherhood, however, gave it a rather suggestive name.

[144] Mahon, *Decline of the Last Stuarts*, p. 76.

Darling' had been heard issuing from the Cocoa Tree and wafting over Pall Mall.[145]

The best known strictly Jacobite society in England was the Cycle Club of the Welsh borders; but its history is shrouded in webs of romantic nostalgia. The tradition that it was founded on 10 June 1710 dates from the 1780s and is improbable. The earliest surviving club minutes are from 1722–3, and it is likely that the Cycle was founded then, in the aftermath of the Atterbury Plot. It was from the beginning a closed society, and the place of its meetings rotated monthly around the houses of its members. All of its early members were very high Tories and Jacobites; none was a Hanoverian Tory.[146]

In a splendid dissertation on the Tory party in Lancashire and Cheshire, Stephen Baskerville has pointed out that two Cycle Club members, Sir Robert Grosvenor and Philip Henry Warburton, assisted the government during the '45 rebellion; but the nervous reactions of many Jacobite sympathizers in that crisis must be balanced against their actions in more placid times. In fact, the Cycle Club may have been in session during the rebellion. According to an informant, Grosvenor, Warburton, Sir Watkin Williams Wynn and other Cycle members met in November 1745 with Lord Barrymore and Sir Rowland Stanley, a recusant baronet, in a Chester tavern, and afterwards gathered secretly at Sir Thomas Longueville's seat in North Wales. They held a hunt club every Thursday at Hawarden, where their toast was 'Down with the Rump'. The rector of Hawarden, who was arrested about this time for drinking Prince Charles's health with Sir John Glynne on the bowling green, was questioned by the government about these allegations, as was George Hope of Broughton, Flint; they admitted the existence of the club, but denied the secret meetings.[147] The story soon spread, however, that Williams Wynn and his friends had been waiting in North Wales, ready to ride out and join the rebels.[148]

[145] Paton, ed., *Lyon in Mourning*, vol. iii, p. 324; see also Stirling, *Coke of Norfolk*, pp. 87–8.

[146] The minutes are printed in William Llewellyn, 'David Morgan, the Welsh Jacobite', *The Cambrian Journal* (1861), pp. 305–6. Stephen W. Baskerville, 'The Management of the Tory Interest in Cheshire and Lancashire 1714–47', unpublished D.Phil. dissertation, Oxford University, 1966, Appendix C, pp. 371–2, lists members of the club for 1722–3 and 1746–8. See also Donald Nicholas, 'The Welsh Jacobites', *T.H.S.C.* (1948), pp. 469–70. A similar club existed in South Wales. See Maj. Francis Jones, 'The Society of Sea Serjeants', *T.H.S.C.* (1967), pp. 57–91.

[147] P.R.O., S.P. 36/75, fos. 89–90.

[148] Vaughan, 'Welsh Jacobitism', p. 33. In fact, for most of this time Sir Watkin was in London, from whence the famous letter to Derby was sent.

By the early 1750s, the Cycle was advertising its meetings in Mrs
Adams's Jacobite *Courant*, but around 1760, with Pitt and then
George III drawing off Jacobite support, the club disappeared.[149] It
was revived in 1770 by the second Sir Watkin Williams Wynn, after his
return from the Grand Tour. This second Cycle was not merely a
drinking society. The politics of its members remained thoroughly
independent; Sir Watkin, no friend to George III, defeated Lord
North's attempt to recover rent arrears on crown lands in Wales during
the American War, and Lord Grosvenor, in spite of accepting a peerage
from the King, had soon returned to opposition. Richard Barry,
Watkin Williams and Thomas Cholmondeley all sat in Parliament as
Tory back-benchers, who had no truck with any administration.[150]
The style of the reinvigorated Cycle, moreover, was outrageously
Jacobite. White roses were embossed on its minute books, while its
rosters showed a snake devouring its tail, a star copied from Charles
Edward's 'MICAT INTER OMNES' medal, and a 'true lover's knot', such
as appeared in many Jacobite prints. When Lady Wynn was made
'Lady Patroness' of the club in 1780, she was given a jewelled badge
showing a white rose and the founding date of 10 June 1710.[151]

The most interesting of these symbols is the snake devouring itself. It
is also found on a broadside of 1717 in Hearne's papers at Oxford,
which was derived from an original of the Restoration period. The
snake represents 'The Old Serpent of Spirit of Resistance'; inside it are
inscribed the 'many Revolutions' of 1649 to 1660, from number one,
'Rump', to number seventeen, 'THE RESTORATION'.[152] The image of the
self-devouring snake, in other words, symbolizes the circular course of
events that will bring back the rightful king. The Cycle's practice of
meeting in rotation had the same significance. The idea of a Jacobite
restoration, in short, was rooted from the beginning in the structure of
the club.

In the 1930s and 1940s, M. T. Steevenson's fascinating papers for
the Glass Circle rescued the memory of many Jacobite clubs from
oblivion by examining sources far more fragile than documents –
namely, glassware. As she demonstrated, the famous 'FIAT' and rose

149 *Adams's Weekly Courant*, no. 1046, 1–8 May 1753.
150 Grant Francis, *Romance of the White Rose* (London, 1933), plate XIII, facing
    p. 229, showing the 1770–2 roster. For Wynn, see Pritchard, *Wynns at Wynnstay*,
    esp. pp. 76, 84. For the M.P.s mentioned, see Namier and Brooke, eds., *History of
    Parliament*.
151 Francis, *Romance*, plate XIII; Hartshorne, *Old English Glasses*, p. 367.
152 Bodl. Hearne Diary, vol. 62, fo. 7a.

glasses were not monopolized by the Cycle Club, and their discovery in far-flung country houses argues for the existence of similar drinking societies in other areas. Henry Jones of Chastleton, Gloucestershire, Sir Roger Newdigate of Arbury, Warwickshire, German Pole of Radbourne Hall, Derbyshire, and the Catholic Bedingfields of Oxburgh Hall, Norfolk, all owned 'FIAT' glasses – Jones possessed eleven of them, and Newdigate no fewer than twenty. Other surviving rose glasses belonged to Sir Matthew Hale of Shrewsbury, and the Price family of Worcester preserved for two centuries the Jacobite glasses of a 'Friendly Society' that met in the town around 1750.[153] Thus, Jacobite clubs like the Cycle may have existed throughout the West Midlands and in East Anglia.

Most of them probably died out around 1760, with the general waning of Jacobitism. It seems to have been in the gloomy first decade of George III's reign that a club of gentlemen was founded at the Mourning Bush tavern in Aldersgate Street, London, whose members vowed to wear mourning, 'not ... for the dead, but for the living', until the Stuarts returned.[154] The partial revival of Jacobite hopes in the late 1760s and early 1770s, however, stimulated the reappearance of the Cycle, the formation of a Jacobite Royal Oak Society in Edinburgh, and the creation in 1773 of the Oyster and Parched Pea Club at Preston.[155] The last of these was a closed society of old Tories, including the Pedders, who met to choose annual officers, such as an 'Oysterius' and 'Clerk of the Peas', and to consume oysters, the traditional food of St James's day. They celebrated marriages of members and births of children, perhaps reflecting a concern with the fertility of Charles and Louisa; in any case, the club historian coyly suggested that 'possibly now and then a Jacobite toast [was] honoured with a bumper'.[156]

The custom of choosing grandly titled officers was not peculiar to this curious dining club. It was also practised in the so-called 'mock corporations' that flourished in Staffordshire and Lancashire throughout the eighteenth century. Five of these organizations are known, of which only one, the corporation of Sefton, founded in the

[153] M. T. Steevenson, 'Jacobite Clubs', Circle of Glass Collectors, Paper no. 7 (1939), pp. 3–6, and her 'Some Jacobite Clubs', Circle of Glass Collectors, Paper no. 60, pp. 3–4. See Plate 13.

[154] Timbs, Clubs and Club Life, p. 152.

[155] For the Royal Oak Society, see Paton, ed., Lyon in Mourning, vol. iii, pp. 309, 330–1.

[156] [William Dobson], Records of the Preston Oyster and Parched Pea Club, 1773–1841 (Preston, 1861), pp. 3–7.

1760s, had no apparent Jacobite associations. The other four appeared at Cheadle in north-west Staffordshire (1699–1729), Walton-le-dale (1701–96), Rochdale (1712–37) and Ardwick, a suburb of Manchester (1746?–present). The idea of a 'mock corporation' (although they never called themselves 'mock') was derived from the popular custom, found throughout England, of electing a 'mock mayor', as a protest against the loss of plebeian voting rights.[157] Although the post-1688 'mock corporations' were exclusive gentlemen's clubs, they may have been inspired by an analogous opposition to Whig domination of corporation boroughs in the late 1690s. The satirical character of the 'mock corporations' was preserved in the titles of their officers, such as 'house-groper', 'slut-kisser' and 'Custard-eater'; but they also had serious sounding positions like mayor and recorder, strict rules imposing fines for non-attendance, and sometimes even elaborate paraphernalia, like the mace and staves of the Walton corporation, now preserved in the Harris Museum. As clubs, they were formal and well organized, as well as convivial.

Significantly, the records of these 'mock' bodies, in spite of numerous references to charters, freedoms, privileges, even 'fundamentall Lawes', never mention the ruling monarchs until the late 1770s, when the Walton corporation was reformed by local Whigs. At Cheadle, only 'honest gentlemen' were to be admitted; in 1707–9, the word 'Loyall' was added to the title of this 'mock corporation', but it was not clear to whom the officers owed their allegiance. In December 1714, at a special meeting, the Cheadle club admitted Ralph Sneyd, who was later accused of leading the meeting-house riot at Newcastle-under-Lyme, in which another corporation member, John Ghent, was also implicated. Another special session of the corporation was held on 6 October 1715, the week of the planned Jacobite insurrection, when six 'persons of Loyalty & sound principles' were admitted. John Dearle, a Stafford schoolmaster, became an alderman at Cheadle in 1718/19; six years later, he was arrested for handing around a copy of the Pretender's declaration, and was only rescued from punishment by the exertions of William Leveson Gower, who was mayor of Cheadle in 1725.[158]

In its early days, the Walton-le-dale corporation included Roman

157 For 'mock mayors', see Michael Mullett, 'Popular Culture and Popular Politics: Some Regional Case Studies', in Jones, ed., *Britain in the First Age of Party*, pp. 142–4.
158 T. Pape, 'The Ancient Corporation of Cheadle', *North Staffordshire Field Club Transactions* (1929–30), pp. 69, 73, 75, 77, 79–80, 83; P.R.O., S.P. 35/25/53, (1)–(3); S.P. 35/25/54; S.P. 35/25/68, (1); P.R.O. Assi. 2/7, Stafford Qua. 7 G. I.

Catholics as well as High Churchmen from the Preston area. James Radcliffe, Earl of Derwentwater, became mayor in 1711, and donated to the corporation the short stave that is its oldest relic. In November 1715, perhaps while the rebel army was at Preston, the Walton officers were 'continued for the year ensuing'; sixteen members of the organization, almost all of them recusants, took part in the rebellion. After 1715, however, Catholics were purged from the corporation, and after 1722, a few Whigs were admitted as freemen, including Daniel Pulteney and the Dissenter Sir Henry Houghton. This 'Country alliance' endured for several years, reflecting the Parliamentary politics of Preston; but in 1740, the election as mayor of Caryll, Viscount Molyneux, a Catholic Jacobite, represented the end of 'mixed government' in the Walton corporation. No Whig entered the society from then until its first demise in 1768. Among the new corporation leaders were Edmund Starkie, at whose house Charles Edward stayed in 1745, and Evelyn Francks, who was arrested in Manchester in 1747 for crying 'Down with the Rump'.[159] In February 1745/6, the mayor paid 2s 6d for refixing the silver name plates on the corporation staves, 'which were taken off on Acc[tt] of the Rebels Coming hither'. The word 'Rebels' is written over something that has been carefully excised, perhaps 'Duke' – meaning the corporation feared the arrival of government troops – or 'Prince' – a too friendly term for Charles Edward.

In its last years, the Walton corporation was joined by Charles Towneley, the recusant antiquary, and Robert Moss, mayor of Preston during the riots of 1768. The last Tory mayor of Walton was Arthur Barry, son of Lord Barrymore and future member of the Cycle Club, who held office in 1766–7. The next page of the minute book, for the election year 1767–8, has been torn out. The 'mock corporation' was revived in 1778 by some local Whigs, and survived until 1796; but in its original form, it died in 1768. Its longevity may have been due to a connection with some local festival, such as a wake. It was always, however, a political organization, and it followed the fortunes of local Toryism exactly. Although it was not consistently Jacobite, it was strongly imbued with the Jacobitism of the local gentry, especially before 1715 and after 1740.[160]

[159] Parkinson, ed., *Remains of Byrom*, vol. ii, part ii, p. 388; P.R.O., P.L. 26/36, Sept. 1747, indts. of E. Francks for riot and scandalous words.
[160] The Harris Museum in Preston possesses the Minute Book of the corporation of Walton-le-dale, as well as the corporation regalia. Lists of members from 1701 to 1714 are published in Frank Coupe, *Walton-le-Dale: A History of the Village*

The Rochdale corporation was extremely high Tory, and some Manchester Jacobites served as its officers, including John Byrom and Reverend Thomas Cattell.[161] No records of the Ardwick corporation survive before 1763, but its traditions hold that it was born after Charles Edward marched through Manchester, and that an empty chair was kept for the Prince at corporation meetings, where his health was drunk 'over the water'. By the 1780s, the society had lost its political character, but still counted a few old Jacobites in its ranks, like Edward Hall, the physician who had stolen the rebel heads from Manchester Exchange in 1748/9.[162] All of the 'mock corporations' mixed conviviality with a remarkably formalized organizational structure and a strong tinge of Jacobitism. Like the Cycle or the Oyster and Parched Pea Club, they were founded on an attitude that did not separate sociability from politics. It is not surprising that men with this outlook became so captivated by the hierarchy and mysticism of Freemasonry.

Recent historical work on Masonry has concentrated on its often radical contribution to the 'rationalism' of the Enlightenment.[163] Yet Masonic lodges were also the purveyors of a quasi-religious mysticism, and encouraged a fascination with some bizarre avenues of spiritual and scientific endeavour. As they began to spread in England under the Restoration, they acquired an association with the Stuarts, through the supposed Grand Mastership of Charles II, and attracted an increasing number of gentlemen and peers. Even in the early eighteenth century, however, lodges of 'operative' stone-masons existed alongside those of 'speculative' brethren who were not of the trade. At Alnwick in Northumberland, an 'operative' lodge survived until 1757 without affiliating with the Grand Lodge of England. The independence of the Alnwick Masons may have been strengthened by the Jacobite tendencies for which the area was notorious, and which resulted in the capture of six Northumbrian stone-masons among the rebels at Preston in 1715.[164]

(Preston, 1954), pp. 144–7, and a slightly inaccurate account of the society appears in T. D. Whittaker, *History of Richmondshire* (2 vols., London, 1823), vol. ii, pp. 428–9.

161 J. P. Earwaker, 'The Mock Corporation of Rochdale', *Transactions of the Historic Society of Lancashire and Cheshire*, 40, New Series, 4 (1888), pp. 93–120. For Cattell, see Parkinson, ed., *Remains of Byrom*, vol. ii, part ii, pp. 393–4.

162 Richard E. Knowles, 'The Ancient and Loyal Corporation of Ardwick', typescript in Manchester Central Library, Archives Room, BR F 369 242 A3.

163 See Margaret C. Jacob, *The Radical Enlightenment: Pantheists, Freemasons and Republicans* (London and Boston, 1981).

164 Province of Northumberland and Durham, Societas Rosicruciana in Anglia, *The Alnwick Manuscript, No. E 10: Reproduction and Transcript, Copy No. 2* (New-

The foundation of the loyalist Grand Lodge of England in 1717 did not solve the perceived problem of Masonic Jacobitism, because the brotherhood was not subsequently purged. In fact, the Grand Lodge itself chose the Duke of Wharton as Grand Master in 1722–3; his Jacobite proclivities may not have been widely known among the members. Wharton's wardens were a stone-mason and a blacksmith, suggesting that he was supported by 'operative' brothers, and by the small tradesmen who had not yet been driven out of Masonry. The band at Wharton's inaugural feast reportedly played 'The King shall enjoy his own again'. Loyalist Whigs regained control of the Grand Lodge in 1723, however, and the disgruntled Wharton formed a new society, the Gormogans, assuring its members that he would exclude 'the Usurper Merryweis' – the code name for George I, later used in the 'Persian Letter'.[165]

English Masonry now entered two decades of respite from internal quarrels. On the continent, however, disruptive developments were taking place. Although the influence of Jacobite exiles on early continental Freemasonry may have been overestimated, it was nonetheless significant. Charles Radcliffe, Earl of Derwentwater, may have founded the first Paris lodge in 1725, and he became Grand Master of the French lodges in 1736.[166] In the same year, a Jacobite lodge was set up at Avignon, and another existed at Rome from 1735 to 1737, headed by the exiled Lord Wintoun. Its English members included William Howard, Viscount Andover, Sir James Dashwood, the Oxfordshire M.P., the Nonjuror John Cotton, Thomas Twisden of Twysenden, Kent, and several Roman Catholics like William Sheldon, Thomas Lisle and a Mr Constable; the Scottish portrait painter Allan Ramsay junior was one of the last members admitted before the lodge was suppressed by a 1737 Papal edict against Masonry.[167]

castle-upon-Tyne, 1895), intro. by W. J. Hughan; Wilhelm Begemann, *Vorgeschichte und Anfänge der Freimaurerei in England* (2 vols., Berlin, 1909), vol. i, pp. 420–44. None of the rebel prisoners was named in the Alnwick lodge minute book, but it contains a mysterious gap between 1710 and 1735.

[165] For the politics of the Grand Lodge, see J. M. Roberts, *The Mythology of the Secret Societies* (New York, 1972), pp. 21, 27; for Wharton's tenure, see Begemann, *Vorgeschichte*, vol. ii, pp. 142, 251–6; Blackett-Ord, *Hell-Fire Duke*, pp. 88–90, 100. The Gormogans (from 'gore Mogans', i.e. Dutchmen) survived until the 1790s; they are mentioned in G. D. Henderson, *Chevalier Ramsay* (London, 1952), pp. 166–7.

[166] Roberts, *Mythology of the Secret Societies*, pp. 29–34.

[167] William James Hughan, ed., *The Jacobite Lodge at Rome, 1735–7* (Torquay, 1910). In the spirit of Masonic brotherhood, Howard and Dashwood did not use their titles within the lodge.

302 Two faces of treason

Charles Edward Stuart was not a member of this Roman lodge; nevertheless, he had been tutored briefly by a prominent Scottish Mason, the Chevalier Michael Ramsay. Like his friend and fellow Mason Sir Isaac Newton, Ramsay advocated a tolerant religious attitude, and was interested in both science and the occult. In 1738, he published his famous *Discours*, in which he argued that the Masons were descended from the chivalric orders of the Middle Ages. This was undoubtedly an attempt to invent an aristocratic heritage for what had begun as a plebeian society; but Ramsay was not anti-egalitarian, and he wished men of all classes to become brothers within the Masonic movement.[168] Nevertheless, the main effect of the *Discours* was to establish Masonry as a pursuit worthy of the noble classes of Europe. It soon gave birth to strange offshoots that Ramsay could not have imagined, beginning with the creation in France of the 'Scottish rite', an extremely mystical and rigidly hierarchical system which claimed to be the pristine practice of the medieval Masonic knighthood. Among the symbols of its higher or Rose-cross grades was the self-devouring snake. By the 1760s, another variant, the rite of 'Strict Observance', had emerged in Germany. It was propagated by the Baron Karl Gotthelf von Hund, who was part fantasist and part charlatan; he claimed that the forefathers of Freemasonry were the Knights Templar of the Middle Ages, that he had been initiated into this 'Order of the Temple' by Jacobite exiles at Paris, and that the secret Grand Master, or 'Unknown Superior', of the order was none other than Charles Edward Stuart himself.[169]

'Strict Observance' or Templar Masonry spread rapidly throughout Germany and other parts of Europe. In England, meanwhile, the brotherhood had followed very similar paths towards aristocratization. In 1751, a group calling itself the 'Ancients' split from the Grand Lodge; it favoured less emphasis on deism and more ritual, as well as greater independence for individual lodges. Toryism, perhaps even Jacobitism, may have been at the bottom of this schism. In any case, decreasing centralization was accompanied by the entry of a large number of Tory gentlemen into the Masonic brotherhood. Philip

---

168 Henderson, *Chevalier Ramsay*, esp. ch. 14, pp. 168–72. Historians of French Masonry have tended to stress the 'democratic' aspects of Ramsay's thought, and have ignored its highly elitist assumptions.

169 See René le Forestier, *La Franc-Maçonnerie Templière et Occultiste au XVIIIe et XIXe siècles* (Paris, 1970); also Wilhelm Begemann, *Die Tempelherrn und die Freimaurer* (Berlin, 1906), and Peter Partner, *The Murdered Magicians: The Templars and their Myth* (New York and London, 1982).

Jenkins has proposed the intriguing hypothesis that Tory Jacobites, disillusioned by the decline of their cause, turned from the Stuarts to Freemasonry as a focus for sociability.[170] While South Wales provides plenty of evidence for this, England was a more complicated case; for example, while five lodges were founded in the 1760s in Jacobite Staffordshire, most of the lodges that sprang up in Lancashire between 1750 and 1770 were located in Whiggish Liverpool.[171] The profusion of new lodges after 1750, however, is undeniable, and many of the novice Masons were certainly old Jacobites, some of whom may have retained their allegiances. In the 1770s, Sir Watkin Williams Wynn initiated a lodge at Wynnstay, whose meetings were held on the nights after those of the Cycle Club. The Cheshire Grand Lodge met on 10 June in 1760 and 1771; on the latter occasion, someone made the curious mistake of recording the name of the Earl of Cholmondeley as Charles James instead of Charles George.[172]

On the continent, the Templar Masons had at last approached their 'Unknown Superior'. In 1776, the Comte d'Albanie, as Charles Edward called himself, was visited by the Duke of Ostrogotha, brother of the King of Sweden, to whom he granted a patent as Vicar of the Northern Lodges; and in September of the following year, the Comte was host to Charles Everard, Baron de Waechter, a deputy of the united Templar lodges of Germany.[173] A fanatical enthusiast of the now-tottering myths of 'Strict Observance', and an enemy of the new 'Swedish system', Waechter wanted some evidence that Hund had been right about the 'Unknown Superior'. Charles Edward completely disproved the story of Hund's Jacobite initiation ceremony; but he brazenly maintained that the secret Grand Mastership of the Masons *was* hereditary in the house of Stuart, and that papers hidden at St Germain would affirm it. The gullible Waechter kept writing to the Pretender for the next decade, even after the Convent of Wilhelmsbad of 1782 had finally rejected 'Strict Observance'. He begged Charles to find the papers, offering him the support of Frederick the Great of

170 Jenkins, 'Jacobites and Freemasons', pp. 396–9.
171 See John Lane, *Masonic Records, 1717–1894* (2nd edn, London, 1895).
172 John Armstrong, *A History of Freemasonry in Cheshire* (London, 1901), pp. 26–33. Because 10 June was two weeks before the main Masonic festival of 24 June, the date of the meetings may have been innocent; but would it have seemed so to men like Wynn, Thomas Cholmondeley, Richard Barry or Philip Egerton, all Masons and Cycle Club members?
173 See Mahon, *Decline of the Last Stuarts*, pp. 77–82. Duke Charles, the future King of Sweden, contacted the Pretender again in 1780 – R.A., Stuart, 497/198, 498/189. Three years later, his brother King Gustavus III arranged Charles Edward's separation from his wife.

Prussia in a mysterious 'Entreprise', although he rejected a proposal for a restoration attempt made to a Masonic emissary by '[q]uelques Anglais du Parti Opposé à la Cour'.[174]

Did these Englishmen of the opposition party really exist? Waechter would hardly have invented them if he disagreed with their views. They might have been English Templars; and there hangs an interesting tale. In 1761, the Grand Lodge of York, which had been active in the north earlier in the century, was revived at York in the house of Henry Howard, probably a cousin of the Duke of Norfolk and son of a Jacobite exile; its founding members included Dr John Burton and the Nonjuring antiquarian Francis Drake. On 10 June 1762, the York Masons licensed their first lodge, called 'French Lodge No. 1'; by 1780, they had granted warrants to ten others, three of them in London, and had chartered the 'Grand Lodge of England, South of the River Trent'. The master-mind of this 'Grand Lodge' was William Preston, a Scottish printer living in London, who had been apprenticed to Thomas Ruddiman of Edinburgh, the notorious Jacobite antiquarian and newspaper publisher.[175] The name given to one of the London lodges, 'Perfect Observance', points to the adoption of the 'Strict Observance' system, and in 1780 the grade of Knight Templar was officially added to the York Grand Lodge hierarchy.[176] Clearly, the fantasies of Baron Hund were taking root in England at precisely the moment they were being challenged in Germany. Given the backgrounds of the founders of the York Grand Lodge and its southern offspring, it is more than likely that the York Templars accepted Charles Edward Stuart as their 'Unknown Superior'. In fact, the only surviving Masonic glasses that bear portraits of Prince Charles belonged to a gentry family of North Yorkshire.[177]

Baron Waechter's English contacts were probably York Masons. Why, then, did he identify them as members of the opposition? The Grand Master of the York Grand Lodge in 1771–2 was Sir Thomas

---

174 Waechter's correspondence with Charles is in R.A., Stuart, 491/123, 493/19, 493/152, 493/179, 494/43, 498/188, 498/248, 506/131, 513/44. Le Forestier, *La Franc-Maçonnerie Templière*, pp. 244, 536–8, and Begemann, *Tempelherrn*, pp. 66–75, ignore the fact that Charles did not reject all of Baron Hund's claims.

175 Lane, *Masonic Records*, pp. 26–7; Begemann, *Vorgeschichte*, vol. ii, pp. 417–42; William James Hughan, ed., *Masonic Sketches and Reprints: 1. History of Freemasonry in York. 2. Unpublished Records of the Craft* (London, 1871); Robinson, *Dukes of Norfolk*, pp. 185–7. Burton, Drake, Preston and Ruddiman are noticed in *D.N.B.*

176 Le Forestier, *La Franc-Maçonnerie Templière*, p. 610; Begemann, *Vorgeschichte*, vol. ii, p. 431.

177 Hartshorne, *Old English Glasses*, p. 361.

Gascoigne, a recusant baronet who later converted and entered Parliament as a supporter of Charles James Fox. Other former Jacobites who became Foxites included Francis Plowden and Joseph Ritson; Fox's friend Sir Thomas Bunbury was the descendant of Jacobites. During the French Revolution, Fox himself was accused of being part of a mythical international Templar conspiracy.[178] Like the Grenvillites in 1769–71, Fox may have used a connection with the vestiges of the Stuart cause to enhance his appeal to ex-Jacobites; this would have been very useful to his ally Lord Fitzwilliam, who managed the Foxite interest in Yorkshire.

It would be a mistake to exaggerate the link between Masonry and Jacobitism, but it was undeniably real. Why did it exist? The answer may lie in the meaning of the central mystery which all Masons share – the tale of Hiram Abiff, the legendary architect of the Temple of Jerusalem, who was murdered by his companions, but is reborn in the person of every Master Mason. Hiram's story resembles that of Christ and of all risen gods, and could easily be interpreted, as the Bavarian Illuminati pointed out in the 1780s, as symbolic of the exile and return of the Stuarts. The cycle of death and rebirth, of revolution and restoration, was represented in the 'Scottish Rite', as in the Cycle Club, by a self-consuming snake. Did the Cycle and other Jacobite clubs have Masonic origins? Was the 'MICAT INTER OMNES' star a Masonic device? Did the Jacobite 'FIAT' refer to the enlightenment offered by Masonic initiation? The shroud of Hiram Abiff is not as impenetrable as these mysteries.

Yet Jacobite sociability, whether it was found in sporting events, clubs, 'mock corporations' or masonic lodges, had a certain intellectual consistency, centred on an image of genteel separation, seclusion or retirement. Safely detached from Whiggish knavery, ensconced in a hidden withdrawing room, surrounded by trustworthy friends and protected by the rules and regulations of their secret societies, Jacobite gentlemen could indulge themselves in the dream of a Stuart restoration. Their reverential toasts, drunk while bowing on a bare knee, or later while passing their glasses 'over the water', were ways of acting out their emotions.[179] They were unwilling to confront reality directly,

---

[178] Namier and Brooke, eds., *History of Parliament* vol. ii, p. 486; Le Forestier, *La Franc-Maçonnerie Templière*, p. 853.
[179] Drinking 'over the water' apparently developed in England around 1745; it may have originated much earlier in Scotland – Hibbert-Ware, *Foundations in Manchester*, vol. i, pp. 97–8. After some Jacobites used this gesture at King George III's

and their intricate and self-involved world of Jacobite invention ended where it began, in the imagination, like the closed circle of the self-devouring snake.

Jacobite leaders often bemoaned the reluctance of the English gentry to do much more than drink the health of the exiled King; but historians should not disregard the Jacobitism of the landed elite for this reason. In their college frolics, their tartan masquerades, their secret clubs, the Jacobite gentry may have accomplished something more than they might have done if they had appeared in arms, to be mowed down by the government's troops or sent to a grisly fate on Tyburn. In their quieter lives, they managed to maintain an important sub-culture, a pattern of existence and of expression that informed their upbringing, education, activities, habits and sociability. The social history of a large segment of the English landed classes was intimately bound up with the development and preservation of Jacobitism.

In search of elite Jacobitism, this chapter has wandered to the ends of many long roads, but for committed adherents of the Stuarts, the road ended only with death – their own deaths, and the deaths of princes. Some carried their principles to their graves, or rather, on them. The epitaph of the Nonjuror Robert Phelips asserted in 1707 that '[t]he times changed, but he did not change with them'.[180] Godfrey Clarke, a Derbyshire Tory, had it inscribed on his monument in 1734 that 'manfully contended that in every matter, those things which belonged to them, should be rendered to the King, the Church and to the State'. The Latin original of 'rendered' is 'redeat'.[181] The Nonjuring bishop Richard Rawlinson went further when he died in 1753; he was buried with a skull in his right hand which he believed to be the disembodied head of Christopher Layer. In fact, it was a fake. The story prompted a malicious wit to comment that when he and his companion awoke at the day of judgment, Rawlinson would be 'amazed and mortified on his perceiving that he had been taking to his bosom, not the head of the Counsellor, but the worthless pate of some strolling mendicant, some footpad, or some superannuated harlot!'.[182]

Many Jacobites passed on their allegiance to their children. On his deathbed in 1692, Sir Coplestone Bampfylde of Poltimore, Devon,

coronation, finger-bowls were abolished from royal banquets until 1905 – Hughes, *Table Glass*, pp. 297–8.
180 Henning, ed., *History of Parliament*, vol. iii, p. 238.
181 Eardley-Simpson, *Derby and the Forty-Five*, p. 30.
182 Nichols, *Literary Anecdotes*, vol. v, p. 498.

instructed his family to be loyal 'to the right heirs to the Crown'; his grandson, who bore his name, was imprisoned during the '15 and sheltered Thomas Carte during the Atterbury Plot.[183] Wives often outlived their husbands, and became the carriers of family political traditions. At times they might even create new traditions, like the widow of Walpole's crony Lord Hervey, who decided to raise her daughters as 'rank Jacobites'.[184]

The Stuart cause had lost any real hope of success by the death of George II in 1760, and Charles Edward's demise in 1788 extinguished what was left of its political importance. Nevertheless, ancient loyalties continued to linger in some hearts. Thomas de Quincey recalled that Charles Lawson, headmaster of the Manchester Grammar School from 1764 until 1807, was still considered a Jacobite when the future opium-eater was his pupil in 1801.[185] Through individuals like Lawson, parts of Jacobite political culture were handed down to the Tories of the nineteenth century. When the abdicated King of Sardinia, heir to the Stuart title, died in 1824, Lord Liverpool informed George Canning that the English court must mourn for him, because 'there are those who think that the ex-King was the lawful King of Great Britain to the day of his death'.[186] The times changed, but they did not change with them.

[183] Henning, ed., *History of Parliament*, vol. i, p. 588; Sedgwick, ed., *History of Parliament*, vol. i, pp. 30–1.
[184] Robert Halsband, *Lord Hervey: Eighteenth Century Courtier* (Oxford, 1974), p. 307. Her son Frederick, Lord Bristol and Bishop of Derry, became a friend of Louisa Stuart – Vaughan, *The Last Stuart Queen*, p. 381.
[185] Alfred A. Mumford, *The Manchester Grammar School 1515–1915* (London, 1919), pp. 168–9, 192, 233.
[186] Quoted in Petrie, *The Jacobite Movement: The Last Phase*, p. 171.

Chapter 10

By a principle of duty: the Jacobite rebels

My motive for serving in the Prince's army was the duty I owe to God, the King and the country, in endeavouring the restoration of King James the Third and the royal family; which I am persuaded is the only human means by which this nation can ever become great and happy

Speech of Thomas Syddall at his execution, 30 July 1746[1]

Rebellion might be regarded as a sort of acid test of Jacobite adherence, and a phenomenon quite separate from the less dangerous manifestations of disaffection described in the last chapter. Yet it was legally indistinct from other forms of high treason, such as recruiting, conspiracy or even publishing, which were sometimes treated with equal severity. In some ways, rebellion was as much a symbolic statement as rioting or posting anonymous letters, and its greater 'seriousness' in comparison to other seditious practices can be questioned. It was one of a variety of hazardous Jacobite activities, not an entirely unique and higher category. Nevertheless, most Jacobites were too timorous to take up arms. They feared for their own lives, and for their estates – after all, except for Monck's coup in 1659–60 and the Revolution of 1688, which was more of a foreign invasion, there had been no successful insurrections in England since 1485. Even the 'Great Rebellion' of 1642 had ended in failure with the Restoration. The memory of that conflict, moreover, fostered a second fear that held Jacobites back from commitment to a rising. The idea of rebellion conjured up images of civil war, confusion and the possibility of anarchy or dictatorship; so Tory gentlemen preferred to dream of a repetition of the 'miracle' of 1660, or of a painless coup on the model of 1688.

Some, however, nursed a more aggressive loyalty, and were prepared to risk all in a single bold show of force. They were not a random

[1] Paton, ed., *Lyon in Mourning*, vol. i, p. 28.

group; their sentiments were determined by specific circumstances. Down to the rebellion of 1715, they were numerous among the northern Catholic community; and the same rebellious spirit persisted among the High Churchmen of Manchester in the '45. This chapter will discuss these belligerent Jacobites in order to discover why some Englishmen did not eschew the odious name of rebel.

The secret army, 1689–1714

The Glorious Revolution was not bloodless in Scotland or Ireland, and even in England there was a show of armed resistance to it. Late in November 1688, as James II's Protestant subjects were deserting him, a regiment of armed Catholic gentlemen, headed by William Molyneux, son and heir of Viscount Molyneux, Lord Lieutenant of Lancashire, rode into Chester to hold it for the King. Realizing the hopelessness of their situation, however, they soon laid down their arms.[2] This incident was both an echo of the Civil War, when so many Lancastrian recusants had rallied for King Charles I, and a foreshadowing of the military zeal that was to be shown by northern Catholics after the Revolution.[3]

James II fled to France on 23 December, but landed at Kinsale less than three months later to lead Ireland's resistance to William and Mary. At the end of March, 1688/9, as James formulated his strategy at Dublin, the Williamite government began to receive reports of meetings at the houses of the Howards, Warwicks and Salkelds, Roman Catholic gentlemen in Cumberland.[4] Within a few weeks, John Graham of Claverhouse, Viscount Dundee, had begun the first Jacobite rebellion in the Scottish Highlands. Local authorities in the border regions became acutely sensitive to any hint of rebellious activity there. From Northumberland in April came word of seventy or eighty armed horsemen meeting thrice weekly at the homes of the Earl of Derwentwater and Lord Widdrington; it was further alleged that the Anglican Jacobite Sir Theophilus Oglethorpe had attended these gatherings.[5] In the following month, a Catholic ex-soldier was apprehended in Cum-

---

[2] David H. Hosford, *Nottingham, Nobles and the North: Aspects of the Revolution of 1688* (Hamden, Ct, 1976), pp. 104–5; Gillow and Hewitson, eds., *Tyldesley Diary*, p. 25.

[3] For the Civil War, see B. G. Blackwood, *The Lancashire Gentry and the Great Rebellion, 1640–1660*, Chetham Society, 3rd Series, 25 (1978), esp. p. 63. My treatment of Lancashire Catholics owes much to Albers, 'Seeds of Contention', ch. 10.

[4] *C.S.P.D., W. & M.*, vol. i, pp. 40–1.   [5] *Ibid.*, p. 71.

berland, and confessed that he was going north to enlist for King James. His guide claimed to have encountered sixty men on 'large Trooping horses, with Pistalls, and all accoutrem^{ts} for Warr' at Hagg on the Scottish border. Edward Charlton of Hesleyside, Northumberland, was taken up in May on suspicion of holding meetings at his house; he had also written a letter containing a rumour of the landing of King James in the Highlands with 6,000 men.[6]

In these minor episodes can be detected the shadows of an emerging pattern. The secret meetings on country estates, the mysterious envoys from the south, the movement of armed men and horses along the borders – it was like a dress rehearsal for something yet to come. The raising of the curtain, however, was postponed by the defeat of the Highland rebels at Dunkeld in August. As long as King James remained in Ireland, the authorities in the far north remained alert, and as late as May 1690, a Scot was arrested at Carlisle for predicting an imminent invasion by a Highland army; but the real threat along the borders had passed.[7]

A different situation prevailed in Lancashire, where the Catholic community was constantly harassed by the government from 1689 until the mid-1690s. Lancashire had the largest recusant population in England, and was closer to Ireland than any other English county, so King James's Irish expedition prompted swift action by the government. The leading Lancastrian recusants were rounded up in June 1689, and kept in detention at Manchester until the following January.[8] It was not a strict confinement – the prisoners were free enough to distribute copies of King James's Dublin declaration about the town – and the government was unable to prosecute them collectively.[9] In the following decade, however, local justices were assiduous in having individual recusants indicted for seditious words. To the cases of Cuthbert Threlfall and George Carus, mentioned in Chapter 8, may be added those of William Clifton of Lytham, charged in June 1689 with damning William and Mary, Richard Shuttleworth of Garstang, accused in the West Riding in 1693 of drinking King James's health, and Charles Towneley of Towneley, tried in 1697 for laying a wager that King James would land in England before the spring.[10] Neverthe-

---

6 P.R.O., Assi. 45/15, part 3, infos. 1, 12–14, 24; C.S.P.D., W. & M., vol. i, pp. 153–4, 162.
7 P.R.O., Assi, 45/15, part 4, info. 46.
8 H.M.C., *The Manuscripts of Lord Kenyon* (London, 1894), pp. 313–14.
9 Bodl. Carte MS 228, fos. 202–3.
10 P.R.O., P.L. 26/26, indt. 2; P.L. 28/1, fo. 22; P.R.O., Assi. 45/16, infos. 73–4; P.R.O., P.L. 26/27, 1697 bundle, indt. C. Towneley.

less, northern juries were apparently better disposed towards recusants than were judges, and most of these prosecutions ended in acquittals. The government was no more fortunate in the famous trial of seven Catholic landowners at Manchester in 1694, which ended in a dismal failure.

Reports that the Lancashire recusants had received military commissions from King James were circulating as early as 1689, and the charges made by John Lunt in 1694 were not original.[11] Greed was undoubtedly a major factor in Lunt's accusations: hoping to obtain part of their estates as a reward, he had previously testified against the same gentlemen in an Exchequer case concerning donations for 'Superstitious Uses'.[12] In fact, historians have not dissented much with the view expressed by Jacobite writers at the time, that the main purpose of the Manchester trial was the confiscation of a number of rich estates, for the profit of greedy Whig ministers and their minions.[13] William Beamont, who first edited an account of the trial, was cautious enough to conclude simply that the allegations were not sufficiently proven; but a later editor, Reverend Alexander Goss, virulently denounced 'the cupidity of hungry Whigs' who sought to indict 'the most honoured gentry of the country ... on the evidence of a gang of ruffians'.[14] Paul Hopkins, who has most recently examined the trial, decries the 'Jacobite drivel' of Lunt, 'a young fantasist', although he notes that there was some factual basis for his inventions.[15]

There is little point in defending Lunt, who was clearly prepared to say anything in order to have the defendants condemned. His evidence was easily refuted; for example, his story of a meeting at Croxteth with Lord Molyneux and others in June or July 1689, which he embellished with a touching description of the Catholic gentlemen kissing their commissions on their knees, was impossible because most of those named were at that time under arrest at Manchester.[16] Nevertheless, it it worth noting that Lunt was remarkably tenacious in his accusations, even after the case had been decided against him. He may have invented

[11] C.S.P.D., W. & M., vol. ii, pp. 22–3; Beamont, ed., Jacobite Trials, pp. xvi–xxxiii.
[12] Paul Hopkins, 'The Commissions for Superstitious Lands of the 1690s', Recusant History, 15, 4 (1980), pp. 271–5.
[13] For contemporary Jacobite opinion, see [Ferguson], A Letter to Mr. Secretary Trenchard, and [Thomas Wagstaffe], A Letter out of Lancashire (n.p., 1694).
[14] Rev. Alexander Goss, ed., 1. Abbot's Journal. 2. The Trials at Manchester in 1694, Chetham Society, 61 (1864), p. v.
[15] Hopkins, 'Superstitious Lands', p. 266, and his 'Sham Plots and Real Plots in the 1690s', in Cruickshanks, ed., Ideology and Conspiracy, p. 95.
[16] Beamont, ed., Jacobite Trials, pp. 69–71.

his own role, but he also may have had connections with others who knew more. He lived in the same clandestine, semi-criminal under-world as did many Jacobite messengers and agents, a fact emphasized, to the damage of Lunt's credibility, by the main defence witness, Robert Taaffe.[17] If Lunt was lying, some of his associates may not have been; John Womball the carrier may have been telling the truth when he claimed to have carried arms and kettle-drums to the house of Lancashire recusants.[18]

In fact, there really was an insurrectionary conspiracy in Lancashire in 1689–94. The evidence of this was provided in 1757 by the dis-covery of Jacobite documents hidden in a wall at Standish Hall. They included a declaration of loyalty to James II, signed by Charles Town-eley, Tom Tyldesley, William Standish and six other northern recu-sants in November 1693, promising 'Obedience to whatsoever Com-mands Your Majesty shall lay upon Us', and affirming that arms and men had been gathered for a rising.[19] Although none of those accused in 1694 put their signatures to the declaration, the letters of Colonel John Parker, also found at Standish Hall, mention a large number of unnamed persons who had received commissions from King James.[20] A list of these commissions has survived among the Nairne Papers, and it implicates all but three of the Manchester defendants. Virtually all of those who were offered commissions were northern Roman Catholics. Lord Molyneux was to command a regiment of horse, in which Sir Rowland Stanley and Sir Thomas Clifton were to have cap-taincies, while William Dicconson of Wrightington was a captain in another regiment – all were later accused by Lunt. The Lancastrian names of Towneley, Tyldesley, Dalton, Standish, Gerrard, Butler, Winckley and Hothersall appear on the list; in Northumberland, the officers included Lord Widdrington, Edward Charlton, a Clavering, a Haggerston and an Errington; and among the Yorkshire contingent were Hugh Smithson, Simon Scroop (both of whom signed the 1693 declaration) and Charles Fairfax, James II's choice for mayor of York in 1688.[21]

Lunt did not know of this list of King James's officers, and he accused two recusants who were apparently innocent – Philip Langton and William Blundell. A third defendant, Bartholomew Walmesley of Dunkenhalgh, had been in France from 1689 until 1694, and could

---

[17] *Ibid.*, pp. 83–94.   [18] *Ibid.*, pp. 35–9.
[19] Porteous, 'New Light on the Lancashire Jacobite Plot', pp. 46–7.
[20] *Ibid.*, pp. 30–45.   [21] Bodl. Carte MS 181, fos. 558, 561–2.

not have received a commission at his Lancashire estate.[22] Lunt was, after all, a scoundrel, and the charges he made were fabricated; but they rested on a basis of truth.

The Manchester trial did not upset the real plans of King James's secret army. In December 1694, instructions were sent from St Germain to Charles Towneley, directing him to inform the friends of the exiled King that he was aware of the pains and hazards they had suffered, and instructing them to remain in readiness.[23] The rising they were expecting, however, never came. By the late 1690s, the secret officers had taken up other pursuits in support of the cause. William Dicconson became under-governor to the Prince of Wales at St Germain in 1699, and was later treasurer to Queen Mary. He was attainted and outlawed for treason in 1701 when he briefly returned to England.[24] In 1710, his former servant, Edward Rigby, informed the government that Sir Nicholas Shireburn and Sir William Gerrard were collectors of revenue for Dicconson in Lancashire, and that Viscount Molyneux was collecting arms at Liverpool. His allegations were dismissed by the Attorney General, who called him a 'foolish fellow'.[25] The Tory government, remembering High Church sympathy for the defendants tried in 1694, was not willing to investigate new allegations against the Lancashire Catholics.

The fears of the early 1690s, however, had been justified. Many northern recusants had been prepared to support an armed Jacobite insurrection, and had accepted military commissions from the exiled King. Why was this aggressive bent so pronounced among Catholics in Northumberland, Cumberland, Lancashire and Yorkshire? There were far more recusants in the north than in the Midlands or the south, and they had lost a great deal in the Revolution. Under James II, Catholics had held 44 per cent of the commissions of the peace in Northumberland, and 57 per cent in Lancashire, although Lord Molyneux found in 1688 that many of the new commissions there had not been put into effect.[26] Proximity to Scotland and Ireland added to the restiveness of northern recusants in 1689–90. Yet these explanations alone do not suffice. The northern Catholics were not the only large recusant

---

[22] Mary Brigg, 'The Walmesleys of Dunkenhalgh: A Family of Blackburn Hundred in the Elizabethan and Stuart Periods', *T.L.C.A.S.*, 75–6 (1965–6), p. 94.

[23] Bodl. Carte MS 181, fo. 427.

[24] Porteous, 'New Light on the Lancashire Jacobite Plot', pp. 27–8.

[25] P.R.O., S.P. 34/12, fos. 138, 141, 150–1; S.P. 34/13, fos. 2, 21, 114; S.P. 34/17, fo. 103.

[26] Miller, *Popery and Politics*, pp. 251, 271.

community; there were other sizeable concentrations along the Hampshire–Sussex border and in Monmouthshire, where Catholics comprised no less than 64 per cent of J.P.s under James II. After 1691, moreover, it was likely that the French would land in the south than that another rising would take place in Scotland or Ireland. Few southern recusants, however, were given commissions. Conversely, not all northerners were organized for a rebellion. Only four commissions were sent to the heavily Catholic West Derby hundred around Liverpool – two to the Molyneux family, one to Sir William Gerrard, another to John Harrington of Aigburth. The Blundells, Fazackerleys, Ecclestons and Urmstons, all prominent and ramified clans in the hundred, were not mentioned on the list of officers.

In fact, numerical strength, political influence and geographical location were not the principal factors that motivated the militant Jacobitism of some northern Catholics; rather, these were aspects of a wider social and cultural situation. James II's secret officers were mostly gentlemen of ancient families, who lived in relatively isolated areas – the Northumbrian valleys, the Yorkshire dales, or Lancashire north and east of the Ribble. They were sometimes enterprising, especially in developing coal mines, but they were less integrated into market economies than were their coreligionists who farmed the arable fields of West Derby hundred. They were fiercely independent and hostile to assimilation; their social lives were focussed not on large towns like Newcastle or Liverpool, but on smaller centres like Hexham, Richmond or Preston, where they could enjoy an environment that was less stridently Protestant. Even the Standishes, who lived just north of Wigan, were pulled more into the orbit of Preston than of West Derby; consequently, they usually married into northern upland clans, like the Heskeths, Tyldesleys or Howards.[27]

Historians are fortunate in possessing the diaries of two early eighteenth-century gentlemen who epitomized the contrasts within the Lancashire Catholic community. Thomas Tyldesley of the Lodge, Myerscough, which lay between Preston and Garstang, kept a diary in 1712–14 that reveals much about the attitudes of a northern uplands recusant squire, while the Great Diurnall written by Nicholas Blundell

[27] See Foster, Lancashire Pedigrees, 'Standish'. For more information on Lancashire Catholic families, see Sherborn, History of the Family of Sherborn; Joseph Gillow, The Haydock Papers: A Glimpse into English Catholic Life (London, 1888); John Wilson, The Chorleys of Chorley Hall (Manchester, 1907); and John Lunn, The Tyldesleys of Lancashire: The Rise and Fall of a Great Patrician Family (Altrincham, 1966).

of Little Crosby, in Sefton parish near Liverpool, between 1702 and 1728, illustrates the mind of a Catholic landowner of West Derby hundred. Their economic priorities were markedly different. Tyldesley paid little attention to his estate, and was finally in danger of losing it; Blundell, on the other hand, was an extraordinarily diligent farmer, and an enthusiastic pioneer of new agricultural techniques. The most important aspect of Tyldesley's existence was conviviality – sporting, gambling, drinking, making visits to the neighbours. Blundell was also very sociable, but he was not as outgoing or exuberant as Tyldesley. Although both men had numerous contacts with Protestant society, Blundell was constantly venturing into the mixed religious atmosphere of Liverpool. At the same time, his house was more liable to be searched by the authorities than was Tyldesley's, and he had to contend with the local authority of the Earls of Derby, traditional Tories who nonetheless strove to ingratiate themselves with Whig governments. Tom Tyldesley was free of such restraints.

Tyldesley and Blundell were both Jacobites, but in different ways. The squire of Little Crosby was undemonstrative about his allegiance. He could be so naive as to write in 1708 to his sister, a nun in Ghent, of 'a Report of King James landing in Skotland' – the phrase was very unwise in a letter that might have been opened by the authorities, but it was typical of Blundell, who had more understanding of grass seed than of politics.[28] This does not mean that he had no interest in political developments; his grasp of them, however, was not very sophisticated. In July 1719, for example, soon after the defeat of a small Jacobite rebellion in the Highlands, Blundell 'paisted a Large Map of Scotland upon a Linnen Cloth', which he put 'into a Fraime and Hung it up in the Paintry'.[29] Now at least he would know where King James's friends were fighting.

Tom Tyldesley was far more intense in his Jacobite loyalty. His political sentiments even impinged upon his religious observances. In October 1712, he was outraged that a priest at Nateby 'did not pray for our master', that is, for James III, and two days later he was delighted to find a different priest giving Mass there, 'honest Mr. Gant being very loyall'. In December 1713, he 'had occation to chide Mr. Jo. Swarbrick for disloyalty'; Swarbrick was the chaplain at Crow Hall.[30] Tyldesley gave 10s 'pro Prince of W.' on the feast of St James the Great in 1713 –

[28] Tyrer and Bagley, eds., *Great Diurnall*, vol. i, p. 166, n. 15.
[29] *Ibid.*, vol. ii, p. 264.
[30] Gillow and Hewitson, eds., *Tyldesley Diary*, pp. 59, 128.

his discreet fashion of referring to James Francis Stuart as Prince of Wales was in keeping with Anglican Jacobite practice, and demonstrated more of an awareness of political niceties than did Blundell's 'King James'.[31] For Tyldesley, Jacobitism was also linked to sociability. 'Dr. Thomas Tyldesley' was 'tester' to the 'mock corporation' of Walton-le-dale in 1704–6, and became 'slut-kisser' to that august body in 1708. He celebrated 10 June 1714 at the cock-fights with several Catholic friends, 'itt being ditto's birthday'. On 4 August 1714, he was in company with Edward Winckley, Gabriel Hesketh and Henry Whittingham when they received the news of Queen Anne's death. Instead of mourning, the four men 'spent 2s. each, being invitted to a pige feast'.[32]

Tom Tyldesley's day was at last dawning. He had been at Chester with Caryll Molyneux in November 1688; he had been detained at Manchester in 1689; he had received a commission as colonel of a dragoon regiment from St Germain in the 1690s. In August 1714, Colonel Thomas Tyldesley must have been very excited. Further south, Nicholas Blundell was probably apprehensive. He could have foreseen another search of his house; he could not have known that in November 1715 he would be hiding in the priest's-hole at Little Crosby for six days, alongside a 'Bed-Fellow' who may have been a Jacobite refugee from the battle of Preston. He could not have predicted that fear of reprisals against recusants would cause him to flee to Flanders in March 1715/16, and remain there for eighteen months.[33] For him, the day of rebellion brought unmitigated disaster. Poor Tom Tyldesley never saw it. He died in January 1714/15, before he had any opportunity to exercise his military commission; but his son Edward, along with Edward Winckley, Gabriel Hesketh and Henry Whittingham, heeded the call to arms when it came. So did scores of other Lancashire recusants, like the Towneleys, Cliftons, Standishes, Caruses, Butlers, Andertons, Walmesleys, Daltons, Gerrards, Shuttleworths, Chorleys, Winckleys, Hothersalls and Cuthbert Threlfall of the Ashes. They were joined by their Northumbrian cousins, the Charltons, Radcliffes, Widdringtons, Erringtons, Claverings, Scarisbricks and Haggerstons, and by the Salkelds, Dalstons and Howards of Cumberland. The secret army was at last revealed; it had come out for the '15.

---

[31] *Ibid.*, p. 102.   [32] *Ibid.*, pp. 13, 154, 164.
[33] Tyrer and Bagley, eds., *Great Diurnall*, vol. ii, pp. 152, 159–206.

The English rebels of the '15

The '15 was the last great rebellion in England, and bore some
resemblance to the greatest northern Catholic rising of all, the Pilgrimage of Grace.[34] Nevertheless, it would be erroneous to represent the
planned insurrection of 1715 as no more than a northern recusant
affair. It had been concocted by Anglican Tories, and its main blow was
to have fallen in the south. The scheme of Sir William Wyndham, Lord
Lansdowne and other Tory leaders called for the seizure of Bristol,
Oxford and Portsmouth, as well as a French landing in the west,
commanded by the Duke of Ormonde. The capture of Newcastle-
upon-Tyne was to be a side-show, facilitated by the collaboration of Sir
William Blackett, the Tory mayor of the town. Unfortunately for the
Jacobites, the plan went completely awry when the French refused to
send troops, which caused Wyndham to have second thoughts. While
he dithered, the government pounced, arresting him and other chief
conspirators on 21 September.[35] On receiving this news, the thirty
Tory gentlemen who had gathered at Bath dispersed, but a group of
former army officers at Bristol continued with their preparations until,
in the early hours of 5 October, General Pepper made a lightning raid
on the town. The leading plotter, Colonel Owen, escaped in his
night-gown; three of his principal associates were captured and executed at Tyburn.[36]

The situation was no better in the north. On 6 October, the
Northumbrian rebels met at Greenrigg, near Lord Derwentwater's
seat, hoping to proceed into Newcastle; but Sir William Blackett had
panicked, and turned himself over to the authorities.[37] Unsure of what
to do next, the Jacobite insurgents galloped around the Northumbrian
countryside, picking up recruits along the way. They rode at last into
Scotland, where the Earl of Mar had raised the Stuart standard.

[34] The Towneleys and the Thornboroughs were involved in both rebellions. See
Christopher Haigh, *The Last Days of the Lancashire Monasteries and the Pilgrimage
of Grace*, Chetham Society, 3rd Series, 17 (1969), pp. 75, 81.

[35] See Petrie, 'Jacobite Activities in South and West England', pp. 95–101; Handasyde,
Granville the Polite, pp. 139–50.

[36] Lady Llanover, ed., *The Autobiography and Correspondence of Mary Granville, Mrs.
Delaney* (3 vols., London, 1861), vol. i, p. 17; Rae, *History of the Rebellion*,
pp. 216–17; Boyer, *Political State*, vol. ix, pp. 335–41, 392–5, 585–6; *St. James's
Evening Post*, no. 76, 22–4 Nov. 1715, no. 82, 6–8 Dec. 1715.

[37] Patten, *History of the Rebellion*, pp. 29–30; Sedgwick, ed., *History of Parliament*,
vol. i, pp. 464–5.

Bolstered by two contingents of Scottish rebels, they hung around the border for several days, trying to decide whether to march north and assist Mar, or turn into Lancashire and Cheshire. Foolishly, they chose the latter course, and advanced into Preston, where they met a larger government force under General Wade. After a brisk fight, in which they inflicted ten times as many casualties as they suffered, the Jacobite army was surrendered by its leaders, who had lost heart in the struggle.[38]

The mainly Catholic rebels had hoped to reach their Tory allies in southern Lancashire and Cheshire; but if they had succeeded, they might have been given little succour. The High Church gentry of Cheshire had been warm for a rebellion in August, when Lord Barrymore, Charles Cholmondeley and Sir Henry Bunbury had convened to plot a rising; they had toasted 'our absent friends and that they may return with honour, prosperity and glory'.[39] Robert Cholmondeley of Holford had been among the conspirators at Oxford.[40] After the arrival of General Pepper's dragoons, he came scurrying back to Cheshire, where he gathered with the leading Tory gentlemen of the county, including Barrymore, Sir Richard Grosvenor, Peter Legh, Henry Legh, Charles Hurleston, Amos Meredith, Alexander Radclyffe, John Warren and Thomas Assheton, in order to decide upon a common course of action. By a majority of one vote, they chose not to support the rebellion in the north.[41]

In spite of the fickleness, hesitation and uncertainty of so many Tories, however, the rebel army contained a strong Protestant element. One of them was the ship's captain Francis Legh, brother of Peter Legh of Lyme, who escaped to France after the battle of Preston; another Protestant gentleman, the Northumbrian J.P. 'Mad Jack' Hall of Otterburn, eventually died on the scaffold as a Nonjuring martyr.[42] In contrast to Hall, Roger Muncaster of Goosnargh, an Anglican attorney

---

[38] The best military analysis of the '15 is John Baynes, *The Jacobite Rising of 1715* (London, 1970).

[39] Sedgwick, ed., *History of Parliament*, vol. i, p. 551.

[40] H.M.C., *Stuart*, vol. iv, p. 422.

[41] Egerton, 'The Cheshire Gentry', pp. 5–21. For further details about Cheshire during the rebellion, see the diary of Henry Prescott, a Jacobite who was deputy registrar of the diocese of Chester, in W. F. Irvine and J. H. E. Bennett, eds., 'Cheshire and "The Fifteen" ', *The Cheshire Sheaf*, 3rd Series, 37 (1942). See also J. H. E. Bennett, 'Cheshire and "The Fifteen" ', *Journal of the Chester and North Wales Archaeological and Historic Society*, New Series, 21 (1915), pp. 30–46.

[42] Newton, *Lyme Letters*, pp. 293–310; H.M.C., *Eleventh Report, Appendix, Part IV. The Manuscripts of the Marquess Townshend* (London, 1887), p. 168; Patten, *History of the Rebellion*, pp. 142–4; P.R.O., S.P. 35/5/64b; S.P. 35/2/11.

and friend of the Tyldesleys, declared himself repentant in his dying speech.[43] Thomas Forster, the Tory M.P. for Northumberland, commanded the Jacobite troops; he later absconded from Newgate and fled into exile.[44] Humbler Protestants were also found among the rebels, like James Gregson, a shoemaker of Preston, or Roger Isherwood of Pleasington, a labourer.[45] From the south came Robert Cotton of Conington, Huntingdonshire, a staunch Nonjuror, who brought with him his son John and his nephew, Lionel Walden of Christ Church, Oxford.[46] Other southern Protestant rebels included two Derbyshire bricklayers and a Staffordshire engraver.[47] Three Church of England ministers accompanied the rebels – Robert Patten, curate of Allendale in Northumberland, Thomas Buxton, a clergyman of Derbyshire, who left the Jacobite army at Lancaster to carry letters into the south, thus avoiding capture at Preston, and William Paul, vicar of Horton-on-the-Hill, Leicestershire. As a lesson to his fellow clerics, the unhappy 'Parson Paul' was later executed in London.[48]

The less conscientious Robert Patten turned evidence against his former comrades, and wrote the most important account of the rising. In its preface, he attempted to justify his behaviour in 1715; he traced the origin of the insurrection to the Sacheverell trial, and 'the licentious Freedom of some in their publick Discourses, and others in their Addresses, to cry up the old Doctrines of Passive Obedience, and to give Hints and Arguments to prove Hereditary Right'. This had led to 'ill-natured Distinctions and Designations', and had incited riots. Patten admitted that he had been taken in by the popular cry of the Church in danger.[49] In an attempt to please his new Whig masters, however, he did not mention the expulsion from office of the Tory party as an inducement to rebel. This had been the critical factor for Thomas Forster, who revealed in an examination soon after his capture that 'in general he look'd upon the whole body of the Torys to be in it'.[50] While this was an exaggeration, it showed the extent to which the High Church insurgents saw themselves as acting in the interests of their party.

[43] Samuel Hibbert-Ware, Lancashire Memorials of the Rebellion, 1715, Chetham Society, 5 (1845), pp. 199–200.
[44] Sedgwick, ed., History of Parliament, vol. ii, pp. 45–6.
[45] P.R.O., K.B. 8/66, part 1, fos. 72–3.
[46] Patten, History of the Rebellion, pp. 92, 149–50; Foster, Alumni Oxonienses 1500–1714, vol. v, p. 1554. Walden's father and grandfather had been supporters of James II – Henning, ed., History of Parliament, vol. iii, pp. 649–51.
[47] P.R.O., K.B. 8/66, part 1, fo. 38, no. 138, fo. 70.
[48] Patten, History of the Rebellion, pp. 22, 25–6, 28, 33, 96–9; P.R.O., S.P. 35/5/64b.
[49] Patten, History of the Rebellion, preface.   [50] H.M.C., Townshend, p. 171.

In fact, the collapse of the southern conspiracy meant that these Tory rebels were embroiled in something quite different from a High Church national uprising. Most of them soon realized that they were mixed up in a mainly Catholic rebellion. This revelation made them lose their nerve; it incited Forster to surrender hastily at Preston, made Hall pretend at first that he had been abducted, induced Muncaster to repent, transformed Patten into an ardent Hanoverian, and almost turned Reverend Paul into an informer. None of these Anglicans wished to die for the sake of a bunch of overly aggressive recusants. No matter how strong their attachment to the Stuart King – and some, like Forster, were firmly loyal to him long after 1715 – they felt little affinity with the aspirations of the English Catholic community. Because they placed small value on the recusant contribution to the rebellion, Anglicans who participated in the '15 tended to underestimate its scope. Reading the accounts of Robert Patten or of the Jacobite lawyer Peter Clarke, one is left with the impression that the rising was a minor affair that attracted few persons of social standing, and was doomed from the start.[51] This is a misleading picture, which can be corrected by examining the various government documents relating to the rebel prisoners. Surprisingly, no use has hitherto been made of them by historians.

The so-called *Baga de Secretis* in the records of the court of King's Bench contains lists of the rebel prisoners held at Wigan, Lancaster and Chester after the '15, as well as an alphabetical index of persons against whom informations were taken at Preston.[52] These materials do not include the names of all those involved in the rising. A substantial number managed to escape from Preston after the battle; some of them can be traced from other sources. Charles Beswicke of Manchester, for example, fled from the town before the surrender, and made off to Italy; he was eventually rehabilitated, and became British consul at Algiers.[53] In Northumberland, the authorities were still arresting escapees from Preston as late as 1718.[54] On the other hand, the *Baga de Secretis* papers implicated a few who aided or abetted the rising, without taking up arms themselves, like Viscount Molyneux of Sefton,

---

[51] See 'Peter Clarke's Journal', in Hibbert-Ware, *Lancashire Memorials*, pp. 69–112; a manuscript copy is in Bodl. Rawl. MS D. 87.

[52] P.R.O., K.B. 8/66, part 1, fos. 17, 38–48, 69–77. All uncited information in this section is from this source.

[53] Hibbert-Ware, *Lancashire Memorials*, p. 86. Edward Beswicke of Manchester, chapman, who may have been his brother, was among the prisoners at Preston.

[54] 'Diary of John Thomlinson', in Hodgson, ed., *Six North Country Diaries*, p. 148.

the same man who had tried to defend Chester in 1688, and who sent some of his servants and horses to join the rebels at Preston.[55] The aged and sickly Sir Nicholas Shireburn of Stonyhurst entertained thirty recusants at a supper on 10 November; they spent the night casting bullets, and rode off the next morning with Sir Nicholas's guns, a blunderbuss, a sackful of pistols and four coach-horses.[56] The government did not hesitate to include men like Molyneux and Shireburn on its lists of rebels. Several of those accused of assisting the rebellion were prosecuted. Albert Silvertopp of Stella, Durham, a recusant coal magnate, was presented at the Palatinate Assizes in 1716 on a charge of high treason in waging war on the King, because he had helped to raise men for the rising.[57] The bill was found *ignoramus*, but it shows that the definition of a rebel was flexible.

How reliable are the *Baga de Secretis* lists? There can be little doubt that prisoners from outside the vicinity of Preston were really rebels; no one would have wandered innocently into the town from another county while it was held by the Jacobites. Nevertheless, it is possible that some natives of Preston or its region were taken up by accident; Lord Carlisle feared that 'severall of the country people were in the disorder and confusion hurried into the church, with the rebells, that being the place where they are at present secured'.[58] The government, however, took care to weed out the innocent, and it should be noted that almost every prisoner against whom informations were taken had more than one witness against him. Anthony Barlow, a gentleman of Preston, was implicated in the testimony of no fewer than sixteen persons. More typically, Thomas Birches, a joiner of the town, was accused by six of his fellow citizens.[59] The chances of a prisoner being wholly guiltless were slight.

The *Baga de Secretis* lists contain the names of 688 English rebels. Seventeen rebels were killed, perhaps two or three hundred escaped, and a few had probably deserted or left the rebel force before the battle. The total number of English rebels, therefore, may have been around 1,000. Combined with 1,500 Scots, and entrenched behind barricades, it is easy to imagine how they could have beaten off attacks by 5,000 soldiers. Of the listed prisoners, 227, or almost exactly one third, were Northumbrians, while Lancashire provided over half of the total

---

[55] B.L., Stowe 750, fo. 158.
[56] John Orlebar Payne, ed., *Records of the English Catholics of 1715* (London, 1889), pp. 145–7.
[57] P.R.O., P.D. 17/1A, indt.   [58] H.M.C., *Townshend*, p. 169.
[59] P.R.O., K.B. 8/66, part 1, f. 69.

recruits, 366 men. The remainder were from diverse counties: twenty-two from Durham, nineteen from Cumberland, twelve from Yorkshire, eight from London (some northern gentlemen gave this as their place of residence), four each from Westmorland and Derbyshire, three each from Cheshire and Cambridgeshire (the Cottons were listed as from this county), two from Leicestershire, one from Staffordshire, six from Ireland and eleven from unidentified places.

The alphabetical list of Preston informations gives the religious affiliations of prisoners, revealing that 75 per cent of them were Roman Catholics. Almost all of those named on this list, however, were from Lancashire; the Northumbrians may have been even more Catholic, although almost all the southerners were Protestants. There was a higher percentage of Catholics among those of lower social standing on the informations list than among gentlemen; about 70 per cent of the gentry were recusants, compared to 90 per cent of 'husbandmen'. The other prisoner lists do not record religion, so it is difficult to be conclusive about the number of Catholics in the rebel force. Nevertheless, it is likely that they constituted between two-thirds and three-quarters of the insurgents.

In Northumberland, two Lords, Derwentwater and Widdrington, and sixty-one gentlemen or esquires rallied to the uprising, along with ninety-nine men listed as 'servants'. Thus, 28 per cent of the Northumbrians were of the landed classes, and 44 per cent were probably their retainers. To the latter category might be added a coachman, two gardeners and, most exotic of all, two bagpipers. Northumberland sent only two professional men to the rising – a doctor and the Reverend Robert Patten. Eight were referred to as 'farmers', which probably meant a yeoman freeholder; two others were marked 'yeoman', and a third simply 'freeholder'. The rest, 18 per cent of the total, were assigned specific trades. Some of them – a mercer, a chandler, a surgeon, a wigmaker – may have been 'middling' men. The others included six masons, six weavers, four carpenters, four smiths, four skinners, four butchers and twenty-two men with assorted occupations.

Geographically, the Tyne valley was the main recruiting ground for the Northumbrian and Durham rebels. Newcastle provided thirteen recruits; ten more came from the Ryton–Whickham area south of the river. The Radcliffe estates in Tynedale contributed twenty-two men, and the market town of Hexham, centre of Northumbrian recusancy, sent out nineteen, including ten tradesmen. From Woodhorn, between the Tyne and the Coquet valleys, came three of the Widdringtons with seventeen servants. Further west, eight servants and ten tradesmen were recruited at Hartburn, home of the Thorntons. A number of Catholic landowners lived in Coquetdale and the interior uplands, but most did not seem to have many servants. The Ords, Robinsons, Lisles and Talbots had few retainers with them, and the Claverings of Callaly brought only themselves. George Collingwood of Whittingham and Alnham, however, compensated for them all by riding out with nineteen servants and a carpenter. The Holy Island of Lindisfarne, briefly seized in a daring Jacobite raid, contributed an impressive troop of thirteen men to the rising.[60]

It is tempting to envision the Northumbrian rebellion as a sort of feudal parade, led by a host of squires, followed by a crowd of retainers, with a few artisans and tradesmen in the rear. The bustling industry of Tyneside has no place in this picture; in fact, only one collier joined the rebels, a miner from Chester-le-Street. This feudal appearance, however, is misleading. Even in the Northumbrian valleys, feudalism was long dead; no legal bond required servants to fight for their masters, and had they been forced, they would have run away at the first shot. They rode with the gentry because they, too, were Catholics; they shared the political loyalties that stemmed from their religion. As for the relative absence of labouring folk, Patten provided an explanation when he wrote that the Northumbrian rebels were

all Horse; for they would entertain no Foot, else their Number would have been very large: But as they neither had nor could provide Arms for those they had mounted, they gave the common People good Words, and told them that they would soon be furnished with Arms and Ammunition, and that then they would List Regiments to form an Army: This was upon the Expectation they had of surprising *Newcastle*; in which case, they did not question to have had as many Foot as they pleased.[61]

The paucity of ordinary workmen, especially coal miners, in the rebel force was caused partly by the refusal to enlist foot soldiers, and partly by the failure to take Newcastle. The Tyneside keelmen, in whom great Jacobite hopes had been placed, exemplified the reactions of Protestant

[60] Information on families and landholding in Northumberland has been derived from John Hodgson, *A History of Northumberland* (6 vols., Newcastle-upon-Tyne, 1827–58); Northumberland County History Committee, *A History of Northumberland* (15 vols., Newcastle and London, 1893–1940); and D. D. Nixon, *Upper Coquetdale, Northumberland: Its History, Tradition, Folk-Lore and Scenery* (Newcastle, 1903).
[61] Patten, *History of the Rebellion*, pp. 26–7.

labourers to the rebellion. Although a few of them marched out to join the insurgents, the majority declared their allegiance to King George after hearing of Sir William Blackett's defection.[62]

The Lancashire rebels were as high-born as their north-eastern cousins; 28 per cent of them were gentlemen. They brought with them, however, only thirty-one servants, about 9 per cent of the Lancastrian contingent. On the other hand, ninety-two rebels from the county, or about one in four, were listed as 'husbandmen', meaning probably small tenant farmers or agricultural labourers. One of the Scottish Jacobite leaders commented upon the large number of 'rustics' who entered Preston from the surrounding countryside.[63] All but nine of these 'husbandmen' were Roman Catholics. Twenty 'yeomen', eleven 'labourers' and seven 'farmers' were also taken. Artisans and tradesmen accounted for 27 per cent of the Lancashire rebels; they included thirty-four weavers, six carpenters, six blacksmiths, five shoemakers, five tailors and three innkeepers. Among those from Preston itself were a few representatives of trades that have been associated by Peter Borsay with the 'urban renaissance' in the town – a glazier, an ironmonger, a silversmith, a hatter and two barbers. Three of them were Catholics, demonstrating that the 'urban renaissance' in Preston was not an entirely Protestant phenomenon.[64]

The geography of the Lancashire rebellion is already familiar. Few adherents of the Stuarts rode in from West Derby hundred, while the Catholic communities north and east of the Ribble turned out in strength. None of the Lancashire gentlemen brought with them many retainers. Richard Towneley of Towneley was accompanied by his coachman, his butler and his postillion; Edward Tyldesley was escorted by three servants, but he also had twelve other residents of Myerscough with him.[65] From Standish came the squire, Ralph Standish, as well as a tanner, a carpenter, a miller, a farmer and a 'husbandman'. John Dalton of Thurnham rode in with his brother and a single 'husbandman'. Indeed, the Lancashire gentry tended to bolster the rebel ranks with members of their own families rather than their servants. William and John Brockholes of Claughton, Richard and Charles Chorley of Chorley, Gabriel and Cuthbert Hesketh of Goosnargh,

[62] Ibid., pp. 31, 36–7.
[63] Annals of King George (London, 1715), p. 136, quoted in Baynes, Rising of 1715, p. 113.
[64] Peter Borsay, 'The English Urban Renaissance: The Development of Provincial Urban Culture, c. 1680–c. 1760', S.H., 5 (1977), pp. 581–603.
[65] Nicholson, 'Lancashire in the Rebellion of 1715', p. 83.

Thomas senior, Thomas junior and Charles Carus of Halton, and four Walmesleys of Preston testified to the fact that the '15 in Lancashire was a family affair.

The familial nature of the rebellion in Lancashire was not limited to the gentry. James, George, Thomas and Lawrence Cowp of Walton-le-dale, all weavers, joined the rebels at Preston; although they owned 20 acres of land in the area, worth £3, the Cowps cannot be considered gentlefolk.[66] Their village of Walton-le-dale was full of rebellious Catholic textile workers; eighteen weavers and sixteen 'husbandmen' (at least five of whom are listed elsewhere as 'weavers') crossed the river to Preston, as did a shoemaker, an innkeeper and a 'yeoman'. Burnley, a weaving village near Towneley in the Calder valley, was home to fifteen rebels, including two jersey combers and four weavers; most of them, interestingly enough, were Protestants. Five recruits came up from Wigan, and three – two chapmen and a silk dyer – reached the rebel army from Manchester. If the rebels had reached south-east Lancashire, they might have been greeted warmly by the weaving community there.

The Lancashire insurgents were more diverse than the Northumbrians, reflecting both the varied economy of the county and the wide social spread of the Catholic community there. Both rebel contingents were top-heavy with gentry, a pattern true of English Catholicism in general; but in Lancashire, recusancy also had some appeal among the labouring classes. The comparative absence of 'servants' among the Lancastrians, and the prominence of 'husbandmen', may be explained by different methods of farming. In the Northumbrian uplands, Catholic 'servants' were probably employed to tend the herds and flocks belonging to recusant landlords. In Lancashire, however, Catholic gentlemen may have taken on copyhold tenants of their own religion, the 'husbandmen' or 'rustics' who were so notable at Preston. In both cases, an economic relationship was complemented by religious ties.

Edward Hughes, citing the poverty of many Northumbrian Catholic gentry after the '15, has argued that this was the rebellion of a declining class.[67] Not all recusant landowners, however, were in dire financial straits. The Earls of Derwentwater, far from being poor, were models

---

[66] Rev. Edgar E. Estcourt and John Orlebar Payne, eds., *The English Catholic Nonjurors of 1715* (London and New York, n.d.), p. 90.
[67] Edward Hughes, *North Country Life in the Eighteenth Century: The North-East, 1700–1750* (London, 1952), pp. xvii–xviii.

of the kind of aggressive capitalism of which Hughes is so enamoured. They enclosed, consolidated and improved their estates and coal mines with as little tenderness towards their tenants as was shown by their Protestant counterparts. By 1715, they were one of the richest families in the north, and the plundering of their estates by Whig politicians became a major source of administrative corruption.[68] The perception that Roman Catholic landowners were impoverished rests too heavily on the registers of recusant estates drawn up in 1717, pursuant to an Act obliging all Catholics to surrender two-thirds of their property.[69] It is easy to understand why sensible recusants made every effort to appear destitute. The Commissioners of Forfeited Estates faced enormous difficulties in determining the real wealth of Catholics. The Standish family, for example, reported that their colliery at Shevington 'was wro't out and no Stock left', but an official who inspected it in 1717 found 'great pyles of Coal ready for sale, and a good quantity of Charcoal made'.[70]

It was not financial distress that brought the northern recusants out in the '15. Their belligerent Jacobitism was rooted in their religious and political identity, and had become part of their social existence. At times, the rebellion was as much a social event as a military expedition. At Lancaster, the Jacobites 'dressed & trimmed themselves up in their best clothes for to drink a dish of Tea with ye Ladys of the Town', and at Preston the ladies were 'so very beautifull & so richly attired y^t ye Gentlemen Soldiers from Wednesday to Saturday minded nothing but courting and feasting'.[71] The nature of northern Catholic allegiance was reflected in the banner carried by the rebels: a pelican feeding her young with her own blood.[72] A traditional family emblem of the Tyldesleys, this was also a symbol of Christ in the role of martyr and sustainer, a representation of the sacrifices made by the exiled Stuarts for the nation, and a depiction of the hardships suffered by recusants for the sake of their religion.[73] The banner showed that

---

[68] Ralph Arnold, *Northern Lights: The Story of Lord Derwentwater* (London, 1959), pp. 34–6.

[69] See Estcourt and Payne, eds., *English Catholic Nonjurors*, and R. Sharpe France, ed., *The Registers of Estates of Lancashire Papists, 1717–1788*, Record Society of Lancashire and Cheshire, 98, 108 (2 vols., 1945, 1960).

[70] Patrick Purcell, 'The Jacobite Rising of 1715 and the English Catholics', *E.H.R.*, 45, 175 (1929), p. 421.

[71] Bodl. Rawl. MS D. 87, fos. 5, 7; Hibbert-Ware, *Lancashire Memorials*, pp. 96–7, 107.

[72] Hibbert-Ware, *Lancashire Memorials*, p. 143.

[73] For the Tyldesley pelican, see Gillow and Hewitson, eds., *Tyldesley Diary*, drawing facing p. 129.

the Catholic rebels were fighting for their God, their King, and themselves.

Not all of them rose enthusiastically; Lord Derwentwater was very reluctant to act, because he was aware that the rebellion had little chance of success without a landing and insurrection in the south. Yet it is unlikely that fear of arrest prompted him to take up arms, as historians have suggested.[74] He could have fled overseas, remained in hiding, or joined Mar's army in Scotland; even arrest would have been less dangerous than the course he chose to follow. An old Northumbrian legend maintains that his wife scorned him into coming out for the Stuarts; if not literally true, this story at least makes psychological sense. The pressures of family, religion and tradition sent the Catholic rebels to their destiny. Derwentwater, a grandson of Charles II, grew up at St Germain as a companion of James III, and the whole Catholic community in the north looked to him as its leader. In his dying speech, the unhappy Earl claimed that he had

never any other but King James III for my rightful and lawful sovereign: him I had an inclination to serve from my infancy, and was moved thereto by a natural love I had to his person, knowing him to be capable of making his people happy. And though he should have been of a different religion to mine, I should have done for him all that lay in my power, as my ancestors have done for his predecessors, being thereto bound by the laws of God and man.[75]

In the end, his hesitation was forgotten; he had done his duty to his religion, to his King and to himself.

The aftermath of the '15

The government took swift revenge on Derwentwater and the other insurgents, although apprehension about the reactions of Tory Anglicans may have prevented a worse blood-bath. Twenty-six English rebels were executed, including twelve commoners, thirteen gentlemen and one unrepentant Earl. Twenty-one estates in Lancashire, and a similar number in Northumberland, were forfeited. The Registration Act was passed to facilitate the confiscation of two-thirds of all recusant lands. It proved a failure, but another new Act, allowing any two justices of the peace to administer the oath of supremacy at any

[74] Arnold, *Northern Lights*, pp. 81–9.
[75] *Ibid.*, p. 58. A reverential view of Derwentwater's life and death is found in F. J. A. Skeet, *The Life of the Right Honourable James Radcliffe Third Earl of Derwentwater* (London, 1929).

time to Catholics, on pain of imprisonment and fines, brought a crushing legal burden on many recusants.[76]

In light of such hardships, it is astonishing that the spirit of militant Jacobitism was not completely crushed in the north. True, there could never be another rising of the Catholic community — too many had been ruined by the first attempt. When Prince Charles Edward and his Highlanders marched down from Scotland in 1745, however, they found that some embers of recusant loyalty were still smouldering. At Brampton in Cumberland, he dined with the Catholic Warwicks of Warwick Hall. His hostess was the daughter of Thomas Howard of Corby Castle, who had been imprisoned at Carlisle along with the Warwicks and other Catholic landowners during the '15 rebellion. In spite of this, thirteen men from Wetherall beside Corby were out in the rising, including Thomas Howard's huntsman.[77] Mrs Warwick's warm reception of Charles Edward was in keeping with the principles of her forebears. So was the behaviour of Henry Salkeld of Whitehall, who met the Prince at Carlisle, and sent one of his servants to carry a message from the Jacobite army to Lord Barrymore in Cheshire.[78] In Lancashire, Charles Edward's army was joined by Francis Towneley, whose brother Richard had been out in 1715, and by Tom Tyldesley's grandson James.[79] At Ormskirk on 25 November 1745, about 200 plebeian Catholics gathered with a drum and proclaimed the Pretender, before being dispersed by a Hanoverian mob.[80]

Nor had the north-eastern recusants forgotten their allegiance. After the battle of Prestonpans, Charles Edward received a letter from William 'Bowrie' Charlton of the Bower, a rebel of the '15, offering assistance in case of a march on Newcastle.[81] At about this time, a Catholic gentleman of Chamboise in Durham, George Turnbull, was arrested for trying to recruit his steward to meet the Highlanders at

---

[76] It was seen as the worst of the penal laws by Catholics — see Purcell, 'Jacobite Rising', p. 432. See also Baines, *County of Lancaster*, vol. ii, pp. 451–2, and Hibbert-Ware, *Lancashire Memorials*, pp. 192–5.

[77] G. G. Mounsey, *Authentic Account of the Occupation of Carlisle in 1745, by Prince Charles Edward Stuart* (London and Carlisle, 1846), pp. 45–6; P.R.O., K.B. 8/66, part 1, fos. 38–49; William Hutchinson, *The History of the County of Cumberland, and some Places Adjacent* (2 vols., Carlisle, 1794), vol. i, pp. 153–4, 163–5.

[78] P.R.O., T.S. 20/33, fo. 22; T.S. 20/39, fo. 11; T.S. 20/112, no. 5; P.R.O., S.P. 36/78, fos. 92–7.

[79] See the next section for Towneley; for Tyldesley, see P.R.O., S.P. 36/81, fos. 163, 315–17; Gillow and Hewitson, eds., *Tyldesley Diary*, p. 183.

[80] Speck, *The Butcher*, p. 63.

[81] P.R.O., S.P. 36/85, fo. 38; Edward Charlton, 'Jacobite Relics of 1715 and 1745', *Archaeologia Aeliana*, New Series, 6 (1865), pp. 29–34.

Morpeth.[82] Although the Prince chose to invade England by the western route, a few Northumbrians managed to reach his army, as will be seen. After the Jacobite retreat, moreover, a serious plot developed at Newcastle. In April 1746, the authorities were informed that the steward of the Erringtons of Beaufront, supported by money from Sir John Swinburne, Thomas Riddel, the Charltons and the Thorntons, was trying to recruit keelmen for an attempt to seize the town.[83] The keelmen were still smarting from their defeat in the violent strike of 1740; furthermore, many of them were Scots. A few days after the information was laid, some soldiers on guard in Newcastle were menaced by forty keelmen who reportedly said 'they did not Care for the Mayor or any Officer in the Regiment for that in two Days Time they would make a second Sheriff Moor [Sheriffmuir] of it, that they would find a Body of Men and arms to make passage for themselves at any time'.[84] The government was alerted, and no rising took place. In July, however, the Tynedale Catholics met for a hunting expedition on the moors, as they had in October 1715; their well-armed sport was seen as 'an Indiscreet if not an Insolent Action in them at this Particular time'.[85]

'Bowrie' Charlton, who had been taken into custody during the rebellion, remained attached to the Stuart family after its suppression. He wrote in 1750 to a missionary priest, enquiring about the habitation of 'the young Goodman of Bellnagih', a nickname for Charles Edward. Charlton's illegitimate daughters preserved his loyalty, and after 1766, when the Vatican ordered that George III be prayed for at Mass, the unmarried Charlton sisters adopted the habit of leaving the chapel as soon as the 'usurper's' name was mentioned.[86] Their attenuated allegiance was matched by Thomas Clifton of Lytham in Lancashire, who celebrated his first marriage on the notable date of 10 June 1750, and who sheltered for many years two Jacobite veterans of the '45. According to the scandalized Anglican minister of the parish, writing in 1778, these enemies of the ruling monarchs had been treated 'as if they had been some great men, who had deserved well of the public'.[87]

Nevertheless, Jacobite leadership in the north had been transferred

[82] P.R.O., S.P. 36/70, fos. 70, 320; P.R.O., P.D. 17/5, gaol order, 1 Oct. 1745.
[83] P.R.O., S.P. 36/83, fos. 46, 70–1.
[84] P.R.O., S.P. 36/83, fos. 145, 147.
[85] P.R.O., S.P. 36/85, fo. 37; also S.P. 44/133, pp. 137–8.
[86] Charlton, 'Jacobite Relics', pp. 31, 34.
[87] Cheshire Record Office, EDV7/Mf44/4. I owe this reference to Jan Albers. One of Clifton's guests may have been Edward Barrow of Westby Hall – see P.R.O., S.P. 36/81, fos. 303–4.

330 Two faces of treason

from the Catholic gentry to other groups by 1745. Charles Edward did not try to raise the recusant squires of Lancashire; he knew that they had not recovered from the devastation wrought upon them after 1715. Instead, he headed straight for the hottest Jacobite town in England, where he was sure to find men eager to join him – not Catholic landowners, but the High Church manufacturers and warehousemen of Manchester.

The English rebels of the '45

Compared to the impressive Jacobite turnout of 1715, the '45 in England seems anti-climactic. Its failure to attract English support has often been interpreted as a sign of the debility of Jacobitism.[88] Yet the situation was more complicated than this. The Tory Jacobite leaders had encouraged a French landing; they saw the '45 as a wild attempt on which only a reckless gambler would have staked his life. The staid, circumspect Anglican Jacobite gentry were alarmed, confused and often terrified by it. Some of them, however, made contact with the rebel army as it advanced south. An ancient Tory lady, Mrs Skyring, who as a baby had seen Charles II land at Dover, watched Charles Edward cross the Mersey in 1745, in the company of several of her neighbours; she later died of shock on hearing of the Jacobite retreat.[89] The Radclyffes of Fox Denton, Lancashire, came out to welcome the Prince, as did the Burdetts and Poles of Derbyshire.[90] Dr Burton of York met the Prince at Lancaster, and William Massingberd of Ormsby, Lincolnshire, was said to have ridden all the way to Derby to see him.[91] All of these men may have carried the same message: that their counties could not rise for the Stuarts.

No prominent Tory gentleman took up arms for the Prince in 1745. The Englishmen who did serve him are generally unknown to historians.[92] About eighty people living along the rebel route to Derby

88 See Speck, *The Butcher*, pp. 183–203. Lenman, *Jacobite Risings*, ch. 10, provides a good assessment of the Scottish side of the rebellion. For local responses to the '45 in England, see Rupert C. Jarvis, *Collected Papers on the Jacobite Risings* (2 vols., Manchester, 1971).
89 Mahon, *History of England*, vol. iii, ch. 28, pp. 403–4.
90 Hampson, *Radclyffes*, p. 194; M. W. Patterson, *Sir Francis Burdett and His Times* (2 vols., London, 1931), p. 4.
91 P.R.O., K.B. 33/4/1, exams. of J. Holland, W. Glover and H. Bracken; P.R.O., S.P. 36/75, fos. 212–14; S.P. 36/77, fos. 143–4; Hill, *Georgian Lincoln*, p. 27 n. 1.
92 This is in spite of the availability of Sir Bruce Gordon and Jean Gordon Arnot, eds., *The Prisoners of the '45*, Publications of the Scottish Historical Society, 3rd Series, 13–15 (3 vols., 1928–9). A recent exception to the lack of scholarly interest in the

were later accused of aiding the Highlanders in some way, by voluntarily providing them with information, helping them collect excise taxes, fraternizing with them or expressing support for them verbally. A few of these culprits marched with the Jacobite army for a day or two. Most of them were Protestant tradesmen or artisans, although John Cupid of Lymm, who accompanied the rebels on their trek through Cheshire, was a gentleman.[93] At least two dozen Englishmen were recruited into Scottish units, including some captured Hanoverian soldiers; a number of them stayed with the Prince until Culloden.[94]

The largest group of Englishmen in the rebel army was found in the regiment created in Manchester on 29 November 1745. Its total effectives were estimated by contemporaries at between 100 and 300.[95] In fact, 160 men of the Manchester regiment can be identified from government sources: 27 officers, 10 sergeants and 123 privates.[96] The total number who served in the force may have been around 200. Unlike the rebels of the '15, they were organized into a regular military unit, and drilled for action. This time, there was no dreaming of an easy stroll to London; the soldiers of the '45 were fully aware that they would have to fight their way to victory, a fact that must have discouraged many from joining them. The military realism of the expedition was further revealed in the choice of a colonel for the Manchester regiment. The 'political' candidate was David Morgan, an Anglican barrister from

English rebels is F. J. McLynn, *The Jacobite Army in England, 1745* (Edinburgh, 1983), which provides a day-by-day chronicle of the Jacobite expedition.

[93] See the cases found in State Papers and in the Treasury Solicitor's Papers, as well as the examinations in P.R.O., K.B. 33/4. A computation of the number of persons imprisoned in the north and Midlands for seditious behaviour during the rebellion is in P.R.O., S.P. 36/81, fo. 78.

[94] For the story of a Preston man who served in two Scottish regiments, see 'A True Account of Mr. John Daniel's Progress with Prince Charles Edward in the Years 1745 and 1746 Written by Himself', in Walter Biggar Blaikie, ed., *Origins of the Forty-Five and Other Papers Relating to that Rising*, Publications of the Scottish Historical Society, 2nd Series, 2 (1916), pp. 165–224.

[95] David Morgan told the government that 100 men had been enlisted at Manchester, but he was trying to minimize the regiment's importance – see B.L., Add. MS 29,913, p. 49, which is printed in 'The Forty-Five in Staffordshire', *North Staffordshire Field Club Transactions* (1923–4), pp. 88–9. The Chevalier Johnstone reckoned that 180 men were recruited at Manchester, and that the regiment eventually had 300 members – Charles Winchester, ed., *Memoirs of the Chevalier de Johnstone* (3 vols., Aberdeen, 1870), vol. i, p. 42.

[96] These figures have been derived from Seton and Arnot, eds., *Prisoners of the '45*, who unfortunately make no attempt to eliminate double or even triple entries resulting from alternate spellings of names, from P.R.O., K.B. 33/4, and from lists in P.R.O., S.P. 36/79, fo. 35, and B.L. Add. MS 29,913, p. 17.

Monmouthshire who had connections with the Duke of Beaufort. His qualifications, however, were less necessary to the rebels than those of Francis Towneley, a former French army officer and veteran of the War of the Polish Succession, who was picked over Morgan as Colonel of the Manchester men.[97]

Towneley was not the only Catholic officer in the regiment. William Vaughan of Courtfield, Herefordshire, rode to Preston with his brother Richard to join the Prince, and became Lieutenant-Colonel of the Manchester unit. He remained with the Prince on the retreat and escaped after Culloden to become a general in the Spanish army.[98] Andrew Blyde, a captain in the Manchester regiment, was described as the steward to a considerable landowner in Yorkshire, apparently the Duke of Norfolk.[99] Captain John Sanderson was a Catholic colliery overseer from Northumberland, who may have been sent as an envoy from his employer, Walter Calverley Blackett. After the rebellion, he became the Duke of Norfolk's master of horse.[100] John Hunter, another Northumbrian, was probably related to the Hunters of Bellingham, a recusant family ruined by the '15, while Christopher Taylor of Wigan, a young regimental ensign, had just returned from schooling in France, a traditional path for the recusant gentry.[101]

The Manchester regiment officers, however, were not predominantly Catholics or landowners. Most were products of the great changes that had occurred in south-east Lancashire in the first half of the eighteenth century. The textile manufactures of Manchester, particularly the fustian trade, had expanded rapidly, and the town's population had doubled to about 20,000.[102] At least nine of the Manchester regiment's officers had connections with the textile industry. James Bradshaw and Thomas Furnivall were warehousemen, George Fletcher and John Berwick were linen-drapers, William and Peter Moss were woollen-drapers, John Holker was a cotton callen-

---

[97] For Towneley, see his notice in *D.N.B.* and Hibbert-Ware, *Foundations in Manchester*, vol. ii, pp. 97–8.

[98] He is noticed in *D.N.B.*; see also Price, 'Side Lights on Welsh Jacobitism', pp. 146–7.

[99] Hibbert-Ware, *Foundations in Manchester*, vol. ii, p. 101; Cruickshanks, *Political Untouchables*, p. 91; P.R.O., S.P. 36/85, fos. 442–3.

[100] P.R.O., S.P. 36/81, fo. 161; S.P. 36/99, fos. 76–9; P.R.O., T.S. 20/49, fo. 15; B.L., Add. MS 28,231, fo. 179.

[101] P.R.O., T.S. 20/102, fo. 130; P.R.O., S.P. 36/107, fo. 132.

[102] See Alfred P. Wadsworth and Julia de Lacy Mann, *The Cotton Trade and Industrial Lancashire, 1600–1780* (Manchester, 1931, 1965), and Baines, *County of Lancaster*, vol. i, pp. 327–9, 347.

derer, James Wilding was the son of a scarlet dyer and Richard Jackson was a mercer.[103] Captain James Dawson, hero of Shenstone's poem, had studied at St John's College, Cambridge; he was the grandson of a Barnsley draper and the son of a Manchester apothecary.[104]

Dawson exemplified local social mobility, generated by the prosperity of the textile trades. Reverend Thomas Coppock, chaplain of the regiment, was a similar case; his father was a tailor, but he had been educated at Brasenose College, Oxford.[105] Thomas Syddall, Colonel Towneley's adjutant, presented another story of social advancement. Syddall inherited the principles of his father, the blacksmith who led the riots of 1715, but he chose a profession more suited to the growing wealth of his town. He became a barber and perruque-maker, catering to the increased demand for luxury hair-pieces. By 1745, Syddall was reputedly worth £2,000, had become a friend of John Byrom and had married the sister of Robert Thyer, librarian at Chetham's hospital, to whose father he had been apprenticed.[106] Syddall was a fine representative of Manchester's growing middle classes, who depended on the wealth and new consumer tastes generated by the textile industry. The young ensigns of the regiment were also aspiring 'middling' men; they included James Betts, a music master, William Bradshaw, a barber's apprentice, Samuel Maddocks, an apothecary's apprentice, and William Brettargh, a lawyer's clerk, son of an attorney of Leigh.[107] All of the regiment's junior officers were Protestants, except James Wilding and possibly John Holker.[108] Thomas Syddall was a member of Thomas Deacon's Orthodox British Church. Three of Deacon's sons – Thomas Theodorus, who was being trained by his father as a physician, Robert Renatus and Charles Clement – were officers in the

[103] Baines, *County of Lancaster*, vol. i, p. 332; Seton and Arnot, eds., *Prisoners of the '45*; Hibbert-Ware, *Foundations in Manchester*, vol. ii, pp. 101–2; Albert Nicholson, 'Lieutenant John Holker', *T.L.C.A.S.*, 9 (1891), pp. 147–54; Parkinson, ed., *Remains of Byrom*, vol. ii, part ii, pp. 390–1, 408–9; P.R.O., T.S. 20/74, fo. 19; T.S. 20/89, fos. 4–9; T.S. 20/102, fo. 120.

[104] Beatrice Stott, 'James Dawson and Thomas Syddall', *T.L.C.A.S.*, 46 (1929), pp. 1–4.

[105] Stott, 'Parson Coppock', pp. 45–9.

[106] Stott, 'Dawson and Syddall', pp. 5–7. For his portrait, see Plate 14.

[107] Beatrice Stott, 'Charles Clement Deacon and William Brettargh', *T.L.C.A.S.*, 41 (1924), p. 1; P.R.O., T.S. 20/89, fo. 5; T.S. 20/102, fo. 131; Parkinson, ed., *Remains of Byrom*, vol. ii, part ii, p. 390 n. 1, which confuses James and William Bradshaw.

[108] One informer, however, reported that Holker was a Nonjuror – Stott, 'Informations', p. 46.

regiment. All were devout Nonjurors, as was Lieutenant Thomas Chaddock, a tallow-chandler from Staffordshire who had migrated to Manchester.

A well-defined class distinction separated the two superior officers in the regiment from their subordinates. Towneley and Vaughan were landed gentlemen; the junior officers were from 'middling' professions. Yet it is misleading to contrast them too sharply. In fact, many of the textile manufacturers were descendants of gentry families. John Aikin pointed out in 1795 that '[i]n George I's reign many country gentlemen began to send their sons apprentice to the Manchester manufacturers; but ... the young men found it so different from home that they could not brook this treatment, and either got away before their time, or ... entered the army or went to sea'.[109] Hibbert-Ware dissented with the view that these high-born apprentices did not remain long in trade, and maintained that some of Manchester's foremost manufacturing families had landed origins.[110]

Most of the Manchester regiment officers were not young apprentices; although some of the ensigns were teenagers, the lieutenants and captains were generally in their mid-twenties. Nevertheless, they do lend support to the opinions of Aikin and Hibbert-Ware, because many of them were the offspring of gentry clans. The Moss brothers were related to the lords of the manor of Bolton-le-Moors; Reverend Thomas Moss, chaplain to the Collegiate Church, may have been their brother.[111] John Holker's ancestors had been granted land at Monton, near Eccles, by James I; he was later ennobled by Louis XV for his service to the French textile industry, a distinction that would have been facilitated by a previous claim to gentility.[112] John Berwick was reportedly related to the Beswicke family, High Church gentry who had gone into trade early in the eighteenth century, and had fought in the '15.[113] George Fletcher's ancestors were the proprietors of Broughton in Furness; his mother was a Holland of New Hall, Pendleton. Regarding Hibbert-Ware's criticism of Aikin, it might be noted that Fletcher was one of the wealthiest manufacturers in Salford.[114] Thomas

---

109 John Aikin, *A Description of the Country from Thirty to Forty Miles Round Manchester* (London, 1795), pp. 182–3.
110 Hibbert-Ware, *Foundations in Manchester*, vol. ii, pp. 70–1.
111 Parkinson, ed., *Remains of Byrom*, vol. ii, part ii, pp. 408–9 n. 5.
112 Nicholson, 'Holker', pp. 147–54.
113 Parkinson, ed., *Remains of Byrom*, vol. i, part i, p. 271 n. 1.
114 James Frederick Beever, *Captain James Bradshaw of the 'Manchester Regiment' of 1745* (Manchester, 1876), p. 17. Fletcher paid £50 for his commission – Hibbert-Ware, *Foundations in Manchester*, vol. ii, p. 101.

Furnivall, on the other hand, was 'in very indifferent Circumstances', although his older brother owned a Cheshire estate, and his cousin was a steward of the Earl of Harrington.[115] James Bradshaw was the cousin of John Bradshaw of Darcy Lever, a wealthy Whig who became high sheriff in 1753; Bradshaw's mother was a Towneley of Dutton, and his brother-in-law was a clergyman. Bradshaw, Fletcher, Berwick, the Mosses and James Dawson were all related to the Bayleys of Withington, the staunchest Whigs in Manchester.[116]

These officers inherited their Jacobitism from their gentry ancestors; but their convictions were strengthened by Manchester's peculiar circumstances. Isolated from national politics by its lack of a borough charter, dominated by independent institutions of ancient foundation, Manchester was a town in which the power of Westminster was not much felt. It was also bitterly divided between religious factions, and the Civil War was still being fought in its streets. The Manchester officers had been well prepared for the rising. Many were educated in Jacobite principles; James Dawson and the Deacon brothers were taught by Reverend John Clayton at the Salford Grammar School. The spiritual guidance of the town was in the hands of Jacobites like Clayton and his Collegiate Church colleagues. Secular society as well was fragmented by religious differences. The Bull's Head tavern in the market-place, principal rendezvous for local Tories like Byrom, Thyer and the Dickinsons, became the recruiting centre for the Manchester regiment. It was there that Thomas Coppock sat drinking with the other Jacobite officers on the day of rebel occupation; the parson later stated that they had been joined in their libations by Oswald Mosley, son of the lord of the manor of Manchester.[117]

The Manchester Jacobite officers were not unique in their principles, but the hot-house atmosphere of their town, coupled with the social tensions of industrialization, caused political resentments to bloom monstrously. The statements made by the Manchester officers at their executions show that they remained absolutely convinced of the moral and religious necessity of their actions. Bradshaw maintained that he had joined the rebels 'by a principle of duty only', and observed that the friends of Hanover had 'let in Infidelity, which is almost become ... the religion established'.[118] Similarly, Thomas Chaddock assured his

[115] P.R.O., S.P. 36/107, fos. 129–30; Stott, 'Deacon and Brettargh', p. 15.
[116] Beever, *Captain Bradshaw*, pp. 7–12, 16–18.
[117] P.R.O., K.B. 33/4/1, exam. of T. Coppock.
[118] Paton, ed., *Lyon in Mourning*, vol. i, pp. 48–50.

listeners that 'True Religion can never florish Under an Unlawful Governm^t.'[119] Thomas Deacon saw his death as 'being little Inferiour even to Martyrdom itself', while James Dawson quoted the gospel of Matthew: 'Blessed are they that suffer Persecution for Righteousness Sake, *for theirs is ye Kingdom of Heaven.*'[120] If these speeches seem preoccupied with an almost mystical conception of divine mission, they were nonetheless consistent with the reality of Manchester, where Jacobites took it for granted that their cause was God's own.

The Jacobite officers, whether recusant gentry or Protestant manufacturers, also shared a commitment to Country or 'patriot' ideals. Their regimental flag was inscribed with 'LIBERTY AND PROPERTY' on one side, 'CHURCH AND KING' on the other – the two slogans were inseparable. Francis Towneley summed up this position in his dying speech, in which he commented upon 'the Oppression of a German Hanoverian Usurper ... I already see him Assending Step by Step, till at last he will Arrive at the very Summit of Arbitrary Power and Despotick Sway.'[121] Towneley's words were echoed by his condemned comrades. 'Poor old England', Thomas Chaddock lamented, was 'hourly expiring under a German Usurper, ruling with a Rod of Iron'; but Charles Edward, Thomas Deacon observed, would protect 'your laws, religion and liberties'.[122] David Morgan, who had written a long poem decrying despotism and praising Country principles, was eloquent in his condemnation of the 'ungrateful avarice' of the Hanoverians, and scourged their Parliaments for having 'given additional power to the Usurper to suspend the bulwarks of liberty'. Happily, the nation could be saved by restoring the Stuarts. 'A lawful king', Morgan declared, 'is a nursing father who would protect us.'[123]

Unfortunately, the ordinary soldiers of the Manchester regiment, in contrast to their officers, left little evidence about themselves. Nervertheless, it is clear that they were very different from their officers.[124] Five of the ten sergeants and forty-three of the privates in the regiment were Roman Catholics; only one sergeant and ten privates were Anglicans. Two other privates, Roger Fulthorpe, who was apprenticed to Thomas Syddall, and the learned barber Thomas

[119] P.R.O., S.P. 36/85, fo. 41.
[120] Chetham Library, Raines MSS, vol. 25, pp. 364, 366, 370.
[121] *Ibid.*, pp. 360–2.
[122] P.R.O., S.P. 36/85, fo. 41; Paton, ed., *Lyon in Mourning*, vol. i, p. 25.
[123] *Ibid.*, pp. 43–7.
[124] The statistical information that follows is based on Seton and Arnot, eds., *Prisoners of the '45*, and on the examinations in P.R.O., K.B. 33/4.

Podmore, were Nonjurors, and one man, rather incongruously, was an Irish Presbyterian. In their occupations, the lower ranks of the rebels reflected the artisanal character of popular Jacobitism. The sergeants included a Wigan barber, a Manchester weaver and a Rochdale clothworker, as well as two shoemakers and an Irish carpenter. There was a small agricultural element among the privates, consisting of six farm servants and two husbandmen; but most were village tradesmen or textile workers. The government later apprehended five carpenters, four shoemakers, four tailors, a butcher, a whitesmith, an anchorsmith, a saddler, a combmaker, a tallow-chandler and an alehouse servant who had served in the Manchester regiment, as well as five 'labourers', some of whom may have been farm workers. By far the most common rebel occupation, however, was weaving. At least twenty-nine weavers, plus a woolcomber and a callenderer, joined the regiment; they made up almost half of the sixty-eight men whose form of employment is known.

Like their officers, the sergeants were mostly recruited in the Manchester area; two were Irishmen resident in Manchester, one was from Wigan, one from Northumberland and one was a Scot. The privates, on the other hand, were a geographically heterogeneous group. Fourteen of them came from outside Lancashire – three from Cheshire, two from Northumberland, two from Derby and two from Cumberland. Nine were listed as Irishmen, two as Scots. The remaining eighty-one men whose places of habitation can be discovered were natives of Lancashire, who generally lived within one of three areas. Eleven were from the textile towns of Manchester, Rochdale, Bury and Ashton-under-Lyne; sixteen lived in the vicinity of Wigan; and another fifteen were from the Ribble valley. Three men, from Lancaster, Myerscough and Warrington, lived outside these areas; and thirty-six were listed simply as being 'of Lancashire'. Surprisingly, this geographical distribution suggests that the majority of recruits did not come from Manchester or the south-east; most were enlisted around Wigan or Preston, where numerous Catholics resided. Moreover, almost all of these men joined the rebellion on the retreat from Derby, which indicates that they were taken on as replacements for deserters. It also shows that some people did not regard the withdrawal of the Jacobite army as final; those who joined the rebels in retreat doubtless hoped to see their homes again.

The ordinary soldiers of the Manchester regiment were a little younger than their officers. Eleven of the privates are known to have been apprentices, and four were under seventeen. John Newton, a cotton weaver from Oldham, claimed under examination to be only twelve years old and therefore too young to hang, but another source, more plausibly, calls him sixteen. The bulk of the regiment's soldiers, however, were more mature; twenty-one of them, over half of those whose age is known, were between nineteen and twenty-four. These were the years in which young men were likely to join the regular army, and many of them no doubt saw the rebellion as presenting a similar career option.

The typical sergeant or private of the Manchester regiment was a native Lancastrian artisan, Roman Catholic in religion, about twenty years old; but this is an artificial construct. The real soldiers of the regiment were men of diverse experiences. Some glimpses into their lives are provided by the examinations given by about forty of them to the authorities, after the fall of Carlisle. These documents, however, are full of fabrications about the examinants' motives. The most incredible yarn was narrated by Philip Hunt of Standish, a barber and peri-wigmaker, who maintained that the Highlanders had stolen his uncle Henry's horse, and that he had trailed them all the way to Carlisle in order to retrieve it, only to find himself locked into the town during the siege.[125] In fact, Hunt had enlisted at Wigan as a sergeant in the Manchester regiment, and had been in charge of a company of about a dozen men. At his trial, he pleaded guilty and was executed.

Many of the stories told by the prisoners seem at least partly factual. Valentine Holt, a clothworker of Rochdale, admitted that he went to Manchester when the Jacobite army arrived there with the intention of seeing them. He met a co-worker of his who had enlisted with them, and the two men drank all night with some Highlanders at an ale-house. The next morning, Holt marched on with the rebels to Derby.[126] A recusant like most of the Manchester regiment's soldiers, Holt was apparently led to become a rebel by his religion, by the example of his friend and by the generous treating of the Highlanders in their all-night drinking bout. A similar tale was told by Hugh Johnson of Euxton, a Roman Catholic weaver. When the Scots returned to Preston, he went there with some work, and encountered two acquaintances of his who were out with the rebels. Johnson went drinking with them, and while inebriated, they put a cockade in his hat. He was enlisted the next morning.[127] The combination of relig-

<hr/>

[125] P.R.O., K.B. 33/4/1, exam. of P. Hunt.   [126] Ibid., exam. of V. Holt.
[127] Ibid., exam. of H. Johnson.

ion, pressure from friends and heavy drinking was typical of many recruits.

The younger soldiers in the regiment may have been seeking adventure, or trying to escape from the miseries of apprenticeship. John Pendleton was a fourteen-year-old apprentice to a worsted weaver in Manchester; he was honest enough to tell his examiners that he ran off with the rebels because he had a bad master. He became a regimental drummer, but never learned how to play his instrument.[128] Pendleton was a Protestant; he lacked the strong religious incentive to follow the Prince that was found among Catholics, but compensated for it with personal reasons. Robert Singleton, however, was both an unhappy apprentice and a recusant. A sixteen-year-old Manchester weaver, Singleton fell out with his mistress and 'was afraid of being beat when his Ma^r came Home', so he fled. He was persuaded to join the Manchester regiment by a Scot who promised him 'he sho^d not want'.[129]

The regiment's privates were occasionally paid 1s by their sergeants; they were fed through requisitioning, and billeted in private homes. It was not an easy life, but it must have had attractions for dissatisfied young weavers. Nevertheless, only four men pleaded poverty or unemployment as excuses for their behaviour, and all of them were Irish. Austin Coleman, alias Augustus Cullinan, had come from his native County Mayo to work as a weaver in Manchester, but was out of work when the Scots arrived on the scene.[130] Thomas Joy, a weaver from Dublin, had been in Manchester only a few days when Charles Edward entered the town; 'having neither Money nor ffriends', he enlisted for 1s.[131] Ormsby McCormack of County Antrim also complained of trade in Manchester being 'at a Stand', and of having nothing to do.[132] It must have been difficult for outsiders, particularly Irishmen, to find work in the town. The demand for labour was growing, but fitfully, and employment probably continued to depend on social and family connections.

The government examinations do not provide much sense of the enthusiasm with which the Jacobite army was greeted by some who enlisted in it. Information from other sources offers a few examples. William Crosby, an Irish weaver, reportedly reacted to the rebel occupation of Manchester by leaping up and down in a Key Street

[128] *Ibid.*, exam. of J. Pendleton.   [129] *Ibid.*, exam. of R. Singleton.
[130] P.R.O., K.B. 33/4/5, exam. of A. Coleman.
[131] *Ibid.*, exam. of T. Joy.   [132] *Ibid.*, exam. of O. McCormack.

tavern, crying 'now is our time ... my Jemmy, my Jemmy, my Jemmy is comeing home again at which he Expressed a Great deal of Joy'.[133] A weaver from Wigan named Edward Roper was said to have kissed the ground as the Highland army approached, declaring 'Now my Prince is come I dare appear in Wigan'.[134] The reasons for his previous agoraphobia are unknown, but probably had something to do with his Catholicism. John Daniel, who met the rebels near Garstang, was overwhelmed by his vision of 'the brave Prince marching on foot at their head like a Cyrus or a Trojan Hero, drawing admiration and love from all those who beheld him'.[135] The prospect of setting eyes on royalty also excited Lewis Barton, a Catholic apprentice weaver of Wigan. He had a bad master, and his uncle was out with the rebels, but what most motivated him, as he told a friend, was that 'he was going to see the King'.[136]

Lewis Barton did not see his King; Jemmy never came home again. The '45 ended in defeat and disaster for most of its participants. Of the twenty-seven officers of the Manchester regiment, one died in prison, one was acquitted, one was pardoned, four escaped, two gave evidence and were released, two were banished, three were transported, and eleven were executed. Dr Deacon lost all of his sons: Robert succumbed to illness at Carlisle, Thomas was executed, and Charles died soon after transportation to Antigua. The government believed that these severe punishments would crush Jacobitism forever. King George could not have suspected that 'Towneley's Ghost' would come back to haunt him in a popular song, or that David Morgan's spirit would reinvigorate the Independent Electors of Westminster, of which body he had been a member.[137] As Thomas Deacon had hoped, the deaths of the Jacobite officers made them martyrs for the cause, and helped to inspire the renewal of Jacobite activity after 1745. In the end, it was Charles Edward's failings, not the brutal executions at Kennington, that led to the disillusionment of his adherents.

The soldiers of the Manchester regiment, however, suffered in obscurity. The sergeants were butchered almost to a man; seven out of ten of them went to the scaffold. At least seven privates were executed; a few died in prison, and most of the rest were transported to Antigua,

133 P.R.O., S.P. 36/81, fo. 207.   134 B.L., Stowe 255, p. 96.
135 'John Daniel's Progress', in Blaikie, ed., *Origins of the Forty-Five*, p. 168. These images were borrowed from Jacobite poetry.
136 P.R.O., K.B. 33/4/1, exam. of L. Barton.
137 See Grosart, pp. 82–3, and Chapter 7 for the Independent Electors.

which was virtually a death sentence. Some escaped punishment by enlisting in King George's army, and a few were discharged or acquitted. Unlike their officers, the sergeants and privates of the regiment left no dying speeches, and were generally forgotten. Nevertheless, the names of sergeants Brady, Holt, Hunt, Park, Rowbotham and Swan, and of privates Matthew Matthews, William Hunter and Edward Roper, appear on a pin-cushion inscribed 'MART: FOR: K: & COU: 1746', which was found in Northumberland.[138] Among Lancashire weavers, the memory of their rebellious forebears may have endured for many years. When the Manchester Blanketeers of 1817 marched towards London, carrying their petition for trade reform, they chose to follow Charles Edward's route through Leek and Ashbourne to Derby, rather than the easier road through Staffordshire.[139] The English soldiers of the Manchester regiment, like all Jacobite rebels, were unusual men; but they could inspire others who were less militant with a renewed spirit of opposition to existing authority.

[138] Charlton, 'Jacobite Relics', p. 33. A similar pin-cushion is now owned by Ushaw College, Durham. For an engraved version, attributed to Robert Strange, see Chambers, ed., *Book of Days*, vol. ii, p. 235.

[139] This fact was commented upon by Archibald Prentice in his *Historical Sketches and Personal Recollections of Manchester* (London, 1851), p. 93.

Conclusion: Jacobitism in history

The invention of a man who did no work with his hands, but merely existed and acted on his environment at a distance, like a sun, was one of the most momentous in the history of man; it was nothing less than the invention of government, and if we cannot always find a scientific justification for the forms which the doctrine of the sun man has impressed upon the institution of monarchy, yet the extraordinary persistence of those forms and their amazing vitality suggest that they are less to blame than the imperfections of our moral science, and that monarchical government has a psychological value we are not yet in a position to understand.   A. M. Hocart[1]

Charles Edward Stuart expired at Rome on 31 January 1788.[2] With his death, the surviving shreds of Jacobite political influence disintegrated. His brother Henry, who became 'King Henry IX' but preferred his title of Cardinal York, apparently enjoyed some residual popularity in Ireland, and was interested in the issue of Catholic emancipation in England, but he made no attempt to oppose King George III – after 1801, in fact, he was a pensioner of the English government.[3] His death in 1807 ended the direct Stuart line. Charles Edward's daughter Charlotte died of cancer in 1789; his wife Louisa lived on in Florence until 1823, an object for the eccentric curiosity of romantic tourists. The so-called Comte de Roehenstart, who was probably Charlotte's illegitimate son, kept Stuart pretensions alive until the 1850s, while with far more flamboyance and success, the 'Sobieski-Stuart' brothers, a pair of brilliant charlatans, milked the Jacobite legend throughout the

---

[1] A. M. Hocart, *Kingship* (London, 1927), p. 46.
[2] It was rumoured that he had actually died one day earlier, on the anniversary of his great-grandfather's execution, but that this was kept secret by his family. See Chambers, ed., *Book of Days*, vol. i, p. 199.
[3] See Chapter 4, n. 49, and H.M.C., *Braye*, pp. 243–6, 248.

mid-nineteenth century.[4] After 1889, English legitimism underwent a strange anti-democratic revival, resulting in the creation of two 'neo-Jacobite' political journals, a host of 'White Rose' clubs, and even a 'Radical Jacobite' Parliamentary candidacy in Hertfordshire.[5] By 1914, however, this bizarre resurgence, which championed the claims of the King of Bavaria to the throne, had been stifled by anti-German sentiment; its only existing offshoot, the present Royal Stuart Society, is non-political.

Notwithstanding its later incarnations, Jacobite political culture in England really succumbed along with Charles Edward Stuart. What were its dimensions in the century of its birth, growth and long decline? When the multifarious evidence is considered as a whole, certain consistent patterns emerge. Most Jacobite activity was concentrated in three periods: 1689–97, 1714–24 and 1745–54. In the first of these, support for the exiled King was limited to Roman Catholics, Non-jurors, a small number of juring High Churchmen (although many more were sympathetic to James) and a group of Pennite Quakers. In social terms, Jacobitism in the 1690s was top-heavy with aristocrats, but had little appeal to the common people, except in places where politics were viciously polarized, as in Bristol. Gentry adherents of King James were spread thinly throughout the country; they were powerful only in places where Catholicism was strong. Just as it lacked a firm social basis, Jacobitism was intellectually confused at this time; the highest-flying doctrines of divine right coexisted with the Country rhetoric of the 'Whiggish' Jacobites.

By 1714, however, Jacobite political argument had coalesced around the ideas of hereditary right and moral reform. Furthermore, the party conflicts of Queen Anne's reign had broadened the exiled King's popularity among Tories. George I's ejection of the Tory party from office produced a massive backlash, and the sudden emergence of a widespread popular Jacobitism. For the next decade, while the Tory leadership veered between conspiracy with James III and attempts to win a measure of favour from King George, their supporters in the port cities, market towns and industrial villages of England remained warmly attached to the exiled claimant. A thriving press spread the message of the Stuart cause to a large audience. The south-east,

4 See Tayler, *Prince Charlie's Daughter*, and George Sherburn, *Roehenstart, a Late Stuart Pretender* (Chicago, 1960); the 'Sobieski-Stuarts' are noticed in *D.N.B.*
5 See Ruvigny, *Jacobite Peerage* (reprinted edn, London, 1972), pp. ix–xliii; also *The Legitimist Kalendar for 1895* (London, 1895), pp. 59–62; *The Royalist*, vols. 1–4 (1890–4); and various issues of *Notes and Queries* throughout the 1890s.

however, had been won back for the Hanoverians by the early 1720s, and turmoil had ceased in Whig-controlled towns like Liverpool, although other areas remained disaffected. The vitality of Jacobite sentiment depended largely on encouragement from the elite, and when the Atterbury Plot was foiled in 1722, the resulting chaos in the Tory party led to a general collapse of anti-Hanoverian protest in the nation.

For the next two decades, Jacobitism remained submerged. The Tories turned to a Country alliance with dissident Whigs, and the prospects for a restoration seemed bleak. Support for the Pretender shrank, although it occasionally emerged in popular disorders. By the late 1730s, however, the continued frustration of Tory ambitions began to motivate new approaches to James III, and the bitter disappointment that followed the fall of Walpole stirred up a major conspiracy in 1743–4. It failed, and English Jacobitism would most likely have withered away, had Prince Charles Edward not decided to embark on his daring attempt in 1745. The frightened Tories did nothing to help the Prince, but they redeemed themselves in the next few years by reviving the Stuart cause. As their desperation grew after the rebellion, the High Churchmen sought to reinvigorate their flagging hopes through embracing the young Prince and the old principles. Seditious riots were fomented, disaffected journals and cartoons were circulated, secret clubs proliferated. Yet in the late 1740s, Jacobitism was restricted to its provincial bastions: the north-west, the West Midlands, Oxford, Norwich, Bristol, Exeter. The government's control over the capital was unshaken, even by the efforts of the Independent Electors of Westminster. Between 1754 and 1760, with Prince Charles sinking into drunken despair, most of his Tory adherents gave up the struggle. To be sure, a vestige of popular Jacobitism endured into the late 1770s, and sympathy for the exiled house may have lingered among the Tory gentry until the early 1780s, but Charles Edward was never again a threat to Hanoverian rule.

The most obvious conclusion to be drawn from this tangled story is that Jacobitism was important. It should no longer be possible to ignore it, or stigmatize it as a reactionary vice, restricted to a tiny band of half-crazed zealots. Few areas of political, social or intellectual history can be cited that did not have any connection with Jacobite political culture. If it was never dominant, it nevertheless had far more influence over almost every aspect of English life than any other seditious form of opposition in the period after 1660. While it would be a mistake to represent Jacobitism as the central factor in English party formation, it was undoubtedly crucial in separating Whigs from Tories, if only because the latter were willing to countenance Jacobite sentiments among many of their colleagues. Popular politicization owed much to the Stuart cause; the sophisticated strategies of the Wilkites developed out of half a century of plebeian unrest over the dynastic issue. Jacobitism left a dual legacy to English politics. It helped to create a framework for extra-Parliamentary radicalism, even as it nurtured forms of elite sociability that would later become bulwarks of conservatism.

Jacobite political culture also deserves attention for the reactions it elicited from the English government. The growth of centralized state power in the late seventeenth and eighteenth centuries was to a large extent made necessary by the threat of the exiled Stuarts and their adherents. Standing armies were maintained to keep guard over England and its restive population. The judiciary was constantly interfered with, especially in counties where justices and juries might be suspect. Every agency of government, from the post office to the munitions works, was thoroughly purged in order to weed out malcontents. The proliferation of customs and excise officials was a means of countering an increase in smuggling that was encouraged by Jacobites. Paradoxically, the greatest impact made by the supporters of the banished Stuarts on English government may have been to accelerate the centralizing tendencies which they so bitterly opposed. Nevertheless, they also provided a barrier to the growth of state authority. Even in the 1690s, the existence of an alternative monarch, who might gain popularity through the abuse of power by the government, motivated the observance of certain limits. The protection of English 'liberties' by Whig regimes in the period after the Revolution was due in some measure to the awareness that, if pushed too far, the Tories could easily fall into Jacobitism, with violent consequences.

As J. C. D. Clark has rightly argued, the acceptance of Jacobitism as a significant feature of the English historical landscape requires a certain amount of restructuring of other features. One does not have to accept all of Clark's revisionism to recognize that Jacobite political culture does not fit easily into the well-ordered garden built by generations of English historians since Macaulay. The Stuarts, Catholicism and the divine right of kings have always been seen as alien growths that had no place in a scenery defined by the concepts of 'reason', 'liberty' and 'progress'. In spite of long-standing dissatis-

faction with Whig historiography, it has continued to exercise a large
degree of control over what is seen as important, and has co-opted
historians of every political persuasion. To some extent, Whig attitudes
are rooted in English national consciousness, and have provided a
foundation for national identity in the United States. To question them,
therefore, is to run the risk of being branded an outcast, or worse, a
foreigner.

Whig historiography was not completely wrong. The Glorious Revolution did ensure the permanency of Parliament, and brought some
alteration in the position of the monarch, who now had to govern
through political parties. The eighteenth century saw changes towards
a more tolerant society, and the gradual expansion of the idea of
'improvement' or 'progress'. The growth of English trade and manufacturing was accompanied by an increased consumption of luxury
goods among the middling classes. In 1788, England was richer and
more powerful economically than it had been in 1688; its government
was more representative of the will of the landed elite than in any
European nation except Poland; its people were exposed to more
diverse political ideas than at any time in its history; and several
religions were able to coexist within its borders. These were remarkable achievements.

Yet they should not be exaggerated. From the Jacobite point of view,
the century after 1688 had not been a happy one. The Revolution itself
was the victory, not of timeless conceptions of 'liberty', but of virulent
anti-Catholicism, and the Toleration Act was a step backwards for
freedom of religion compared to James II's Declaration of Indulgence.
The post-Revolutionary judiciary seemed as pliable as ever, and *habeas
corpus* was suspended so many times between 1689 and 1723 that it
seemed to be in an almost permanent state of abeyance. Freedom of the
press meant little to the executed William Anderton in 1694 or John
Matthews in 1719. In fact, the 'despotism' of James II appears
amateurish beside the measures of George I and his Whig ministers,
when one considers the Riot Act, the Registration Act, the Constructive
Recusancy Act, the Septennial Act, the Smuggling Act, the Peerage Bill
and the Black Act. The execution of James Shepheard in 1717/18 was
among the most atrocious examples of judicial murder in English
history. The situation did not alter much under George II. The
treatment of the English rebels of the '45 differed little from that of
Monmouth's supporters, and the virulence of anti-Catholic rhetoric

during Prince Charlie's attempt exceeded even the level of 1688–9. Whig principles do not look very 'libertarian', or very attractive, from this angle.

Of course, the Jacobite point of view is distorted; but so is the Whig perspective. Both of them are based upon the acceptance of absolute moral values; above all, they are hostile to ambiguity or contradiction. Yet the history of England between 1688 and 1788 was not straightforward or 'rational'. Nobody planned it out in advance. In many ways, this century witnessed not the resolution, but the deepening of social and intellectual contradictions. In spite of political change, England remained a monarchy, with a strong executive, and the middling classes did not attain even a modicum of power. The perfection of the English constitution was not incompatible with a violently repressive legal code. In 1715 and 1780, furthermore, this tolerant nation was rocked by the worst religious riots seen in Western Europe in the eighteenth century. These facts are not anomalous; they typify the complexities of the period.

Yet they threaten to turn the placid English garden into a wilderness. Historians insist upon order – either a sense of movement towards a fixed goal, or an overall constancy. J. H. Plumb's concept of 'political stability' emphasizes the second option. The party strife of the late seventeenth and early eighteenth centuries, according to Plumb, masked the development of a secure, oligarchical government. The elimination of the disruptive and reactionary Tories in 1714 made possible the fulfilment of this process, through the one-party Whig regime of Sir Robert Walpole.[6] The persuasiveness of this interpretation cannot be denied; after all, no opposition movement was successful in overthrowing Whig hegemony. Nevertheless, Linda Colley has shown that the Tory party was a potent force in politics long after 1714, and that party conflict was as disruptive under the first two Hanoverians as it had ever been. Of course, it is not clear from Plumb's definition whether or not this kind of opposition would entail instability. The failure of Jacobitism may indicate that England was fundamentally stable; on the other hand, its persistence may show that turmoil was never far from the surface. Certainly, Walpole himself was constantly apprehensive that the Jacobites were going to subvert his system. Yet how many riots would have to be chronicled in order to

---

[6] J. H. Plumb, *The Growth of Political Stability in England, 1675–1725* (London, 1967). For more recent perspectives on the Walpolean regime, see Jeremy Black, ed., *Britain in the Age of Walpole* (London, 1984).

show that 'the people' did not 'accept' their rulers? 'Political stability' is not self-evident; it has to be better defined. Moreover, it may be a sterile notion. Instead of inspiring a flood of bold ideas, as Plumb had hoped it would, it has imposed a new kind of rigidity.

English political and social history between 1689 and 1760 may be better characterized by dynamic tension than by 'stability'. Two great parties, based on religious animosities, vied together in what was often perceived as a battle to the death; but neither was strong enough to destroy the other. Consequently, party conflict had to be waged according to strict rules, so that it would not result in civil war. The party in opposition became a watch-dog against abuses of traditional rights and liberties; the party in power was constrained to respect these privileges. James II violated this system by trying to create his own party, and to promote unpopular religious goals. His successors were more careful; but they also lacked traditional legitimacy, and had to extend their executive power in order to maintain themselves. As a minority party with fewer ties to the old system of monarchical rule, the Whigs were more prepared to support the growth of central authority; and this attitude kept them in office for almost fifty years.

The Whig regime was neither 'progressive' nor 'reactionary'; it was mainly pragmatic. Jacobitism opposed it in almost every detail. Supporters of the exiled Stuarts believed that parties and factions represented selfish interests; national government required selflessness and sacrifice. Parliament was not denied a role in government by Jacobites, but it was not to be trusted with ultimate authority, because it was vulnerable to corruption. Only a single detached arbiter, without personal interests, responsible only to God, and acting on the highest moral principles, could legitimately head the state. Christ-like, imbued with a divine as well as a human nature, he was the sacred and hereditary king. His power might be restricted by law or convention – in fact, Jacobites tended to favour such limitations – but his sanctity could never be questioned.

Jacobitism was a response to the decline of unity in the state. Paradoxically, although they were the sources of much dissension and party rancour, Jacobites believed that division would lead to ruin. The Whigs were not altogether different in their views; they simply substituted one-party rule for divinely sanctioned monarchy. In fact, Jacobites, Tories and Whigs shared a common anxiety about the future of their society. How was a nation riven by political divisions to survive? Without traditional monarchical legitimacy, on what grounds could the structure of government and the social hierarchy be justified? These questions were to become universal; they have plagued the rulers of every nation in modern times. The creation of wealth on an unprecedented scale in sixteenth- and seventeenth-century Europe weakened centralized authority and consequently exacerbated divisions of all kinds – religious, ethnic, class. By the late seventeenth century, a solution to disorder had been found in the continental absolutist state; but England's severe disunity made this an impossibility. Instead, the English government muddled through on a mixture of centralization and constitutional traditionalism, of expediency and myth. Yet this did not prevent political and religious strife from reverberating in England for a century after the Restoration.

The Jacobites did not seek to impose order on a divided nation by establishing absolutism on continental lines; rather, they wished to strengthen the mythic component of the English constitution, by exalting kingship as a guarantee of unity. Theirs was not an anachronistic strategy; it was later adopted by George III, Queen Victoria and several of Britain's twentieth-century monarchs, and it has parallels in the reverence shown for the Presidency in Western republics, or the elevation of the party in communist regimes. All states abhor divisions, and combat them through myths – myths of origins, of ancient foundations, of divine or popular sanction, of kingship or republican virtue, of the inevitability of socialism. Perhaps that is why King James III, in his portrait from the studio of Belle, is smiling at us so benignly. He recognizes us, and seems to suggest that, if his own titles and authority are no more than myths, so too are ours.

Bibliography

MANUSCRIPT SOURCES

PUBLIC RECORD OFFICE, CHANCERY LANE
State Papers, Domestic
34	Anne
35	George I
36	George II
43	Regencies, 1716–60
44	Entry Books, 1715–60

State Papers, Foreign
78	France

Treasury Solicitor's Papers
11	Various Briefs
20	Rebellion of 1745
23	Various Briefs

Court of King's Bench
1	Affidavits
8	*Baga de Secretis*, 1715
10	Indictments, London and Middlesex
11	Indictments, Out-Counties
33	Miscellaneous Affidavits

Assizes
2	Oxford Circuit, Crown Minute Books
4	Oxford Circuit, Process Books
5	Oxford Circuit, Indictments
21	Western Circuit, Minute Books
23	Western Circuit, Gaol Books
35	South-Eastern Circuit, Indictments
41–2	North-Eastern Circuit, Minute Books
44	North-Eastern Circuit, Indictments
45	North-Eastern Circuit, Depositions, ed. by J. S. Cockburn

Palatinate of Chester
   5   Assizes Crown Book, William & Anne
  24   Assizes Gaol Files, Writs, etc.
Palatinate of Durham
  16   Assizes Crown Book
  17   Assizes Indictments
Palatinate of Lancaster
  26   Assizes Indictments
  27   Assizes Depositions
  28   Assizes Minute Books

BRITISH LIBRARY
Additional Manuscripts

5,853	Strype Letters
17,677	State Correspondence, England–Netherlands
22,202	Strafford MSS
28,230–6, 28,249–52	Caryll Papers
29,913	Jervis Correspondence
29,981	'Loyal Poems'
32,096	Malet Papers: George Harbin
32,686, 32,703–4, 32,867, 32,874 32,884, 32,992, 33,050	Newcastle Papers
33,286	Hickes Papers
35,600	Hardwicke MSS
37,660–1	Melfort Papers
37,662	Brown Letter-Book
38,507	Townshend Papers
39,923	Jacobite Papers
62,558	Caesar Diary

Egerton
3,436, 3,440	Duke of Leeds Papers

Stowe
158	Scottish MSS
232	Jacobite Letters
255	Rebel Trials, 1745
750	Macclesfield MSS

Lansdowne
817	'Case of Thomas Wells', 1715

BODLEIAN LIBRARY, OXFORD
Rawlinson Manuscripts

A	311, 333
B	376
C	376, 735, 986

D   87, 91, 178, 198, 361, 367, 383, 400, 404, 680, 832, 835, 842,
             847, 849, 890, 924, 1003, 1079, 1081, 1094, 1128, 1133, 1179,
             1232, 1238, 1251, 1305, 1361, 1489
Poet.   81, 155, 169, 181, 203, 207
Q.   f. 5
Carte Manuscripts
  76, 79, 181, 208–9, 228, 233, 239, 240
Hearne Diary
  vol. 62

ROYAL ARCHIVES, WINDSOR
Stuart Papers

CAMBRIDGE UNIVERSITY LIBRARY, CAMBRIDGE
Cholmondeley (Houghton) MSS

CITY OF LONDON RECORD OFFICE, CLERKENWELL
Middlesex Quarter Sessions Records, 1690: MJ/SR 1751–67

CHETHAM LIBRARY, MANCHESTER
Raines Manuscripts

CENTRAL LIBRARY, MANCHESTER
Typescript of Richard E. Knowles, 'The Ancient and Loyal Corporation of
  Ardwick', BR F 369 242 A3

HARRIS MUSEUM, PRESTON
Minute Book, Corporation of Walton-le-dale

LANCASHIRE RECORD OFFICE, PRESTON
Quarter Sessions Records, DDke/2/2: Indictment Book, 1686–91/2
                          QJI/2/10: Indictment Book, 1700–19
                          QSI/1/89–120: Indictments, 1689–1746

OXFORDSHIRE RECORD OFFICE, OXFORD
Quarter Sessions Rolls, 1687–1783. Transcribed by Canon J. Oldfield.
Quarter Sessions Minute Books, 1688–1768. Transcribed by Canon J.
  Oldfield.

BEINECKE LIBRARY, YALE UNIVERSITY, NEW HAVEN, CONNECTICUT
Osborn Files: 'Seers', 'Mallet', 'Lavington Box'
Osborn Shelves,   b. 111;   'Loyal Poems'
                  f. c. 58:   'Poems'

COLLECTIONS OF ARTEFACTS

British Museum, London: Jacobite medals, ceramics
City Museum and Art Gallery, Hanley, Stoke-on-Trent: Jacobite ceramics
Harris Museum, Preston: local Jacobite memorabilia
Lyme Park, Cheshire: Jacobite glassware
Stanford Hall, Leicestershire: Jacobite portraits
Victoria and Albert Museum, London: Jacobite jewellery, ceramics, glassware,
fans, clothing, etc.

PAMPHLETS AND BROADSIDES

These are all Jacobite works. They have been arranged by year, then alphabeti-
cally within each year, with items of dubious date listed at the end of the
probable year of publication. It is not a complete list; for example, it presents
only a sampling of the vast Nonjuring literature. Broadside ballads are not
included. I am grateful to Paul Hopkins for information on authorship and
dating of works in the 1690s. The location of some very rare tracts is given at
the end of the entry. Two accessible collections are:

Walter Scott, ed., *A Collection of Scarce and Valuable Tracts, on the most
Interesting and Entertaining Subjects: but chiefly such as relate to the
History and Constitution of these Kingdoms. Selected from an infinite
number in print and manuscript, in the Royal, Coton, Sion and other
public, as well as private, libraries; particularly that of the late Lord
Somers* (2nd edn, 13 vols., London, Cadell and Davies, 1813), and *A
Choice Collection of Papers Relating to State Affairs: During the Late
Revolution* (2 vols., London, n.p., 1703). See also Mark Goldie, 'The
Revolution of 1689 and the Structure of Political Argument: An Essay and
an Annotated Bibliography of Pamphlets on the Allegiance Controversy',
Bulletin of Research in the Humanities (1980), pp. 473–564. This des-
cribes thirty-three additional Jacobite pieces not listed here.

James II, *His Majesties Letter to the House of Lords and Commons, Writ from
St. Germain the 3d of February 1688* (n.p., n.p., 1688/9).
  *His Majesties Letter To the Lords and Others of His Privy Councel. St.
Germain-en-Laye, 4/14 Jan. 1688/9* (n.p., n.p., 1688/9).
[Collier, Jeremy], *Vindiciae Juris Regii: or, Remarques upon a Paper, Enti-
tuled, An Enquiry into the Measures of Submission to the Supream
Authority* (London, n.p., 1689).
*A Letter from a Gentleman in the Country to his Correspondent in the City,
concerning the Coronation Medal, distributed April 11th, 1689* (n.p., n.p.,
1689).
A Letter from an Absent Lord to one of his Friends in the Convention (n.p.,
n.p., 1689). B.L. 1,484.g.5.
Min Heer T. Van C.'s Answer to Min Heer H. Van l.'s Letter of the 15th of

March, 1689; representing the true interests of Holland, and what they have already gained by our Losses (n.p., n.p., 1689).

[Pendergrass, Sir Thomas], *A Short History of the Convention; or, New Christened Parliament* (London, n.p., 1689).

A Speech to his Highness the Prince of Orange, by a true Protestant of the Church of England, as established by Law (n.p., n.p., 1689).

[Collier, Jeremy], *Animadversions upon the modern Explication of II Hen. 7. Cap. 1. Or a King de Facto* (n.p., n.p., 1689?). B.L. 1,484.g.5.

England's Crisis: Or, the World Well Mended (n.p., n.p., 1689?). B.L. 1,484.g.5.

A Letter to a Member of the Committee of Grievances, containing some Seasonable Reflections on the present Administration of Affairs, since Managed by Dutch Councils (n.p., n.p., 1689?). B.L. 1,484.g.5.

Observations upon the late Revolution in England (n.p., n.p., 1689?).

A Remonstrance and Protestation of all the Good Protestants of this Kingdom, against Deposing their Lawful Soveraign K. James II (n.p., n.p., 1689?). B.L. 1,484.g.5.

Five Questions Propounded to the People of England (n.p., n.p., 1689/90?). B.L. 1,484.g.5.

Lettre du Roy de la Grande Bretagne au Lord Comte Portland. A Letter from the King of Great Britain to the Earl of Portland (n.p., n.p., 1689/90?).

To the Right Honourable Lords, and to the Gentlemen Convened at Westminster (n.p., n.p., 1690). B.L. 1,484.g.5.

[Johnston, Nathaniel], *The Dear Bargain, or, A True Representation of the State of the English Nation under the Dutch. In a Letter to a Friend* (n.p., n.p., 1690?).

A Copy of Mr. Ashton's Paper, Delivered to the Sheriff at the Place of Execution, January 28, 1690/1 (n.p., n.p., 1690/1).

[Hickes, George], *An Apology for the New Separation: In a Letter to Dr. John Sharpe, Archbishop of York; Occasioned by his Farewell-Sermon, preached on the 28th of June, at St. Giles's in the Fields* (London, n.p., 1691).

[Jenkins, Robert], *The Title of a Thorough Settlement Examined; In Answer to Dr. Sherlock's Case of the Allegiance Due to Sovereign Powers, etc.* (London, J. Wells, 1691).

[Kettlewell, John], *The Duty of Allegiance Settled upon its True Grounds, According to Scripture, Reason, and the Opinion of the Church: In Answer to a Late Book of Dr. William Sherlock, Master of the Temple* (London, n.p., 1691).

[Lawton, Charlwood], *The Vindication of the Dead: or, Six Hours Reflection upon the Six Weeks Labour in Answering Mr. Ashton's Speech published by Authority* (n.p., n.p., 1691).

The Substance of King William's Discourse to his Cabinet-Council (n.p., n.p., 1691?).

The Substance of King William's Second Discourse to His Cabinet-Council (n.p., n.p., 1691?).

[Hickes, George], *A Vindication of Some among Our Selves against the False Principles of Dr. Sherlock* (London, n.p., 1692).

James II, *His Majesties most Gracious Declaration to all His loving Subjects, commanding their Assistance against the P. of Orange, and his Adherents. St. Germain, 20 April 1692* (n.p., n.p., 1692).

Lawton, Charlwood, *The Jacobite Principles Vindicated, In Answer to a Letter sent to the Author. Dedicated to the Queen of England* (London, n.p., 1692).

[Montgomery, Sir James], *Great Britain's Just Complaint for her late Measures, present Sufferings, and the future Miseries she is exposed to* (n.p., n.p., 1692).

[Wagstaffe, Thomas], *His Majesty's gracious Speech to both Houses of Parliament, with Additions and Explications: Directed to the House of Commons, by the Free-born People of England* (n.p., n.p., 1692).

[Lawton, Charlwood], *Honesty is the Best Policy* (n.p., 1692?).

Some Remarks upon our Affairs (n.p., n.p., 1692?). B.L. 1,484.g.5.

[Montgomery, Sir James], *The People of England's Grievances offered to be enquired into, and redressed by their Representatives in Parliament* (n.p., n.p., 1692?).

An Account of the Conversation Behaviour and Execution of William Anderton Printer . . . on Friday the 16th of June 1693 (London, J. Wallis, 1693).

[Grascome, Samuel], *An Appeal of Murther from certain unjust Judges, lately sitting at the Old Baily, to the righteous Judge of Heaven and Earth; and to all sensible English-men, containing a Relation of the Tryal, Behaviour, and Death of Mr. William Anderton, Executed June 16, 1693, at Tyburn for pretended High Treason* (n.p., 1693).

James II, *His Majesties most Gracious Declaration to all his Loving Subjects. St. Germain en Laye, April 17, S.N. 1693* (n.p., 1693).

[Lawton, Charlwood], *A French Conquest neither Desirable nor Practicable. Dedicated to the King of England* (London, n.p., n.p., 1693).

Remarks upon the Present Confederacy, and Late Revolution in England, etc. (London, [W. Anderton], 1693).

[Ferguson, Robert], *A Letter to Mr. Secretary Trenchard, Discovering a conspiracy against the Laws and ancient Constitution of England: With Reflections on the Present Pretended Plot* ([London], [R. Ferguson], 1694).

A Letter to the Right Honourable, My Lord Chief Justice Holt, occasioned by the Noise of a Plot ([London], [R. Ferguson], 1694).

Querela Temporum: or, the Danger of the Church of England. In a Letter from the Dean of — to —, Prebend of — (n.p., n.p., 1694).

[Wagstaffe, Thomas], *A Letter out of Lancashire to a Friend in London, Giving some Account of the Late Tryals there: Together with some Seasonable and Proper Remarks upon it. Recommended to the Wisdom of the Lords and Commons Assembled in Parliament* (n.p., n.p., 1694).

A Letter out of Suffolk to a Friend in London, giving some Account of the last Sickness and Death of Dr. William Sancroft, late Archbishop of Canterbury (n.p., n.p., 1694).

[Ferguson, Robert], *A brief Account of some of the late Incroachments and Depredations of the Dutch upon the English; and of a few of those many Advantages by which Fraud and Violence they have made of the British Nation since the Revolution, and of the Means enabling them thereunto* ([London], [R. Ferguson], 1695).

Whether the Parliament be not in Law dissolved by the Death of the Princess of Orange? And how the Subjects ought, and are to behave themselves in relation to those Papers emitted since by the Stile and Title of Acts? With a brief Account of the Government of England. In a Letter to a Country Gentleman, as an Answer to his second Question ([London], [R. Ferguson], 1695).

Whether the Preserving the Protestant Religion was the Motive unto, or the End, that was designed in the Late Revolution? In a Letter to a Country Gentleman, as an Answer to his First Query ([London], [R. Ferguson], 1695).

[Grascome, Samuel], *An Appeal to all True Englishmen (If there be any such left;) Or, A Cry for Bread* (n.p., n.p., 1695?).

Quaeries (n.p., n.p., 1695?). B.L. 1,484.g.5.

[Wagstaffe, Thomas], *A Letter to a Gentleman elected a Knight of the Shire to serve in the present Parliament* (n.p., n.p., 1695?).

A True Copy of the Papers Delivered by Sir John Frend [sic], and Sir William Parkyns, to the Sheriffs of London and Middlesex, at Tyburn, the Place of Execution, April 3d. 1696 (n.p., n.p., 1696).

[Wagstaffe, Thomas], *An Account of the Proceedings in the House of Commons, In Relation to the Recoining of the Clipp'd Money, and Falling the Price of Guineas. Together with a Particular List of the Names of the Members consenting and dissenting. In Answer to a Letter out of the Countrey* (London, n.p., 1696).

A True Copy of the Paper Delivered by Sir John Fenwick, Baronet, to the Sheriffs of London and Middlesex, on Tower-Hill, the Place of Execution, on Thursday, Jan. 28 1696/7 (n.p., n.p., 1696/7).

[Hickes, George], *The Pretences of the Prince of Wales Examin'd, and Rejected. In a Letter to a Friend in the Country* (London, n.p., 1701).

Right To those that Suffer Wrong: Or, a Full Confutation Of the Assertions of that Grand Imposter Fuller, al' Fullee, al' Fouler, al' Elleson, al' — etc. Concerning the Birth of the Pretended Prince of Wales (London, n.p., 1701).

[Wagstaffe, Thomas], *The Present State of Jacobitism in England. A Second Part. In Answer to the First* (London, n.p., 1702).

Gandy, Henry, *Jure Divino: Or An Answer To All that Hath or Shall be written by Republicans Against the Old English Constitution* (London, n.p., 1707).

[Leslie, Charles], *Beaucoup de Bruit pour une Aumelette, or, Much a Do about Nothing, Being a Tryal of skill betwixt the Jacobite's Hopes Reviv'd, And the Good Old Cause. By a True Trojan* (London, n.p., 1710).

An Oath to an Invador, and Abjuring the Invaded, dissected and examin'd upon the following Queries (n.p., n.p., 1711). B.L. 1,484.g.5; P.R.O., S.P. 34/17/48.

Reasons to prove the Complying Clergy, and those that Adhere to them, guilty of Schism (n.p., n.p., 1711).

Memoirs of the Chevalier de St. George: With some private Passages of the Life of the Late King James II (London, n.p., 1712).

[Harbin, George], *The Hereditary Right of the Crown of England Asserted: The History of the Succession since the Conquest clear'd; and the True English Constitution Vindicated from the Misrepresentations of Dr. Higden's View and Defence* (London, G. James, 1713).

[Leslie, Charles], *The Right of Monarchy Asserted; Wherein the Abstract of Dr. King's Book, With the Motives for the Reviving it at this Juncture are fully considered* (London, J. Morphew, 1713).

[Hickes, George], *Seasonable Queries Relating to the Birth and Birthright of a Certain Person* (n.p., n.p., 1714).

James III, *Proclamation, 29 August 1714* (n.p., n.p., 1714).

Manifeste Touchant les Droits du Roy Jacques III. Aux Royaumes d'Angleterre, d'Ecosse & d'Irlande (n.p., n.p., 1714). P.R.O., S.P. 35/1/31a.

James III, *To his Subjects of England … 25 Oct. 1715* (Perth, R. Freebairn, 1715).

[Leslie, Charles], *Mr. Lesley to the Bishop of Sarum* (n.p., n.p., [1715]).

A Letter to Richard Steele, Esq. (n.p., n.p., 1715). Bodl. Rawl. MS D. 1081.

[St John, Henry, Viscount Bolingbroke], *The True Copy of a Letter From the Right Honourable the Lord Viscount Bolingbroke* (London, J. Roberts, 1715).

[Welton, Richard], *The Clergy's Tears: or, a Cry against Persecution. Humbly offer'd in a Letter to the Lord Bishop of London, in our Present Great Distress and Danger* (n.p., n.p., 1715).

Reasons for Committing the Duke of Ormond To The Tower (n.p., n.p., 1715?). Bodl. Rawl. MS D. 383.

Reflections upon a late Declaration of the Bishops, submitted to their Consideration (n.p., n.p., 1715?).

[Howell, Lawrence], *The Case of Schism in the Church of England truly Stated* (n.p., n.p., 1716).

'Miners, Willowby', i.e. Mynors, Willoughby, *True Loyalty; or Non-Resistance the only Support of Monarchy. A Sermon Preach'd at St. Pancras, Middlesex, on Sunday, June 10, 1716* (London, J. Morphew, 1716).

A True Copy of the Paper Delivered to the Sheriffs of London, by Colonel Henry Oxburgh, Who was Drawn Hang'd and Quarter'd at Tyburn for High Treason against His Majesty King George, Monday the 14th Day of March 1716 (n.p., n.p., 1716). P.R.O., S.P. 35/5/48b.

A *True Copy of the Paper delivered to the Sheriffs of London by Richard Gascoigne* (n.p., n.p., 1716). P.R.O., S.P. 35/5/48b.

A *True Copy of the Papers Delivered to the Sheriffs of London, by William Paul a Clergyman, and John Hall Esq.; late Justice of the Peace in Northumberland Who were Drawn, Hang'd and Quarter'd at Tyburn, for High-Treason against his Majesty King George; July the 13th, 1716* (London, A. Bell and J. Phillips, 1716). P.R.O., S.P. 35/5/64b.

The Character of Sultan Galga, the Present Cham of Tartary. Drawn by a Wallachian who had been his Favourite for several Years (n.p., n.p., 1716?). B.L. 1, 484,g.5.

A *Letter of a zealous Quaker to one of the Canons of the Cathedral Church at Worcester, Concerning the Birth of the Pretender* (n.p., n.p., 1716?). B.L. 1, 484.g.5.

To a Thing they call Prince of Wales (n.p., n.p., 1716?). B.L. Tracts 1541.

'Rt. W.', *To Mr William Thomas* (n.p., n.p., 1716?). B.L. Tracts 1541.

'William Thomas', *To Sir Robert Walpole Esq.* (n.p., n.p., 1716?). Bodl. Rawl. MS A. 311.

To the Army and People of England (n.p., n.p., 1716?). B.L. Tracts 1541.

Earbery, Matthias, *The History of the Clemency of our English Monarchs. the Usage Prisoners who Surrender'd at Discretion have met with from their Hands. Compar'd with Several Matters of Fact which have lately occurr'd in this Kingdom* (London, n.p., 1717).

[Ferguson, Robert], *The History of all the Mobs, Tumults, and Insurrections in Great Britain, From William the Conqueror to the present time* (London, J. Moore, 1717).

The History of the Revolution (n.p., n.p., 1717).

James III, *His Majesty's Letter to the Reverend Mr. Charles Lesley. Urbino, Nov. 29, 1717 N.S.* (n.p., n.p., 1717).

The Necessity of a Plot (n.p., n.p., 1717?). P.R.O., S.P. 35/10/84.

The Father's Letter to the Son, and the Son's Answer (London, M. Jenour, 1717/18?). P.R.O., S.P. 35/11/12.

The Dying Speech of James Shepheard. An Hymn to the Holy and Undivided Trinity. A true Copy of a Prayer found in his Pocket, soon after he was Executed, Write by his own Hand (n.p., n.p., 1718). Bodl. Rawl. MS D. 383.

An *Hymn to the Holy and Undivided Trinity, Written by James Shepard, During his Imprisonment in Newgate* (London, n.p., 1718). P.R.O., S.P. 35/11/53.

Shippen, William, *et al.*, *Three Speeches against Continuing the Army, etc. As They were Spoken in the House of Commons the last Session of Parliament* (London, W. Johnson, 1718).

The Copy of a Paper Deliver'd by Mr. John Matthews to a Friend of his before his Execution (n.p., n.p., 1719). P.R.O., S.P. 35/19/50.

The Last Dying Words, Characters, Portraiture, Prison Prayers, Meditations, and Ejaculations of Mr John Matthews; Printer (London, F[rancis] C[lifton], 1719). P.R.O., S.P. 35/19/47.

The Letter of the Duke of Or—nd, To All True Lovers of the Church of England and their Country (n.p., n.p., 1719). P.R.O., S.P. 35/18/69b.

A Letter from Mr. John Matthews, After his Condemnation, to Mr. John Broderick (n.p., n.p., 1719). P.R.O., S.P. 35/18/78.

A Letter from a Whigg at Rome, March the 11th, 1718/19 N.S. to a Lord of the Same Party in London, writ originally in French, and Translated into English (n.p., n.p., 1719).

Ex Ore Tuo Te Judico: Vox Populi, Vox Dei (n.p., n.p., 1719?) Bodl. 4° Rawl. 536; Beinecke C.P. 1616 (corrected version).

James III, *Proclamation to all his loving Subjects of what Rank and degree soever ... 10 Oct. 1720* (n.p., n.p., 1720).

The Whole Life and Character of that beautiful, pious and illustrious Princess Sobieski who is by Proxy espous'd to the Chevalier. Containing Her Family, Birth, Education, Fortune and Nuptial Ceremonies (London, F[rancis] C[lifton], 1720?). P.R.O., S.P. 35/24/68.

A Letter from a certain Man Somewhere, to an uncertain Great Man Here ([London], [J. Lightbody], 1720/1). P.R.O, S.P. 35/25/90.

'M.T.', *A Letter from a Gentleman at Rome, to his Friend in London; Giving An Account of some very surprising Cures in the King's Evil by the Touch, lately effected in the Neighbourhood of that City* (London, A. Moore, 1721).

[Rialton, Viscount], *A Letter from a Whigg at Rome* (London?, n.p., 1721?).

A certain Clergyman's Letter, from St. Andrews-Holborn, to the Lord Bishop of Rochester, In the Tower of London (n.p., n.p., 1722). P.R.O., S.P. 35/33/53.

Counsellor Layer's Letter To His Grace the D. of N—le And the Right Honourable the Lord Viscount T—d ([London], [F. Clifton], 1722). P.R.O., S.P. 35/34/98.

Councellor Layer's Second Letter Deliver'd by his Wife, To his Grace the D. of N—le With the Manner of his Grace's receiving the Same ([London], F. Clifton], 1722). P.R.O., S.P. 35/34/117

Counsellor Lear's [sic] Humble Petition to His Majesty For a Pardon, with His Majesty's Answer (London, Mary Hynde, 1722). P.R.O., S.P. 35/34/89.

[Earbery, Matthias], *An Historical Account of the Advantages that have Accru'd to England, by the Succession in the Illustrious House of Hanover* (London, n.p., 1722).

The Second Part of the Historical Account of the Advantages that have Accru'd to England, by the Succession in the Illustrious House of Hanover (London, n.p., 1722).

[Granville, George, Lord Lansdowne], *A Letter from a Noble-Man Abroad, To his Friend in England* (London, n.p., 1722).

James III, *Declaration ... Sept. 10 1722* (n.p., n.p., 1722).

The Last Dying Words of the Late King James to his Son and Daughter, and the French King (n.p., n.p., 1722).

The Lord Bishop of Rochester's Answer to a Letter, sent him by a certain

Clergy–man, at St. Andrew's Holborn (n.p., n.p., 1722). P.R.O., S.P. 35/33/53.

To the King's Most Excellent Majesty The Humble Petition of Christopher Layer Esq; Now Lying under Sentence of death, in the Tower of London. For High Treason (London, n.p., 1722). P.R.O., S.P. 35/34/89.

The exact Effigies, Life, Character and Case of Francis Atterbury, late Lord Bishop of Rochester. To which is Added the Learned Speech made at his Promotion (London, Fra. Clifton, 1723). P.R.O., S.P. 35/43/85.

[Wharton, Philip, Duke of Wharton], The Duke of Wharton's Reasons for Leaving his Native Country, and Espousing the Causes of His Royal Majesty King James III. In a Letter To his Friends in Great Britain and Ireland (n.p., n.p., 1726).

[Earbery, Matthias] The Occasionall Historian (4 parts, London, J. Wilford, A. Dodd, W. Wells, J. Parker, W. Pepper, E. Nutt, 1730–2).

The Chronicle of Charles, the Young Man ([Edinburgh], n.p., 1745).

Considerations Addressed to the Publick ([Edinburgh?, n.p., 1745?]). Beinecke Bz 25. 22.

A Full Collection of All the Proclamations and Orders published by the Authority of Charles Prince of Wales ([Edinburgh], n.p., 1745).

A Letter to the Archbishop of York (n.p., n.p., 1745). Grosart.

Stuart, Charles Edward, Unto all His Majesty's Subjects, of what Degree soever ... 10 October 1745 ([Edinburgh], n.p., 1745).

A True Copy Of a Scandalous Paper, which was thrown in the Face of His Majesty King George, on Saturday last the 26th of this Instant October, by James Corbet a Romish Priest; as his Majesty was Reviewing the City Militia on the Terrace Walk in his Garden at St. James's. The Manner of his being Seiz'd His Examination before Justice Burges, and his Commitment to Newgate ([London], [—Fowler], 1745). P.R.O., S.P. 36/72, fos. 348–50.

A Full and True Collection of All the Orders, Proclamations, and Papers, etc. Published by the Authority of Charles Prince of Wales, Regent of Scotland, England, France and Ireland, and Dominions thereunto belonging, Since his Arrival in Scotland to this present Time (Glasgow, n.p., 1746).

[Griffiths, Ralph], Ascanius: or, The Young Adventurer; A True History (London, G. Smith, 1746).

[Macdonald, Alan, of Kingsborough], Alexis; or, The Young Adventurer. A novel (London, T. Cooper, 1746).

A Letter to the Author of the National Journal (n.p., n.p., 1746?). Beinecke Bz 25.22.

A True Copy of the Paper read by Mr. James Bradshaw, And delivered by him to the Sheriff of Surry Just before his Execution at Kennington-Common on Friday, November the 28th 1746 (London, T. Meighan, 1746/7).

Podmore, Thomas, The Layman's Apology for returning to Primitive Christianity (Manchester and London, J. Lister and M. Cooper, 1747).

A Familiar Instructive Dialogue, Which happened last Week at a Tavern near the Royal Exchange, Between An eminent Merchant of Dunkirk, one of their great Politicians there, and An English Member of Parliament; who became acquainted with him in that Town, when their Embarkations were so much talk'd of, in Favour of the Young Chevalier, etc. . . . Designed for the timely Information of the Publick, against the next Meeting of the Parliament. And Humbly Addressed to all true English Members (London, n.p., 1748).

'Michell, M.', pseud., Young Juba: or, the History of the Young Chevalier from His Birth, to His Escape from Scotland, after the Battle of Culloden (London, n.p., 1748).

A Remarkable Dialogue, Which lately happened In the Gardens of Luxembourg at Paris, Between An Old Impartial English Whig, and A Nonjuror of the Church of England, Concerning the Young Chevalier; and Several other Affairs regarding Great-Britain, etc ... By a Prussian Officer (Edinburgh, n.p., 1748).

A Letter from H[enry] G[oring], Esq; One of the Gentlemen of the Bed-Chamber to the Young Chevalier, and the only Person of his own Retinue that attended him from Avignon, in his late Journey through Germany, and elsewhere: containing Many remarkable and affecting Occurences which happened to the P— during the Course of his mysterious Progress. To a Particular Friend (London, n.p., 1750).

A True Copy of the Letter from Birmingham To the Publisher of the Daily Advertiser, Concerning the almost Instantaneous Cure of David West of that Town, Who had been for many Years most grievously afflicted with the King's Evil (n.p., n.p., 1751?). R.A., Stuart Box 6, no. 82.

Elegy upon the Death of the Heroic Charles Edward Stewart (n.p., n.p., 1788). R.A., Stuart Add. 7/28.

NEWSPAPERS AND PERIODICALS

Adams's Weekly Courant (Chester, E. Adams, 1753–4).

[Byrom, John and Thyer, Robert], Manchester Vindicated: Being a Compleat Collection of the Papers Lately published in Defence of that Town, in the Chester Courant. Together with All those on the other Side of the Question, Printed in the Manchester Magazine or elsewhere, which are answered in the said Chester Courant (Chester, E. Adams, 1749).

A Collection of Political and Humourous Letters, Poems and Articles of News, Publish'd in an Evening Paper, intitled, The National Journal, or, Country Gazette (London, J. Clarke, 1748).

A Collection of Political Essays and Letters in the Freeholder's Journal (London, T. Payne, 1722).

[Earbery, Matthias], The Universal Spy: Or, the Royal Oak Journal Reviv'd (London, W. Hinton, 1732).

[Flint, George], Robin's Last Shift: Or, Weekly Remarks and Political Reflections Upon the most Material News Foreign and Domestick. Part I (London, Isaac Dalton, 1717).

The Shift Shifted: Or, Weekly Remarks and Political Reflections Upon the most Material News Foreign and Domestick (London, Isaac Dalton, 1716).

The Flying Post: or, the Post-Master (London, R. Tookey, 1715–16).

Fog's Weekly Journal (London, J. Wilford and J. Purser, 1728–37).

The Gentleman's Magazine (London, Edward Carr, 1731–58).

[Leslie, Charles], 'Philalethes', *A View of the Times, their Principles and Practices: in the . . . Rehearsals* (6 vols., London, W. Bowen, 1750).

The Loyal Observator Reviv'd; or, Gaylard's Journal (London, Dr Gaylard, 1723).

Mist's Weekly Journal (London, N. Mist, 1725–8).

The Orphan Reviv'd: or, Powell's Weekly Journal (London, E. Powell, 1718–19).

[Osborne, George], *The Mitre and Crown; or, Great Britain's true Interest* (London, J. Fuller, 1748–50).

[Osborne, George and Caryll, John], *The True Briton* (London, J. Fuller, 1751–3).

St. James's Evening Post (London, J. Baker, 1715–46).

The Weekly Journal, or Saturday's Post (London, R. Mawson, N. Mist, 1715–25).

[Wharton, Philip, Duke of Wharton], *The True Briton* (London, T. Payne, 1723 – 4).

The Whisperer (London, W. Moore, 1770–1).

PUBLISHED LETTERS, MEMOIRS, DIARIES, ETC.

Blaikie, Walter Biggar, ed., 'A True Account of Mr. John Daniel's Progress with Prince Charles Edward in the Years 1745 and 1746 Written by Himself', in *Origins of the Forty-Five and Other Papers Relating to that Rising*, Publications of the Scottish Historical Society, 2nd Series, 2 (1916).

[Bowdler, Thomas], *Memoir of the Late John Bowdler, Esq.* (London, Longman, 1825).

Brady, Frank and Pottle, Frederick A., eds., *Boswell on the Grand Tour: Italy, Corsica and France, 1765–1766* (New York, McGraw-Hill, 1955).

Brockbank, W. and Kenworthy, F. eds., *The Diary of Richard Kay, 1716–51, of Balsingstone, near Bury, a Lancashire Doctor*, Chetham Society, 3d Series, 16 (1968).

[Buckley, W. E., ed.], *Memoirs of Thomas, Earl of Ailesbury. Written by Himself* (2 vols., Westminster, Nichols and Son, 1890).

Chapman, R. W., ed., *The Letters of Samuel Johnson* (3 vols., Oxford, Clarendon Press, 1952).

Clark, Andrew, ed., *The Life and Times of Anthony Wood, Antiquary of Oxford 1632–1695, Described by Himself*, Oxford Historical Society, 24–6 (3 vols., 1892–4).

Clarke, J. S., ed., *The Life of James the Second, King of England, &c. Collected out of Memoirs Writ of his Own Hand. Together with the King's Advice to his Son, and His Majesty's Will* (2 vols., London, Longman, Hurst, Rees, Orme and Brown, 1816).

Coxe, William, *Memoirs of the Life and Administration of Sir Robert Walpole, Earl of Orford. With Original Correspondence and Authentic Papers, Never Before Published* (3 vols., London, Cadell and Davies, 1798).

Cozens-Hardy, Basil, ed., *The Diary of Sylas Neville 1767–1788* (London, Oxford University Press, 1950).

Crawfurd, Gibbs Payne, ed., 'The Diary of George Booth of Chester and Katherine Howard, his Daughter, of Boughton, near Chester, 1707–1764', *Journal of the Chester and North Wales Architectural, Archaeological and Historic Society*, New Series. 28, 1 (1928), pp. 5–96.

Doble, C. E., *et al.*, eds., *Remarks and Collections of Thomas Hearne*, Oxford Historical Society, 2, 7, 13, 34, 42–3, 48, 50, 65, 67, 72 (11 vols., 1884–1918).

Fitzmaurice, Lord, *Life of William, Earl of Shelburne* (2 vols., London, Macmillan, 1912).

'The Forty-Five in Staffordshire', *North Staffordshire Field Club Transactions* (1923–4), pp. 87–96.

Gent, Thomas, *The Life of Mr. Thomas Gent, Printer of York; Written by Himself* (London, T. Thorpe, 1832).

Gibbon, Edward, *Memoirs of my Life*, ed. G. A. Bonnard (London, Nelson, 1966).

Gillow, Joseph, and Hewitson, Arthur, eds., *The Tyldesley Diary. Personal Records of Thomas Tyldesley ... During the Years 1712–13–14* (Preston, A. Hewitson, 1873).

Herbert, Lord, ed., *Henry, Elizabeth and George (1734–80): Letters and Diaries of Henry, Tenth Earl of Pembroke and his Circle* (London, Jonathan Cape, 1939).

ed., *Pembroke Papers (1780–1794): Letters and Diaries of Henry, Tenth Earl of Pembroke and his Circle* (London, Jonathan Cape, 1950).

Hill, George Birkbeck and Powell, L. F., eds., *Boswell's Life of Johnson* (6 vols., Oxford, Clarendon Press, 1934–64).

Historical Manuscripts Commission, *Tenth Report, Appendix, Part VI. The Manuscripts of the Lord Braye* (London, H.M.S.O., 1887).

Eleventh Report, Appendix, Part IV. The Manuscripts of the Marquess Townshend (London, H.M.S.O., 1887).

Eleventh Report, Appendix, Part VII (London, H.M.S.O., 1889).

Fourteenth Report, Appendix, Part X. The Manuscripts of the Earl of Dartmouth (2 vols., London, H.M.S.O. 1895).

Calendar of the Stuart Papers Belonging to His Majesty the King, Preserved at Windsor Castle (7 vols., London, H.M.S.O., 1902–23).

The Manuscripts of His Grace the Duke of Portland (10 vols., London, H.M.S.O., 1891–1920).

The Manuscripts of Lord Kenyon (London, H.M.S.O., 1894).

Manuscripts of the Earl of Egmont. Diary of Viscount Percival, afterwards Earl of Egmont (3 vols., London, H.M.S.O., 1920–3).

The Manuscripts of the Marquess of Downshire. Papers of Sir William Trumbull (1 vol., 2 parts, London, H.M.S.O., 1924).
Report on the Manuscripts of Allan George Finch (5 vols., London, H.M.S.O., 1913–   ).
Report on the Manuscripts of the Earl of Verulam, Preserved at Gorhambury (London, H.M.S.O., 1906).
Report on the Manuscripts of the Late Reginald Rawdon Hastings, Esq., of the Manor House, Ashby de la Zouche (4 vols., London, H.M.S.O., 1928–47).
Hodgson, J. C., ed., *Six North Country Diaries*, Surtees Society, 108 (1910).
Irvine, W. F. and Bennett, J. H. E., eds., 'Cheshire and "The Fifteen" ', *The Cheshire Sheaf*, 3rd Series, 37 (1942).
James, G. P. R., ed., *Letters Illustrative of the Reign of William III. From 1696 to 1708. Addressed to the Duke of Shrewsbury, by James Vernon, Esq. Secretary of State* (3 vols., London, Henry Colburn, 1841).
King, William, *Political and Literary Anecdotes of His Own Times* (London, John Murray, 1819).
Lewis, W. S., gen. ed., *The Yale Edition of Horace Walpole's Correspondence* (41 vols., New Haven, Ct, Yale University Press, 1937–84).
Llanover, Lady, ed., *The Autobiography and Correspondence of Mary Granville, Mrs. Delany* (3 vols., London, R. Bentley, 1861).
Manchester, Duke of, *Court and Society from Elizabeth to Anne. Edited from the Papers at Kimbolton* (2 vols., London, Hurst and Blackett, 1864).
Matthews, William, ed., *The Diary of Dudley Ryder, 1715–1716* (London, Methuen and Co., 1939).
Newton, Lady, *The House of Lyme* (London, Heinemann, 1917).
Lyme Letters, 1660–1760 (London, Heinemann, 1925).
Oliver, Andrew, ed., *The Journal of Samuel Curwen, Loyalist* (Cambridge, Mass., Harvard University Press, 1972).
Parkinson, Richard, ed., *The Private Journal and Literary Remains of John Byrom*, Chetham Society, 32, 34, 40, 44 (4 parts in 2 vols., 1854–7).
Paton, Henry, ed., *The Lyon in Mourning or A Collection of Speeches Letters Journal etc. Relative to the Affairs of Prince Charles Edward Stuart by the Rev. Robert Forbes, A.M., Bishop of Ross and Caithness 1746–1775*, Publications of the Scottish Historical Society, 20–2 (3 vols., Edinburgh, 1895–6).
Singer, S. W., ed., *The Correspondence of Henry Hyde, Earl of Clarendon and of his brother Laurence Hyde, Earl of Rochester* (2 vols., London, H. Colburn, 1828).
Thicknesse, Philip, *Memoirs and Anecdotes of Philip Thicknesse, late Lieutenant Governor of Land Guard Fort, and unfortunately Father to George Touchet, Baron Audley* (2 vols., n.p., 1788).
Thompson, E. M., ed., *Letters of Humphrey Prideaux sometime Dean of Norwich to John Ellis sometime Under-Secretary of State 1674–1722*, Camden Society, 15 (1875).
Thomson, W. H., ed., *Beppy Byrom's Diary. An Eye-Witness Account of*

Bonnie Prince Charlie in Manchester (Manchester, W. H. Thomson, [1945]).

Tyrer, Frank and Bagley, J. J., eds., *The Great Diurnall of Nicholas Blundell of Little Crosby, Lancashire*, Lancashire and Cheshire Record Society, 110, 112, 114 (3 vols., 1968–72).

Watson, Robert, *The Life of Lord George Gordon: With a Philosophical Review of his Political Conduct* (London, Symonds and Eaton, 1795).

Whiting, C. E., ed., *Two Yorkshire Diaries*, Yorkshire Archaeological Society Record Series, 107 (1951).

Wilkinson, C. H., ed., *The King of the Beggars: Bampfylde Moore Carew* (Oxford, Clarendon Press, 1931).

Winchester, Charles, ed., *Memoirs of the Chevalier de Johnstone* (3 vols., Aberdeen, D. Wyllie and Son, 1870).

OTHER PUBLISHED PRIMARY SOURCES

An Account of the Riots, Tumults, and other Treasonable Practices; since His Majesty's Accession to the Throne (London, J. Baker, 1715).

Beamont, William, ed., *The Jacobite Trials at Manchester in 1694. From an Unpublished Manuscript*, Chetham Society, 28 (1853).

Bennett, J. H. E. and Dewhurst, J. C., eds., *Quarter Sessions Records with Other Records of the Justices of the Peace for the County Palatine of Chester 1559–1760*, Record Society of Lancashire and Cheshire, 94 (1940).

Boyer, Abel, *The History of the Reign of Queen Anne, Digested into Annals* (11 vols., London, T. Ward, 1703–13).

The Political State of Great Britain (40 vols., London, J. Baker, 1711–40).

Earwaker, J. P., 'The Mock Corporation of Rochdale', *Transactions of the Historic Society of Lancashire and Cheshire*, 40, New Series, 4 (1888), pp. 93–120.

Estcourt, Edgar E. and Payne, John Orlebar, eds., *The English Catholic Nonjurors of 1715* (London and New York, Burns and Oates, n.d.).

France, R. Sharpe, ed., *The Registers of Estates of Lancashire Papists, 1717–1788*, Record Society of Lancashire and Cheshire, 98, 108 (2 vols., 1945, 1960).

'Gentleman of Chichester, A', *A Full and Genuine Account of the Inhuman and Unparalleled Murders of Mr. William Galley, A Custom-House Officer, and Mr. Daniel Chater, A Shoemaker, by Fourteen Notorious Smugglers* (6th edn, Chichester, n.d.).

Gilbert, John T., ed., *Narratives of the Detention, Liberation and Marriage of Maria Clementina Stuart* (Shannon, Irish University Press, 1894, 1970).

Goss, Alexander, ed., *1. Abbott's Journal. 2. The Trials at Manchester in 1694*, Chetham Society, 61 (1864).

Grosart, Alexander, ed., *English Jacobite Ballads, Songs and Satires, etc. from the Mss. at Townley Hall, Lancashire* (Manchester, S. E. Simms, 1877).

Hardy, William John, ed., *Calendar of State Papers, Domestic Series, of the Reign of William and Mary* (13 vols., London, H.M.S.O., 1895–1924).

ed., *Notes and Extracts from the Sessions Rolls, 1581–1850*, Hertford County Records, vols. i–ii (2 vols., Hertford, Clerk of the Peace Office, 1905).

ed., *Notes and Extracts from the Sessions Books, Sessions Minute Books and Other Sessions Records, 1658–1752*, Hertford County Records, vols. vi–vii (2 vols., Hertford, Clerk of the Peace Office, 1930–1).

Hibbert-Ware, Samuel, *Lancashire Memorials of the Rebellion, 1715*, Chetham Society, 5 (1845).

The Historical Register, containing An Impartial Relation of all Transactions, both Civil and Military, Foreign and Domestick (2 vols., London, C. Meere, 1724).

Horwitz, Henry, Speck, W. A., and Gray, W. A., eds., *London Politics 1713–1717*, London Record Society Publications, 17 (1981).

Howell, T. B., ed., *A Complete Collection of State Trials* (33 vols., London, T. C. Hansard, 1816–26).

Hughan, William James, ed., *The Jacobite Lodge at Rome, 1735–7* (Torquay, Lodge of Research, 1910).

ed., *Masonic Sketches and Reprints. 1. History of Freemasonry in York. 2. Unpublished Records of the Craft* (London, G. Kenning, 1871).

Johnson, H. C. and Williams, N. J., eds., *Quarter Sessions Records, Easter 1690 to Michaelmas 1696*, Warwick County Records, vol. ix (Warwick, Sir Edward Stephens, 1964).

Le Hardy, William and Reckitt, Geoffrey L., eds., *County of Buckingham: Calendar to the Sessions Records* (5 vols., Aylesbury, County Hall, 1936–58).

Lord, George deF., gen. ed., *Poems on Affairs of State: Augustan Satirical Verse, 1660–1714* (7 vols., New Haven, Ct, and London, Yale University Press, 1963–75).

Luttrell, Narcissus, *A Brief Historical Relation of State Affairs from September 1678 to April 1714* (6 vols., Oxford, Oxford University Press, 1857).

Macpherson, James, ed., *Original Papers; Containing the Secret History of Great Britain, from the Restoration to the Accession of the House of Hannover* (2 vols., London, W. Strahan and T. Cadell, 1776).

Mahaffy, R. P., ed., *Calendar of State Papers, Domestic Series, of the Reign of Anne, Preserved in the Public Record Office* (2 vols., Hereford and London, H.M.S.O., 1916, 1924).

Mahon, Lord, *The Decline of the Last Stuarts. Extracts from the Despatches of British Envoys to the Secretary of State* (London, W. Nicol, Shakespeare Press, 1843).

Pape, T., 'The Ancient Corporation of Cheadle', *North Staffordshire Field Club Transactions* (1929–30), pp. 52–88.

Patten, Robert, *The History of the Late Rebellion: with Original Papers, and the Characters of Principal Noblemen and Gentlemen Concern'd in it* (2nd edn, London, T. Warner, 1717).

Payne, John Orlebar, ed., *Records of the English Catholics of 1715* (London, Burns and Oates, 1889).

Phillips, William, ed., 'William Cartwright, Nonjuror, and his Chronological History of Shrewsbury', *Transactions of the Shropshire Archaeological and Natural History Society*, 4th Series, 4 (1914), pp. 1–70.

Porteous, T. C., 'New Light on the Lancashire Jacobite Plot, 1692–4. An Account of the Plot Papers Found at Standish Hall, 1757, now Preserved in the Wigan Public Library', *Transactions of the Lancashire and Cheshire Antiquarian Society*, 50 (1934–5), pp. 1–64.

Province of Northumberland and Durham, Societas Rosicruciana in Anglia, *The Alnwick Manuscript, No. E 10: Reproduction and Transcript, Copy No. 2* (Newcastle-upon-Tyne, n.p., 1895).

Rae, Peter, *The History of the Rebellion, Rais'd against His Majesty King George I. By the Friends of the Pretender...* (2nd edn, London, A. Millar, 1746).

A True and Particular Narrative of the Disturbances and Outrages That have been committed in the City of Norwich, Since November to the present Time (London, n.p., 1752).

The Whole Proceedings upon the Arraignment, Tryal, Conviction and Attainder of Christopher Layer, Esq.; for High Treason in Compassing and Imagining the Death of the King (London, S. Buckley, 1722; Dublin, 1723).

REFERENCE WORKS

Beaven, Alfred B., *The Aldermen of the City of London Temp. Henry III.–1912* (2 vols., London, Eden Fisher, 1908–13).

Chambers, Robert, ed., *The Book of Days* (2 vols., Edinburgh, W. and R. Chambers, 1863).

[Cokayne, G. E.], *The Complete Baronetage* (5 vols., Exeter, W. Pollard, 1900–6).

The Complete Peerage of England, Scotland, Ireland, Great Britain and the United Kingdom, Extant, Extinct or Dormant (14 vols., London, St Catherine's Press, 1910–59).

Foster, Joseph, *Alumni Oxonienses: The Members of the University of Oxford, 1500–1714* (5 vols., Oxford, Clarendon Press, 1891–2).

Foxon, D. F., *English Verse 1701–1750* (2 vols., Cambridge, Cambridge University Press, 1975).

Gillow, Joseph, *A Literary and Biographical History, or Biographical Dictionary of the English Catholics. From the Breach with Rome, in 1534, to the Present Time* (6 vols., New York and London, Burns and Oates, 1885).

Hawkins, E., *Medallic Illustrations of the History of Great Britain and Ireland* (2 vols., London, Spink and Son, 1885; reprinted 1969).

Henning, Basil Duke, ed., *The History of Parliament: The House of Commons 1660–1690* (3 vols., London, Secker and Warburg, 1983).

Lane, John, *Masonic Records, 1717–1894: Being Lists of all the Lodges at*

Home and Abroad Warranted by the Four Grand Lodges and the 'United Grand Lodge' of England, with their Dates of Constitution, Places of Meeting, Alterations in Numbers, etc., etc. (2nd edn, London, Freemasons' Hall, 1895).

Lillywhite, Bryant, *London Coffee Houses: A Reference Book of Coffee Houses of the Seventeenth, Eighteenth and Nineteenth Centuries* (London, George Allen and Unwin, 1963).

Namier, Sir Lewis and Brooke, John, eds., *The History of Parliament: The House of Commons, 1754–90* (3 vols., London, H.M.S.O., 1964).

Nichols, John, *Literary Anecdotes of the Eighteenth Century; comprizing Biographical Memoirs of William Bowyer, Printer, F.S.A., And Many of his Learned Friends; An Incidental View of the Progress and Advancement of Literature in this Kingdom during the last Century; and Biographical Anecdotes of a Considerable Number of Eminent Writers and Ingenious Artists* (6 vols., London, J. Nichols, 1812).

Ruvigny and Raineval, Marquis of, *The Jacobite Peerage, Baronetage, Knightage and Grants of Honour* (Edinburgh, T. C. and E. C. Jack, 1904).

Sedgwick, Romney, ed., *The History of Parliament: The House of Commons 1715–54* (2 vols., London, H.M.S.O., 1970).

Seton, Sir Bruce Gordon and Arnot, Jean Gordon, eds., *The Prisoners of the '45*, Publications of the Scottish Historical Society, 3rd Series, 13–15 (3 vols., 1928–9).

Stephen, Leslie and Lee, Sidney, eds., *The Dictionary of National Biography* (63 vols., London, George Smith, 1885–1900).

Stephens, Frederick George, ed., *Catalogue of Political and Personal Satires Preserved in the Department of Prints and Drawings in the British Museum* (3 vols., London, British Museum, 1870–7).

SECONDARY WORKS: LOCAL SOURCES

Aikin, John, *A Description of the Country from Thirty to Forty Miles Round Manchester* (London, J. Stockdale, 1795).

Aveling, J. H. C., *Catholic Recusancy in the City of York 1558–1791* (St Albans, Herts., Catholic Record Society, 1970).

Northern Catholics: The Catholic Recusants of the North Riding of Yorkshire 1558–1790 (London, G. Chapman, 1966).

Baines, Edward, *The History of the County Palatine and Duchy of Lancaster*, ed. James Croston (6 vols., Manchester, J. Haywood, 1893).

Bennett, J. H. E., 'Cheshire and "The Fifteen"', *Journal of the Chester and North Wales Archaeological and Historic Society*, New Series, 21 (1915), pp. 30–46.

Blackner, John, *The History of Nottingham* (Nottingham, Sutton and Son, 1815).

Brigg, Mary, 'The Walmesleys of Dunkenhalgh: A Family of Blackburn Hundred in the Elizabethan and Stuart Periods', *Transactions of the*

Lancashire and Cheshire Antiquarian Society, 75–6 (1965–6), pp. 72–102.

Briggs, J. H. Y., 'The Burning of the Meeting House, July 1715: Dissent and Faction in Late Stuart Newcastle', *North Staffordshire Journal of Field Studies,* 14 (1974), pp. 70–3.

Burton, Alfred, *Rushbearing* (Manchester, Brook and Crystal, 1891).

Charlton, Edward, 'Jacobite Relics of 1715 and 1745', *Archaeologia Aeliana,* New Series, 6 (1865), pp. 29–34.

Collyer, Cedric, 'Yorkshire and the "Forty-Five"', *Yorkshire Archaeological Journal,* 38 (1955), pp. 71–95.

Coupe, Frank, *Walton-le-Dale: A History of the Village* (Preston, Guardian Press, 1954).

Dent, Robert K., *The Making of Birmingham: Being a History of the Rise and Growth of the Midland Metropolis* (Birmingham, J. L. Allday, 1894).

Dobson, William, *History of the Parliamentary Representation of Preston* (2nd edn, Preston, W. and J. Dobson, 1868).

Records of the Preston Oyster and Parched Pea Club, 1773–1841 (Preston, W. and J. Dobson, 1861).

Doran, [John], *London in the Jacobite Times* (2 vols., London, R. Bentley, 1877).

Eardley-Simpson, L., *Derby and the Forty-Five* (London, Philip Allan, 1933).

Egerton of Tatton, Earl, 'The Cheshire Gentry in 1715: Drawn from the Ashley Hall Portraits at Tatton', *Journal of the Architectural, Archaeological, and Historic Society for the County and City of Chester and North Wales,* New Series, 15 (1909), pp. 5–21.

Fitts, James, 'Newcastle's Mob', *Albion,* 5, 1 (1973), pp. 41–9.

George, M. Dorothy, *London Life in the Eighteenth Century* (New York, Capricorn Books, 1925, 1965).

Gillow, Joseph, *The Haydock Papers: A Glimpse into English Catholic Life* (London, Burns and Oates, 1888).

Greaves, R. W., *The Corporation of Leicester, 1689–1836* (Leicester, Leicester University Press, 1939, 1970).

Hampson, Charles P., *The Book of the Radclyffes* (Edinburgh, T. and A. Constable, 1940).

Henson, Gravenor, *The Civil, Political, and Mechanical History of the Framework-Knitters, in Europe and America...,* vol. i (Nottingham, Richard Sutton, 1831).

Hibbert-Ware, Samuel, *History of the Foundations in Manchester of Christ's College, Chetham's Hospital, and the Free Grammar School* (2 vols., Manchester, T. Agnew and J. Zanetti, 1830).

Hill, Sir Francis, *Georgian Lincoln* (Cambridge, Cambridge University Press, 1966).

Hodgson, John, *A History of Northumberland* (6 vols., Newcastle-upon-Tyne, various publishers, 1827–58).

Holmes, Geoffrey, 'The Sacheverell Riots: The Crowd and the Church in Early Eighteenth Century London', *Past and Present,* 72 (1976), pp. 55–85.

Homeshaw, Ernest James, *The Corporation of the Borough and Foreign of Walsall* (Walsall, County Borough, 1960).

Hughes, Edward, *North Country Life in the Eighteenth Century: The North-East, 1700–1750* (London, Oxford University Press, 1952).

Hutchinson, William, *The History of the County of Cumberland, and some Places Adjacent* (2 vols., Carlisle, F. Jollie, 1794).

Jarvis, Rupert C., *Collected Papers on the Jacobite Risings* (2 vols., Manchester, Manchester University Press, 1971).

'The Forty-Five and the Local Records', *Transactions of the Lancashire and Cheshire Antiquarian Society*, 65 (1955), pp. 70–90.

[Jenkins, Alexander], *Jenkins's Civil and Ecclesiastical History of the City of Exeter and its Environs, from the Time of the Romans to the Year 1806* (2nd edn, Exeter, W. Norton, 1841).

Jenkins, Philip, 'Jacobites and Freemasons in Eighteenth-Century Wales', *Welsh History Review*, 9, 4 (1979), pp. 391–406.

The Making of a Ruling Class: The Glamorgan Gentry, 1640–1790 (Cambridge, Cambridge University Press, 1983).

'Tory Industrialism and Town Politics: Swansea in the Eighteenth Century', *Historical Journal*, 28, 1 (1985), pp. 103–23.

'A Welsh Lancashire? Monmouthshire Catholics in the Eighteenth Century', *Recusant History*, 15, 3 (1980), pp. 176–88.

Latimer, John, *The Annals of Bristol in the Eighteenth Century* (Bristol, J. Latimer, 1893).

Lunn, John, *The Tyldesleys of Lancashire: The Rise and Fall of a Great Patrician Family* (Altrincham, St Ann's Press, 1966).

Mander, Gerald P. and Tildesley, Norman W., *A History of Wolverhampton to the Early Nineteenth Century* (Wolverhampton, City Borough Corp., 1960).

Mitchell, A. A., 'London and the Forty-Five', *History Today*, 15, 10 (1965), pp. 719–26.

Mounsey, G. G., *Authentic Account of the Occupation of Carlisle in 1745, by Prince Charles Edward Stuart* (London and Carlisle, Longman, 1846).

Mumford, Alfred A., *The Manchester Grammar School 1515–1915* (London, Longmans, Green and Co., 1919).

Muskett, Paul, 'Military Operations against Smuggling in Kent and Sussex, 1698–1750', *Journal of the Society for Army Historical Research*, 52, 210 (1974), pp. 89–110.

Nicholson, Albert, 'Lancashire in the Rebellion of 1715', *Transactions of the Lancashire and Cheshire Antiquarian Society*, 3 (1885), pp. 66–88.

'Lieutenant John Holker', *Transactions of the Lancashire and Cheshire Antiquarian Society*, 9 (1891), pp. 147–54.

Northumberland County History Committee, *A History of Northumberland* (15 vols., Newcastle and London, County History Committee, 1893–1940).

Owen, Hugh and Blakeway, J. B., *A History of Shrewsbury*, vol. i (London, Harding, Lepard and Co., 1825).

Petrie, Sir Charles, 'The Jacobite Activities in South and West England in the Summer of 1715', *Transactions of the Royal Historical Society*, 4th Series, 18 (1935), pp. 85–106.

Pritchard, T. W., *The Wynns at Wynnstay* (Caerwys, Old Court Press, 1982).

Robson, R. J., *The Oxfordshire Election of 1754: A Study in the Interplay of City, County and University Politics* (London, Oxford University Press, 1949).

Rogers, J. P. W., 'John Oldmixon in Bridgwater 1716–30', *Proceedings of the Somersetshire Archaeological and Natural History Society*, 113 (1968–9), pp. 86–98.

Rogers, Nicholas, 'Aristocratic Clientage, Trade and Independency: Popular Politics in Pre-Radical Westminster', *Past and Present*, 61 (1973), pp. 70–106.

'Popular Disaffection in London during the Forty-Five', *London Journal*, 1, 1 (1975), pp. 5–27.

'Popular Protest in Early Hanoverian London', *Past and Present*, 79 (1978), pp. 70–100.

Rowlands, Marie B., *Masters and Men in the West Midlands Metal Trades before the Industrial Revolution* (Manchester, Manchester University Press, 1975).

Rudé, George, *Hanoverian London 1714–1808* (London, Secker and Warburg, 1971).

Paris and London in the Eighteenth Century: Studies in Popular Protest (New York, Viking Press, 1971).

Sharp, Richard, '100 Years of a Lost Cause: Nonjuring Principles in Newcastle from the Revolution to the Death of Prince Charles Edward Stuart', *Archaelogia Aeliana*, 5th Series, 8 (1980), pp. 34–55.

Sherborn, C. D., *A History of the Family of Sherborn* (London, Mitchell and Hughes, 1901).

Slocombe, I. M., 'A Bridgewater Riot, 1717', *Proceedings of the Somersetshire Archaeological and Natural History Society*, 106 (1961–2), pp. 66–76.

Stephens, W. B., ed., *A History of Congleton* (Manchester, Manchester University Press, 1970).

Stott, Beatrice, 'Charles Clement Deacon and William Brettargh', *Transactions of the Lancashire and Cheshire Antiquarian Society*, 41 (1924), pp. 1–39.

'The Informations Laid Against Certain Townsmen of Manchester in 1746', *Transactions of the Lancashire and Cheshire Antiquarian Society*, 42 (1925), pp. 25–52.

'James Dawson and Thomas Syddall', *Transactions of the Lancashire and Cheshire Antiquarian Society*, 46 (1929), pp. 1–31.

'Parson Coppock', *Transactions of the Lancashire and Cheshire Antiquarian Society*, 40 (1923), pp. 45–75.

Timbs, John, *Clubs and Club Life in London* (London, J. Camden Hotten, 1872).

Trease, Geoffrey, *Nottingham: A Biography* (London, Macmillan, 1970).

Tyndale, O. M., '"Manchester Vindicated" and the later Nonjurors', *Transactions of the Lancashire and Cheshire Antiquarian Society*, 53 (1938), pp. 119–30.

Victoria County History of Hampshire and the Isle of Wight (5 vols., London, Constable, 1900–12).

Victoria County History of Lancashire (8 vols., London, Constable, 1906–14).

Victoria County History of Leicestershire (4 vols., London, Constable, Oxford University Press, 1907–).

Wadsworth, Alfred P. and Mann, Julia de Lacy, *The Cotton Trade and Industrial Lancashire, 1600–1780* (Manchester, Manchester University Press, 1931, 1965).

Ward, W.R., *Georgian Oxford: University Politics in the Eighteenth Century* (Oxford, Clarendon Press, 1958).

Wedgwood, Josiah C., *Staffordshire Parliamentary History from the Earliest Times to the Present Day, vol. 2*, William Salt Archaeological Society (1922).

Whittaker, T. D., *History of Richmondshire in the North Riding of the County of York* (2 vols., London, Longman, Hurst, Rees, Orme and Browne, 1823).

Whittaker, W. E. B., *The Glynnes of Hawarden*, Flintshire Historical Society Publications (Chester, 1906).

Wilson, John, *The Chorleys of Chorley Hall* (Manchester, Sherratt and Hughes, 1907).

SECONDARY WORKS: GENERAL

Arnold, Ralph, *Northern Lights: The Story of Lord Derwentwater* (London, Constable, 1959).

Ashley, Maurice, *James II* (London, Dent and Sons, 1977).

Atherton, Herbert M., *Political Prints in the Age of Hogarth* (Oxford, Clarendon Press, 1974).

Aveling, J. H. C., *The Handle and the Axe: Catholic Recusants in England from the Reformation to Emancipation* (London and Tiptree, Essex, Blond and Briggs, 1976).

Baynes, John, *The Jacobite Rising of 1715* (London, Cassell, 1970).

Beattie, J. M., *Crime and the Courts in England, 1660–1800* (Princeton, Princeton University Press, 1986).

Begemann, Wilhelm, *Die Tempellherrn und die Freimaurer* (Berlin, Mittler, 1906).

  Vorgeschichte und Anfänge der Freimaurerei in England (2 vols., Berlin, Mittler, 1909).

Beloff, Max, *Public Order and Public Disturbances, 1660–1714* (London, Frank Cass, 1963).

Bennett, G. V., 'English Jacobitism, 1710–1715: Myth and Reality', *Transactions of the Royal Historical Society*, 5th Series, 32 (1982), pp. 137–52.

The Tory Crisis in Church and State, 1688–1730: The Career of Francis Atterbury, Bishop of Rochester (Oxford, Clarendon Press, 1975).

Black, Jeremy, ed., *Britain in the Age of Walpole* (London, MacMillan, 1984).

Blackett-Ord, Mark, *Hell-Fire Duke: The Life of the Duke of Wharton* (Windsor, Kensal Press, 1982).

Bles, Joseph, *Rare English Glasses of the XVII and XVIII Centuries* (London, Geoffrey Bles, 1924).

Bloch, Marc, *Les Rois Thaumaturges* (Strasbourg, Istra, 1924).

Bongie, L. L., *The Love of a Prince: Bonnie Prince Charlie in France, 1744–1748* (Vancouver, University of British Columbia Press, 1986).

'Voltaire's English, High Treason and a Manifesto for Prince Charles', *Studies on Voltaire and the Eighteenth Century*, 171 (1977), pp. 7–29.

Bossy, John, *The English Catholic Community, 1570–1850* (London, Darton, Longman and Todd, 1975).

Bradshaw, Peter, *Eighteenth Century English Porcelain Figures, 1745–1795* (Woodbridge, Suffolk, Antique Collectors' Club, 1981).

Brewer, John, *The English Satirical Print, 1600–1832: The Common People and Politics, 1750–1790s* (Cambridge, Chadwyck-Healey, 1986).

Party Ideology and Popular Politics at the Accession of George III (Cambridge, Cambridge University Press, 1976).

Brewer, John and Styles, John, eds., *An Ungovernable People? The English and their Law in the Seventeenth and Eighteenth Centuries* (New Brunswick, N.J., Rutgers University Press, 1980).

Bronson, Bertrand H., *Joseph Ritson, Scholar-at-Arms* (2 vols., Berkeley, University of California Press, 1938).

Broxap, Henry, *A Biography of Thomas Deacon, the Manchester Non-Juror* (Manchester, Manchester University Press, 1911).

The Later Non-Jurors (Cambridge, Cambridge University Press, 1924).

Burke, Peter, *Popular Culture in Early Modern Europe* (New York, Harper and Row, 1978).

Bushaway, Bob, *By Rite: Custom, Ceremony and Community in England, 1700–1880* (London, Junction Books, 1982).

Campbell, George, *Imposter at the Bar: William Fuller, 1670–1733* (London, Hodder and Stoughton, 1961).

Carson, Edward, *The Ancient and Rightful Customs: A History of the English Customs Service* (London, Faber and Faber, 1972).

Chambers, Robert, *History of the Rebellion of 1745–6* (London and Edinburgh, W. and R. Chambers, 1869).

Cherry, George L., 'The Legal and Philosophical Position of the Jacobites, 1688–1689', *Journal of Modern History*, 22, 4 (1950), pp. 309–21.

Childs, John, *The Army, James II, and the Revolution* (Manchester, Manchester University Press, 1980).

Christie, Ian, 'The Tory Party, Jacobitism and the "Forty-Five": A Note', *Historical Journal*, 30, 4 (1987), pp. 921–31.

Clark, J. C. D., *English Society, 1688–1832: Ideology, Social Structure and*

Political Practice during the Ancien Regime (Cambridge, Cambridge University Press, 1985).

'The Politics of the Excluded: Tories, Jacobites and Whig Patriots, 1715–60', *Parliamentary History*, 2 (1983), pp. 209–22.

Revolution and Rebellion: State and Society in England in the Seventeenth and Eighteenth Centuries (Cambridge, 1986).

Clark, Peter, *The English Alehouse: A Social History, 1200–1830* (London, Longman, 1983).

Clifton, Robin, *The Last Popular Rebellion: The Western Rising of 1685* (London and New York, Maurice Temple Smith, 1984).

Cockburn, J. S., *A History of English Assizes, 1558–1714* (Cambridge, Cambridge University Press, 1972).

Coleridge, E. H., *The Life of Thomas Coutts, Banker* (2 vols., London, John Lane, 1920).

Colley, Linda, 'Eighteenth-Century English Radicalism before Wilkes', *Transactions of the Royal Historical Society*, 5th Series, 31 (1981), pp. 1–19.

In Defiance of Oligarchy: The Tory Party, 1714–60 (Cambridge, Cambridge University Press, 1982).

'The Loyal Brotherhood and the Cocoa Tree: The London Organization of the Tory Party, 1727–1760', *Historical Journal*, 20, 1 (1977), pp. 77–95.

Cranfield, G. A., *The Development of the Provincial Newspaper* (Oxford, Clarendon Press, 1962).

Crawfurd, Raymond, *The King's Evil* (Oxford, Oxford University Press, 1911).

Cruickshanks, Eveline, ed., *Ideology and Conspiracy: Aspects of Jacobitism, 1689–1759* (Edinburgh, John Donald, 1982).

'Lord Cornbury, Bolingbroke and a Plan to Restore the Stuarts, 1731–1735', *Royal Stuart Papers*, 27 (1986).

Political Untouchables: The Tories and the '45 (London, Duckworth, 1979).

Cruickshanks, Eveline and Black, Jeremy, eds., *The Jacobite Challenge* (Edinburgh, John Donald, 1988).

Cruickshanks, Eveline and Erskine-Hill, Howard, 'The Waltham Black Act and Jacobitism', *Journal of British Studies*, 24 (1985), pp. 358–65.

Daly, James, 'The Idea of Absolute Monarchy in 17th Century England', *Historical Journal*, 21, 2 (1978), pp. 227–50.

Sir Robert Filmer and English Political Thought (Toronto, University of Toronto Press, 1979).

De Krey, Gary S., *A Fractured Society: The Politics of London in the First Age of Party, 1688–1715* (Oxford, Clarendon Press, 1985).

'Political Radicalism in London after the Glorious Revolution', *Journal of Modern History*, 55, 4 (1983), pp. 585–617.

Dennistoun, James, *Memoirs of Sir Robert Strange* (2 vols., London, Longman, Brown, Green and Longmans, 1855).

Dickinson, H. T., *Bolingbroke* (Constable, London, 1970).

Liberty and Property: Political Ideology in Eighteenth-Century Britain (New York, Holmes and Meier, 1977).

Earle, Peter, *Monmouth's Rebels: The Road to Sedgemoor, 1685* (London, Weidenfeld and Nicolson, 1977).

Ellestad, Charles D., 'The Mutinies of 1689', *Journal of the Society for Army Historical Research*, 53, 213 (1975), pp. 4–21.

Erskine-Hill, Howard, 'Alexander Pope: The Political Poet in his Time', *Eighteenth-Century Studies*, 15, 2 (1981–2), pp. 123 8.

The Social Milieu of Alexander Pope: Lives, Exampl and the Creative Response (New Haven, Ct, Yale University Press, 1ᶴ 5).

Farquhar, Helen, 'Royal Charities. Part III. Continuation of Touchpieces for the King's Evil. James II to William III', *British Numismatic Journal*, 14, New Series, 4 (1920), pp. 89–120.

'Royal Charities. Part IV. Continuation of Touchpieces for the King's Evil. Anne and the Stuart Princes', *British Numismatic Journal*, 15, New Series, 5 (1921), pp. 141–84.

'Some Portrait Medals Struck between 1745 and 1752 for Prince Charles Edward', *British Numismatic Journal*, 17, New Series, 7 (1923–4), pp. 171–225.

Ferguson, James, *Robert Ferguson the Plotter or the Secret of the Rye House Conspiracy and the Story of a Strange Career* (Edinburgh, D. Douglas, 1887).

Figgis, J. N., *The Divine Right of Kings* (2nd edn, New York, Harper and Row, 1914; reprinted 1965).

Flinn, M. W., *Men of Iron: The Crowleys in the Early Iron Industry* (Edinburgh, Edinburgh University Press, 1962).

le Forestier, René, *La Franc-Maçonnerie Templière et Occultiste au XVIIIe et XIXe Siècles* (Paris, Aubier-Montagne, 1970).

Forster, Margaret, *The Rash Adventurer: The Rise and Fall of Charles Edward Stuart* (St Albans, Herts., Panther, 1973).

Francis, Grant, *Old English Drinking Glasses: Their Chronology and Sequence* (London, Herbert Jenkins, 1926).

Romance of the White Rose (London, John Murray, 1933).

Fritz, Paul, 'The Anti-Jacobite Intelligence of the English Ministers, 1715–1745', *Historical Journal*, 16, 2 (1973), pp. 265–89.

The English Ministers and Jacobitism between the Rebellions of 1715 and 1745 (Toronto, University of Toronto Press, 1975).

Garrett, Jane, *The Triumphs of Providence: The Assassination Plot, 1696* (Cambridge, Cambridge University Press, 1980).

Goldie, Mark, 'The Roots of True Whiggism, 1688–94', *History of Political Thought*, 1, 2 (1980), pp. 195–236.

Goulden, R. J., 'Vox Populi, Vox Dei: Charles Delafaye's Paperchase', *The Book Collector*, 28, 3 (1979), pp. 368–90.

Greenwood, David, *William King, Tory and Jacobite* (Oxford, Clarendon Press, 1969).

Gregg, Edward, *Queen Anne* (London, Ark, 1980, 1984).

Gunn, J. A. W., *Beyond Liberty and Property: The Process of Self-Recognition in Eighteenth-Century Political Thought* (Kingston and Montreal, McGill-Queens University Press, 1983).

Halsband, Robert, *Lord Hervey: Eighteenth Century Courtier* (Oxford, Oxford University Press, 1974).

Handasyde, Elizabeth, *Granville the Polite: The Life of George Granville, Lord Lansdowne, 1666–1735* (Oxford, Clarendon Press, 1933).

Harris, Michael, *London Newspapers in the Age of Walpole: A Study of the Origins of the Modern English Press* (London and Toronto, Associated University Presses, 1987).

Harris, Tim, *London Crowds in the Reign of Charles II: Propaganda and Politics from the Restoration until the Exclusion Crisis* (Cambridge, Cambridge University Press, 1987).

Hartshorne, Albert, *Old English Glasses* (London and New York, Edward Arnold, 1897).

Hatton, Ragnhild, *George I: Elector and King* (London, Thames and Hudson, 1978).

Hawkins, L. M., *Allegiance in Church and State: The Problem of the Nonjurors in the English Revolution* (London, Routledge, 1928).

Hay, Douglas, Linebaugh, Peter, Rule, John G., Thompson, E. P. and Winslow, Cal, *Albion's Fatal Tree: Crime and Society in Eighteenth Century England* (New York, Pantheon, 1975).

Hill, Patricia Kneas, *The Oglethorpe Ladies and the Jacobite Conspiracies* (Atlanta, Cherokee, 1977).

Holmes, Geoffrey, *Augustan England: Professions, State and Society, 1680–1730* (London, Allen and Unwin, 1982).

The Trial of Doctor Sacheverell (London, Eyre Methuen, 1973).

Hopkins, Paul, *Glencoe and the End of the Highland War* (Edinburgh, John Donald, 1986).

Horwitz, Henry, *Parliament, Policy and Politics in the Reign of William III* (Manchester, Manchester University Press, 1977).

Hughes, G. Bernard, *English, Scottish and Irish Table Glass, from the Sixteenth Century to 1820* (New York, Bramhall House, 1956).

Insh, G. P., *The Scottish Jacobite Movement* (Edinburgh, Moray Press, 1952).

Jacob, Margaret C., *The Radical Enlightenment: Pantheists, Freemasons and Republicans* (London, Allen and Unwin, 1981).

Jones, Clyve, ed., *Britain in the First Age of Party, 1680–1750: Essays Presented to Geoffrey Holmes* (London and Ronceverte, Hambledon Press, 1987).

Jones, G. H., *Charles Middleton: The Life and Times of a Restoration Politician* (Chicago, University of Chicago Press, 1967).

'The Jacobites, Charles Molloy, and *Common Sense*', *Review of English Studies*, New Series, 4, 13 (1953), pp. 144–7.

The Mainstream of Jacobitism (Cambridge, Mass., Harvard University Press, 1954).

Jones, J. R., 'James II's Whig Collaborators', *Historical Journal*, 7, 1 (1960), pp. 65–73.

The Revolution of 1688 in England (New York, Norton, 1972).

Kantorowicz, Ernst, *The King's Two Bodies: A Study in Medieval Political Theology* (Princeton, Princeton University Press, 1957).

Kenyon, J. P., *Revolution Principles: The Politics of Party, 1689–1720* (Cambridge, Cambridge University Press, 1977).

Kramnick, Isaac, *Bolingbroke and his Circle: The Politics of Nostalgia in the Age of Walpole* (Cambridge, Mass., Harvard University Press, 1968).

Lang, Andrew, *Pickle the Spy or the Incognito of Prince Charles* (London, Longmans, Green and Co., 1897).

Prince Charles Edward Stuart: The Young Chevalier (new edn, London, Longmans, Green and Co., 1903).

Lathbury, Thomas, *A History of the Nonjurors: Their Controversies and Writings* (London, W. Pickering, 1845).

Lenman, Bruce, *The Jacobite Clans of the Great Glen, 1650–1784* (London, Methuen, 1984).

The Jacobite Risings in Britain, 1689–1746 (London, Eyre Methuen, 1980).

Lewis, Lesley, *Connoisseurs and Secret Agents in Eighteenth Century Rome* (London, Chatto and Windus, 1961).

Macaulay, Lord, *The History of England from the Accession of James II*, ed. C. H. Firth (6 vols., London, Macmillan, 1913–15).

McKendrick, Neil, ed., *Historical Perspectives: Studies in English Thought and Society in Honour of J. H. Plumb* (London, Europa, 1974).

McKendrick, Neil, Brewer, John and Plumb, J. H., *The Birth of a Consumer Society: The Commercialization of Eighteenth-Century England* (Bloomington, Indiana University Press, 1982).

McLynn, F. J., *France and the Jacobite Rising of 1745* (Edinburgh, Edinburgh University Press, 1981).

'Issues and Motives in the Jacobite Rising of 1745', *The Eighteenth Century*, 23, 2 (1982), pp. 97–133.

The Jacobite Army in England, 1745 (Edinburgh, John Donald, 1983).

The Jacobites (London, Routledge and Kegan Paul, 1985).

Mahon, Lord, *History of England from the Peace of Utrecht to the Peace of Versailles, 1713–1783* (7 vols., London, John Murray, 1839–54).

Malcolmson, Robert, *Popular Recreations in English Society, 1700–1850* (Cambridge, Cambridge University Press, 1973).

Melville, Lewis, *The Life and Writings of Philip, Duke of Wharton* (London, John Lane, 1913).

Midgley, Graham, *The Life of Orator Henley* (Oxford, Clarendon Press, 1973).

Miller, John, *James II: A Study in Kingship* (Hove, Wayland, 1978).

Popery and Politics in England, 1660–1688 (Cambridge, Cambridge University Press, 1973).

'The Potential for "Absolutism" in Later Stuart England', *History*, 59 (1984), pp. 187–207.

Monod, Paul, 'Jacobitism and Country Principles in the Reign of William III', *Historical Journal*, 30, 2 (1987), pp. 289–310.

Ollard, Richard, *The Image of the King: Charles I and Charles II* (New York, Atheneum, 1979).

Overton, J. H., *The Nonjurors: Their Lives, Principles, and Writings* (London, Smith, Elder and Co., 1902).

Partner, Peter, *The Murdered Magicians: The Templars and their Myth* (New York and London, Oxford University Press, 1982).

Perry, Ruth, *The Celebrated Mary Astell: An Early English Feminist* (Chicago, University of Chicago Press, 1986).

Plumb, J. H., *The Growth of Political Stability in England, 1675–1725* (London, Macmillan, 1967).

Petrie, Sir Charles, 'The Elibank Plot, 1752–3', *Transactions of the Royal Historical Society*, 4th Series, 14 (1931), pp. 175–96.

The Jacobite Movement: The First Phase, 1688–1716 (London, Eyre and Spottiswoode, 1948).

The Jacobite Movement: The Last Phase, 1716–1807 (London, Eyre and Spottiswoode, 1950).

Pocock, J. G. A., *The Machiavellian Moment* (Princeton, Princeton University Press, 1975).

de Polnay, Peter, *Death of a Legend: The True Story of Bonny Prince Charlie* (London, Hamish Hamilton, 1952).

Price, Jacob M., *France and the Chesapeake: A History of the French Tobacco Monopoly, 1674–1791, and of its Relationship to the British and American Tobacco Trades* (2 vols., Ann Arbor, University of Michigan Press, 1973).

Purcell, Patrick, 'The Jacobite Rising of 1715 and the English Catholics', *English Historical Review*, 44, 175 (1929), pp. 418–32.

Reay, Barry, ed., *Popular Culture in Seventeenth-Century England* (New York, St Martin's Press, 1985).

Reynolds, Myra, *The Learned Lady in England, 1650–1760* (Gloucester, Mass., Peter Smith, 1920, 1964).

Roberts, J. M., *The Mythology of the Secret Societies* (New York, Scribner, 1972).

Robinson, J. M., *The Dukes of Norfolk* (Oxford, Oxford University Press, 1982).

Rogers, Pat, 'The Waltham Blacks and the Black Act', *Historical Journal*, 17, 3 (1974), pp. 465–86.

Roth, Cecil, *A History of the Jews in England* (3rd edn, Oxford, Clarendon Press, 1964).

The Royalist, 1–4 (1890–4).

Rudé, George, *The Crowd in History: A Study of Popular Disturbances in France and England, 1730–1848* (revised edn, London, Lawrence and Wishart, 1981).

Sachse, William L., 'The Mob and the Revolution of 1688', *Journal of British Studies*, 4, 1 (1964), pp. 23–40.

Schochet, Gordon J., *Patriarchalism in Political Thought: The Authoritarian Family and Political Speculation and Attitudes, Especially in Seventeenth-Century England* (Oxford, Clarendon Press, 1975).

Schwoerer, Lois, *The Declaration of Rights, 1689* (Baltimore, Johns Hopkins, 1981).

'Women and the Glorious Revolution', *Albion*, 18, 2 (1986), pp. 195–218.

Seddon, G. B., 'The Jacobite Engravers', in R. J. Charleston, Wendy Evans and Ada Polak, eds., *The Glass Circle*, 3 (Surrey, 1979), pp. 40–78.

Sherburn, George, *Roehenstart, A Late Stuart Pretender* (Chicago, University of Chicago Press, 1960).

Shield, Alice, *Henry Stuart, Cardinal of York and his Times* (London, Longmans, Green & Co., 1908).

Shield, Alice and Lang, Andrew, *The King over the Water* (London, Longmans, Green and Co., 1907).

Skeet, F. J. A., *The Life of the Right Honourable James Radcliffe Third Earl of Derwentwater* (London, Hutchinson, 1929).

  ed., *Stuart Papers, Pictures, Relics, Medals and Books in the Collection of Miss Maria Widdrington* (London, John Whitehead and Son, 1930).

Speck, W., *The Butcher: The Duke of Cumberland and the Suppression of the '45* (Oxford, Blackwell, 1981).

Steevenson, M. T., 'Jacobite Clubs', Circle of Glass Collectors, Paper no. 7 (1939).

  'Some Jacobite Toasts', Circle of Glass Collectors, Paper no. 17 (1940).

  'Some Jacobite Clubs', Circle of Glass Collectors, Paper nos. 59–61 (1945).

  'More Clubs', Circle of Glass Collectors, Paper no. 107 (n.d.).

Stevenson, John, *Popular Disturbances in England, 1700–1870* (London, Longman, 1979).

Stirling, A. M. W., *Coke of Norfolk and his Friends* (London, John Lane, 1912).

Straka, Gerald M., *Anglican Reaction to the Revolution of 1688* (Madison, Wisconsin, University of Wisconsin Press, 1962).

  'The Final Phase of Divine Right Theory in England, 1688–1702', *English Historical Review*, 77, 305 (1962), pp. 638–58.

Szechi, Daniel, *Jacobitism and Tory Politics, 1710–14* (Edinburgh, John Donald, 1984).

Tayler, Alistair and Tayler, Henrietta, *The Old Chevalier* (London, Cassell, 1934).

  1715: The Story of the Rising (London, T. Nelson, 1939).

Tayler, Henrietta, *Prince Charlie's Daughter: Being the Life and Letters of Charlotte of Albany* (London, Batchworth Press, 1950).

Thomas, Keith, *Religion and the Decline of Magic* (New York, Scribner, 1971).

Thompson, E. P., 'Eighteenth-century English Society: Class-Struggle without Class?', *Social History*, 3, 2 (1978), pp. 133–65.

  Folklore, Anthropology and Social History (Brighton, Sussex, J. L. Noyce, 1979).

  'Patrician Society, Plebeian Culture', *Journal of Social History*, 7, 4 (1974), pp. 382–405.

  Whigs and Hunters: The Origins of the Black Act (revised edn, Harmondsworth, Middlesex, Penguin, 1977).

Vaughan, Herbert M., *The Last Stuart Queen: Louise Countess of Albany: Her Life and Letters* (London, Duckworth, 1910).

Western, J. R., *The English Militia in the Eighteenth Century* (London, Routledge and Kegan Paul, 1965).

Monarchy and Revolution: The English State in the 1680s (London, Blandford, 1972).

Wiles, R. M., *Freshest Advices: Early Provincial Newspapers in England* (Columbus, Ohio, Ohio State University Press, 1965).

UNPUBLISHED DISSERTATIONS

Albers, Jan, 'Seeds of Contention: Society, Politics and the Church of England in Lancashire, 1689–1790', Ph.D. diss., Yale University , 1988.

Baskerville, Stephen W., 'The Management of the Tory Interest in Cheshire and Lancashire, 1714–47', D.Phil. diss., Oxford University, 1976.

Chapman, Paul, 'Jacobite Political Argument in England, 1714–1766', Ph.D. diss., Cambridge University, 1983.

Findon, J. C., 'The Nonjurors and the Church of England, 1689–1716', D.Phil. diss., Oxford University, 1978.

Goldie, M. A., 'Tory Political Thought, 1689–1714', Ph.D. diss., Cambridge University, 1977.

Hopkins, Paul A., 'Aspects of Jacobite Conspiracy in England in the Reign of William III', Ph.D. diss., Cambridge University, 1981.

Monod, Paul, 'For the King to Enjoy His Own Again: Jacobite Political Culture in England, 1688–1788', Ph.D. diss., Yale University, 1985.

Szechi, Daniel, 'Parliamentary Jacobitism and its Influence in the Tory Party, 1710–1714', D.Phil. diss., Oxford University, 1982.

Wilson, Kathleen, 'The Rejection of Deference: Urban Political Culture in England, 1715–1788', Ph.D. diss., Yale University, 1985.

Index

English place names that are mentioned only once in the text are listed under the counties in which they are situated. The entries for major cities and towns include references to civic institutions, neighbourhoods and suburbs (e.g. Newgate prison, St Andrew's Holborn and Whitechapel are under 'London'). For individual clubs and societies (except Masonic lodges and mock corporations), see 'clubs'. Taverns, alehouses and inns are found under 'taverns', but coffee-houses are in a separate entry. The names of individuals who took part in the riots and demonstrations described in Chapters 6 and 7 are listed under 'rioters'. Persons accused of seditious words whose names appear in Chapter 8 are indexed under 'seditious words'.

Lever family, 281
Leveson Gower, John, 1st Earl Gower,
  199
Leveson Gower, Richard, 206
Leveson Gower, William, 298
Lévi-Strauss, Claude, 8
Lewis, Anne, 213
Lewis, John, 136
Lewis, Mr, 136, 292
Lexinton, Lord, see Sutton, Robert, 2nd
  Baron Lexinton
Lichfield: races at, 199, 207, 209, 293,
  294; riots at, 198, 199, 201, 207, 219,
  237, 259
Lichfield, Earl of, see Lee, George Henry,
  3rd Earl of Lichfield
Lightbody, John, 47, 53n
Lincolnshire, 238n; places in: Boston,
  275, Lincoln, riots at, 201, Ormsby,
  330, Stamford, 169
Linebaugh, Peter, 110, 162n, 206
Lisle, Thomas, 301
Lisle family, 323
Lister, Thomas, 221
Little Crosby, Lancs., 315, 316
Littleton, Sir Edward, 207
Liverpool, 225, 303, 314, 315, 345
Liverpool, Lord, see Jenkinson, Thomas
  Banks, 2nd Earl of Liverpool
Locke, John, 16, 21, 32, 42, 84
London, 47, 64, 74n, 78, 81, 84, 97,
  101, 105, 108, 109, 110, 114, 116,
  121, 122, 129, 136, 142, 143, 150–1,
  154, 169, 170, 176, 178, 207, 209,
  217, 230, 231–2, 238, 244, 251, 253,
  280, 281, 286, 295n, 297, 304, 319,
  321, 331; aldermen of, 130, 228, 231,
  281–2; charity schools in, 150;
  Common council of, 226, 227, 228,
  281; Common Hall of, 227; Jacobite
  periodicals in, 29, 30n; Jacobite songs
  printed in, 47–8; medieval foundations
  of, 226–8, 231–2; places in and
  around: Aldersgate Street, 143,
  Bishopsgate, 149, Blackfriars, 221,
  Bridewell Hospital, 221, 227, 282,
  Cheapside, 181, Clare Market, 151,
  167, 168, Clerkenwell, 183, Fleet
  Street, 143, 231, Goodman's Fields,
  156, Gray's Inn, 149, Holborn, 143,
  167, 223, Lincoln's Inn, 40, Lincoln's
  Inn Fields, 151, Lyons Inn, 230,
  Middle Temple, 280, Newgate Market,
  180, Newgate prison, 230, 319,
  Portsoken, 227, Queen St, 181,
  Salisbury Court, 206n, 227, 228, St

Alban's Woodstreet, 150, St Andrew's
  Holborn, 143, 180–1, 227, 258, St
  Bartholomew's Hospital, 282, St
  Giles-in-the-Fields, 108 (riots at), 201,
  St Leonard's Shoreditch, 221, St
  Mildred's Breadstreet, 149, Smithfield,
  181, Snow Hill, 180, Stepney, 255,
  Stock Exchange, 181, Spa Fields, 119,
  'the Temple', 280, Tyburn, 120, 206,
  306, Wapping, 108, 155n,
  Whitechapel, 72, 143, 183, 227; riots
  and demonstrations in, 47, 98, 99,
  143, 163, 164–6, 166–8, 171, 172,
  173, 180–1, 183, 185, 204, 206n, 210,
  221, 222, 223, 225–8, 231; Sessions,
  252, 253; weavers' strike in, 197; see
  also clubs; coffee-houses; Middlesex;
  Mug-houses; Southwark; taverns;
  Westminster
London Chronicle, 60
London Evening Post, 131
Longueville, St Thomas, 295
Louis XIV, King of France, 74, 99, 147
Louis XV, King of France, 108, 109,
  111, 115, 130, 334
Louisa of Stolberg, Countess of Albany,
  88–90, 278, 285, 297, 307n, 343;
  medal of, 89; portraits of, 89
Louise-Marie Stuart, 'La Consolatrice',
  portraits of, 73, 74, 290n
Lovat, Lord, see Fraser, Simon, 11th
  Lord Lovat
Lovel, Christopher, 130
Lowick, Maj. Robert, 100
Loyal Observator Reviv'd; or, Gaylard's
  Journal, The, 29
Lucas, Catherine, 109
Lunt, John, 103, 113, 311, 312, 313
Luttrell, Narcissus, 112
Lutwyche family, 142
Luxmoore, Charles, 277
Lyme Hall, Cheshire, 77, 272, 283, 289,
  291, 318

Macaulay, Thomas Babington, 1st Baron
  Macaulay, 2, 96, 97, 142, 155, 346
McCormack, Ormsby, 339
Macdonald, Alaistair, alias 'Pickle the
  Spy', 102
Macdonald, Flora, 85
McLynn, Frank, 3
Maddocks, Samuel, 333
Mahon, Lord, see Stanhope, Philip
  Henry, Viscount Mahon
Mainwaring, Arthur, 55
Malcolmson, Robert, 203